THE BOOK OF
JARGON

THE BOOK OF
JARGON

DON ETHAN MILLER

COLLIER BOOKS

A DIVISION OF MACMILLAN PUBLISHING CO., INC.

NEW YORK

Macmillan Publishing Co., Inc.
866 Third Avenue, New York, N.Y. 10022
Collier Macmillan Canada, Inc.

Library of Congress Cataloging in Publication Data
Miller, Don Ethan, 1947–
The book of jargon.
Includes index.
1. English language—Jargon.   2. English
language—Terms and phrases.   3. Professions—
Terminology. I. Title
PE1585.M48   1982b 423′.1   82-4528
ISBN 0-02-080970-0   AACR2

DESIGNED BY JACK MESEROLE

FIRST COLLIER BOOKS EDITION 1982

10   9   8   7   6   5   4   3   2   1

PRINTED IN THE UNITED STATES OF AMERICA

The excerpt from "Author's Prologue" is reprinted from *The Poems* of Dylan
Thomas. Copyright 1952 by Dylan Thomas. Reprinted by permission of New
Directions.

"Cat's Nap" is reprinted from *Under Milkwood* by Dylan Thomas. Copyright
1954 by New Directions Publishing Corporation. Reprinted by permission of
New Directions.

The Book of Jargon is also published in a hardcover edition
by Macmillan Publishing Co., Inc.

Contents

VI   SCENES AND SUBCULTURES

Acknowledgments

My own Herculean (and at times Sisyphean) efforts notwithstanding, several thousand hours of research and dozens of preliminary drafts were contributed by the following individuals, whom I wish to publicly thank and acknowledge:

Mike Silverstein (Real Estate, Fashion, Business Management); Robert Epstein (Jazz, Drugs); Julian Miller (Wine, Auto Mechanics); Mike Shoob (Motion Pictures, Gambling); Sigmund Miller (Wine, Medicine); Charles Wyzanski (Law); Tom and Ray Maggliozzi (Auto Mechanics); Randi Barenholtz (Sailing); Tim Patterson (Television); Joe Mayr (Computers); Scott Allen (Computers); Bob Ryan (Tennis); Michelle Satter (Ballet); Leslie Long (Advertising); and Bernice Schneider (Ballet). Special thanks also to Don Davis, Laura Snowdon, J. D. Sloan, Donna Parker, Steven Hall, and Cheri Sheaff.

Finally, my gratitude immeasurable to Phyllis, Sigmund, and Julian, who have bolstered my spirit through many a dark nadir; to my son Jason, for his enthusiasm and his laughter; and to Michelle Eve Satter, for her love.

Introduction

The idea for this book was conceived some three years ago, after a friend of mine returned from a meeting at which she had received the disappointing news that her application to a graduate program at an Extremely Prestigious Eastern University had been rejected as below certain unstated "standards." I asked her to show me the application, and it seemed that she was eminently qualified for the program. She had, however, written the narrative sections of the application in a friendly, discursive style, much as one might write a letter to a distant cousin to whom one had not spoken for many years.

"You just haven't used the jargon," I told her. "You've got to use the language *they* use in order to become one of them." To illustrate, I wrote down fifteen or twenty of the key terms, the buzzwords that I knew were current in that particular field at the time; alongside each I wrote its equivalent in Plain English.

"Look," I said, "let's make an experiment. Just plug these buzzwords into your application—don't change anything else, not even the sentence structure—just substitute these jargon terms for yours, retype it, and send it in. Let's see what happens."

If you have some sense of how the world works these days you can probably guess the end of the story: Several weeks later, on the basis of the newly jargonized application, my friend was admitted to the program—with a scholarship.

This story revealed something that I had acknowledged previously but had never seen so starkly exposed: that language has assumed an exceptional importance in our society today, not only defining the basic technology and concepts (or **hardware** and **software**, as the computer people would say) of scores of different fields, from auto mechanics to wine tasting, but also forming the basis for admission and access to those fields—or exclusion from them. Who among us, after all, has not stood glassy-eyed during a mechanic's abrupt yet arcane explanation of an insanely expensive car repair? Or strained to decipher the Latinate crypticisms of a doctor's pronouncements? Or sighed at a bureaucrat's interminable terminology? We are all at least subliminally aware that professionals, or any group of people in a closed organization or society, use a specialized version of the language—not only to communicate with each other but to effectively exclude outsiders, whether these be customers, clients, applicants, or simply laypersons. We sense, even if we do not consciously understand, that language is power; and that, not knowing the language when we are in the other party's territory, we are powerless.

This was my initial perspective on the subject, engendered not only by the incident I have described but by years of linguistic encounters with doctors and lawyers, repairmen and therapists, not to mention several bouts of government employment. I determined to write a book that would empower consumers to do battle with the professionals by knowing their language—in order to prevent both the abuse of their rights and their pocketbooks and the abuse of language that the rampancy of jargon represented. I knew that jargon—or, to be more precise, specialized and nonpublic language of any kind—was a distortion, an illness, a corruption of Mother English. This is a viewpoint shared by many learned writers on the language today, and certainly familiar to anyone who has been exploited at the hands of a jargon-toting professional. I was in full agreement with George Bernard Shaw, who wrote: "Every profession is a conspiracy against the layman."

As I worked on the book, however—hiring researchers who had worked in different fields, interviewing professionals and specialists of all kinds, reading hundreds of books, trade magazines, and "internal communications"—I started to see things differently. I found that each variation on the language, much as it might be abused, contained something fascinating that I had not expected: It revealed the basic mind-set, the underlying style of thinking and perceiving, of each singular discipline and the people who inhabit it.

When a group of people witness, for example, an automobile accident, how each of them perceives the event will be in some measure determined by the language each regularly employs. The doctor will observe **contusions** and **lacerations** and **hemorrhage**; the attorney will consider **civil liabilities** and **criminal negligence**; the mechanic will see crushed **fenders** and bent **axles**; the psychologist will think of *stress reactions, trauma,* and *guilt.* This is not to imply that each of them will not also view the event on a purely human scale, as injury and pain caused by some error of judgment or lapse of skill. Each of these people, however, views the event from a specialized, professional point of view at least in part because each of them *has a language with which to do so.* Much of what we call thought is a kind of internal verbalization, and when we have used a particular variation of the language frequently and fluently enough, it shapes our way of seeing the world, of experiencing events, of *thinking.*

Thus I began to feel that there was something to be learned from the jargons, and that in fact it was much more interesting to have these different dialects in existence than to live in a perfectly homogeneous linguistic universe. The *existence* of jargon, I came to believe, is not the problem, but rather the *abuse* of jargon: the deliberate barriers set up to keep others from learning it, the exploitative uses of specialized terminology, and the sheer lack of knowledge on the part of most people.

In this spirit I continued on, my purpose now being not to destroy jargon but to open it up, to make it available to all those who would want or need to know. To those who would "defend" the language from specialization and change, moreover, I can only point out that all the greatest users of our language, from Chaucer to Shakespeare to Dylan Thomas, have changed it in the service of their art. When Thomas writes, "The cats nap in the slant corners or lope sly, streaking and needling, on the one cloud of the roofs," or

> This day winding down now . . . In the torrent salmon sun,
> In my seashaken house
> On a breakneck of rocks
> tangled with chirrup and fruit,

he may be "ungrammatical" or "incorrect" from one point of view, but it is just such creative uses of the language that make it stronger; the innovation and change that make it not moribund, but alive. And, similarly, when a jazz musician says, "Did you **dig** the **lines** that **cat** was **running**? That **horn** can **wail**!" this is a style of language use I would not want to try to eliminate—but only to appreciate and understand.

It is not only the major professions and subcultures that have their own styles and vocabularies; many much smaller social units do, as well. Often within a single family, between brothers and sisters, or between lovers or old friends there exists a special, secret language, unknown to the rest of the world, which carries an intimate set of meanings and associations. In my own experience I have found these to be among the most beautiful forms in which language can be used.

For the purpose of language is nothing more or less than *communication:* and I am proposing, therefore, that language is "good" only when it communicates, and "bad" only when it does not. I have attempted in this book to provide the means by which we can all communicate with each other more effectively, more knowingly, and more joyfully—to move through all the different territories of the language, to play with the many variations on the theme of English. My own personal image for the book is that of the Rosetta Stone—the great archeological discovery of the late eighteenth century that provided the key to translating the theretofore undecipherable hieroglyphics of ancient Egypt; except that here we are seeking to unlock not the mysteries of forgotten civilizations but the realities of modern American life.

Finally, I want to justify, or at least explain, the inclusion of certain subjects in the book and the exclusion of others. My primary set of standards held that the topics included should be timely and current; involve large numbers of people or have significant impact on our society and the rest of the world; and have a clearly defined sublanguage that many people would benefit from understanding. Beyond this, several sections were included solely because they interested *me* greatly and I chose to exercise my author's prerogative to write them for that reason alone. Also, I was obliged to eliminate quite a few chapters that were valid by one or the other of these criteria, but which due to the implacable march of time and the constraints of the publishing business simply didn't get on the ark before the rains came.

In the hope, then, that you will use and enjoy this book, and the language itself, with boldness and good spirit, I take my leave.

Cambridge, Massachusetts
February 8, 1981
Just before dawn

I

TERMS THAT EVERYONE NEEDS TO KNOW

[1]

Medicine

The language of the medical profession is almost a foreign tongue, replete with tens of thousands of words and phrases that do not appear anywhere else in the general vocabulary, but which suddenly intrude into the layperson's language on the occasion of someone's illness.

Medicalese is predominantly based upon Latin and Greek, though in its usage classically derived polysyllabisms (see below) are sprocketed with abbreviations, acronyms, jargon, and slang. Thus one **resident** might say to another, "That **cholecystectomy** in the **OR** had an **MI** and boxed"—blithely mixing technical terms, abbreviations, and med-school slang to describe the death by heart failure of a person who was undergoing a routine gall-bladder operation.

Medicalese characteristically describes patients in terms of their disorders and their (diseased) organs and parts. To some extent this is the natural and inevitable shorthand for a profession whose practitioners see many sick and injured patients each week and cannot possibly afford the time or emotional energy to relate personally to each one of them—after a while learning to see only the broken arms and inflamed throats, but not the faces of the people they belong to.

Thus a doctor will refer to a **myasthenic anorexic** when describing a weak and frightened fifteen-year-old girl who has eaten no solid food for over a month and is wasting away because of some unnamed emotional trauma. This style of language and perception is necessary but also reflects the profession's tendency to regard the magnificent and complex human being as a machine. The doctor, in this way of thinking, must be a precise and logical technician—fueling, lubricating, maintaining, repairing—even, in these days of transplants, bypass grafts, and prostheses, replacing worn or damaged parts.

This depersonalized professionalism is established and sustained

3

effectively through the use of medical terminology and jargon. The inside language also serves to insulate medical professionals from their patient/clients, maintaining the mystique of the doctors' omniscience and infallibility, and denying to all but the most resolutely self-educated very much choice in determining the nature and extent of and possible alternatives to their treatment.

In the interest of more evenly sharing the knowledge inherent in medical language, and to enable the nonmedical person to converse intelligently with doctors and nurses—in short, in the interest of better medical care—we present this section.

On the Construction of Medical Terms

The vast majority of medical terms are constructed from a relatively small group of Latin (and in some cases, Greek) roots, prefixes, and suffixes. The suffix *-itis,* for example, meaning inflammation, can be combined with scores of roots that refer to body parts or organs, to form such terms as **arthritis** (inflammation of the joints), **nephritis** (of the kidneys), gastritis (of the stomach), and so on. The prefix *hyper-,* meaning excessive or extreme, combines with root words to produce such terms as **hyperglycemia** (high blood sugar), **hypercholesteremia** (excessive cholesterol in the blood), and **hyperthyroidism** (overfunction of the thyroid gland). The following list of major suffixes and prefixes will enable the reader to have some understanding of medical terms he or she may hear, even if they have never been encountered before. ❧

COMMON PREFIXES	MEANING	EXAMPLE
a-, an-	without, lacking	asymptomatic (lacking symptoms)
dys-	painful, difficult	dyspnea (labored breathing)
derm-	skin	dermatitis (inflammation of skin)
gastr-	stomach	gastroscopy (visual inspection of stomach)
hem-, hema-, hemo-	blood	hemorrhage (bleeding)
hyper-	excessive, over	hyperkinetic (showing excessive movement)
hypo-	diminished, deficient	hypoglycemia (low blood sugar)
hystero-	uterus	hysterectomy (surgical removal of uterus)
myo-	muscle	myocardium (heart muscle)
neuro-	nerve	neuralgia (pain along nerve)
nephr-	kidney	nephrologist (kidney specialist)
therm-	heat, temperature	thermoplegia (sunstroke)

COMMON SUFFIXES	MEANING	EXAMPLE
-algia	pain	dentalgia (toothache)
-dynia	pain	arthrodynia (joint pain)
-ectomy	surgical removal of	appendectomy (removal of appendix)
-emia	blood	hypercholesteremia (high cholesterol in blood)
-genic, -genetic	caused by	psychogenic (caused by the mind)
-gram	picture, measure, tracing	cardiogram (tracing of heart activity)
-graph	recording instrument	electromyograph (device to record muscle activity)
-itis	inflammation	bursitis (inflammation of a bursa)
-oid	resembling	chancroid (resembling a chancre)
-ology	science of, study of, specialty	cardiology (study of heart function and disease)
-oma	tumor, growth	carcinoma (cancerous tumor)
-ostomy	surgical opening	colostomy (opening created in the colon)
-otomy	surgical incision	laparotomy (incision into abdominal wall)
-plegia	paralysis	paraplegia (paralysis of lower body)
-rhage, -rhagia	sudden flow, discharge	hemorrhage (bleeding)
-rhea	flow	rhinorrhea (runny nose)
-uria	urine	polyuria (excessive urination)

Medical Personnel

The medical profession has become increasingly specialized, with very few doctors practicing general medicine as did the old "family doctor" of times past. Modern medical knowledge and technology have become so complex that no single physician can keep up with the advances in every field. Thus it is imperative that the layperson understand both the various specialties within the medical profession, and the other types of medical personnel (nurses, technicians, etc.) who may be encountered at a hospital or clinic. The following guide will enable you to distinguish one *-ologist* from another. 🐛

allergist: A doctor who treats allergic conditions.

anesthesiologist: A doctor who specializes in administering **anesthesia**, and the study of anesthesiological science.

anesthetist: One who administers **anesthesia**, often a nurse or technician who is not a physician.

attending: The senior physician responsible for a patient.

cardiologist: A specialist in the treatment of heart disease.

clinician: A practicing physician, expecially one who devotes most of his time to treating patients (as opposed to doing research, for example).

dermatologist: A specialist in skin disorders.

endocrinologist: A specialist in the study and treatment of endocrine-gland disorders.

family practitioner: A doctor trained to treat the majority of ailments and illnesses, except for those that require the skills of a specialist (**cardiologist, surgeon, gynecologist,** etc.).

fellow: A physician in an advanced stage of medical training, following **internship** and **residency**, usually in a subspecialty such as heart disease.

gastroenterologist: A specialist in disorders of the stomach and intestines, and related organs (esophagus, pancreas, etc.).

G.P.: General practitioner, a **family** or **primary care** physician.

gynecologist: A specialist in disorders specific only to women, especially those of the reproductive/sexual organs. Gynecologists are frequently **obstetricians** as well and are referred to by the combination abbreviation OB/GYN.

hematologist: A specialist in disorders of the blood and the blood-forming organs.

hepatologist: A specialist in liver disorders.

house officers, house staff: The **interns** and **residents** of a hospital, who are physicians-in-training, one–three years out of medical school.

intern: A recent medical school graduate serving in a hospital to receive training by treating patients under the supervision of medical staff. (Not to be confused with **internist**, below.)

internist: A specialist in internal medicine, which is the diagnosis and treatment of disorders of the internal organs not requiring surgical procedures.

L.P.N.: Licensed practical nurse, trained to care for patients but not a diplomaed graduate of a school of nursing.

M.D.: Medical doctor, commonly called a doctor or a physician. A person who has successfully completed medical school and is licensed to practice medicine.

nephrologist: A specialist in kidney function and disorders.

neurologist: A specialist in disorders of the nervous system.

N.P.: Nurse practitioner; a trained but unlicensed nursing staffperson.

obstetrician: A physician who treats women during pregnancy and childbirth; responsible for the actual delivering of babies. Abbreviation OB/GYN for obstetrician/gynecologist.

oncologist: A specialist in the study and treatment of tumors; a cancer/specialist.

ophthalmologist: The ophthalmologist is an M.D. who is licensed to perform surgery and treat all medical problems involving the eyes; not to be confused with an *optometrist,* who measures and tests the eyesight, or an *optician,* who makes or sells glasses and contact lenses. Neither of the latter two is a physician.

orthopedist: A specialist in diseases and conditions of the locomotor structures of the body, such as muscles, bones, joints, tendons.

otolaryngologist, otorhinolaryngologist: A specialist in disorders of the ear, nose, and throat. Commonly called an ENT.

pathologist: A specialist in diagnosing diseases through the examination of tissue removed from the patient's body.

pediatrician: A specialist in treating children.

physical therapist: A person (usually not an M.D.) trained to administer **physical therapy** (massage, heat, exercise, etc.) as prescribed by a physician. Abbreviated P.T.

podiatrist: A specialist (generally not an M.D.) in treating disorders of the feet.

positive test result: A result which indicates the presence of the disease or condition being tested for. For example, a *positive* **Glucose Tolerance Test** result would indicate the presence of a **hypoglycemic** condition.

primary care: Referring to the physician or medical facility from which one receives basic, everyday medical treatment: routine checkups, vaccinations, treatment for minor disorders. Generally a **G.P.** or local health clinic.

proctologist: A specialist in diseases of the colon, rectum, and anus.

psychiatrist: A specialist in disorders of the mind who, unlike most psychologists and psychotherapists, is a licensed medical doctor.

radiologist: A specialist in the use of X-rays and radioactive substances, for both diagnostic and therapeutic purposes.

resident: A doctor continuing his training after **intern**ship as part of a hospital staff; usually learning a specialty.

rheumatologist: A specialist in arthritic conditions and other disorders involving the joints.

R.N.: Registered nurse; a person who has graduated from an accredited school of nursing and is licensed to care for the sick, wounded, and infirm.

surgeon: A specialist in treating patients through operative procedures (surgery). Surgical subspecialties include, among many others, thoracic (chest) surgery, plastic surgery, and orthopedic surgery.

urologist: A specialist in treating disorders of the urinary tract in both sexes and the genital tract in the male (including kidneys, ureter, bladder, prostate, penis, urethra, and testes.)

visit: A senior physician who makes teaching **rounds** in order to supervise cases and instruct **interns** and **residents**.

300 MEDICAL TERMS THAT EVERYONE NEEDS TO KNOW

abscess: A localized collection of pus, caused by the disintegration of surrounding **tissue**.

acute: Severe; sharp; developing rapidly. *acute abdomen:* any abdominal condition requiring immediate operation. (See **chronic**.)

ambulatory: Able to walk; not confined to bed (referring to a patient or injured person).

amniocentesis: Tapping a small amount of amniotic fluid from the womb of a pregnant woman to test for abnormalities of the fetus (unborn child).

anemia: A condition in which there is a reduction in the number of red blood cells or the amount of **hemoglobin** in the blood, producing weakness, pallor, and fatigue.

anesthesia: Partial or complete loss of sensation (feeling), usually induced to make surgery easier. *General anesthesia* affects the entire body, including the brain and produces loss of consciousness. *Local anesthesia* eliminates sensation in a specific part of the body, while the patient remains conscious and awake.

aneurysm: Abnormal dilatation (stretching) of a portion of a blood vessel. An extremely dangerous condition.

angina pectoris: Tightness, pain, or oppression in the chest, sometimes radiating to the left arm. Most commonly caused by coronary artery disorder.

angiogram: The injection of radiopaque material (dyes) into a blood vessel, followed by a series of X-rays, which reveals the size and shape of the veins and arteries.

anorexia: Lack or loss of appetite.

anorexia nervosa: Chronic loss of appetite due to psychological causes; primarily occurring among young women.

antibiotic: Any of a variety of substances (both natural and synthetic) that inhibit the growth of or destroy bacteria; commonly employed to treat a wide variety of infectious diseases. The best-known antibiotic is penicillin.

antihistamine: A medication to counteract an allergic condition.

antiseptic: Preventing decay, putrefaction, or sepsis; any agent that inhibits or destroys bacteria.

Apgar score: A system for scoring an infant's condition one minute after birth. Heart rate, respiration, muscle tone, color, and response to stimuli are scored 0, 1, or 2; highest score is 10. Infants with low Apgar scores require immediate attention in order to survive.

aphasia: Loss of ability to express oneself verbally or to comprehend speech.

apnea: Cessation of breathing, usually temporary.

arrhythmia: Absence or irregularity of rhythm; especially, *cardiac arrhythmia,* irregular heart beat.

arteriosclerosis: Thickening, hardening, and loss of elasticity of the walls of blood vessels, especially arteries. (See **atherosclerosis.**)

arthritis: Inflammation of a joint, usually painful and often producing actual structural change in the joint.

articulation: The connection of two or more bones; a joint.

asphyxia: A decrease in the amount of oxygen and an increase in the amount of carbon dioxide in the body as a result of some interference with normal breathing; suffocation.

aspiration: The drawing of a fluid or solid into the respiratory tract; also, removal of fluids *from* the body, by suction.

atherosclerosis: A form of **arteriosclerosis** marked by fatty deposits on the inner lining of the arteries. One of the major causes of arterial **occlusion** (blockage).

auscultation: Listening for sounds in some of the body cavities (especially the chest and abdomen), in order to detect abnormal conditions. Generally accomplished with a stethoscope.

autoimmune disease: Disease in which the body produces a disordered response against itself, reacting to its own **tissues** as if they were foreign substances such as bacteria or toxins.

autonomic nervous system: That part of the nervous system that controls involuntary bodily functions: the actions of the glands, all internal organs, the circulation of blood, and digestion.

barium enema/upper G.I. Series: A procedure used to determine if there is cancer or any other irregularities of the **gastrointestinal**

tract. The barium enema is followed by an X-ray of the large intestine.

benign: Not dangerous; not **malignant**; not recurrent; mild. Used most commonly in referring to **tumors** that are not cancerous.

biopsy: Surgical removal of a piece of live **tissue** for microscopic examination.

blood count: See **CBC**.

blood pressure: Abbreviated BP; the force or pressure exerted by the heart in pumping blood from its chambers; also, the pressure exerted by the blood on the walls of any vessel. Each BP reading ("120 over 80," for example, written 120/80) consists of two figures: 1. the **systolic** pressure (the upper figure, indicating the greatest force exerted by the heart during contraction); and 2. the **diastolic** pressure (the lower reading, indicating the arteries at rest between heartbeats). Systolic pressures above 140 and diastolic above 90 are considered abnormally high.

BMR: Basal Metabolic Rate; a measurement of the amount of energy expended by the body when at rest. A basic test of thyroid gland function.

brachycardia, bradycardia: Abnormally slow heartbeat.

bubo: An inflamed, swollen, or enlarged lymph node.

B.U.N.: Blood Urea Nitrogen; a basic test for kidney function.

bursa: A padlike sac or cavity found in connecting **tissue**, usually in the vicinity of joints.

bursitis: Inflammation of a **bursa**, especially between bony prominences and muscle or tendon (shoulder, knee, etc.).

CABG: Coronary Artery Bypass Graft; a heart operation in which a blocked artery to the heart is bypassed by the attachment of a vein which has been grafted from the patient's leg.

calcification: The depositing of calcium salts in the body **tissues**, producing abnormal hardness.

calculus: An abnormal, hard, stonelike mass

within the body, usually composed of mineral salts; commonly called a stone. (For example, *renal calculus:* kidney stone.)

calor: Heat; moderate heat of fever. Along with rubor (redness), tumor (swelling), and dolor (pain), it is one of the four classic signs of inflammation.

carcinogenic: Causing cancer. In the past few years, the number of known and suspected cancer-causing agents (*carcinogens*) has multiplied dramatically, to the point where many scientists now feel that the vast majority of cancers are caused, or triggered, by environmental toxins such as asbestos, cigarette smoke, and a host of industrial and agricultural chemicals.

carcinoma: A **malignant tumor** of organ-lining cells. May affect almost any organ or part of the body and spread through the bloodstream.

cardiac: Of or pertaining to the heart. *Cardiac arrest* is heart failure.

cardiogram: A graph of the electrical activity of the heart muscle, which provides important information on heart function and disorder. Also called **electrocardiogram** and commonly abbreviated **ECG** or **EKG**.

cardiovascular: Pertaining to the heart and blood vessels. Cardiovascular fitness is best achieved through a program of prolonged, moderate exercise such as walking, running, swimming, or bicycling.

catalepsy: A trancelike, immobile state with loss of voluntary movement and power of speech.

cataract: A condition in which the lens of the eye or its enclosing membrane becomes opaque; i.e., light cannot travel through it. Usually treated by surgical removal of the lens.

catatonia: A psychological condition in which the patient is unresponsive, does not talk, move or react. Also, a condition of stupor or immobility.

CAT scan: Computerized Axial Tomography; a technique of advanced computerized photography which takes a large number of X-ray photographs of the body in parallel slices and thus produces accurate information in three dimensions.

cautery, cauterization: A means of deliberately destroying **tissue** through electricity, heat, or use of corrosive chemicals.

CBC: Complete Blood Count; a set of five tests to determine the red and white blood cell content of the blood, **hematocrit** and **hemoglobin** levels, and the distribution of various types of white blood cells.

CCU: Coronary Care Unit; a specially equipped area of a hospital for providing intensive care for **coronary** patients.

cerebellum: The lower portion of the brain, involved in the coordination of voluntary muscular movements and balance.

cerebrum: The largest part of the brain, consisting of two hemispheres separated by a deep longitudinal fissure. The cerebrum interprets sensory impressions, directs voluntary muscular activities, and is the center for all higher mental functions: learning, memory, reasoning, consciousness, creativity.

Cesarean section: The delivery of a child by means of incision into the uterus, usually through the abdominal wall.

chancre: A hard genital sore that is the first sign of syphilis.

chemotherapy: The use of **cytotoxic** (poisonous to cells) drugs to treat diseases, especially cancer, based on the premise that the drug will have a more destructive effect on the cancer cells than on the normal cells of the body.

chronic: Prolonged; drawn out; not **acute**, as, for example, chronic bronchitis.

CNS: Central nervous system; consisting of those parts of the brain, spinal cord, various nerves, and organs that control consciousness and voluntary movement. Also referred to as the **voluntary nervous system** and the **cerebrospinal system**.

cobalt therapy: A particular form of radiation

therapy (employing radioactive cobalt-60) used to combat **malignancies**.

coma: An abnormal deep stupor occurring as a result of illness or injury. The patient cannot be roused by external stimuli.

congenital: Present at birth; as a congenital defect.

coronary: Pertaining to those blood vessels that supply blood to the heart. Used as medical shorthand for *coronary occlusion,* or blockage of a coronary artery. Coronary occlusion, also referred to as *coronary thrombosis,* is the primary cause of a heart attack.

cortisone: A hormone naturally secreted from the cortex of the adrenal gland and important in the regulation of metabolism; also prepared synthetically and widely prescribed for a great variety of disorders. A powerful and often dangerous drug.

crisis: The turning point of an illness, often indicated by a long sleep with profuse sweating. Also, a severe or painful period in the course of a disease.

critical: 1. At the turning point of a disease. (See **crisis**.) 2. In extreme danger; at a point where survival is in question.

cumulative drugs: Those which, after being taken into the body in repeated small doses, are not eliminated, but tend to accumulate in the system and eventually produce symptoms of poisoning.

curettage: The scraping of a cavity. (*Uterine curettage* is the scraping of the uterus, done following an abortion or to obtain specimens of **tissue** for use in diagnosis.)

CVA: Cerebrovascular accident, also known as a **cerebral hemorrhage**; commonly called a **stroke**. The result of a **sclerosed** or diseased blood vessel in the brain; often associated with high blood pressure. May result in death, or in partial paralysis, with speech and memory loss.

cyanosis: Bluish, grayish, slatelike, or dark purple discoloration of the skin due to poor circulation or insufficient oxygen in the bloodstream.

cyst: A closed sac or pouch containing fluid or semifluid material; usually an abnormal structure.

D and C: Dilatation (stretching) of the cervix and **curettage** of the uterus; a surgical procedure often performed to see if there is any cancer of the uterus.

D. C. Van Dissel: A mnemonic device used by doctors to check off all the necessary procedures in admitting a patient to a hospital: *Di*agnosis, *C*ondition, *V*ital signs, *A*mbulation, *N*ursing orders, *D*iet, *I*ntake and output, *S*ymptomatic drugs, *S*pecific drugs, *E*xaminations, *L*aboratory.

deciduoma: A uterine tumor, thought to arise from portions of the uterine lining cells retained in the uterus following an abortion.

dehydration: A dangerous condition occurring when the body's intake of water does not equal water loss. May occur through actual deprivation of drinking water, water loss from severe sweating or diarrhea, or reduction in quantity of body salts and electrolytes.

diabetes mellitus: Usually abbreviated to **diabetes**. A **chronic** and serious disease, in which insufficient insulin is produced by the pancreas to **metabolize** (burn up) carbohydrates, resulting in dangerously high blood sugar levels and other complications if untreated.

diagnosis: 1. The accurate description and naming of a disease or disorder. 2. The process by which a physician determines the nature and the cause of a disease, employing the patient's history, signs and **symptoms**, special tests, lab results, etc. The diagnosis then becomes the basis for treatment.

diastolic pressure: See **blood pressure**.

dyspnea: Difficult, painful, or labored breathing.

ECG or **EKG: Electrocardiogram**; also known as **cardiogram**; a graph of the electrical activity of the heart muscle. The ECG is one of the most basic tools in the diagnosis and monitoring of patients with heart disorders.

echo: Short for **echography**; the use of ultrasound to "bounce" sound waves off body tissues of different density, for diagnostic purposes.

eclampsia: A major **toxemia** (blood poisoning) of pregnancy, which endangers both mother and child. Accompanied by high blood pressure, convulsions, and **coma**.

ectopic pregnancy: A pregnancy taking place in the fallopian tube (or elsewhere), rather than in the uterus. Surgical termination is usually required.

edema: Excessive accumulation of fluid in the body tissues, causing swelling.

EEG: Electroencephalogram; the recording of electrical activity of the brain (brain waves), giving a picture of brain function and disorder.

embolism: The obstruction of a blood vessel by a blood clot or by foreign substances.

EMG: Electromyogram; a recording of electrical impulses that pass through a muscle as it contracts and relaxes.

emphysema: A condition in which the air spaces in the lung become distended or ruptured, making breathing more difficult.

endocrine glands: Glands that secrete their hormones into the bloodstream. Three major endocrine glands are the pituitary, the thyroid, and the adrenals.

endoscopy: Observation of the inside of a body cavity or organ by means of various instruments (for example, a proctoscope).

episode: An attack of an illness that tends to recur at intervals.

epithelioma: A cancerous tumor of the skin.

ER: Emergency room, also, *EW:* emergency ward. Special room(s) in a hospital where immediate treatment is given for serious ailments. Often the only facility in a hospital that is open on a twenty-four-hour basis.

erythrocyte: A red blood cell. The major function of the red blood cells is to carry oxygen to, and carbon dioxide from, the cells.

ESR: Erythrocyte Sedimentation Rate, also, **Sedimentation Rate** or **Sed Rate**; a laboratory test of the rate at which red blood cells settle. ESR results are important in diagnoses of many infectious diseases, pregnancy, and cancer.

estrogen: The female sex hormone, produced by the ovaries.

etiology: The study of the causes of disease; also, the causes of a specific disorder.

excision: The surgical cutting away or taking out of any tissue.

fibrillation: Irregular quivering action of a muscle. Fibrillation of the heart usually indicates a failing heart which requires support. (See **ventricular fibrillation**.)

fibroids: Benign tumors of the uterus, often removed surgically.

frozen section: A technique for analyzing a **biopsy** specimen obtained at surgery to determine within minutes—while the patient is still in surgery—whether any **malignancy** is present.

FUO: Fever of unknown origin.

gastric: Pertaining to the stomach.

gastric lavage: Washing out of the stomach (to empty it of poisons, or in preparation for surgery).

gastroenteritis: Inflammation, usually acute, of the stomach and intestines.

gastrointestinal: Abbreviated **G.I.**; pertaining to the stomach and intestines.

generic-name drug: A drug sold under its technical name; a nonpatented drug. A generic drug is almost always cheaper than the same drug sold under a brand name.

geriatrics: The study and treatment of diseases affecting old people. Also known as *gerontology*.

G.I. Series: See **barium enema**.

glaucoma: An eye disease characterized by unusually high pressure within the eyeball. May be mild, **acute**, or **chronic**.

Glucose Tolerance Test: Abbreviated **GTT**; a blood test performed to determine the body's ability to **metabolize** sugar; a specific test for **diabetes** and **hypoglycemia**.

gonad: A sex gland, either male (testicle) or female (ovary).

Guaiac Test: A test for occult (hidden) blood in the stool.

Hematocrit Test: A blood test to determine the relative proportion of red blood cells to **plasma**. In **anemia**, the relative number of red blood cells is decreased.

hematoma: A swelling or tumor underneath the skin that contains blood; usually resulting from an injury such as a direct blow.

hemoglobin: The pigment in red blood cells. Hemoglobin is the substance that carries oxygen from the lungs to the tissues.

hemorrhage: Bleeding; the escape of blood from the blood vessels, either externally or internally.

hepatic: Of or pertaining to the liver.

herpes: An acute viral inflammation of the skin, characterized by small pustular blisters. *Herpes Simplex I* is a "cold sore." *Herpes Simplex II* affects the genital organs and is transmitted through sexual contact. It is one of the most rapidly proliferating venereal diseases today, and may have severe consequences if present in a woman at the time of childbirth.

histology: Study of the minute structure of body tissue; generally refers to examination of material under the microscope.

hypercholesteremia: Excess cholesterol in the blood.

hyperglycemia: Excessive sugar in the blood, as found in **diabetes mellitus**.

hyperkinetic: Showing excessive movement.

hypertension: High blood pressure. In general, a **systolic** pressure above 140 or a **diastolic** above 90 is considered high.

hypoglycemia: Low levels of glucose (sugar) in the blood. Also referred to as *hyperinsulinism*.

Symptoms may include fatigue, restlessness, malaise, irritability, weakness. Commonly called "low blood sugar."

hysterectomy: The surgical removal of the uterus.

I and D: Abbreviation for **incision and drainage** (of an **abscess**).

iatrogenic: Caused by medical treatment (such as the side effects of a prescribed drug), or through medical error or incompetence. The Public Interest Health Research Group statistics show some 16,000 iatrogenic deaths per year.

ICU: Intensive Care Unit; a specially equipped area of a hospital in which critically ill patients are carefully monitored and attended around the clock.

idiopathic: Of unknown cause, such as an idiopathic infection.

IM: Intramuscular(ly); into the muscle. Usually shorthand for an injection of fluid into some muscle mass of the body, commonly the upper arm or buttock.

immune: Protected or exempt from a disease (as by vaccination, immunization, or heredity).

incubation period: The time between exposure to a disease and its appearance.

induration: An area of hardened tissue, such as might be found around the edges of an inflamed wound.

infarct, infarction: The death of an area of tissue due to the stoppage of its blood supply. (See **myocardial infarction**.)

infusion: The injection of a solution into a vein or beneath the skin.

innervation: The nerve supply to an organ or part of the body.

insult: Damage to an organ or part of the body; **trauma**.

in utero: Unborn; within the uterus.

irradiation: See **radiotherapy**.

ischemia: Temporary lack of blood supply to an organ or body part due to spasm of the artery or other obstruction of circulation.

IV: Intravenous(ly); generally used to refer to any injection of fluid directly into a vein.

jaundice: A condition characterized by yellowness of the skin and eyes; a symptom of several disorders, including hepatitis.

KUB: Kidneys, Ureter, Bladder; an X-ray of the abdominal area.

laparotomy: An incision into the abdomen; also, an abdominal operation of any kind.

LD: Lethal dose.

lesion: A widely used medical term, applied to almost any area of altered, wounded, or infected tissue. Examples are **chancres**, **pustules**, **tumors**, rashes, **ulcers**, **abscesses**, and scars.

leukocytes: White blood cells, used by the body to combat infection.

ligation: The tying off of a blood vessel (or other structure), usually as part of a surgical procedure. The thread or wire used is called a *ligature.*

lipids: Fats or fatlike substances found in the body that are not soluble in water (for example, cholesterol).

lipoma: A commonly occurring, non**malignant** fatty **tumor**.

lithotomy: The surgical removal of a stone (for example, a kidney stone).

lordosis: Excessive arching of the lower back; swayback.

lumbar puncture: Abbreviated **LP**; the insertion of a needle into the spinal canal to withdraw a small amount of spinal fluid for diagnostic purposes. An LP is also used to inject fluid (e.g., an anesthetic solution) into the spinal canal. Generally called a *spinal tap.*

lymph: The fluid derived from connective tissue and in tissue spaces between organs, traveling through lymph *ducts* and *nodes.*

malignancy: A cancerous **tumor** or growth.

malignant: Harmful; deadly; virulent. Usually refers to cancerous **tumors**. The opposite of **benign**.

mammography: An X-ray examination of the female breasts, especially for the possible detection of breast cancer. Excessive mammography, however, has in some cases been considered itself the cause of such cancers.

masking of symptoms: The concealment of a disorder or its real cause, due to the effects of drugs or to other factors.

massage, cardiac: An emergency measure undertaken when the heart has stopped; the chest is opened and the heart is actually squeezed by hand.

mastectomy: Surgical removal of a breast. A *radical mastectomy* involves removal of the breast and some of the chest-wall muscle and the **lymph** nodes under the arm.

Master Two-Step Test: An exercise test for coronary circulation. The subject steps up on and down from a nine-inch-high stool at a given pace. The heart rate and **EKG** measurements are taken.

melanoma: A serious form of cancer derived from pigmented cells; a mole that has become **malignant**.

membrane: A thin, soft, pliable layer of tissue that lines, covers, or separates an organ or other part of the body.

metabolism: All energy and material transformations that take place within living cells; especially, the process by which foods are transformed into useful elements for energy and growth.

metastasize: To spread from one part of the body to another, generally referring to the spreading of cancer.

mitoses: Literally, cell divisions; now a euphemism for cancer.

morbid: Diseased; pertaining to disease.

morbidity rate: The incidence of disease in a population, usually expressed as the number of cases per 1,000 or 100,000 persons per year.

murmur: A heart sound heard during **auscultation**, caused by turbulent blood flow. Some murmurs are quite harmless, while others may indicate heart disease (such as a leaking heart valve).

myalgia: Tenderness or pain in the muscles.

myasthenia: Muscular weakness. *Myasthenia gravis* is a serious, debilitating disease associated with the wasting of muscles.

myeloma: Cancer of the bone marrow.

myocardial infarction: Abbreviated **M.I.**; damage to the heart muscle, usually caused by a blockage of the blood supply due to **coronary** artery **occlusion**. This is the typical cause of a heart attack.

narcosis: Deep stupor or unconsciousness, produced by a drug.

necrosis: The death of areas of body tissue or bone, surrounded by healthy parts.

negative test result: Result indicating the absence of the disease or condition being tested for, as a negative **Wassermann test** result indicates no sign of syphilis.

neoplasm: Any new, abnormal growth of tissue. Although some neoplasms are **benign**, the word is often used as a synonym or euphemism for cancer.

neurasthenia: Lack of energy, weakness, fatigue, exhaustion, and other physical symptoms, usually associated with depression or another neurotic emotional condition.

NPO: Not by mouth, from the Latin, *non per ora.*

objective signs: Those conditions that can be seen, felt, observed or measured by a physician (such as pulse rate, temperature, blood pressure); as distinct from subjective **symptoms** (pain, itching, etc.), which only the patient experiences.

occlusion: A closure or shutting off, as of the blood flow in a clotted blood vessel.

occult blood: Blood loss concealed (in the stool, for example) and revealed only by chemical or microscopic examination.

operative risk: An estimation of how well or poorly a patient can be expected to withstand surgery. A bad or poor operative risk may not survive surgical treatment.

orthopedics: The branch of medicine concerned with disorders of the locomotor structures of the body: muscles, joints, bones, tendons, etc.

orthopnea: The inability to breathe except when sitting or standing up; often associated with severe heart conditions.

ossification: The transformation of nonbony tissue (e.g., cartilage) into bone.

osteoarthritis: Degenerative inflammation of joints, with damage to cartilage and bone.

otitis: Inflammation of the inner ear.

P and V: Pyloroplasty and vagotomy; the basic anti**ulcer** operation.

palliative treatment: Treatment that relieves symptoms but does not cure the disease.

palpation: Feeling a body organ or part by hand in order to make a diagnosis.

papilloma: A *benign* (noncancerous) growth of skin or mucous membrane, such as warts, polyps, etc.

Pap Test, Pap smear: Papanicolaou test; a test for the early detection of cancer. Shed cells, especially from the cervix and vagina, are stained and examined under the microscope.

papule: A pimple, or other red elevated area on the skin, such as those occurring in measles, chicken pox, eczema, syphilis, etc.

paresis: Partial or incomplete paralysis.

pathological: Diseased; caused by or pertaining to disease.

pathology: 1. The study of the nature and causes of disease. 2. An abnormal condition produced by a disease (as in blood pathology, or muscular pathology).

peptic ulcer: An ulcer of the stomach, duodenum, or lower end of the esophagus.

peritonitis: Infection of the abdominal lining following rupture of the appendix or other intestinal organ.

PFT: Pulmonary Function Test; any of several breathing tests used to determine whether the lungs are functioning properly.

phlebitis: Inflammation of a vein, with pain and

swelling. May lead to the development of a clot (**thrombus**).

phobia: An abnormal or excessive fear (as *acrophobia,* fear of heights).

physical therapy: Abbreviated **PT**; treatment using natural physical agents and methods (such as heat, light, water, massage, and exercises), as distinct from drugs, radiation, or surgery.

placebo: A medicine with no actual useful ingredient (often just a sugar pill), which is given in order to please the patient, or to act as a control in the "double-blind" testing of new medicines. The discovery that placebo drugs or treatments often engender real, significant improvements in patients' conditions has caused many medical professionals to look more deeply into the effect of the mind and emotions on the process of disease and healing.

plasma: The fluid portion of the blood in which the red and white blood cells are suspended; the clear liquid portion of the blood.

pneumonia: Inflammation of the lungs (fatal in 30 percent of those cases not treated with antibiotics); may be caused by bacteria, viruses, dust, and chemical irritants.

PO: By mouth, from the Latin, *per ora.*

poliomyelitis: Inflammation of the gray matter of the spinal cord; also known as *infantile paralysis, epidemic paralysis,* and *polio.* Certain forms of the disease produce muscular paralysis and atrophy, others do not.

polyp: A growth with a kind of stalk (*pedicle*), deriving from the mucous membranes—especially in the nose, uterus, or rectum. Polyps are usually noncancerous.

precancerous: Referring to a **benign** condition that will probably become **malignant** (cancerous).

prep: Short for preparation, or prepare; usually of a patient before surgery.

process: A projection or outgrowth of tissue, especially bone. Generally refers to normal body structures, such as *maxillary process,* the upper jaw.

prognosis: A prediction of the course and outcome of a disease; outlook.

progressive: Advancing; as, a disease going from bad to worse.

prolapse: A falling or dropping down of an organ from its normal position.

prophylaxis: Measures carried out to prevent disease before it occurs. In dentistry, the cleaning and scaling of teeth.

psychosomatic: Pertaining to the mind-body interaction. The term has traditionally been applied to a disorder that is generated and sustained, at least in part, by emotional factors; however, modern medicine has become increasingly cognizant of the psychosomatic nature of many diseases including all those now thought to be caused by stress.

ptosis: The dropping or drooping of an organ or part.

puerperal: Pertaining to or caused by childbirth.

pulmonary: Of or pertaining to the lungs.

purpura: A bleeding into the skin, producing purplish discoloration; there can be several causes.

purulent: Forming or containing pus.

radical treatment: Extreme or extensive treatment (especially surgery) that seeks an absolute cure or elimination of the disease. The opposite is *conservative treatment.*

radiotherapy, radiation therapy: The treatment of disease with radiation (e.g., X-rays) or with radioactive substances. Not to be confused with the use of X-rays for diagnostic purposes (*radiography*).

RBC: Red Blood Count; a measurement of **erythrocyte** levels in the blood.

reduction: Restoration to a normal position, as of a fractured bone.

reflex: An involuntary (uncontrollable) response to a certain stimulus. For example, the "knee-jerk" or *patellar reflex,* which occurs when the knee tendon is struck lightly.

remission: The clearing up of a disease or lessening of its symptoms.

renal: Of or pertaining to the kidneys.

resection: The surgical removal or **excision** of part of a bone or other structure.

Respiratory Distress Syndrome: A condition accounting for more than 25,000 infant deaths per year in the U.S., in which the newborn has serious difficulty breathing due to a membrane covering the air sacs in the lung.

Rh factor: A blood factor present in about 85 percent of all humans, who are designated *Rh Positive* (Rh +). Those without the factor are designated *Rh Negative* (Rh −).

rounds: Part of the daily hospital routine in which one or more doctors tour the hospital to check on every in-patient. *Grand rounds* are conferences at which a group of physicians discuss specific cases.

saline solution: A solution of salt and distilled water; normally 0.85 percent salt.

sarcoma: A cancer arising from underlying tissue such as muscle, bone, and connective tissue.

sclerosis: A hardening of an organ or tissue, especially due to the excessive growth of fibrous tissue.

scoliosis: Abnormal lateral curvature of the spine, usually consisting of two curves, the original one and a compensatory curve in the opposite direction.

section: 1. The process of cutting, as in surgery. 2. A surface or slice of tissue made by cutting. (See **frozen section**.)

sedation: The process of allaying nervous excitement, usually by means of a drug. Also, the resulting state of being calmed.

Sed Rate: See **ESR**.

sepsis: A reaction of the body to bacteria and poisonous products in the bloodstream, including chills, fever, etc.

septicemia: Blood poisoning; a serious condition resulting from the presence of large amounts of bacteria or **toxins** in the blood.

sequela (plural, **sequelae**): A condition following and resulting from a disease.

seroreaction: Reaction to an injection of **serum**, marked by rash, fever, and pain. Also known as *serum sickness*.

serum: The liquid, clear portion of the blood that remains after the blood has clotted— **plasma** minus *fibrinogen* (a clotting agent). Also, any similar fluid in the body that moistens lining membranes. Serum from an animal immune to a specific disease may be injected as protection into a patient with that disease.

shock: A dangerous disturbance associated with reduced oxygen supply to the tissues and reduced blood return to the heart. Shock may be caused by a variety of conditions including bleeding, infection, drug reaction, injury, poisoning, heart attack, and dehydration. Signs of shock are: weak, rapid pulse; pale, clammy skin; drop in blood pressure; extreme thirst.

SIDS: Sudden Infant Death Syndrome; the unexplained death of young infants, usually during unobserved sleep. A variety of explanations have been suggested but none is completely satisfactory. Commonly called *crib death.*

sinus: A canal or passage inside the body; a cavity within a bone; a dilated channel for venous blood; or any other cavity having a relatively narrow opening.

sperm count: A procedure for calculating the number of sperm per ejaculation. Sixty to 120 million per milliliter is considered normal (the average ejaculation is two to six milliliters, or .066 to .2 ounce). Low sperm count may be an indication of infertility.

sphygmomanometer: A device that measures **blood pressure**.

spur: A sharp or pointed growth on a bone, often seen on the heel; not **malignant**.

stenosis: Constriction or narrowing of a passage or opening.

Stress Test: A method of determining the ability of the heart to function under conditions of moderate to extreme exertion. The subject walks, then runs on a continuously moving treadmill (or pedals a stationary bicycle) while his heart function is monitored. Often heart conditions and anomalies show up in the stress test that do not appear in the resting condition.

subacute: Of a condition between **acute** and **chronic**, possibly with some acute characteristics.

subdural hematoma: A blood clot on the brain as a result of head injury.

suture: As a verb, to sew or stitch tissue together. As a noun, the thread or wire used in suturing. Also, the seam or line of union made by such stitching, or in an unmovable **articulation,** such as the skull bones.

sympathetic nervous system: That part of the **autonomic nervous system** which responds to stress and emergency demands by producing **vasoconstriction**, raised **blood pressure**, accelerated heart rate, and depression of **gastrointestinal** activity.

symptoms: Evidences of disease, especially those subjectively experienced by the patient, such as pain, dizziness, weakness, nausea. Often distinguished from *signs*, which are objective manifestations such as a fever or a visible rash.

systemic: Involving the entire body; not localized.

systolic pressure: See **blood pressure**.

tabes: Gradual progressive wasting in any chronic neurological disease; especially, the locomotor discoordination caused by late stages of syphilis.

tachycardia: Abnormally rapid heartbeat. May be caused by disease, fever, drugs, lack of oxygen, or simple exertion.

tachypnea: Abnormally rapid breathing.

TAH-BSO: An operation in which the uterus, both ovaries, and both fallopian tubes are removed.

T and A: Tonsil and adenoidectomy; the surgical removal of the tonsils and adenoids.

tenesmus: Pain, spasm, and strain experienced when attempting to urinate or defecate.

terminal illness: An illness that can be expected to cause the patient to die.

testosterone: The male sex hormone, manufactured and secreted by the testes. It is responsible for the normal growth and development of the male sex organs, male characteristics and sexual activity, and other metabolic functions.

therapeutic trial: The experimental use of a certain treatment on a patient to determine its effectiveness.

thermography: The measurement and depiction in graphic form of the temperature of various parts of the body. Body surfaces emit slightly different amounts of heat, and extremely sensitive equipment can detect such temperature differentials between areas of the body, indicating tumors and other circulatory obstructions.

thrombosis: The formation or development of a blood clot (*thrombus*).

thrombus: A blood clot obstructing a blood vessel or cavity of the heart.

tinea: Any fungal skin disease, especially ringworm, occurring on various parts of the body.

tinnitus: Any subjective sound, such as a ringing or roaring in the ears.

tissue: Any group or collection of similar cells that act together in the performance of a particular function; for example, muscle tissue, nerve tissue, connective tissue.

TNM classification: A method of classifying **malignant** tumors (cancers) with respect to primary *tumor*, involvement of regional lymph *nodes*, and presence or absence of *metastases* (tumors spread to other regions).

tonicity, tonus: Muscle tone; the state of normal tension of muscle fibers while at rest.

toxemia: The distribution of poisonous products or bacteria through the body, producing generalized symptoms.

toxin: A poisonous substance of plant or animal origin.

tracheotomy, tracheostomy: Surgery involving cutting into the trachea (windpipe), usually to insert a tube for air to pass through when the trachea is obstructed or the patient is suffocating.

traction: Pulling or exerting force to stretch a part of the body.

trauma: An injury or wound.

tumor: A swelling or enlargement, particularly a spontaneous new growth of tissue forming an abnormal mass that performs no physiologic function. May be **benign** (noncancerous) or **malignant** (cancerous).

TURP: Trans-Urethral Resection of the Prostate; surgical removal of the prostate through a tube passed into the urethra of the penis.

ulcer: An open sore or **lesion** of the skin or mucous membrane lining of the body, with loss of substance, sometimes accompanied by the formation of pus.

uremia: A serious toxic condition caused by the inability of the kidneys to eliminate waste products.

urinalysis: Abbreviated **UA**; the chemical analysis of the urine for diagnostic purposes.

vaccine: A solution of killed or weakened bacteria, given for the purpose of establishing resistance to an infectious disease (such as mumps, polio, rabies, measles).

vaginismus: Painful spasm of the vagina due to contraction of the surrounding muscles.

vasoconstrictor: A nerve (or drug) that constricts or narrows the blood vessels.

vasodilator: A nerve (or drug) that relaxes or dilates the blood vessels.

ventricular fibrillation: Rapid, tremulous, weak heart ventrical contractions, generally due to injury, drugs, electric shock, or **coronary occlusion**. Can be fatal if fibrillation continues for any length of time.

vertebra: One of the bones forming the spinal column. The thirty-three vertebrae are divided into five sections: the *cervical* vertebrae (neck), the *thoracic* (upper back), the *lumbar* (lower back), the *sacral* (fused to form the sacrum), and the *coccygeal* (forming the coccyx).

viable: Capable of living; generally referring to a fetus twenty-eight weeks or older, which can survive outside the mother's womb.

virulent: Powerful, capable of causing disease (as a virulent bacterial infection).

virus: A microorganism, smaller than a bacterium, that can grow in the human body and cause a variety of diseases.

vital capacity: The (measured) volume of air that can be forcibly exhaled from the lungs after a full inhalation. An average-size male has a vital capacity of four to six liters of air.

vital signs: Measurements of heart rate (pulse in beats per minute), respiration (breaths per minute), and temperature.

Wassermann test: A blood test for syphilis.

workup: A complete series of tests performed in order to reach an accurate **diagnosis**.

One of the more frustrating facets of medical language is its inclusion of hundreds of special terms for which there are perfectly good words already in use by the lay public. To say **deglutition**, for example, instead of "swallowing," or **pyrexia** for fever, or **rhus dermatitis** for poison ivy, seems unnecessary; yet learning these terms is part of the education of every medical student and their use remains the habit of almost every physician. The following section lists several hundred of the most common of these terms, and is followed by an example of short-story writing in Pure Medicalese—with simultaneous translation into common English. ❦

Medicalese for Common English Words

adipose	Fatty	**coxa**	Hip, hip joint
aerophagia	Swallowing air	**cranium**	Skull
afebrile	Without fever	**cutaneous**	Relating to skin
affect	Emotion, feeling	**decubation**	Lying down
alopecia	Baldness	**decubitus ulcer**	Bedsore
anacusis	Deafness	**defurfuration**	Scaling skin
analgesic	Painkilling	**deglutition**	Swallowing
anterior	At or toward the front	**diaphoresis**	Profuse sweating
antitussive	Cough medicine	**diplopia**	Double vision
arrest	Stoppage	**dolor**	Pain
axilla	Armpit	**dorsal**	Back, rear
bleb	Blister	**dyspepsia**	Indigestion
bromidrosis	Foul-smelling sweat	**dysphagia**	Difficulty in swallowing
buccal cavity	Mouth	**dyspnea**	Shortness of breath
bulla	Large blister	**ecchymosis**	Black-and-blue mark; bruise
byllosis	Clubfoot		
cacodontia	Bad teeth	**emesis**	Vomiting
calcaneus	Heel bone	**enuresis**	Bed-wetting; incontinence
calculus	Stone (*renal calculus:* kidney stone)	**epistaxis**	Nosebleed
		erythema	Red patch on skin
cardiac	Heart	**femur**	Thighbone
caries	Decay	**flatulence**	Gas
carpus	Wrist	**flexion**	Bending
cathartic	Laxative	**furunculus**	A boil
cephalalgia	Headache	**gingiva**	Gum
cerumen	Earwax	**gluteus**	Buttock
cicatrix	Scar	**halitosis**	Bad breath
claudication	Lameness, limping	**hallux**	Big toe
clavicle	Collarbone	**hemoptysis**	Coughing up blood
climacteric	Menopause	**icterus**	Jaundice
coccyx	Tailbone	**incision**	Surgical cut
comedo	Blackhead	**inspiration**	Breathing in, inhalation
contusion	Bruise, injury	**keratoma**	Callus; horny growth
coryza	Head cold	**labia**	Lips; vaginal folds of skin

laceration	Wound, cut, or tear of flesh	**pyrexia**	Fever
		pyrosis	Heartburn
lacrimation	Shedding of tears	**recrudescence**	Relapse; return of symptoms
lactation	Secretion of milk		
larynx	Voice box	**renal**	Pertaining to the kidneys
libido	Sexual energy or desire	**respiration**	Breathing
lumbago	Low back pain	**retroflexed**	Bent backward
lumbar region	Lower back	**retroverted**	Turned or tipped back
menses	Menstruation	**rhinorrhea**	Runny nose
miliaria	Heat rash; prickly heat	**rhus dermatitis**	Poison ivy
moribund	Dying	**rubella**	German measles
multiparous	Having borne more than one child	**rubeola**	Measles
		rubor	Redness caused by inflammation
myocardium	Heart muscle		
myopia	Nearsightedness	**scapula**	Shoulder blade
nares	Nostrils	**scarlatina**	Scarlet fever
nasus	Nose	**sclera**	White of the eye
neonate	Newborn infant	**senescence**	Old age, aging
nevus	Birthmark, mole	**singultus**	Hiccups
nictation	Winking, blinking	**sinus rhythm**	Normal heartbeat
nulliparous	Never having borne a child	**sternum**	Breastbone
		syncope	Fainting
occiput	Back of the head	**tachycardia**	Rapid heartbeat
ocular	Pertaining to the eye or vision	**talus**	Anklebone
		tarsus	Ankle
parturition	Childbirth, delivery	**therapy**	Treatment
patella	Kneecap	**thorax**	Chest (adj.: *thoracic*)
pertussis	Whooping cough	**tibia**	Shinbone
phalanges	Bones of fingers or toes	**tinea cruris**	Jock itch
plantar	Relating to the sole of the foot	**tinea pedis**	Athlete's foot
		trachea	Windpipe
polydipsia	Excessive thirst	**tussis**	Cough
polyuria	Excessive urination	**tympanic**	
popliteal region	Back of the knee	**membrane**	Eardrum
posterior	Toward the back, rear	**umbilicus**	Navel
postpartum	After childbirth	**urticaria**	Hives, nettle rash
postprandial	After eating	**uterus**	Womb
prenatal	Before birth	**varicella**	Chicken pox
presbyopia	Farsightedness due to age	**variola**	Smallpox
		verruca	Wart
procedure	Treatment	**vesicle**	Small blister containing fluid
prosthesis	Artificial limb, organ		
pruritus	Itching	**viscera**	Internal organs; "guts"
pulmonary	Pertaining to lungs	**zygoma**	Cheekbone

NOCTURNAL REMISSION

Torporous but ahypnic, G. ambulated in the algid nocturnal atmosphere. His pruritic nasus generated a sudden sternutation. "Coryza spasmodica," he cerebrated, though his anergia was symptomatic of incipient rhinits. He was not prone to neurasthenic disorders.

Within the tenebrosity, he discerned a threshold-level auditory stimulation, reminiscent of laryngeal susurri and human tussis. Cutis anserina developed antebrachially, with associated sudoresis and cardiac arrhythmia. Hyperbouliate, he sedated himself and respirated maximally. A triadic unit manifested itself from the opaque environment.

The primary was ectomorphic, cacodontiac, with a zygomatic cicatrix. The secondary was a hirsute, alopeciac endomorph, with buccal comedos and furunculi. The tertiary was mesomorphic, with keratomous dactyli and partial anodontia. He was bromopneac and bromidrosic.

The ectomorph verbalized: "Our fee or we'll concuss your cranium." G. responded reflexly, from sustained prior operant conditioning: He levorotated his coxae and synergistically combined the resultant centrifugal force with a right quadriceps contraction, impelling his calcaneus into the endomorph's patella.

The mesomorph approached posteriorly and, interdigitating, vigorously contracted biceps and pectorali around G.'s thorax, to which action angina and dyspnea were direct sequelae. Contracting his longus capitis forcefully, G. accelerated his occiput into the mesomorph's nasal cartilage. Lacrimating, the aggressor emitted a spontaneous hyperphonesis of algetic etiology.

The ectomorph struck G.'s mandible dextromanually; G. responded to this stimulus with a sinistro-ulnar concussion to the temporal region, causing instantaneous cataplexy. The endomorph advanced, holding an incisionary

NIGHT CURE

Tired but unable to sleep, George walked in the chilly night air. His itchy nose suddenly exploded in a sneeze. "Touch of hay fever," he thought to himself, though his sluggishness indicated that he was getting a cold. He wasn't the type to feel ill for no reason.

In the darkness, he barely made out what sounded like the murmur of voices and someone coughing. Gooseflesh rose on his forearms, he started to sweat, and his heart pounded erratically. By an extreme effort of the will he calmed himself and breathed as deeply as he could. Three figures appeared out of the gloom.

The first man was thin, with bad teeth and a scar across his cheekbone. The second man was fat, bald, and extremely hairy, with blackheads and boils on his face. The third man was muscular, with calloused fingers and several teeth missing. He had a foul, offensive breath and body odor.

The thin man spoke: "Your money, man, or we'll bust your head." George acted automatically, the result of many years of karate training: He twisted his hips to the left, straightening his leg to lash his heel viciously into the fat man's kneecap.

The muscleman came up from behind and clasped his hands together, locking his arms around George's chest in a steely grip. George felt an oppressive, suffocating pain in his chest and could hardly breathe. George snapped his neck back, smashing the back of his head into the man's nose. His eyes watering, the attacker howled in pain.

The thin man hit George with a hard right to the jaw; George countered with a left elbow strike to the temple, which dropped him like a stone. The fat man advanced, holding a knife, but George grabbed his wrist and twisted it,

NOCTURNAL REMISSION

instrument, but G. grasped his carpal articulation and rotated, retroflexing the antebrachium and causing severe orthrodynia. The mesomorph, epistaxic, was no longer hyperdynamic. To insure no recrudescence, G. drove his metatarsals into the man's inguinal region.

He addressed the ectomorph: "Take Bromidrose and Adipose and discharge yourselves. Before my negative affect becomes acute!" The triad claudicated into the umbras.

G. suspirated, reverting to parasympathetic innervation as his cenesthesia was restored. He ambulated to his primary-care unit, generally myalgic, with anapeiratic systremmae. He was contused and ecchymosed, with stomatodynia and cephalalgia. "But my rhinitis symptoms have abated," he thought, as he decubated pronate on the bed and descended into a sonorous sopor.

NIGHT CURE

bending the forearm backward and causing severe pain. The muscleman, bleeding from the nose, had no appetite for further violence. Just to be sure, George kicked him in the groin.

He turned to the thin man: "Take Stinky and Fatso and beat it. Before I get really mad!" The three men limped away into the shadows.

George sighed, his nerves finally relaxing as his normal feeling of well-being returned. He walked home, all his muscles aching, with cramps in both calves from his exertions in the fight. He was battered and bruised, his mouth hurt and his head ached. "But at least my cold seems to be going away," he thought, as he lay facedown on his bed and fell into a deep, snoring sleep.

|2|

Law

Law pervades every aspect of our lives. Legal **contracts** determine the terms and conditions of our employment, home rental or ownership, purchase of goods and services, insurance policies, product warranties, bank loans; disputes of all kinds are settled in light of the rules of law involved—both informally and through **litigation**; even the most fundamental events of birth, marriage, and death are defined and certified through legal documents. The entire criminal justice system, imperfect as it is, protects the average citizen from the rampant crime that would ensue without it, keeping at least some of the dangerous criminals off the streets and providing a kind of order to the society that is, in principle at least, fair and humane.

Law embodies, in fact, all those rules which a society deems critical enough to enforce with the power of the state. Some system of law and justice has been a central element of almost every human culture—from the most primitive tribal societies to the ancient civilizations of the Near and Far East, Classical Greece and Rome, through to the present day. In America today, law is one of the fastest-growing professions, with 30,000 men and women graduating from law schools each year to join an estimated half million practicing attorneys. We now have one lawyer for every 480 people: Lawyers outnumber police, bus drivers, bank tellers, or doctors. There are twice as many **courts** in the United States as there are hospitals.

The use of language is the lawyer's basic tool—or weapon. His or her ability to think in legal concepts (such as **tort**, **liability**, **negligence**, **due process**) and to apply the terminology that expresses them—both in and out of the courtroom—is the very real skill a lawyer has to sell, for very real amounts of money. **Contracts** are made, and hinge upon, specific legal wording; **civil** and **criminal** cases are tried *verbally*, in open court, in a contest of words between two opposing sides; thus the ability to use and manipulate language is the lawyer's greatest asset. Arcane Latin phrases (**mens rea**, *coram nobis*, **amicus curiae**) and terms obscure to the layperson (**subrogation**, **tortious**, **M'Naghten Rule**) are the lawyer's stock in trade.

The lay population, though immersed in a sea of legal relationships and responsibilities, and called upon with increasing frequency to retain the services of the legal profession, remains woefully ignorant of the law and the process of legal thinking. The average college-educated person today cannot explain so simple a thing as the purpose and function of a **grand jury**, or name the several levels of **courts** in his own state judiciary system, or define so basic a concept as **habeas corpus** or **jurisdiction**. Yet knowledge of these things is becoming a necessity in our highly legalized, overlitigated society. If words are power, as in the legal system they most assuredly are, to learn the language is to become empowered. The following section is devoted to that purpose.

Courts

The term **court** refers both to the physical locus of, and the legal forum created by, a **judge** or judges in session to administer justice. Courts have varying degrees of legal **jurisdiction**, including **original**, **appellate**, **general**, and **limited** or **special jurisdiction**. A court of **original jurisdiction**, or **trial court**, has initial authority to try a case and pass a judgment on the law and facts. A court of **appellate jurisdiction**, or **appellate court**, has authority to review cases and hear appeals on the law, or the law as applied to the facts found by the trial court. A court of **general jurisdiction** is a trial court of unlimited original jurisdiction in civil and criminal cases, while a court of **special** or **limited jurisdiction** is a trial court with legal authority over only a particular class of cases, such as **probate**, **juvenile**, or traffic cases, or cases involving only a limited amount of money (**small claims**) or minor criminal offenses.

As the diagram indicates, American courts are divided into two complete systems, **federal** and **state**; each of these systems is composed of various levels of courts arranged in a hierarchical structure. The federal courts are organized in a simple and logical arrangement, with one or more of the ninety-four trial courts known as **U.S. District Courts** located in every state and one each in the District of Columbia, Puerto Rico, the Virgin Islands, the Canal Zone, and Guam. For judicial purposes, the country is divided into eleven numbered **circuits**, each of which has a single **Federal Court of Appeal**, with a twelfth such court sitting in the District of Colum-

---

FEDERAL JUDICIAL SYSTEM

Supreme Court of the U.S.
9 Justices
‖
U.S. Courts of Appeal
12 Circuits, 97 judges
‖
U.S. District Courts
94 Courts, 400 judges
‖
Quasi-Judicial Agencies
Tax Court, FTC, NLRB, FCC, etc.
‖
Courts of Special Jurisdiction
Court of Claims, Customs Court,
Court of Customs and Patent Appeals

STATE JUDICIAL SYSTEM

State Supreme Court
Also called Court of Appeals,
Supreme Court of Errors,
Supreme Judicial Court, etc.
‖
Intermediate Appellate Courts
(In 20 out of 50 States only)
‖
*Trial Courts of Original and
General Jurisdiction*
Highest trial courts.
Variously termed Circuit Court,
District Court,
Court of Common Pleas,
and Supreme Court [NY]
‖
Courts of Limited Jurisdiction
Handle minor civil and criminal cases.
Include Family Courts, Juvenile Courts,
Probate Courts, Small Claims Courts,
Traffic Courts, Municipal Courts,
Magistrates, Justices of the Peace, etc.

---

bia. The courts of special jurisdiction in the federal system include the **Customs Court,** and the **Court of Claims** (for claims against the United States).

No such uniformity exists among the fifty separate state judicial systems. They are products of their differing historical evolutions, originating often in models and assumptions of the eighteenth century or earlier. They tend, however, to provide neighborhood courts at the lowest level in the widespread **justice of the peace** system. These lowest courts are typically not courts of **record,** however, and if their decisions are appealed, an entirely new trial must be held in the higher trial court. As will be noted from the diagram, an **intermediate appellate court** exists in twenty states, as a tribunal midway between the highest trial court and the **State Supreme Court** (by whatever name it is called). ❧

Legal Terminology

ABA: The American Bar Association; a voluntary national association of lawyers, which, however, wields considerable power: setting minimum standards for **plea bargaining** and other aspects of criminal justice, evaluating judges, and the like.

ab initio: From the beginning; from inception.

accessory: A person who, while not actively participating in committing a crime, facilitates, assists, or otherwise contributes to it. An *accessory before the fact* is one who plans, instigates, or orders the crime (but does not personally commit it); an *accessory after the fact* is one who knowingly conceals or harbors a criminal or otherwise helps to prevent his being brought to justice.

accomplice: A person who actively and knowingly participates in committing (or attempting to commit) a crime. The accomplice (unlike the **accessory**) is thus liable for the same offense as the original **defendant**.

accused: A person who has been charged with a crime; the **defendant** in a criminal proceeding.

acquit: To declare innocent of the offense charged; to set free. Following an *acquittal,* the **party** may not be prosecuted again for the same crime—under the principle of **double jeopardy**.

action: A legal proceeding in which one **party** prosecutes another; a **lawsuit**.

actionable: Applies to conduct capable of provoking or causing an **action**; legally wrongful; giving rise to a *cause of action.* (For example, the unconsented to application of physical force on another person is actionable conduct; as is a **breach of contract**.)

actus reus: The criminal act; the physical deed itself—as distinguished from **mens rea**, the mental intent to commit the crime.

adjourn: To postpone, delay, put off. Trials, hearings, and other legal proceedings may be adjourned for meals, overnight, or for other specific reasons.

adjudication: A judgment; the judicial determination of a legal controversy.

admissible evidence: Material or **testimony** that a **trial court** may allow either of the **parties** to introduce. Rules of evidence determine admissibility, but the **judge** in his **discretion** may not necessarily permit all such evidence to be introduced.

adversary proceeding: The process of reaching a decision based upon the presentation of opposing views by contesting **parties**. The adversary system is the basis of American legal justice; however, it is not the only system of law practiced in other countries, nor obviously are all non**litigated** controversies settled by adversary proceedings. In schools, corporations, closed societies, etc., other methods of decision-making are more common.

affidavit: A written statement made under oath and signed before a duly authorized officer of the court (such as a **notary public**). The person giving the statement is termed the *affiant.*

agency: 1. The relationship in which one person (the **agent**) acts on behalf of, and with the authority of, another (the **principal**).

2. An administrative division within the executive branch of government which may be authorized to exercise certain limited judicial functions (enforce regulations, hold hearings, etc.). Examples of agencies with such functions include the Federal Trade Commission (FTC), the Federal Communications Commission (FCC), the Interstate Commerce Commission (ICC), and the Federal Aviation Administration (FAA).

alibi: A verifiable claim that a **defendant** (or suspect) was in a different or distant place at the time a crime was committed and thus could not possibly have committed it.

allegation: An assertion of fact by a **party**, which he later expects to prove is true.

amicus curiae: Latin, "a friend of the court." One not a **party** to a **lawsuit**, but having sufficient concern or interest in its outcome to be allowed to present argument or introduce **evidence**—usually by way of an *amicus brief.* For example, the NAACP might file an amicus brief in a school desegregation case that has ramifications for the black population in general.

answer: The **defendant**'s major **pleading** in response to the **complaint** against him. May include a refutation of the facts that the **plaintiff** alleges and/or the **allegation** of additional evidence that controverts the plaintiff's claims.

appeal: As a verb, to seek modification or reversal of a decision by going to a higher **court** or tribunal. As a noun, the procedure of seeking such a reversal. The **party** seeking the appeal is termed the **appellant**; the party against whom modification or reversal is sought is termed the **appellee**.

appellate court: See "Courts" section.

arbitration: A less formal method of dispute resolution than that of a **court,** wherein one or more impartial **arbitrators,** agreed to by both **parties,** render a decision—which may either be binding or *appealable* in court.

argument: That portion of a lawyer's presentation in **court** which is intended to convince on the basis of certain facts, which are established separately. In a typical **trial** sequence, there is a short *opening statement* preceding the presentation of **evidence,** and a more extensive *closing argument,* which follows the evidence. In an **appeals** case, however, there is only argument, as no new evidence is to be presented.

arraignment: An early stage in a criminal case, following the filing of an **indictment,** when the **defendant** is brought before the **court** to have the charges against him presented and to be informed of his constitutional rights and the **pleas** he may enter (**guilty**, not guilty, or **nolo contendere**).

arrest: The act of a law enforcement officer (or other) to deprive a person of his liberty in order to answer for a crime of which he is suspected.

assault: An attempt or threat to inflict bodily harm on another person, with the apparent ability to do so (if not prevented). (Compare **battery**.)

attachment: Seizure of a **defendant**'s property by the **court** in a **civil** controversy, to ensure satisfaction of a debt should the **judgment** be found for the **plaintiff**. Attachment can occur before or during the progress of a **lawsuit**. (Compare **garnishment**.)

attorney-at-law: A person authorized to prepare, manage, and try cases in **court**, by virtue of having passed a state **bar** exam and having met any other state requirements (usually a law degree, etc.) to practice law.

attorney general: The highest law officer of a state or nation, who is charged with representing and counseling the government in **litigation** and other legal matters.

bail: The deposit in **court** of a sum of money (or other **security**) as condition for the release of an **arraigned** prisoner pending trial. In the event the prisoner fails to appear, the bail is forfeited. The amount of bail is set by the **judge** at his **discretion**.

bail bondsman: A person who acts as a **surety** for a **defendant** in a criminal case and effects his release by posting the *bail bond.* Without collateral, the bondsman's fee is usually 10 percent of the sum at risk.

bailiff: A uniformed **court** attendant whose duties may include keeping the peace in the courtroom, guarding prisoners, and assisting the **judge** and **jury** as required.

bait and switch: A deceptive retail practice, now outlawed in many states, wherein a low-priced product is used to "bait" the customer into the store only so that the seller can "switch" him to a higher-priced product on which the profit is greater.

bankruptcy: A process under federal law that may be begun voluntarily by an insolvent individual or corporation, or at the instigation of unpaid creditors, to liquidate assets for division among the creditors, thereby allowing the *bankrupt* to begin anew.

bar: 1. The railing that separates the general courtroom audience from the area in which **court** business is conducted.

2. Lawyers as a body (*the bar*), so called because they are privileged to enter beyond the court railing to participate in the court proceedings.

3. Short for the **bar exam**, a comprehensive test of legal knowledge, typically lasting over several days, which must be passed in order to practice law. Different states have somewhat differing bar exams; there is also a multistate bar exam, which confers simultaneous qualification for practice in several states.

battery: The unconsented to use of physical force (touching, grabbing, pushing, striking, beating, etc.) on another person. A criminal act that may also give rise to **civil** liability.

bench: 1. The place in a courtroom where the **judge** or judges sit. (To "approach the bench" means to confer with the judge.)

2. The **court.** Thus, a *bench warrant* is a **warrant** for arrest issued by the court as opposed to the police or other law enforcement agency, used generally to compel appearance in court for **contempt** or to answer an ignored **subpoena**.

bequeath: To make a gift of personal property (not real property) through a will. The property thus bequeathed is called the *bequest*.

bill: Any of a variety of formal written statements, complaints, or other documents. A *bill of particulars* is a complete statement of all specific charges and facts, requested by the **defendant** to obtain information and limit the scope of the trial. A *bill of attainder* is a legis-lative act prohibited by the Constitution, which would punish named individuals or members of a group without a hearing.

boilerplate: Standardized provisions of certain legal documents, such as **contracts**, **wills**, **pleadings**, which are reproduced verbatim without any specific material included.

bona fide: In good faith; genuine; honest. A bona-fide purchaser is one who buys something in good faith, with no knowledge of any other claim outstanding on the purchased item, or any dispute or wrongdoing connected with it.

bond: A written promise of the performance of specified acts; or statement of certain obligations; or acknowledgement of a required payment or debt. A *bondsman* is one who guarantees such performance by another. (See **bail bondsman**.)

breach: Violation of, or failure to fulfill, any law or obligation. *Breach of contract* is the nonperformance of any duty forming all or part of a contract, without a valid legal excuse for such failure. It is an **actionable tort**. Other breaches include: *breach of promise, breach of warranty, breach of the peace*.

brief: A written submission to the **court** containing a **party**'s statement of the facts of the case, the questions of law involved, and the arguments in support of the law that party believes should be applied. A *Brandeis brief* is one that marshalls its arguments not only on the basis of legal reasoning and precedent but also from learning in allied fields, such as economics or sociology.

burden of proof: The necessity of substantiating one's **allegations** in order to prevail in a legal case. In criminal law, the burden of proof upon the **prosecution** is higher than in civil cases—being the standard **beyond a reasonable doubt**. In **civil** cases, the standard of substantiation is the **preponderance of the evidence**.

burglary: Traditionally defined (in **common law**) as the breaking and entering of a dwelling in the nighttime with the intent to commit a **felony**. Many state **statutes** have expanded the definition, however, to include any breaking and entering of any building at any time to commit a crime.

case: Any dispute, controversy, **action**, or **cause** capable of legal action before a **court**. *Case law* is a body of **adjudicated** cases, particularly those having to do with a particular subject or type of dispute, as distinguished from **statutes** and regulations.

cause of action: Facts which give rise to the right to sue; the existence of a **breach** or other wrong which entitles the **plaintiff** to institute **litigation**.

caveat: Latin, "let him beware." A caution or warning. *Caveat emptor,* "let the buyer beware": A principle that the purchaser of goods and services does so at his own risk; now modified by consumer protection laws and **implied warranties**.

chambers: The office(s) of a **judge**; or, more generally, any place out of open **court** where a judge can confer privately. "See me in chambers" is the judge's usual statement when he wishes to meet privately with **counsel**.

charge: 1. As a noun, the accusation of an offense in criminal cases. Also, as a verb, for example "to *be charged* with manslaughter."

2. The verbal directions given by the **judge** at the close of the **parties**' presentations, instructing the **jury** as to what principles of law to apply to the facts of the case in reaching their decision.

cite: To quote, as authority, any reference to written law (**statute**, **ordinance**, **court** case, or section of a constitution).

civil action, matter, or **suit:** A controversy (not involving criminal law) over the respective rights and duties of two **parties** to each other. Most common civil actions involve **tort** or **contract disputes**.

claim: The assertion of a right (as to money or property); also, those facts which, taken together, comprise a legal right that might be enforceable in **court**. The person making a claim is termed the *claimant*.

class action: A **lawsuit** brought by one or more specific individuals on behalf of themselves and a larger group of persons who are in some way similarly affected by the issues to be settled. For example, parents of children in a state institution might bring a class action against the state for negligent treatment; or one stockholder of a large corporation might bring a class action on behalf of all other stockholders.

collusion: Secret cooperation for an improper or illegal purpose. *Collusive action* refers to a situation in which presumably opposing **parties** in a **lawsuit** seek a **judgment** in their mutual interest—an improper purpose since **courts** are empowered only to decide **cases** in controversy.

common law: That portion of law derived from **case law**, that is, the precedent of previous **judgments** and decrees, and based upon general principles of reason and justice; as distinguished from legislative enactments and other abstract codes. Common law originated in the rigid codes of medieval England, but has been adapted and continuously developed since then; it is used in all states but Louisiana, whose Civil Code is largely derived from the law of Napoleonic France.

complainant: The person who initiates a legal **action**. Usually synonymous with **petitioner** or **plaintiff**; however, in some criminal matters, the complainant might appeal to the **district attorney**, who would press **criminal charges**, in which case the state would be the plaintiff.

concurrent sentences: Multiple sentences (as, for several crimes of which the **defendant** is found guilty at the same time) that will run together over the same course of time, as opposed to running consecutively.

condemn: 1. To declare legally useless, as a building found unfit for human habitation, or land that has been declared convertible to public use under **eminent domain**.

2. To sentence to death for a **capital** offense.

consideration: Something given in return for something else, or the promise of something else, in order to form a **contract**. The consideration, which may be of real value or only symbolic (e.g., one dollar, or one peppercorn), is what distinguishes a contract from a **gift**.

conspiracy: An agreement or concerted action by two or more people to achieve an unlawful purpose, or a lawful purpose by unlawful means.

contempt of court: Disrespect for or interference with the **court** or its orders; punishable by fine and sometimes imprisonment. Failure to answer a **subpoena**, or refusal to **testify**, or to obey an **injunction** are typical infractions that may be considered contempt of court.

contingent fee: A type of fee, common in **civil suits**, in which the attorney's payment is premised upon winning the **case** and is usually some percentage of the amount recovered for his client. In some major corporate law cases, for example, involving settlements of millions of dollars, a contingent-fee basis will prove far more lucrative than any hourly fee or flat rate.

continuance: A postponement of **trial**, granted by the **court**. Rarely granted to the **prosecution** (the state) in a criminal case due to the constitutional guarantee of a speedy trial; however, continuances are routinely granted, on almost any pretext, to both sides in **civil** cases; probably 50 percent or more of such suits involve at least one continuance.

contract: A legally binding agreement between two (or more) **parties** in which each commits to certain obligations (e.g., to perform services, to make payments). The law recognizes the fulfillment of the terms of a contract as a lawful duty, and **breach of contract** as entitling the injured party to a **remedy**.

contributory negligence: Conduct below the standard of care prescribed by law and for which the **plaintiff** in a **negligence** case has been responsible; thereby reducing or preventing his monetary recovery.

copyright: An exclusive right to reproduce, publish, or sell any original literary, artistic, or musical work—protected by both federal **statute** and **common law**.

coroner: An official who investigates deaths, through postmortem examination of the body and other elements of a *coroner's inquest* (judicial inquiry).

corpus delicti: Latin, "the body of the crime." The objective proof that a **crime** has been committed—including the actual injury or **evidence** thereof (such as the burned house or the wrecked car) *and* proof of criminal intent or other **mens rea** (criminal state of mind).

counsel: Attorney, lawyer; particularly refers to one engaged to represent a **party** in **court** (most often used without articles or possessive pronouns: "**Counsel** will approach the **bench**.").

count: Each separate **allegation** or **charge** in a **civil complaint** or **criminal indictment**. (For example, a man who went on a violent rampage might be charged with several counts of **assault**, **battery**, and attempted **homicide**.)

counterclaim: A claim made by the **defendant** in a **civil** suit that is more than an answer or denial of the **plaintiff**'s claim in that it alleges wrongdoing by the plaintiff and asks monetary or other relief from him.

court: A legal forum wherein controversies are heard and decisions rendered. (See "Courts" section for details and types.)

covenant: 1. *n.* A written and signed agreement or promise, often part of a deed or contract—for example, *restrictive covenants, covenant of quiet enjoyment.*

2. *v.* To enter into an agreement; to promise.

crime: An act or behavior that the government

has determined is wrongful or injurious to the public and is the subject for a **prosecution** in criminal court (*criminal action*); any violation of criminal laws or statutes. Crimes can be either **felonies** (more serious) or **misdemeanors** (less serious).

cross-examination: The questioning by **counsel** of a **witness** whose **testimony** has been introduced by the opposing **party** (in **direct examination**).

damages: Money awarded by a court to compensate for injury done to the person, property, or rights of another. *Actual damages* are compensation for the injury itself. *Consequential damages* are compensation for the indirect but foreseeable results of the injury. *Double (treble) damages* are two (or three) times what would otherwise be awarded, specially provided by statute to discourage certain conduct (such as, violation of antitrust laws).

de facto: In fact; actual; in reality. For example, a situation of *de facto discrimination* might exist although not sanctioned officially (**de jure**, by law).

default judgment: A decision against the **defendant** for his failure to answer a **complaint** or to appear in **court** at the appointed time.

defendant: In **civil actions**, the **party** who is sued by, and must **answer** the **plaintiff**; in **criminal** proceedings, the **accused** who is **prosecuted** by the **state**.

defense: The facts and/or argument introduced to oppose the **charges** brought by the **plaintiff** or **prosecution** against the **defendant**. An *affirmative defense* is one that does not merely deny the plaintiff's **allegations** but seeks to establish new facts or introduce new evidence that will cause the **case** to be settled in his favor.

de novo: Anew; new; for the second time; as in a *de novo hearing*, in which a reviewing court suspends the original judgment of a trial court in order to make a new judgment (which may or may not uphold the original finding).

deposition: A written record of the sworn **testimony** of a **witness** taken before **trial**, usually in response to questions from **counsel** (with an opportunity for **cross-examination** by the opposition). A common form of **discovery.**

derivative tort: A **civil action** deriving from a **crime** committed by the **defendant** for which injury the **plaintiff** now seeks compensation.

direct examination: In a **trial**, the questioning of a **witnees** by the **party** who has called him to testify.

disbar: To take away a lawyer's license to practice law, as a result of illegal or unethical conduct.

discovery: The opportunity for one **party** to learn about the opponent's case before trial, through **depositions**, **interrogations**, and requests for production of relevant documents.

discretion: The latitude of choice legitimately possessed by a public official; the ability to make decisions within an official role. For example, *prosecutorial discretion* entitles the **prosecutor** (in **criminal** cases) to decide whether to prosecute, what offenses to charge, whether to accept certain **pleas** or **plea bargaining**. Also, *judicial discretion* and *legal discretion*.

dismissal: Termination, denial, rejection. A **case** may be dismissed by the **judge** without a complete **trial** (if, for example, the **plaintiff** has presented completely insufficient **evidence**); a **motion** made by counsel may be dismissed by the judge—i.e., rejected; while an **appeal** dismissed is merely denied but might be resubmitted. *Dismissal with prejudice* implies a bar to future consideration; *dismissal without prejudice* leaves the **party** free to pursue further **action** at a later time.

dissent: This may occur in a **court** comprised of several **judges** (such as the Supreme Court), when one or more judges disagree with the conclusion of the majority. Those in disagreement (said to dissent) will commonly write a *dissenting opinion* to express the minority viewpoint and reasons for it.

district court: See "Courts" section.

docket: A **court's** schedule of **cases**. A case is said to be "on the docket" for a certain date and time.

double jeopardy: A second **prosecution** for the same (**criminal**) offense—forbidden by the Constitution, except when the result of a **mistrial** or an **appeal** by the **defendant**.

due process of law: Fundamental fairness and justice in the government's treatment of the individual; guaranteed by the Fifth and Fourteenth amendments to the Constitution ("Nor shall any state deprive any person of life, liberty, or property without **due process of law**") and interpreted through the decisions of the Supreme Court.

duress: Threat, force, or other wrongful acts that compel a person to do something he would not otherwise do; duress thus constitutes a valid **defense** to both **civil** and **criminal actions**. For example, if a **contract** were signed under the threat of bodily harm, the person who was made to sign under such duress would not be held liable for a **breach** of that contract.

embezzlement: The unauthorized use of funds of which one has lawful possession but not ownership. Applies typically to bank tellers, public officials, bookkeepers, and the like, who have legitimate access to funds that they then misappropriate for their own use.

eminent domain: The right of government to take private property for public use (i.e., to **condemn**), without the consent of the owner but (as required by the Fifth Amendment) with the payment of **just compensation**.

encumbrance (also **incumbrance**): Any claim, interest, or right to property, other than that of the owner or **title** holder: for example, a **mortgage** or a judgment **lien**.

enjoin: To order or command officially that something be (or not be) done. For example, a **court** might enjoin a company from selling stock pending resolution of a **complaint** by the SEC. (See **injunction**.)

entrapment: A criminal **defense** maintaining that the conduct of the police (or FBI) persuaded or lured a **defendant** into doing something which he otherwise would not have done.

equal protection: A constitutional guarantee against laws that arbitrarily discriminate against a certain class or group of persons.

equity: 1. Generally, fairness, justice, impartiality of law. Specifically, a body of law that was administered by special courts established by the King of England to supplement the more rigid original **common law courts** and provide a **remedy** for every **injury**. Today the courts of **equity** and **law** are merged, although the principles remain distinct.

2. An owner's interest in his property—that is, its total value minus all **liens** and **encumbrances**.

estate: All that a person owns and may leave at death. Also, more specifically, any of several types of interest in land, such as *estate at will* and *estate in common*.

estoppel: An **equitable** doctrine that precludes a **party** from asserting in **court** a position inconsistent with what was represented previously, and from denying his own act or deed —upon which position or act the other party has relied.

eviction: The legal expulsion or dispossession of a person from lands or dwelling (as of a tenant from a rented apartment by a landlord).

evidence: All varieties of proof used to establish factual **allegations** in a **trial**, including the **testimony** of **witnesses**, documents, **records**, **exhibits**, and the like.

exception: An **objection** to a **judge's** ruling or action during a **trial**, stated in the **court** record, reserving the right to seek a later **reversal** of that ruling.

exhibit: An object, document, or other item produced and identified at a **trial** as evidence; for example, the murder weapon or a threatening letter.

expert witness: A person having specialized knowledge or experience not possessed by the ordinary person, and whose **testimony** will shed some light on the facts of a **case**. May be called by either **party** or by the **court**.

ex post facto: Latin, "after the fact." Retroactive. Ex post facto laws, which would make punishable (or more punishable, or more difficult to defend) **crimes** committed before the passage of those laws, are prohibited by the U.S. Constitution.

extenuating circumstances: Special factors or considerations that explain or mitigate the seriousness of an illegal act, and which are presented to the **court** to reduce a **defendant's** punishment or payment of **damages**. For example, a driver's rushing to get his sick child to the hospital would constitute the extenuating circumstances that could reduce his penalty for speeding.

extradition: The delivery of an accused criminal from one country, state, or **jurisdiction** back to another for the purposes of **trial**, which often occurs when a criminal has fled from one locale to another in order to escape **prosecution**.

fair trade laws: State laws that permit manufacturers to set minimum wholesale or retail prices, thus constituting an exception to the prohibition on price-fixing in the federal antitrust laws.

federal courts: See "Courts" section.

fee simple also **fee simple absolute:** An estate owned completely and unconditionally, which the owner may convey or leave to his heirs without any restrictions.

felony: A serious, major, or "high" **crime**, as variously defined by state **statute** and **common law**; usually referring to those crimes punishable by imprisonment or death; distinguished from less serious crimes called **misdemeanors**. A *felony murder* is a **homicide** committed during the course of a felony (or attempted felony) and is considered *first-degree murder*. Adjective: *felonious*.

Fifth Amendment: A provision of the Constitution that in its most general clause prohibits the federal government from depriving any person of life, liberty, or property without **due process of law**. To **plead** the Fifth Amendment refers to invoking the specific clause that prohibits the federal government from compelling anyone in a **criminal case** to be a **witness** against himself.

finding: The decision of judge or jury on issues of fact. Often part of a **special verdict**; however, even **general verdicts** may be stated in the form "we **find** for . . ." or "we **find** the defendant . . ."

foreclosure: An **equitable action** available to a creditor with a **lien**, **security interest**, or **mortgage** on some property. The action cuts off or terminates the owner's rights to the **encumbered** property, leading to its sale to satisfy the debt.

forensic medicine: That branch of medicine relating medical knowledge to legal issues. Examples include determining causes of death or injury or, competency to stand trial.

fraud: An intentional misrepresentation, deceit, artifice, concealment, or cheating, relied upon by another person to his detriment. Examples of *fraudulent* acts are as innumerable as man's criminal imagination, but some common examples include: selling a car with falsified mileage; selling a forged painting as an original; or inducing people to buy nonexistent tracts of land.

garnishment: A **statutory** procedure wherein a **plaintiff** can require a third party holding property of the **defendant** to withhold it from him and to dispose of it as the **court** directs in order to satisfy a **judgment** against the defendant. Commonly, wages, bank accounts, stock holdings and the like may be **garnished** to repay a debt.

gift: A voluntary transfer of anything to another person (or legal entity) without anything given or promised in return (that is, without **consideration**).

Good Samaritan doctrine: The principle that a person who helps another in distress or imminent danger (for example, a doctor with an accident victim on the street) cannot be held liable for any harm caused to that person—unless the result of intentional malice or **negligence**.

grandfather clause: A provision that exempts persons already engaged in a certain business from new, more stringent requirements imposed subsequently. For example, if a police force in the past has not required high school diplomas for its officers, those without such diplomas do not need to meet the requirement demanded of candidates applying currently.

grand jury: A group of citizens (usually numbering twenty-three) convened by law to receive **complaints** in **criminal cases**, and to decide whether there is sufficient **evidence** to warrant **indictment** on criminal **charges** for later **trial**.

grand larceny: See **larceny**.

guardian: The person legally responsible for the well-being and property of another person (termed the **ward**), due to the ward's age or inability to care for himself.

guilty: Having confessed to, or having been found by **judge** or **jury** beyond a **reasonable doubt** to have committed, the **criminal** offense with which one is charged. Persons found guilty of a crime are then **convicted** and **sentenced**.

habeas corpus: Latin, "you have the body." A **writ** employed to bring a person held in custody or imprisonment before a **court**, in order to challenge the legality of that person's detainment. Often used when **due process of law** may have been violated in a person's arrest or **conviction**.

hearing: A proceeding held before a **judge** or **magistrate** without a **jury** (or before other officials with judicial functions), in which facts or arguments are presented and a decision is rendered or information is obtained.

hearsay: A statement by a **witness** about something he or she has not experienced, but only heard about from another person. Generally excluded as **evidence** from a **court** of law.

homicide: Any killing of one human being by another. Not all homicide is unlawful, however: Killing in appropriate self-defense is considered *justifiable homicide*. The four categories of homicide (in declining order of seriousness) include **murder**, **manslaughter**, *excusable homicide* and *justifiable homicide*.

hung jury: A **jury** that cannot reach a **verdict** due to differences of opinion. (In some cases a verdict requires unanimity of all members of the jury; in others only a significant majority.)

implied: Not expressed directly, but nonetheless to be inferred or deduced from surrounding facts. An *implied warranty* exists when one purchases a new watch or clock or household appliance that the item be in good working order and not defective.

indictment: A formal written **criminal** accusation presented to a **grand jury** for it to decide if there exists sufficient evidence for the indictment to be approved and a **trial** to follow.

injunction: A **court** order commanding a person to do something or (more commonly) to refrain from doing something. A *temporary injunction* may be issued to maintain a situation without change during the course of a **trial** —for example, a company may be enjoined from selling a product the safety of which is being questioned.

injury: Any **damage**, wrong, or violation to a person or his legal rights or property. Injury in the legal sense need not involve any bodily harm. An injury is redressed through a **remedy**.

in pais: French, "in the country." Outside of court.

inquest: A **court**-authorized inquiry, conducted

by either a **grand jury** or a **coroner**, to determine inssues of fact in **criminal cases**. The group thus constituted, and its **finding**, are also termed the inquest.

instrument: A written legal document, such as a **contract**, a **bond**, a **deed**, or a **will**.

intent: Purpose; deliberateness; the knowing state of mind that desires and intends to accomplish an act. *General intent* must be established in any **criminal conviction**. *Specific intent* (as in **assault with intent to kill**) is a component of certain crimes and must be proven beyond a reasonable doubt.

interest: 1. A partial share in something, such as land or a business.

2. A personal concern or stake in a **lawsuit**; it is grounds for disqualifying a **judge** or **juror**.

interrogatories: A written set of questions served on the opposing **party** in a **civil action**, which must be answered in writing and under oath. A means of pretrial **discovery**.

intestate: Having died without leaving a will, the consequence of which is that the deceased's **estate** is distributed according to state law.

ipso facto: Latin, "by the fact itself." In and of itself.

issue: 1. A disputed question of law or fact.

2. Offspring; descendants.

joint custody: A resolution in some child custody **cases** in which both parents, though living apart, are awarded equal legal control of the child's upbringing and equal responsibility for his care.

judge: A public official, authorized to decide questions of law and fact, usually in a **court** of law.

judgment: The final determination of a **case** by the **court** to which it has been submitted; the **judge's** pronouncement of the court's decision. Not the same as a **verdict**. (See also **N.O.V.**)

jurisdiction: 1. The legal authority for a **court** to consider and decide upon a particular **case** —depending upon location, subject matter of the dispute, presence of and notice given to the **parties** involved, etc. *Appellate jurisdiction*, for example, is the power of an appellate court to revise or correct judgments made in lower court.

2. The geographical territory within which a court has the power to function. (See the section "Courts.")

jurisprudence: Law; the science of legal systems, practice, and philosophy; the overall pattern or trend of judicial decisions (as distinct from legislation).

jurist: A legal scholar or expert, often a **judge** or retired judge.

jury: A group of citizens, drawn from a cross-section of the community, summoned and sworn to decide the facts of a **case** in a **court** of law. (See also **hung jury**, **grand jury**, **petit jury**.)

juvenile: One who is under the age of legal majority as defined by state law—usually eighteen. *Juvenile courts* hear only cases relating to minor-age children (both **criminal** offenses and custody). A *juvenile delinquent* is a minor who has been **convicted** of a criminal offense; although in most cases the juvenile will not be punished with the same severity as an adult convicted of the same crime.

larceny: The taking of property from its rightful owner with the intention of not returning it. *Grand larceny* and *petit (petty) larceny* are distinguished in state law by the value of the property taken.

lawsuit: Also **suit**. A **case** that is **litigated** in **court**; more properly refers only to **civil actions**.

liability: Legal responsibility for one's conduct. *Strict laibility* is the responsibility at law for one's conduct and its consequences regardless of fault or carelessness, as for example when using explosives. *Vicarious liability* is the responsibility at law for someone else's conduct, such as that of an employer for an employee in the course of business.

libel: Any published or broadcast statement that is both injurious to the reputation of another *and* false. Truth is a **defense** for the individual charged with libel, and in the case of defamatory statements about public figures, the absence of malice or reckless disregard of the truth is also a defense. (See also **slander**.)

lien: A monetary **claim** registered against a piece of property and which can be satisfied by the sale of the property, if necessary. (See also **mechanic's lien**.)

litigation: Controversies that are destined for, or have reached, court. One who is **party** to such a controversy is termed a **litigant**.

magistrate: A lower judicial officer; or a public official with limited judicial powers who is not a **judge**—such as a justice of the peace or a mayor.

malfeasance: The commission of an intrinsically wrongful, unlawful act (such as extortion), especially in an official capacity or public office. Distinguished from *misfeasance* (the improper doing of a lawful act) and **nonfeasance** (the omission of, or failure to perform, a legal duty).

malice: The mental **intent** to cause harm to another, or the wanton, willful or reckless disregard of the likelihood that such harm shall occur. The unjustified, unmitigated intention to injure or do evil.

malpractice: Professional misconduct (or, as some would have it, "unprofessional conduct") due to wrongdoing, incompetence, **malice** or neglect. Usually applied only to doctors and lawyers.

mandamus: Latin, "we command." A **writ** compelling the performance of a certain act by a public official, usually employed only after all other legal **remedies** have failed or proven inadequate. For example, a higher court might order a school system to desegregate, or a policemen's union to return to work, via a *writ of mandamus.*

manslaughter: The unlawful killing of another without malice or premeditation. Classified as a less serious crime than **murder**. *Involuntary manslaughter* is an accidental killing, resulting from grossly negligent or reckless conduct (as, typically, in the operation of an automobile). *Voluntary manslaughter,* while an "intentional" killing, is one that is committed in a heat of passion (rage, fright, terror, or desperation) provoked by the deceased.

material: Significant, relevant, important—either in terms of the issues presented (as in *material evidence* or *material allegation*), or in terms of the overall purpose of a **contract** (as in *material breach of contract*).

M'Naghten Rule: The principle of criminal responsibility which holds that a **defendant** is not legally **liable** for his acts if it can be proven that he did not know what he was doing or could not distinguish right from wrong, or was otherwise insanely deluded.

mechanic's lien: A claim that secures payment to a workman (on a car, house, or other property) by **attaching** or holding the property worked on.

mens rea: Criminal **intent**; a guilty mind. The intentional, knowing, reckless, or grossly negligent state of mind that engenders a criminal act. (See **actus reus**.)

merits: The substance of a **case**, based on the **pleadings** and **evidence;** the basic elements of each **party**'s judicial cause. A *judgment on the merits* is thus one based on substantive issues, rather than procedural or technical matters.

meritorious: Deserving of judicial consideration. (*Not* synonymous with commendable!)

ministerial act: An act that an official must perform given certain circumstances and in which he has no **discretion**.

Miranda Rule: By the mandate of a 1966 U.S. Supreme Court decision (*Miranda* v. *Arizona*), the requirement that no statement of a person taken into custody can later be introduced against him in **court** unless he has been warned that he has the right to remain silent; that any statement he makes may be used against him in court; that he has the right to speak to an **attorney**; and that if he cannot afford to hire one, an attorney will be appointed for him if he so desires.

misdemeanor: A **criminal** offense less serious than a **felony**, as defined by **statute**. To be **charged** with a misdemeanor, no **grand jury indictment** is required, nor does **conviction** serve to disqualify a person from voting or engaging in licensed occupations. Generally refers to minor crimes punishable by a fine or short jail term.

misprision of felony: Failure to prevent a **felony** of which one is aware, or concealment of it—without any **accessory** role. A **misdemeanor**.

mistrial: A **trial** that has been terminated and declared void because of external circumstance (such as the death of an **attorney**, a **judge**, or a necessary **juror**); or due to some prejudice that cannot be cured (improperly inflammatory remarks in the **prosecution**'s closing statement, for example); or, most commonly, because the requisite number of jurors cannot agree on a **verdict** (**hung jury**). A mistrial does not constitute a **judgment** of any kind.

mitigating circumstances: Factors that, although not completely excusing unlawful conduct, may cause a reduction in the **charge** or the penalty for a committed **crime**, or of the **damages** awarded in a **civil case**.

moot: Abstract or academic, not representing an actual, practical **case** or controversy. A *moot point,* for example, might be the guilt of a person who has already died. A *moot court* is a tribunal established as part of an academic or learning exercise, usually in law school.

motion: An oral or written application to a **court** by a **party** to act in his favor, as a matter of either **discretion** or law. For example, *motion to dismiss, motion to set aside judgment.*

motive: A need or desire that causes one to act.

Unlike **intent**, it is not a necessary element for **criminal conviction**.

municipal courts: City **courts** vested with limited authority, hearing **cases** related to the **breach** of city **ordinances**, lesser **crimes**, and **civil** suits for smaller amounts of money. (See "Courts" section.)

murder: The unlawful killing of another with **malice** and premeditation. Modern state **statutes** vary, but most distinguish between *murder in the first degree,* which is characterized by a premeditated intent to kill or to commit a **felony** that results in death (*felony murder*); and *murder in the second degree,* in which there is malice but no premeditation.

negligence: Failure to exercise the care that the law sets as a minimum and which a reasonable and prudent man would exercise in the same situation. This failure is not intentional or so flagrant as to be reckless. *Comparative negligence* is a doctrine found in some state laws, which allows a **plaintiff** to recover damages against a negligent **defendant** even though he himself was negligent. In such cases, the amount of damages is diminished in proportion to the plaintiff's negligence. (See also **contributory negligence**.)

no fault: 1. In the context of divorce, **statutes** permitting the dissolution of a marriage upon a showing that the relationship is no longer viable instead of the traditional requirement that one spouse prove the other to have committed certain acts, such as adultery or desertion.

2. In the context of automobile **negligence**, a statutory scheme that removes smaller **claims** from the **courts** by providing that the policy holder will be compensated by his own insurance company irrespective of who caused the accident.

nolo contendere: Latin, "I do not wish to contend." Without pleading **guilty**, this is an admission by a **defendant** to the facts of a **criminal indictment** for the purposes of the particular **case** and is accepted within the **dis-**

cretion of the **judge** who will then **sentence**. Unlike a **plea** or **verdict** of guilty, this admission cannot be used as the basis of any **civil liability** or other related **action**.

non compos mentis: Latin, "not of sound mind." Not in control of oneself; insane; not legally competent.

nonsuit: A **judgment** against the **plaintiff** for failing or neglecting to prove sufficient basis for his **claim**. Since this is rendered before the **defendant** puts on his **case**, it is not a **judgment on the merits**, and the plaintiff is not prevented from reinstituting **suit** at a later time.

notary public: A minor public official who is authorized to perform certain functions, such as administering oaths, attesting and certifying legal documents, etc.

N.O.V. (Non obstante verdicto): Latin, "not withstanding the verdict." A *judgment N.O.V.* is rendered by the **court** (i.e., the **judge**) reversing the determination of the **jury**'s **verdict** when that verdict either has no reasonable support in the **evidence** or is contrary to law, or both.

notice: Legally valid communication of information concerning a fact, condition, or **action**. *Actual notice* is the knowledge of such information without the necessity of its being communicated. *Constructive notice* is legally presumed knowledge as, for instance, after the mailing of a **complaint** to another **party** or the publication in a newspaper of a prospective name change.

objection: In **trial** practice, the assertion that a piece of **evidence** or argument should not be allowed into evidence by the **court**. Accomplished by the objecting **party**'s standing up and/or stating "I object," or "Objection, your honor," sometimes with the grounds for objection added.

obstruction of justice: A **crime** at **common law** as well as by **statute**, involving the intentional interference with the judicial process, as, for instance, the deliberate destruction of **sub-**

poenaed documents or the attempted bribe of a **witness** or a **juror**.

opinion: A statement by the **court** expounding the law as applied to the facts of the **case** and the reasons for its decision. Judicial decisions are not always accompanied by opinions, particularly in trial courts. A *dissenting opinion* is a statement of one or more **judges** as to why he (they) disagreed with the reasoning and result of the *majority opinion*. A *concurring opinion* is a statement of one or more judges of their different or additional reasons for arriving at the same decision as the majority of the other judges.

ordinance: A law enacted by local authorities (a city council or the like) to deal with matters of particularly local concern: such as zoning, parking, garbage disposal, and lesser-grade offenses such as loitering. (Compare **statute**.)

overrule: The **court**'s rejection of an assertion by **counsel** (e.g., "**Objection overruled**") or **reversal** of the decision of a lower court.

parole: Permission to serve the balance of a **criminal sentence** outside of prison, on the condition that the *parolee* complies with certain restrictions during the term of his parole. (Compare **probation**.) Also, verb, *to parole* a convicted offender.

party: A person (or organization) who is one of the **litigants** in an **adversary court** proceeding, or who enters into a legal transaction. Often used to refer to either "side" in a legal controversy, including in some sense the **attorney**; although strictly speaking, it is only the client. A *third party* is a person or organization not directly involved or affected by a given court proceeding or transaction.

patent: Exclusive right to the making and selling of an invention, granted by the federal government for a period of years. *Patent pending* means that an application for protection has been made and, if subsequently granted, will exclude those who have been given prior notice.

per curiam: Latin, "by the court." A unanimous

decision or **opinion** in which no judge is identified as author.

peremptory challenge: The right each **party** has at the time of **jury** selection to reject a specified number of **jurors** for no stated reason. Distinguished from *challenges for cause.*

perjury: The criminal offense of making a false statement under oath in a **court** proceeding; now also expanded in some statutes to include other false swearings in legal matters.

petition: A formal, written request to a **court** setting forth the relevant facts and circumstances and the relief sought, such as, *petition for review of administrative order.*

petit jury, also **petty jury**: The standard trial jury, employed to decide issues of fact in criminal and some civil cases. Traditionally composed of twelve citizens, but reduced to six in some **jurisdictions**.

petty larceny: See **larceny**.

plaintiff: The **party** who initiates a **civil lawsuit** against one or more **defendants**. The equivalent in a **criminal case** is the state.

plea: In *criminal procedure,* the response of the **defendant** to an **indictment: guilty, not guilty,** or **nolo contendere.**

plea bargaining: The process whereby a **defendant** agrees to admit to certain criminal **charges** in exchange for the dropping of certain other charges or the recommendation of a lighter punishment by the **prosecutor** to the **court** than might otherwise be made.

pleadings: Papers filed with the **court** by **plaintiff** and **defendant** setting forth their opposing **allegations** of fact and desired **relief**. Typically, the plaintiff's first filing is denominated the **complaint**, followed by the defendant's **answer**, and, where permitted, the plaintiff's **reply**. This process serves to define the **issues** for **trial**. Pleadings may be either *peremptory* (i.e., substantive, **on the merits**) or *dilatory* (dealing with procedural or technical matters).

power of attorney: Written authority given by one person to another to act as his or her agent for either limited or unlimited purposes.

precedent: Previously recorded judicial decisions that **courts** consider when making decisions or interpretations of law in similar **cases**. *Binding precedent* refers to decisions of courts of equal or higher authority in the same **jurisdiction** which, to the extent they present the same question of law, must be followed under the principle of **stare decisis**. *Persuasive precedent* or *persuasive authority* refers to decisions from courts of other jurisdictions whose reasoning may be followed.

preponderance of the evidence: The standard of proof necessary to prevail in **civil actions**: That amount of evidence which persuades the **court** or **jury** that a contested **claim** is more likely justifiable than not. (Compare **beyond a reasonable doubt**, the **criminal** standard of proof, which requires "moral certainty" and not mere likelihood.)

presumption: The legal assumption that follows after the establishment of certain facts, unless proven otherwise. (The *presumption of innocence* in criminal cases is a major tenet of the Anglo-American legal system.) The effect of any legal presumption is to shift the **burden of proof** to the other side.

prima facie: Latin, literally "at first view." That which appears to be true; on the face of it; apparently valid. A *prima facie case* is a case that, in the absence of any contradictory **evidence**, is legally sufficient to prevail in **court**.

privileged communications: Confidential communications that are protected by **statute** from forced disclosure in **court**; these include the communications within specified relationships such as doctor-patient, husband-wife, attorney-client, priest-penitent, and counselor-client. The communications of journalist-source have recently been adjudicated as *not* privileged in several controversial cases.

probable cause: The existence of sufficient facts

and circumstances to legally justify search or arrest.

probate: As a verb, to prove that a document purporting to be a **will** meets all the requirements of applicable state **statutes** to be given effect. As a noun, the process by which the validity of the will is determined and the estate parceled out. *Probate court* is a court whose limited **jurisdiction** includes proceedings relating to a decedent's estate, and may include divorce and custody matters as well.

probation: A nonprison sentence imposed in certain criminal cases after the **defendant** has been found guilty; the criminal is not incarcerated but will be supervised by a *probation officer*. Sometimes a *split sentence* is given, in which a short term in prison is combined with a larger period of probation.

pro bono (publico): Latin, "for the public good." Legal representation provided by lawyers without compensation, for some publically beneficial cause.

procedure: The method and manner by which a **case** is brought to **court** and tried; and the rules which govern the legal process. Distinguished from the substance of the law, the **merits** of a case, and so on. An example of a *procedural* defect in a case would be when the **statute of limitations** had already expired for the offense charged.

process: The means by which a **court** obtains compliance with its orders. Usually refers to a formal **writ** (or **summons**) requiring the attendance of the **defendant** in a **civil suit**. The person employed to deliver such court papers is termed the *process server*.

pro se: Latin, "for himself." A **litigant** who appears in **court** without the services of a lawyer.

prosecution: 1. A **criminal action;** the act of pursuing a **lawsuit.**

2. The government as **party** to a lawsuit, seeking to enforce the criminal laws.

prosecutor: The public official charged with handling **prosecutions;** variously termed **district attorney, county prosecutor,** or **U.S. attorney,** depending upon his **jurisdiction.**

punitive damages: A monetary award made not to compensate the **plaintiff** for **injury** sustained but to discourage the offending **party** from engaging in such activity in the future.

qua: Latin, "as." In the capacity of. For example, a lawyer may occasionally sit **qua judge,** by specific designation.

quasi: Latin, "almost." As it were; to some degree. A *quasi-contract* is not a contract, but a relationship to which a **court** will give similar meaning in the interest of fairness.

reasonable doubt: The standard beyond which the factfinder (the **jury** or **judge**) must be convinced in order to convict a **defendant** of a **criminal** offense.—*Beyond a reasonable doubt* is construed as "moral certainty," less certain than absolute certainty, which is not realistically possible, but significantly more certain than a **preponderance of the evidence,** which is the standard in **civil trials.**

reasonable man: The hypothetical personification of the legal standard of intelligence and care expected in the community, a violation of which is **negligence.** For example, a reasonable man would be expected to stop his automobile if he saw a child running out into the middle of the street in front of him.

rebuttal: The stage of **trial** at which **evidence** is introduced to counter, explain, or otherwise diminish the force of the other side's **witnesses** or **evidence.** *Rebuttable evidence* is that which can be contradicted or disproven.

recess: A temporary **adjournment** in **court** proceedings, usually not for the consideration of other business, but for lunch or overnight. (Compare **continuance.**)

recognizance: Agreement by a person to appear in **court** at a later date to answer **criminal charges** without the requirement of posting **bail.** A person will generally be granted a *release on personal recognizance (ROR)* when it is deemed highly unlikely that he will fail to appear in court.

record: The written compilation of all **pleadings**, transcribed **testimony**, and other **evidence** introduced, as well as the **findings** of the **court**. Only material on the record may be considered in an **appeal** to a **reviewing** court.

relief: A nonmonetary **remedy** sought from or awarded by a **court** in the form of an **injunction**, **specific performance**, or the like.

remedy: In **civil cases**, the judicial means by which to enforce or preserve a right, usually by the award of monetary **damages** after a violation of such a right, but also through such **equitable remedies** as **injunctions** or **specific performance**.

reply: A response by the **plaintiff** to new matters or **counterclaims** introduced in the **defendant's** answer.

representation: The relationship of attorney to client; the engagement of the services of a lawyer. Every citizen **charged** with a **crime** is entitled to representation.

res ipsa loquitur: Latin, "the thing speaks for itself." A situation in which the fact that a certain accident happened can only be attributed to **negligence**. An example would be a surgical scalpel remaining in a patient after an operation; the **burden of proof** would then be upon the **defendant** to show that this was *not* caused by negligence.

respondeat superior: Latin, "let the master answer." A **civil** doctrine that holds an employer (or other executive) responsible for the acts of his employees or agents when in the course of his business.

respondent: The **party** answering a **petition** or **appeal**. The converse of a **petitioner** or **appellant**.

restitution: A legal **remedy** that endeavors to return the **parties** to their original position. In **contract**, for example, this would mean the return of monies received by the party who failed to perform; in **criminal** law, the

return by the thief of goods which he had stolen.

restraining order: Temporary **court** order issued in extraordinary circumstances at the request of one of the **parties** without a **hearing** or notice to the other side, to prohibit any change in the status quo until such time as a hearing can be held on more permanent **relief**. Often called a *temporary restraining order*, abbreviated *TRO*.

restrictive covenant: An agreement, usually incorporated in the **deed**, to limit the use or sale of land. If for the purpose of racial exclusion, however, it will be unenforceable in the **courts**.

retainer: A fee paid a lawyer in advance of service, either as a first installment or to ensure the availability of **counsel** when required.

reversal: The overturning or setting aside of a lower **court** or agency decision, by a higher body.

review: Reexamination of the decision or **record** made by a lower **court** or agency. The review may be by the original body but more often refers to the examination made by an **appellate court**.

robbery: Taking the property of another by force or the threat of force. (Compare **burglary**, **larceny**.)

rule of law: The result of a substantial number of **cases** involving essentially similar facts being decided the same way. Distinguished from **legislation**.

search and seizure: A law-enforcement practice whereby a person or place is searched (by police, sheriff, FBI, etc.) for **evidence** that is then confiscated for later use at **trial**. The practice is limited by the federal and state constitutions, and evidence not lawfully obtained will be excluded.

search warrant: Judicial authorization to search a specified person or place for contraband, stolen goods, or other specific persons or things.

self-defense: The lawful use of force to protect

oneself, one's family, or one's property. A complete **defense** to a **criminal charge** or a **civil suit** if there is a real or apparent need to use force, the need was not a result of provocation, and it could not have reasonably been avoided by retreat or otherwise.

self-incrimination, the right against: A constitutional right under the Fifth Amendment to refuse to answer questions in **court** because they might subject one to **criminal prosecution**. ("I refuse to answer that question on the ground that it would tend to incriminate me" is referred to as *pleading the Fifth*.) This right ceases to exist if the witness has been granted immunity from criminal prosecution.

sentence: The punishment imposed following a **criminal conviction**, usually in the form of a fine or term of **probation** or imprisonment. A *concurrent sentence* is an order of imprisonment that is to be served at the same time as another order of imprisonment, thereby resulting in no additional time. A *consecutive sentence* is an order of imprisonment that is not to start running until after the expiration of an earlier term. See also **probation**.

set aside: To annul, **overrule**, or **reverse** a judgment, thereby making it of no effect.

shepardize: To find all the instances in which the **opinion** in a case has been subsequently **cited** by use of volumes for that purpose called **Shepard's Citations.**

sheriff: An elected county officer charged with assisting the **civil** and **criminal court** process in such ways as serving court papers, summoning juries, and holding judicial sales.

show-cause order: Upon application of a **party**, an order of **court** compelling the other side to appear in expedited fashion and argue why a certain thing should not be done or permitted. It is an accelerated method of bringing a **case** to court.

solicitor general: The third-highest official in the **attorney general**'s office, whose duty it is to represent the United States in **actions** in which it is involved before the U.S. Supreme Court.

specific performance: A **court**-ordered **remedy** requiring that a **contract** be performed exactly as promised, rather than that monetary **damages** be awarded for its **breach**. Available only in extraordinary circumstances where the subject of the contract cannot be purchased elsewhere, as with a particular piece of land or specific object of art.

standing: The legal right to bring an issue to **court**; or sufficient stake in the subject matter to be **party** to its resolution in court.

stare decisis: Latin, "to stand by what has been decided." The judicial doctrine of following **precedent**. The doctrine is not, however, inviolable.

state's evidence: **Testimony** given by a **convicted criminal**, or one who could be **charged** with crime, and used by the state to convict someone else. Often given in exchange for leniency or immunity from **prosecution**.

statute: Law that has been enacted by (state or federal) legislation, as opposed to unwritten and judge-made rules of law. *Statutory:* Arising out of legislatively enacted law.

statute of frauds: Legislatively enacted law requiring that in order for certain **contracts** to be enforceable in **court** they must be in writing, so as to reduce **fraud** and **perjury**. Typically covered are those contracts which entail the payment of more than a certain amount of money (e.g., $500), the sale of a piece of land, or which take place over more than a year's time.

statute of limitations: The law defining the length of time during which a given offense is prosecutable. Every type of **civil** or **criminal action**, with the exception of **prosecution** for **murder**, may be brought for only a limited period of time. These limits vary with the action, but are uniformly intended to protect potential **defendants** from endless fear of **suit** and the difficulty of maintaining **evi-**

dence of innocence over a long period of time.

stay: An order of **court** halting judicial proceedings until the occurrence of some later event.

subpoena: Latin, "under penalty." A **court**-authorized **writ** requiring the attendance of a **witness** at a judicial proceeding under penalty of **contempt of court** proceedings. (*Subpoena duces tecum:* Latin, "under penalty you shall take it with you." Attendance is required with certain specified documents under the individual's control.)

subrogation: One **party**'s succession to the rights of another by payment of a debt or third-party obligation. A typical such instance occurs when an insurance company pays its insured for injuries caused by a third party and then seeks reimbursement from that third party.

suit: A legal proceeding to obtain a **remedy**. More properly used in connection with **civil actions** only.

summary judgment: A judicial determination of a **case** with **argument** but without a full **trial** because the essential facts are undisputed and the **issue** or issues relate only to the law.

summation: Counsel's right, after the presentation of the **evidence**, to address the **jury** and explain his theory of the **case** in relation to that evidence.

summons: Written notification to the **defendant** that he has been sued and that his failure to appear in **court** on the appointed date to answer the **charge** against him will necessarily result in a **judgment** against him.

supreme court: The highest **court** of a state or the entire nation (U.S. Supreme Court). (See "Courts" section.)

sustain: To uphold or approve, as for example, when a **court sustains** a lawyer's **objection** to the admission of some **evidence** and refuses to accept it.

tenancy: The right of a tenant to possess premises in subordination to ownership by the landlord, created by a written or oral lease. *Tenancy for years* is the right of possession for a fixed duration, to end after a specified number of weeks, month, or years. *Tenancy at will* is the right of possession for indefinite duration, which may be ended by either the landlord or tenant by statutorily sufficient **notice** of termination. *Tenancy at sufferance* exists after the right of possession has terminated and the lease is no longer in effect. The tenant is subject to **eviction** but not **prosecution** as a **trespasser** since his original entry onto the premises was with consent.

testimony: An oral statement given by a **witness** under oath. One type of **evidence**, distinguished from documentary evidence or "real" evidence such as a gun.

title: Legal ownership—for example, to land or a motor vehicle; the right to possess something.

tort: A violation of **civil** law (as opposed to **criminal** law), which does not arise out of **contract** and which results in damage or **injury** to another. Common torts are **negligence** and **libel**. A *tort-feasor* is the person who commits a tort. *Tortious* means referring to that type of conduct that constitutes a tort.

trespass: A wrongful or **tortious** interference with another person's property.

trial: A judicial examination of a **criminal** or **civil case**, including the taking of **evidence**, for the purpose of making a decision as to the rights of the **parties**, based on the facts and law.

ultra vires: Latin, "beyond or in excess of powers." In excess of the powers conferred, as on an agency by **statute**, or on a corporation by articles of incorporation.

unconstitutional: Contrary to either the federal or a state constitution.

variance: An exception granted in individual cases by the zoning board to the strict application of the zoning law in order to avoid undue hardship.

venue: The place of **trial**. Any one of a number of places where a **court** has authority to hear the **case**. *Change of venue* may be granted if the court finds the scheduled place of trial the subject of too much prejudicial publicity.

verdict: A factual determination by a **jury** or **judge**. A *directed verdict* is rendered by a jury by the instruction of the judge (e.g., to **acquit** a **defendant** where insufficient **evidence** has been presented by **prosecution**). A *general verdict* simply declares which **party** has prevailed in the **case;** while a *special verdict* involves a **finding** on specific facts within a case.

void: Legally null; unenforceable in a **court** of law; empty.

voidable: Capable of being challenged and annulled in court, but otherwise enforceable. A **contract** with a minor is voidable, for example, and may be either repudiated or ratified when the child reaches the age of majority.

warrant: A written order issued by a **court,** authorizing someone's **arrest,** the search of premises or property, or other acts.

will: A person's written disposition of his property to be given effect at death. Requirements as to form are prescribed by **statute**, but the **instrument** is in all cases revocable by the maker during his lifetime, provided he is competent.

witness: A person who testifies in **court** as to the existence of a fact or facts. Also, someone who sees and can authenticate that a person has signed his signature.

writ: A written order issued by a **court** to a **sheriff** or another of its officers that something be done. Examples include *writ of habeas corpus, writ of mandamus, writ of coram nobis, writ of execution, writ of certiorari.*

[3]

Auto Mechanics

There is no one who has not, at one time or another, looked under the hood of a car and stared in confusion or dismay at one of the most ubiquitous, frustrating inventions of the twentieth century. The large majority of Americans, who depend so heavily upon the automobile, understand little or nothing of what goes on beneath the steering wheel, beyond the brake and gas pedals, behind the instrument panel. Though we spend over $30 billion yearly on automobile repairs and parts, few of us actually comprehend how this magical machine works, or what to do if it stops running.

The person who does understand (or at least claims to understand) the metal labyrinth beneath the hood is the auto mechanic, an individual cloaked in mystical grease and coveralls, who seems to speak (and occasionally write) a completely foreign language.

CUSTOMER: A hundred and eighty-seven fifty! Didn't you say you thought this bill was only going to run me fifty dollars?

MECHANIC: Yup. But I hadn't seen the car then.

CUSTOMER: What's this charge for the **starter**? Didn't you fix the starter for me last month?

MECHANIC: [*Condescendingly*] Last month we replaced the *armature* on the starter. That wasn't the problem this time.

CUSTOMER: [*Taking the cue*] What was it this time?

MECHANIC: **Solenoid**. We **pulled** it and the **points** were all burned up. Had to **R and R** the Bendix, too.

CUSTOMER: [*Trying to sound knowledgeable*] The Bendix? How could that . . . ?

MECHANIC: All chewed up. [*Shouts*] Hey, Charlie, still got that Bendix drive from Smith's car? [*Walks off into the shop and disappears. Returns almost fifteen minutes later holding an unrecognizable hunk of grimy metal*] See? Wasn't hitting right. Lucky we caught it now,

45

before it chipped the **flywheel** teeth. Gotta **yank** the engine if that goes.

CUSTOMER: [*In alarm*] The flywheel's O.K., isn't it?

MECHANIC: Looked all right, as far as I could tell. These teeth here're all chewed up, though, see? [*Holds out the part for inspection*]

CUSTOMER: [*Recoiling from the part, but relieved about the flywheel*] Oh, yeah, that looks terrible. I'm sure glad you caught that in time. [*Pause while Customer studies the repair bill further in the hope of finding something he can understand*] Hey, wait a minute, what's this? [*He tries to make out the writing on the bill*] "COMP. TEST. ADJ. VALVES, TORQ. HEAD." I didn't ask for any of that! And look at what you charged me—!!

MECHANIC: [*Scathingly*] Mr. Smith, you said the power was low, so we did a **compression test**. Figured either you had **burnt valves**, or else they was way out. But after I **adjusted** 'em, they read O.K., so we left it at that. Now, you also complained of smelling oil, so I *torqued* the *head*, and replaced a *valve cover gasket*. That seems to have cleared up the leak.

CUSTOMER: [*Mouth agape*] Oh. Ah, well, I guess that's O.K. then.

MECHANIC: And one other thing, Mr. Smith.

CUSTOMER: [*Weakly*] Yes?

MECHANIC: That squeak in the **front end**.

CUSTOMER: Squeak? Oh, yes, the squeak. Horrible sound. Did you find out what was causing it?

MECHANIC: [*Nods*] **Bushings**.

CUSTOMER: Pushing? Pushing what?

MECHANIC: *Bushings*. Worn out. Had to replace four of them. That road salt sure eats up the rubber.

CUSTOMER: [*Wistfully*] Yes, it sure does. [*Takes out his checkbook*] Who do I make this out to?

The following is a guide through the linguistic haze that surrounds the world of the automobile, like the blue smoke billowing from the rusty tailpipe of a **sled** in dire need of a **ring job**. In the interests of clarity, read on.

Note: After most of the repair jobs listed in this section, the approximate price range of the job, *including parts*, has been noted. A single dollar sign ($) denotes a minor job, up to $50 or $60. Two dollar signs ($$) mean a medium job, in the $75–$150 range. Three dollar signs ($$$) mean a major job, denoting those consummations devoutly to be unwished, repairs costing several hundred dollars or more. While there is always some variation and continued inflation may alter the figures somewhat, the mechanics consulted on this section have agreed that the jobs listed *should* fall within the ranges indicated; if not, you are most likely being ripped off. Forewarned is forearmed.

In addition to an extensive technical vocabulary (discussed below), mechanics have a slang that they employ among themselves. A smattering of these terms will make the speaker appear to be at least a peripheral member of the mechanical community—provided you've got the greasy hands to back it up. ❧

Mechanics' Slang

blown: Ruined; also, bored out; also, cleaned. **Head gaskets** can be blown (ruined); **cylinders** can be *blown out* (enlarged); an air **jet** in the carburetor can be *blown out* (cleaned).

boat: Also **ark**, **canoe**, **sled**. A large, unwieldy, usually older American car, such as a Cadillac, Oldsmobile, or Chrysler. ("Picked up this **boat** for seventy-five bucks.") Such cars are not purchased for their high EPA mileage ratings.

boneyard: Junkyard, where cars go to die and from which their usable parts are "recycled."

chop shop: An illegal car-parts operation that takes stolen cars and cuts them up, selling the separate parts at a high profit.

clunker: Also **junker**, **shitbox**, **dog**, **heap**. A car in terrible condition, needing extensive body work or mechanical work, or probably both. ("That **clunker's** headed straight for the **boneyard**.")

frozen: Also **froze up**. Jammed, locked on, no longer movable. Used mainly to refer to threaded couplings, such as nuts and bolts, etc. (Not the same as **seized**, which usually refers to a movable part or system.)

howler: A car that makes a howling noise when it moves forward. It may have something wrong with the **differential**, causing it to howl only when the foot is on the gas pedal, but not when coasting. Or it may have **singers** for tires, usually snow tires with poorly designed treads, which set up a resonance pattern and produce a singing noise.

junk a car: To send it to the junkyard; or to send it *from* the junkyard to the *crusher*, which reduces it to a small package of concentrated metal.

midnight acquisition: The unfortunately all too common practice of stealing parts out of sound cars to install in vehicles that are under repair. See also **chop shop**.

on the hook: On the back of a tow truck.

pull: Also **yank**. To remove. ("That's right, mister, eighty bucks to **pull** the **tranny**.")

R and R: Remove and replace an auto part. Formerly meant (and in some rare situations may still mean) remove and repair. It is always easier for the mechanic to replace an item than repair it, and sometimes it may be cheaper for the customer as well.

rubber: Tires. *Good rubber* means new or almost-new tires; also tires that have worn evenly, indicating good **front end** (**ball joints** and **alignment**).

run it into the ground: Drive a car without bothering to spend any money to repair it, until it is ready to be **junked**. Common advice given to the owner of a **clunker**.

seized: Rigid; immovable; effectively ruined. A seized engine is one in which the metal parts have become so hot they have actually welded together. ("Ran out of oil and the engine **seized**.")

stripped: Applied to a damaged or nonfunctioning screw-thread on a nut, a bolt, a screw, or on any other threaded part. A **spark plug**, for instance, can be stripped if it is screwed in too tightly into the **cylinder head**.

wall job: Also, **sunbath**. An unscrupulous dealer will often receive a car for warranty work and give it a wall job—that is, parking it in his lot and doing no work on it. Then he will return it to the customer, perhaps with some minor repairs performed, hoping it will last until the warranty expires—at which point he gets fully paid for the repair work he should have done for free.

AUTO MECHANICS TERMINOLOGY

air cleaner: A large cylindrical or pie-pan-shaped device that sits on the top of the **carburetor** on most American cars and some foreign ones.

air filter: Located inside the **air cleaner** to screen out dirt and other impurities from the air that is drawn into the **carburetor**. (Replacement: $)

alignment: Also, **wheel alignment**. A series of adjustments to position the front wheels relative to each other and to the road, in order to create optimum handling and tire wear. Alignment adjustments include: *camber, caster, toe-in, toe-out,* and *steering axis inclination.* ($)

alternator: A device run by belts that converts mechanical energy to electrical energy and continuously charges the battery while the engine is running. Replaces the **generator**, which performed a similar function in older cars. (New alternator: $$)

axle: Solid metal shaft or rod that spins and transfers the engine power from the **differential** to the drive wheels.

ball joint: Any of several ball-and-socket arrangements used to create movable joints in the **suspension system** and **steering linkage** of the car; used for cushioning and relieving stress while providing free turning movement of the front wheels. (Replace two ball joints: $$)

barrel: The main body of the **carburetor**, a thick tubelike metal channel in which air is mixed with fuel. Carburetors can be made with more than one barrel: *dual carbs* (two barrels) or *quads* (four barrels). Some of the older high-performance gas guzzlers (such as the famed Pontiac GTO) used to feature three two-barrel carburetors, known as *trips* or *three deuces.*

bearing: A device that lowers the friction between two moving parts, usually through a ball-bearing effect. Front *wheel bearings* (which are of the roller type) should be repacked with grease and rear wheel *axle bearings* replaced if a grinding noise emanates from the front or rear wheels. ($)

bleeding: The process of removing air bubbles from a hydraulic (liquid-filled) system, most often the **brakes**. ($)

block: Also, **engine block**. The main body of the engine, which encloses the **cylinders** and **pistons** and sits over the **crankcase**, and through which both coolant and lubricating oil circulate. A *cracked block* occurs when the engine coolant freezes, or occasionally when cold water is poured into an overheated engine that is not running. Usually the entire engine must be replaced. ($$$)

blown head gasket: A situation in which the **gasket** between the **cylinder head** and the **engine block** no longer creates an adequate seal. This causes loss of power, overheating, and can eventually ruin the engine. (Replacing **head gasket** if no other complications: $$)

brake line: Steel, rubber, or plastic tubing that

connects the **master cylinder** and the **wheel cylinders**, and contains the brake fluid,

brakes: Devices used to slow down the car by applying pressure through friction against a moving part of each wheel. There are two kinds of brakes: *disc* and *drum*. In *drum brakes,* hydraulic pressure forces the curved *brake shoes* against the inner surface of the round, hollow metal drums to stop the car. In *disc brakes,* the hydraulic pressure (transmitted from the action of the brake pedal) causes the *pads* on pincerlike **calipers** to be squeezed against flat metal discs, creating the friction that stops the car. Many cars today have disc brakes on the front wheels and drum brakes on the rear.

burn oil: Also, **throw oil** or **pump oil**. Occurs when oil escapes from beyond the **piston rings** onto the **cylinder** wall, indicated by a cloud of foul-smelling blue or black smoke coming from the exhaust pipe. Usually indicates the need for a **ring job**.

bushing: A hollow, cylinderical **bearing**, often a rubber "doughnut," which allows metal parts to move against one another without grating.

butterfly nut: Also, **wing nut**. Not an aficionado of Lepidoptera, but a nut with two extended "wings" so that it can be easily turned and tightened by hand. Often one is located on top of the **air cleaner**.

butterfly valve: A metal plate or disc that opens and closes to admit more or less air into the **carburetor**. Combined with an automatic or manual method of control, it comprises the **choke** mechanism.

calipers: A device found only on **disc brakes**; a kind of pincers, which squeeze the *disc pads* against the disc to slow or stop the car.

cam: An irregularly shaped metal disc attached to a rotating shaft; used on the **camshaft** to open and close the **valves**, and in the **distributor** to open and close the **points**. *Cam lobes* are the curved extrusions of the cams that periodically make contact with other mechanical parts. Terms such as *SOHC* and *DOHC*

stand for *single* and *dual overhead cams*, and describe camshafts situated above the **cylinders** in the engine. (See **OHC**.)

camshaft: A shaft with **cams** attached that causes the **valves** to open and close; usually located below the **cylinders**, and connected by **push rods** to the valves.

carburetor: A device that mixes fuel and air in the correct proportions, producing a fine misty gasoline vapor, which is then passed to the engine to be ignited in the **cylinders**.

catalytic converter: A pollution-control device found in most newer cars. Located between the **exhaust manifold** and the **muffler**, it converts exhaust hydrocarbons and deadly carbon monoxide (combined with oxygen) into carbon dioxide and water.

catch: *v.* When the engine suddenly turns over on its own power (as opposed to that of the **starter motor**), burning gasoline and emitting a consistent exhaust vapor.

charging system: The system that restores energy to the battery after it has been depleted (by starting the car), and which also provides the electricity for lights, horns, and accessories while the car is running. It consists basically of an **alternator** (or **generator**), which is run by a **fanbelt**; and a **voltage regulator**. Often a "dead" battery is caused by some fault or loose connection in the charging system.

chassis: The frame of the car which remains after you take away the outer shell (body and fenders).

choke: 1. *n.* The device in the **carburetor** that alters the air/gas mixture, as the car goes from cold to warm. (See **butterfly valve**.) Chokes may be *manual* or *automatic*.

2. *v.* To decrease the relative amount of air coming into the carburetor so that the engine burns a richer gas mixture; necessary when starting a cold engine.

clutch: A device situated between the engine and the **transmission** to enable the changing of gears. When the clutch pedal is pushed in, the transmission is disengaged from the engine, allowing the gears to be shifted. A clutch may *drag* (not fully disengage, making gear shifting difficult); *slip* (not fully engage engine with transmission, creating slippage and loss of power); *grab* (making the car lurch or jerk forward as you release the clutch pedal); or *chatter* (grab in a staccato fashion, causing the car to shudder). Terms related to the clutch include: **throw-out bearing, free play, pressure plate**, and **flywheel**. (Clutch replacement: $$$)

coil: Also, **ignition coil**. A part of the **ignition system** that looks like a small solid cylinder, and whose purpose is to amplify the current from the battery into a "jolt" strong enough to create a powerful spark in the **spark plugs**. (Replacement: $)

combustion chamber: The small space at the top of the **cylinder**, where the fuel/air mixture, having been compressed by the **piston**, is ignited by a spark from the **plug.**

compound: To rub the car with an abrasive compound, removing superficial scratches and often renewing the car's shine. Compounding a car is the last attempt at renewal before a paint job. After compounding, which removes the surface layer of paint, a car is usually waxed.

compression test: A fairly simple test used to diagnose the power-providing functions of the engine. A *compression gauge* is inserted into each **spark plug** hole in turn, and the engine **cranked** several times; the resulting reading indicates the maximum compression produced in each **cylinder**. Normal compression readings are 120–150 psi, with no more than a 10 to 15 percent difference between any two cylinders. (Test: $)

condenser: A small electrical device in the **distributor** that keeps the **points** from burning by sponging off excess current.

cooling system: Consists of the **radiator, thermostat, water pump, fan, water jackets,** hoses, and *coolant* mixture. The cooling sys-

tem circulates a liquid mix of water and antifreeze (or coolant) through the **engine block** in order to keep it from becoming overheated.

cooling system flush: See **flush.**

core plugs: Also, **freeze plugs**. Small brass or steel plugs inserted into the **engine block**, designed to pop out and relieve excessive pressure, to prevent the block from cracking.

crank: Also, **turn over**. The engine cranks if, after turning the ignition key on, one hears the sound of the **crankshaft** rotating, **pistons** pumping, and so on, indicating that both the battery and **starter motor** are functioning. ("**Crank** the engine and let's see what she sounds like.") (See **catch**.)

crankcase: Section of the engine below the **block**, which houses the **crankshaft** and **oil pan**.

crankshaft: The main power output shaft of the engine, which receives power from the **pistons** (via *connecting rods*) and transmits it, through the **transmission**, to the **driveshaft** and eventually, the wheels.

creeper: A board on wheels, used by mechanics to work under cars. It enables one to move around freely and avoid lying on the invariably grease-covered garage floor.

cylinder: The part of the engine where the power to drive the wheels is created. Each cylinder is a kind of hollow metal pipe with one end closed, and houses a moving **piston**. The upward action of the piston compresses the air/gas mixture, which is ignited by the **spark plug** and explodes, driving the **piston** down—which turns the **crankshaft** and ultimately powers the drive wheels. Most cars built today have four, six, or eight cylinders.

dieseling: Also, **postignition**. A condition in which the engine continues to "run on" after it has been turned off. Usually caused by an excessively **lean** fuel mixture, or incorrect **timing**. (Correction: $)

differential: Also, **rear end**. A mechanical device, situated between the two *drive wheels* of the car, which transfers energy from the **driveshaft** ninety degrees to the rear **axle**, and which also enables each of the rear wheels to turn at a different speed when the car is turning.

disc brakes: See **brakes**.

distributor: A device that sends electricity (received from the **coil**) to each of the **spark plugs** in the correct sequence and at the right time, in order to ignite the fuel-air mixture in one **cylinder** after another.

distributor cap: A hard plastic covering that fits over the **distributor**, with little "towers" for each of the **spark plug** wires to fit into, and a center "tower" for the wire from the **coil**.

double-clutching: A method of shifting gears whereby the driver depresses the **clutch**, shifts into neutral, releases the clutch, steps lightly on the accelerator, then depresses the clutch again before shifting into the next gear. The technique is used to equalize the speeds of the engine and **clutch disc**, thereby reducing wear on these parts. Double-clutching can only be done with a manual transmission, and is usually used with cars or trucks that do not have synchromesh.

driveshaft: A thick metal shaft that runs from the **transmission** to the **differential**, transmitting the power from the engine to wheels by spinning rapidly. It is a major element of the **drive train**.

drive train: All the critical components of a car that cause it to move; or the path through which power is transferred from the engine to the *drive wheels* (which are usually the rear wheels on an American car). Sequentially, the drive train consists of the **engine**, **clutch**, **transmission**, **driveshaft**, **differential**, and rear **axle**. (On **front-wheel-drive** cars, it consists of **engine**, **clutch**, **transaxle**.)

dwell: Also, **dwell angle** or **cam angle**. A measurement of how long the distributor **points** stay closed—measured in degrees of rotation of the **distributor** shaft. This is an exact index of correct gapping (see **gap**) of the points, or the correct timing of firing the **spark plugs**.

dwell meter: An electronic device that measures the actual **dwell angle** of the **distributor points**, which, when compared with the **specifications** for that car, will indicate whether the points have been gapped (see **gap**) correctly and deliver electricity in the correct timing.

electronic ignition: A so-called breakerless ignition, meaning there are no breaker **points** in the **distributor,** and no **condenser**. Instead, a magnetic or optical sensor triggers the spark. A feature on some more advanced late-model cars.

engine block: See **block**.

exhaust manifold: Or simply **manifold**. The very beginning of the **exhaust system** in a series of pipes (one for each engine **cylinder**) that lead the exhaust gases out of the engine, toward the **muffler**.

exhaust system: The series of pipes and devices that carry the waste gases from the engine into the air. Along the way, **mufflers**, **resonators**, and pollution-control devices dampen noise and absorb harmful substances.

fan belt: A long continuous rubber belt that runs due to the turning of the fan (which is connected to the engine) and which in turn runs the **alternator**. In some cars, additional fan belts are used to drive air conditioning and power steering. (Replacement: $)

feeler gauge: Also, **gapper**. A set of flat metal strips, or round metal wires, of varying thicknesses, used to measure and set the **gap** (space) between ignition **points**, **spark plug** electrodes, or **valves**.

firewall: The insulated wall separating the engine compartment from the driving compartment. The firewall keeps noise, fumes, and fire from the car's interior.

flat rate: A method of computing labor costs from a book published by Chilton's or the manufacturer, with suggested times indicating how long each job should take. (See also **on the clock**.)

flat time: Same as **on the clock**.

flooding: "Drowning" the engine with too much gasoline; the **spark plugs** become wet and cannot fire. This often occurs from trying to start a car with the **choke** stuck closed.

flush: To circulate liquid through a system in order to clean it out. Flushing the **cooling system** is done by emptying the old water-and-coolant and running clean water through the system to remove rust, dirt, and other accumulated debris. ($)

flywheel: A thick, heavy plate attached to the **crankshaft** and moving with it. When the car is in gear, the flywheel is in contact with the **clutch disc**, and engine power is transmitted through the **drive train**.

free play: The distance the **clutch** pedal will move before beginning to disengage the clutch, which indicates how far the **throw-out bearing** is from engaging the **pressure plate**. If there is too much free play, it is difficult to disengage the clutch and shift (the gears will grind); if too little free play, the clutch is never fully engaged, causing it to **slip** and wear out prematurely.

freeze plug: See **core plug**.

front end: All those mechanisms in the front of the car concerned with steering: **ball joints**, **tie rod ends**, **pitman arm**, **idler arm**, **center linkage**.

front-wheel drive: An alternative **drive train** system in which power is transmitted almost directly to the front wheels, which "pull" the car rather than "push" it, as do rear-wheel-drive systems. Front-wheel drive eliminates the need for **driveshaft** and **rear end** (**differential**) and also confers certain advantages in handling and performance, especially on snow and ice.

fuel filter: A small cylindrical filter, about the size of an egg, which absorbs dirt and impurities from the fuel before it reaches the **carburetor**. (Replacement: $)

fuel injection: A system of delivering fuel/air mixture to the **cylinder** combustion chambers without a **carburetor**. An electronic device senses fuel demand and injects it in the correct quantity.

fuel pump: A device that draws fuel from the gas tank and pumps it through the gas lines to the **carburetor**. This is one item typically replaced by "overzealous" mechanics when the actual problem is somewhere else in the fuel system—and repair a lot less expensive. (Replacement: $$)

fuse: An electrical safeguard that melts or *blows* if any electric circuit is overloaded; the fuse will burn out instead of the wires. Fuses are easily replaced (*fuse box* is located under the dashboard) and should be the first place to check when encountering *any* electrical malfunction.

gap: The distance between electric **points**, such as the ignition points, or between any two pieces of metal. To *gap the points* means to gauge the distance between them (using a **feeler gauge**) and adjust it to the proper tolerance.

gapper: See **feeler gauge**.

gasket: A shaped insert, made of rubber, paper, cork, or other substance, that seals the space between two metal parts, making them airtight, gastight, or watertight. (See **blown head gasket**.)

gearbox: See **transmission**.

generator: The device that runs off the **fan belt** and delivers direct-current electricity to the battery; usually only found in older cars. (Newer cars have an **alternator**, which performs the same function.)

grease fitting: A device that enables grease or some other lubricant to be added to a **ball joint** or other cushioning mechanism to prevent wear and friction in the joint. Lubricant is added to those grease fittings that require it in a **lube job**.

ground: Electrical connection between the battery and the metal car frame. The automobile battery has two *terminals:* a *positive terminal,* from which a cable leads to the various electrical devices of the car; and a *negative terminal,* from which a cable leads to some metal bolt on the **chassis**, or frame, thus completing the electrical circuit. This latter connection is called the ground.

head: The **cylinder** head, a large metal engine component just above the **block**, which forms the top of the **combustion chamber** and within which the **valves** are located.

head gasket: The seal between the **head** and the **block**, usually made of rubber. (See **blown head gasket**.)

heater core: A small radiator that heats air as it is blown into the passenger compartment.

hydraulic: Referring to any system operated by the pressure of a liquid (water, oil, brake fluid, etc.) through a tube or other small opening. **Brakes** and **transmissions**, for example, are hydraulic systems.

idle: When the engine is running without moving the car—i.e., in neutral (or park) with no pressure on the accelerator pedal—the car is said to be idling. The speed of the engine in such a condition is its *idle speed.* There are several *idle adjustments* that should be made as part of every **tune-up**.

idler arm: The passenger-side equivalent of the **pitman arm**. It supports the right side of the **center link** and is part of the **steering linkage**.

ignition coil: See **coil**.

ignition system: All those electrical parts of the automobile that serve to generate the spark in the **cylinder combustion chamber** that will ignite the fuel/air mixture. It includes the battery, **coil**, **distributor**, **points**, **plugs**, and numerous wires.

intake manifold: An array of iron pipes that serve as passageways for the gas/air mixture from the **carburetor** to the **combustion chambers** of the **cylinders**.

intake valve: The engine **valve** which opens and closes to admit the fuel/air mixture into the **combustion chamber**—at the right time and in the right amount. There is one intake valve per **cylinder**. (See also **valve**.)

jet: A small opening that allows a controlled fuel flow to enter the **carburetor** barrel. Jets often look like thick, hollow brass screws.

knocking: Rapid rattling or pinging sound from the engine (especially while going uphill), caused by low-octane gasoline or improper engine **timing**. (Also called **pre-ignition air**.)

lean: Indicates too little gas (per given volume of air) in the fuel/air mixture created in the **carburetor** for optimal engine performance. *Rich* indicates too much gas (per given volume of air).

lifters: Devices that open and close the **valves**, using the circular energy of the rotating **camshaft**.

line: Any tube or hose device that carries a fluid: e.g., *brake line, gas line,* etc.

linkage: Any mechanism of metal rods, levers, or cables that transmit motion from one place to another. Common linkages include: **clutch pedal** to **clutch**; gas pedal to **carburetor**; steering wheel to front wheels; stick shift to **transmission**, and so on. The large majority of linkages go from inside the driving compartment to outside it.

lube: Also **lubricate**. To pump grease into all the ball-and-socket joints of the **steering linkage** (and some other movable parts) to reduce friction and wear. A *lube job* should be done once or twice a year. ($)

lug nuts: Large hexagonal nuts that hold the wheels (tire **rims**) onto the car. Tires are fitted onto the rims, and, in order to change a tire, you must first remove the rim by loosening the lug nuts, with a *lug wrench.*

mags: Fancy magnesium-alloy wheels, used for

show, and because they dissipate heat faster and are stronger than other wheel alloys.

manifold: A pipe that connects a series of passageways to one passageway. The **exhaust manifold** connects the **cylinder** exhaust ports with the **exhaust** pipe.

master cylinder: The main unit in any **hydraulic** system, which creates a fluid pressure that is then transmitted along the **line**. When you press on the brake pedal a **linkage** transfers this force to the *master cylinder piston,* which compresses the brake fluid. This pressure is transmitted by means of the **brake lines** out to the brakes at each wheel. (Replacement: $$)

misfiring: Condition that exists when one or more **cylinders** fails to achieve combustion of the fuel/air mixture. There can be many causes, ranging from fouled or faultily gapped plugs, to bad wiring, to incorrectly gapped points, to worn **piston rings** and **valve** problems. (See also **gap**.)

muffler: Literally, a device to muffle the sound of the engine before it leaves the tailpipe. Usually, an expanded **cylinder** between the exhaust pipe and the tailpipe with a number of baffles to absorb engine sounds and cool exhaust gases.

needle valve: Small **valve** that regulates the mixture of air and gas in the **carburetor**.

octane: A numerical rating that stands for the ability of a specific gasoline to resist detonation or **knocking**. The higher the number, the greater the proportion of antiknock substances per gallon of gas. High-performance engines usually require *high-octane* gasoline, also called *high-test*.

OHC: Overhead cams; a **camshaft** that runs above the heads rather than below the **cylinders** as is customary, thus eliminating the need for **push rods**.

oil filter: A device that filters and cleans the oil as it circulates through the engine. Most oil filters look like small cans and screw into the side of the engine.

oil pan: The storage compartment for engine oil, located at the bottom of the **crankcase**. The *oil-drain plug,* which is used to empty the old oil during an oil change, is located on the bottom of the oil pan.

oil pump: A device that pumps the oil from the **oil pan** through to all rotating and moving parts of the engine, providing lubrication and reducing wear.

on the clock: Also called **flat time**. A labor charge based on exactly how long it takes the mechanic to fix the car (e.g., two hours at $15 an hour). Not to be confused with **flat rate**, which is a fixed charge for a particular repair regardless of how long it takes.

oscilloscope: Also called a **scope**. An electronic testing instrument used to diagnose engine problems and give accurate indication of **ignition-system** performance.

overhead cams: See **OHC**.

oversteer: The tendency of a car to turn more and more sharply into a curve with very little steering effort. Only a small amount of pressure on the steering wheel, or a small turn on the wheel, will produce a tendency to turn quite sharply.

PCV valve: Positive crankcase ventilation valve. A device that takes unburned fuel/air and exhaust fumes which have escaped past the **piston rings** into the **crankcase** and reroutes them back to the **carburetor** to be reburned. This reduces pollution emission and increases fuel economy.

piston: The major mechanical component of a **cylinder**. Pistons are shaped like thick, smooth cans, with a rod extending from the bottom surface; they receive and transmit energy by sliding up and down inside the cylinder. The word most often refers to the part of the engine that transmits the power of the explosions in the **combustion chamber** to the **crankshaft**; however, there are also pistons in the brake **cylinders**, for example.

piston rings: See **rings**.

plugs: See **spark plugs**.

points: Also, **contact points**, **breaker points**, or **ignition points**. Metal terminals located within the **distributor** that open and close rapidly, thus alternately breaking and closing a circuit which delivers electricity to the **spark plugs**. *Gapping* the points is a critical element of every **tune-up** (see **gap**).

positraction: Limited-slip **differential**, a factory option not found on most cars. Positraction basically delivers mechanical power to the wheel with most traction. Thus, if one of the driving wheels is spinning (on ice, mud, etc.), it will power the other one.

pre-ignition: See **knocking**.

pressure plate: Part of the **clutch** mechanism, a disc that presses against the **clutch disc**, forcing it into contact with the **flywheel**, when the car is in any driving gear.

push rods: Metal rods that connect the **lifters** to the **rocker arms**, thus enabling the rotation of the **cams** to open and close the **valves**.

radiator recore: The job of removing and replacing the water tubes in a radiator; required when the tubes have been damaged in an accident or are hopelessly clogged. ($$)

rear end: Also, **differential**. A device that transfers energy from the **driveshaft** to the **axles** (a 90-degree turn). It is a large casing situated at the juncture of the driveshaft and rear axles. The term is also sometimes used to mean the *final drive ratio*, which is the number of turns the driveshaft must make to produce one full turn in the axle or drive wheels.

rebuild: To take a worn or malfunctioning part or device, disassemble it, clean it, replace all worn or malfunctioning parts, and then reassemble it. **Starters**, **clutches**, **brakes**, **carburetors**, **fuel pumps**, and even engines can be rebuilt, and, although the job may be expensive, it is always cheaper than buying a new part.

regulator: See **voltage regulator**.

reline brakes: To replace the asbestos lining of the *brake shoes* in *drum*-type brakes. However, the shoes and lining are usually sold as a unit, hence, to reline the brakes is now synonymous with installing new brake shoes. (Front or rear brakes only: $; all four brakes: $$)

resonator: A kind of secondary **muffler** found on some foreign cars, which provides additional noise reduction.

ring job: Replacement of the **piston rings** in the engine; one of the most serious of all repair jobs. A ring job is required when the rings wear out or break—indicated by low **compression** or severe **burning of oil**. ($$$)

rings: Also, **piston rings**. Metal rings that fit into parallel grooves around the sides of the **piston**, and which act as a seal to keep fuel/air above the piston and oil below it. The rings insure a snug, smooth fit between pistons and **cylinder** walls.

rocker arms: Small levers that connect the **push rods** and the **valves**. They make the valves open and close by transmitting the pressure from the **cam lobes**.

rocker panel: The section of a car's body that runs under the door or doors on one side of the car, and extends from the front to the rear-wheel well. Often this is the first area in which rust appears.

rotor: A device found inside the **distributor cap** that spins around, delivering electric current to each **spark plug** terminal in the correct order. Usually replaced as part of a **tune-up**. The term is also sometimes used to refer to the **brake discs**.

scope: See **oscilloscope**.

shimmy: Uncontrollable vibration of the **front end**, usually perceived through a shaking or oscillation of the steering wheel. Caused by out-of-balance tires, worn or loose **wheel bearings**, worn **ball joints**, or bad **alignment**.

shocks: Also, **shock absorbers**. Hydraulic devices (usually a telescoping tube) that reduce bouncing on uneven road surfaces and improve a car's handling on turns or rough roads. One per wheel. (Replacing all four: $$)

spark plugs: Also **plugs**. Small devices (approximately four inches long) that deliver the spark of electricity that ignites the fuel/air mixture in the **cylinder**. Each plug has two electrodes with a **gap** between them; as the current passes across this gap, the spark is created. Spark plugs are usually replaced at every tune-up, or whenever they are fouled or burned. ($)

specs: Specifications. The manufacturer's list of sizes and measurements for the various parts and adjustments for each model car. For example, one must know the correct specs in order to **gap** the **points** and **plugs** on a car.

springs: Major components of the **suspension system**. Located between the body and the **axles**, springs cushion the shock of bumps and reduce swaying. There are two main types: *coil springs* and *leaf springs*.

starter: Also, **starter motor**. A small electric motor (run by the power of the battery) that turns the **flywheel** and thus starts the engine. (Replacement: $$)

starter solenoid: A switch that activates the flow of current to the **starter motor**. It is engaged when the key is turned in the **ignition switch**. (Replacement: $)

steering linkage: Those mechanisms which transmit steering-wheel movement to the front wheels. Includes the steering column, **idler arm**, *pitman arm, tie rods,* and **ball joints**.

suspension system: Those mechanisms which support the weight of the car, cushion and absorb shocks, and maintain stability. Includes **springs** and **shock absorbers**, and often such features as torsion bars, roll bars, etc.

thermostat: A small device (located inside the radiator hose) that opens to allow circulation of coolant-and-water only when the engine has reached a certain temperature. The thermostat thus enables the engine to warm up more quickly; but if it should become stuck, the engine will overheat. (Replacement: $)

throttle: A "butterfly" device similar to the **choke** but located at the bottom of the *carburetor barrel*. It controls the amount of fuel and air entering the carburetor by opening to create a richer mixture when the accelerator pedal is pressed down.

throwing a rod: A disastrous situation wherein a **connecting rod** becomes detached from the **crankshaft**, often ramming right through the **block**. A major repair! ($$$)

throw-out bearing: A device activated when the **clutch pedal** is pressed; it in turn causes the **pressure plate** to move, disengaging the **clutch** from the **flywheel**. The throw-out bearing can wear quickly from "riding" the clutch or **idling** with the pedal depressed while still in gear. (Replacement: $$)

tie rod ends: Joints in the **steering linkage** whenever two parts meet; they are filled with grease to prevent friction and maintain free movement.

timing: Also, **set the timing**. Adjusting the **spark-plug** firing so that it occurs at exactly the correct moment in the **piston**'s up-and-down movement; this enables the engine to operate smoothly and efficiently. The timing is set with a *timing light,* a gunlike device that emits a stroboscopic light. Checking and setting the timing must be a part of every **tune-up**.

torque the heads: To tighten the **cylinder head** bolts to a specific tension, using a device called a *torque wrench*. Often these bolts have to be tightened in a specific order. ($)

transmission: Also, **tranny, gearbox**. A multiple-gear unit that controls the changing relationship between the engine speed (rpms) and the speed (and direction) of the drive wheels. Transmissions may be *manual* (operated through a **clutch** system) or *automatic*. (Replacement: $$$)

tune-up: A periodic check and adjustment of the **ignition system** and related devices. At the very minimum, a tune-up must include: replacing and gapping **plugs** and **points** (see **gap**); setting the **timing**; replacing **rotor** and

condenser; adjusting the **idle**. A "major" tune-up will also include check or replacement of: **PCV valve**, **distributor cap**, **spark-plug wires**, **air filter**, etc. Tune-ups should be performed approximately twice a year. (Basic tune-up: $; major tune-up: $$)

turning drums or rotors: A process in which the *brake drums* or *disc rotors* are removed from the car and machined (on a lathe) to smooth out their surface. The purpose of this job is to give the *brake shoe* or *pad* a smooth surface to rub up against. Pulsing or shuddering when the brakes are applied is often an indication that the drums or rotors need to be turned. (All four brakes: $$)

universal joint: Also, **u-joint**. Flexible coupling, located at each end of the **driveshaft**. Together the two u-joints allow the rotational energy to be transmitted from **transmission** to **rear end**, while still absorbing up-and-down movement as the car moves over varying terrain.

valve: There are many valves in the modern automobile—*tire valves, carburetor valves*, **PCV valve**, etc. However, the term is generally used to refer to the *engine valves*. These are small devices, two to a **cylinder**, that open and close in response to the rotation of the **camshaft** (transmitted through the **cam** lobes, **push rods**, and **rocker arms**). The *intake valve* opens to admit the fuel/air mixture into the **combustion chamber**; the *exhaust valve* opens to release exhaust gases into the **exhaust manifold**.

valve adjustment: Adjusting the clearance between the **valve** and *valve seat* in order to get maximum compression and to reduce valve wear, as well as the likelihood of valves burning. The need for a valve adjustment is often indicated by a steady, rapid tapping noise in the engine. An inexpensive job, usually no more than $25, and not to be confused with a **valve job**. ($)

valve job: Replacing or resurfacing (grinding down) the engine **valves** so that they form an airtight seal when closed. (Valves mate with their *valve seats* in order to form such a seal.) Not nearly as serious as a **ring job** and less than half the cost. ($$)

vapor lock: The vaporization of gasoline inside the fuel line. Such a condition prevents a smooth flow of fuel to the **carburetor** or engine, causing the car to run roughly or not at all. Occurs usually in very hot weather.

venturi: A narrowed section of the *carburetor barrel* that creates a vacuum as air passes through it—thus drawing fuel from the float bowl.

voltage regulator: A small box-shaped device that regulates the current flow from the **alternator** to the rest of the *electrical system*. (Replacement: $)

water jackets: Channels in the **engine block** through which water-and-coolant circulate to keep the engine from overheating.

water pump: A device that forces the water-and-coolant mixture through the **water jackets**, radiator, and hoses. If it malfunctions, the car will overheat; however, the water pump is often replaced needlessly when overheating has been caused by something much simpler. (Replacement: low $$)

wheel balancing: Adjusting the weight of the tire-and-wheel assembly so that the tire rotates evenly and smoothly. Out-of-balance wheels will produce excessive and uneven tire wear and a bouncing or vibrating ride. There are *static* and *dynamic wheel-balancing* procedures; the dynamic (done with the tires spinning while on the car) is more reliable. (All four wheels: $)

wheel cylinder: A small **hydraulic cylinder** located in each **brake** assembly (*drum*-type brakes). The cylinder pushes the **brake shoes** out against the drum to stop the car. If the cylinder leaks, braking power will be lost. (Rebuild or replace: $$)

zerk fitting: The place where the grease gun is inserted when adding grease to a **ball joint** during a **lube job**.

[4]

Real Estate

Real estate is the largest industry in the country: Buying, selling, trading, improving, developing, subdividing, and syndicating land and buildings provide full-time work for hundreds of thousands of Americans, and a part-time vocation for millions more. Owning real estate has traditionally been the security blanket for the aspiring middle class, a key element of the American dream of upward mobility, and (for quite a few years now) categorically the best hedge against inflation. But the game has gotten tougher and more complicated to play, however, between the relative scarcity of affordable **properties**, the wildly fluctuating **mortgage** rates (and mortgage availability), the complexities of varying **assessment** and taxation systems, **zoning** ordinances and **variances**, **covenants**, **easements**, and **encumbrances**.

The language of real estate is both extensive and highly specialized, yet it is one employed by a broad spectrum of people who work in the field: not only **real estate agents** but builders and **developers**, **property managers**, **subcontractors**, speculators and investors, **assessors**, **zoning boards**, and a host of self-appointed "real estate experts." This entire cast of characters seem to know exactly what they're talking about when they speak of **air rights**, **fee simple**, **rent multipliers**, **plats**, and **net net leases**—but the layperson, trying to do something simple like find, buy, or sell a house or **condominium**, is most often hopelessly bewildered by the plethora of technical terms with which the professionals are only too delighted to besiege him. In order to keep that person—*you*—from becoming the innocent lamb thrown to the realty wolves, we offer this section.

absentee ownership: Possession of property one does not occupy; property owned for investment rather than for personal use. The term has a negative connotation in the residential real estate market, where it is sometimes assumed that if an owner lives in his own building, it will be better maintained.

abstract of title: A summary of all recorded

documents relating to a property's past ownership. A biographical synopsis, or history, of a given piece of real estate.

abutting: Adjacent, bordering, touching, or joined to (another property). A fairly broad term that indicates some connection between one piece of property and another. (See **adjacent, adjoining**.)

access: A means of getting to a property, which in cities is generally over public walkways. Where no public ways lead to a piece of property, its owner must secure permission from others or get an **easement** (right of way) from public authorities. A fair share of world history revolves around attempts by individuals or governments to acquire or improve access to desirable chunks of land.

acre: A measure of land equal to 43,560 square feet. A *square acre* measures 208.71 feet on each of its four sides. Acres are a standard unit of land measure in the English-speaking world.

adjacent: Near, but not necessarily touching (another piece of property). For example, "Prime location, **adjacent** to town recreation facilities" (translation: There's a schoolyard full of drunk teenagers across the street.)

adjoining: Actually touching or sharing a boundary (with another property). For example: "Three **adjoining** acres are also available with the property."

adverse possession: A legal way for one person to take possession of another's property without going through the formality of making a purchase or passing a **deed**. If a person has "open and continuous" occupancy of the property for a time period specified by the local government, he takes **title**. This legalism acts as a check against abandonment or nonuse of property by providing means to get unworked property into new hands.

air rights: The right to build aboveground on undeveloped property, or to add new floors or other structures to existing buildings. The growth of solar energy has focused public attention on air rights because high buildings can cut off the amount of sunlight available to lower buildings. The possibilities here for future litigation and lawyers' fees are immense.

alienation: The transfer of property from one person to another. This term harks back to the time when bonds between people and land were stronger and loss of land ownership, whether through sale or **foreclosure**, made one "alien" to his roots.

amenities: Features of a property that indirectly increase its value. For example, "The solid construction of the house and the extensive stand of wood out back are this property's major selling points; the fine people living nearby and the view of Old McIntosh Peak are **amenities** that make it even more saleable."

amortization: Reduction of the total cost of property (**principal** and **interest**) over a period of years through regular installment payments. As an individual's debt on property is *amortized* (gradually paid), his **equity** (share of ownership) increases.

apportionment: The division of a property's outstanding debts and income between its buyer and seller. On a selected day—usually the **closing** date, when property **title** is transferred—everything due creditors, such as taxes and fuel bills, and everything owed the property owner, such as rent, is *apportioned*.

appraisal: The process of estimating the value attributed to a piece of property at a given time, by a disinterested party not involved in buying or selling the property. Appraisals can be made using any one of several bases, including the amount of income a property generates, its replacement value, and comparison to similar properties.

appreciation: The increased value of a piece of real estate over its original purchase price. This increment may be due to inflation, improvements made on the property, or the sheer luck of being in an area that has become more desirable. Appreciation that matches the rate of inflation is a hedge against changing economic conditions. Appreciation exceeding the rate of inflation can be transformed into real profit.

appurtenances: Additional rights, benefits, or physical possessions that are extras to the actual purchase of a property. These could include anything from the right to use a neighbor's pond to an **option** to buy future properties as they become available.

arrears: Overdue debts. When a **tenant's** rent is *in arrears*, he may be subject to **eviction.** When a homeowner's **mortgage** payments are in arrears, he can be **foreclosed.**

as is: A transaction condition in which the buyer accepts property **title** without expecting any changes or improvements, and without regard to any statements that may have been made about the property. Barring illegal elements in the sale, when you buy as is, you own what you get with no recourse from the property's past owner.

assessed valuation: The value of a property for tax purposes as determined by an official of local government. Since these evaluations are often considerably below the true market value of a property, they bear only a fractional relationship to *appraised valuation* (see **appraisal**).

assessment: A special or additional tax on real property to pay the cost of some local improvement like repairing a school, fixing streets, building a new sewage plant, etc. As in the board game Monopoly, assessments on "all houses and hotels" can be devastating for owners of large amounts of property who happen to be cash poor.

attachment: The seizure of property by a court in settlement of a debt or to pay legal obligations such as alimony. "When Hank's business failed, he tried to avoid paying off his loan to the People's Trust, which was ultimately forced to *attach* his home and land."

auction: A public sale at which property is sold to the highest bidder in accordance with terms announced before the auction starts. *Voluntary auctions* take place when an owner wishes to sell his property. This person often sets an *upset price*—a minimum sale price—which must be met before the sale takes place. *Involuntary auctions* are usually the result of creditors forcing a property sale through the sheriff's office to satisfy their claims.

balloon clause: A financing innovation that permits people to make exceptionally large payments at the end of a **mortgage**—like second down payments—instead of larger installment payments during the whole course of the mortgage. The practical consequence of this ballooning is usually to generate a need for a new loan at the end of a mortgage's term, thus perpetuating the eternal indebtedness which is a central feature of our modern economic system.

benchmark: A post used by surveyors to delineate boundary lines. By extension, a benchmark has become a term that describes any fixed point or standard against which other things are measured, such as *benchmark legislation.*

bill of sale: A document that notes the transfer of ownership of personal property. In the real estate market, the equivalent for land or buildings is a **title** or a **deed.** Bills of sale are for dishwashers, carpets, tractors, and other *chattel.*

binder: A small payment that holds a piece of property for one buyer (often for a specified period of time) and keeps it from being sold to another—clearly distinguished from *down payments,* which are the first formal payments on a piece of property.

blanket mortgage: Sometimes called **budget financing.** A **mortgage** that covers property to be divided and sold in parcels. An owner or developer has pieces of the property released from the blanket as he sells them, then repays the lender a part of the total mortgage based on the size of the property sold.

bona fide prospect: A potential property buyer who shows serious interest and has the resources to close a deal. Such people are definitely a minority in the real estate market, where *tire kickers*—people who like just to shop or enjoy chatting—constitute an overwhelming majority.

breach of conditions: Usually, a violation of some part of a **lease** agreement, brought about by failure to pay rent, by causing damage to the property, or by using it in a manner contrary to either written provisions of the lease or common custom. Establishing gambling dens or raising livestock in a loft space, for example, are breaches.

broker: Someone who is licensed by a state to represent others in buying and selling real estate. A broker may simply be a go-between for two parties in a transaction, but the exceptionally competitive nature of the real estate market today generally requires that this individual possess the memory of a computer, combined with the sales hype of a Hollywood press agent.

building codes: The body of laws, regulations, and standards that govern how any structure in a town or a city may be put together. These rules touch on everything from materials to principles of assembly and siting, and are one reason why the construction industry is so conservative and resistant to change; creative architectural visions often do not survive the logic of part-time town selectmen.

cancellation clause: The "out" in a real estate contract; a provision that permits one party to back out of the contract if the other party does not meet some specific condition. ("Jack exercised the **cancellation clause** of his agreement when the Jones House Building Company was unable to get him the 11 percent mortgage money they had promised.")

caveat emptor: Latin, "Let the buyer beware." An admonition that applies especially to transactions in which the value of what is sold is susceptible to different interpretations or rapid change. This, of course, is the situation with many pieces of property, especially those sold **as is**. What you see is what you get.

certiorari proceeding: Latin, "to be informed." A legal review proceeding, often used as a last-ditch effort by a homeowner to protect himself from the depredations of the town **assessor**. After the assessor has reevaluated his property upward, the owner of property may ask a court for a certiorari proceeding and a change of the assessment decision.

chain of title: A sequential list of owners that also notes the various rights and claims that have attached themselves to a property at various times. (See also **abstract of title**.)

chattel mortgage: A special contract that obligates someone to repay a debt on money borrowed against *chattel*—personal, movable property (rather than **real** (fixed) **property**) which is not covered by ordinary **mortgage** agreements.

closed mortgage: A **mortgage** that cannot be paid off early. "When Amy inherited a large sum of money from her grandmother, she wanted to pay off her parents' *mortgage* in full, but found it was **closed** and could not. The friendly man at the bank, however, hinted something could be done if she were willing to pay a penalty."

closing: The legal ceremony of passing **title** on a piece of property. It assumes that all disagreements between buyer and seller have been reconciled, and all income and debts on the property settled.

closing costs: Sometimes outrageous fees exacted by banks and lawyers in order to take care of simple work associated with consummating a real estate transaction. These little extras now often run to 20 percent of sizable down payments. They include: *application fees, loan discounts, credit report fees,* **title-search** *fees, prepaid interest, insurance premiums,* and *recording fees.*

cloud of title: A flawed ownership document that makes it impossible to sell a piece of property. A *color of title* is a defect like a cloud, but one that is not as readily noticeable in looking over a title.

commissions: Brokerage fees; what a **broker** charges buyers, sellers, or both for his or her services. Though rarely fixed by law, most commission structures are standardized by custom for given services within given parts of the country. A broker is also usually required to inform clients of his fees before doing work for them.

community property: Property owned jointly by a husband and wife. In some states, this ownership is determined directly by the two parties, while in others (like California) it is an automatic consequence of marriage. Community-property ownership has various tax, legal, and usage ramifications that differ from individual ownership.

condemnation: A legal ruling that allows government to take over private property after paying its owner fair market value. "In order to build the new Civic Center, the city had several tracts of old three-family residences *condemned* and then demolished."

condominium: Also, **condo**. A form of co-ownership in which each owner has exclusive rights to use and dispose of a certain portion of a property (usually one apartment in a multi-unit building), and also a proportional interest in common property of the building. As **mortgage** and construction costs have risen steeply since the late 1970s, condominiums and **cooperatives** have been rapidly replacing the detached, single-family house as the mode of home ownership most affordable by the American middle class.

contractual limitation: In a real estate purchase, restrictions in a **deed** that outline what a new owner may or may not do with his property. These limitations often take the form of **covenants**.

conventional mortgage: A **mortgage** not insured by a government agency like the FHA or the VA. "After discovering all the paperwork involved in getting a loan from the Veterans Administration, Dudley decided to get a **conventional mortgage** with a slightly higher interest rate but lower up-front **points** to pay."

conversion: Changing the physical structure or layout of property to accommodate a new use. Conversion is the step that precedes the developmental rebirth of a piece of property. *Condo conversion,* for example, takes apartments that were previously rental structures, or large private homes, and makes them into **condominium** units.

conveyance: A transfer document, such as a **bill of sale**, a **deed** or some other "carrying instrument" that changes a property's ownership.

cooperative: A form of joint ownership of property in which each buyer purchases shares in a company that owns a building. It differs from **condominium,** in which a person buys part of a larger property and shares in its common area. A cooperative has different tax benefits and limits on disposing of property features than does a condominium.

covenant: Limitation on how a property may be used or disposed of. In a *deed with full covenants* a seller provides a buyer with certain standard legal assurances that no untoward surprises will come with the newly purchased property.

deed: A document transferring (*conveying*) ownership of property, according to various legal standards which must be met for the document to be binding. Limits on how property may be used are sometimes incorporated in the deed through **covenants** (agreements between the parties) or through restrictions conforming with local laws or regulations.

deficiency judgment: A legal action that seeks to collect the difference between what a person owes for a debt and the amount collected through sale of the assets that had secured this debt. For example, "Jane's house was put up for auction when her loan was called.

When the proceeds of this sale didn't cover all she owed, the court issued a **deficiency judgment** to get the rest of the money due to her creditors."

depreciation: For tax purposes, the "writing off" of a certain portion of a property's worth each year because the value is supposed to be declining (*depreciating*). This often is an accounting myth upon which many a real estate fortune has been built. This depreciation may either be the same amount each year for a fixed number of years (*straight-line depreciation*) or may be concentrated into early years (*accelerated depreciation*). In an inflationary economy, of course, most property does *not* decline in value—but increases. The combination of write-offs on depreciating real estate and the **appreciation** the property is actually undergoing is what produces profits for investors in real estate.

descent: The filtering down of property ownership to heirs of a person who dies without leaving a will (*intestate*).

displacement: The eviction of poor people from a building or neighborhood because property improvements (often associated with *condo conversion*) have made the rents or **mortgage** payments too high for existing **tenants**. Displacement lowers an area's "indigence quotient," and is the price a community "pays" for **gentrification**.

dispossess proceedings: The full legal process of **eviction**, often quite lengthy and expensive for the **landlord**. (Compare **summary proceedings**.)

duplex: A two-story, two-unit building in which each occupant shares part of the first and part of the second stories. A *duplex apartment* is one in which the space extends over two stories of a building.

earnest money: A **binder** fee, or deposit, on a piece of property showing that a person is truly willing and able to buy it. Few professions put more emphasis on the importance of being earnest (see **qualifying**) than real estate. Sincerity here often finds its expression in the form of money—such as earnest money.

easements: Rights to use or pass through another's property. Easements grow out of necessity (for example, a driveway into land not accessible by public road) or out of special contractual arrangements between owners of two separate properties.

eminent domain: The right of government to take property from an individual without his or her consent. Just compensation for the property based on market value is usually paid. "Though Farmer Brown sat on his porch with a loaded shotgun and threatened to blow away anyone who tried to demolish his home so the new highway could be built, **eminent domain** was finally exercised and he was removed."

encroachment: Illegal intrusion on another's property or on public land. For example, "A new survey found that Jackson's barn **encroached** nearly two feet on the land of his neighbor Jones, who immediately demanded that a portion of the barn be removed."

encumbrance: Any legal restriction that limits the way an owner can use his property. Includes **liens**, **mortgages**, **deed** restrictions, unpaid taxes, and **zoning** limitations.

equity: That percentage of the cost of a piece of property actually paid for by its owner. This sum is usually represented by the amount of down payment made on the property plus the amount of **principal** retired through **mortgage** payments. Equity increases as mortgages are *amortized,* or paid off. (See **amortization**.)

escalator clause: A standard feature in many modern **mortgages**, permitting upward changes in the terms of the mortgage so that a bank can get higher monthly payments in the future. This cushions the bank against future inflationary pressures. An escalator clause is also found in some **leases**, enabling the landlord to raise the rent contingent upon inflation rates or the like.

escape clause: Generally, a clause by which a buyer can get out of an agreement without losing money when the **mortgage** he thought he could get doesn't materialize; otherwise known as the "out."

escrow account: A fund set up to pay a debt that is due at a later date, or to pay a debt after some condition is met. Banks that grant **mortgages** often collect homeowners' property taxes and put them *in escrow* for cities and towns to whom they are due. A **tenant** may sometimes refuse to pay rent directly to a **landlord** until the heat comes on, while putting his rent *in escrow* until it does.

estate: The total value of a person's **real property**.

eviction: The legal act of expelling a tenant from a rented property. Eviction may be a relatively simple process (**summary proceedings**) or a more complex affair (**dispossess proceedings**).

extender clause: An interesting element of many contracts negotiated between real estate **brokers** and would-be home sellers, that provides the broker with a **commission** even if a sale is made after his agreement with the seller expires (within a specified period). The commission provision is thus extended beyond the ordinary life of the contract.

fee: Also **fee simple, fee absolute**. The absolute right to control property and do with it as you will. An outmoded concept in today's world, unless you own the bank.

FHA: Federal Housing Administration; the government agency that insures banks for **mortgages** they extend to the public; one of the numerous government entities that in one form or another seek to assist the building and real estate industries.

first refusal: The right of a person to have first crack at buying a piece of property. "Myles offered his **tenant** the right of **first refusal** when the apartment went **condo**. When the offer was not accepted, he sold the unit at a higher price to an outsider."

foreclosure: The seizure and sale of a piece of property to satisfy a debt, usually owed to a bank. For various reasons, the foreclosure process has become more difficult to execute in recent years. Creditors now generally try to get their money in more "benevolent" ways.

gentrification: Property improvement that leads to bringing a more prosperous group into a building or a neighborhood. The term has different connotations to different people, depending on whether one has the money to buy in (the *gentry*) or is forced to move out (the *displaced*).

grace period: Extra time in which to perform some requirement or duty before a penalty is assessed. For example, "Bank policy allows fifteen days after the first of the month as a **grace period** for **mortgage** payments before tagging on a late charge."

graduated lease: A **lease** that provides for automatic rent increases at specified times. These increases are not tied to special circumstances (as in the case of **escalator clauses**).

ground lease: A long lease on unimproved land, often entered into with the idea of building on the property. **Tenants** then have use of the property without having to buy it. For the **landlord**, the advantage lies in having an undeveloped property developed.

incorporeal realty: The intangible elements of property and the nonmaterial rights that go with property, such as **right of way** or **air rights**.

interest rate: The "cost" of money; the yearly percentage charged by a bank to extend a loan. Since repayment of the **principal** of a **mortgage** loan is usually spread out over twenty or thirty years, the bulk of mortgage payments is for interest. Interest payments are deductible from federal income taxes, which gives a major stimulus and indirect subsidy to the nation's real estate industry.

joint tenancy: Ownership of property by more

than one person. This type of ownership is similar to an arrangement called *tenancy in common,* except that joint tenancy has a survivor clause—if one of the tenants dies, the other inherits.

junior mortgage: Also called a **second mortgage**. An additional borrowing against a piece of property. The first mortgage, however, has prior claims on the proceeds of selling the property in case of **foreclosure.**

landlord: A property owner who charges rent to **tenants** for the privilege of occupying a house, an apartment, or other property.

lease: A document that permits one party (the *lessee*) to occupy the property of another party (the *lessor*) for a specified period of time at an agreed-upon price (the rent). Leases may have *fixed rents,* which don't change with time, or *graduated rents* that provide for raises at specified intervals. Leases are highly flexible documents that can accommodate the different needs of different **landlords** and **tenants.** (See **net lease** and **net net lease.**)

lien: A creditor's claim on the property of a person who owes him a debt. A lien is a kind of **encumbrance** which limits how a person may dispose of his property.

listing: Property registered for sale with a **broker** or put up for rent by a **landlord.** In the former case, the property may be listed exclusively with one broker or *open-listed* with several brokers, who then presumably vie to sell it first and get the **commission.**

lot: A subdivision of land; a building site; the debris- and bottle-infested area that occupies space before it becomes a ranchero or highrise. A *regular lot* is one shaped like a square or a triangle, with front and back edges of equal lengths.

market value: The price a piece of property will fetch in the real world. "The house meant a good deal to Maude because it had been her parents' home. But when she tried to sell it, she found its **market value** was considerably lower than its sentimental value."

mechanic's lien: The claim of a builder, a contractor, or a general repairman (the "mechanic") on the land portion of a property. This lien usually derives from work done (but as yet not paid for in full) on the building portion of the property.

misrepresentation: Falsely describing a piece of property; making deceptive statements about real estate, its characteristics, condition, or state of ownership.

model home: An idealized version of what a home in a development or unit in a **condominium** will look like after it has been bought and put into shape. Model homes or *model units* are real estate sales aids, meant to entice potential buyers with the possibilities of the property being sold.

month-to-month tenancy: A way to rent an apartment without a **lease.** In this form of occupancy, there is no agreed-upon date when the **tenant**'s stay will run out or come up for renewal. Rent is offered to a **landlord** monthly, and if he accepts the check, the tenant can stay another thirty days.

more or less: A term that sometimes appears on a land **deed** for property that has not been exactly surveyed and may include a bit more or a bit less area in some places than is noted in the deed.

mortgage: A debt secured by **real property**. Mortgages are generally held by banks that make loans toward the purchase of land or buildings. The buyer contributes some of his own money to the purchase (the *down payment*) and takes on a debt (the mortgage) for the balance of the property's cost. A *conventional mortgage* is one that is not backed by a government agency (VA, FHA). An *open mortgage* is one that is overdue and may soon be **foreclosed**.

net lease: An agreement between **landlord** and **tenant** that provides for the latter to pay some of the upkeep costs of a rented property (such as fuel bills or maintenance) along with the rent. This arrangement partially insulates the landlord against the rising costs of running his property.

net net lease: An agreement between **landlord** and **tenant** that provides for the latter to pay *all* upkeep costs of a rented property (such as heat, insurance, maintenance, taxes), plus rent. This formula is common in **sale-lease-back** arrangements.

operating expenses: Costs involved in keeping a rental property usable. These include heat, repairs, and cleaning, but not such other overhead expenses as taxes.

option: The right of a buyer (usually the **tenant** in an apartment) to purchase a given property at a future date at a set price. This price includes a fee called a *consideration,* which goes to the seller.

parcel: One part of a larger piece of land. "Pa Thompson set aside a choice **parcel** of land for his grandson, **title** to pass when the boy reached his majority.")

participation mortgage: A shared **mortgage,** in which several people get together to share in a property package that requires they all repay the debt (though all the parties in this arrangement are not necessarily committed to paying an equal amount of the debt).

PITI: Principal, **interest,** **taxes and insurance;** an acronym for the major expenses in owning property.

plat: A proposal concerning a subdivision of land from a surveyor which may be submitted to county authorities; it describes how a property is to be divided and laid out.

plottage: Connected plots; a collective term for more than one plot of land, which collection for one reason or another has its own distinct identity and value.

points: The fee charged by a **mortgage** lender (over and above regular **interest**) for making a loan; a prepaid fee charged at the time of **closing.** Each point is equal to one percent of the total mortgage. In periods when mortgages are hard to obtain, points tend to increase. ("The bank charged Bob three **points**

when he closed on his **condo,** an out-of-pocket outlay of $1,200 on the $40,000 mortgage.")

prepayment clause: In a mortgage agreement, allowing a borrower to repay a debt early *without* paying full interest as a penalty. Since lenders such as banks prefer to collect fixed sums at regular dates over long periods, they tend to discourage early repayment of loans by not including a prepayment clause and by collecting all the interest from a loan's full term, even if the loan is repaid early.

principal: 1. Principal sum; the actual amount borrowed; the basis on which **interest** is computed in a loan arrangement.

2. The main party in a real estate transaction—either buyer or seller.

property: Something owned; or in a legal sense, the right to own something. Property may be *real,* that is, fixed and immovable, as land or buildings; or it may be *personal,* which means it can be moved.

property management: A profession involving activities such as maintaining land and buildings, collecting rents, finding and dealing with **tenants,** and the like. As the real estate field has become more specialized, these functions have been taken over more and more by people who do not own the property they manage, a "professionalization" that has had both good and bad effects on tenants.

prospectus: A description of a real estate development prepared for prospective buyers. Also, the document used to describe a public real estate tax shelter investment.

puffing: Exaggerating the attractions of a piece of property without actually misrepresenting it (which constitutes fraud). The line between puffing and sound salesmanship is often rather thin.

purchase money mortgage: A mortgage given the buyer by the seller. This occurs in cases when an owner finds it hard to sell his property; he may "take back" some of the **mortgage** himself—the amount a bank won't finance or a buyer won't borrow at high interest rates—and extend it himself to the buyer.

qualifying the prospect: The process by which real estate **brokers** try to get rid of the sightseers as expeditiously as possible while determining the **bona fide prospects**. This is done because not everyone who looks at property is actually interested or in a position to buy it.

quiet enjoyment: The right to live in or enjoy the use of property without being bothered; a right guaranteed in most binding legal documents pertaining to real estate ownership.

quit notice: A **landlord**'s notice to a **tenant** asking him or her to leave his property. If the tenant refuses to comply, the landlord can go to a court and seek an **eviction** notice.

real estate: See **real property**.

real estate syndication: A limited partnership investment in which a syndicator (the *sponsor*) gets people to pool their money to buy property that is professionally managed and later sold. There are often interesting tax advantages in this arrangement.

real property: Fixed property such as land or buildings. Real property, **real estate**, and *realty* are often used interchangeably.

realtor: A real estate **broker** affiliated with the National Association of Realtors, a professional group that requires that he or she conform to certain standards before acquiring realtor status. The term is a trademark of the association.

reconditioning: A nebulous term that covers various levels of improvements to a property, ranging from top-to-bottom repairs to merely cosmetic ones.

recording: Placing facts affecting a property's ownership into the public record. When you *record a* **deed**, you are making sure that the provisions of that deed are on file and ownership rights cannot be challenged.

redemption: A quaint, biblical-sounding term that is real estate talk for second chance. Or possibly, last chance. Redemption is the right of a **foreclosed** property owner to reclaim his

own, or a dispossessed **tenant** to get back an apartment. There is a time limit involved and certain specific legal steps are required in this process.

rent multiplier: The constant used in determining the rent-related value of a building. ("Bill netted $5,000 a year in rent from an apartment. The accepted **rent multiplier** in his area was eight years, so he calculated he could sell the unit for $40,000.")

replacement cost: The price to construct a new building comparable to one that has been destroyed. "Comparable" is the key word here, because replicating structures built some years ago is more difficult (and usually much more expensive) than simply replacing them.

reproduction costs: The price of rebuilding a destroyed structure to its original appearance using authentic materials. Such restoration has been assisted in recent years with very generous restoration tax credits.

restrictions: Legal limits on what one can do with property. Restrictions are the result of laws and regulations, not agreements between individuals (**covenants**).

right of way: The right to get to one's own property by using or traversing someone else's.

sale-leaseback: A way to have your real-estate cake and eat it, too. A large company will construct a building to its own specifications, then sell it to a group of investors. (See **real estate syndication**.) The investors lease it back to the company (usually with a **net net lease**). The company gets to rent a made-to-order site without having to tie its money up in real estate, an investment it would probably rather avoid. The investment group that bought and leased the property receives regular rental payments plus a chance for later capital gain if the property **appreciates** in value.

sandwich leasehold: A three-way relationship created among a **landlord**, a tenant-cum-landlord, and the apartment's new **tenant**, when the original tenant **sublets** his or her apartment. A rental ménage à trois.

satisfaction of mortgage: Payment of a **mortgage** in full. The document that records this state of grace is the *satisfaction piece.*

section: A unit of land that measures 640 acres, or one square mile.

securing mortgages: Obtaining mortgages. In smaller transactions, most people go to their banks and secure their own mortgage. In larger or more complex property purchases, specialists who are experts in obtaining money or getting the best loan terms are often used for this purpose. These specialists take their fees in **points**.

security deposit: Money paid a **landlord** by a **tenant** when he or she first moves into an apartment, to cover the cost of any potential damage done to the unit by the tenant. At the end of the tenancy this deposit is to be returned, with accrued interest.

servient estate: The party that gives up an **easement** to the property of another. The latter, who benefits from the easement at the expense of the first party, is called the *dominant estate.*

situs: Location; setting; usually refers to the economic merits of the area in which a property is located. ("The house would be worth $30,000 anywhere else. But in that **situs**—a little block of brownstones—it should bring at least $75,000.")

squatter's rights: One way to acquire property without a **deed**. If an uninvited resident (the *squatter*) lives on the premises for a certain time without challenge and meets certain other qualifications, he gains **title**.

straight fee: Money paid to someone who finds listings for a **broker**; the fee a licensed broker pays an unlicensed supplier of leads.

straight-line depreciation: See **depreciation**.

straw man: A nonexistent person used as a front in a real estate transaction. ("When the seller realized that there was no Jon Endsworth, and that the name was simply a **straw man** for the big development firm that had been trying to buy his property, he called off the deal.")

subdivision: The process of dividing a large piece of land into smaller pieces, or the actual smaller pieces that result. A developer usually acquires a large property, improves it, perhaps builds on it, then sells the subdivisions to several other people.

subletting: The **leasing** of a piece of property to a second **tenant** by the person who leased it directly from a **landlord**. (See **sandwich leasehold**.) Most leases have provision for this sort of arrangement, which is a commonplace in our mobile society. Subletting is often the best way to avoid the tedious business of having to break a lease.

subordination clause: A clause in a contract outlining the rights of second-tier creditors in obtaining the proceeds from a **foreclosure**, after first-**mortgage** holders or other prior-claim creditors have been paid. See **junior mortgage**.

summary proceedings: A faster, less expensive **eviction** process than **dispossess proceedings**, to which a landlord is entitled under certain conditions (such as nonpayment of rent).

survey: A process involving checking the physical boundaries and other characteristics of a piece of property; work done by either a surveyor or civil engineer to define legally the boundaries of property.

tax sale: The sale of property to collect money in **arrears** for taxes. "No taxes were paid on the house for four years and it was taken over by the county. When the owner still failed to pay up or make a claim within another four months, a **tax sale** was held and money was collected to pay the debt.")

tenancy at will: An arrangement that allows either **landlords** or **tenants** the right to break a **lease** arrangement at any time without notice.

tenancy in common: See **joint tenancy**.

tenant: A renter; one who has a **lease** with a property owner (**landlord**) and pays for the right to occupy a living or working space.

tenement: 1. A property in its entirety including all land and buildings.

2. A slum building; a run-down urban property housing people in substandard or dangerous dwellings.

"time is of the essence": A phrase appearing in some contracts, indicating that certain key times mentioned in the document (such as the **closing date**) must be met without fail for the contract to be binding or satisfied.

title: Property ownership; evidence of property ownership; to *have title* is to own a piece of property legally.

title search: A check through public records to ascertain who owns a piece of property and whether any **encumbrances** exist that might be attached to it. This is a very necessary precaution in any real estate transaction to avoid the possibility of **clouded titles** and other problems.

upset price: See **auction**.

usufructory right: The right to use an inland waterway (such as a stream or a pond); the right to be protected from someone's changing the course of such a waterway.

utilities: The producer/supplier of piped-in or wired-in energy used in buildings; usually refers to natural gas companies that supply gas for cooking and heating, and electric companies that supply electricity for light, cooking and/or heating. Utility bills are often paid by tenants separately from rent, though some **leases** read "utilities included."

valuation: The worth of a piece of property as determined by an **appraiser**.

walk-up: A multistory apartment building that does not have an elevator. Sometimes used synonymously with **tenement**—a run-down building without the amenities, or *cold-water flat*, both indicating a generally deteriorated apartment.

warranty deed: A **deed** containing assurances from the seller to the buyer about such things as freedom from **liens** and other **encumbrances**, and **clear title**. This is the most desirable sort of deed to get.

zoning: Government regulations that limit the ways in which property can be used in a given area. These regulations are outlined in laws called *zoning ordinances*. When a particular building in an area is exempted from zoning rule, it is an example of *spot zoning*. The way in which a property is zoned can often make the difference between an increased or decreased **valuation** over the years.

II

MEDIA, ARTS, AND ENTERTAINMENT

[5]

Motion Pictures

Chaplin. Bogart. Cagney. Garbo. Hepburn and Tracy. Gable and Lombard. Monroe. Brando. Lancaster. Olivier. Mastroianni. Redford. Fonda. De Niro.

Hitchcock. Capra. Welles. Truffaut. Fellini.

Modern Times. Casablanca. Citizen Kane. The Wizard of Oz. Duck Soup. Gone with the Wind. Singin' in the Rain. On the Waterfront. 8½. Midnight Cowboy. The Godfather. Rocky. Star Wars. Close Encounters of the Third Kind. Kramer versus Kramer. Ordinary People.

In three-quarters of a century, the motion picture has become deeply engrained in our national psyche. Its images and heroes and stories form a kind of collective memory, a common stock of myths and dreams that for many of us holds almost as much potency as real events. There is something unique in the nature of the medium —its sheer size, the intimacy of sitting in a darkened movie theater, the capacity of the art to shift and transpose images and sounds, similar to the shifting inner images of dream and imagination—that gives it an extraordinary power to affect the viewer. It is an art form that contains within itself almost all the other arts—theater, visual composition, writing, music, photography, choreography—and, when fully realized, it is a medium more engaging, more compellingly potent than any other.

Although the world of film encompasses many forms—**animation**, **documentaries**, educational and business films, home movies, experimental films, **shorts**—we will concentrate here on the terminology and jargon of **feature films**. For it is through these full-length fictional creations, shown in movie theaters across the country, that the medium continues to have its greatest impact upon our lives.

When we talk about feature films, we are speaking the language of **Hollywood** (or, as they say in the business, **the Coast**). It is here

73

that most major motion picture **studios** and production companies are located, where most multimillion-dollar **deals** are consummated, and where a large number of films (even in this era of **location shooting**) are still made. The reputation of Hollywood as the scene of epic struggles between conflicting personalities is not unfounded, for the movie business is inherently stormy, unpredictable, and problematic. The *average* American movie now costs $10 million to produce (its **negative cost**), and another $6 million to market. The industry as a whole invests one and a half billion dollars in feature film production yearly. This is big money, and as one might expect, it is controlled by massive, multibillion-dollar conglomerate corporations, which have (over the last decade or so) assumed greater influence in the direction of all aspects of the film business.

To oversimplify somewhat, these conglomerates see motion pictures as *product,* to be turned into as much revenue as possible, in the safest way possible: through massive advertising and promotion of a handful of big **blockbuster** pictures; and the "preselling" of ancillary rights to network television (which average $3 or $4 million and may run as high as $20 million for a big hit), pay and cable TV, videocassettes and videodiscs; and foreign TV and foreign theatrical distribution. Profits from all these sources may greatly exceed the domestic **box-office** profit. The inclusion of **bankable** stars and **director**, a script adapted from a best-selling novel in a **package** that appears to be **commercial**, regardless of quality, all help insure financial success both here and abroad.

Against this tendency we find a large number of talented and creative people, **directors**, **producers**, writers, actors, **editors**, and **cinematographers**, who like money as much as anyone else, but who also are devoted to making motion pictures as artistically excellent as possible. Once again, this is an oversimplification, as there are plenty of venal "artists" and more than a few "business" people concerned with the quality of the movies they finance; but the struggle between the two sensibilities is real indeed. Does one cast a bland but well-known TV actor for the lead (insuring the **bankability** of the project) or an exciting, fiery, but unknown new actor? Does one temper a controversial script to make it palatable to network television and foreign sales, or leave it intact?

Add to this cast of characters the film **exhibitors** (theater owners), who are in constant conflict with the **distributors** (mostly, the **major studios**) about almost everything; the **talent agents** and **agencies** (who have become increasingly important in packaging projects on a multimillion-dollar scale); and a host of other hopefuls—**stunt** men and **starlets**, **PA**s and **AD**s, cameramen and **publicists**, **story analysts**, **gaffers**, **gofers**, and **extras**—and you have a veritable cauldron of ambitious, often conflicting personae. Nonetheless, somehow, the vast array of people, resources, and technical considerations come together to produce several hundred new films every year; and miraculously, every year, some beautiful, moving, important, and utterly entertaining movies emerge. When the film-maker succeeds at this, despite the complexities of the medium and the industry, he or she is indeed the consummate magician: a choreographer of disparate realities, a weaver of dreams.

At movie-industry meetings, **story conferences**, lunches at the **Polo Lounge** or the Palm Restaurant, there is a patois employed over and around the technical terms which are defined later in this section. The following is a brief glossary of this insider's talk.

Hollywood Talk

baby: A general term for any person, even your worst enemy, or someone you are about to fire. ("Harry, **baby**! Of *course* we want your script!")

between projects: Out of work.

distributor's costs: Every penny a **distributor** can keep from a **producer**.

ex-ex New Yorker: Someone who has not only moved to **the Coast** physically, but spiritually as well. *Ex-New Yorkers* still yearn for crisp fall days, Lincoln Center, and Sunday brunch at Zabar's. Ex-ex New Yorkers have gone the way of Jacuzzis and the year-round tan. From this there is no return.

film: What graduates of **film schools** call a **picture**.

hot: Someone whose last picture made money. A *genius* is someone whose last picture made a *lot* of money.

house nut: Every penny an **exhibitor** can squeeze from a **distributor**.

in development: Stymied, lost, becalmed, suffocated.

message: In the classic dictum of a Hollywood mogul, this is what you send by Western Union—not by motion picture.

on spec: Working for nothing. Pie in the sky. The opposite of **deal**, contract, **option**, salary, or money.

paying dues: What every cabbie in L.A. with a film script under the seat, and every waitress with a stack of eight-by-ten glossies in her bag, is doing.

producer's profits: A fiction, some percentage of which is always proffered to the unwary neophyte. ("Always get it off the *gross*, **baby**.")

story conference: A sophisticated form of torture in which a screen writer must witness the utter destruction of his script, in order to render it more **commercial**.

take a meeting: To have, or go to, a meeting. A cliché, but still very much in use.

turnaround: A project is *in turnaround* when its **option** with a particular **studio** or **producer** has expired, and the author (or **agent**, or **director**) is then "free" to take it elsewhere.

MOTION PICTURE TERMINOLOGY

above-the-line costs: That portion of a film **production** budget which covers all the major nontechnical creative labor: expenses to **option** a **property** and for **script development**, the fees of **director** and **producer**, and the salaries of all actors, **stunt men**, and **extras**. (See also **below-the-line costs**; **negative cost**.)

A.C.E.: Association of Cinema Editors; a professional society of film and television **editors**. Membership in the association is honorary, by invitation only.

action: The **director**'s order (to actors, **extras**, et al.) to begin playing a scene; follows shortly after "**roll it**."

A.D.: assistant director; the title usually accorded the individual who carries out most of the non-artistic, administrative tasks of the **production**, including budget and time control; in this respect the A.D. is really more like an assistant **producer**. Often there will be a *second assistant director*, who handles the movements of **extras**, crowd scenes, and the like.

A.F.I.: The **American Film Institute**; a nonprofit organization founded in 1967. Its Washington branch contains an immense film archive and a theater sponsoring retrospectives, and is the publishing locus for the magazine *American Film*. Its Greystone mansion in Beverly Hills houses a film school, processes grants for independent film-making, and sponsors film internships in **Hollywood**.

agent: A person who represents an actor, writer, or **director**; the agent attempts to get work for his (or her) clients and to negotiate the most favorable possible contracts. The agent's share for these services is 10 percent of whatever the client earns. Agents may operate individually but are usually associates of a larger organization, a *talent agency*. Major multiparty motion picture **deals** are often put together (as a **package**) by the action of a powerful agent or agency.

angle: The direction from which the camera views the main subject in a given **shot**. There are *high* and *low angles, side angles, subjective angles,* and the like. The selection of angle in any shot is a key factor in determining the mood, tone, or impression that it will make upon the viewer.

animation: Any of several processes by which static objects (or drawings, cut-outs, puppets) are filmed one frame at a time, with slight changes from each frame to the next, giving the illusion of movement. Animation includes but is not limited to traditional screen *cartoons*.

answer print: Also called **check print**, **trial print**, **first answer print**. The first composite (sound *and* picture) motion picture **print** from the laboratory, with **editing**, **score**, and **mixing** completed. Usually color values (and other factors) will have to be corrected before a **release print** can be ordered.

Arri: Arriflex; a lightweight, portable 35mm camera, especially useful for **hand-held** and **cinema-vérité**–type filming.

art director: The individual who designs the **sets** and conceives the visual environments to be used in **location** shooting; responsible (along with the **director** and **cinematographer**) for the look of a film—especially backgrounds, costumes, furnishings, architecture, and the like.

art film: A motion picture, usually foreign, usually **low-budget**, deemed to have a limited appeal—limited mostly to the devotees of **art houses**. Refers more accurately to films made with artistic values predominating over commercial considerations. In **Hollywood**, needless to say, "art film" is one of the worst epithets one can employ.

art house: A movie theater that specializes in showing foreign films, film classics, offbeat or experimental films, or other movies that are not receiving wide commercial **distribution**. The art house is the second home of every serious film buff—often the only place to view the work of great film-makers such as Hitchcock, Kurosawa, Godard, Truffaut, Welles, Rossellini, and Ford.

ASC: Americal Society of Cinematographers; the professional organization of film and TV **cinematographers**.

aspect ratio: The ratio of width to height of a screen, or film. Formerly standardized at 1.33:1; but **wide-screen** formats (Cinemascope, Panavision, etc.) extend the ratio anywhere from 1.66:1 to 2.55:1.

assistant director: See **A.D.**

auteur: A French term for the total film-maker. The *auteur theory* holds that the **director** is the true creator of a film, bringing together script, actors, **cinematographer**, **editor**, and all **production** factors and molding them into a work of cinematic art. In some cases this holds true, and the style and themes of certain directors (Fellini, for example, or Godard) are as discernible throughout their body of work as any painter's or composer's. On the other hand, especially in certain sectors of the American film industry, the **producer** or **studio** head is considered more fundamentally the film-maker; and the director merely one more person hired to work on the film. This conflict is at the heart of more than a few battles that rage and have raged in **Hollywood**.

back lot: Site of the major, permanent **sets** (depicting, for example, city streets and Old West towns) located on the grounds of the major **studios** where almost all exterior **scenes** were filmed in the old days. Now that most movies are shot on **location**, the back lots are rarely used.

bankable: To have "hit it" so successfully in a previous film (or films) that one is considered a good risk for investing money; the best thing to be in **Hollywood**. The term may apply to star actors, **directors**, **producers**, or entire project **packages**.

below-the-line costs: The costs of technical expenses and labor in the **production** of a film: set construction, technicians' salaries, equipment rental, transportation, **special effects**, wardrobe, film stock, developing and printing, **editing**, sound **mixing**, and **location** costs. (See also **above-the-line costs**; **negative cost**.)

best boy: The assistant to the **gaffer**.

bit part: A small but identifiable speaking role in a movie; less than a **lead** or supporting character, but more than an **extra** or **walk-on**.

blacklist: An odious practice of the film industry during the 1950s, in which writers, **directors**, and other workers were denied employment because of suspected association with Communist or left-wing causes. Lives and careers were ruined for those who refused to recant their convictions and "name names" of others to blacklisted. **Hollywood**'s darkest hour.

blind bidding: The film **distributors'** practice in which **exhibitors** are required to submit competitive bids to rent a motion picture without having had the chance to view it beforehand. This practice has been prohibited in several states, although it is frequently relied upon by distributors to raise additional monies before the film has completed production.

block booking: An illegal practice wherein **exhibitors** are required to rent several (usually mediocre) films from a given **distributor** in order to receive one (highly desirable) product. In a recent block booking scandal, rental of *The Other Side of Midnight* was made a prerequisite for showing the more lucrative *Star Wars*.

blockbuster: A major film—costly to produce, heavily promoted and advertised, and expected to do well at the **box office**. When such a film goes down in flames, more than a few people go down with it.

blue movie: Also, **nudie**, **porno movie**, **skin flick**. A movie whose major appeal is the graphic depiction of sexual acts; usually **low-**

budget. A surprisingly high percentage of "name" **directors** got their start doing such pictures.

booking: Film rental or showing at a given theater. ("It was kind of an arty picture—got great reviews, but they couldn't get enough **bookings** to break even.")

box office: Also, **B.O.** The revenue generated by the ticket sales of a film. The *box-office gross* is the total cash received by the showing of a given film, usually computed per theater per week. *Variety* will typically report: "*Body Snatchers* swift $20,000; *Moment by Moment* dim $3500; *Superman* whammo $88,000; *Warriors* torrid $26,000."

"B" picture: A relatively low-budget film, with few artistic aspirations—or pretensions. Many "B" pictures have proceeded to earn a great deal of money, and some (the early Bogart films, for example) have gone on to become classics. The term originated in the thirties and forties, when double features were common; the "B" picture was supposed to be the second feature, something like the flip side of a hit record.

burn in, burn out: Two types of transition in which a normal **shot** either becomes visible from a totally white screen (burns in) or gradually washes out to total white (burns out). The opposite of **fade in**, **fade out**.

can: A container for film. When shooting has been completed, a film is said to be *in the can.*

Cannes: The most famous **film festival** in the world—variously described as glamorous, ridiculous, prestigious, intolerable, frenzied, or simply—as the French would say—*incroyable.*

casting: The process of selecting and hiring actors and actresses for a motion picture, often handled by a *casting director,* who works for the **producer** or **studio**. Major casting decisions are more often determined by whether the lead actors are **bankable** than by whether they are suitable for their roles.

cinematographer: The director of photography, who is creatively responsible for all the camera work and lighting of a film. The cinematographer is not the person who actually operates the camera (usually called the *cameraman* or *second cameraman*); however, certain individuals may perform both functions. (Claude Lelouch, the famous French **director**, also acts as cinematographer and cameraman on his own films.) The cinematographer defines the distinctive visual style of a film and is—along with the writer, **director**, and **editor**—one of the true "creators" of the motion picture.

cinematography: The picture-making art, especially the distinctive visual style of a motion picture. (See also **cinematographer**.)

cinéma-vérité: French, literally "truth cinema." A **documentary** technique of recording people and events "as they are," using **hand-held** camera, natural sound, and no rehearsal or manipulation of the subject in shooting. The term also refers to a similar, quasidocumentary style used in such fictional dramatic films as Bergman's *Scenes from a Marriage,* and the work of John Cassavetes in the 1960s and 1970s.

close-up: See **C.U.**

commercial: Capable of making money at the **box office**. Along with **bankable**, this is the term of highest approbation in the movie business. ("We think you've got a very **commercial** idea here. There are just a few changes we'll have to make. . . .")

concept: The basic idea of a film, which should ultimately be expressed not only in the **screenplay**, but also in the directing style, the **cinematography**, **casting**, and **editing**. Says the great American director, John Huston: "The most important element to me is always the idea I'm trying to express, and everything technical is only a method to make the idea into clear form. I'm always working on the idea whether I am writing, directing, choosing music, or **cutting**."

conforming: See **negative cutting**.

continuity: The exact matching of details from

one scene to another or one **take** to another. Flowers must be arranged the same way in a vase, a tie must be loosened to the same degree from one **shot** to the next, and so on. Also, the subjective impression that action is proceeding continuously, as in real life, although shots may be discontinuous (with **inserts**, **cutaways**, etc.).

coverage: 1. Film shot of a particular scene in addition to the main, or **master shot**(s). A **director** may want **close-ups**, shots from various **angles** or with varying lighting effects, some of which may then be used in the **cutting** of that scene after filming is concluded.

2. The synopsis and commentary on a submitted **screenplay** or story idea, made by a **story analyst** (or **reader**). Most scripts are not read by **producers** or other **studio** executives without their accompanying coverage.

crane: A mobile camera mount that enables the camera to be moved up and down and also horizontally when high above the ground. Used especially for *high-angle shots*—as of battle scenes, crowd scenes, or lovers embracing in the street as camera pulls up and away.

credits: The names of cast and crew shown at the beginning (*opening credits*) and/or end (*closing credits*) of a film.

crossover: A film which has been "targeted" for a specific audience that draws other segments of the movie-going public—for example, a children's movie that attracts a large number of adults.

C.U.: close-up; a **shot** in which the camera is so close to the subject (e.g., a person's face) that the subject almost fills the screen. When not overused, the close-up can be one of the motion picture's most intense and revealing techniques.

cut: 1. As a noun, any change of scene or **shot** in a motion picture. There are **jump cuts**, **match cuts**, **dissolves**, and so on.

2. As a verb, to trim down and rearrange shots in the **editing** process. Used synony-mously with edit. ("The **studio** wanted him to **cut** it to one hundred minutes but he said it had to run at least two hours.")

3. **Director**'s signal to halt actors, camera, and sound recorder. ("**Cut**! Let's try it again.")

cutaway: A **shot** inserted between segments of the main action of a **scene**. For example, during a Western fight scene the **director** might introduce a brief cutaway of a child watching from behind a tree, or a horseman riding in from out of town.

dailies: The results of the previous day's shooting, viewed as soon as they have been printed. Also called **rushes**.

day for night: A technique by which a nighttime **scene** is shot during daylight, using special filters.

day player: An actor who works a day at a time on a motion picture. Refers usually to actors with **bit parts**.

deal: A consummation of negotiations resulting in (at least the promise of) some monetary payment. Where deals are concerned, any combination of parties suffices to play the game: **producers**, **directors**, writers, actors, **studio** executives; but the efforts of at least one **agent** are almost always involved as well. The making of deals is probably *the* major activity in **Hollywood**, exceeding by a large margin the making of movies. See also **package**, **points**, **bankable**, and **agent**.

deep focus: A method of shooting in which all objects seen by the camera will appear in sharp, clear focus, from the closest to the most distant.

deferred payment: In a great many **low-budget productions** (and in not a few expensive ones as well), writers, **directors**, actors, and others accept only a portion of their salary or fee, in order to reduce the **negative costs** of production; the remainder of the money to be hypothetically paid back from **box-office** and other revenues that will accrue later. (A variation of this scheme is to accept **points**.) Unfortunately, in a high percentage of cases the deferred payment is deferred forever.

development: The process by which an initial idea (the **concept**) is turned into a finished **screenplay**, usually going through several stages along the way. (See **outline** and **treatment**.) When a project has bogged down and is stymied for one reason or another, the euphemism is "It's in **development**." Most **major studios** have at least a hundred script ideas in development over the course of a year but actually produce only a handful of them. The odds are not good.

DGA: Directors Guild of America; the professional guild that represents **directors**, **assistant directors**, **unit production managers**, and others, in both the motion picture and television industries. The DGA establishes minimum salaries and working conditions for its members, and gives awards for achievement in the directorial field.

director: The person who is primarily responsible for turning a **concept** and a **screenplay** into a fully realized motion picture. The director has ultimate artistic responsibility for a film, coordinating the efforts of writer, actors, **cinematographer**, technical crew, composer, **editor**, etc. While some directors have greater or lesser control over the totality of their films' **production**, the director is, at all times, the person in command of what happens on the **set** while a film is actually being shot.

dissolve: A common transition between two **scenes** in which one shot gradually disappears as the new shot gradually appears on the screen. Also called **lap dissolve**.

distribution: The marketing of a motion picture by a **distributor**.

distributor: A company that markets a motion picture, placing it in theaters, advertising and promoting it. The **major studios** are now mostly in the business of financing and distributing films, leaving the majority of **production** efforts to **independent** companies.

In the most prevalent arrangement, the distributor takes a percentage (anywhere from 50 to 90 percent) of the **box-office** net (gross ticket sales minus the **exhibitor**'s fees); from this sum the distributor takes *distribution costs,* followed by a 30 percent *distribution fee,* followed by some percentage of the remaining profit. Anything left over from all this goes to the **producer**, the person or company that actually made the picture. The power of the distributor—not only in controlling the finances but in determining how, when, and where a film will be released, advertised, and promoted—is enormous.

documentary: Loosely, any nonfiction film. The subject materials of the documentary—characters, dialogue, settings, events—are not invented but are "real life"; they may be selectively and creatively woven, however, to tell a story or deliver a message. John Grierson's definition of a documentary: "The creative treatment of actuality."

dolly: A mobile cart with wheels that carries the camera and camera operator. Also used as a verb, to *dolly in* toward the subject. A *dolly shot* —also called **tracking** or **trucking**—is one in which the camera is moving (forward, backward, alongside a moving subject, etc.) while the film is being shot. The crew member who pushes the dolly around is called the *dolly grip*.

double: One who takes the place of a featured actor at certain points during **production**. *Stunt doubles* perform dangerous feats that the actor cannot accomplish (fight scenes, car wrecks, or falls); *photo doubles* (also called **stand-ins**) replace the actor for **extreme long shots** (**ELS**), during set lighting and other technical preparations.

double system: Separate but simultaneous recording of sound (on tape or film) and picture (in the camera). This is the method employed in almost all **feature film** production.

downer: Also **downbeat**. A story, script, or film that ends unhappily; or is concerned uncom-

promisingly with serious subjects; or shows a great deal of human suffering (as distinct from violence). Despite the fact that most of the great works of human literature—from the Greek tragedies to *Hamlet* to *Sophie's Choice*—have fulfilled this definition, **Hollywood** avoids the downbeat story like the plague; or changes the ending.

dropping dead: The condition of total failure for a film—both financially and critically. In **Hollywood**, making a comeback from a picture that has dropped dead is extremely difficult: "You're only as good as your last picture." Also to **bomb**, to **flop**, to **die**.

dubbing: 1. Re-recording sound in another language (as, when a French film is dubbed into English).

2. Recording or re-recording dialogue in a studio after the film has been shot. The sound is not the original sound recorded during shooting. (See also **looping**.)

duping: Short for **duplicating**. Specifically, the printing of multiple copies of a finished motion picture **print**.

ECU: Also **XCU**; **extreme close up**; a **shot** in which the camera is very close to the subject, which is usually itself rather small—for example, a hand, a mouth or part of a face, a child's toy seen from inches away.

editing: Also known as **cutting**. The process of transforming a mass of raw **footage** (film that has been shot) into a coherent, polished final product that can be reprinted and shown. Film is literally cut and **spliced** together, certain **shots** being reduced, eliminated, or rearranged; **special effects**, **titles**, and **credits** are added; the **sound track** (including music, sound effects, **dubbed** dialogue) is **mixed** and coordinated with the edited footage. In major **Hollywood** films, there may have been up to eighty times as much film shot as will be used; thus, in a very real sense, the movie is "made in the cutting room." The film **editor** is thus one of the most critical, influential talents in the final creation of a motion picture.

editor: The person responsible for the important process of **editing** raw film into a final motion picture.

ELS: Also **XLS**; **extreme long shot**; a **shot** taken at a great distance from the subject(s)—as in a panoramic view of a mountain range, the towers of a distant castle, etc. In ELS, human figures are so small as to be nearly indistinguishable.

establishing shot: Abbreviated **est**; usually the first, or one of the first, **shots** in a **scene**, generally a **medium**-to-**long shot** that gives the entire setting where the action is taking place: a slow **pan** of a crowded bar, for example, or a **crane shot** of a deserted waterfront.

exhibitors: The owners and operators of commercial movie theaters. They rent the film from its **distributor** for some percentage of the **box-office** take, plus expenses. In some cases, the exhibitor may rent the theater to the distributor, a procedure called **four-walling**.

exploitation films: Low-grade, **low-budget** films generally without artistic or social redemption. Major ingredients of exploitation films include violence, sex, car chases, horror, and gore. *Blaxploitation* films—featuring black actors, racial hostility, and plenty of macho violence—were a popular genre in the early 1970s. *Sexploitation* films are a continuing source of revenue and, curiously, have been the training ground for many young film-makers who have gone on to become famous.

extra: A person employed to play a nonspeaking, background role in a motion picture—part of a mob or army, passerby on the street, or the like.

fade in: A transition effect in which the image gradually appears from complete darkness.

fade out: An effect in which the perceived image gradually fades to complete blackness. Often written at the end of a **screenplay**.

feature film: A full-length motion picture (usually seventy-five minutes or longer, the standard being around one hundred minutes) that is made to be shown commercially in theaters. Other types of films include **shorts**, **documentaries**, *industrials* (business films) and *educational films*.

film festivals: Any of a wide variety of affairs in which an array of films are screened for critics, movie industry personnel, and the public. Most often the festivals are devoted to showcasing new films from different countries, although some may be devoted to a single **genre**, or include retrospectives. The best known film festivals include **Cannes**, New York, Venice, Chicago, Edinburgh, and Montreal. In several of these (Cannes and Venice, for example) awards are given—which are taken with varying degrees of seriousness.

film noir: Dark, violent, urban, **downbeat** films, many of which were made in America in the late 1940s and early 1950s. Not a popular **genre** in modern-day **Hollywood**, though it is occasionally tried—*Taxi Driver* (1976) being perhaps the best-known recent example.

film school: One of over two hundred universities in the United States offering degrees in film, though not all of them contain genuine film schools—graduate divisions equivalent to law school or business school. The most notable and serious American film schools are those at UCLA, USC, and NYU, but even there, the connection between a graduate degree and employment in the industry is tenuous at best. However, entry into the film profession from *any* direction is illogical and chancy.

final cut: The last stage in the **editing** process, resulting in that version of the film that will be released and shown in theaters. The right of final cut determines who has the ultimate artistic control over a picture, and is frequently a source of bitter contention between **director** and **producer**, or director and **studio**.

fine cut: One of the last stages in the **editing** process, at which point the film is shown to **producers**, **distributors**, and **preview** audiences. Various personae at this point will start jockeying for positions for the **final cut**.

first run: The first engagement of a new film at a limited number of theaters in a given area. The **exhibitor** thus has the opportunity to reap the largest profits from a newly released picture. Following its first run, a film will go into **general release**, being shown at several theaters in the same area at the same time.

flashback: The presentation, within a motion picture, of a time period prior to the present tense of the main story. Usually the flashback is a **scene** (sometimes just a single, brief **shot**) inserted within the main action, but some films have told almost the entire story in flashback.

follow shot: A type of **dolly** or **tracking shot** in which the camera moves along with the moving subject (a person walking or a speeding car, for example).

four-walling: A **distribution** arrangement in which the theater is rented outright for a flat fee from the **exhibitor**, with no percentage arrangements or exhibitor costs deducted.

frame: 1. As a noun, a single image on film. The normal motion picture is actually a succession of changing frames, projected at a speed of twenty-four per second, giving the illusion of actual movement. In the work of a master film-maker or **cinematographer**, virtually every single frame can stand by itself as a complete and telling visual composition.

2. As a verb, to compose a **shot**—to select a camera **angle**, distance, and lens that will feature the main subject and background in the visually most effective way.

freeze-frame: Also **stop frame**. An **optical** effect in which one frame is reprinted many times in succession, giving the impression (when projected) of a moment "frozen" in time.

front office: The top executives of a **studio** or **production-distribution** company; the people who control the money. ("Listen, baby, we *love* your *picture!* But we've got some problems with the **front office**. . . .")

full shot: Abbreviated **FS**; a **shot** that includes an actor's whole body but not much else.

gaffer: The chief electrician on the motion picture **set,** responsible particularly for lighting. Also known as the **juicer**.

gag: A stunt or other effect achieved through physical action (for example, a car plunging off a cliff, apparently with the driver in it), as opposed to **optical special effects**.

gauge: The width of a given type of film. The major gauges are 8, 16, and 35mm; 70mm is "wide-screen." In general, the wider films are shot with more sophisticated and expensive equipment. Most documentaries and non-theatrical films are shot in 16mm, while most **feature films** (and TV commercials) are shot in 35mm.

general release: The showing of a film in a large number of theaters at the same time—usually following the **first run**, though certain pictures may go immediately into general release. A major, **blockbuster** Hollywood movie may have as many as 1,500 prints showing in general release at the same time.

genre: A familiar, identifiable type or category of motion picture; many movie genres have existed with only minor changes since the advent of "talkies" in the 1930s. Among the better-known movie genres are: the *musical;* the *Western;* the *war* movie; the *horror* movie; the *sci-fi* movie; the *comedy;* the *disaster* movie; the *caper* movie; the *detective/gangster/cop* movie; the *swashbuckler* (historical romance and adventure); the *martial arts* movie (called a "chop-socky" by *Variety*); the *sports* movie; the *tearjerker;* and so on. Of course, many movies combine several genres, while some —the exceptional ones—transcend their genre or defy categorization.

gofer: The lowliest member of the movie **production** crew. This is the person whom everyone else tells to "go for" coffee, or deliver messages, or find a ten-gallon hat at two in the morning. In many instances, a job as gofer has been a talented young person's entrée into the film business.

grip: A manual laborer on the set. Grips build, move, load, dig, push, and carry; they are indispensable to any large-scale production.

guilds: The trade unions of the "talent" in the motion picture industry: specifically, **SAG**, **DGA**, and the **Writers Guild**.

hand-held: A lightweight, 35 or 16mm camera that the cameraman carries individually, without using a tripod, **dolly**, **crane**, or the like. Also the type of images thus produced —having a deliberately rough, jerky, subjective or **cinéma-vérité** quality.

heavy: 1. The bad guy, the villain, the antagonist in a motion picture. Some actors have made their entire careers out of playing convincing heavies.

2. Authoritative, compelling, confident, centered. A heavy **producer** (or **agent, director**, actor) is direct, definite, respected (whether his last picture was a **hit** or not), a prime mover who is concerned with getting things done, rather than playing games. The opposite is a **junior** or a **lightweight**, a person who doesn't return phone calls, strings others along through endless rounds of meetings without coming to a decision, and is afraid to take risks.

In terms of films and performances, "The openings of films that are **heavy** seem to be energized by something that has gone on before the film started; when such films are over, one feels that there is sufficient energy left to continue the story, if the filmmaker so desired. Light films, on the other hand, crank up while you look at them, and die when they are finished" (Bill Bayer).

hit: A movie that makes a lot of money, earning back at least five times its **negative cost** at the **box office**. **Hollywood** has the rather short-sighted habit of attempting to follow up on every hit with an array of sequels, imitations, and spinoffs; thus, we have had a spate of occult movies following the success of *The Exorcist,* a slew of expensive musicals after *The Sound of Music,* a batch of sci-fi and space epics chasing after *Star Wars.* With only rare exceptions, these imitations never come up to the standard of the original, nor do they make as much money.

Hollywood: Also known as **the Coast.** The center of the American film industry, where all the major **studios** are located, and where most production decisions (even for films shot elsewhere) are concluded. Hollywood has the highest concentration of working (and nonworking) screen actors, writers, **directors, editors,** and film technicians of any city in the world. Though almost everyone has something bad to say about Hollywood, it remains nonetheless the place to be for anyone serious about being involved with making **feature films.**

hot: An adjective applied to **directors, producers,** writers, and actors whose last picture made a lot of money; or, to anyone who has recently won an Academy Award; or, to anyone who is currently being lionized by the media. Seeming to have momentum, the "magic touch," the commercial pulse of the nation in entertainment. People who are hot one year may be cold as the tomb the next. Steven Spielberg, for example, was hot after *Jaws,* even hotter after *Close Encounters;* after the expensive debacle of *1941,* however, he cooled off considerably. (See **bankable.**)

hyphenates: Persons who fulfill two (or more) major roles in the making of a motion picture: *producer-director, actor-director, writer-director,* etc. To do so takes tremendous talent, or prior success, or chutzpah.

IATSE: (Pronounced YAH-tzee.) The **International Alliance of Theatrical Stage Employees and Motion Picture Machine Operators.** A trade union for **grips, editors,** camera operators, lab technicians, and other behind-the-scenes employees in films, theater, and television.

independent: A **producer** or **production** company not directly employed by a **major studio.** The independent may or may not receive some financial backing from the studio, however. The term also applies to films thus produced, as in a (hypothetical) *Variety* headline: *Indie Features Nab B.O. Bonanza.*

insert: A detail **shot cut** into the main action, usually showing a static object such as a newspaper headline, a bomb ticking away, a map of Mexico, a pair of smashed eyeglasses, or the like.

intercutting: Also **crosscutting.** Alternation (usually rapid) between two or more separate lines of action; achieved through interweaving the different sequences in the **editing** process. (See **parallel action.**)

internegative: Also **dupe negative** or **printing master.** A negative printed from the original film, used to make the multiple **release prints** that will be shown in theaters.

iris-in, iris-out: Transition effects in which the image expands circularly outward from a central point on a dark screen (*iris in*), or is gradually reduced to darkness by contracting inward to the center (*iris out*). The latter was often used at the end of cartoon **animation** shorts.

jump cut: An abrupt, sometimes jarring transition in which one **shot** is cut directly to another with a break in **continuity,** either because the **angle** remains the same but time jumps forward, or because the scene is shifted without smoothness or explanation. Sometimes an error (especially among inexperienced film-makers) and sometimes deliberate—as in Jean-Luc Godard's *Breathless* (1959).

lap dissolve: Abbreviated **LD.** See **dissolve.**

lead: The most important role or roles in a motion picture. Having a major star playing the lead is often enough to make the project

bankable, especially if he or she is **hot** at the moment.

legitimate: Live (theatrical) productions as distinguished from film or television—which are not, however, called "illegitimate." Many actors and **directors** cross over from legitimate projects to the movies—and occasionally return the other way.

location: Any place outside the confines of a **studio** where a film is being shot. While at one time films were almost universally shot in the studios and their extensive **back lots** (with recreations of frontier towns and medieval castles), the trend of the past ten or fifteen years has been increasingly toward the greater realism and atmosphere of films shot *on location*.

long shot: Abbreviated **LS**; a **shot** in which the main subject is at a significant distance from the camera—for example, a couple coming down the aisle seen from the opposite end of the church.

looping: A type of **dubbing** in which an actor re-records dialogue in a sound studio while watching a section of film (the *loop*) which replays continuously; thus, he is able to synchronize his lines precisely with the lip movements of the original film.

low-budget: Applied to film-making at low cost. Although definitions vary considerably, it is safe to say that, in the early 1980s, a film produced by one of the major **studios** for less than $6 or $7 million was low-budget. For an established **independent** production company the standard might be $2 or $3 million; and for any **feature film** produced by *any* company, anything less than a million dollars now constitutes a low-budget. In general, costs are cut in low-budget films either by quick shooting (whole porno movies, for example, have been shot in one day); or by using a script, a **director**, actors, and **locations** that cost little—in some cases, nothing at all. Contrary to a prevailing notion in Hol-

lywood, the outlay of enormous sums of money to produce motion pictures ($60 million for *Superman*, $23 million for *1941*) guarantees neither quality nor success; and on the other hand, some wonderful and successful movies have been made on extremely low budgets. Some examples: *Breaking Away* (1979), *Faces* (1968), *American Graffiti* (1973), *Nothing but a Man* (1964), *Harlan County, U.S.A.* (1976), *Airplane* (1980), and *Best Boy* (1979).

majors: The major **studios,** which today number exactly seven: Paramount, United Artists (*UA*), Columbia, Twentieth Century–Fox (*Fox*), Universal, Warner Brothers, and Metro-Goldwyn-Mayer (*MGM*). These companies are the major sources of financing for the **production** of **feature films**, and are also the major **distributors** today. Although they deal in as variable and mysterious a commodity as movies, the studios are quintessentially large corporations, and like all large corporations, they are in business for one reason only: to make money. Further, each studio (as of this writing) either is owned by a huge, multibillion-dollar conglomerate (Gulf and Western owns Paramount, MCA owns Universal), or is itself a diversified conglomerate that makes a large percentage of its revenues from nonfilm ventures (Fox owns Aspen Skiing Corporation, Columbia Pictures owns Arista Records, for example). This has inevitably changed both the style and the substance of the industry—leading to an emphasis on the **packaging** of a *product* through several interlocking media (a novel that becomes a movie which is then renovelized *and* sold to television *and* spun off into a series, for example) and massive advertising campaigns behind a smaller number of big-budget **blockbuster** movies.

master shot: A single, continuous **take** of an entire **scene** (into which **close-ups**, **inserts**, **cutaways**, and **medium shots** can later be woven); or, the main **shot** which reveals the important action of a scene.

match cut: A transition from one **shot** to another that maintains the viewer's sense of **continuity** in time and space, such as a **medium shot** of a man arguing with his girl-friend inside a car, **cut** to a **long shot** of the car crossing a bridge, back to a **close-up** of the man's face behind the wheel; if these are match cut, it will appear that there has been no break in the scene's action whatsoever. Match cuts can also be used to attain an apparent continuity when in fact there is none, for example, the pounding of a judge's gavel, match cut to (the next shot) a convict's sledgehammer breaking rocks in a prison work gang.

medium shot: Abbreviated **MS**; a **shot** roughly in between a **long shot** and a **close-up**. If a person is the subject of a medium shot, the camera should take in most or all of his body. Slightly longer than this is a *medium long shot* (*MLS*); slightly closer is a *medium close shot* (*MCS*) or *medium close-up* (*MCU*).

MIFED: A major, international film "market," held in Milan each fall, where film-makers, **distributors**, and **exhibitors** gather to view each other's *product* and make **deals**.

Mitchell: The most common 35mm motion picture camera, used in a majority of **feature-film** productions.

mixing: The process of putting together the **sound track** of a motion picture: specifically, combining various audio elements—original dialogue, **dubbing**, sound effects, background noise, music—onto one track, which will be used on the **release print**. The audio equivalent of **editing**.

montage: A sequence in which various related images overlap and flow into each other—through **superimpositions**, **dissolves**, and **jump cuts**—to give a subjective impression or to quickly imply a whole story. For example, a montage may show a performer's rise to stardom through a succession of **shots**—newspaper clippings, speeding trains, cheering audiences—each one dissolving into the next.

MOS: Without sound. A direction (on a **shooting script**, for example) that indicates a **scene** is to be shot silently, without sound track. Supposedly an abbreviation for "Mit Out Sound," a Germanic **director**'s mispronunciation in the early days of **Hollywood**.

Moviola: The trade name of the traditional, portable upright **editing** machine, which enables film and sound to be run together or separately. Term is also used to mean any editing machine.

MPAA: The **Motion Picture Association of America**; an organization of movie **distributors** that assigns **ratings** (G, PG, R, X) to films to be released in the U.S.

negative cost: The cost of producing the finished version of a film—not including printing copies, advertising and publicity, **distribution**, and **exhibition** expenses. The negative cost of a film is the sum of its **above-the-line** and **below-the-line costs**.

negative cutting: A final stage in the **editing** process. After the **final cut** has been made using various positive **work prints**, the original negative is cut to match the positive exactly. This negative will then be used to produce **release prints**.

New Wave: In French, *La Nouvelle Vague*. Generic term for a loosely connected but divergent group of innovative French **directors** who attained prominence in the early sixties. The "breakthrough" year widely held to have inaugurated the New Wave is 1959; in this year Jean-Luc Godard made *Breathless*, François Truffaut made *The 400 Blows*, and Alain Resnais made *Hiroshima, Mon Amour*.

non-theatrical film: A film made primarily for showing elsewhere than in commercial movie theaters. The term thus includes educational films, industrial films, training films, and medical films. Also refers to the **distribution** of films to schools, churches, clubs, and other organizations—usually on a flat rental fee basis rather than any **box-office** percentage.

on spec: On the speculation of success. The term is applied to work performed on a film project (usually writing but also acting, **directing**, camera work) for no immediate payment but only the hope of future sale or the promise of future profit. (See **deferred payment**, **points**.) The bars on **the Coast** are filled with writers who worked on spec, only to have their hopes dashed against the realities of ruthless **readers**, jaded **agents**, and **producers** interested only in what's **bankable**.

opticals: The more common **special effects** that can be produced by manipulation of film (not people or buildings) in the camera or by an *optical printer* machine. Also called *optical effects*, these include **fades, dissolves, wipes, freeze-frames, split-screens**, and **superimpositions**.

option: The right to use a literary **property** (a screenplay, an adaptation of a novel, a dramatic play or musical) for a specified period of time. A **producer** or **studio** will option the work (for much less than the projected purchase price) in an attempt to put together a **package** and make the film. If the option expires without the film having been made, the author may sell the property elsewhere.

original: A **screenplay** neither adapted from a novel, updated from an old movie, expanded from an article, nor otherwise spun off from some other property. Given that the conglomerated **studios** like to invest in stories that are "pre-sold" due to their previous success in other media, there is increasingly less room for the original in **Hollywood** these days.

Oscars: The Academy Awards, selected through balloting of the three thousand-member Academy of Motion Picture Arts and Sciences. The Oscars have been called everything from political and nepotistic to pure industry self-aggrandizement, but it is nonetheless true that the best films sometimes *do* win the awards they deserve. Not to mention the overwhelming sight of Charlie Chaplin receiving his long-overdue honorary Oscar in 1971.

outline: A short written description of a (projected) motion picture, usually only three to ten pages long. The outline is the briefest possible explication of the storyline of a film, and is often the basis on which a **studio** or **production** company commits money to develop a **treatment** and commence to put together a **package** for production.

out-takes: Takes that have been shot but not used, or other portions of a film which have been **cut** in the final **editing**.

package: A combination of **concept, screenplay** (or **property** to be adapted), **director** and star (or stars) that appears **commercial** enough to interest **studios** or other financial backers. The package is usually put together by an **agent** or **producer**; the more **bankable** elements there are included in the package, the more likely the film is to be made.

pan: The movement of the camera on the horizontal plane. ("**Pan** across the conference room to Patton in front of the wall map of Europe.")

parallel action: Two (or more) storylines or sequences that are presented as occurring simultaneously—through alternating shots from each line of action. (See **intercutting**.)

pickups: Movies acquired for **distribution** by **major studios**, which are already shot and **edited:** the studio's only investment is thus for printing and advertising. The risk on such projects is minimal; the profit may be great.

picture: What **directors** and **producers** call a movie; also what **distributors** (studio execs) call it, unless they are dealing with **exhibitors** or corporate honchos to whom they are accountable—in which case it becomes simply *product.*

points: A percentage of the income from a film, often included in a star's or **director**'s contract in lieu of a larger salary.

Polo Lounge: The bar in the Beverly Hills

Hotel, where many of the biggest movie **deals** are made. Every table has a phone.

post-production: Everything that goes on after the conclusion of **principal photography** but prior to a film's release: including **editing**, **dubbing**, **mixing**, creating **opticals** and other **special effects**, and **printing**.

pre-production: That stage in the development of a motion picture from its inception to the start of **principal photography**. This includes script **development**, **casting**, hiring of the technical crew, and, of course, raising the money to pay for the whole **production**.

press tour: A standard element of modern motion picture publicity: the **director** and/or lead actors of the new movie make a whirl-wind tour of a major city where their film is opening, giving newspaper interviews, appearing on talk shows, and otherwise making themselves as visible as possible.

preview: 1. A showing of a film to some segment of the public prior to its actual opening, used to gauge audience response and, often, to obtain feedback that will determine final changes in the version of the film to be released. Francis Ford Coppola is actually supposed to have polled preview audiences as to which of several endings they preferred to his *Apocalypse Now* (1979) and to have made his **final cut** accordingly.

2. A synonym for **trailer**.

principal photography: The actual shooting of the main body of a film—as distinct from **pre-** and **post-production** efforts, and **special effects** shooting. Principal photography is the only stage in a movie's creation that is correctly called "in **production**."

print: 1. As a noun, any positive version of a film, at any stage in its creation. Also, a copy of the completed version of a film. (See also **answer print**, **release print**.)

2. As a verb, part of the **director**'s command ("Cut! **Print**!") when he has completed a **take** that he feels is a satisfactory version of the **shot** or **scene** he is working on, indicating

that the film is to be sent to the lab for developing.

process shot: A **special effect** achieved in the laboratory, including both **opticals** and several methods by which footage of actors can be combined with images of backgrounds that have been shot separately.

producer: The administrative and business executive of a motion picture. The producer raises money to finance the picture, hires the other major personnel (**director**, stars, and so on), and negotiates all business transactions involved in making the movie and getting it distributed. Generally, the producer leaves artistic responsibility to the director—though there are countless cases of bitter conflict over this issue. In **pictures** produced by **major studios** or large **production** companies, there may be several individuals with this title: The **executive producer**, for example, is often the **studio** chief, who may have little actual contact with the project other than to approve its financing.

production: 1. Any film enterprise; the making of a motion picture.

2. The period of **principal photography**.

production designer: See **art director**.

production manager: The person who handles all the non-creative details of the movie-making company, arranging such details as food, transportation, housing, scheduling and payment of cast and crew, obtaining of proper equipment and props. The equivalent of a stage manager in the theater.

property: Any material that may form the basis for a movie; generally refers to a written work in another medium which will be adapted into a film—a play, a novel, a short story, or a newspaper article. (*Saturday Night Fever*, for example, was derived from a nonfiction article on the Brooklyn disco scene that appeared in *New York* magazine.)

publicist: The person whose responsibility is to generate publicity about a movie, its stars, **director**, and **production**. Publicists arrange junkets for reviewers, develop press packets, **press tours**, and press releases, arrange interviews and appearances, set up special contests and other promotional gimmicks, and do everything—other than paid-for advertising—to get their picture into the public consciousness.

rack focus: Shifting the camera's focus from one subject to another within the same **shot**.

rating: MPAA classification of a motion picture according to its sex and violence content: either G (suitable for all ages); PG (Parental Guidance Suggested); R (Restricted—children under eighteen must be accompanied by parent or guardian); or X (no one under age eighteen admitted).

raw stock: Unexposed film.

reaction shot: A **shot** that shows a person's response to something—usually a short, soundless expression such as surprise, terror, or amusement. One second of the attentive interviewer inserted in countless news segments is a typical reaction shot.

reader: See **story analyst**.

reel: A spool of film, holding a standardized 1,000 feet of 35mm film or 400 feet of 16mm. This provides approximately twelve minutes of showing time. Also used to refer to the length of film or the time taken to project it, one reel usually being taken to equal ten to twelve minutes in 35mm. (See **two-reeler**.)

release print: The final, approved version of a film, which is then copied and shown in theaters.

rentals: Arrangements between the **exhibitor** and **distributor** for the showing of a film (the exhibitor "rents" it from the distributor); also, the number of such showings (the number of theaters in which the film will be seen); also, the amount of revenue received by the distributor through such arrangements. ("We **dropped dead** in the domestic markets, but we pulled $50 million in foreign **rentals**!")

repackaging: A film may be released and promoted heavily but die at the **box office**.

Rather than abandoning it as a total failure, the **distributor** may quickly withdraw the *product* from all theaters, completely revamp the marketing strategy, redo all the posters, print advertising and publicity—often changing the title as well—and reopen the "new" film at different theaters. On more than a few occasions, this repackaging pays off. A notable recent example was *Walking Tall,* which bombed in its initial run but made enormous profits in its repackaged version.

re-release: Showings of a film subsequent to the end of its first **general release**. Often a popular movie will be **exhibited** several years later in re-release and return a healthy profit, without any further expense to the **distributor** other than advertising and publicity. (See also **repackaging**.)

reverse shot: A **shot** that shows the opposite point of view from the previous shot. Thus, if shot 83 is a **close-up** of Fred from Mary's point of view, shot 84 is a reverse shot if it shows Mary from Fred's point of view.

"Roll it!": Also **"Roll," "Roll 'em." Director**'s order for the camera and sound recording to begin operating: several seconds later, when they have reached operating speed, he will call **"Action"** and the playing of a **scene** will commence.

rough cut: The first assembled version of the film in the **editing** process. It affords the earliest sense of what the film will actually look like—although there remains an immense amount of **editing** work to be done.

runaway production: A production that is shooting out of the United States in order to escape the high costs of labor and **locations**.

rushes: See **dailies**.

SAG: The **Screen Actors Guild**, with some 50,000 dues-paying members (1981). SAG negotiates minimum wages and working conditions for screen actors and **stunt persons** (but not extras, who are represented by **SEG**). Although the SAG **scale** may appear generous, the majority of SAG members make only a minimal income from movie acting: In 1979, more than half the membership made less than $2,500 from movies; 33,000 out of 47,000 made less than $15,000. The fabulous few who made over $100,000 in 1979 numbered a mere 560.

scale: The minimum salary set by the guilds (**SAG**, **DGA**, etc.) for work on a motion picture. For an actor with a speaking part in a **feature film**, the 1981 scale was $259 per day.

scenario: See **screenplay**.

scene: A group of **shots** depicting a unit of the story, usually taking place in one location. In some films (*Citizen Kane* a notable example) an entire **scene** of several minutes' duration might be filmed in one extended shot; but this is rare.

score: The music used on a motion picture **sound track**. Also used as a verb: "I'm **scoring** a picture for Coppola right now." The person who scores a film is known as the *composer*.

screening: A private showing of a motion picture. This may be a *press screening* attended by a large audience of critics and invited guests; or an intimate viewing for two or three **studio** execs in a plush, secluded *screening room*.

screenplay: Also **scenario**. The written script for the movie, including all dialogue, some description of setting and mood, and a minimum of camera directions. When the screenplay has been broken up into numbered **shots** and includes all major camera directions (**close-up**, **long shot**, **pan** to . . . , for example), it is called the **shooting script**.

screen ratio: The ratio of screen width to height. Trouble develops when this is not the same as the **aspect ratio** in which a film was shot—as, for example, a **wide-screen** movie shown on television.

screen test: An audition performed before the motion picture camera, in order to see what the actor or actress looks like on film and whether he or she has a quality that projects itself through the film medium.

second A.D.: The person who organizes **extras** for crowd scenes. (See **A.D.**)

second unit: An auxiliary film crew that shoots car chases, chariot races, crowd **scenes**, forest fires, and other exterior sequences that do not require the **director** or stars to be present.

SEG: Screen Extras Guild; the union for all **extras** involved in motion picture work.

send-up: A satirical take-off or comical exposé. *Airplane* (1980), for example, was a superb send-up of a whole **genre** of airline disaster movies.

set: The place where a film is being shot. It may be an interior or an exterior, in the **studio** or on **location**, a battlefield filled with a thousand extras, or a room with a bathtub and some toy boats. Though rarely behind the camera himself, the **director** is absolute master of what takes place on the set.

setup: A single arrangement of camera, scenery, and lighting to film a **shot**, a whole **scene**, or several shots from different scenes. Every change of the camera's position constitutes a new setup.

shooting ratio: The ratio between the amount of film shot in making a picture and the amount in the final version after **editing**. Shooting ratios vary widely: from as little as 4 or 5 to 1 (as in the documentary recording of a rock concert or other live event) to as much as 80 to 100 to 1 (in high-budget films where the same **scene** may be shot from several different camera **angles** and positions, and many **takes** are made of each **shot**).

shooting script: A later version of the **screenplay** in which each separate **shot** is numbered and camera directions (**C.U.**, **dolly in**, **pan** across, and so on) are indicated. The working document from which the filming is effected.

short: A nonfeature film, usually less than three **reels** (approximately thirty minutes) in length. At one time, the showing of a short in commercial theaters before the **feature film** was commonplace; now, lamentably, it is almost nonexistent. The medium of the short, however, remains an excellent vehicle for student and experimental films.

shot: The basic unit of movie-making; a single piece of action captured on a single, continuous (un**spliced**) section of film. There are **master shots**, **long shots**, **medium shots**, **close-ups**, **two-shots**, **panning shots**, and so on. Very often, **directors** will shoot the same **scene** at several distances and at different **angles**, in order to have **coverage** when it comes time for film **editing**. The opposing tendency is reflected in the *designed shot,* which has been so carefully and deliberately chosen by the **director** that there is little or no need for additional shots of the same **scene**.

16mm: A narrow **gauge** of film (relative to 35mm), which is commonly used in shooting educational films, **documentaries**, television, and other **nontheatrical** motion pictures. Occasionally a **feature film** has been shot in 16mm and then blown up to 35mm for commercial release (Cassavetes' *Faces* [1968] or Wadleigh's *Woodstock* [1970], for example).

slateboard: Also **clapboard**, **clapper**. The traditional slate attached by a hinge to a thin board which is clapped down at the beginning of each **take**. The visual image of the board closing can then be synchronized with the sound of the clap. On the slate is written the **scene** number and the take number. The slateboard has been replaced on some more sophisticated systems by an electronic marker.

sleeper: A film that was not expected to make a lot of money, but which for some reason captures the imagination of the public and becomes a major success. A recent example: *Animal House.*

SMPTE: The **Society of Motion Picture and Television Engineers**.

soft focus: A hazy, blurry, or slightly out-of-focus image, which can be achieved either through a deliberate minor unfocusing of the lens, or by shooting through a diffusing medium such as gauze or Vaseline. Used for a romantic or dreamlike effect—or to minimize the truth of an actress's age.

sound effects: Pre-recorded tapes of sounds (such as birds chirping, horns honking, waves crashing, church bells ringing) that can be used on a sound track, eliminating the need to record them "live."

sound stage: An acoustically controlled room or hall used to shoot (usually interior) **scenes** in a motion picture; the sound stage enables the clear, accurate recording of dialogue and may obviate the necessity of **dubbing** those scenes shot there.

sound track: 1. Literally, the thin band along the side of the film strip, which carries the entire audio component of a movie.

2. More generally, the complete sound aspect of a film, including dialogue, **sound effects**, environmental sounds, and music.

special effects: Abbreviated **SFX** or **SP-FX** or **SP-EFX**; the whole array of visual images in motion pictures that have been created through some deliberate manipulation, other than the direct filmic recording of people and places. Special effects include **opticals** and other laboratory or camera "tricks" (**freeze-frames**, **wipes**, **dissolves**, slow motion and fast motion, time-lapse, **fades**, **superimposition**); the use of miniatures, models, mock-ups, mechanical beasts, and other illusionary constructions; and the generation of "actual" events such as fog, rain, explosions, bullet holes, collapsing buildings, spurting blood, flying nuns, or talking aliens.

splice: As a verb, to join together two separate pieces of film, by means of glue, heat, or tape.

As a noun, the connection thus formed. (There are several types: *lap splices, butt splices, negative splices.*) Splicing is the quintessential act during the **editing** process, and the number of splices made (on **rough cuts**, **fine cuts**,

internegatives) on a **feature film** runs well into the thousands.

split-screen: A **special effect** in which the screen appears divided into two, four, or other multiple separate sections, each with a separate image (which may be totally distinct **shots** or repetitions of a single shot). The technique became popular in the late sixties but is seen more in TV-show **credits** now rather than in **feature films**.

stand-in: A **double** who replaces the actor during light-setting, blocking, and other technical preparations.

Steenbeck: A modern **editing** machine with more flexibility than the older **Moviola**.

step deal: An arrangement by which a screenwriter is contracted to produce the **screenplay** for a movie but must pass through several stages of approval to receive full payment. Usually these steps include: **outline**, **treatment**, **screenplay**, and conclusion of **principal photography**. No figures are available, but it is common industry knowledge that more stories are dropped (or shifted to another writer) than make it to the "big money" at the end of the step deal. (See also **development**.) This fact has been known to provoke profound feelings of insecurity in some screenwriters.

stills: Publicity photographs, either reproduced from single **frames** of the film or (more commonly) shot by a still photographer on the **set**.

stock footage: Also **stock shot**, **library shot**. Sequences taken from a film library of old newsreels, **documentaries**, nature films, and **features** to save **production** time and expense, or to provide authenticity. For example, most war movies use stock footage of WW II bombing scenes, as the cost of recreating these realistically would be prohibitive.

story analyst: Also **reader**. A person employed by a **major studio**, **producer**, or talent **agency** to read submitted scripts (and other **properties**), synopsize and evaluate them. More

often than not the reader, who has little or no power and is probably a bright, frustrated **film school** graduate, savages the material he or she reads, which—taken with the fact that a single major studio may receive several thousand submissions a year—makes for a lot of savagery.

studio: The company which produces or distributes a film; generally, the term refers only to the seven major **Hollywood** companies. (See **majors**.) Once the independent oligarchy of picture-making, most **studios** are now subsidiaries of multinational corporations like Gulf and Western and Transamerica. With the emergence of many **independent** production companies, the studios now function increasingly as financing and **distributing** companies and less as actual movie-makers. The term is also used to refer to the physical plant or working area owned by the company, replete with **sound stages**, **back lots**, **editing** rooms, and the like.

stunt man/woman: A person who **doubles** for an actor in dangerous or demanding **scenes**. Stunt men or women are the ones who actually fall off the cliffs, smash up the cars, dive through the windows, and get thrown over the bar.

Super 8: A type of improved 8mm film with a wider frame and the capacity to hold a **sound track**. The most inexpensive **gauge** of film that can be used to make passably professional-looking movies.

superimposition: Two images occupying the screen at the same time, an effect achieved by exposing the same footage twice, or through a laboratory process. Used in "ghost" sequences, **titles** and **credits**, subtitles, **dissolves**, and **montages**.

swish pan: Also **flash pan** or **blur pan**. A fast horizontal pivot of the camera, which produces a blurred image to the viewer, similar to the sensation of turning one's head rapidly to one side.

synopsis: An extremely brief description of the

plot of a motion picture, often as short as a paragraph, never longer than a few pages.

take: A single filming of a **shot** or **scene**; one uninterrupted running of the camera. "**Scene 41B, take 8**" announced before the shot (and sometimes still written on the traditional **slateboard** with clapper) indicates that this is the eighth time that shot B of scene 41 has been filmed. Dozens of takes may have to be made of a given shot or scene before the **director** is satisfied enough to say "**Cut! Print!**"

talent: The word used by business people in the film industry to describe those involved in the "artistic" aspects of film-making—**directors**, actors, and screenwriters. ("It's a youth picture goddammit, so get me some young **talent** on it!")

teaser: The opening sequences of a film, usually preceding the **titles** and **credits**; often an unexplained but dynamic or unusual sequence that will engage the audience's interest.

theatrical: A motion picture designed to be shown commercially in movie theaters; distinguished from educational films, **TV movies**, business films, training films, and other **nontheatricals**.

tilt: Upward or downward rotation of the camera on its axis, or the **shot** thus effected. A vertical **pan**.

time-lapse photography: A **special effect** in which a large expanse of "real" time is condensed into a very short amount of screen time. The complete life-cycle of a plant, taking several months to sprout, blossom, and die, could be presented, through time-lapse photography, in less than a minute. The effect is achieved through exposing one **frame** of film at regular, infrequent intervals (such as once per day) while the camera remains fixed in exactly the same position.

titles: Any printed words appearing on the screen. Types of titles include the film's **credits**, *subtitles* for foreign-language films, *crawling* or *creeper titles* (that move slowly across the screen), *main titles* (the name of the film and opening credits), and *end titles*.

tracking: Movement of the camera on wheels, rails, or other device. (See **dolly**.)

trades: The daily and weekly periodicals of the film industry, the most widely read of which are *Variety* (daily and weekly versions), *Box-office*, and the *Hollywood Reporter*. **Box-office** figures, major **deals**, and the comings and goings of important movie personalities are all reported within the pages of the trades.

trailer: Also **coming attractions**. Brief advertisements for motion pictures, shown in theaters, usually employing excerpted scenes from the film. Called trailers because they used to follow the main feature; now, of course, they precede it.

treatment: A medium-length, present-tense prose account of the storyline of a film. Usually somewhere between twenty-five and eighty-five pages, the treatment is a stage in the **development** of a script and is frequently the piece of work upon which a writer is commissioned to produce a **screenplay**.

trucking: See **dolly**, **tracking**.

two-reelers: Short comedy films, two **reels** in length (twenty to twenty-four minutes) that were a popular medium from the early days of silent movies through to the thirties and forties. Many of the early Chaplin gems, as well as the work of Laurel and Hardy, Buster Keaton, and other great comics of the silent era, were two-reelers.

two-shot: A fairly close **shot** of two persons, usually including the bodies from the waist up. If the shot is closer, showing just the heads and shoulders, it is called a *tight two-shot*.

TV movies: Also **made-for-TV movies**, also **120's** or **90's**. Films produced for television primarily—although quite a few are subsequently sold for theatrical release in other countries. TV movies run the gamut from schlock detective stories and cheap copies of noteworthy theatrical films to more ambitious and meaningful projects—such as *Roots, Friendly Fire, Holocaust, Shogun*. With rare exceptions, however, **production** values are lower, **cinematography** less imaginative, and scripts more constrained than in **feature films** made for theatrical release. Most TV-movie **directors** would probably rather be doing feature films, but there is a vastly greater volume of work available in television.

unit production manager: Also **production unit manager**, **unit manager**. The person who is in charge of all logistical details of a film company shooting on **location**—arranging food, lodging, transportation, supplies, crew's salaries, legal matters, and liaison with the local population.

voice-over: Abbreviated **V.O**. Speech by an unseen narrator while the visuals (with or without additional **sound track**) proceed.

walk-on: An extremely minor role in a picture, usually without spoken lines but with some identifiable piece of action: a shocked look, a sexy walk, a snappy salute, etc. One step up from an **extra** role.

WGA: Writers Guild of America; the union of writers in motion pictures and also TV, radio, and theater. It registers **properties**, negotiates minimal salaries, working conditions, and (as recently disputed in a lengthy strike), royalties on works sold to other media (e.g., cable TV).

wide-angle lens: A camera lens with a shorter than normal focal length that takes in a wider image from the same distance. Used for an all-inclusive or distorting effect.

wild track: Any sound recorded at a different time from the visual filming. A sound crew may be sent out to get wild sound of a busy intersection, helicopters flying, or any dialogue or other sound effects.

wipe: An **optical** transition wherein one **shot** gradually replaces the preceding shot by "wiping" it off the screen—usually horizontally but also vertically, diagonally, by flipping over, and the like.

work print: A positive **print** of the film that includes all the **takes** to be used and which the **editor** works on after getting the project, from the first assembly to the **final cut**.

zoom: A **shot** in which the subject seems to come rapidly closer (*zoom in*) or move farther away (*zoom out*). Achieved with a variable focus *zoom lens*, which enables the subject to be brought (apparently) closer or farther without moving the camera itself.

[6]

Television

INTERIM REPORT TO INTERGALACTIC COUNCIL
Subcommittee on Primitive Cultures, Intelligence Level 3
Preliminary Observation of Solar System 3146-X2L
Planet 3/9, Indigenous Appellation: EARTH

Our initial investigations of the dominant life form on this planet have focused on one specific national unit, indigenous appellation America, and specifically upon what appears to be the most salient element of the rather strange proto-civilization (TECHNO LEVEL 4.9, NUCLEAR/ELECTRONIC) existing there. With extremely rare exceptions, the entire population of this geopolitical unit spends an average of 4.1 hours (out of a 24-hour diurnal period which is the basic time-frame for all their activities) in passive auditory-visual reception of information emanating from a crude electronic projection device (official appellation "Television," more frequently termed TIVI, possibly an acronym as yet undeciphered), at least one of which is situated in a central location in 97.6 percent of all dwellings and many of which are also located in other settings. The device appears to have a critical socialization function, as physiologically immature EARTH inhabitants (termed "kids") occupy a plurality of all conscious time (NOTE: This species has the unusual habit of periodic unconsciousness called "sleep," probably for regenerative purposes) in TIVI reception, beginning within one or two solar revolution periods years after birth. EARTH inhabitants of all ages and both sexual dimorphic aspects, however, also spend extensive periods of time receiving outputs from TIVI. A preliminary hypothesis concluded that this behavior is some form of bizarre worship ritual, akin to the Vashra Cult on Planet 2/12 of Sigma Centauri. This hypothesis was strengthened by the prevalent habit of intense viewing frequency at certain hours of the day, especially the first few hours after apparent solar decline. Further, the typical viewing TV-behavior pattern —consisting of low levels of motility and speech, and limited inter-entity interactions—appears to substantiate the conclusion that there is a strong religious, or at least psychic subordinacy, component to the TIVI phenomenon. However, a statistically significant amount of response behavior, including both positive and negative effects, and control-tuning adjustments made by viewers, indicates that EARTH inhabitants also exert some measure of volition and interaction with respect to TIVI outputs. Thus, it is apparent that whatever the exact nature of this mass-behavior phenomenon, it does not conform to any of our usual Communications or Religions modules, and requires further study.

* * *

The statistical aspects of American television viewing are, by now, widely accepted: The average household has at least one set on for 6½ hours a day, the average adult watches about 27½ hours a week. Children watch even more—over 30 hours a week for preschoolers, which amounts to about *one-third* of their waking hours. More time is spent in front of the TV set, in the aggregate, than in school, outdoors, in direct contact with parents, or in any other activity besides sleep. These are average statistics, moreover; which means that a significant proportion of the population, both young and old, watch even more. The net result is that, for good or evil— though most assuredly a mixture of both—television has become the "major transmitter of our culture" in modern times. Our sense of what is happening in the world comes from TV news and documentary shows; our ideas of what products we should be consuming (and our desire for them) emanates from TV advertising—an average of 20,000 commercials seen by every person each year; our concepts and myths about success, sexuality, and power, even our sense of humor—all are imparted, more than by any other medium, and possibly more than by all the others combined—through the electronic shrine of television.

The language of the television industry is a mixture of technical terms, advertising and big-business lingo, and show business. We have focused in this section on the language of those persons in charge of TV programming and production—basically, network executives who determine what shows millions of Americans will be exposed to. Many of the technical production terms are identical to those of motion pictures (as a large percentage of TV product is shot on film rather than videotaped), and are not contained here but may be found in the Motion Pictures chapter. Finally, a subsection has been included on the new TV technology—the **VCRs** and **videodiscs** and **cable** setups that are revolutionizing the medium and expanding tremendously the amount and kinds of shows that will be available to the viewer. This may prove to be a positive development, as the loosening of the networks' hegemony may afford a greater degree of personal control and choice.

The central "problem" however, of the medium—as observed

by our extraterrestrial visitor—is not likely to diminish; if anything, American TV viewing has increased over the past few years and will probably continue to do so. We cannot escape the fact that television is now the most important cultural element of our society, a shared ritual of entertainment, information, and imagery which our population observes with a curious passive intensity. It is essential that we understand the medium, learn its inner language and procedures, and become more able to accept or reject its offerings with some independence of thought. The tube, in truth, becomes Big Brother only to the extent that we let it.

*   *   *

The 1980s are witnessing a radical expansion of the technology of home video use, an explosion of new systems that will undoubtedly transform the TV industry and the average person's viewing experiences. The introduction of **cable**, **paycable**, **VCR**s and **videodiscs** in the late 1970s has sparked an enormous growth industry—both in the sale of these systems to the general public, and in the creation of new product (or *software* for VCR and disc) to be viewed on them. By the beginning of 1981, cable TV reached some 20 percent of all television households, and, along with **paycable**, formed a $3-billion-dollar industry; VCRs, selling at a thousand dollars or more per system, had been purchased by hundreds of thousands of Americans. In both these areas, and in virtually every other aspect of the "New Television," revenues and **penetration** (i.e., the percentage of homes using the new technology) are expected to at least double by the end of the decade. Inevitably, viewing patterns will change: Using VCRs to record shows and replay them, people will watch television on their own schedules; with an array of forty or fifty cable stations, they will have a massively expanded range of programming choices (many of them *"narrowcasted"* to appeal to smaller, more highly defined audiences); and with the capacity to purchase and play non-broadcast shows via **videocassettes** and **videodiscs**, the individual's control over what he views will be even greater. Herewith, a brief guide to the most important terms of the new era in video technology. 🍂

The New TV Technology

cable: Also **CATV (community antenna television)**. A method by which a much larger number of stations (as many as fifty) can be received, with better reception, through wires connected to a single large antenna site. Cable service is available from any of three thousand cable companies, for an installation payment plus a small monthly fee (averaging around $8 in 1980). As of early 1981, approximately 20 per cent of all U.S. homes with television subscribed to cable—some 16 million households—and the number is growing rapidly. Cable industry revenues topped $2 billion in 1980, and are expected to hit $8 billion by the middle of the decade.

paycable: Also **feevee.** An optional service available to cable subscribers, by which an additional channel or channels can be made available, for an additional monthly fee (average around $9). Paycable channels feature Hollywood movies (shown without commercial interruption), live sports events, variety shows, and the like. Paycable is a major growth industry, with well over 6 million subscribers and revenues expected to reach $3 billion by 1985. Home Box Office, a paycable service owned by Time, Inc., dominates the market, with some 4 million subscribers in 1980.

pay TV: Synonymous with **paycable,** except when referring to certain subscription services not requiring **cable** hookups but offering a special channel which can be received by the installation of a signal-unscrambling device.

superstation: A broadcasting system in which programming is beamed off satellites, and received through **cable** service, enabling the simultaneous transmission of dozens of programs on a nationwide basis. The first, and to date the largest of the superstations is Ted Turner's WTCG in Atlanta, which reaches viewers in forty-six states.

two-way cable: Also **interactive television.** Any of several systems in which the viewer can interact or communicate with the broadcasting system. One major use is in certain **paycable** systems, where selected programs are chosen for viewing (by the insertion of a special card into the set), and fees are paid on a per-usage basis. Another type of two-way cable is that represented in the Qube system of Warner Amex Cable, through which viewers can indicate their responses to various polling questions by pressing buttons at home that are instantly transmitted to the broadcast headquarters for tabulation; and in which a computer "sweeps" the viewing audience every few minutes for precise tabulation of viewing patterns.

VCR: Videocassette recorder, a device that attaches to a television set and enables one to record any program onto videocassettes and to replay it at any future time. The widespread acceptance of VCRs in American homes (probably by the mid 1980s) may threaten both the programming and advertising system of television as it has been, because viewers can now: tape a program and view it later (called *time-shift viewing* in the industry); tape one show for later viewing, while watching its competitor in the same time-slot on another network "live"; skip the commercials altogether with a simple press of a *fast-search* button. VCRs also enable the viewing of **videocassettes** of nonbroadcast programs; see next entry.

videocassette: A recording of a film, TV program, or other production on cassette, similar in appearance to a conventional audio cassette but larger. An industry has sprung up to provide videocassettes for the owners of **VCR**s, and the major motion picture and television companies have entered the market in the early 1980s with lines of home video products including feature films, sports-event shows, music concerts, and documentaries. These "legitimate" enterprises will undoubtedly overtake the already-thriving business of pornographic movies on videocassette. Videocassettes, as well as **videodiscs** are referred to as the *software* of the home video industry.

videodisc: Also **vidisc.** A twelve-inch flat plastic record, similar in appearance to a conventional sound LP, which is played on a *videodisc system* that translates into a high-quality picture and sound on a TV set. The videodisc systems are (as of this writing), priced at around half the cost of the **VCR**s (around

$500 compared to $1,000 and up), and individual discs are similarly less expensive (under $20 per record compared with $40 and up for **videocassettes**). Industry experts expect the videodisc technology to achieve a 40 percent penetration of American homes by 1988, as major networks and film companies begin to produce an extensive line of films, shows, and original programming on disc.

TELEVISION TERMINOLOGY

above-the-line: Referring to the production costs for artistic and creative work: scripting, directing, casting, acting, and the like. Also refers to those jobs and the people who do them: People who do above-the-line work on a show are called **staff**, as opposed to the **crew**, who work **below the line**.

ACT: Action For Children's Television; a consumer group that has lobbied (in many cases successfully) for a reduction in commercial advertising on children's programs and a major upgrading in the quality of programming during child-viewing hours.

A.D.: Associate director (in tape) or **assistant director** (in film); the second person in charge in the **control room**, and the person responsible for communicating most noncreative instructions to cast and crew.

affiliate: A locally owned TV station that has an arrangement with one of the three major **networks**, by which it shows only their product —in addition to any shows it may produce locally itself. Affiliates generally carry (at least) network national news, **prime-time** shows, and late-night programming. As of 1980, each of the three major networks claimed slightly over two hundred affiliates.

AFTRA: The **American Federation of Television and Radio Artists**; the union representing all radio and TV performers, announcers, and commercial actors.

below-the-line: Referring to production costs for technical services and equipment: camera, sound, editing, lighting, and the like. Also, the persons who perform such technical jobs: collectively called the **crew**.

bicycling: The method by which most **syndicated** programs are distributed. Each station after airing the program, passes the print along (by mail or express delivery) to the next station on the *bicycle route*, which plays it a week later, then passes it on to another station.

billboard: The identification of a show's sponsor, or other announcement made (usually by **voice-over**) before or after the show, or before a commercial break. (" 'Great Moments in Fly-Casting' has been brought to you by . . .")

Black Rock: The CBS-TV New York headquarters, at Fifty-second Street and Sixth Avenue.

call a taping: To create a show through the orchestration of several live videotape cameras, pretaped footage, **remote** cameras, slides and credits, and other elements. In the **control room**, the **director** views upward of half a dozen **monitors** (TV screens), and "calls" which of the images is to be fed onto the single **master tape**, which will form the basis for the show. In the case of a live taping—as of a rock concert, sports or news event, or Academy Awards ceremony—the director actually creates the broadcasting as the event is happening. This is one of the most hectic, demanding, and exciting processes in television.

casting director: The staff member on a dramatic show or series who is responsible for finding and auditioning new acting **talent**.

Century City: The location of ABC-TV executive offices in Hollywood.

control room: The place where the **director calls a taping**. Seated at a console and flanked by **A.D.**, **T.D.**, and other assistants, the director watches a bank of **monitors**, selecting the images he wants to employ from one moment to the next. When a show is being taped outside the studio, a mobile *control booth* replaces the control room.

counterprogramming: Scheduling programs to counter the appeal of another **network**'s programs in the same time slot. For example, ABC schedules a two-hour "Charlie's Angels" special against an installment of NBC's "Holocaust."

CPM: Literally, **cost per thousand** (*M* in Latin). A critical unit of TV commercial time-buying, based upon how many people are watching a given program (derived from the **ratings**), and the price of an advertising spot (say, $60,000 for thirty seconds of network **prime time**). A sponsor can then compute the commercial's cost for every thousand people who will (hypothetically) view it.

crew: Those who work on a show in a technical capacity: **associate director** (**AD**), **technical director** (**TD**), lighting director, stage manager, production manager, cameramen, sound men, prop personnel, stagehands (**grips** in film), electricians (**gaffers**), **gofers**, costumers, makeup people, and the like.

DB: Delayed broadcast. The practice by **network affiliates** of taping a network program and broadcasting it later, rather than at the same time as all the other network stations (which is called **networking**). "Cincinnati **DB**'d 'Happy Days' for a *beauty contest?*"

DGA: The **Directors Guild of America**, representing **directors**, **A.D.**s, and stage managers in TV, film, and radio.

director: The person who **calls the taping** of all shows in video, and creates the visual images and sound of the final product the TV audience will view. Though less important than in film-making, the role of director in TV production is a central one. He realizes the concept and script, but otherwise has far less

hegemony over the program than the **producer**.

docudrama: A combination of documentary and drama, usually a semifictionalized reconstruction of a historical event or personality. Docudramas such as "Roots" and "Holocaust" had a major impact on TV programming in the late 1970s.

dub: To copy (a print or a tape of a program); also, as in film, to copy a program with a different language sound track, for distribution to foreign countries. Travelers abroad may be surprised to see Tarzan speaking fluent Italian, or Baretta emoting in Japanese.

edit plan: A comprehensive description of how the raw materials of a program (tape, film footage, stills, titles, voice-overs, sound effects) are to be edited and put together to achieve the final version of a show to be broadcast on the air. The edit plan will describe each shot, the sound track accompanying it, and the transitions (such as dissolve, wipe, fade) between them.

ENG: Electronic news gathering; the process of recording news events with portable, lightweight video cameras (as opposed to motion-picture film cameras); often enabling the tape to be instantly transmitted via microwave equipment, to create "live" coverage of news events, reported as they are happening. ENG was introduced in the early 1970s and has become a major element in modern broadcast journalism.

executive producer: Generally, the person who puts together (**packages**) a show and is its administrative overseer, but is not involved in actual creative production activities. Occasionally, the executive producer is nothing more than a "paper position," a title with no responsibilities whatsoever, granted to someone important who has the clout to demand it.

FCC: The **Federal Communications Commission**; established in 1934 as the government agency responsible for regulating the broadcast media. Among other things, the FCC has the power both to grant and to revoke a station's license to broadcast; sets guidelines for commercial time limits (a maximum six minutes of commercials per hour in **prime time**); requires a certain amount of children's and **public-affairs** programming, in reasonably accessible time slots; and attempts to maintain the standard that broadcasts must operate "in the public interest, convenience, and necessity."

format: 1. A detailed breakdown of a TV show, indicating the various **segments** and breaks, the locations or shots involved, and the exact time (in minutes and seconds) of each element.

2. More generally, the structure of a program—as **magazine format**, *talk-show format;* or of a series of programs—series, **miniseries**, serial, and so on.

fringe: Late afternoon and late night hours, just before and just after **prime time**, during which local stations usually run their non-network shows, such as local news and old series reruns.

FTC: The **Federal Trade Commission**; the government agency that regulates trade practices, including broadcast advertising and its effects. (See entry in ADVERTISING chapter.)

general manager: The administrative head of a TV station, responsible for all aspects of that station's management, including budget, programming, hiring of personnel, sales, and compliance with federal broadcast license regulations.

gofer: The person who "goes for" coffee, locates strange props, and generally performs any sort of odd jobs during production.

hyphenates: **Producer-director**, writer-producer, actor-director, etc. In television (and film) today, this is an increasingly common phenomenon, as talented people take on several responsibilities in order to have greater artistic control over their work.

IATSE: The **International Alliance of Theatrical and Stage Employees**; a union which represents technical crews, sound people, stagehands and other **below-the-line** employees. (See also **NABET**.)

independents: Local stations that are not directly affiliated with any of the major **networks**. (See **affiliates**.) Of approximately 750 licensed commercial stations in the United States in 1980, over 600 were network affiliates, leaving less than 150 classified as independents.

ISO: Literally, **isolated setup**. Having an additional, completely separate videotape recording system, which is continuously taking the "second best shot" available; used especially during sports coverage or live event shooting where no retakes can be made. Thus while the main unit may be recording the entire stage scene during a music concert, the *iso unit* may be zeroing in on one performer, or on faces in the audience, which will later be intercut with the main-unit material. The iso unit is controlled by an *iso director*.

kidvid: children's television. The average American child between the ages of two and five (according to the A. C. Nielsen company) watches 33 hours of television per week and views more than 28,000 commercials per year. (Ages six to eleven watch somewhat less: 29 hours per week in 1980.) The competition for this audience—concentrated especially on Saturday mornings—is particularly fierce, though the fervor seems more focused on high-power commercials selling candy bars, sugary breakfast cereals, and overpriced toys than on imaginative or socially responsible programs for kids, of which there are precious few. The average American child will have seen some 20,000 hours of television by age sixteen—more time than is spent in school, or outdoors, or reading, or almost anything besides sleeping: this makes kidvid (and TV in general, as kids watch a wide variety of "adult" shows as well) one of the most important cultural forces in our society.

Have *you* watched "Godzilla" or "Plasticman," or even "Mr. Rogers" lately?

lead time: The length of time required from the decision to produce a show to its actual first airing. While this may be as little as a few months for "live" entertainment shows or **segments**, lead time for major **network** series can be as long as one to two years.

magazine format: A program structure in which a variety of **segments**, often of differing lengths and always with differing subjects, are combined into a single program. Weekly news programs such as "60 Minutes" and "20/20" employ a magazine format, as do entertainment nonfiction shows such as "Evening Magazine," "P.M.," and "Real People."

minicam: A small, portable transistorized video camera used for location shooting, especially in electronic news gathering (See **ENG**.)

miniseries: A series of programs shorter than a full thirteen-week **season**; usually refers to major **network** productions that extend over three to six evenings and are highly advertised, such as "Roots," "Holocaust," "Rich Man, Poor Man," "The Godfather."

monitor: A special television set or screen. In a modern **control room**, there may be as many as ten or more different monitors, labeled "Preview" (showing the next shot to be used), "Line" (the shot being taped at the moment), "Film" (prerecorded shots to be inserted); "1,2,3,4,5" (showing what each of five different cameras is shooting), "Slide," "Remote" (out-of-studio camera), and others.

MNA: (Multi-Network Area Report); A **Nielsen** rating report, which gives detailed information on viewing patterns in the seventy largest cities in the country. The MNA arrives a week after programs have aired—slower than the **overnights** (but more informative), faster than the **nationals**.

NAB: The **National Association of Broadcasters**; a trade organization of radio and TV stations and **networks**, whose Code outlines industry standards for program content, morality, limits on commercial time, and the like.

NABET: The **National Association of Broadcast Employees and Technicians**; representing technical personnel, NABET is a competitor union with **IATSE**.

nationals: The Nielsen Television Index, or NTI, released every two weeks—the most comprehensive and influential of all the rating services. Not only are **ratings** and **shares** included, but figures are further broken down demographically: for example, numbers of women aged eighteen to thirty-four; numbers of children aged six to nine. These breakdowns are critical for advertisers targeting their product appeal to specific markets (household products as opposed to toys as opposed to beer, for example).

networking: The standard distribution of **network prime-time** shows. For example a program originating in New York is broadcast simultaneously (with time-zone variations) on all network **affiliate** stations. A 9:00 P.M. show emanating from New York will be held for three hours in Los Angeles, for example, to be shown there at 9:00 P.M. Pacific Time.

networks: ABC, CBS, and NBC, the three major commercial broadcasting companies, each of which owns several major television stations, a dozen radio stations, and other concerns; and **PBS**, the **Public Broadcasting System**. Through hundreds of network **affiliates**, each network controls a distribution system for the programs they produce each year (or have previously produced and now rerun). Each of the three commercial networks has executive offices in New York City, and major production facilities (with more executive offices) on the West Coast. Although the situation may now be changing with the advent of **pay TV**, **cable**, and successful independent stations (especially UHF), and **videodisc** and **videocassette** (see p. 98), the three networks have dominated the industry for thirty years and have almost totally created the medium as we know it today. With yearly sales of several billion dollars each (CBS the leader, $1.7 billion sales in 1980 and $248 million profits), the networks remain the most powerful force in television and are themselves major conglomerate corporations with dozens of subsidiaries. (See also **PBS**.)

Nielsens: Also **the numbers**, **the ratings**. The A. C. Nielsen Company is a Chicago-based research company one of whose major operations is estimating how many people are watching the respective offerings of the **networks** (and other stations) at any given time. The Nielsen **ratings**, of which there are several varieties, are the critical factor upon which networks create, sustain, or drop programs—largely because advertisers place their commercials in accordance with **the numbers** (of viewers) indicated by the ratings. Although the validity and accuracy of the Nielsen surveying method (the service is based mainly upon a recording device installed in only 1,170 homes) has been called into question, it remains a most potent force in TV programming.

non-program time: The broadcast time not devoted to the actual, scheduled program within a given time slot. This includes commercials, **PSA**s, station identification, **billboards**, and the like. **FCC** guidelines have limited non-program time to 9½ minutes per hour in **prime time** and children's programming; and to 16 minutes per hour in all other time periods.

numbers: The **ratings**, or (via the ratings) the actual number of people thought to be viewing a particular show. "Norman's not pulling down the kind of **numbers** he did last season."

O and O: Short for **owned and operated**, referring to the five VHF stations each **network** is allowed by law to own directly (as distinct from its **affiliates**). All the network O and O's

are located in the major urban areas such as New York, L.A., and Chicago.

off-network reruns: Shows which once aired on the major **networks** but have now been **syndicated** and are shown in **station time** on local stations all across the country and the world. There are hundreds of such reruns airing constantly, from afternoon replays of last season's "M*A*S*H" to midmorning reruns of "I Love Lucy" from 1957.

one-twenty: Also **120**. A TV show that takes up two hours of air time, meaning it is in actuality somewhere between 88 and 101 minutes long. The 120 is a common format for made-for-TV movies and for extended **pilots** for proposed series.

overnights: The most immediate of the **Nielsen ratings**—the results of the previous night's viewing in New York, Los Angeles, and Chicago (the three largest markets), released the following morning. "How'd we do in the **overnights**?" is the classic query in **network** executive offices around 10 A.M.

P.A.: Production assistant; a production **crew** member who may not be much more than a glorified secretary or may in fact have real responsibility for continuity, time-keeping, script changes, location scouting and other production arrangements.

package: A combination of concept, script, **producer**, **director**, and stars, which becomes a viable product for production money investment. The **executive producer** is most often (but not always) the packager.

pass: As a verb, to reject a show, either in the concept stage or even when fully produced. Also, as a noun, "I'll take a **pass** on this one," or (according to Bob Shanks in *Cool Fire*), "It's *El Paso*" or *Pasadena*.

PBS: The **Public Broadcasting Service**; the national **network** of the more than 200 **public television** stations, which distributes programs among and between its member stations. PBS is not truly analogous to the three commercial networks, however, as it has neither the massive resources nor the centralized control over **affiliates** that CBS, NBC, and ABC have; it is rather a confederation of independent public television stations which make their own programming decisions and use the network to provide them with shows or distribute ones they have produced. See **public television.**

pilot: A sample show of a projected series, produced to gauge its viability and audience appeal. Most pilots are now ninety- or one hundred twenty-minute made-for-TV movies aired in the spring to determine if they should be part of the regular **network** schedule in the fall. A *busted pilot* is one which fails this test and never becomes a series.

prime time: The period of peak television viewing and thus also of peak advertising rates. Originally considered 7:00 to 11:00 P.M., but after the passage of the **Prime Time Access Rule**, it is now held to run from 8:00 to 11:00 P.M. (except for the Midwest, where prime time occurs an hour earlier). Although news, sports, daytime, late night, and morning programming are all essential parts of a **network**'s or station's schedule, it is in prime time that virtually all major shows are aired and where the competition for viewers is the most fierce.

Prime Time Access Rule: An **FCC** regulation, passed in 1970, under which **networks** may supply their **affiliates** only three hours of **prime-time** programs per night—not including the national news. This has obliged local stations to fill the remaining half hour (usually, 7:30 to 8:00 P.M.) with either locally produced or more often, **syndicated** programming.

producer: Far more than in the movie industry, the producer is the major creative and controlling force (what the French would call the *auteur*) of a television show. He (or she) has developed a concept, through the talents of selected scriptwriters, **director**, cast, and technical crew; has overseen virtually all facets of the making of the show, dealing with the **network** (or other distributor) on one end and actual production personnel on the other. It is the producer who takes the blame when a show bombs—and gets at least a good share of the credit when it succeeds.

production house: Also **production company**. An independent company that produces shows for television—as distinct from "in-house" **network** or station production units. The majority of network **prime-time** fare is now supplied by these independent production houses (mostly located in Los Angeles), such as Norman Lear's Tandem Productions, MTM, Quinn Martin, Goodson-Todman, and the TV divisions of Universal, Warner's, Paramount, and other film studios.

program department: The division within a station or **network** responsible for scheduling, purchasing, and producing the programs it will air (usually not including news, which comprises a separate department).

program flow: The tendency of TV viewers to continue watching the same channel from one show to the next; also, the tendency to keep watching the same *kind* of show from one hour to the next, even if they are on competing stations. Thus **networks** will schedule an evening's programs around one major hit show, hoping to keep the audience on their stations; and conversely, networks will try to lure audiences away from their competitors, to a similar type of show in the next time-slot (from one detective show to the next, for example) on their stations.

program manager: Also **program director**. The person at a TV station responsible for planning the entire broadcast day: scheduling shows, purchasing and/or overseeing production of shows (including news), coordinating the **program department,** and the like.

PSA: Public service announcement; A noncommercial message (for the Boy Scouts, cerebral palsy, or other charities and organizations) aired during nonprogram time-slots. All stations are obliged by law to carry a certain amount of PSAs during a given programming day, but generally schedule them late at night or early in the morning, when the losses in advertising revenues will be far less than in **prime time**.

public affairs: Programming, though not news reportage per se, concerned with issues and events affecting the general population. All TV stations are required by law to broadcast a certain amount of public affairs programs.

public television: Non-commercial television, broadcast on the more than 200 stations of the **PBS network**, and funded by the federal government (through *CPB*, the Corporation for Public Broadcasting), state governments, individual subscribers, corporations, foundations, and colleges. Without the pressure to program in response to **ratings** and the desires of advertisers, public television has been free to create alternative, "quality" programming that would otherwise not be available to the public. To some extent it has done so, with shows ranging from "Sesame Street" to "The Great American Dream Machine" to "I, Claudius." Its full potential has never been realized, however, due to chronic financial problems, deep internal conflicts (especially between CPB and PBS), political conflicts, bureaucratic duplications, and lack of strong public support.

ratings: The estimate of how many people are watching a particular show at a particular time. Specifically, the term usually refers to the **Nielsen** ratings and, even more specifically, to the index of what percentage of all television sets in the country are tuned to a given show or station. (See also **share**.) A rating of 20 percent or more probably constitutes a network "hit," though this may vary. The ratings (in their general meaning) are the most significant factor in determining whether a show will survive on television or "go down in flames."

reality programming: Also **actuality program-**

ming. A genre of nonfiction TV shows based on the actual exploits of real people (and animals), but which emphasize entertainment over news or information. The genre became extremely popular in the late 1970s with "Real People," quickly followed by a spate of **spin-offs**: "That's Incredible," "Those Amazing Animals," "Games People Play," and others.

real time: The actual time at which something is being broadcast; used particularly to refer to news reports, press conferences, concerts, and the like that are broadcast as they are happening, i.e., "in real time."

remote: Originating from outside the television studio or a show's major location. For example, a remote camera during the filming of a sports event might be picking up faces in the crowd, or capturing locker-room interviews with players and coaches.

residuals: Payments to actors, writers, **directors** when their programs (or commercials) are rebroadcast. The TV equivalent of royalties in publishing. What the show-business populations of Hollywood and New York check their mailboxes for each morning.

SAG: The **Screen Actors Guild**; the union representing all movie actors and also all performers in TV programs which are shot on film. (Performers in videotaped shows are represented by **AFTRA**.)

scale: Union minimum wages for broadcasting-industry artists—actors, **directors**, writers, musicians, and others.

season: That period in the fall during which the three commercial **networks** introduce their major slate of new programs. Originally thirty-nine weeks, the TV season has been reduced over the years to its present thirteen weeks—that is, a regular **prime-time** series will air thirteen original episodes, followed by six or nine months of reruns. While some shows are scrapped from the lineup and replaced by others in October or November, and some original programs are aired in spring and summer, nonetheless the only real season in terms of network competition is the fall.

segment: A discrete portion of a larger show, such as an interview with a celebrity on a morning news-and-information program, or a single "story" in a **magazine-format actuality** show. One piece of a composite program.

share: A specific TV audience **rating** that indicates the percentage of all TV sets *in use* at a given time which are turned to a specific program. It indicates the popularity of a show in competition with other programs airing at the same time. A *30 share* is the standard for survival of major network **prime-time** shows. See also **ratings**.

shoot: As a verb, to film or videotape. As a noun, the period or process of filming or videotaping. "He's on a **shoot** in Montana, one of those macho beer commercials again."

single delay: Airing a **syndicated** show two weeks after its original taping.

sitcom: Situation comedy; probably the mainstay of **network prime-time** programming for the past twenty years.

soaps: Afternoon serial melodramas, usually sponsored by the major soap-cleanser-household-products companies (such as Procter & Gamble, which owns and sponsors five soaps) and targeted primarily toward housewives (though now increasingly popular with other groups as well). When similar programs appear in **prime time** (usually in a weekly as opposed to daily format), they are called "dramatic series."

S.O.T.: Sound on tape; a designation for the recording of dialogue and sound effects on the videotape machine that is capturing the visuals; as distinguished from *synch-sound* recording with a separate sound tape recorder.

spin-off: A program that derives its main character or theme from another (usually very successful) show. Spin-offs are a major source of "new" TV programming, especially **sitcoms** ("Laverne and Shirley" spun

off from "Happy Days," as did "Mork and Mindy"; "The Jeffersons" from "All in the Family"; "Knots Landing" from "Dallas"; and so on.)

staff: Production personnel who perform **above-the-line jobs**—writers, **directors**, actors, **casting director**, and the like. (See also **crew**.)

standards and practices: A department of each major **network** that oversees the "moral standards" of that network's products, and their compliance with federal regulations.

station group: Any company that owns a number of TV stations; although the term technically includes the big three **networks**, it is generally applied to **independent** companies, whicy may by law own up to seven separate stations.

station time: Also, **local time**. Those periods of day or night when no **network** shows are airing, and local **affiliates** can air their own programs or **syndicated** shows. **Independent** stations, obviously, have nothing but station time.

strip: A show scheduled at the same time every day, Monday through Friday—such as the major talk shows, variety shows, and **soaps**.

sweeps: The special, comprehensive **Nielsen ratings** compiled by a diary-keeping method during three key periods each year—November, February, and May. The sweeps give detailed viewing information for each separate television station in the country, and are thus the occasion for a major effort to attract large audiences. **Networks** compete by scheduling their most lavish specials and most popular guest stars during this period.

syndication: The major method of distributing shows other than **networking**: An independently produced show, or a rerun of a former **network** show, is sold to local stations, which pass it from one to the next through the process called **bicycling**. Syndication is a major source of TV programming, and accounts for most of what is seen on the average local station besides network **prime-time** shows and news.

talent: Generic term for actors, singers, **voice-over** narrators, and any other performers. The person who books guests for a variety or talk show ("The Mike Douglas Show," "The Tonight Show," for example) is called the **talent coordinator**.

talent coordinator: The person who seeks out, auditions, and hires performers for variety or talk shows. The equivalent position in dramatic shows is the **casting director**.

talking head: The screen image of a person or persons seen only from the shoulders up, talking, as in an interview or panel discussion. This is held to be the most boring way to shoot TV interviews and is to be avoided if at all possible—or spiced up with intercut shots from different angles and distances.

T.D.: Technical director; the person who accomplishes electronically what the **director** calls for during a videotaping session. The T.D. is the top **below-the-line** position.

tease: Any broadcast announcement that promises something "coming up" or "coming up next"—usually just before a commercial break to ensure that the audience will stay tuned to the same program.

telecine: A system through which filmed material can be transferred to videotape for television broadcasting. Much of the material used on television has been originally shot on motion-picture film—but all TV broadcasts must be on videotape before they can be aired.

Thirty Rock: NBC-TV headquarters in New York City, at Thirty Rockefeller Plaza.

TV City: The CBS West Coast production center, in Hollywood.

TV-Q: A measurement of a performer's (hypothetical) popularity with the viewing public, expressed in a dual score: a *familiarity rating*, which is that percentage of people polled who knew who the performer was; and a *Q rating*, which is that percentage of people who knew the performer who also said that they liked him or her. The two scores together comprise the TV-Q.

UHF: Ultra-high frequency; the designation for that range of the electromagnetic spectrum used for television stations having channels numbered 14 through 83. UHF broadcasting was officially introduced in 1953 but did not gain widespread acceptance until the 1960s. At present there are about 400 UHF stations in the United States.

VHF: Very high frequency, the designation for the range of electromagnetic frequencies employed by TV stations numbered 2 through 13 (and by FM radio). There are over 600 VHF stations broadcasting in the United States today.

voice-over: Abbreviated **V.O.**, a spoken narration or announcement heard "over" the visual images of a program or commercial; any voice not represented by a person seen in the visual component.

WGA: The **Writers Guild of America**; the union representing TV and motion-picture writers.

zero delay: Showing of **syndicated** programs one week after their original taping.

|7|

Ballet

Dance in America is experiencing an unprecedented surge of popularity: In 1964, one million Americans paid to see dance performances, while fifteen years later, over 20 million Americans attended dance performances—more than the number that saw all that year's NFL football games combined. The United States is now home to over 850 professional dance companies, covering a wide range of styles including modern, jazz, folk, and tap; yet by far the majority of these companies have ballet as their primary, if not their exclusive, dance modality.

In almost all performing dance (as distinct from social dancing such as ballroom, jitterbug, and disco) the vocabulary of movement, position, and technique is the language of ballet. Instructors in Afro-jazz classes and **dance masters** with Broadway musicals alike will refer to **second position**, **demi-plié**, and **relevé**—using the vocabulary of classical dance although the style to which it is applied is entirely different.

The language of ballet is 99 percent French, stemming from the seventeenth to nineteenth centuries, when French schools of ballet were paramount in the world of dance. Later, Russian, Danish, English, and other systems of training developed and expanded the art—but the universal language of dance remained French.

The following section will enable the reader to converse intelligently with **balletomanes** and other dance enthusiasts; to make his or her way through a beginning dance class (as increasing numbers of people are doing, including many professional athletes); and to be able to attend the ballet, confident that when your less well-read companion says, "Didn't you love that thing Baryshnikov did, you know, where he jumps way up, from one leg to the other, sort of turning around while he makes a big circle around the stage?" you can blithely respond, "Oh, you mean that **enchaînement** of **grand jetés en tournant**? Yes, his **elevation** and **ballon** were exceptional."

adagio: A slow, lyrical combination of movements done to slow music, stressing the beauty of **line**, **technique**, and **aplomb**. Also used to describe the slow section of partnering in a **pas de deux**. All ballet classes follow the strenuous **barre** work with an adagio, which begins the **center floor work**.

allegro: A series of movements in fast tempo, stressing lightness, smoothness, and **ballon**. The allegro follows the **adagio** in the **center floor work** of a ballet class.

aplomb: Ability to hold balance with the weight correctly centered during a movement; poise.

arabesque: Defined by the ancient Moors and Greeks as an ornament of fantastic geometric design; in ballet, a position in which the dancer stands on one leg with the other leg extended behind in a straight line. The arms are stretched to make the longest possible **line** from fingertips to toes. This basic pose has many variations.

arrière: Backward direction in the execution of a step, or direction of movement away from the audience. (For example, *jeté en arrière*—a leap backward.)

assemblé: A basic step of **allegro** combinations, in which the dancer brushes the **working leg** outward on the floor into the air and springs upward with the **standing leg**. Both feet come to the ground simultaneously in the **fifth position**.

attack: Movement performed in a strong, clear, decisive manner. ("He has good **attack**, but lacks balance.")

attitude: Inspired by Bologna's statue of the god Mercury, a position in which the dancer stands on one leg while the other leg is raised behind the body at an angle of ninety degrees, with the knee bent. Traditionally, the arm of the side of the raised leg is held over the head in a curved position, while the other arm is extended to the side. A leg extended to the front with the same spatial design is also referred to as an attitude. To achieve the perfect attitude requires years of hard work.

avant, en: Forward direction in the execution of a step; indicating movement done toward an audience.

ballerina: A principal female dancer or soloist in a ballet company. Colloquially (but incorrectly) used to refer to any female ballet dancer. See also **prima ballerina**.

ballet master or mistress: A teacher who is responsible for the training of dancers in a ballet company. The ballet master or mistress usually teaches the company class, works with each dancer on **technique** and execution, and tours with the company.

balletomane: A person addicted to ballet, who can be found at ballet theaters all over the world; a devoted fan, an appreciative and critical member of the audience. The term was first used in Russia in the nineteenth century to describe men who attended every performance sitting in the front of the stalls.

ballon: Elasticity in jumping and ability of the dancer to remain in the air for a length of time, rising easily, and descending lightly; bounce.

barre: A bar, usually of wood, fastened horizontally to the walls of a dance studio, 3 to 4 feet from the floor, roughly at waist height. It serves as a support for the dancer during **warm-up** exercises. Every ballet class begins with barre work, usually called simply barre. ("She gives a great class—a half-hour ballet **barre** and a half hour of jazz combinations.")

battement: A kick or beating action of the extended leg, done in any direction, either high (*grand battement*) or low (*petit battement*). The grand battement is done to loosen the hip joint and the petit to warm up the feet. Both are an essential exercise at the **barre**.

batterie: All movement in which the legs beat together or one leg beats against another, usually while in the air. The *cabriole, brisé,* and the **entrechat** all exemplify this beating movement.

breathe into it: A common correction that emphasizes the need for the dancer to control breathing in order to elongate a movement and keep it flowing. A ballet class isn't complete without hearing the teacher say "**Breathe into it**."

broken wrists: Allowing the hand either to drop or bend back, "breaking" the smooth line from arm to fingertips.

center: As in, "Find your **center**!" "Move from your **center**!" The center is the internal point or line where all movement should begin and is the dancer's inner source of energy. Moving from the center gives the dancer complete control, and is essential in working the correct parts of the body. It takes many dancers years of work to find their center.

center floor work: In a ballet class, exercises and combinations done without the support of the **barre**, in the center of the studio or across the floor. The command "Come center" follows the **warm-up** exercises that have just been completed at the barre. **Adagio, allegro**, across-the-floor combinations, and turns are all part of the center floor work.

chaînes: A series of chainlike turning steps in **first position**, usually done on **pointe** across the floor.

changement de pieds: Literally, "change of the feet." Changements are springing steps from the **fifth position**, changing feet in the air, and landing in the fifth position with the opposite foot in front.

chassé: A sliding step in which one foot displaces another out of its position as if "chasing" it. Used frequently in **allegro**.

choreographer: The composer or creator of a ballet or dance piece; the one who invents, selects, and designs the movements. There are hundreds of great dancers in the ballet world today, but few exceptional choreographers.

"Connect your legs to your arms": A common correction to emphasize the imagery of extended **lines** in all movements.

corps de ballet: The chorus or members of a ballet company who do not have principal roles; the rank and file of the company. The competition among members of the corps de ballet for principal dancer status is fierce.

coryphée: A performing rank higher than **corps de ballet** but not of principal status; a leading dancer of the corps; one who performs movement distinct from the corps, but does not perform a complete solo.

croisé: A position in which the **working leg** is crossed over the **standing leg**, and the body is diagonally turned with the head looking over the forward shoulder.

danse d'école: Dance based upon the traditional techniques of classical ballet.

danseur: A principal male ballet dancer in a company; a male soloist. The *premier danseur* is the leading male dancer and a partner to the **prima ballerina**. Rudolf Nureyev, for example, is a premier danseur of the American Ballet Theater.

dedans, en: Inward movement; used to describe steps or exercises in which the leg moves in a circular direction from back to front, either in the air or on the floor.

dégagé: Disengaged; the pointing of the foot in an open **position** with a fully arched instep.

dehors, en: Outward movement; used to describe steps or exercises in which the leg moves in a circular direction from front to back.

demi-plié: Half-bend of the knees. A demi-plié begins and ends all steps of **elevation**.

derrière: Behind, back. Refers to a movement, step, or placement of a particular limb in back of the body. ("**Battements derrières**.")

développé: The slow unfolding movement of the **working leg** as it is raised in an **extension** from the floor into any desired position. It begins in the knee, which bends as the working leg is taken from the floor and straightens when the extension is achieved. It is usually practiced in every direction as part of the **barre** work.

devant: Front. Refers to movement or placement of a limb in front of the body. ("**Assemblé devant**.")

divertissement: A ballet or series of dances inserted into a ballet, that have no plot, theme, or mood, but serve to display the individual dancers' talents to their best advantage.

échappé: A step in which the dancer's feet spring out simultaneously from a closed to an open **position**, from soles flat on the floor to **demi-pointe** or **pointe**, traveling an equal distance from the original position. The step is **executed** from **first** or **fifth position**, to **second** or **fourth position**. (See **position**.)

elevation: The ability of the dancer to attain height in jumps and to move easily in the air. Nijinsky was famous for his extraordinary elevation.

enchaînement: A combination or series of steps put together for use on stage or in the classroom.

entrechat: A jump in which the dancer springs straight up, beating and changing the legs while in the air.

épaulement: The placing and movement of the shoulders and head to add style and artistry to a pose or movement.

equipment: A well-proportioned body. "She has good **equipment**, but lacks **technique**."

extension: The ability of a dancer to raise and hold his or her leg in the air. It also applies to a stretching of the leg at any angle to the body. A dancer has *good extension* when consistently able to hold the **working leg** at a 135-degree angle from the **standing leg**.

focus: Directing one's attention—through use of the eyes, head, or full body—to a particular place. Focus can be inward or outward and is an important quality in performance, requiring intense concentration. "**Focus** downstage!"

fondu: Sinking down, melting. A lowering of the body made by bending the knee of the **standing leg**.

footwork: Fast steps in a combination that shift weight from one foot to another. "The new combination contains some delightful **footwork**."

frappé: A beating of the toes of the **working foot** against the ankle of the **standing leg**.

gesture: Subtle movement or **mime** that expresses emotion or signifies an object or conception; used in dance to reveal character or situation.

glissade: A traveling step executed by gliding the **working foot** from the **fifth position** in any direction, and closing into fifth position with the other foot. Usually a preparatory movement for leaps.

grip: Constricting muscles of the foot to hold a difficult **position**. When a dancer is gripping, she is not properly **placed**, is holding tension, is not **pulled up**, or not **breathing into** the movement.

gypsies: Chorus girls or boys who dance in Broadway shows, going from one show that closes to try out for a new one. Also, dance students who make the rounds of different studios and teachers. ("It's difficult to maintain continuity because I get so many **gypsies** in my class.")

heave: To jump incorrectly, landing with the body forward and the hips back.

hyperextended: Swayback; with the knees pushed back and the joints extended beyond a straight line.

jeté: A leap from one leg to the other. In a *grand jeté* (great leap), the dancer seeks the highest **elevation** possible, and may often achieve a near split in the air.

leg warmers: Also called **warm-ups**. Knit stockings or socks worn over tights to keep the leg muscles warm and avoid injury. Leg warmers, sometimes topped by plastic sweat pants, are the fashionable attire in most ballet studios.

line: The visual form created by the dancer's position and movement. "Her **arabesque** displayed an exquisite **line**."

mark it: To walk through a dance or combination without full energy. ("We're **spacing** this afternoon, girls, so just **mark it**—and don't forget it!")

mime: 1. A narrative sequence in a classical ballet.

2. The stylized gestures used to communicate plot, emotion, and character to the audience. Most **choreographers** develop themes that can be expressed entirely through movement and do not use formal mime passages.

notation: A script method of recording **choreography** by graphic symbols so that complete ballets can be revived or reproduced. Laban developed a system called *Labanotation* which is the most commonly used form today. It has now been recognized as a means for copyrighting choreography.

pas de deux: A dance for two. A classical pas de deux, performed by a **prima ballerina** and a **premier danseur** contains five sections: entrée, **adagio**, two variations, and a coda. Colloquially referred to as **partnering** or **doublework**.

passé: To pass through. An auxiliary movement in which the foot of the **working leg** passes the knee of the **standing leg** moving from one position to another. "Starting from **fifth position**, **passé**, **développé** to the front, keeping your standing leg straight."

pirouette: A complete turn, spinning in place on one foot. The free leg may be held in any of several positions. The pirouette is performed by a **ballerina** on **pointe** and by a **danseur** on *demi-pointe*.

placing: Proper alignment. ("Your placing is off—drop those shoulders! *Turn out!*")

plié: A bending of the knees with the hips, legs, and feet **turned out**. A *demi-plié* is a small knee-bend, and a *grand-plié* is a deep knee-bend. The plié is used as a preparation for most steps and movement of ballet. It lends lightness and softness to all movement and precedes **elevation**.

pointe: The tip of the toe. The **ballerina** dances *en pointe*, pivoting on the tips of her toes and wearing special toe slippers for extra support.

The slipper is constructed to provide support for the arches and comfortable cotton or lambswool cushioning for the toe. Dancing on pointe requires extensive training and tremendous strength of the feet, ankles, and calves. *Demi-pointe* refers to the ball of the foot.

port de bras: 1. Traditional arm positions, corresponding to the five **positions** of the legs.

2. A series of fluid, circular arm movements usually practiced as part of the **barre** exercises.

position: Placement of the feet; specifically one of five traditional arrangements of the feet that form the foundation of all movement of the legs. Each has a related arm position.

first position: Heels together, feet and legs turned out.

second position: Heels wide apart, feet and legs turned out.

third position: Feet turned out and partially crossed, the front heel at middle of near foot.

fourth position: Feet crossed, with one foot a step forward.

fifth position: Feet turned out and fully crossed, completely overlapping (right heel by left toes, and vice versa).

prima ballerina: The leading female dancer in a ballet company, distinguished from other female soloists, who are termed simply **ballerinas**.

project: To **focus** outward to the audience, while performing.

pull up: A common correction that means to shift the weight upward, lift from the waist, and move from the **center**. Pulling up achieves lightness, grace, and mobility.

relevé: To raise the body by going up to **pointe** or **demi-pointe**.

reverence: A curtsey or low graceful bow, given at the end of a class or a performance.

rond de jambe: Rotation of the **working leg** in a large circle, either on the floor or in the air.

saut: A jump. When added to a particular step, the movement is performed while jumping. ("**Saut pirouette**.")

sickle foot: A foot that is turned in from the ankle, breaking the **line** of the leg.

spacing: Becoming familiar with a new space and readapting movement to work in that particular space. A typical performance rehearsal schedule involves spacing, technical rehearsal, and dress rehearsal.

spotting: A rapid, controlled movement of the head during turns to maintain direction, balance, and avoid dizziness. The dancer chooses a spot (point or object in the room) and while turning holds his gaze upon it while the body turns. When the neck has reached its limit (about half a turn), the dancer snaps his head and refocuses immediately upon the same spot.

standing leg: The leg which supports the body weight and remains still while the **working leg** moves. Also called the **supporting leg**.

technique: The execution of all movement according to a precise method of ballet training. ("Before you can dance as if you hadn't a care in the world, you must spend many years—hard years—mastering **technique**!")

tendu: A basic foot exercise that involves stretching the foot and pointing the toes sharply, in various directions.

tour: A turn; usually describes a movement that is done while turning in the air; *tour jeté,* for example.

turned in: Positioned with the feet parallel, the legs rotated inward, the knees and ankles aligned.

turnout: The most important body position of ballet and the first basic principle of ballet training, in which the legs are rotated out from the hips, while the heels are together. The perfect turnout forms a 180-degree angle. Good turnout is accomplished through the hips and *not* from the knees.

tutu: A short conventional petticoat or ballet skirt worn by the female ballet dancer in performance.

warming up: A series of stretches or exercises a dancer will do before class or performance to make certain that the limbs and muscles are pliable and limber.

winging the foot: Distorting the angle of the foot to give the impression of a better **line**.

working leg: The leg that is stretching and visibly moving during a given movement or exercise; the non-**supporting leg**.

|8|

Jazz

Jazz is a music difficult to define but easy to identify: It is Louis Armstrong in Chicago, 1922, **punching out** the clearest, most inventive **horn solos** anyone had ever heard. . . . Jazz is Earl Hines, pianist, a contemporary of **Satchmo**'s in the twenties, at a small New England **club** half a century later, playing with an easy grace and stunning force, watching his own hands, listening to himself play, magically riding his own music. . . . Jazz is **Bird** (Charlie Parker), blowing that new **bebop** sax in '47, breaking all the rules. . . . Jazz is Duke Ellington. . . . And **Diz jamming** with Ray Charles and Kenny Burrell at Montreux. . . . Benny Goodman, Count Basie, Jimmy Lunceford, and the infectious beat of **swing**. . . . **Trane** and **Miles**, Mingus and **Monk**, the insistent, demanding energy of the **avant-garde**. . . . Jazz is the sound of a saxophone coming from an unseen window in the city on a summer night, that both bespeaks and defies despair. . . .

Jazz is a music that is always to some degree created by the musician. **Improvisation** distinguishes and defines jazz, giving it an alive, spontaneous, "real" quality. (Jo Jones, quoted by Nat Hentoff: "Jazz is playing what you feel.") One can analyze at great length the rhythmic patterns, harmonic structures, melodic **lines**, and tonal qualities that typify jazz—but all these can, and have been, altered in the evolution of jazz styles and the creative work of jazz artists. What marks jazz, above all, is its authenticity, the feeling of the music being *created as it is being played*—thus telling the listener something real about the men and women who are playing it.

The major (though not the only) stream of creative energy that has generated jazz has been the black experience in America. Thus, it is no surprise that the language of jazz overlaps considerably with black English: such jazz "standards" as **dig**, **cool**, **jive**, **gig**, **hip**, and **lame** have long ago become entrenched in the black patois, many of them making it into white urban argot as well.

The language of jazz is a vocabulary of sounds, the words and phrases short but malleable, like musical notes themselves: **playing the changes**, **cutting your chops**, **running lines**, **blowing riffs** and **licks**, and can you **dig** that **cat's sense of time**? The ethos of jazz, again, values authenticity above all—the ability to *say* something with your music, to know what your message is and **blow** the **sounds** you hear inside. To be real in jazz you must not only have the **chops** to play with technical proficiency, you must also have **paid your dues**; it cannot have come too easily. But if there is some pain in the music—and there almost always is—there is also a tremendous energy, and freedom, and joy, and humor. Jazz is playing what you feel.

accent: An increase of volume on a single note, giving it emphasis over another. The placement of accents largely defines the **rhythm** of a **tune** or a style.

against the grain: Unfamiliar; dissonant; unusual.

avant-garde: Jazz that has departed from the **mainstream**, especially in the post-**bop** era. The avant-garde of the sixties was called *free jazz;* that of the late seventies and early eighties is often synonymous with **loft jazz**. Fundamentally, avant-garde jazz is characterized by an extremely high degree of **improvisation** by the artists—to the point where recognizable melodies and chord progressions have been obliterated, in favor of a directly expressive, often discordant rendering of the player's intention; in many ways the musical equivalent of abstract art.

ax: Originally, a guitar; now, any instrument. ("Good to see you, **man**! Bring your **ax**?")

ballad: A slow **tune**, usually languorous or sensual, often with nostalgic or sentimental significance. For example, "My Funny Valentine."

beat: The basic **rhythmic** pattern of a **tune**. Several related phrases describe the overall rhythmic style of an **improvisor** in relation to the rhythm of the piece he is playing.

1. *On top of the beat:* The improvisor attacks the **accents** of the rhythm with precision and directness. There is a sense of being right on target, even more so than is normal.

2. *Behind the beat:* There is a sense of sneaking the **lines** in just after the accents.

3. *Ahead of the beat:* The improvisor arrives with his accents before the pulse of the overall rhythm gets there; a surprising and driving style.

4. *Pushing the beat:* Similar to "ahead of the beat"; as the expression implies, there is a sense of pushing the rhythm of the piece on ahead, through accenting a beginning note consistently a little before it arrives in the pulse and driving through after it. It gives the feeling that the piece is being sped up, even though it is really not.

bebop: See **bop**.

big band: A large jazz band, usually with twelve to twenty players, characterized by a dense, driving **sound**. Although the *big band sound* means **swing**, contemporary big bands may play **bop**, modern jazz, or **fusion**. Big bands typically contain trumpets, trombones, **reeds**, guitar, piano, bass, and drums.

Bird: Charlie Parker (1920–55), a brilliant, innovative **bop** alto saxophonist, whose tragic death from drugs at the age of thirty-four ended a musical life of intense genius, radical creativity, and personal suffering.

bop: Also **bebop**. A fast and complex **improvisational** style of jazz developed in the

1940s, characterized by its intense and tricky **rhythmic** interweavings. Originated and exemplified by Charlie Parker (**Bird**) and Dizzy Gillespie (**Diz**). Much of its material was made up by combining new melodies and rhythms with the **changes** of **standards**, which were often played at breathtaking **tempos**. *Hard bop* was a development of the late 1950s that reinstated the gritty, **driving** quality that had been lost in **cool jazz**; best exemplified in the work of such artists as Sonny Rollins, Cannonball Adderly, and Art Blakey.

blow: Originally, to play a wind instrument; now, to play any instrument. ("He **blows** some dynamite **vibes**.") The connotation is of intense, highly energized **improvised** playing. ("He leads the group firmly, but gives his soloists plenty of **blowing** room.")

blues: A form of music—and a feeling or quality found in that music—which has been a source or key influence in almost all of jazz. *Traditional blues* is a twelve-measure form (as opposed to the eight or sixteen of most popular music), typically played on guitar with vocals and often harmonica (*blues harp*). It features repeating lyrics, a highly defined **beat**, and a I–IV–V⁷ chord progression. Combined with the use of the **blues scale** and **blue notes**, these provide the earthy, nostalgic, soulful, or melancholy **sound** that is the most salient characteristic of the blues.

blues scale: The five-note scale that is the basis for the **blues**. Although it is similar to the Western minor scale, the blues scale in fact originated from African musical forms. In the key of C, the scale is C–E♭–F–G–B♭; the flatted notes (E♭, B♭) are called **blue notes**. A blue note is also any note that is temporarily played a half-step (or less) lower than usual—resulting in the characteristically soulful blues feeling.

break: A short **solo** played during a sudden stop by the rest of the band; or, any solo in general. "**Dig** Dolphy's **break** on this **cut**—it'll knock you out!")

bridge: Also **release**. The "b" or middle section of the **head**, usually eight bars long, part of the typical song form a–a–b–a. In **bebop** and post**bop** styles, players often improvise over the bridge.

cat: Originally, a hot jazz **improvisor**; now, any male. ("That **cat** on **vibes** is smokin'!")

changes: The harmonic structure of a piece, delineated by the transitions (changes) from one chord to the next. *Making* or *running* or *playing the changes* means to follow the given chord sequence with one's particular instrument; while *playing over the changes* means to **improvise** within the same chord structure.

chart: The written sheet music for a **tune**; the arrangement.

chops: Originally, the strength and endurance of a musician's natural physical equipment (chops being literally cheeks or lips); later generalized to mean technical competency and force, residing in the part of the body used to play an instrument (a piano player's hands are his chops). To *cut your chops* means to develop technical and improvisatory ability to a professional level—to become a jazz artist.

chorus: As in folk music, a single playing of the **tune**; usually a **solo**, with some **rhythm section** backup. ("Hawkins takes a **chorus** of "Greensleeves" that will blow you away.")

clam: A musical error, a goof, a misplayed note.

club: An establishment where people gather to listen to jazz, usually a place small enough to ensure some degree of intimacy in listening to the music; characterized by a layout of tables and a bar, with a bandstand for the musicians. Non-electric, or *acoustic*, jazz is usually played in the clubs.

combo: A small jazz group or band, usually three to eight musicians.

comp: Abbreviation for **accompany**; to play the **changes** behind the **solo**. ("Your second **horn man comps** okay, but don't give him no solos.")

cool: 1. Relaxed, laid back, unemotional, in control. ("Be **cool**, man—you've got the **gig**, now don't blow it!")

2. Excellent, sensational.

cool jazz: 1. The more sonorous and smooth **bebop** style developed largely by **Miles Davis** in the middle part of his career.

2. The restrained, riskless, unemotional jazz especially popular in the mid-1950s, also known as *West Coast jazz*, or *Mickey Mouse jazz* by the scornful.

crib: Apartment, house, domicile. Replaces the formerly prevailing *pad*.

cut: 1. As a noun, a single **tune** on a record.

2. As a verb, to *cut a disc:* to make a recording.

3. To do something competently. ("Your **keyboard** man can't cut that **hard bop** shit.")

4. To show one's musical superiority over another musician. See **cutting contest**.

cutting contest: An informal competition between musicians—usually **reed men**—in which one tries to best the other by **blowing** a hotter, or stronger, or more creative **solo**.

dig: To enjoy, understand, appreciate, listen to, hear. ("Did you **dig** the **lines** that **tenor** was laying down?")

Dixieland: See **New Orleans jazz**.

Diz: Dizzy Gillespie (born 1917); trumpeter and bandleader, one of the early **bop** rebels who continues to be a major force in the jazz world today.

drive: Energy, pulsing rhythm, force, aggressiveness, momentum. One of the most common descriptive qualities in understanding jazz.

Duke: Duke Ellington (1899–1974); composer, pianist, jazz orchestra leader; prolific in the creation of some of the most exquisite and memorable jazz music, from the 1920s through to the 1970s.

eight: A phrase of eight bars, usually referring to a section of the **head**. ("The **horns rip** on the opening, drop out on the second **eight**, come in soft on the third.")

exercise: Derogatory reference to work that is technically well performed but devoid of emotional energy or authenticity, merely mechanically competent. ("Great **exercise**—pull my coat when he's got something to **say**.")

fake: To play by ear—i.e., without **reading** the music.

fake book: A book with the collected chord progressions (**changes**) and basic melody for hundreds, even thousands, of popular songs. Many cocktail-bar pianists, small **combos** and groups use fake books as the basis from which to play their own versions of the **standards**, without having to keep hundreds of sheet-music arrangements on hand.

fusion: A contemporary popular music that combines jazz elements (improvised horn **lines**, for example) with **rhythms** and chord structures from rock, funk, and pop music. *Crossover* is generally synonymous, referring to a jazz-funk synthesis. The fusion sound is typified today by such groups as Weather Report, Chick Corea, Herbie Hancock, Spyro Gyra, and others—who have attained commercial success to a degree that "pure" jazz artists rarely achieve.

gig: A playing or recording engagement. The term is usually reserved for musical jobs, as distinguished from other work that is taken just to earn money, which is known as a *slave*.

Hawk: Coleman Hawkins (1904–1969); one of the greatest of all **swing**-era tenor saxophonists. Famous for his 1939 recording of "Body and Soul."

head: The song itself, the theme or actual melody, usually played as written at least once through before the **improvising** over the **changes** begins.

hip: One of the oldest and most enduring of jazz expressions, despite its appropriation and corruption by the non-jazz population.

1. Savvy, wise, able to survive in the world.

2. Artistic, authentic, unconventional, not plugged into the mainstream (**square**) society and its values.

3. OK, good, acceptable. These three

meanings obviously overlap. ("Freddie's **club** is **hip**—like, he lets you *play,* **dig**?"

horn man: A player of any wind instrument, either **reeds** or brass. Often rendered simply **horn**.

ideas: Improvised innovations, or other original musical conceptions. ("He hasn't had an **idea** since 1958, but I still **dig** his **sound**.")

improvisation: The act of creating music as it is being played—which is a special characteristic of many occasions of jazz play. The successful improvisor must have such thorough knowledge of the **rhythmic**, harmonic, and melodic structure of the music that he can "compose" in action without making an error.

inside: Literally, remaining within the **changes** (established chord sequence) of a **tune**. By extension, playing that is without frills or ostentation, motivated by the harmonies and melodies of the song itself.

jam: As a noun, a gathering of jazz musicians to **improvise** together; also called a *jam session*. As a verb, to get together with other musicians to improvise. The tradition of jamming is one of the oldest and most enduring in the subculture of jazz—it is both a method of practice, a group sharing of ideas, and a way in which the music evolves. ("After Bobby's **gig** at the Vanguard, we went up to his **crib** and **jammed** till four!")

jazz singer: In a technical sense, a singer who has the vocal facility to improvise jazz phrasing and dynamics with the competence of a jazz instrumentalist. A modern master of this art is the great jazz singer Ella Fitzgerald.

jive: Inauthentic, insincere, pretentious talk or action. ("I don't care how many **discs** they've **cut, man**, this **fusion** shit is **jive** music!") The word may be used as noun, adjective, or verb.

keyboard: Piano, organ, or any of the electronic keyboard instruments.

Lady, Lady Day: Billie Holiday (1915–1959); universally recognized as the greatest of the **jazz singers** in the 1930s, 1940s, and 1950s.

Her style, **time**, and **blues** feeling have never been duplicated.

lame: Inept, weak, incompetent, **square**.

left hand: Literally, facility at playing jazz piano with the left hand; in usage, it means the ability to **play the changes** authoritatively and interestingly and/or to *walk* through them. ("Love that Fats Waller **left hand**!")

lick: A short musical phrase or **line**, often one that is identified with a particular performer and requires a high degree of technical competency. ("He sat in this little room for a month with a record player and an old Stratocaster electric, learning all of B. B. King's **blues licks**."

lip: Embouchure; the strength of the lips and resultant ability to play powerfully, accurately (especially high notes), and with dexterity; specifically of brass players (trumpet, trombone, cornet). ("The old man may have lost some of his **lip**, but he still **swings**.")

lines: The melody which a jazz musician creates **improvisationally**. ("Okay, here the **rhythm** section lays back, the **keyboard**'s just makin' the **changes**, and Robo will run some **lines** on the tenor. Got it?")

listen: To pay attention, be responsive musically—usually referring to one musician's ability to play **improvisationally** with others. (Bobby Hutcherson, quoted in *Jazz Is:* "Like you're out there, and you know there's no chord pattern where you can say, 'Okay, on this D-minor 7th chord I'm going to play . . . ,' or 'Yeah, I know this **lick**, I can run across that, and then I can do that.' It's not like that. You're out there, and you have to **listen**.")

loft jazz: Also known as **new jazz**, or the **new music**. Contemporary extension of **avant-garde** jazz into a new range of artistic freedom and innovation. This music thrives today in New York and Philadelphia in a jazz subculture that takes place in lofts—less formally organized than **clubs**, serving not only as performance sites but also as meeting places for progressive musicians who want to **jam**.

mainstream: 1. Belonging to the earlier schools of jazz, particularly **swing**-rooted music.

2. **Bebop**-oriented music as opposed to **avante-garde** music; music which is not **outside** of the **changes**.

3. What is current and non-controversial in jazz style; the acceptable or usual music of the present scene.

man: A term of address, often employed for females as well as males. ("Hey, **man**, what's happening?") *My man* is reserved for good friends, or ingratiation. ("Billy, **my man**! Got any **gigs** for me?"). *Main man* refers almost exclusively to one's best friend (male only), mentor, hero, or partner. *The man* means either the establishment, the police, the power structure; or the top person in a given field. ("If you're into bass, Mingus was **the man**.")

Miles: Miles Davis (born 1926); composer, bandleader, **horn man**, on the cutting edge of jazz innovation since the 1950s.

modal: Referring to music which is confined to a non-Western, melodic scale (usually Oriental, "primitive," or minor-related) and its variations within a simple chord structure. Different chords or notes may be interpolated, but the music remains in a constantly returning relationship to the main notes of the modal scale. Modern jazz innovators have experimented with modal music as an alternative to that based on the Western seven-note scale.

modern jazz: A general term for all jazz that uses the post-**swing** innovations in harmonic structure and **rhythmic** complexity; usually refers to the **sounds** developed in the 1960s by such artists as **Miles Davis**, Bill Evans, Charles Mingus, etc.

Monk: Thelonious Monk (born 1918); bandleader, composer, pianist, dynamic innovator of jazz from the **bop** era through the present day.

New Orleans jazz: The original jazz, the first to be called jazz, popular from the turn of the century to about 1935; and constantly revived since then. It is characterized by a pronounced but not harsh beat and the collective **improvisation** of trumpets, trombones, saxophones, and clarinet. New Orleans jazz was originated as an *ear music* (i.e., it was not written down) and differed from Western melodic scales in the use of **blue notes** and a rough, earthy blues timbre. Still popular with many people today, New Orleans jazz is also known as **traditional jazz**, and, in a somewhat less gutsy, more toned-down form, **Dixieland**.

noodle: To play without direction or intention; to ramble musically.

open: Also **open horn**. Played without a mute (refers to trumpets, trombones, etc.).

out, outside: Against the grain, **avant-garde**; music that is the contrary of what is expected in relation to the **changes** or the apparent structure employed. To *go out* means to abandon traditional jazz concepts. ("Some have *gone* **out** because they had something new to **say**, but most have just *gone* **out**.")

pay dues: To suffer and experience hardship in the course of becoming an artist with something to **say**. Paying dues refers to both the specific difficulties of making a living with integrity as a musician, and to the inevitable tragedies of life as a feeling human being—especially (as many jazz musicians are) as a black in the United States. "Their **sound** is empty because they made it too big, too soon—never **paid their dues**."

Pops: Louis Armstrong (1900–71); also called **Satchmo** or simply **Louis**. Armstrong was the first, and to many minds the greatest, of all the jazz giants—trumpeter, bandleader, singer of incomparable spirit, energy, style, and **drive**. The first of the truly great creative **soloists**.

Prez: Lester Young (1909–59); influential tenor saxophonist of the **swing** and **bop** eras.

progressive jazz: Contemporary, **avant-garde** jazz that continues to push the limits of expression—into dynamic, often disturbing new forms; typified in the work of Cecil Taylor, Ornette Coleman, Sonny Rollins, Eric Dolphy, later John Coltrane.

punch out: To perform powerfully and without hesitation. ("He **punched out** a dynamite tenor **solo**.")

read: To play the music as written—as distinguished from playing by ear and **improvising**. ("He can **read** but he can't *play*" [i.e., *improvise*].)

reed: Any wind instrument, especially saxophone or clarinet.

rhythm: Beat, pulse, pattern of **accents** in the music. The characteristic **sound** of each jazz style (**swing**, **bop**, **fusion**, etc.) is at least partly a result of its unique, identifiable rhythm.

rhythm section: Usually the bass, drums, and piano (or rhythm guitar).

riff: A short repeated figure, or familiar **line** by a performer. ("I thought I heard some of **Bird**'s old **riffs** in his **solo**.")

right hand: Literally, the jazz pianist's facility in playing with his right hand; usually refers to the ability to **improvise lines** on piano. ("My **right hand** is loose, **man**, but I can't seem to get my bass **lines** together.")

rip: A fast crescendo **line** (on **reeds** or **horns**) that leaps up to a high staccato note at the top, then cuts off quickly.

say: To play not just with musical accuracy but with clear human feeling; to play meaningfully, importantly, emotionally; to communicate something with one's music. ("**Say** it, man. I hear you talkin'." "He's **blowing** mighty hard but he ain't **sayin'** nothing.")

scat singing: Playing rapid jazz **improvisational lines** with the voice—singing nonsense syllables—as an instrument. The technique's innovation is attributed to **Louis Armstrong** in the 1920s.

scene: The overall state of jazz affairs; what is current in the sound and style of a particular segment of the culture. ("Lotta new **clubs** opening in Philly, **man**—the **scene** down there is really happening!")

set: A series of **tunes** played by a band without a break during a **gig**. The evening is divided into several sets, each set usually lasting forty minutes to an hour. The second set is usually longer, looser and more exciting—this is the one the cognoscenti catch.

sideman: One of the members of the band who back up or complement the leader; any members of the band besides the leader or featured soloist.

sit in: A musician who is not a member of the band may be invited to sit in (play with the group), usually only for a few **tunes**. This is an old jazz tradition, which persists to the present day; it is both the way that young musicians can establish themselves (showing up with their **ax** at some **club** and asking if they can sit in) and an expression of the open, communal nature of jazz, where top musicians, in the audience at other people's **gigs**, may be invited to join in an unrehearsed but frequently spectacular, live collaboration.

solo: A section of music played solely by one instrument; or mainly by one instrument with fairly unobtrusive accompaniment. Also called a **break**.

sound: The overall character and texture of the music being played, or an aspect of that texture contributed by a particular instrument or musician. ("Who else but Basie gets that **sound, man**?" [*Jazz Talk*, p. 254])

space: The intervals of (silent) time between notes, or between musical phrases—employed deliberately by the creative jazz artist. (Johnny Griffin in *downBeat*, 1979: "I use a lot more **space** in my playing than when I was twenty-five or thirty years old. . . . I was in a rush to play everything possible—I got angry when I had to take a breath!")

square: Uncool, un**hip**, inhibited, conventional in style and/or values. "Square" can refer to music, clothes, life-style, or personality—but it is always a derogation in jazz language.

standard: An older tune, familiar to the jazz community; a jazz classic, such as "Summertime," "Fine and Mellow," "Lady Be Good," "Cherokee," "Take the A Train," etc.

straightahead: 1. Not experimental in its form; honest, uncontrived.

2. Having power, drive and continuity; strong, pinpointed on its forward motion. ("Gillespie's **set** was **straightahead** and relentless in its impact.")

Street, The: Also **Swing Street**, **Swing Alley**. Fifty-second Street, between Fifth and Seventh avenues in New York City. From 1935 to 1948, the **swing** era, this was the main locus for **clubs** that played jazz music.

stretch out: To take a long, exploratory **solo**; to play deeply, thoroughly, soulfully without rushing. ("**Trane** wasn't afraid to **stretch out** on a **solo**; he took all the time he needed and **said** everything there was to say.")

studio musician: One who earns his living as a **sideman** at another artist's record dates. Studio musicians are known for their expertise in playing a broad range of music (for instance, pop, country, classical, and jazz equally well), and are excellent **readers**.

swing: 1. As a verb, to play with energy, feeling, and especially the **rhythms** characteristic of jazz music. ("Milton Jackson may **swing** less than Lionel Hampton [the **drive** is not so strong] but he **swings** better [his rhythmic sensibility is more developed]"—from *Jazz Talk*.)

2. As a noun, the pulsing quality of jazz rhythms, especially the triplet quality underlying swing and **bebop** (i.e., thirties and forties jazz). "It Don't Mean a Thing If It Ain't Got That **Swing**."

3. The most popular, dominant jazz style from the mid-thirties to the mid-forties, associated with the **big bands** of Count Basie, Benny Goodman, Jimmy Lunceford, and others. Swing is a fairly stylized form of jazz, although it includes some room for **improvisation**; and tends to be smooth and mellifluous, never grating, though with a palpable, distinctive underlying rhythm.

tag: The coda; the ending bars of a piece when the **head** is played for the last time through; a short epilogue to the **tune**.

take it out: To finish a **tune**; to go into the concluding section—known as the *out chorus*. ("After the third **horn chorus**, we lay back and let the **rhythm section take it out**.")

tenor: A tenor saxophone, or a tenor saxophone player. ("Heard there's a hot new **tenor** down at the Vanguard.")

thin: Superficial, weak, unimpassioned. May refer to someone's **sound** or **ideas**.

third stream: A style that combines elements of both jazz and classical music; best exemplified in the work of bassist-composer Charles Mingus.

time: Also **sense of time**. A feeling for, and control of, **rhythm**, to a degree that surpasses mere technical accuracy. Time is the artist's personal rhythmic style, the apparently effortless ability to be absolutely right in one's timing. (John Hammond, quoted in *Jazz Is:* "I first heard Billie in 1933 . . . her **time** was something else.")

Trane: **John Coltrane** (1926–67); **tenor** and soprano saxophonist, one of the most influential creators of the **avante-garde** jazz of the late 1950s and 1960s.

tune: Any short musical composition, usually a song.

up-tempo: Also **up**. Fast, or with a brisk, lively, or **driving** underlying **rhythm**. ("A whole **set** of **ballads** won't work, **man**—you've got to throw in a couple of **up-tempo** things.")

vamp: 1. As a noun, a short (usually two-chord) repeating pattern; often played behind a **solo**.

2. As a verb, to play a repeating chord pattern behind a solo, or simply to repeat the same thing over and over. ("Just **vamp** on it

for eight bars, and then we'll break back into the **head**.")

vibes: A vibraphone, an instrument like a large metal xylophone. Also applies to related instruments—vibraharp, vibrabells, etc.

voicings: The arrangement of notes in the chords of a piece, played on a single instrument (e.g., piano); or, the harmonic juxtaposition of melodic **lines** distributed through all the instruments of a group as they play together.

wail: To play emotionally, intensely, excellently. ("Here's a **horn** who can really **wail**!")

walking bass: A continuously moving melodic bass **line**, consisting of a series of unaccented single notes (as opposed to chords or rhythmic figures); especially characteristic of the old, "boogie-woogie" piano style of the thirties and forties.

"What's your story?": The classic invitation to **sit in**.

woodshed: 1. To have a private rehearsal or practice session, in order to work on new material or improve technique.

2. To go into retreat, for personal soul-searching and/or musical development. ("Jones? He's been **woodshedding** since '79. But I hear he's coming back with a whole new **sound**.")

[9]

Rock and Pop Music

Popular music pervades our lives—on radio and television, in elevators and department stores, on private tape decks and stereos. And no wonder: The American music business is gigantic. Dominated by a small number of major record **labels**, which collectively sell over $3 billion yearly in records and tapes, the industry also includes thousands of radio stations, tens of thousands of live concert performances, TV and movie soundtracks and appearances. It is peopled by a fascinating cast of characters: **producers** and **promoters**, **engineers** and personal **managers**, **singer/songwriters**, **front men**, **sessionmen**, **jocks**, and **groupies**. And while there are many genres of popular music—**soul**, **disco**, **country**, **fusion**, **MOR** —the **pop charts** today are dominated by **rock** music, that "flash in the pan" upstart music of the fifties that is still going strong twenty-five years later.

The language of the music industry is a mixture of musicians' terms (**bridge**, **lick**, **riff**, **jam**), radio terms (**AOR**, **Top 40**, **jock**), and the specifics of the record-selling business: **hooks**, **rack jobbers**, **white labels**, going **platinum**. The industry is notoriously high pressure, risky, and labile, with trends and personalities rising and falling with an appalling rapidity. One group might find their latest **single** "number 39 on the **country** charts this week with a **bullet**, great potential for crossover to **pop**, definitely heading for **gold**"— only to see their elaborately produced **LP** wind up in the **cutout** bins for $1.59 a few months later. Still, for those with a passion for the music, the excitement, and/or the money, there's no business like it. Herewith, a guide to the most-used terms of the rock and pop music industry.

A and R: Artist and Repertoire: a position in a record company with the general responsibility for finding and signing new talent, and releasing their records at the right time and place.

AC: Adult contemporary; a type of music (and

the radio **format** that plays it) characterized by a fairly soft, mellow sound, including **soft rock**, and especially mainstream (**MOR**) **pop** —such as Barbra Streisand, Neil Diamond, and Barry Manilow.

acid rock: A form of **rock** popular in the late 1960s, named for the obvious influence of psychedelic drug experience in the generation of the music. Typified by such groups as Jimi Hendrix, Big Brother and The Holding Company, The Doors, and the early Grateful Dead, the music includes long, wild **lead guitar** solos and a heavy **bass** and percussion section.

acoustic: Non-electric, "natural"; used primarily in relation to guitar, although it may also apply to piano and other instruments. Acoustic guitar is uniformly used in **folk** and classical music, some of the time in **blues**, **country** and **jazz**; but only very rarely on **rock** or **pop tracks**—for example, John Lennon's guitar work on the Beatles' White Album.

add: The addition of a particular song or album to a radio station's **playlist**. Once a record has gotten an add, its promoters work to get it in rotation—either *light, medium,* or *heavy,* depending upon the number of times it is regularly played each day.

AOR: Album-oriented rock; one of the major identifiable radio **formats**, characterized by the airplay of whole LPs or **cuts** on them that are not necessarily hit **singles**; the other end of the radio spectrum from **Top-40** radio. The connotation of AOR is that less "commercial," more serious music is played; more AOR formats tend to be found on FM radio and more Top 40 on AM, although these distinctions are not as rigid as they once were.

arrangement: A particular version of a song, as modified by a single artist or played by the various members of a group—for example, Henry Mancini's arrangement of Neil Sedaka's "Calendar Girl." May also refer to the specific part played by a single instrument or group of instruments within a larger ensemble, such as "a juicy horn **arrangement** on the new Quincy Jones album."

ASCAP: The **American Society of Composers, Authors, and Publishers**; one of the two major performance rights licensing organizations in the U.S. ASCAP represents some 20,000 music writers and publishers. It collects fees from radio stations, TV, nightclubs, jukeboxes, and the like (usually based on a percentage of ad revenues, as in the case of radio, the major source of income). It distributes advances and royalties to its members on a formula basis, reflecting—at least hypothetically—their fair share of the total incomes.

A side: The more marketable song on a 45 rpm record (or **single**). It is marked "A" on the record, and is promoted heavily to receive radio airplay.

backup: Supporting musicians or singers, especially those who are not part of a group per se, but are hired for a studio session or live appearance.

ballad: Originally, a longish, slower-tempo song that told a (usually tragic) story—such as Dave Van Ronk's "Lazarus," or "Frankie and Johnny," or "It Was a Very Good Year." Currently, the term is applied to any song that has a similar feel—that is, slowish, melancholy songs of love or nostalgia, such as Don McLean's "The Day the Music Died."

bass: 1. The lower, deeper tones of the music range, and the technical sound equipment that communicates them (e.g., *bass pickup*).

2. An electric bass guitar (four strings only), used both as a basic rhythm instrument and as a carrier of melodic/harmonic lines in almost all **rock** groups.

bluegrass: The true old-time **country** music from the South (especially Kentucky and West Virginia, the Appalachian region), featuring banjos, mandolins, and fiddles—typified by Flatt and Scruggs and the "Dueling Banjos" **track** made famous in the movie *Deliverance.* Bluegrass is one of the major sources for modern, commercial **country and western**.

blues: The original black American musical form, which has been the major musical source for **jazz**, **R and B**, and **rock** and which survives as a distinct music of its own today. There are many forms of blues, from the raw, basic guitar/voice/harmonica styles of *Delta* or *country blues*, to the sophisticated, electrified *Chicago blues* or *"blues band"* sounds of Muddy Waters, B. B. King, or James Cotton. In its latest incarnation, blues has become multiracial with such groups as the Paul Butterfield Blues Band and John Mayall's Blues Breakers performing exceptionally powerful versions of this compelling music. Blues invariably involves the use of a five-tone *blues scale,* and the characteristic "bending" or flatting of certain notes to produce the wailing, gutsy blues sound. Contrary to popular (white) belief, however, blues is by no means a music confined to the expression of sadness or hardship, but is as frequently rollicking, bawdy, lusty, and affirmative.

BM: Beautiful music; usually **Top-40** tunes that have been rearranged with less heavy beat and a lot of strings, for play in shopping malls, elevators, dentists' offices, and radio stations that specialize in it. This is what you hear when the secretary at a large corporation puts you on hold. Music to wait by.

BMI: Broadcast Music, Inc.; one of the two giant organizations (see also **ASCAP**) that license the radio airplay and other performance uses of music by its members. BMI represents 40,000 writers and publishers and distributes advances, royalties, and bonuses to them from the revenues it collects from radio stations, TV, nightclubs, concert halls, and the like.

board: Short for *sound board;* an elaborate console of switches and dials, used by the sound **engineer** to control sound levels and tone qualities, when recording, **mixing**, **dubbing**, or amplifying live music (at a concert). Literally scores of disparate sound elements can be controlled and combined at the same time with the most modern sound boards.

boogie: A corrupt verb meaning to dance, to party, to have fun. Used as a noun or adjective (*boogie bands*), it connotates **rock** music with a **blues** or **R and B** quality, suitable for dancing. Not to be confused with *boogie-woogie* (from which the term may have derived), an eight-to-the-bar jazz piano style popular in the 1930s.

bootleg: An illegally produced album (or tape). Often the bootleg album is a recording of a live concert performance, for which the artists are never paid; it is thus a violation of copyright laws, as well as infringing upon whatever contracts the artist and a record **label** may have in effect.

brass pop: A style of **pop** or **pop-rock** music in which the use of trumpets and trombones is emphasized, with a corresponding absence of guitars and reed instruments (such as saxophone). Exemplified by Herb Alpert and The Tijuana Brass, Al Hirt, and some Blood, Sweat and Tears **tracks**.

breakout: A designation in the **trades** for a record that has begun to sell extremely well in one part of the country and may be expected to start selling nationwide and climbing the **charts**.

bridge: The section of a song between any of its major verses; a transitional section, usually invoking a change of key. For example, in "Over the Rainbow", the bridge is the part that goes, "Someday I'll wish upon a star and wake up where the clouds are far behind me . . ."

bullet: A designation in the record-sales **charts** indicating that a record is rapidly gaining popularity and is expected to climb higher in the upcoming weeks. Thus, a **single** might be "48 with a **bullet** on the **soul charts** this week." A *superbullet* indicates that a ten-point jump is expected in the next week.

B side: Also **flip side**. The second side of a **sin-**

gle, generally considered less promotable than the **A side** and less often given airplay. (See **A side**.)

C and W: Country and Western (music). See **country**.

charts: 1. The **trade** magazine (*Billboard, Record World,* et al.) rating charts, which indicate the best-selling **singles**, **LPs**, and tapes overall and in various categories (**soul**, **disco**, jazz, **rock**, **adult contemporary**, Latin), for each week; as well as those receiving the largest amount of airplay. The charts are the most fundamental index of "what's happening" in the music industry.

  2. A musical **arrangement**, as in "Doc's put together some terrific **charts** for Johnny's anniversary special."

CHR: Contemporary Hit Radio. See **Top 40**.

concept album: A **rock** (occasionally **pop**, **jazz**, or **folk**) **LP´** that is not merely a collection of twelve or sixteen **tracks** but is unified by some underlying theme, narrative, idea, or purpose; for example, The Beatles' *Sergeant Pepper's Lonely Hearts Club Band*.

consultant: An individual (or organization) hired by a radio station, basically to tell the station which records to play in order to maximize listenership within a given **format**. The **AOR** field is dominated by the views of three or four very powerful, widely used consultant firms.

country: Also **country music**, **country and western**, **C and W**. A style of music, identified with the South and Southwest (and especially with **Nashville**), and typically merging **bluegrass**, **blues**, **rock**, **folk**, and **ballad** elements in songs of love, love lost, hard times, and individual rebelliousness. Country music's all-time greats have included: Hank Williams, Jimmie Rodgers, Merle Haggard, Chet Atkins, Johnny Cash, and Loretta Lynn; top current stars include Glenn Campbell, Dolly Parton, Crystal Gayle, and Willie Nelson. A modern offshoot of country and western is called *country rock,* which includes typical country elements in a more heavily rock-oriented synthesis. (Examples are the Flying Burrito Brothers, and individual **tracks** of various artists, from Kris Kristofferson to the Rolling Stones.) See also **outlaw country**.

cover: 1. Also **cover version**. A particular group's or artist's rendition of a song written by someone else, as Glen Campbell's cover of Fred Neil's "Everybody's Talking at Me." Also used as a verb (to *cover* a fifties hit) and adjective (a *cover artist*).

  2. An album cover or jacket.

cut: 1. As a noun, a single song or **track** on a record album ("A **reggae**-inspired **cut** on the new Rolling Stones **LP**").

  2. As a verb, to record a song or album ("They're reissuing the legendary **blues** sides Robert Johnson **cut** in 1935 and 1936").

cutout: Also **delete**. A record that has not sold well and has thus been "cut out" of a record company's catalogue; such records are then sold at a discount either through the *cutout bins* at a regular record store or through stores that specialize in old and discontinued records.

date: A live concert performance or a studio recording session.

delete: See **cutout**.

demo: When a group or solo artist is seeking radio airplay, or a recording contract, or a star to **cover** a composition, he (or she or they) will prepare a demo or demonstration tape that can be sent around for review by the powers that be in the music industry.

disco: The major **pop** music phenomenon of the late 1970s, a strictly dance-oriented music with a steady but not heavy beat, and inconsequential lyrics. Although the disco craze has waned considerably in the early 1980s, the music continues to sell and be played—though at nowhere near the rate of the more than ten million copies of the *Saturday Night Fever* album sold in 1978.

DJ copy: A record with only an **A side**, for airplay by radio **disc jockeys**.

DJ: Disc jockey. See **jock**.

doo-wop: Type of fifties **rock** or **R and B** in which the **backup** vocals involved the repetition of such phrases as "doo-wop," "Sh-bop," "Sh-boom," "doo-lang," and the like, utilizing harmonies that were popular among groups of young men who stood around and "harmonized" on city street corners in those days.

dub: Also **overdub**, **dub-over**. To record additional **tracks** on top of the original groups or artist's rendition; often used to add **backup** vocals, **strings**, or double-**tracks** of guitars, voice, sound effects, or other audio elements. An extremely common practice in the production of most **rock** and **pop** records.

easy listening: A general term for **soft rock**, **MOR**, **pop**, and light **disco** or **fusion** music that is mellifluous, nonabrasive, and without a heavy or driving beat. Certain radio stations specialize in this type of sound.

echo: Also **reverb** (for reverberation). The addition of an echo-effect sound, either through a device built into the instrument (especially electric guitar) or, in the recording studio, through an echo-chamber device.

engineer: Also **sound engineer**. The person who operates the *sound board* and is responsible for picking up the **tracks** from various mikes, adjusting their sound levels, and coordinating the technical mix of all elements on a **master** tape. In some recording setups, there may be both a *recording engineer* (responsible for miking and pickup) and a *mixing engineer*.

EP: A record that is played at 45 rpm but contains twice the material of a standard **45**—i.e., usually two **cuts** per side. A popular medium in Europe that is beginning to see distribution in the U.S. as well.

Fender: A major brand of electric guitar (and **bass**) used by **rock** musicians.

folk: The traditional music of rural American and other countries, usually handed down orally for generations, although it may have been transcribed in recent years, and almost always performed on **acoustic** instruments. The term is also applied to music written and performed by more modern artists, often expressing social and political protest, that remains within the folk idiom—relatively simple musically, played on acoustic instruments, with traditional chord progressions. The music of Woody Guthrie, early Bob Dylan, and early Judy Collins is all considered folk although for the most part they wrote and performed original material.

folk rock: A development of the mid and late 1960s, triggered by Bob Dylan's switch to electric guitar; the genre took hold, however, as a fertile blend of the social and emotional elements of **folk** with the heavier beat and higher energy of **rock**. Prime examples of the folk-rock explosion include Dylan, Arlo Guthrie, Simon and Garfunkel, The Lovin' Spoonful, and The Byrds.

format: In radio, a general type of music played at a given station; and, by implication, the listening audience targeted. Thus a **Top 40** format plays only hit **singles** from the **rock/pop charts** and appeals primarily to young people in their teens and twenties; while an **AOR** format attracts an audience in their late twenties and thirties; and an **easy listening** format generally garners listeners in their forties and older.

45: A seven-inch-diameter record, meant to be played at 45 rpm and generally containing only one song on each side. **Top 40** radio stations play 45s almost exclusively, as it is through this medium that the "hottest," most commercial **pop** and **rock** songs are disseminated. See also **single**.

front man: The leader of a musical group, so named because he usually stands in front of the rest of the musicians during live performances. The front man is almost always the lead singer in **rock** and **pop** groups—such as Mick Jagger of the Rolling Stones; but less uniformly in jazz and other genres (Count Basie on **keyboard** fronting his orchestra, or

Sun Ra, on anything, fronting his Solar Arkestra).

funk: A somewhat imprecise term applied to late-seventies and early-eighties "black-oriented" music, characterized by a pronounced, danceable beat, slower than typical **R and B** but "funkier" (sexier, more low-down) than **disco**. The modern equivalent of what was called **soul** in the 1960s. Major funk groups include Parliament-Funkadelic; Earth, Wind and Fire; Rick James and the Stone City Band; Kool and the Gang; and many others.

fusion: A type of music that combines elements of jazz and **rock**, or jazz and **pop**, and has enjoyed far greater commercial success than any of the "pure" jazz musics in recent years. Typifying fusion are such artists as Chick Corea, Weather Report, Spyro Gyra, and Herbie Hancock.

Gibson: A famous brand of electric guitar, especially popular among **blues** and **blues–rock** artists.

gig: A job or musical engagement. ("I've lined up a **gig** at the Paradise for September.")

gold: Having sold 500,000 units (records or tapes) of a given **single** or **LP**. Thus an album is said to have *gone gold* when the Record Industry Association of America (RIAA) certifies that a half million copies have been sold.

gospel: The religious music of certain black American churches, characterized by a steady, pronounced rhythm, exquisite vocal harmonies, and the frequent use of (often syncopated) hand clapping, blues notes, and falsettos. Gospel is closely related to **blues** and forms a major influence on **R and B**, **soul**, and **rock** music in general. Many black **pop** stars—Aretha Franklin is probably the best known—began their careers as gospel singers.

Grammy: The major award of the record industry, given to artists in various categories (**country, rock, jazz**, and so on) every year in a ceremony rivaling that of the motion-picture Oscars.

groupie: An individual, usually a teenage girl (but sometimes older and occasionally male) who follows a **rock** group around, exchanging sex and/or company for the dubious privilege of being associated with rock musicians.

hard rock: A catchall term for all those varieties of **rock** (including **heavy metal, blues rock,** and **punk**) with a powerful driving beat—as distinguished from the "softer" sounds of **folk rock, fusion,** and **soft rock**. The Who, for example, as distinguished from Jackson Browne.

harp: A harmonica, especially in **blues** parlance.

heavy metal: Hard rock with almost total reliance on electric guitars (and **bass**), without piano, sax, horns, or other mollifying influences; a crude, powerful, musically violent **rock** variant, typified in such groups as Iron Butterfly, Kiss, Queen, and Black Sabbath. Also known as *crunch rock.*

hook: A musical phrase, repeated lyric, or other device in a song that "hooks" the listener and is likely to be remembered. The ability to write music with hooks is considered a key element in the **Top 40** artist's commercial success. (Example of a hook from classic fifties **rock**: "Duke, Duke, Duke, Duke of Earl.")

instrumental: A **cut** with no vocals. Extremely common in jazz or **fusion** music, but quite rare in the **pop** or **rock** forms today—except when reduced to so-called **beautiful music** (see **BM**.)

jam: Also **jam session**. A term derived from jazz (see complete definition in JAZZ section), referring to musical improvisation among two or more players. Jam sessions vary widely, from inchoate noodling to spectacular innovation and discovery; when the latter has been captured on disc, it is a rare treat indeed.

jazz rock: See **fusion**.

jock: Also **DJ**. A disc jockey, a radio-station employee who plays records and speaks over the airwaves. Popular jocks on major **Top-40** stations have become personalities almost as well-known (and well paid) as the artists whose music they purvey.

keyboard: A generic term for piano and all other related instruments: electric piano, electric organ, harpsichord, and the like.

label: The record company that is marketing and distributing a record, and whose "label" is thus on the record itself (or the tape, or album cover). The major record labels—RCA, Warner, CBS, Polydor, Capitol, MCA, and Arista—account for over $3 billion a year in sales of records and tapes. They are major corporations (usually divisions of larger conglomerates), with multiple departments (such as **A and R**, **promotion**, advertising, sales, publicity) and thousands of employees. The label itself may or may not actually produce a given record—as independent **producers** account for a significant amount of the record companies' "product" today, in much the same way that independent film and TV production companies sell their works for distribution by the studios and networks.

lead guitar: The guitar (also the player) which carries the melody line in a **rock**, **blues**, or **fusion** group, and which is usually the key instrument in the group's identity. Some of the most notable lead guitarists have been Jimi Hendrix, Eric Clapton, George Benson, and, of course, Chuck Berry.

lick: A short, intense musical phrase, usually of some technical difficulty; especially used in reference to fast runs on the electric guitar.

liner notes: The writing—usually by a music critic or expert, sometimes the artist or **producer**—found on the **jacket** or inside sleeve of an **LP**. Liner notes range from the sublime to the ridiculous, most often falling in the mundane middle.

lip synch: The process by which a performer appearing live on stage or on television apparently "sings" his or her recorded song, while in fact only mouthing the words in synchronization with the pre-recorded **track**. This is how a **Top-40 single** that was elaborately produced in a studio with ten different **tracks dubbed** on top of each other and a **backup** group of twenty-five musicians can be "performed" by the main artist (Donna Summer, or whomever), on a taped-live TV show. Reality is malleable in the entertainment biz.

LP: A long-playing record album, to be played at 33⅓ rpm. The typical LP contains between twenty-five and fifty minutes of music—or approximately ten to fifteen **cuts** of **Top-40 single** length.

manager: Also **personal manager**. An individual (or often an entire staff under one key management figure) who handles all of an artist's affairs—business deals and contracts, musical engagements, schedules, and personal needs. The manager is the artist's link to the rest of the world—dealing with the Machiavellian intrigues of the record industry; promoting and publicizing; and often attending to those personal details that will make the artist comfortable and productive: taking care of friends and lovers, buying clothes and costumes, and a host of activities cynically called "baby-sitting." Nonetheless, the role of the manager is an indispensable one, and one of the most lucrative in the entire music industry: Managers receive a healthy portion of their clients' income—as much as 50 percent—for their services.

master: 1. The **master tape**, the final tape resulting from the mixing process, which will ultimately be transferred onto records or tapes for commercial sale.

2. The vinyl master record cut at a *mastering lab,* which, after several further stages, will result in mass-produced record copies.

3. As a verb, to complete the final stages of the recording process, producing a vinyl record ready for reproduction.

M.D.: Music Director. The person responsible

for specific music decisions (e.g., selection of the **playlist**) at a radio station.

mix: To combine various **tracks** that have been recorded (either simultaneously or separately), emphasizing some ("bring up the **strings** here") and reducing others ("too much **bass**"), to achieve the proper balance of all elements in the final **master**.

MOR: Middle of the road; a generic term for all types of music considered palatable to the mainstream of listeners—that is, music that is not extreme in terms of beat, lyrics, or musical complexity. Includes most **pop** music, and the tamer forms of **rock**, **disco**, **R and B**, and **country**.

Motown: The Detroit-based record **label** that achieved great success in the 1960s with its popularization of the Motown **soul** sound through such artists as The Supremes, The Temptations, The Four Tops, Martha and the Vandellas, and Smokey Robinson and The Miracles. The Motown synthesis of **R and B** with jazz, **gospel**, and **rock** elements (for example, The Four Tops' "Baby I Need Your Lovin'") has never been equaled in American popular music.

moves, the: Also, **the jumps**. Movement of a record up or down the **charts** in the **trades**, or within a given radio station's **playlist**.

Nashville: The major recording center for **country** music, as well as a significant amount of **rock** and **pop** production. The Nashville sound, though not so identifiable as it was fifteen or twenty years ago, is synonymous with a tight, professional, electrified country-style pop music, as exemplified by such artists as Dolly Parton and Glen Campbell.

New Wave: A generic term for a variety of avant-garde **rock** groups that sprang up in the late seventies and early eighties. New Wave is, in general, an aggressively experimental form of rock with either artistic or social/political content—or pretension. Key figures in New Wave include The Clash, The Sex Pistols, Talking Heads, Elvis Costello,

Robin Lane and the Chartbusters, and The Police. (See also **punk rock**, generally considered a subset of New Wave.)

one-stop: One of the three major forms of record and tape distribution (the others being retail record stores and racks; see **rack jobber**). One-stops are music-industry wholesalers, who purchase records direct from the record company and then resell them to retail stores, jukebox operators, and the like.

outlaw country: A branch of **country** music that tends to be more progressive politically, and less tied into the **Nashville pop/country** system; represented by such artists as Willie Nelson and Waylon Jennings.

payola: Illegal payments, in the form of money or gifts, to a **jock** or radio station director, to solicit airplay for specific records. The practice is *not* unknown in the music business.

P.D.: Program Director. The person responsible for overall programming decisions (e.g., **formats**, scheduling of different shows, etc.) at a radio station.

phones: Call-out research done by a radio station or record company. *Getting good phones* means receiving excellent response to a specific record or show or market-research inquiry.

platinum: Having sold a million units (records and/or tapes). A record *goes platinum* when it achieves RIAA-certified sales of one million or more. (See **gold**.)

playlist: A radio-station listing of the songs it has played in a given day or week.

A *frozen playlist* is one with no **adds**, no **moves**, no changes during a given week.

pop: 1. A general term for "popular"—that is, commercially successful—music, which can thus include anything from Dolly Parton to George Benson to The Beatles; with the implication, however, that the music is not extreme either musically (no **heavy metal**, no avant-garde jazz) or socially. Pop thus includes almost everything that is on the **Top-40 charts**.

2. In a more specific sense, **MOR** music, with a fairly mellifluous sound, especially in the non-rock "Tin Pan Alley" tradition of songwriters such as Barry Manilow and Burt Bacharach.

producer: The individual responsible for the overall coordination of a record's creation—similar to a motion-picture producer/director. The producer may be involved with virtually every aspect of a record's production—the matching of artists and materials, selection of **backup** musicians and **sessionmen**, recording studio arrangements, sound **mixing**, orchestration. While some producers may simply act as production administrators without any real creative involvement, the great producers of American music—Phil Spector, Jerry Wexler, Berry Gordy, and the like—have been responsible, in some ways more than the musicians themselves, for creating a certain "sound" that was unmistakable, and supremely successful.

product management: The liaison between the record **label** and a given artist or artist's **manager**.

progressive: A loose and much-abused term that can be applied to any of the major genres (*progressive country, progressive rock,* etc.), to imply a musical or psychological sophistication, the predominance of artistic over commercial values, or any attempt to break out of an established **MOR** mold and create original, meaningful music.

promoter: A person who stages and produces live-music concerts, whether small club appearances or huge, Woodstock-type festivals. Basically, the promoter rents the facility (theater or concert hall or outdoor arena), books the acts (a single rock group or an entire constellation of acts), and advertises the show to get people there. It sounds simple, but in fact concert promotion is an extremely high-pressure, high-anxiety, and high-risk occupation with tremendous amounts of responsibility (for example, 50,000 teenagers turning out to see a **punk rock** concert) and lots of money to be made, or lost. Bill Graham was *the* legendary sixties and seventies rock promoter.

promotion: Efforts made by a record company to get a record played on as many radio stations as many times as possible; and other efforts to keep the record in the public eye (or ear). One of the pivotal marketing functions at a record company; not to be confused with the functions of a **promoter**.

punk rock: A noxious musical phenomenon of the late seventies in England and slightly later in the U.S., which appears to be wearing out in the early 1980s, punk rock is characterized musically by a monotonous, simplistic, heavy beat, dehumanized voices, and angry, violent lyrics. Punk performers also affect a weird, antisocial appearance and personal style, in which any expression of rage, disgust, or hostility is considered artistically valid. Though many rock critics have been eager to show the "social significance" of punk as a progressive force for alienated adolescent youth, the objective observer is more likely to discern pathological, sadistic-fascistic tendencies in both the groups and their fans; certainly there is little or no resemblance to the progressive, **folk-rock** protest music of the late 1960s and early 1970s.

quad: short for **quadrophonic**, sound recorded and reproduced through four separate sources (as opposed to stereo, which has two). Quad sound systems (for example, in some movie theaters) usually place the speakers in all four corners of a room or auditorium, in order to achieve a "natural," sound-surround effect.

rack jobber: A wholesaler who buys records and tapes in quantity from the record company and distributes them to department stores (such as K-Mart, Sears, J.C. Penney, Zayres), where they are sold in record *racks*. Such "racked" accounts represent half of all records and tapes sold in the U.S. today.

R and B: Rhythm and blues; a vital, energetic

style of music developed in the late 1940s and 1950s as a synthesis of elements from traditional **blues**, **gospel**, and jazz, but with a unique, powerful rhythm that makes it one of the most danceable of all American **pop** forms. R and B was, in many senses, the black parallel to early 1950s rock and roll, and provided much of the musical energy that was then "translated" by such white artists as Elvis Presley. Major R and B figures include Fats Domino, Ray Charles, Chuck Berry, Bo Diddley, Little Richard, the Isley Brothers, and James Brown. Sixties **soul**, modern **funk**, and the entirety of **rock** for over twenty-five years have borrowed and absorbed elements of R and B.

reggae: A form of music played by the Rastafarians of Jamaica and now popularized by Jamaican groups in the U.S. and others who have imitated the sound. Reggae is characterized by a distinctive syncopated beat, the use of steel drums, and often highly political lyrics. Well-known reggae artists include Jimmy Cliff, Toots and the Maytals, and the late Bob Marley and The Wailers.

road manager: The coordinator of a traveling musical tour, responsible for all transportation and lodging arrangements, guiding the group or artist to interviews, performances, parties, and the like.

roadie: A crew member of a touring musical group, responsible for transporting and setting up all musical equipment, arranging the stage and instruments, breaking it down after a performance, and moving it again.

rock: An extremely broad classification of music, which includes sounds as disparate as Arlo Guthrie's **folk rock** and the Sex Pistols' **punk rock,** as well as "classic" fifties *rock and roll* of Buddy Holly, Fats Domino, or Elvis Presley. The term was first used in the mid-fifties to denote a kind of "white" **R and B** played by such groups as Bill Haley and the Comets. Over the ensuing decades, rock has expanded and branched out into many forms, some of them sophisticated, some crude, some creative and innovative, many more derivative and banal. Now the term probably applies to any music played on electrified instruments with a pronounced beat that does *not* have an otherwise distinctive identity—thus excluding **country**, **soul/funk**, **disco**, and **fusion**, though some would consider them all subsets of rock. One salient characteristic that defines rock, subjectively at least, is its energy—a pulsing, adolescent drive that, while mindless and chaotic (if not offensive) at its worst, can also prove exhilarating and transportive at its best. But then, any category that includes The Chiffons, The Beatles, The BeeGees, and Kiss defies accurate description.

rockabilly: A combination of "rock" and "hillbilly," referring to a style of music that fused elements of early **rock** with **country and western**—as exemplified in much of Elvis Presley's early work, the incomparable Jerry Lee Lewis, and more recently Jimmy Buffett.

salsa: A form of **rock/pop/disco** music identified with Hispanic artists and generally featuring a distinctive Latin beat; exemplified by such groups as Tito Puente, Julio Iglesias, Salsoul Orchestra, and Gato Barbieri.

session: A recording session at a sound studio.

sessionman: A musician who is not a member of an established group but who is hired to play at the recording **dates** of various groups; sessionmen (and women) tend to be technically excellent, straight-headed players, without the hubris and temperamentality of many "name" artists. They are the artisans of the music industry.

singer/songwriter: An artist who both writes and performs his or her own material. More specifically, the term refers to a genre of performers, starting in the late 1960s **folk** and **folk-rock** era and continuing through the seventies and eighties, who wrote softer, less rabid forms of **rock** and **pop** music, in which the lyrics were held to be of some importance.

Major singer/songwriters of this group include Leonard Cohen, James Taylor, Simon and Garfunkel, Carole King, Joni Mitchell, Cat Stevens, Harry Chapin, and Neil Diamond.

single: The **A side** of a 45 rpm record; a single song marketed to receive radio airplay (especially on **Top-40**-type stations) and sold as the commercial half of a **45** (though a hit **single** may also appear as one **cut** of an album as well).

soft rock: A **rock/pop/folk** hybrid that became especially popular in the 1970s, soft rock tends to be slower paced and with a less harsh or heavy beat than **hard rock.** It is a style of music that includes a wide range of performers, from Jackson Brown to The Eagles to Cat Stevens to Linda Ronstadt.

soul: 1. A style of music developed in the early 1960s (and popular for the next decade), which took **gospel** and **R and B** elements, added more sophisticated instrumentation and production values, and became not only the dominant form of black music but one of the most popular types of music anywhere during that decade. Key soul artists (out of dozens) were Ray Charles, Otis Redding, Wilson Pickett, Aretha Franklin, James Brown, Sam Cooke, The Four Tops.

2. A general music-industry term for "black-oriented music," which may include **R and B, funk, fusion, disco,** "rap" records, and the like.

stiff: A record that does not sell, and heads almost immediately to the **cutout** bins. La bomba.

strings: Violins and other related string instruments (cellos, violas, etc.), especially when added in the studio as an additional **track** to "soften" the sound of a **pop** artist's recording. More than one serious musician has seen his work turned into **MOR** pabulum by the injudicious application of strings; in the hands of a genius group such as The Beatles, however

("All the Lonely People" on *Magical Mystery Tour* comes to mind), the use of strings can be enormously effective.

test: An album run off from a **master** and distributed within a record company for approval by various executives before mass production is undertaken.

Top 40: Literally, the **chart** listing of the forty (or 100, or 200) best-selling **singles,** in a given week, as found in *Record World* and *Billboard* magazines. The term is now used to refer to the most popular, commercial type of music (which tends to be mostly **rock** and **pop,** with little jazz, **country,** or **soul**), and to radio-station **formats** that play such music almost exclusively. Every major city has at least one of these Top 40 stations, usually on the AM band, and it is often the most listened-to station in town. Also known as **CHR,** or **Contemporary Hit Radio.**

track: 1. A single line of recorded sound. Usually each musician is recorded through a separate mike, and the various tracks thus obtained are **mixed**—with additional tracks added—via a multi-track **sound board.**

2. A single **cut** or song on a record album. *Top Tracks* is a relatively new **chart** in some **trades,** indicating the album **cuts** which are receiving the most radio airplay (mostly on **AOR**).

trades: The weekly publications of the record/music business, which in the U.S. refers basically to *Billboard, Cashbox, Record World, Radio and Records,* and the music sections of *Variety.* Other key music publications include *Down-Beat* (heavy jazz orientation) and *Musician/Player and Listener,* which are both monthlies.

12-inch: An album-size record with only one song on each side, mostly used for promotional purposes, to focus attention on a single **cut** off a commercial **LP.**

white label: A promotional or **DJ** copy of a record, not for commercial sale but sent to radio stations to receive airplay.

III

BUSINESS

[10]

Business Management

There is a group—some would call it a class—of people, who form the upper levels of the pyramidal hierarchy in most American **corporations** today. They are business **managers**, and their work, though tremendously varied, is defined by their authority over at least one subordinate (or an entire level of subordinates) and their power to make decisions (of varying magnitudes) by which they will be judged. These are the people who run American business, and as a result, they form one of the most influential groups of people in the world.

Classically, there are three fairly distinct levels of management in the medium to large company: **first-line** or "low-level" **management**, which includes positions usually titled foreman, supervisor, and the like, with the responsibility of directly overseeing production efforts and directly relating to production workers; **middle management**, which typically contains several layers of employees above first-line management, and is devoted to implementing long-range company goals through the administration of specific departments, plant sites, task groups, projects, and the like; and **top-level management** (usually referred to as **executives**, though this term may include some high middle managers as well), which consists of those who set long-range policy for a company and make decisions of major importance. We are concerned in this section fundamentally with the language of the two upper levels of management, as these are the people who wield the real power and who shape the corporate world.

Although there are innumerable theories (expounded in innumerable books) on management methods and executive "leadership styles," the topmost levels of American management are remarkably homogeneous: almost exclusively white, middle-aged males, forceful, intelligent, self-confident, wealthy, and extremely devoted—some would say *obsessively* devoted—to their work. Top execs are

137

also distinguished by their language—a fascinating mix of technical jargon (specific to their business, whether aeronautics or women's fashions); financial and accounting terms; military-sounding acronymns (see p. 206), and pure managementese—a language of decision-making and power.

The individual who wishes to deal successfully with business executives—or merely understand them—would do well to learn their language. For the person immersed in the Machiavellian world of corporate politics, attempting to claw his (or her) way up the **corporate ladder**, knowing the language is indispensable.

Executive Acronyms   One of the things middle and upper-level managers like to do is throw around a lot of acronyms and abbreviations, which not only saves time (efficiency of speech) and indicates the speaker's knowledgeability (leadership validation) but also puts the listener who is not exactly sure what they mean on the defensive (corporate politics). Herewith, a Berlitz guide to twenty of the most common AIUs (Abbreviations in Use). 🍎

APV: Administrative point of view. What the middle level tells the lower level, coming from the higher level; the official position.

AQL: Acceptable quality level; in **quality control**, the proportion of produced or shipped or received items that must meet quality standards or specifications. This is rarely 100 percent. An AQL of .95 means that a shipment will be accepted if no more than 5 percent of the items are substandard or defective.

CEO: Chief executive officer; the person who actually "runs the show" at a large company, usually the president but sometimes the executive vice president or some other titleholder. The term is meant to evoke the same authoritative image as the military designation it resembles and from which it was derived—CO (Commanding Officer).

CPM: Critical Path method; a method of planning or analyzing a problem which indicates the interrelated sequence of tasks and events required to complete the project, with time estimates for each; the critical path includes only those functions that will delay the whole

project if they take longer than planned; other tasks, comprising noncritical paths, are indicated although they are unlikely to affect the overall time sequence (either because there is "slack" in the time required or because they are relatively inessential functions). See **pert**.

EDP: Electronic data processing; the use of computers to store information (such as stock inventories, accounts payable and receivable, client listings) and manipulate it to solve problems or provide fast, accurate "readouts" as required. This rapidly growing phenomenon is causing a revolution in the way that many companies operate. When properly programmed and used in the warehousing and retailing applications where it functions best, EDP can save a great deal of time, cut overhead costs, and reduce instances of human error; where ineptly or unnecessarily applied, it can waste a great deal of money and replace ongoing human judgment with rigid machine-programmed calculations.

FTC: The **Federal Trade Commission**; the federal agency with the responsibility of regulating American business on behalf of free competition and consumer protection. As the agency most likely to interfere with the "freedom" of **big business** to monopolize the market and/or produce harmful products, the FTC is often perceived in corporate circles with less than total enthusiasm.

M.B.A: Master of Business Administration; the basic graduate degree in business and an almost essential ingredient for admission to the **fast track** to corporate success. A Harvard M.B.A. is by far the most valuable.

MBO: Management by objectives; a method and style of management, first expounded by management **consultant** and author Peter Drucker. In MBO, a manager and his subordinates together arrive at a specific set of performance objectives that the employees (or a unit of employees) agree to achieve. The system thus incorporates the participation and opinion of the subordinates, increases their motivation, enables fair and accurate evaluations, and generally improves the work climate. MBO is a popular buzzword and is actually in fairly widespread practice in certain industries in the United States and abroad.

MIS: Management information system; usually a computerized system for delivering information to top management for use in effective planning and decision-making.

OC: Organizational climate; the ambience of a place of business, its "feel." The level of vitality and enthusiasm exhibited by managers and other employees, their attitude toward the company, the image and competence they exhibit to outsiders. Morale. All other things being equal, a "positive **OC**" translates into higher profitability; which is, as they say, the **bottom line**.

OD: Organizational development; the process of engendering change in the structure and/or methods of an organization, either for greater efficiency and profitability, expansion, adaptation to new demands, or the like. OD is not the specifics of implementing the change but the process of diagnosing the necessary changes and planning strategies for achieving them.

OR: Operations research; the use of **quantitative analysis** of various kinds to solve problems or reach conclusions; using simulations, projective models, **PERT** and other scientific methods to analyze complex data and provide analysis of alternative courses of action to achieve company objectives.

PERT: Performance evaluation and review technique; originated by the United States Navy's Polaris missile program, this is a method of analyzing the various factors involved in reaching an objective (say, the national marketing of a radically new automobile). Each event or step in the process is analyzed for its time requirements (optimistic, realistic, and pessimistic), and its relationship to other essential events in the total network of the project is plotted. Using a computer in most cases, an organized, quantified picture of the total project is obtained and specific problems or delays (see **CPM**) can be identified.

R and D: Research and development; the conception, creation, design, initial work, and testing undertaken to produce new products and procedures, or improve on existing ones. Conducted both in-house (i.e., within a corporation) and by large-scale outside **consulting** firms and subcontractors, R and D constitutes a huge, twenty-billion-dollar industry by itself and is now a major facet of the U.S. economy.

ROI: Return on investment; a measure of the profitability of a certain investment, whether in a completely new **start-up** venture, a new retail outlet, a major advertising campaign, or thc like. Basically, ROI is the amount of profit earned within a given period of time, expressed as a percentage of the amount invested. Thus, a store that required a $400,000 investment and returned profits of $80,000 in the first year would have an ROI of 20 percent.

SBA: The Small Business Administration; a federal agency created to help small businesses prosper through organizational and financial advice, loans, referrals, and other forms of assistance. Given the extent to which the American economy is dominated by a relatively small number of giant **corporations** (see **conglomerates, multinationals**), the battle to make small businesses thrive is not one the SBA or its clients are expected to win.

SOP: Standard operating procedure; formal or informal policies that govern the daily activities at a single company. A military-sounding term that managers of that ilk or derivation like to throw around. (See **bureaucratic procedure**.)

TIA: Trend impact analysis; another computerized, **quantitative analysis** technique, used to calculate mathematically the future effects of a variety of possible trends and events.

WSJ: The Wall Street Journal; published by Dow Jones with a daily circulation of 1.6 million, *WSJ* is the ongoing bible of the financial and business communities. To be profiled or even mentioned in the *Journal* for a business person is like a *Time* cover for a politician or a *People* magazine article for the aspiring entertainer.

ZBB: Zero-based budgeting; a relatively recent innovation in budgeting and resource allocation, started in the government and now taken up by some segments of the private sector. In ZBB, the previous year's budget is *not* taken as the basis for the new year's allocations (with new items added, inflationary adjustments, reductions, and modifications,); instead, each department (or agency, or division, or unit) must start from scratch and justify every element of its budget "from zero" —i.e., without prior assumptions.

BUSINESS MANAGEMENT TERMINOLOGY

achievement motive: One of the main engines that fuels executive ambition. While most workers are motivated by financial reward, increased **fringe benefits**, or a desire for security, there is a category of people in the job market—usually in the **executive** ranks—who work to realize a sense of achievement, a personal feeling of having done something significant. For these people, higher pay and larger benefits are simply outward signs of achievement.

adhocracy: From *ad hoc* (Latin, "to this"), meaning for a specific purpose; a temporary organization (distinct from bureaucracy, a permanent organization) set up to accomplish specific tasks—such as the creation of a new product line—and then dissolve. Management theorists predict that the adhocracy is the structure of the future—replacing the

waste and stagnation of huge standing corporate employment structures.

annual report: A written summary of a company's performance in the past year and its hopes and projections for the future. A highly structured and often elaborately produced document that a public company is legally required to prepare and distribute to its **stockholders** each year.

arbitration: The settlement of a dispute by an impartial party, usually chosen by and acceptable to the persons involved in the conflict. The decision reached by arbitration is binding, which makes the process different from *mediation,* in which the parties are not bound to accept the recommendations of the mediator. Arbitration is most commonly associated with labor disputes whose settlement has defied ordinary bargaining procedures. Here, a representative of the federal government is often picked as *arbitrator* (or *arbiter*).

asset: Anything a company owns or has rights to that has value. *Tangible assets* are actual property or physical entities, and are usually subdivided into *current assets* (cash, receivables, and inventory, which can be easily converted into money) and *fixed assets* (factories, equipment, buildings, and the like, which are not readily converted). *Intangible assets* are such factors as copyrights, patents, trademarks, franchises, and **goodwill**, which do not have any concrete existence but are of value to the company nonetheless.

balance sheet: A statement of a company's financial position, with its **assets** listed on one side, and its liabilities and **stockholders'** equity (or other ownership) on the other. A useful index of a company's financial standing, from which various significant figures (such as *net current assets,* which are current assets minus current liabilities) can be extrapolated.

big business: A generally imprecise term referring to major **corporations** that dominate the important industries of a developed country —such as oil, steel, transportation, banking, communications. Big business is also distinguished (usually) by the fact that its corporations are run by a group of professional **managers**, as opposed to owner-managers who typically run smaller businesses. **Small business** is often defined by government standards (of revenues, number of employees, **assets**), which by implication define big business as well.

board of directors: An executive body, elected by the shareholders of a **corporation**, which sets overall policy for the company and appoints its chief officers—president, vice-presidents, and other top **management.** In practice, the board of directors rarely makes any decisions relative to the daily administration of a business, but approves (or disapproves) the actions of the president and his staff. ("The annual meeting of the **board** con-

vened at 11:00 A.M., approved the proposed budget for the following year, congratulated the **CEO** for his fine **turnaround management**, and adjourned by noon. The *chairman of the board* was on the golf course by one.")

bottom line: The final figure on a typical profit and loss statement, indicating the net profit after tax (if any). By extension, the ultimate standard for judging any decision or action; and the criterion of success. This grossly overused term nonetheless retains its vitality. ("Your ideas are clever, Hutchinson, possibly even brilliant, but you've not focused on the **bottom line** here—*sales,* Hutchinson, *sales!*")

break-even analysis: A method of calculating revenues in relation to the factors of production costs, volume of sales, and product price. The *break-even point* is the level of unit sales (at a given selling price) at which costs equal revenue, and there is neither profit nor loss to the company. Break-even analysis is commonly used to determine production levels or set prices and sales targets.

bureaucratic procedures: Corporate activity governed by preset rules or regulations. Hence, actions that can be performed without thought, without individual responsibility and, often, without recourse to common sense. The conversion of "live" **management** decisions into bureaucratic procedures is the goal of **executives** whose business thrives on order and regularity rather than initiative and inventiveness.

capital: The equipment, cash, human talent, or other assets available to a company for its production of goods and services. The basis of a company's wealth. ("When we started the company, our **capital** consisted of a few thousand dollars in the bank, some printing presses, and the paper we had on our shelves. Today, that capital has grown to include ownership of several buildings, a wide variety of printing equipment, and several hundred thousand dollars in **working capital** we use to pay bills and buy new facilities.") *Capital in-*

vestment refers to money put up to purchase an **asset** used in the productive end of a company's business.

cash flow: The cash position of a company; that is, the amount of money collected vis-à-vis what must be paid out. Money available at any given time for expansion, payment of debts, or any other purpose. Cash flow is the chief determinant of a company's ability to carry out day-to-day operations. Even if a company has numerous **assets** and large amounts of **receivables**, it may go under if it cannot collect (or borrow) enough cash to meet its running expenses.

chairman of the board: The person, usually elected by the **board of directors** (or, occasionally, self-appointed), who holds the highest-ranked position in a **corporation**. The chairman of the board is thus more powerful, hypothetically, than the president (unless he *is* the president, which is not uncommon), although the latter is generally a true **management** position with real responsibility for running the show, while the position of chairman may be only a figurehead.

change agent: An individual (or **consulting** company) employed to effect a significant change in a corporate organizational system —or, in the case of *personal change agents,* to help **executives** shift careers, clarify personal goals, or otherwise make moves that will fulfill their personal needs and ambitions.

conglomerate: A large **corporation** that has acquired a variety of diversified companies which are basically unrelated to each other. For example, a major oil company may own a motion-picture studio, an airline, a hotel-resort complex, and a record company, which makes it not an oil company at all but a multimarket conglomerate.

consolidation: Integrating outlying or diverse business structures into a single unit. Generally, business grows and prospers the way armies spread and conquer. A feeler is put out, a beachhead is established in a new market, and there is a rush to exploit the just-opened opportunity. Before any further advance can be made, however, the new territory has to be fitted and worked into a company's existing organization—through consolidation.

consultant: An individual (or, probably more often, a *consulting firm*) hired by a corporation to provide special expertise, technical knowledge, or "outside" perspective on the company's problems. Consultants generally receive extremely high fees ($1,000 a day is not uncommon) and their advice ranges from the invaluable to the ridiculous—including, on some occasions, that rare and most highly prized of all commodities: common sense. From modest beginnings, the consulting business has now grown in to a multibillion-dollar industry in and of itself—with such "think tanks" as Rand Corporation and Arthur D. Little garnering immense contracts from the government and **big business** alike.

contingency approach, contingency management: A modern method of organization in which the behavior and style of the **executive** varies in response to the task at hand, or the technology involved, or the personnel to be dealt with. Thus the contingency approach might impel a **manager** to be highly authoritative, directive, and threatening in certain situations (such as a high-pressure drive to meet a "hard" production goal) and more democratic, informal, and open in the other situations (such as the planning sessions for a new marketing campaign).

control: A **management** function that examines performance in specific areas (such as the rate of production on an auto assembly line) in relation to predetermined goals and objectives, evaluates that performance, and initiates corrective measures if the performance is substandard. The "upward vertical flow of information" (from production areas to the management level responsible for its control) is the critical factor in a corporate control system.

corporate ladder: The ascending sequence of job positions in the hierarchy of most large **corporations**—from the lowest levels of first-line **management** (such as production foreman) through to the highest levels of top management (president and vice-presidents). Higher "rungs" on the corporate ladder accord the climber increasing amounts of prestige, power, and income. The price, for those who choose to play the game, may be similarly increasing amounts of stress, working hours, and responsibility.

corporation: The dominant form of business organization in the American economic system. Corporations are owned by **stockholders**, who are a separate group from the people actually running the corporation (**management**). The stockholders share in the corporation's profits while being personally free of its liabilities, an organizational structure that has allowed corporations to raise the huge amounts of **capital** necessary to carry out major economic projects.

costs: The expenditures necessary to run a business. *Fixed costs* are those that have to be paid regardless of how much work or how much output is turned out by a company; these include rent, interest payments to banks, salaries of top management, and the like. *Variable costs* are expenditures that change, depending on a company's workload or output; these include direct labor wages, raw material costs, sales commissions and so on. *Cost accounting* is a method of figuring how much each product in a company's product line or each service in its service offerings actually costs to make or deliver. Goods and services that cost too much in relation to what they return can thus be spotted and weeded out of a company's **line.**

data base: A store of facts from which various indices and measurements can be extrapolated, and upon which managerial decisions can be made. Today, it usually refers to an electronically stored and rapidly retrievable body of raw information.

Delphi technique: Named after the ancient Greek oracle, this is a method of forecasting future trends and events, planning, or drawing other authoritative conclusions: A group of experts is first polled separately (to avoid their influencing each other's recommendations), then allowed to view the other experts' projections and modify their own on the basis of the rest of the group's opinions. The results of this method, while superior to some other forms of forecasting, are rarely as portentous as the name implies.

distribution: The process of getting goods from companies that make them to retailers who sell them. This may be a one-step process or involve several levels. A major distributor, for example, may have exclusive rights to sell a line of products in a certain region. He buys them in huge lots, stores them in his warehouse, then resells them in smaller lots to subdistributors, who in turn sell them to retailers in their local cities and towns. Each level of distribution boosts the price of an item as distributors cover their own costs and take a profit.

diversification: Expanding into new fields or broadening the scope of a business in which a company is already engaged. Diversification spreads risks and opens possible new markets, but puts an added burden on management because different businesses require different types of managerial expertise. The potential and risks of business diversification are manifested by the performance history of **conglomerates**, **corporations** composed of businesses with no market similarities. Some have done exceptionally well and some have proven to be economic disasters.

down time: A period when people or equipment have no work to do, usually because of some failure in the production cycle or through poor **management** planning. Too much down time in any business can be disastrous: **fixed costs** such as rent and certain salaries must be paid even if no work is done, and down time thus leads to lower levels of productivity and reduced profits.

entrepreneur: The Don Quixote of modern American business, who, in spite of all the evidence to the contrary, still believes it possible to start a new business, sell a new product, or peddle an innovative service outside the protective shield of the corporate umbrella. The chief difference between classic entrepreneurial endeavors and most business in operation today is that the entrepreneur generally owned the business he managed. **Corporations**, contrarily, are owned by a group of strangers and run by visiting professionals.

espionage: Also **industrial espionage**. The pursuit and theft of the financial, marketing, or technical secrets of one **corporation** by one of its competitors. As with governments, corporations in certain fields with fast-shifting market demands (entertainment, women's fashions) or rapidly evolving technologies (computers, semiconductors) sometimes find it convenient to use industrial spies in plants and offices to hasten the success of their own development programs. The penalties for this kind of espionage are rarely as severe as for the more traditional kind, and the rewards can be even greater.

Eurodollar: American dollars deposited in commercial banks outside the United States, or otherwise used as credits for commercial transactions outside the country. The world center for Eurodollar exchange is London.

executive: Used synonymously with **manager**, but also to refer to **top management**—presidents, vice-presidents, and department chiefs who make the major, long-range policy decisions of a company and beneath whom are several layers of **middle** and low **management**. The term carries a connotation of authority, decisiveness, and power (to "execute" as distinguished from to "manage") and is the preferred word in such popular buzz-phrases as *executive stress, executive personality, executive leadership styles, executive search programs,* and the like.

expedite: Getting a job done or making it possible for the job to be done. In production-oriented industries, having supplies of the right raw materials in places where they will be needed is the job of the expediter.

expense account (EA): The right to spend money outside the plant or office, hypothetically in pursuit of company goals, for which monies an individual is reimbursed. The most common outlays covered by EAs are travel and entertainment, and the most diligent users of these funds are usually salesmen trying to impress clients, or **executives** trying to impress each other. In some companies, the privilege of "expensing" is so flagrantly abused that the EA itself is regarded as a major **fringe benefit**—and one that happens not to be taxable. The expense-account phenomenon is what keeps New York restaurants like Lutèce and The Four Seasons in business, allows airlines to maintain first-class sections, and generally supports the luxury goods-and-services sector of the economy. How many people would pay $200 for a lunch out of their own pockets, after all?

fast track: The path to rapid progress up the **corporate ladder**, characterized by frequent changes of position (within a company and from one company to another) and aggressive moves within the complex competitive politics of the corporate world. Talent, brains, ambition, confidence, and an **M.B.A.** from Harvard Business School are the basic prerequisites for the fast track.

feedback: A term adopted from the world of computers, in business usage referring to opinions, information, and other data received back from employees, consumers, or other sources—which information may be used to improve company performance. Replaces the simple English word "opinion."

flow chart: A chart showing the movement of money through a purchasing cycle, materials through a production cycle, or the flow of any other process or procedure. A favorite tool of reports to **managers** from their staffs, or to higher **executives** from their subordinates.

fringe benefits: Compensation for work over and above regular salary, commissions, and "standard" employment benefits like vacations and sick leave. These compensations comprise the *fringe package* a company offers its employees, and may include anything from a company car or limousine to dental insurance, from stock options to personalized stationery.

fulfillment: Currently popular term for the achievement of a specific objective, or completion of a promised task or commitment. ("You're three months late on that ball-bearings market analysis, Henderson. When can we expect **fulfillment**?")

futurists: People who construct models or scenarios of the world of the future by extrapolating from present data or trends. This technique can have important marketing implications for firms that must gauge the demand for their products or services well in advance. ("While the new generation plant was still on the drawing board, the utility called in some leading **futurists** as **consultants** to project electricity demands and public attitudes toward coal-fired plants in the early twenty-first century.")

game theory: A mathematical exercise in which different variables are thrown together and "played out" to come up with the best strategy for meeting a problem. A kind of simulation that was first popular among military people, game theory now is used extensively by some executives who try to anticipate and prepare for situations they may one day face in the marketplace. From the simulated struggles of game theory exercises, **managers** may gener-

ate a real-life *game plan*, which is a strategy for accomplishing specific objectives, especially in relation to "opposing" business entities.

goodwill: An **intangible asset**, consisting of a favorable reputation, a well-known and well-liked location, a brand name or trademark that many people regard positively, a history of good customer relations, or the like.

headhunter: An employment agent (or agency) that specializes in getting job placements for top **executives**. With salaries of their clients frequently in the six-figure range, the fees that headhunter agencies take for their services (often one third of a year's salary) might more properly be called cannibalistic.

horizontal integration: Expanding a business by acquiring other firms engaged in essentially the same line of work; for example, if an eraser manufacturer buys out all the other significant competitors producing erasers, this is benignly termed horizontal integration. (See **vertical integration**.)

human resource administration: Social-scientific jargon for personnel work—hiring, firing, dealing with employee grievances, and the like.

intensive: Suffix in hyphenated phrases, meaning "requiring a large amount of." Thus certain industries are said to be *labor-intensive* (employing many people relative to equipment and capital, such as certain types of farm work), others *capital-intensive, technology-intensive, research-intensive.*

interface: The meeting ground or area of communication between two organizations, groups, industries, or other entities. The term derives from computer terminology, where it means a device for enabling two disparate computer systems to communicate with each other. Also used as a verb: "Our new product line has failed to **interface** with consumer purchasing patterns." (Translation: "They're not buying the damn things!")

leadership: An intangible quality which is nonetheless held in high esteem in corporate circles and considered essential to the ambitious **manager**'s ascent to **executive** success. Once identified as a certain personal charismatic power and authority, leadership is now seen as existing in a variety of *leadership styles*— some of which exert influence through fear and intimidation, others through motivation and encouragement, still others through Machiavellian manipulations or keen insight into human nature.

lead time: The interval between the time a project is conceived (or a request made, a need determined) and the end-product is actually delivered. ("Between the idea and the reality," wrote T. S. Eliot, "falls the shadow.")

line: 1. A group or category of products manufactured by a company, or sold by retailers. Also called *product line*. For example, the Fabergé line of perfumes and cosmetics products.

　　2. **line organization:** The flow of authority in a direct line from top **management** down to the actual production workers. Some companies are completely line-organized, but most have both line and **staff** positions, the latter having no direct authority over subordinates but advising and performing supplemental functions to the line officers. Thus, a plant foreman is a line position, as is a vice-president in charge of production in the West Coast division of a major shoe manufacturer; while an accountant or a **public relations** executive would hold staff positions.

loyalty: Also **corporate loyalty**. The litmus test for elevation to higher posts in certain **corporations**. **Executives** and other employees are expected not only to do their jobs well and faithfully, but to make a commitment to stay with the company and not betray its secrets to outsiders. In general, corporate loyalty in the United States is far less important in getting and keeping work than in other industrial countries. In Japan, for example, it is common for employees to gather first thing in the morning to sing the company song and perform other gestures of loyalty elsewhere associated with nationalistic or religious fervor.

management: The planning, organizing, and running of a business activity. This complex function includes the supervision of production efforts and personnel; the setting of long-range strategies, performance objectives, and short-term goals; allocation of **capital** and manpower resources; and a host of other activities devoted to maximizing a company's profit.

management science: Theories and techniques applied to the operations of business, which allow it to function in a more orderly, predictable and (hopefully) more profitable manner. This branch of study has evolved rapidly since the early part of the century and especially since the Second World War, and is now studied extensively in business schools. (See **M.B.A.**) In modern corporate settings, the principles of management science have replaced **entrepreneurial** instinct in much the same way that automated machinery has replaced hand workmanship.

manager: An employee of a company who holds authority over at least one other person and who has some decision-making responsibility. Managers range from shop foremen and plant supervisors, who directly oversee production work, all the way up to presidents and vice-presidents, who set overall company policy and make long-range decisions on a massive scale. See also **executive**.

marketing: All those business activities devoted to getting a maximum (or maximally profitable) amount of products or services purchased by the consumer. Marketing thus includes such diverse functions as advertising, promoting, pricing, packaging, **market research**, and effective **distribution**.

market research: A technique used to judge the saleability of goods or services to a particular buying public, or to find the best way to reach that public with word about a product or service. Modern market research uses sophisticated selection and interviewing methods to provide market data that is often turned into statistics tabulated by computer. It is the antithesis of the old "seat of the pants" method of gauging customer response, which was based on the intuition of an **entrepreneur**.

market share: Also **share**, **market penetration**. A key measurement in business, referring to the percentage of all sales in a particular market (such as women's underwear sold in the Southwest; bottled beer sold in supermarkets nationwide) captured by a particular company or product **line**. The figure, although given preternatural importance in most corporate meetings, also must be weighed against the growth or decline of the entire market—because a large share of an industry on the way out (such as manual typewriters) may be no victory at all.

maximin: A course of action designed to maximize the chances of incurring the minimum possible loss. Distinguished from the **maximax** strategy, which strives to maximize the maximum possible profit (risky, but a big payoff if successful), and the **minimax** strategy, which seeks to minimize the chances of a maximum loss.

merger: The joining together of two business entities. Mergers are most often accomplished by outright takeover of one company by another, a process known as **acquisition**. The acquiring company absorbs the stock of the acquired company for cash or shares of its own stock, and the latter then becomes a subsidiary or operating division of the former. Mergers are becoming even more common as small business seeks the security of being part of large **conglomerates**, and large firms look to expand their **marketing** base.

merit rating: A way of evaluating and rewarding the work performance of a company's employees, rather akin to the system used in the lower grades of some public school systems. Merit rating usually involves assigning point values to work-related activities and attitudes, then using these values to assess a worker's progress toward a promotion or salary boost.

middle management: Any of a variety of positions midway up the corporate hierarchy, characterized by the responsibility for implementing overall company policy and plans through the administration of specific sectors of the company's business—e.g., a plant manager, a regional sales chief, a local TV station general manager, a newspaper advertising director.

mobicentric manager: The "new" type of **manager**, characterized by a high degree of mobility, both within a company and from company to company, and often from one job area to another as well. Replacing the "old" type of manager (which probably still forms the majority) who was characterized by a certain technical expertise and loyalty to his employer, the mobicentric manager changes geographic location, technical area, and corporate position frequently. He or she is oriented toward the political-administrative-**marketing** kinds of achievement, rather than the specific progress of a single industry or company. Given the fact that 40 percent of those managers who become presidents of **corporations** have entered their companies at top management levels (rather than working their way up through the ranks, in that company at least), it appears that the mobicentric style is certainly the wave of the future.

multinational: A type of **corporation** with major **assets** or facilities in more than one country, and with a **management** team that is generally drawn from several nations. Multinational organizations arouse hostility in many parts of the world today because their policies don't always reflect the interests of their host country, and because their accounting procedures tend to shift money out of the reach of national treasuries with great success.

organization chart: A line illustration showing

the official relationship of one person to another in a company's **management** structure: Who reports to whom, who is responsible for what job function, and the like. The higher up one appears on these charts (i.e., the closer to the top of the pyramid shape of almost all such drawings), the more important one is in the organization. ("When the new **organization chart** was circulated around the office, Dudley found that he no longer reported to the chief of operations; he knew then that it was time to start looking for a new job.") Often, however, the real working relationships, and effective power in a company are quite different from those shown on the organization chart.

organization man: A generally disparaging term for a person who either makes a company (or some other organization) his highest personal priority, or who follows company procedures without question. One of the interesting changes that have taken place in today's business climate is that many organization "men" are now women.

packaging: The enclosing of goods, especially in such a way as to make the product as attractive as possible to the consumer, and to provide a long shelf life in a variety of saleable sizes. The importance accorded to packaging in the total "**marketing** picture" may be gauged by the fact that as much money is spent on packaging efforts as on all forms of advertising combined. "It's not the product, it's the **packaging**" is the operative principle in marketing many products today, from phonograph records to paperback books to potato chips.

perks: Perquisites: fringe benefits, both official and unofficial. In recruiting and retaining top **executives**, it would be hard to overestimate the importance of perks. These tax-free benefits and prestige-imparting prerogatives give many executives the life-style edge they crave and expect as part of their careers in corporate **management**. Perks range from personalized parking spaces to company-paid junkets to visit "potential plant sites" in the Caribbean; estimates have it that all such fringe benefits combined may comprise as much as a quarter to a third of some corporate payrolls.

profit margin: Also **gross margin**. A key business measure used in assessing the profitability of a certain product or retail outlet. The cost of the goods is subtracted from the net sales (gross sales minus returns, losses, etc.) to produce the gross profit figure (e.g., $5,000 cost from $15,000 net sales = $10,000 gross profit). The percentage that the gross profit forms of the net sales (in this example, 66.7 percent) is the profit margin. This figure is never as high as the *net margin*, however, which takes into account retail overhead and other operating expenses.

public relations: See PUBLIC RELATIONS chapter.

purchasing agent: Usually a **middle-management**-level employee, responsible for buying goods and services used by a company in its own operations. This person is the chief target of much sales pressure, and occasionally the recipient of largesse from salesmen peddling a variety of wares used by business. The goods and services ultimately selected by the purchasing agent are bought from people termed the company's "vendors."

quality control: All those activities undertaken to check and maintain the quality levels and standards of a company's products (and its purchases as well); these include the establishment of specifications, the inspection of finished products, the sampling of mass-produced items where examination of each individual piece is unfeasible, and the like. See also **AQL**.

quantitative analysis: Any of a wide variety of methods for analyzing, forecasting, or making decisions that attempt to express factors, conditions, and options in numerical terms. These include sampling and polling, cost-benefit analysis, **PERT** and **CPM**, computations of gross and net **profit margins**, and literally scores of other measures, indices, and statistical devices. With the rapid expansion of computer technology and its availability to businesses, this trend has developed even further, so that it is rare indeed that any corporate decisions of any magnitude are made on purely personal or experiential judgment, without recourse to **market penetration** figures, **trend impact analyses**, **ROI** percentages, profitability ratios, and the like.

receivables: The amount of money owed to a company by its customers for delivered products or services (called *accounts receivable*); as well as the amount owed a company in the form of promissory notes by customers or other debtors (called *notes receivable*). These receivables are considered company **assets**, which are not, however, always convertible into cash because a percentage of them turn into "bad debts." The inability to collect receivables with rapidity hurts a company's **cash flow**, which could lead to expensive borrowing or the need to use those carrion crows of the marketplace—the collection services.

recruitment: The process of seeking out and hiring new personnel, especially on the **executive** level. Most major **corporations** recruit for their **management** "team" from the graduating class of top business schools, through **headhunting** agencies, and from the employees of rival companies. The choice of a military term is in consonance with the quasimilitary structure of many corporate hierarchies—in which **middle-management** positions are, for example, roughly comparable to master sergeants, lieutenants, and captains.

reorganization: A corporate fetish, especially popular in larger concerns, aimed at improving a company's profit picture or operational performance. It involves replacing **executives**, shifting other executives to new slots or areas of responsibilities, or making some

other **management** change that is supposed to make things run more smoothly.

revenue: In business, the income generated by sales of goods and services. In government, the monies collected from direct or indirect taxation. In neither case does revenue represent the actual amount of money available for use because the cost involved in getting it has not been figured in. ("The **revenues** of Acme Plastic increased dramatically in 1979 owing to the company's penetration of several new **markets**. But its net income actually declined that year because of the costs of entering these new markets.")

satisficing: Attempting to attain a specific **market share**, production level, or other figure as opposed to simply trying to maximize profit or production. Most **corporations** (and divisions within corporations) have fairly specific performance objectives, which they seek to **satisfice**, as opposed to the open-ended attempt to "do better."

share: See **market share**.

span of control: The number of employees directly subordinate to a given **manager** or **supervisor**. A *broad span of control* is one involving many direct subordinates (such as that of a production foreman who directs fifty or one hundred workers); a *narrow span of control* involves few immediate subordinates (such as a division chief with three department heads below him).

staff: Those employees who are not directly in the **line** of command from top **management** to production, but who perform auxiliary or adjunctive functions—such as accounting, purchasing, promoting, research, advising, assisting, secretarial, and the like; also, the positions thus held (**staff** versus **line** positions).

start-up: The initiation phase of a new business, production of a new product **line**, opening of a new plant or franchise, or other commercial enterprise; and, by extension, the cost for such initiation. ("Our **start-up** on the Cincinnati outlet was $2 million, but we expect to see a significant **ROI** within eighteen months.")

stockholders: The owners of a publicly traded corporation; people who buy ownership certificates (*stock*) through salesmen (*brokers*) operating on an *exchange* (a securities marketplace). These stocks often provide their owners with returns on investment (in the form of dividends) and the ability (in the case of "common stock" holders) to vote for corporate officers. Stockholders are to **corporations** what citizens are to a commonwealth: the theoretical basic unit of control and chief recipient of benefits. In actuality, however, stockholders exercise little control over the ongoing procedures and decisions of large corporations, which are firmly in the hands of top **management** and the **board of directors**.

stock options: Agreements that permit employees to purchase company stock at a fixed price within a specified period or during the period of their employment. Such options can be a valuable **fringe benefit** because if the market price of the stock is higher than the option price (which is often the case), the employee can "exercise his option," buy the stock, and immediately resell it at a profit.

suboptimization: A trade-off or compromise between multiple, often conflicting objectives. Every **management** decision must take several variables into account, which may conflict: The differing interests of **stockholders**, employees, and consumers, for example, might each dictate differing production/**marketing** choices for a major **corporation**. Or, the concerns for **quality control**, production levels, and **profit margins** may likewise be in conflict. The resolution of these conflicts—through accepting that none of the multiple objectives will have absolute priority, and that some or all will have to be compromised—is called suboptimization.

supervisor: A person who directs or controls the work of other employees. In a sense, any **manager** is a supervisor in that he or she can tell a production or clerical employee what to do in certain instances. But the term is usually reserved for people whose job is heavily involved with directing the efforts of others, especially in actual production work. Supervisors are thus, for the most part, located in the lowest third of the **management** hierarchy.

systems analysis: A method of approaching problems and reaching conclusions, based upon the perception of a business (or a specific aspect of it) as a *whole system*, with both material and informational inputs and outputs, boundaries, and interactions with the outside environment (or *external systems*), and a constellation of internal *subsystems* (i.e., departments, divisions, etc.) interconnected by *feedback loops*. Due to the complexity of multiple factors involved in *systems analysis*, a computer is usually employed to manipulate the data. If you think all this sounds like a high-tech way of describing "looking at the big picture," you may be right; nonetheless, the *systems approach* is a big favorite among execs today, and literally millions of dollars are spent on **consultants** who have convinced them that they need it.

Theory X, Theory Y: Two diametrically opposed conceptions of human nature in relation to work, from which derive two radically different styles and methods of **management**. As expounded by behavioral scientist Douglas McGregor, Theory X maintains that people basically do not like to work, need to be threatened or otherwise coerced into producing, and would rather be told what to do than take responsibility. Theory Y, on the other hand, holds that humans have a natural inclination to be active and productive, can and will choose to take responsibility and be self-directing under the right circumstances, and can be motivated by many other, more positive inducements than threat or force.

time frame: A period of time, length of time. A favorite of **executive** phraseology. ("What's the **time-frame** on the **R and D** here?")

turnaround management: The process of taking a failing business or poorly selling product (or any other unsuccessful business entity) and improving its profitability to the point where it is making money. Some **executives**, such as television's Fred Silverman, are supposed to be geniuses at turnaround management, for which they are understandably well paid; no one, however (Silverman's efforts for NBC being a notable example), succeeds at it all the time.

up or out: The unstated rule in certain organizations that managerial employees—especially at middle and upper levels—are expected to advance up the **corporate ladder** within a certain span of time, or else they will be "let go." The idea is that everyone *has* to be ambitious, dynamic, hard-driving, and competitive; if you are content to stay in one place and simply do a good job, there's something wrong with you.

venture capital: Money invested in new companies or other high-risk business ventures. Given the fact that some three-quarters of all new businesses are doomed to fail within a few years of **start-up**, some prefer to call monies invested in them "*adventure capital.*"

vertical integration: The expansion of a business through acquiring companies or concerns involved in earlier or later stages of the production-**distribution** process. For example, if a dress manufacturer buys up a textile mill that produces the fabric for its dresses,

this is *backward vertical integration*; if a radio and phonograph manufacturer buys up a chain of retail stores that sell such products, that is *forward vertical integration*.

working capital: Money which a company has available to meet its current debts, expand its operations, or otherwise "do business"; generally computed as the total of its current **assets** minus its current liabilities.

working control: Effective control of a **corporation**'s policy and direction, through (individual or collective) ownership of a significant plurality of voting stock. While officially 51 percent of voting stock is required to control a corporation, in reality it is rare for any single person or group to own that much of a major corporation or **conglomerate**, and the party that owns the largest single chunk (which may be as little as 20 or 30 percent) will have working control.

zero-sum game: In **game theory**, a conflict or situation in which any advantage to one "player" results in an equal disadvantage to his opponent(s). Thus, if an institutional investor has $10 million to invest in one or more **start-up** ventures, the competition to gain those particular funds is a zero-sum game: Whatever monies Venture A gets are monies that Ventures B, C, D, will not get. Most competition for a **share** of the **market** in a particular industry is not truly a zero-sum game, however, as the market itself may be expanding (for example, more people buying color television sets in 1982 than in 1980), such that the sum can be greater than zero.

|11|

Advertising

At one time, in the childhood of the free-enterprise system, the scope and function of advertising was quite simple: A man selling copper pots, for example, or shoeing horses needed to inform those who might require his product or service of when and where it was available. He hired a boy to go through the streets, clanging a pan and crying out his location; he hung out a wooden sign that he had paid to have carved and lettered. Skip forward four or five hundred years, and observe how the scope and function of advertising has changed. In the United States alone, corporations and businesses spend over $50 billion a year—not only to inform but to persuade, convince, motivate, seduce, suggest, entice, intimidate, promote, publicize, get "media exposure," improve corporate **images**, make **consumer profiles** and **target** specific **markets**, and *sell*. Often the products being sold, the services being touted, the politicans or entertainers being marketed in the mass media are ones the public has no need of, nor liking for. But no matter. Advertising, as any good **copywriter** will tell you (and public relations, as any flack will attest) shapes opinion. It does not exist nearly as much to inform any more as it does to persuade, to make people do something, buy something, accept something; in essence, to *want* that which they otherwise would not want.

This is not to say that advertising should be construed as coercive; it is not. But in the aggregate, in the 20,000 TV commercial messages that every man, woman, and child witnesses (on the average) every year; in the $50 billion worth of national **spots** and two-page **spreads**, **billboards** and neon signs, **handbills** and **direct-mail** offerings and radio **jingles**, the ubiquity of modern advertising becomes an enormous force, one that affects our lives in an insistent, almost irresistible fashion. Procter & Gamble does not spend $500 million a year, Ford $200 million, Coke $140 million a year on advertising simply by accident: Advertising works.

Although the advertising business in this country is widely diversified, it is dominated by a relatively small number of major advertising **agencies**, all headquartered in New York City: **superagencies** like J. Walter Thompson, with 1980 world **billings** of $2.1 billion, and such accounts as Ford, Burger King, the government of Chile, and Kodak; or Young & Rubicam—$2.27 billion in billings, advertises Sanka Brand coffee, Kentucky Fried Chicken, Oil of Olay. At these agencies, hundreds of **copywriters**, **art directors**, **creative directors**, **jingle** creators, and the like labor mightily to produce the **headlines**, **slogans**, **key visuals**, and **jingles** with jolt, originality, impact, and hooks; the **ad campaigns** and **marketing strategies** that will help their clients capture a larger **market share**, while maintaining a top **brand loyalty index** and a positive **corporate image**.

The language used in the advertising industry is a fascinating mixture of high-tech social research jargon (**demographics**, **reach and frequency**, **brand potential index**), corporate management lingo (**CPM**, **media buy**, **positioning**, **roll-out**), technical ad-production terms (**gutter bleed**, **tight comp**, **storyboard**, **key visual**) and showbiz hype (**beauty shot**, **slice of life**, **talent**). It is a language employed by some of the most creative, intelligent, savvy people in this country, whose brilliance has embedded hundreds of rhymes and jingles, images and messages in our minds, our dreams, our memories; so much talent and energy (and finance) devoted to making us want to drink Coke, be part of the Pepsi Generation, take a break today (at McDonald's), spray our underarms with Right Guard, brush our teeth with Crest, wash our laundry with Tide, drink Bud, wear Jordache jeans, smoke Marlboros.

The little boy no longer clangs the pots as he walks down the street. **Market research** and a **superagency creative team** have transformed him into a seductive teenage fashion model discoing on an Arizona mountaintop, backed up by a fifty-piece orchestra and a singing group playing a catchy Steve Karmen ("When You Say Budweiser") **jingle**, in a $75,000 thirty-second TV **spot**, placed on network prime time for $100,000 a showing, seen in living color by 70 million people an average of 83.4 times over a span of six months, and coordinated with a **pool** of six related spots and a saturation radio, **print**, and **billboard** campaign, designed to double the client's **market penetration** in the cooking utensil "purchaser universe." There's certainly no point in leaving anything to chance, is there?

AAAA: Also **Four A's. The American Association of Advertising Agencies**, a trade organization for independent **ad agencies**.

A and M: Art and mechanical; all the labor and materials necessary to produce the **graphic** portion of an **ad** or **campaign**; also, the cost of such production.

account: The company or person that has hired an advertising **agency** to advertise its services or products. Also called a **piece of business**.

account executive: An **agency** staffperson who is the liaison between the **client** and the rest of the agency, especially the **creative department**. The account executive has more day-to-day contact with the client than anyone else in the agency.

ad: A **print** advertisement in a newspaper or magazine, as opposed to a radio or TV **commercial**.

Ad Council, The: A nonprofit organization that produces **public service ad campaigns** for worthy causes (fire prevention, the Boy Scouts, etc.), with the work rotated among different **agencies**.

ADI: Area of dominant influence; a geographically designated market area in which a television (or radio) station is watched by most people. The term is used by the **Arbitron rating** service; an ADI rating of 24, for example, indicates that 24 percent of all homes in that area watched a given show.

agency: Also **shop**. A company, usually made up of many departments, that creates and places advertising for its **clients**. Some of the largest ad agencies (BBD&O, J. Walter Thompson, Young & Rubicam) are so powerful that they may produce their own television shows, obviously to be sponsored by their own clients. There were over 7,000 ad agencies of varying sizes operating in the U.S. in 1980, with 1,300 of these (including most of the **superagencies**) headquartered in New York City.

agency commission: The commission paid to an advertising agency by the medium that has sold advertising space or time to the agency's **client**. It is usually 15 percent of the amount billed to the advertiser. Thus if McCann-Erickson places its Coca-Cola ads on NBC-TV at a prime-time rate of $100,000 per half-minute, the agency will receive $15,000 of each $100,000 as its commission. Such commissions are the major source of revenue for advertising agencies.

Arbitron: A device used by the American Research Bureau to provide information on television viewing patterns; also refers to the **rating** services supplied by that company, which are the major alternative to the A. C. **Nielsen** Company ratings.

art: The original graphic content of an **ad** in the **print** media—such as photographs, illustrations, diagrams, and the like. Also, a generic term for the visual look and effect of a print ad (or poster, **billboard**, **handbill**) as distinct from its **copy**.

art director: The person who creates the look of an **ad**—choosing photography, designing the ad, deciding on illustrations, **typeface**, style, and **layout**. When working on a TV **commercial**, the art director supervises the **shoot** and is responsible for the overall appearance of the **spot**. The art director usually does not actually do the drawing or illustration himself, however.

attitude study: Any of a variety of surveys made to ascertain public response to a product or organization; often such studies are made before and after an ad **campaign** (or other major event) to assess its impact or effectiveness. See **pre-to-post**.

back of book: That part of a magazine which follows the main body of **editorial** material; used in ordering advertising space. Back-of-book space is typically the least expensive space in consumer magazines.

BC: Back cover, also called **fourth cover**; the outside rear cover of a magazine; used when ordering advertising space.

beauty shot: In television **commercials**, a close-up shot of the product being advertised, set up and lit to enhance its appearance.

billboard: 1. In television and radio, the announcement of a program **sponsor**, usually before the show or on one of its breaks. (" 'All My Birds' is brought to you by the Cackle Chicken Company.")

2. An outdoor advertising panel, often located on the side of major roadways. Also **board**. *Riding the boards* is the practice of driving around to visually inspect a series of billboard displays.

billings: The amount of money charged to a **client** advertiser for communicating its messages, including the media charges for **time** or **space**, expenses for production of **ads**, etc. Also used for any total of advertising expenditure. ("Network radio **spots** are headed for over $160 million in annual **billings**," or "GE is shifting $14 million in appliance **billings** to BBD&O.")

Black Book: The **Creative Black Book**, a yearly manual that lists resources for all the services agency **creative** people might require—including illustrators, photographers, typeshops, retouchers.

bleed: An ad or illustration extended to the very edge of a page in a print medium, without any margin whatsoever. ("We want a **four-color gutter bleed** for this, running for the next three weeks.")

body copy: The main text of a **print ad**; everything written in an ad other than the **headline**, **tag line**, and **logo**.

book: 1. A magazine or other periodical.

2. An advertising **portfolio**—that is, the collected best works of a **copywriter** or **art director**, used as an extended résumé in applying for advertising **agency** jobs. One's book is dropped off and, if well received, generates an interview at the agency.

boutique agency: A smaller **agency** with extremely creative accounts that are advertised in intriguing ways; usually creates advertising but is not involved in **time-buying**, **market re-**search, and other functions of **full-service agencies**.

brand: A group or line of products (or services) distinguished and identified by a special name, symbol, **logo**, or the like. For example, Budweiser, Calvin Klein, Palmolive, Sony, Heinz. Much advertising is devoted to achieving *brand differentiation, brand preference,* and *brand loyalty;* while extensive **market research** is frequently devoted to ascertaining such scientific-sounding figures as the *brand development index* (BDI), *brand name index* (BNI), and *brand potential index* (BPI).

BTA: Best time available; used in ordering television or radio advertising **time**.

bullpen: The place in an agency where **paste-ups** and **mechanicals** are put together.

campaign: A group, series, or array of **ads** (or **commercials**) devoted to a single product (or group of products, or client). The basic **concept** remains the same, and often the **tag line** ("Things go better with Coke"; "Have it your way") as well, through a carefully orchestrated strategy of otherwise varied ads.

card rate: The fees for purchasing advertising **space** from a newspaper, magazine, or TV or radio broadcaster, as listed on that organization's standard **rate card**; from this rate, discounts are often deducted for purchasing a large volume of **time** or space, and **commissions** to advertising **agencies**.

cast: 1. To calculate how much **print** space is required for a certain amount of **copy** in a given type size; or vice versa (how much copy of a certain type will fill a given page space).

2. To hire **talent** for a commercial or show. Also, as a noun, the performers thus hired.

classified advertising: Advertising in newspapers and other periodicals in which **ads** are categorized into subject divisions: Real Estate for Sale, Music Lessons, and so on. Usually such ads are relatively small and composed predominantly of **copy** (as opposed to **art**).

client: The firm (or individual) who hires an **ad agency** to create and/or buy **time/space** for advertising for its products. Often termed the **account**.

clutter: Cynical ad-business term for the frantic array of **commercials**, **PSAs**, and other announcements on television (also radio and **print**); the term implies the difficulty of making one's particular advertising message stand out from all the rest of the clutter.

column inch: A unit of **space** used for ordering advertising in newspapers and magazines: One column inch is a space one inch deep by one column (standard for that periodical) wide.

commercial: An advertisement on radio or television. See also **ad**.

commission: A percentage of **billing** charges paid to an **agent**, **ad** salesperson, or the like by the medium in which the ad appears. See **agency commission**.

comp: Short for **comprehensive** (which is never used); A preliminary version of the artwork or **graphic** design of an **ad**, giving the basic idea of the "look" of the ad. **Rough comps** are an early hand-drawn version; **tight comps** a more finished picture.

comparative spot: A TV or radio **commercial** in which one product (or service) is compared to another: ("Bully's Burgers are bigger than McDonald's—juicier than Wendy's—better than Burger King's. So bite into a Bully Burger today!")

composition: The arrangement of **art**, **copy**, or **type** in a **print** advertisement; also, the process of making such an arrangement.

concept: The central idea of a single **ad** or of an entire ad **campaign**; the image of quality or the product attribute that the ads are designed to express. In creating advertising, the concept is the most critical element. A chewing-gum commercial concept could be almost anything: the Fun of Chewing, the Great Taste of the gum, great for Jaw Exercise, Chewing while Doing (discoers, skateboarders, skiers, writers, et al., all chewing away), and so on—each a distinct concept that would

then express itself in totally different ads or commercials.

consumer goods: Products that people use (underwear, toothpaste, cottage cheese) as distinguished from **industrial goods** (machinery, raw materials, supply stocks, and the like) which are not routinely employed by the public.

consumer profile: A description of the age, sex, income level, life-style and other characteristics of the typical buyer of a product (or user of a service). **Market research** determines such profiles so that advertising can be "targeted" to the specific audience of a product's main consumers.

co-op: Co-operative advertising, in which the manufacturer (or other major advertiser) pays for some portion of an **ad**—ranging from 25 percent to the full 100 percent— while the retailer actually selling the product in a specific location pays the rest. Quite common, for example, in the publishing business, where a major bookstore (or chain of bookstores) may take out co-op ads for its "big" books, for which the publisher pays 50 percent or more.

copy: Writing; the written text of an **ad** or the words that will be spoken in a **commercial**.

copy strategy: The basic "message" of an **ad**, and the means by which it will be imparted: relevant facts and statistics, comparison with other products, celebrity endorsement, evocative images, life-style associations, and so on. Also (when not limited to copy alone) called the **creative strategy**.

copy supervisor: Also **copy chief**. The **ad agency** employee who supervises the work of **copywriters**; this responsibility is more commonly subsumed now under the title of **creative director**, who oversees both **art** and **copy**.

copywriter: The staffperson in an **agency** who writes the **copy** in a **print ad** or the narration of a radio/TV **commercial**. In most large agencies, writers begin as *junior writers*, progress to *copywriter*, then *senior copywriter*, and may ultimately reach a supervisory writing level (variously titled *copy group head,* **copy chief**, or **copy supervisor**).

cover: Any of the four outermost surfaces of a magazine, used when ordering space for **print ads**. *First cover* is the outside front cover; *Second cover* the inside front cover; *Third cover* the inside back cover; and *Fourth cover,* the outside back cover.

CPM: Cost per thousand; the (estimated) cost to the advertiser to reach one thousand persons (or homes, or other audience unit) with a particular **ad** in a given medium. For example, if a full-page ad in a major newspaper costs $5,000 and the circulation of that paper is held to be 500,000 readers, then the CPM would be $5,000 ÷ 500,000 × 1,000 = $10. In TV, the CPM is calculated in relation to the **ratings** of a given show—which is why the ratings are so critical to both broadcasters and advertisers.

creative: Engaged in the actual creation or production of advertising messages, as opposed to the business end of advertising (handling **accounts, market research**, selling services, planning media exposure). In the advertising business, "creative" does not mean imaginative or innovative, but refers solely to the job function in an **agency**. Thus, we also have the *creative department, creative floor, creative* (**boutique**) *agencies*, and so on.

creative director: One of the top **agency** positions, the person who has ultimate control over the nature of the advertising created by **art directors, copywriters**, et al. The person in charge of **creative** production.

creative team: Usually, an **art director** and **copywriter** who work together to create an **ad** or **commercial**.

cume: See **reach and frequency**.

daypart: A subdivision of the broadcasting day for a TV or radio station or network. On TV, for example prime time is the daypart from 8:00 to 11:00 P.M., followed by **late fringe** (11:00 P.M. until signoff). On radio, the first daypart is **morning drive** (up to 10:00 A.M.), followed by **housewife** (10:00 A.M. to 3:00 P.M.), and so on.

demographics: The study of populations, with reference to certain "parameters"; age, sex, geographical location, income, occupation, race, education, etc. In advertising, it refers to the results of such studies pertaining to the audience for a given medium (a trade magazine, a TV show, a radio station) or the consumers of a specific product. ("We're targeting this **campaign** toward the young single professional woman, 25 to 32, mid to upper **demographics**, spends 23 percent of her income on leisure pursuits, 63 percent college-educated, 87 percent white, interested in sex, clothes, and travel.")

direct mail: Advertising sent through the mail directly to the **target audience**—as distinguished from advertising where **time** or **space** is bought in another medium (**print**, broadcast, **billboards**, and so on).

direct response: Advertising in which the prospective customer is solicited to make a purchase directly by responding (e.g., through an attached order coupon) to the manufacturer (or other advertiser). Those late-night TV ads exhorting you to "call now—call collect" to get your "limited-order set of Bicentennial Bookends" (or whatever), "not available in department stores," are common examples of direct-response advertising.

display advertising: Advertising in **print** media that uses **graphics**, illustrations, artwork, or a larger format than the simple type-only **layout** of most **classified advertising**.

downscale: Low-income, or of a lower socioeconomic class; used as a description of a certain **target audience** for certain types of advertising. An **ad** for McDonald's, for example, is targeted for a more downscale audience than one for BMW automobiles. See also **upscale, consumer profile, demographics**.

editorial matter: An advertising term for everything in a newspaper or magazine that is *not* advertising; "the stuff you separate ads with."

face: A designed alphabet (such as Gothic, roman, sans serif, and many others) with associated punctuation marks, numbers, etc., which can often be printed in various sizes of **type**.

fifteen and two: The typical newspaper discount off the **rate card** given to **ad agencies:** 15 percent as **commission** and 2 percent for prompt payment.

flier: A one-page advertising sheet, usually mailed or distributed as a **handbill**.

focus group: An informal research method in which groups of consumers are polled for their reactions to a particular product or advertising pitch. Focus groups may be run by an **in-house** research department or by an outside testing company.

four-color: Abbreviated **4/C**; printing (usually, of an **ad** or illustration) using the three primary colors (yellow, red, blue) and black—thus generating a complete range of colors and tones. (See **two-color**.)

free-standing insert: A preprinted **ad** page or pages that fit loosely into a newspaper but are not part of the numbered pages of the paper. This kind of ad often appears in the Sunday editions of newspapers.

front of book: That portion of a magazine before the main body of articles (the **editorial matter**); used when ordering advertising **space**.

full-service agency: An advertising **agency** that provides a complete range of services to its clients, including **market research**, creation of **ads** and ad **campaigns**, **media buying**, and so on. Distinguished from **boutique agencies** (mainly **creative**), media-buying agencies, and market research firms, all of which have more limited capabilities.

graphics: A general term for the various visual elements in a **print** media **ad**—including **logos** and symbols, drawings, graphs, borders, decorations, lettering, design, but usu-

ally excluding photographs and the actual execution of artwork (called **illustration**).

Greek: An indication of lettering that does not reveal the actual **copy**—using garbled letters, cross-hatching, and the like—used to show the general design of an **ad** or a **package**.

GRP: Gross rating point; a measurement of audience size for a given **ad**, **commercial**, **campaign**, or program. One GRP equals 1 percent of the total potential audience. The GRP is computed by multiplying **reach** times **frequency** of exposure.

gutter: The center area of two facing pages in a newspaper or magazine, composed of the combined margins on either side of the center crease. A *gutter bleed* is an **ad** or illustration that runs uninterruptedly across this area.

halftone: A printing process for reproducing photographs and other colored or shaded areas. The colored areas are produced by the printing of many tiny dots, which may be more or less densely spaced, producing greater or lesser intensity of color.

handbill: An advertising **flier** distributed by hand—either on the street, or to homes and offices. It is one of the least expensive forms of advertising.

headline: Attention-getting or summarizing phrase, sentence, or word, set in bold type, usually (but not always) at the top of a **print ad**. ("What Kind of Man Reads Playboy?")

heavy: An experienced, successful, and usually high-priced person, such as a top TV commercial director.

image advertising: Advertising that sells a product not so much on its specific virtues (effectiveness, cost, superiority), but on its association with a certain positive, appealing image—sexuality, vitality, fun, success. What sells one soft drink over another (or cigarette, or beer, or soap, or toothpaste) is fundamentally the image such advertising has managed to associate with it. ("It's the Pepsi Generation!")

impulse buy: A purchase made on the spur of

the moment (stimulated by the sight of a product or **ad** on display, for example), rather than by planning. **Point-of-purchase** advertising is used to stimulate this kind of buying.

in-house agency: Also **house agency.** An advertising services department that is owned completely by the advertiser, and works only on its products. Many large corporations have their own house agencies and will assign certain projects *in-house*, while going to independent agencies for other projects—major TV commercial **campaigns,** for example.

institutional advertising: Advertising that does not attempt to sell goods or services but rather to improve the image of a company or an industry. Full-page ads by major oil companies "informing" the public of how civic-minded and concerned about the environment they are, are a good example.

jingle: A short musical refrain, usually mentioning the name of the product or company, used in radio and television **commercials.** Some of these jingles have become so successful, they are entrenched in the minds, the subconscious depths, of tens of millions of Americans. You may wake up humming "Brush-a, brush-a, brush-a, with the new Ipana" only to realize that jingle has been off the air for fifteen years; or drive to work singing "At McDonald's, we do it all for you"— even if you have not been to McDonald's in years and have no intention of ever going again. Such is the power of the jingle.

keyline: A layout of a **print ad,** using the exact type proofs of the ad **copy** and reproductions of the artwork. Also called **type mechanical.**

key visual: The most important single image in a TV **commercial,** often used to present the basic idea of the ad (with accompanying copy), rather than a complete **storyboard.**

layout: The visual design of an **ad,** that is, the placement and relative size and position of its various elements—as distinct from the actual artwork, photography, or illustration. Even an ad that is all **copy** (contains no **art** per se) must be laid out.

line: Also **agate line.** A unit of **space** sold for advertising in **print** media. One line is 1/14 of an inch high by one column wide.

live tag: A brief addition at the end of a prerecorded TV or radio **commercial,** in which a live announcer gives some concluding message. ("Yes, folks, and in Lebanon it's Al's Muffler King, on the Miracle Mile.")

logo: The distinctive signature or symbol for a particular company or product (the Coca-Cola lettering, the Cadillac crest), which remains the same despite variations in **ad copy, commercial visuals,** and the like.

Madison Avenue: A street in New York City on which almost all major advertising **agencies** were once located; thus, the term became synonymous with the advertising business. The term has become obsolete, although even now more agencies are located on Madison Avenue than on any other street in America: some 250 in mid-1980.

mail order: Any form of advertising in which purchasers are persuaded to order products through the mails. *Not* synonymous with **direct-mail** or **direct-response** advertising.

make good: Any running of an **ad** or **commercial** free of charge, to recompense the advertiser for an error in the original run. For example, when a radio announcer flubs the reading of a live commercial, or a TV station airs a **spot** at 8:00 A.M. that was scheduled for 8:00 P.M., the advertisers are entitled to make goods.

marketing: All those processes by which a business attempts to maximize the profits from selling its product(s). Advertising is but one element of the total marketing picture—of which the other components include packaging, pricing, selling, promotion, distribution, product development, and **market research.**

market research: The process of determining various factors related to the **marketing** of a product or service; What kind of people buy such a product (their age, sex, income, geographical location, education)? What motivates them to choose one brand or product over another? What is the existing competition in this product (or service) category? What types of packaging, pricing, sizing, advertising, promoting are most likely to enhance sales of the product or service? Market research questions are often quite specific, such as: Will more teenage girls buy Fayva boots if exposed to ads with a musical background of disco or punk rock? Market research may be conducted **in-house**, by a **full-service agency**, or by an independent market research company.

mechanical: The combination of **art** and typeset **copy** such that all elements are in proper position and ready for printing; a **paste-up** that is accurate and ready to be reproduced.

media buyer: An **ad agency** employee responsible for placing **ads** and purchasing **time** or **space** in the communications media. The buyer specifies conditions, arranges dates and times, negotiates costs with the media in which the ads will run. The six major media in which the greatest amount of space or time is bought are: consumer magazines; national newspaper supplements; network TV; **spot** TV; network radio; and **outdoor advertising**.

Nielsen: The **A. C. Nielsen Company**; the nation's largest **market research** firm (annual sales of $400 million), which provides the most widely used system for measuring the number of persons viewing television shows (generally known as the *numbers*, the **ratings** or simply the *Nielsens*); as well as extensive **demographic** breakdowns of audience composition; and many other market surveys and studies. For details of specific Nielsen TV ratings (**share**, **overnights**, **sweeps**), see TELEVISION chapter.

O and O: Short for **owned and operated**; those TV or radio stations that are owned and

operated by one of the networks, as distinguished from independent stations, or **indies**.

orange goods: Products that have a medium rate of consumption, servicing, and profit margin (or markup). Most clothing, for example, falls in this category. See **red goods**, **yellow goods**.

outdoor advertising: Advertising placed on **billboards**, signs, posters, and the like in outdoor locations. Over half a billion dollars is spent on outdoor advertising in the United States each year.

outsert: An advertisement or other printed piece attached to the outside of a product or package.

packaged goods: Products that come in a package, box, tube, or other container—such as cereals, household products, canned goods, toothpaste. The vast majority of all **ads** are for packaged goods, and some of the largest ad **agencies** do most of their business advertising these products.

parity product or service: A product or service that is fundamentally similar to other products or services in the same category. Dishwashing detergents, fluoride toothpastes, club sodas, and flashlight batteries are all examples of parity products; the various taxi services, bus lines, piano tuners, dry cleaners, bank checking accounts are all mostly parity services.

paste-up: The process of assembling the artwork and type proofs for a **print ad**, literally by pasting them into position on heavyweight paperboard. Also used synonymously with **mechanical**.

piece of business: See **account**.

point: 1. A **rating point**; that is, the percentage of people who saw (or heard) an **ad**, **commercial**, or program out of all those who might possibly have done so.

2. A unit of height in **type**, equal to $\frac{1}{72}$ of an inch, or $\frac{1}{12}$ pica.

point-of-purchase: Abbreviated **P.O.P.**; also

point-of-sale. Advertising located at the place where the consumer may actually buy the product (or service); this includes displays in stores, posters, signs, bins with advertising on top or sides, and the like.

pool: Also **commercial pool**. An array of **commercials** for a single product (or service), which are available to be broadcast by the advertiser at any time. Often all the commercials in a pool have a common theme or set of characters—e.g. Madge the Manicurist for Palmolive Liquid.

portfolio: Also called **book**. A collection of the best examples of an **art** or **copy** person's work, used as an extended résumé. The work is usually presented in a large, flat leather case with zippers.

position: 1. The location of an **ad** within a **print** medium (e.g. **front of book**, **back cover**), or of a **commercial** on a radio or TV station's schedule (prime time, early fringe, and so on). *Premium* or *preferred positions* are those which attract more attention and are, of course, billed at a higher rate.

2. To place one's product in the overall market in relation to competing products. See **positioning**.

positioning: A key concept in advertising strategy and in **marketing** in general: creating the public perception of a product or service as having a particular **position** in relation to the competition. For example, Coke is normally positioned as an "industry leader," whereas Avis designed its most successful **ad campaign** around being positioned as number two. Other products may be positioned as being of the highest quality (though exclusive and expensive), the most economical, the safest, the sexiest, and so on. Positioning also refers to targeting one's **marketing** efforts to a certain segment of the population—e.g., advertising Rolls-Royce automobiles only to the highest-income individuals; and to emphasizing certain qualities or aspects of one's product that are different from those of the

industry leader—7-Up's "Uncola" campaign, for example.

pre-to-post: In **market research**, a measurement of how subjects' desire to purchase a product (or service), or their general perception of it, changed from before viewing an **ad** or **commercial** to after viewing. A basic way of attempting to quantify the effectiveness of advertising on a control group of people.

print media: Also simply **print**, or **press**. All those communications media based primarily on the printed page, i.e., newspapers and magazines of all types.

problem-solution: A genre of advertisement (especially common in TV **commercials**) in which a problem is presented (Mrs. Jones can't get her husband's greasy overalls clean) and a solution found—by means of the product being advertised (Wisk detergent gets it out).

proof: Also **printer's proof**, **page proof**. A sample of the impression made by typeset copy or engraving, provided by the printer in order to check that all elements are set correctly and to make alterations if necessary.

PSA: Public service announcement; advertisements for philanthropic causes, nonprofit organizations, and other acceptable civic purposes. TV and radio stations are required by law to run a certain amount of PSAs in their daily broadcast schedule; most of these, of course, wind up somewhere between the late-late movie and the national anthem.

psychographics: A type of **market research**, similar to **demographics**, but focusing on the psychological traits and responses of a **target audience,** e.g., their aggressiveness, patriotism, sexual attitudes, life-style, emotionality, and other psychological factors.

publicity: Anything that gets a product or service—or the company which produces it, or anything connected with these—into the public eye, but which has not been paid for by the purchase of advertising **space** or **commercial time**. Thus, when a famous movie star says he loves his Jaguar more than his mother-in-law in a *Playboy* interview, this comment (referred to as a *plug*) is a form of unpaid publicity for the auto company. See also PUBLIC RELATIONS chapter.

puffery: Exaggerated claims or advertising **copy** statements not meant to be taken seriously. ("Use Snake-o Bath Oil—you'll be irresistible." "Foghorn's Costume Jewelry—worth its weight in gold!")

push money: Abbreviated **PM**; a kind of payoff or kickback paid to salespeople or retail dealers for "pushing" a certain product **line** over the competition. Usually paid as a bonus fee for each item sold.

Q-rating: Also **TV-Q**. A measurement of the popularity of a TV show (or a performer, or product), expressed in a dual score: the percentage of persons polled who recognized the show (or product, etc.), called its *familiarity rating;* and the percentage of these who also said they liked it and regarded it as a favorite (the *Q-rating*). The combination of both scores is called the TV-Q.

rate card: A card listing the standard advertising rates for buying **space** or **time** in a communications medium—especially **print**. Most frequent or major advertisers are given discounts off this **card rate**.

ratings: Any of a variety of measurements by which the number of persons (or homes) watching or listening to a TV or radio show can be estimated. The ratings thus also indicate the number of persons exposed to a **commercial**, and are the major basis for setting the rates for buying **time** in the broadcast media (shows with higher ratings charge more for the same **spot**, naturally). **Nielsen** and **Arbitron** are the two major rating services. See also the TV section for specific types of ratings.

reach and frequency: Two factors used in measuring the exposure achieved by a series of **ads** or commercials. Reach, also known as **cumulative audience** (or **cume**), is a measure of the number of (unduplicated) viewers of a program or advertisement. Frequency refers to the average number of exposures to the same broadcast over a specific period of time. The product of percentage reach times frequency is expressed as **gross rating points** (**GRP**).

red book: Either the *Standard Directory of Advertising Agencies,* or the *Standard Directory of Advertisers*, two volumes used extensively in the advertising business.

red goods: Products that are frequently purchased, rapidly consumed, often replaced, widely available, with a relatively small per-item profit margin. Fresh foods are a prime example. See **orange goods**, **yellow goods**.

rep: **Representative**; a person who represents photographers, illustrators, et al., by showing samples of their work to **art directors** and generally acting as business liaison between an artist and the **agency** or agencies that may employ him.

repro proof: Also, **slick**. A **proof** usually on glossy paper, which has been corrected and is ready for photographic reproduction, in order to make a printing plate.

residuals: Payments made to actors or other performers (e.g., **jingle** singers) for each repeated showing of a radio or TV **spot**.

retouching: Changing or "improving" a photograph (or **repro proof**) to make all elements perfect for publication; this may involve anything from straightening a model's teeth to eliminating the small print from a product package and amplifying the package's color. Almost all photography used in **print** advertising is retouched in some way. (No one's teeth are *that* white!)

roll-out: Also, **roll, launch**. The introduction of a product or service into a new or expanded market (such as, nationwide from a regional **test market**). ("Pillsbury Co.'s consumer group is moving into **test** with a new product, **rolling** national with another, and preparing for early 1980 **roll-out** of another"—*Advertising Age,* Sept. 17, 1979.)

roughs: Also **rough comps**. Before an **ad** is actually illustrated, photographed, or typeset, the visual idea and **headline** are hand-drawn in a rough manner (*comped up*) to give an idea of what the finished ad will look like without incurring the expense of actually producing it. These drawings are the roughs.

sample reel: Also **demo reel**. A film reel containing a number of TV **commercials**, used to present the work of a director (or production studio) to prospective employers (**ad agencies**, producers, advertisers).

scrap: Photos or illustrations cut out of magazines (or other sources), used as a guide to drawing or **laying out** a **comp**; or in picturing what the **visual** images will be like prior to shooting them.

selling idea: A single line that succinctly sums up the major theme or idea of the **ad**. In some TV **commercials**, the selling idea is repeated in **voice-over** at the end of the **spot** or superimposed on the screen; in **print ads**, it is often printed in large type across the page. ("Nikolai Vodka—Kisses . . . but never tells"; "BVD—The Great American Fit for the Great American Male"; "The Cartier Executive—European Style Made Comfortable." See also **slogan**.

share: 1. In television, a **Nielsen rating** that indicates the percentage of homes which were tuned to a given show out of all those sets in use at that time.

2. *Share of market,* a measure of what percentage of total sales in a given category (e.g., cigarette sales in the Northeast) is captured by a certain **brand**.

shop: Ad-industry term for **agency**. ("After ten years at BBD&O, he left and started his own **shop**, an exclusive **boutique agency** on East Sixty-third Street.")

shoot: A photographing or filming session, especially one that is on location as opposed to in a photography studio.

shooting board: A more detailed version of a **storyboard**, in which every second of a TV **spot** is accounted for. A shooting board for a thirty-second **commercial** would consist of thirty separate drawings.

sixty: A sixty-second **commercial**. Relatively rare these days, when prime-time slots on network TV can cost over $200,000 a minute.

slice of life: A type of **commercial** that seems to be realistic, involving everyday people in ordinary life situations: the housewife serving dinner to her family, the commuter on a crowded subway, and so on. Of course, in almost every case these are professional actors and actresses reading painstakingly prepared scripts, but the slice of life is a distinct genre of advertising, quite different from elaborately produced, special-effects **spots** such as luxury automobiles on remote mountaintops and extravagant Busby Berkeley musicals regaling canned soup.

slogan: A phrase that is repeated or emphasized throughout an **ad** or **campaign**, designed to "hook" into the audience's consciousness. ("You deserve a break today"; "When you say Budweiser, you've said it all"; "The Good Hands people"; "We're American Airlines, Doing What We Do Best.")

space: The area in a **print** medium (also used in **outdoor advertising**) which may be purchased for advertising purposes.

spec book: A collection of hypothetical **ads**, **storyboards**, or **copy** created by a prospective **art director** or **copywriter** when he or she has not had actual work experience to present to employers.

split run: In **print** advertising, the use of several different versions of the same product advertisement; usually done to appeal to different populations who may read different editions of a paper, or to test reader responses to each version.

sponsor: An advertiser who buys some or all of the **commercial time** within and around a given TV or radio program. In its most extreme form sponsorship involves an arrangement in which the advertiser itself produces the show, during which its products will be advertised.

spot: A TV or radio **commercial**. *Spot advertising* (as opposed to *network advertising*) refers to the purchase of specific air time slots on specific stations where the commercials will hypothetically have the greatest effect.

spread: A **print ad** that runs across two facing pages.

still life: Also, **table top**. A photograph, usually in **print ads**, showing the advertised product or several inanimate items (such as the various ingredients that go into a cereal) without depicting people or events.

storyboard: Also called simply **board**. A hand-drawn representation of a TV **commercial**, with a separate drawing for each scene. Beneath each picture (drawn in a TV-screen-shaped frame) are written video instructions (such as zoom, or pan) and accompanying audio (narration, music, sound effects). The storyboard is the major form in which a TV **spot** idea is presented to a **client** or **agency** supervisor.

super: Short for **superimposition**; usually a group of words (or **logo**) that appears "printed" over the background visual image on a filmed or taped **spot**.

superagencies: The huge, multimillion-dollar **ad agencies**, which produce thousands of **ads** and commercials yearly and dominate the ad industry. The top ten agencies in terms of United States business, together account for over $6 billion in yearly domestic **billings** (and considerably more if foreign business is added). The number-two agency, for example, (J. Walter Thompson) employs over 1,300 **copywriters**, **art directors**, and TV producers, and creates advertising for 800 different **client** companies. The ten largest superagencies (in domestic business), the colossi of American advertising, are: Young & Rubicam; J. Walter Thompson; Ogilvy & Mather; Ted Bates; Foote, Cone & Belding; Leo Burnett; Batten, Barten, Durstine, & Osborne; Grey; Doyle Dane Bernbach; and McCann-Erickson.

table top: See **still life**.

tag line: Also called **logo line**, **theme**, or **base**. The key phrase in an **ad** which sums up the impression the ad (or an entire **campaign**) wishes to create. ("Good to the Last Drop"; "Coke Adds Life"; "Ford has a better idea.") In **print** ads, tag lines are most often found at the bottom of the ad in bold type.

talent: Actors and actresses, singers, dancers, announcers, models, and other performers employed in TV and radio **commercials**. ("Bring in the **talent**.")

target audience: The prospective audience toward which an **ad**, **commercial**, or **campaign** is oriented; the people one wishes to reach with an advertising "message."

team: An **art director** and **copywriter** who work together to create a complete **ad** or **commercial**. The art-copy team is one of the most common working units in advertising.

tearsheet: An extra copy of a printed page or **ad** or article from a newspaper or magazine, used as a file copy or to check for accuracy; may be sent to an advertiser as proof that his ad was run correctly.

teaser campaign: A series of **ads** and/or **commercials** which do not give complete information but serve to rouse the audience's curiosity; often used to stimulate interest in a major motion picture well in advance of its actual release.

ten: Also **10**. A ten-second radio or TV **spot**.

test market: Also simply **test**. The introduction of a product into a (relatively small) market area—e.g., three selected cities in the Southeast—in order to gauge the effectiveness of the **marketing** strategy chosen and/or the saleability of the product. A new product or service is almost always test-marketed before it *rolls national* (is marketed all over the country).

thirty: A thirty-second **commercial**. For a network airing in prime time on a top-rated show, one thirty-second time slot will cost over $100,000.

throwaway: Any simple, printed advertisement, such as a **handbill** or a supermarket discount sheet, which is expected to be read only for a few moments and then thrown away.

tight comp: A more finished version of a **rough comp**, in which the visual idea is very carefully drawn and the **headline** finely hand-lettered. A *very tight comp* may utilize scrap or photos from a test **shoot**, and have typeset **body copy**.

time: **Commercial** air time on radio or television stations, which can be bought by advertisers for their messages. A *time-buying agency* is one that specializes in arranging such purchases in the broadcast media (as distinct from a **full-service agency**).

Top 100: The one hundred largest markets, as ranked by their sales in a specific area (e.g., new automobile purchases), total population, or some other factor.

trade advertising: Advertising that is aimed not at the public but at businesses, who will in turn sell or distribute a product. For example, trade ads in *Publishers Weekly* (the major trade publication of the book industry) are placed by publishers to persuade booksellers and wholesalers to stock their latest titles.

two-color: An **ad,** magazine page, **handbill**, or poster printed in two colors—usually black and one color, sometimes two different colors.

typeface: Also called **face** or **type**. Any one of the thousands of different styles of printing that may be employed in an **ad**.

up-cutting: The practice of cutting out part of a TV or radio program to give more time for **commercial** messages. Often seen on syndicated off-network reruns shown in non–prime time where more commercials are allowed per hour.

upscale: An industry term for consumers who are on the higher end of the socioeconomic scale, who have money and can be pitched for more expensive products.

vertical publication: A magazine (or other periodical) aimed at people in a specific field, with a certain interest or life-style, or some other common element. For example, a skate-boarding magazine, an airline industry magazine, a show-business weekly. Distinguished from *horizontal publications* (such as *Time, Newsweek, Life*), which are aimed at the general public rather than special-interest groups.

vignette: 1. An illustration, photograph, or camera shot with deliberately faded or blurry edges; achieved in filming by means of an opaque-edged lens.

2. A type of TV **commercial** with several little scenes (vignettes), each of which presents a similar message about the product.

visual: The **graphic** and artistic material in an **ad** (illustrations, photos, fancy lettering, design), as distinguished from the **copy**; also, the video component of a TV **commerical**, as distinguished from the audio.

voice-over: Abbreviated **V.O.**; narration or other voice track in a **commercial** by a person who is not seen on camera. Often famous voices—or imitations of famous voices—are employed for effect. (The "Groucho Marx" voice for Vlasic pickles, for example.)

white coat rule: The rule prohibiting advertisers from using real or apparent medical professionals (doctors, dentists, nurses) as spokesmen in their **commercials**; imposed by the FTC to prevent abuse of the medical professions' authority to sell products.

yellow goods: Products that are consumed and replaced quite rarely, and have a relatively high profit margin—for example, refrigerators, television sets, automobiles. See **red goods**, **orange goods**.

|12|

Public Relations

The range of activities undertaken under the general rubric of public relations would come as a surprise to most Americans. The old image of a show-business **flack** sending gossipy tidbits to newspaper columnists is as outmoded as the Model-T Ford. Today's PR is a $3-billion-a-year industry, employing over 130,000 people, using the most sophisticated methods of research and communications to shape and alter public opinion. For the most part, the clients who spend the greatest amount of this total PR budget are the major corporations, the United States and some foreign governments, and other powerful organizations and interests.

What defines and unites all PR efforts is the intent to change the attitudes and perceptions of certain **publics** (which may be an entire population or a limited "target group" such as corporation stockholders, state legislators, congressional committee members) in a direction beneficial to the client's interests. To these ends, an astonishing array of activities may be generated: from **press conferences** for aspiring politicians to arranging author appearances on TV talk shows; from **press releases** about museum exhibits and other nonprofit events to the preparation of slick corporation **annual reports**; from **junkets** to exotic locations for movie reviewers to private **image consulting** for top executives. Although traditional definitions of PR distinguished it from advertising—in that advertising involves the paid purchase of media time and space while PR seeks unpaid publicity through other means—in the 1970s and 1980s PR has expanded to the point where it incorporates certain forms of advertising (such as the full-page **advertorials** placed in major newspapers by oil companies to counter consumer and environmental critics) and has established separate PR **wire services** that stand alongside the AP and UPI machines in many media newsrooms. In its overall impact on public opinion, modern public relations work may actually exceed the more obvious, and more costly, efforts of paid advertising campaigns.

There are three major categories of modern PR work: (a) the "in-house" PR departments of major corporations, unions, and organizations, which handle their general community relations, **internal communications**, publicity, and media contact requirements; (b) the PR **agencies** (many of which are subsidiaries of the major ad agencies) and **consultants**, who serve accounts such as Coca-Cola, ITT, and the government of Chile with high-power campaigns to achieve well-defined PR objectives (for example, to convince the public that there was no serious danger from the "incident" at Three Mile Island); and (c) the public relations and public information personnel of nonprofit organizations such as the Red Cross, the Boy Scouts, the Metropolitan Museum of Art, various state and federal agencies, and so on. The people who work in these areas may be known by different names: **publicists**, **press agents**, **PRO**s, **PIO**s, **executive counselors**, **image consultants**, or media representatives, but they fundamentally speak the same language. Herewith, a verbal guide to the world of the image-makers and opinion-shapers: the basic vocabulary of public relations.

advertorial: A combination of "advertisement" and "editorial"; a form of paid PR in which major companies (such as Exxon, Mobil, Chrysler) present their views on political, social, and ecological matters—usually in the form of full-page statements in major daily newspapers.

angle: Also **slant**, **handle**, **peg**. The aspect or element of a **press release** (or other story fed to the news media) that makes it "newsworthy." For example, the report of a new scientific study disproving the effects of smoking on lung cancer might provide the angle (in this case, controversy) for a newspaper to run a story based on PR material emanating from the American Tobacco Institute.

annual reports: Also **annuals**. Reports to stockholders (and the general public) that all publicly traded companies are required to send out at least once a year. Frequently the job is given to an outside PR agency, for which it can be one of the most demanding, ego-

involved projects in **financial/corporate** PR, but also one of the most profitable.

APR: Accredited in Public Relations; a designation indicating that a person has practiced PR for five years and has passed an examination given by the **Public Relations Society of America** (**PRSA**).

attitude management: A basic premise of modern PR—that people's attitudes can be managed (that is, manipulated) to further specific interests. A pertinent quotation from *Lesley's PR Handbook* (1978): "It is important to recognize that, in the arena of present '**attitude management**,' not the facts but the *impression* people get of a situation is the real reality."

backgrounder: A **press release**, briefing, or other factual communication to the news media in advance of some event—such as, a backgrounder on the situation in El Salvador prior to the president's announcement of stepped-up military involvement.

book: PR agency term for a magazine or a periodical. A *key book* is the magazine in which a client passionately wishes to appear—often *Forbes, Fortune,* or *Business Week.*

bylined article: An article, usually for the trade press, that appears to be written by one of the top executives of a client firm, thus enhancing the **image** of that company as an industry leader and authority in the field. The article, of course, is almost invariably "ghost-written" by agency writers and "sold" by strenuous PR efforts.

clipping bureau: Also **clipping service**. A company that culls all articles, features, and news reports mentioning a client (organization or individual) from hundreds of newspapers and magazines, and sends them to the client or PR agency. It is also used to collect reviews of movies and books that may have appeared in somewhat more obscure publications.

clipsheet: A single-page **press release** that combines a variety of separate items—press photos, short **filler** squibs, a longer story—arranged in newspaper-column format. The newspaper editor can then clip out whichever of these items he or she wishes to use.

communication: The central buzzword of the PR industry. Although public relations as a whole involves hundreds of distinct functions —from research/analysis and PR policy formulations through postprogram assessments, the essence of the business (as PR professionals are only too happy to repeat) is communication. By this is meant the actual process of delivering a message to the public, *and achieving a desired effect* with that message. Critics of the industry would prefer to call this manipulation, but no communications professional would ever use such an unpleasant word.

corporate PR: PR efforts that are devoted to enhancing the **image** of a corporation—as dynamic, profitable, stable, socially responsible, and the like—in the mind of the public (or several **publics**); as distinct from PR which attempts to promote specific products, services, or programs of that company.

counseling: Telling a client how to improve his corporate or marketing **image**, without actually doing anything concrete (such as composing and mailing *press releases*) to expedite that improvement. For the PR agency, counseling is one of its most profitable ventures— billed at high rates and requiring no effort beyond an energetic and informed conversation. For the individual PR practitioner, to become a private PR consultant whose business it is to counsel—without the burden of executing the plans suggested—is the dream of kings. (See also **image consultant**, **PPR**.)

credibility: The believability of an organization's statements, or, more importantly, of statements *about* the organization. Thus, while the public may be skeptical when a corporation advertises its own products or denies its culpability in an environmental catastrophe, when a respected news medium or other third party states something favorable about it, they tend to be believed more readily. A key concept in public relations practice. See also **third-party credibility**.

crisis communications management: Handling the "public relations problem" that arises when a company (or individual) is faced with a major fiasco, scandal, or other disaster that the press has found out about. For example, a major oil spill, the near-meltdown at Three Mile Island, and the revelation of the Ford Pinto's explosive gas tank all constituted crises in which communications management became a prime objective of the companies (and industries) involved. That is to say, it was considered critical to control the way the public *perceived* these events—often more important than actually doing something concrete about remedying them.

distribution services: Organizations that serve the PR industry by sending out **press releases** (or other PR materials) to selected media, thus saving their clients the time and effort of developing an appropriate **press list** and mailing to everyone on it. Typically, the customer merely checks off what kind of audience he wishes to reach (for example, apparel editors at metropolitan dailies and major magazines), encloses the release, and the distribution service does the rest.

Dow-Joneser: An interview by Dow Jones. The Dow Jones company runs a service that sends financial information to investment houses and other key sectors of the financial community; and also publishes the *Wall Street Journal*. An interview by its staff—a Dow-Joneser—can thus provide an extremely well-respected, high-**credibility** vehicle for transmitting information about a client company. ("The account was hurting till we hit the **long-bomb**, a **Dow-Joneser** that kept the **CEO** smiling for a month.")

filler: Small space-filling news items distributed as a form of PR. Many publications, especially small-town and suburban newspapers (and the second and third sections of large metro dailies), use small, non-news "items" to fill space left in their layout after the features and advertising have been put together. Many **press releases** and other PR materials are used—sometimes verbatim—as *filler copy* for these spaces. (When you see a short paragraph on page forty-eight describing the amount of feed grain it takes to produce a single quart of fresh milk, this is probably a filler that emanated from the PR department of the American Dairy Institute.)

financial PR: Communications aimed at persuading stockholders, investment bankers, stockbrokers, investment counselors, and other **publics** within the financial community of the viability and profitability of a company or organization. Financial PR thus includes everything from the preparation of **annual reports** to the careful placement of articles and items in the business press to personalized presentations to important security analysts and investment advisers. Financial PR emphasizes the economic potency of the client, as distinct from the quality or value

of his products or services. (See **marketing PR.**)

flack: A disparaging term for a PR person. Originally applied to show-business **press agents**, who were perceived as willing to make a lot of noise about any subject, the word has been extended to PR personnel in general but is a distasteful term within the industry.

government relations: A branch of PR that focuses on the communication between government (especially the federal government) and the client company or organization. The government relations person is typically based in Washington, D.C., and communicates the latest legislative and administrative developments to his client company, and attempts to influence government officials (senators, congressmen, agency chiefs, et al.) in the interests of his client. This is not exactly synonymous with lobbying, but it's close.

hand-holding: An important activity of account executives and account supervisors at public relations agencies, consisting of reassuring nervous or angry clients of the value of a PR agency's services. The best hand-holders have warm, dry hands, an infinite pliancy, and an American Express Gold Card.

image: A central buzzword and concept in modern public relations, image is the perception of an individual, a product, or a company that is held by the public and can be created or changed through **communication** efforts. Thus, an old, well-established travel agency might have its image "updated" to capture the young singles travel market through a carefully planned communications strategy of advertising, contests, **promotions**, and **press releases**. A chemical company might place a series of **advertorials** in major newspapers to give it an image of environmental concern. As with most public relations practice, the emphasis is on perception rather than fact. (See also **image consultant.**)

image consultant: A PR professional who specializes in teaching executives, politicians, and other important types how to dress, speak, socialize, and otherwise project an **image** of success, dynamism, leadership, and power. This may include anything from giving advice on a "positive power executive vocabulary" to employ whenever possible (verbs like *conglomerate, initiate, endorse, acquire*), to ghost-writing **bylined** articles for publication in trade journals, to selecting ties and cufflinks with the appropriate "power look." Fees for these services may run $1,000 a month and up. See also **PPR**.

industry leadership programs: Stories "placed" in the press that portray a company (or its chief executive officer) as the leader in a given field. Such programs may be put into effect for a variety of purposes—from a need to justify price raises of the client's products to the personal desire of an executive to raise his status in the professional community.

internal communications: Methods by which the management of a company (or the executives of a trade union, hospital, university) can communicate with their employees (or members). Most often this takes the form of a company newspaper or newsletter, but may also encompass such communications as training films, public-address-system announcements, and management-employee meetings.

issue management: Preparing the public to view an issue in a way that serves the interest of a client. For example, a tremendous PR effort has been made on "**managing** the nuclear power **issue**"—which is to say, persuading the public and the government that nuclear power is safe, necessary, and inevitable if we are to be self-sufficient in energy production. Given the actual facts, the widespread public acceptance of nuclear power must be seen as a major PR "achievement."

junket: A publicity trip for reporters, critics, or other media persons, paid for by the company whose product they are going to review or report on. Especially common in the mo-

tion-picture business, where many thousands of dollars are spent flying movie reviewers to exotic locations where the reviewers can "get a closer look" at the filming. The basic premise is that the more lavishly treated the media people are on a junket, the more favorably they will report.

kill a story: A form of "reverse" PR in which the public relations agent strives to keep the press from running a story that will depict his client in an unfavorable light. Thus, a mayor's press corps might exert its influence to keep the story of municipal contract kickbacks out of the local papers—or at least delayed until after the election.

list: Also **press list, media list, contact list**. A PR person's most basic tool—a list of all the persons in the communications media who should be sent **press releases**, **press photos**, or **press packets**, or otherwise contacted on behalf of a certain client or for a specific PR campaign. A motion-picture **publicist**'s list, for example, would include all the movie reviewers on all the major newspapers, magazines, TV and radio stations. The list is the PR person's stock in trade and, given the changeable nature of the mass media, needs to be updated almost daily.

long-bomb: Taken from football terminology, a PR long-bomb is a **score** in a key **book**, that saves an account from dropping an agency's services, usually at the last minute.

marketing PR: Public relations aimed at improving the **image** of a company's products or services—for either the general public, or distributors and sellers.

media event: An event created fundamentally as a device to gain media attention for a client or an issue—with the implication that the event would not occur on its own, without media coverage. A **press conference** is the most obvious example, but hundreds of other media events are engineered by enterprising PR people every month: gala openings, corporation-sponsored contests, special days and weeks, ground-breaking ceremonies, carefully planned "demonstrations," sudden appearances of important politicians in news hot spots, ribbon-cutting affairs, and the like.

media packet: Also **media package, media kit.** A compilation of various PR components distributed to media people, especially in the context of a "major event"—a weeklong trade fair, a presidential candidate's declaration of candidacy, a "blockbuster" movie release. The packet may include basic fact sheets, photos, and other visual materials (tapes or film clips if broadcast media are involved), biographies of major personnel, brochures, short and long **press releases**, suggested feature news stories, and the like.

media relations: Public relations work devoted to gaining media coverage for one's client(s); much of the work involves establishing personal connections with a large number of "contacts" in the press and broadcasting. As increasing numbers of former newspersons move into the (generally more lucrative) field of PR, these connections get increasingly cozy.

news advisory: An announcement to the news media from a PR person or office that an event of importance is going to take place. Much briefer and more factual than the average **press release**, the news advisory is designed to get press coverage, rather than to indicate what the actual content of a story should be.

news peg: The truly newsworthy or important element in a **press release**, that will motivate a news editor to take it seriously and run a story based upon the release.

news release: A more current term for **press release**, with the additional connotation of including the broadcast as well as print media.

newsroom: Also **media facility.** Λ temporary "communications headquarters," set up by PR staff to accommodate large numbers of news reporters on or near the site of a major event. Thus, when the released U.S. hostages from Iran arrive in West Germany, or the Democratic party holds its National Convention, a newsroom is established on location to facilitate reporting and enable PR persons to distribute **press kits** and the like to a concentrated group of news people. Also refers to the news-gathering and writing center of a newspaper or TV news department.

opinion leaders: Also **influentials.** Persons who are considered to be significantly more powerful or influential than the average person, and are thus targeted as high-priority audiences for PR efforts. Opinion leaders include government officials—legislators, agency chiefs, judges; mass media figures—newspaper editors and publishers, TV commentators, reviewers, radio DJs; and vocal activists or celebrities—such as Ralph Nader, Robert Redford, Jerry Falwell, or William Buckley.

peripherals: Smaller, secondary, or off-the-beaten-track media: suburban weekly papers, **trade** journals with extremely limited circulation, minor radio stations, and the like.

photo opportunity: A chance for a newspaper or TV station to cover an event where striking or intriguing photographs (or film) can be shot—according to the PR person who is "generous" enough to notify them of this opportunity.

photo syndicates: Organizations that distribute photos to thousands of newspapers and periodicals—in much the same fashion as the major **wire services** distribute stories. (In fact, two of the five largest photo syndicates are AP Newsphoto and UPI News Pictures.) It is much easier, however, to get a **pickup** for a clever photograph than for a feature story or **news release;** thus, many PR agencies send **press photos** (with captions) that depict their clients or something about their clients to the photo syndicates and have a good chance of seeing them published. Look at the photos in your daily newspaper and guess how many of them emanated from PR sources.

pickup: Also **placement**. The acceptance or use of a **press release** or some other PR communication by the media.

PIO: Public information officer; usually an employee of a state or federal agency, or a nonprofit organization, who performs public relations functions such as sending out **news releases**; preparing brochures, newsletters, and exhibits; arranging speeches, tours, and conferences; creating and placing public service announcements (**PSAs**). For some reason, government and the nonprofit world do not like the connotations of public relations and have substituted this term instead.

positioning: Term derived from advertising (see also ADVERTISING chapter), referring to the creation of a specific **image** for a client—especially in relation to the acknowledged industry leader. Thus, a PR campaign might be undertaken with the aim of positioning the company as being in the forefront of community-oriented corporations (e.g., Kodak in Rochester, N.Y.) or as being an old-fashioned, traditional-values type of organization ("The Basic Things We Used to Know").

PR: Public relations.

PPR: Personal public relations; a subindustry within the world of PR, which focuses on attaining "visibility" and improved **image** for individuals, usually politicians and Hollywood celebrities, but now, with increasing frequency, top corporate executives and ambitious people in almost every field. PPR involves not only **image consulting** but the full range of other PR activities—**press releases, media events**, arranged interviews and talk-show appearances, **bylined articles** —that will thrust the client into the public eye.

press advisory: See **news advisory**.

press agent: A mostly archaic term for a PR practitioner, still in use mainly to refer to show-business **publicists**, whose clients are actors, singers, entertainers, Broadway plays, and Hollywood movies.

press conference: A **media event** in which a politician, celebrity, or other public figure makes a statement and is interviewed by an assembled corps of news reporters. What most of us do not realize is that every press conference is arranged by a professional PR staff and that, in many respects (timing, location, procedures, and even the **image** to be projected by the important person) it is *their* show.

press kit: 1. See **press packet**.

2. An extended blueprint for the way a local-area publicity campaign is to be conducted, usually prepared by a national headquarters (e.g., of the Republican party) and distributed to local PR representatives. The kit will contain sample **releases**, suggestions for events, and methods of procedure, to be adapted by the local staffpersons.

press liaison: Keeping in touch with the press. This is of course a necessary element of almost all effective public relations work, but it is also a handy device for a PR agency when it needs to reach a specific "billing objective": The agency charges the difference between work actually done and the total sum billed to press liaison, and keeps its fingers crossed.

press list: A PR person's list of all contacts at newspapers, magazines, and other news media. Probably the most vital tool to effective PR practice, and constantly updated as media people change jobs and positions. See **list**.

press packet: Also **press book**, **press kit**, **media packet**. A collection of PR materials, often distributed to news reporters on the occasion of a major or extended event, such as a movie opening, the launching of a new product line, the start of a large convention, trade fair or charity drive. The press packet usually includes long and short articles, schedules of events, fact sheets, photos and other visual materials, brochures and biographies.

press photos: Black and white, eight-by-ten glossies that can be sent to newspapers and magazines to accompany a **press release** or as supplemental material provided to reporters working on a story. See also **photo syndicates**.

press release: The most basic tool of PR practice: a typed statement that gives information about a company (or organization or individual, or product) and which is sent to the print and broadcast media in the hope that some or all of it will be used—thus gaining an unpurchased and highly credible piece of publicity that will reach thousands, even millions of people. Press releases typically start with the heading FOR IMMEDIATE RELEASE (occasionally FOR RELEASE ON a certain future date), and include the PR person to contact for further information. Although news editors will tell you that they really don't use very much of what comes in as press releases, and while the very high-level, high-power PR people accomplish everything through personal contacts and private meetings, nonetheless the press release remains the mainstay of the profession and forms the basis, if not the substance, for a surprisingly large percentage of what appears in the news media.

press tour: A modern version of the traveling road show, in which a movie star (or author, director, politician) flies from city to city, to be interviewed by the local news people, appear on the radio and TV talk shows, and generally get as much media coverage for the new movie (or play, or product, or campaign) as possible.

PR news wires: Information-distribution services that function in much the same way as the major news **wire services** (AP, UPI, Reuters), except that the material emanates not from (hypothetically) objective, disinterested reporters, but from the press secretaries, PR officers and contracted PR agencies of major corporate and institutional clients. Nonetheless, there is a clacking teletype machine printing out the latest PR releases alongside the UPI and Reuters reports in the newsrooms of many major newspapers and TV network news offices.

PRO: Public relations officer; generally the "in-house" public relations position in a large corporation, with responsibilities for day-to-day media contact, company newsletters and publications, and the like. Usually the more glamorous high-profile PR work is contracted to an outside PR agency or **consultant**.

promotion: A special type of **publicity**, in which special events are arranged in order to gain public attention and favor. Promotions include contests ("Win a free trip to Disneyland!"), *stunts* ("Elephants in Adidas on Fifth Avenue"), tie-ins with other media (WXYZ Radio runs a drawing for some company's "big prize giveaway"), live shows, attention-getting *gags*, fund-raising dinners, and the like.

PRSA: The **Public Relations Society of America**; a trade organization that grants accreditation to some PR practitioners (see **APR**) and generally acts as a PR agency for the PR industry. The 7,000 PRSA members, however, constitute only a small fraction of the 130,000 Americans who work at PR in some capacity.

PSA: Public service announcement; a radio or TV "commercial" for a nonprofit organization (e.g., United Cerebral Palsy), which is broadcast free by local stations, in accordance with federal regulations. PSAs form an extremely effective and usually inexpensive form of PR for nonprofit groups.

public affairs: The branch of public relations that deals with political and social issues and events—specifically, such areas as (in PR jargon) **government relations**, *minority relations, community relations,* and *political relations.* Public affairs can include anything from high-level lobbying in Washington to publicizing the hiring of a black middle-manager to deluging an environmentally threatened community with "expert" testimony on the harmlessness of nuclear wastes. It is clearly distinguished, however, from the other major types of PR function (**marketing PR**, **financial relations**, etc.), and in many companies there is an executive for public affairs different from the one in charge of general public relations.

publicist: The general name for a public relations practitioner in the motion picture–entertainment business, where getting **publicity** for new films, movie stars, shows, and performers is the major focus of attention. Long-term corporate **image** work, for example, or **government relations** PR is of little significance in marketing *Star Wars* or *Endless Love;* immediate impact is the key. See **publicity**.

publicity: That type of public relations which has an immediate impact—e.g., the appearance of a client on "Donahue" or "The Tonight Show," the favorable mention of a company or its product in a daily newspaper, a photo of a movie star about to appear in a new movie. Publicity generally involves the mass media (newspapers and magazines, TV and radio) but can also include such methods as direct mailings, auto bumper stickers, lapel buttons, leaflets, contests, **promotions**, and other special events.

publics: A key buzzword in modern PR. Sophisticated and costly **communications** efforts are rarely directed indiscriminately at the general public, but are targeted at specific, well-defined groups of people, or publics. Thus we have large-category publics such as adolescents, black Americans, residents of metropolitan Chicago; and smaller, more precise publics such as the stockholders of a single corporation, or the owners of a certain recalled automobile, or the members of a congressional investigating committee. It is a tenet of modern public relations that every communciations effort must be created specifically for its intended public.

score: Also **hit**. Getting favorable material about a client printed in a desirable publication. ("The VP loved our **score** in *Forbes* and has agreed to double the company's **financial relations** account for next year.")

success stories: Also **case histories**. Tales of how a client's products or services were used —by other companies or individuals—with good results. These stories are usually "sold to" (i.e., placed in) the **trade press**, and thus have the advantage of two **third-party credibilities**—the users and the publication's.

third-party credibility: The rationale behind most public relations, as distinguished from advertising: The premise is that when someone else—a theoretically objective, disinterested third party such as a newspaper editor or magazine writer—comments favorably upon an individual, a product, or an organization, he will be more readily believed by the public than if the company or individual buys advertising space to convey the same message.

trade press: Also **the trades**. Publications directed at specialized audiences, especially in one industry or field of business. Distinguished from the *consumer press,* which is aimed at the general public, and the *business press* (such as *The Wall Street Journal, Forbes, Fortune*), which is directed at the entire business and financial community. Examples of trade press publications include *Publishers Weekly, Aviation Week, Road and Track, Variety,* and *Billboard.*

value billing: Charging a client for a **placement** based on its worth to him, rather than the standard monthly fee plus out-of-pocket expenses.

wire services: The major international news

distribution networks—Associated Press (AP), United Press International (UPI) and Reuters. If a PR agent can get a **pickup** from one of these wire services, it virtually guarantees that the story will reach thousands of newspapers and TV and radio newsrooms. Sending an excessive amount of less-than-earthshaking material to or through these services is known in the trade as *abusing the wires*.

[13]

Fashion

Fashion is change. Fashion is "an intensely personal performance art." Fashion is communication. Fashion is "what's happening now." Before considering these profundities (likely to be encountered in the latest fashion ads or articles) with any seriousness, it's important to get the facts straight: First and foremost, *fashion is big business*. Figures vary, but it is generally agreed that something over $50 billion is spent every year in the U.S. on clothing alone—not to mention shoes, lipstick, jewelry, handbags, and other fashion **accessories**. Taken together, the apparel and **textile industries** are the largest field of employment in the country—providing jobs for some 2.5 million people. A single "name" **designer**, such as Yves St. Laurent or Calvin Klein, will do several hundred million dollars of business every year. (Klein, for example, sold $70 million worth of jeans alone in 1979!) Each year the American apparel industry produces over 200 million dresses, 170 million pairs of men's pants, 200 million blouses. The industry is considered the third largest in our economy—exceeded only by the food and·fuel industries.

In order to maintain—and expand—such a huge volume of business, fashion **styles** must be constantly changed in order to induce people to buy. While it is true that in the last few years there has been a relaxation of the hegemony of the fashion "leaders," and that what is **in** or **out**, acceptable or not, can no longer be rigidly dictated—either by the designers or the fashion publications—nonetheless there is a constant stream of new **items** being manufactured and put on the market every **season**. And the most strenuous, imaginative, determined efforts are made to convince the public that they simply *must* have them.

While it is also true that the way one dresses *is* a personal statement, a form of immediate artistic communication, nonetheless the greater weight of such factors as fabric availabilities, style creation, and price determination derive from economic and technological realities rather than aesthetic concerns. Oil-based synthetics rise sharply in price, or are in short supply—and suddenly garments made of natural fibers such as cotton or wool become "the" things to wear. A popular fabric can absorb one dye color better than another—and lo, fabric of the more easily taken color is featured in all the major fashion magazines. It is not all beautiful models swirling down the runways of **couture salons.**

Beneath the level of the top designers, the well-established **manufacturers** and **retailers**, the world of fashion, or the *rag trade*, as they call it on New York City's **Seventh Avenue**, can be a tough place to survive: a world of **knock-offs** and markdowns, **price points** to be met, with **Chapter XIs** always right around the corner. A voluble, changeable, risky world where glamour, art, and sex blend not so neatly with high-pressure business, hype on all fronts, and a sort of institutionalized plagiarism. It's nothing that one could discern from turning the pages of *Vogue,* **GQ**, or *Mademoiselle.*

The vocabulary of the fashion world is a linguistic hodgepodge, a mixture of high French, low Yiddish, and the romantic novel—with a healthy dose of twentieth-century Big Business thrown in. Fashion terms are created or altered constantly as designers reach out for new ways to describe the same thing. Thus, "old-fashioned" becomes *camp,* which becomes **retro.** Sales pitches are disguised as philosophical ruminations, or factual reportage of the current scene. Words like "wonderful," "revolutionary," "clever," "heavenly," "outrageous" are rendered meaningless from overuse. **Gonifs** and **couturiers** mingle and do business—if in fact they are not one and the same. Herewith, a linguistic guide to this fabulous! outrageous! wonderful! world of fashion. For fall, it's a must!

accessories: Items of attire, other than major pieces of clothing; including jewelry, handbags, shoes, hats, scarves, gloves, belts, and hosiery.

adaptation: A copy of an original garment design; a more generous, classier term for **knock-off.**

apparel: In common usage, any type of **clothing** whatsoever; in the **retail** clothing business, however, the term refers only to major outerwear for women—that is, dresses, suits, and coats.

atelier: In French **couture**, a workroom where skilled needle-trades workers make duplicate models of the latest **designer fashions**.

Bloomie's: Bloomingdale's; the New York–based department store chain regarded as a **fashion** and merchandising leader. Bloomie's is *the* place to find what is fashionable in the middle-to-upper levels of **mass fashion**.

body clothes: Also **body-conscious clothing**. Form-fitting attire, which clearly accentuates and outlines the wearer's figure. Dancers' leotards were the prototypical body clothes, but the term now includes a much wider variety of jumpsuits, male *body shirts,* even some forms of evening wear.

boutique: A **retail** store usually selling a higher quality or more specialized line of clothing than that found in larger department stores. Used as an adjective, boutique implies something very much in **fashion**, distinctive, out of the ordinary.

BP: The **Beautiful People**; those whom the media have declared the elite in **fashion**, status, and social importance. Usually these are wealthy jet-setters who are prominent in the entertainment, political, or business worlds, and are supposed to lead exciting, fashion-making lives.

buying syndicate: An organization, usually located in New York City, that keeps out-of-town **retailers** abreast of the latest **fashion** trends and may actually purchase **clothing** or **accessories** for these retailers.

Carnaby Street: A major London clothing **fashion** center, now synonymous with English fashion.

Chapter XI: A legal proceeding undertaken when a company is on the verge of bankruptcy—a last-ditch attempt to save a business, in which a court sets up terms of payment to the company's creditors and appoints someone to see that they are honored. Though Chapter XI mechanisms are available in all industries, they are so common in the high-pressure, make-it-or-break-it **fashion** and apparel field that the term has become an integral part of the **trade** vocabulary. ("Harry? He's on a **Chapter XI** again—just like last year!")

classic: An enduring **style** in clothing, usually a conservative compromise between extreme swings of **fashion**; a look that does not change much from year to year, is not trendy but may still be "dressed up"; an item of attire that always sells well. Crew-neck sweaters or herringbone jackets for men, for example, are classics, as is a simple shirtwaist dress or pantsuit for women.

clothing: Besides its general meaning, in the men's clothing business this refers to suits, sportcoats, and dress pants—as distinct from casual male apparel.

collection: A **line** of apparel (usually 30 to 150 different pieces) created in a particular **season** by a **designer**.

contemporary: A **classic** or traditional look that has been updated with some new **fashion** element to give it an up-to-the-minute feel. Such changes might include a new **in** color, a slightly wider or narrower lapel, a higher or lower hemline.

contractor: In the apparel manufacturing field, a business whose employees cut pieces of fabric or sew and assemble finished garments, but which does not produce any entire garment from start to finish.

coordinates: Matching pieces of **sportswear** that can be combined to make an **ensemble**, but may also be worn separately with other pieces.

copy: Any reproduction of a piece of clothing made by someone other than the original **designer**'s company; at major **couture** showings, visiting **trade** buyers and **manufacturers** are charged a high "caution fee" and higher than normal prices for original **models**, because it is assumed that they will be making their own **copies** of those designer pieces they think will catch on.

couture: French, "sewing." The term fundamentally applies to all design houses, particularly those of high **fashion** in Paris and New York. By extension, any of the elite and extremely expensive, usually custom-made clothing, produced in small quantities for the "fashion leaders" who are willing to pay thousands of dollars for a single Givenchy or Courrèges or Chanel original. The line between couture and **ready-to-wear** (**RTW**) has blurred somewhat in recent years as the number of "name" **designers** has increased and as more of these have begun to reach out directly to a **mass fashion** market. Couture in its broadest sense now refers to the origination of a design and the elite world of expensive custom-made high fashion.

couturier (couturiere): Male (female) **designer** or dressmaker.

cutting: The actual cutting of fabric in accordance with a specific clothing design; also, the number of pieces ordered for manufacture. ("Let's go with a **cutting** of 500 on that Dior **copy**.")

cycles: Fashion is a uniquely seasonal, time-bound business and every fashion trend or change goes through a three-part cycle, which may last anywhere from weeks to years. Basically, the cycle runs: introduction-acceptance-regression (to obsolescence). Roughly corresponding to this fashion cycle are buying and promotion cycles, in which **styles** are first tested and the public informed; then fully stocked and the general public persuaded to buy; and finally, reduced through sales, markdowns, clearances, and closeouts.

designer: A person who conceives and executes a new (or pseudo-new) article of clothing or **fashion line**. There are the famous **haute couture** designers (Givenchy, Courrèges, Yves St. Laurent, Pierre Cardin); and others, less exclusively haute, who design for the **RTW (ready-to-wear)** market (Calvin Klein, Anne Klein, Halston); as well as a host of less prestigious designers who create clothing that is bought in the **mass fashion** market.

designer clothes: Apparel that bears the name of a "known" **designer** in its label. Buying designer clothes implies an interest in the latest **fashion** trends, and a willingness to pay more for such items than for ordinary **ready-to-wear (RTW)**, in order to look fashionable. Often the only discernible difference *is* the label, however—and the price tag.

disco: A highly stylized **fashion look**, made popular through the dance phenomenon of the late 1970s and continuing into the early 1980s. The look includes elements of 1930s and 1940s nostalgia, black, Latin, and formal styles, emphasizing flashiness, mobility, and youthful sexuality.

ensemble: An outfit consisting of separate pieces that combine together into an aesthetically pleasing, effective whole, though not in as formalized a way as would be found in a suit.

fashion: 1. The prevailing **style** of clothing at any given time.

2. The system or process of marketing and other influences by which particular **styles** of attire are communicated.

3. That portion of the apparel industry concerned with creating and convincing the public to buy an ever-changing array of "new" **items** and styles.

4. The total effect of a concatenation of clothing, jewelry, and other **accessories**, and additional visual-textural elements including (we are told) furniture, environmental design, packaging, art, auto design, etc.

5. A group of interrelated industries, including clothing **designers**, **textile** and fabric **manufacturers**, clothing manufacturers, **retail** clothing outlets, and related services such as fashion magazines, and modeling and advertising agencies.

fashion market: Any of several occasions when new **lines** of apparel are displayed to the *retail trade* (store owners, managers, buyers, etc.), who agree to buy certain amounts of the **items** they think will "move." The fashion markets are held seasonally, at least twice a year, approximately six to eight months before the actual retail buying **season**. The major fashion markets are in New York, Los Angeles, and Dallas, although there are many smaller regional markets. The markets are hectic, tense, excited, and suffused with nervous tension on all sides.

fashion statement: The "message" communicated by one's **clothing** (and jewelry, shoes and boots, hairstyles), indicating socioeconomic status (or trying to give the impression thereof), sexual availability and preference, and cultural values. Do you want to appear as a rising young executive? Hot and heavy swinger? Premier athlete? Established professional? Countercultural radical? Disco queen? The clothes you wear can make any of these statements, and more.

fill-in buying: Purchasing apparel in the middle of a *fashion season* to replace sold-out stock or to have on hand **items** that had not been ordered but are now in great demand.

FIT: The **Fashion Institute of Technology**; the most widely recognized and respected school of **fashion** design and production in the United States, located (of course) in New York City.

flash: An attention-getting, gimmicky, bright, extravagant **look** (e.g., an electric blue jumpsuit with knee-high silver sequined boots).

Ford: Also **runner**, **bestseller**. An item of **clothing** or general **style** (e.g., the miniskirt) that sells extremely well for quite a period of time —longer than a *fad* (which lasts only a **season** or two), but shorter than a **classic** (which endures for years, even decades).

garment district: See **Seventh Avenue**.

gonif: Thief; crook. The Yiddish term is widely used in the **rag trade**, which has traditionally included many Jewish people in all phases of business. ("You'd buy from a **gonif** like him? He'll shortchange you and what's more, he won't deliver!")

GQ: Gentlemen's Quarterly; a men's **fashion** publication aimed at the male consumer. The success of this publication is significant in that it reflects the growing interest of men in fashion (changing **styles**, greater latitude in creating an individual **look**), which used to be an almost exclusively female domain.

greige goods: Also **gray goods**. Fabric that has not yet been dyed at a mill or patterned by a finisher; fabric at a middle stage of the finishing process.

GWP: Gift with purchase; a promotional gimmick usually employed to introduce a new clothing or *accessory item* in a department store. The cost of the gift (a lipstick, pair of stockings, etc.) is generally borne by the **manufacturer**.

hand: The feel of a fabric, its texture or touch.

haute couture: French, "fine sewing." The most exclusive, prestigious **designers** and design houses; the high **fashion** created by the top designers; the world of high fashion, including the designers, the **clothing** itself, and the elite customers who are able to pay thousands of dollars for custom-made clothing.

house: A dressmaking firm, usually referring to one of the **couture** concerns, including a **designer** (or designers), several sewing rooms (**atelier** in French), a showing **salon**, business offices, sales department, etc.

ILGWU: The **International Ladies' Garment Workers Union**; the major labor union representing apparel-industry workers of all kinds.

in: In **fashion**. The term itself is no longer in vogue, having been replaced by such terms as "now," "today," or simply forms of the verb "to be" ("For elegant evenings this fall, it's . . ."). Fashion is built upon the notion that certain **styles**, **items**, and **looks** are in at any given time, while others are **out** (**passé, obsolete**). This enables the fashion industry to generate a kind of anxious excitement to buy them—in order to be in (which will make you admired, popular, successful, prestigious, or sexy) as opposed to out (God forbid!).

integration: The expansion of an apparel company into other areas of the business, usually applied to a **manufacturing** company that expands into **retail** selling (*forward integration*) or fabric production (*backward integration*).

item: A piece of clothing or **accessory**. ("There wasn't an **item** in his entire **line** that hadn't been seen before, but they're selling like crazy . . . it's the label.")

jobber: An apparel industry firm that may perform various partial roles in the total **manufacturing/retailing** process: **style** designing, or storing and shipping finished garments, or subcontracting **cutting** and sewing.

junior: Clothing sizes for young girls and women with youthful figures, indicated by odd-numbered sizes from 1 through 15. Size categories like junior (others include *missy, petite,* and *half-sizes*) are based on the ratios of bust to waist to hips.

keystoning: The general **retail** practice of doubling a **manufacturer**'s wholesale price for a garment before offering it to retail customers.

knock-off: As a verb, to copy the **styles** of another **designer** or **manufacturer**. As a noun, the **item** resulting from such copying. Knock-offs usually sell for considerably less than the original garment, and are a more or less institutionalized method by which **couture fashion** is trickled down through the socioeconomic ladder, until Zayre's and K-Mart are selling for $14.95 their knock-off of a dress that sold for $59.00 at Macy's, which was a knock-off of a Bergdorf Goodman $400.00 item—which may itself have been a high-class knock-off (more genteelly termed an **adaptation**) of a French designer original that sold for $5,000.00

layered look: An **ensemble** consisting of pieces of **clothing** deliberately placed one atop the other to create a visual or textural sense of depth.

leave paper: To place an order. When **retail** buyers attend showings of **designers**' or **manufacturers**' latest **collections**, they are there to purchase quantities of the styles they think will sell. These purchase orders are called **paper**. The apparel thus ordered is then shipped directly from the manufacturer to the retail outlet.

leisure wear: A category of **clothing** that includes items people wear for play or fun activities, jeans being undoubtedly the best example. Leisure wear is less formal than sportswear but usually does not encompass *active wear* items such as tennis shoes and running outfits.

line: A **collection**. The complete array of different **clothing** pieces (usually 30 to 150) that a particular **designer** is selling in a given **season**.

line for line: An exact **copy** (of another **designer**'s **model**).

lines: Specifically, the lines the eye tends to follow when looking at a garment; more generally, the **style**, design, or visual effect of clothing, especially its outline.

look: Undoubtedly the most overused word in the **fashion** business, referring to *any* identifiable aspect of **clothing** or appearance, and often combined with almost any adjective: a **classic** look, a sexy look, the look for fall, the latest look, the look of suede, and so on.

manufacturer: The company that actually produces a given **item** of apparel. Manufacturers usually purchase fabric, design the patterns, show their **styles** to buyers, **cut**, sew and assemble the finished garments, and ship them to the **retailers**—though any of these functions may be subcontracted to another firm. Also (see **integration**), the fabric production and retailing aspects may be undertaken by the larger manufacturers.

market, the: The **garment district**, also known as **Seventh Avenue** or **SA**.

mass fashion: The **style** or styles which are being purchased by a large number of people, and are thus being promoted and sold in large volume.

menswear: Attire for men, usually divided into *men's clothing* (suits and coats only) and *men's furnishings* (shirts, separate trousers, ties, jackets, underwear). The "**fashion** revolution" in menswear, beginning in the late 1960s, has opened up the field to a much wider array of possible **styles**, colors, fabrics, and to the idea of change in men's fashion similar to the changing styles of women's fashion.

merchant: A term of approbation in the **fashion/retailing** world signifying someone who does not just buy and sell, but does these things extremely well. ("Pinsky—now there's a **merchant**!")

mill: The place where fabric that will ultimately become **clothing** is produced. Mills obtain their raw stock from fiber manufacturers, and then produce the fabric through spinning, weaving, knitting, dyeing, and other processes.

model: In **couture fashion**, the garment itself —as opposed to the person who is wearing it at a showing. ("Our next **model** is a bold chiaroscuro design, with the feeling of Matisse. . . .")

number: The American equivalent of **model**; also called **item**. A particular piece of **clothing**. ("Here's a hot little **number** for those steamy disco nights.")

opening: The first public showing of the latest **designer collections**. ("You missed the Rome **openings**? Darling, what a shame. . . .")

open-to-buy: The amount of money a **retailer** has available to spend on apparel for the upcoming **fashion season**. Women's fashions are usually bought about six to eight months ahead of season (in spring for fall, for example), men's **apparel** even farther ahead. A number of factors, including the perceived state of the upcoming economy, determines how large the collective open-to-buy will be, and hence how successful a season will be for most **manufacturers**.

original: A design created for showing in a **collection**, or a duplicate garment made to order for a specific customer. The word gets watered down a little as so-called **designer originals** are increasingly mass-produced for **RTW (ready-to-wear)**.

out: Also **passé, obsolete**, **unfashionable**. A general term for anything that is not part of the current **style** or which is otherwise lacking in a well-conceived sense of dress **fashion**. The fear of being out—far more even than the desire to be **in** fashion—motivates millions of women (and men) to change and ex-

pand their wardrobe constantly—which is exactly what the purveyors of apparel advertising have in mind.

paper: Signed orders for a certain number of pieces, left at **manufacturers' showrooms** by **retail** buyers. Getting retailers to **leave paper** is the whole point of the **fashion markets**.

Paris: Traditionally the **fashion** center of the world, and still the locus of the major **couture** houses and the prestige center of the fashion world. Paris is synonymous with high fashion.

prêt-à-porter: French for **ready-to-wear**. Use of the term carries the patina of **couture**, even when undeserved.

price points: Predetermined **retail** prices (or price scales) that **manufacturers** feel will maximize the sale of certain **items** to certain types of buyers. In many cases, **retailers** will not even display garments that do not fit into the price range favored by their prime shoppers. To a large extent, price points determine the fabric blends and **styles** of apparel available on the **mass fashion** market.

prints: Fabrics that are stamped or imprinted with a particular design. Individual prints per se rarely come into prominence, but prints in general are usually either **in** or **out** of **fashion** in any given **season**. The traditional alternative to prints is *solids* (single color, no design).

punk: An "anti-**fashion**" **look** consisting of such niceties as rolled up T-shirts, closely chopped hair, and safety pins through earlobes. The look enjoyed a brief but highly publicized popularity in the late seventies and early eighties, associated with the success of punk rock music.

rags: **Fashion** industry slang for clothes. The *rag trade* is the garment business; a *rag merchant* is someone who buys or sells clothing.

ready-to-wear: Abbreviated **RTW**. Any **apparel** that is not custom-made; mass-produced **clothing**. The once great difference between custom-designed clothes and RTW has been blurred in recent years, with the entry of "name" **couture designers** into the RTW market.

resource: Someone who provides a **retailer**, distributor, or **manufacturer** with essential goods or services. A **mill** is the manufacturer's resource; the manufacturer is the retailer's resource. ("It's understood that your **resource** will extend you a little extra credit when you need it—if they didn't, everyone in the **rag trade** would go out of business!")

retailer: Any store, firm, company, or individual that sells materials directly to the consumer. Generally used to refer to clothing stores, or department stores that have apparel departments.

retro: Short for **retrograde** or **retrospective**; **fashion looks** that take their inspiration from **styles** of the past—especially those of the thirties, forties, and fifties.

salon: A large room where **collections** are shown, especially in the **couture** world; in America, less pretentiously called a **showroom**.

season: The time of year during which a certain kind of **fashion** is typically sold. For the most part, fashion seasons match the calendar seasons, with some variations; in places with extreme climates, like the Southwest, there may be only one or two seasons; and, in stores catering to classes of people who usually take extended winter vacations to warmer climes, there is a definite winter holiday season of tropical-weather attire. Further, the term sometimes refers to that most intense, concentrated **retail** period of the year, the six weeks between Thanksgiving and just after New Year's.

sell-off: The unloading of otherwise unsaleable goods at discount prices.

Seventh Avenue: Synonymous with the **garment district**, that area in New York City between Thirty-sixth and Fortieth streets, Sixth Avenue and Broadway, that has long been the center of the industry. With scores of manufacturers and markets, showrooms and apparel concerns small and large, this area is a frantic, seemingly chaotic jumble of narrow streets with racks of clothes being moved constantly. The fact is that over 60 percent of all American apparel is designed and produced in New York City, almost all of it in this small area.

shaped: Characterized by the highly structured use of materials to achieve and maintain a desired **silhouette**; shaped clothing does not so much follow the wearer's body contours as have its own shape that will create a **look** or image: broad, square shoulders and narrow waist, for example.

showroom: The area where **retailers** come to view the wares of the **manufacturer** or **designer**. Depending on the showroom operator, the decor will vary from tasteful to flashy, from elegant to downright seedy. Almost all, however, feature undersized dressing rooms for the models and cabinets stocked with J&B and Canadian Club for the buyers.

silhouette: The overall **look** breaking in a **market** during a **fashion season**; specifically, the external **lines** of a garment that form its characteristic outline. Silhouettes may be straight and narrow, triangular, hourglass-shaped, etc.

sportswear: The category of apparel that includes items that are neither "dress" wear (suits, evening dresses) nor *basics* (undershirts, bras, socks). Sportswear has almost nothing to do with athletics, most clothing worn for exercise being usually termed *active wear*. Typical sportswear **classic**: the Banlon shirt.

style: In its narrowest meaning, a certain characteristic or combination of characteristics in clothing—the **line**, **silhouette**, design, or **look**, that identifies it: bellbottom pants, cowl collars, and the like. In its wider sense, style is an overall quality or feeling made up not only of the specifics of clothing design, but also reflected in hairdo, makeup (or lack of it), jewelry and other accessories, music, furniture and architecture. Style is the total effect of the consciously generated personal environment.

tailored: Custom-made; also, cut to body-hugging contours. ("John made his appearance in a jumpsuit that was **tailored** to the point where his circulation at certain critical junctures was imperiled.")

textile industry: The general label that includes all those businesses producing the fabrics which are made into clothing (by the **apparel** industry). In the United States alone, the textile industry employs over 1 million workers in over 7,000 plants.

theater retailing: Enticing customers to browse and buy **clothing** by creating an entertaining shopping environment. This may be accomplished through bold graphics, innovative lighting and fixtures, audio and visual effects, celebrity appearances, or any of a thousand other approaches. The theater element comes in, in making the customer feel that she is truly a part of that exciting and dramatic world in which she is about to spend her cash.

tops: Any garments (except for coats and other outerwear) worn above the waist: such as shirts, blouses, and turtlenecks.

trade: Usually **the trade**. The garment business.

trading up: Buying, or selling, a more tasteful and/or more expensive type of **clothing**. ("After getting his suits at K-Mart for the past ten years, he started **trading up** and was last seen in an elegant three-piece from Louis.")

trend: The direction in which current **fashion** seems to be moving; those **styles** which are prevalent in the upcoming **retail season**. Many trends occur, however, that do not make it to become the full prevailing fashion.

unisex: A **clothing style** especially popular in the mid-seventies that sought to dress men and women in almost identical-looking garments. It grew out of the universal popularity of jeans but extended to many other types of apparel.

WWD: Women's Wear Daily; a newspaper generally considered to be the bible of the women's (and children's) apparel industry, both in the United States and Europe. *WWD* discusses **retail** happenings, **manufacturing** techniques, and government regulations, along with giving complete coverage of the latest **fashion trends** and trend-setters.

[14]

Computers

With reference to **computers**, there are basically two groups of people: those who understand them and those who don't. In the first group fall probably half a million computer **programmers**, **hardware** designers, systems analysts, silicon-**chip** mavens, and electronics wizards, along with those business, military, academic and lay persons who, for one reason or another, have become informed users or cognoscenti of the new "information revolution" technology. In the other camp fall the rest of us, who couldn't tell a **loop** from a **floppy**, and wouldn't know an **algorithm** if we fell on one. All this stuff about **integrated circuits** and **microprocessors** seems not only impossibly technical and futuristic, but remote from our lives and experience. *What* information revolution?

What is fascinating is that in this field of endeavor, more than any other, there are so few people with a moderate amount of knowledge. Most ordinary people have a modicum of understanding about medicine, say, or law; plenty of people who are not tennis pros know the difference between a cannonball serve and a lob or volley. But in relation to computers there seems to be no middle ground: You're either in or out, informed or ignorant. (Coincidentally, it is exactly this **binary** [two-state] mode that is the essence of how a computer stores and processes information: in a multitude of 0-1, yes-no, true-false **bits** of data represented by tiny electrical circuits being either on or off.)

The problem with this dichotomous situation is that there really *is* an information revolution taking place, one that astute observers consider as massive in its impact as the Industrial Revolution of the eighteenth and nineteenth centuries—and equally transformative of our society. Computers and associated technologies are indeed all around us, they are involved in almost every sector of modern life, and their penetration has only begun. Computerized filing and accounting systems, vast computerized data banks that can record everything from credit ratings to sales figures to political "watch lists," computer-directed air traffic control and missile guidance systems, **word processors**, hand calculators, **digital** alarm clocks and watches, electronic toys and adult computer games, computerization of Stock Exchange trading and check clearing and Dow Jones reporting systems, computer-controlled laser surgery and traffic lights and subway systems, auto ignition microprocessors, retail sales register-bar graphics, computerized billing systems and Defense Department early warning systems and airline ticket counters and banking services and horse-racing results and market analysis and newsroom **VDT**s and . . .

These are only a sampling of the current applications of computer technology. And this is only the beginning. Like it or not, the Computer Age is upon us. The section that follows is designed for the lay person, the "techno-peasant," for whom at least some knowledge of what computers are—and are not—has already become a necessity. Herewith, a basic vocabulary lesson in computerese.

Computer Slang   Computer "jocks" employ not only an extensive technical vocabulary, but also an array of pithy argot to describe the common hassles and major disasters of computer operation. Here are some examples. 🍏

bomb: Also **barf**. When a piece of **computer** equipment (especially **software**) ceases to function, or begins to function erratically.

bug: A wrinkle, a hitch, a fault, a boner, a loose nut, a problem, an *erratum;* that is, anything that stands between a **program** and absolute perfection.

crash: A **program bombs**, but a an entire **computer** system **crashes**. Why all the fighter-pilot jargon, no one knows.

cybercrud: Attributed to Theodore Nelson, a good word to describe the less professional aspects of the **computer** boom; the electronic equivalent of "hype" or "bull." Because computers were for so long mysterious and awesome machines, a mystique grew up around them—much of which is, of course, false. Computers *can't* evaluate sketches for matchbook art schools, *never* go on monomaniacal rampages, and *rarely* speed up your tax return.

FIFO: First in, first out; a simple—but not always efficient—way to deal with a list of tasks, meaning that the list is treated as a line of people at a bank teller's window. Also called **first come, first served**.

GIGO: Garbage in, garbage out; regardless of the sophistication of a system, this acronym reminds us that its weakest link is the **data** and assumptions that a system operates upon. Whether the system is the Internal Revenue Service, or a **microcomputer** accounts-payable system, what comes out is absolutely dependent on what goes in.

glitch: A source of malfunction. The glitch is a rather vague critter that may prove to be anything from a loose wire to a statewide power failure. Its essence is that it is unexpected.

kluge: Also **kludge**. Probably from the German *kluge*, meaning clever. A *kluged* solution to a problem is an improvised *patch-up* (usually of **software**) that always seems to last longer than it has any right to, or than anyone would have expected. When a kluge fails, however, everyone says, "Well, what did you expect?"

LIFO: Last in, first out; Another method by which **computers** deal with a list of tasks, but not a method humans like to be a part of.

moby: A very large and seemingly malevolent group of devices (or **kluges**), which threaten to come apart violently at any moment.

mung: Acronym for **mushed until no good**. **Programs** can mung up **files** if, due to some undiscovered **bug**, they run amok.

number crunching: Tasks that require not insight but seemingless endless repetitive calculations. **Computers** are absolutely vital to such scientific endeavors as the space program, more for their routine (rather than exotic) applications. **Digital** machines can perform thousands of numerical operations per second, thus resolving tedious problems in planetary mechanics, fuel use, materials stress, and the like.

nybble: Half a **byte**.

scrub: To clean **a file** of data that isn't needed, such as data that is out of date or redundant. This is distinct from **garbage collection**, as files are usually scrubbed only once, while their garbage is collected periodically.

wetware: Not a swimsuit, but the organic **hardware** that conceives of and writes the abstract **software** which drives the mineral hardware. In other words, wetware is the human brain —or, by extension, any organic intelligence.

COMPUTER TERMINOLOGY

ACM: Association for Computing Machinery; a professional society for **computer** manufacturers, **programmers**, and the like.

Ada: A **programming language** to end all programming languages—or such was its intent when the Department of Defense started on the project several years ago. Ada was meant to be a standardized language for use with **real-time** control devices, mechanisms that must perform calculations and then use the results to alter some operation in progress, such as rocket guidance controls. Very little of Ada, however, has made its way into the civilian or business **computer** markets. (The name derives from Lady Ada Lovelace, the daughter of Lord Byron, who supported Charles Babbage, the inventor of a mechanical **analog** computer called an "analytical engine.")

a/d converter: Any device that translates **analog** information (such as a wave form) into **digital** information (all 1's and 0's). It can also be called a *digitizer*.

address: Every space (or location) in a computer's **memory** is numbered. Any data stored in that location is then associated with that location's number; this is called the data's address.

ALGOL: ALGOrithm Language (1960); intended as the Esperanto of international **programming languages**, put together by a committee from several industrial nations. ALGOL is good at mathematical formulations, and is widely used in Europe, though it has largely given way in this country to newer languages and newer **hardware** that performs many of ALGOL's operations automatically.

algorithm: A systematic method or strategy for attacking and solving a problem in a finite number of steps. A simple example: To find the average cost of gasoline over the past month, you (1) compile the prices on each day of that month; (2) Add these together; (3) divide the total by the number of days in the month. The sequence of steps used to arrive at the result is an algorithm.

analog: When we represent an event that normally occurs in one medium in terms of some other medium, we have created an analog of that event. For example, the grooves in a phonograph record are an analog of the variations in air vibration that comprise certain sounds; on a tape, these sounds are represented by a different analog: the continuous fluctuations of magnetic fields. Early **computers** were analog computers that used variations in electrical current or mechanical movement to represent *all* information. Analog computers are not as flexible or reliable as **digital** computers, however, and are used today almost exclusively in the analysis of sound waves and other continuously varying properties.

AND: One of several **logic** operations a **computer** performs. The computer compares two quantities, yielding a positive result *only if* the quantities are the same; i.e., both 1's, both true, both positive, etc.

ANSI: American National Standards Institute; an organization something like the FTC for **computer languages**, that works for uniformity of commercial computer **software**.

APL: A Programming Language (1962); a serious **programmer**'s language; concise to use, difficult to learn. APL has its own symbols for many operations (⌐means "then," ← means "equal to," □ means "read from"), and is in direct conflict with languages like **COBOL** and **BASIC**, which strive to look as much like English sentences as possible. APL is very good at handling **arrays**.

applications programs: Programs, usually written in a high-level **computer language**, designed primarily to manipulate data, not to govern the operation of the **computer** itself (see **operating systems**). An accounts-

payable system, for example, uses different applications programs for each specific function: purchase-order entry, vendor maintenance, check-writing, and so on.

array: A set of related quantities that are numbered (or subscripted). Tables of information are typically set up as arrays, for instance:

DAY	TEMPERATURE
1	55
2	52
3	60
4	57
5	61

We might call the array "DAY," and store the table as DAY(1) = 55, DAY(2) = 52, and so on. This is a *one-dimensional* array. We could expand the table to include time of day:

DAY	TIME	TEMPERATURE
1	12:00	55
	5:00	54
2	2:00	52
	3:00	53
3	8:00	56
	10:00	58
	1:00	60

The table could then be stored as DAY(1,12) = 55, DAY(1,5) = 54, DAY(2,2) = 52. This is called a *two-dimensional array,* or a *matrix.* Setting up and handling arrays is a central part of efficient **computer programming**.

artificial intelligence: A much used and much abused term, referring to a branch of **computer** research aimed at getting computers to think like people. Computers can mimic human thinking, as with chess-playing or pattern-recognition programs, but lack the flexibility and learning capacity to truly *reason.*

MIT has developed a *computer program,* called, succinctly enough, DOCTOR, which converses with a person through a **CRT** as if it were a psychiatrist—with many of its patients unaware they were dealing with a machine. The program is designed to recognize and pursue key words, much as in Rogerian, nondirective therapy. An exchange might proceed as:

PATIENT: I saw my mother today.
COMPUTER: Yes?
P: She was angry.
C: Angry?
P: Well, she looked angry.
C: Looked angry? Tell me about that.

And so on. Such programs, which are actually far simpler than those which, for example, direct the Voyager spacecraft, bring into question long-accepted beliefs about just what is and what is not "intelligence." (See **Turing Test**.)

ASCII: The **American Standard Code for Information Interchange**, pronounced ASK-ee. When you enter the letter "A" into a computer, it stores this symbol as the **binary** number "1000001." Every symbol used by **computers** has had a binary number assigned to represent it, so that computers made by different companies can speak to each other, and to us, without constant translation. This series of binary numbers is standard throughout nearly all computer equipment (with the significant exception of IBM machines; see **EBCDIC**).

assembler: A **program** which translates *assembly language* into **machine language**. (See **computer languages**.)

backplane: To keep the complex wiring of **computer** devices as accessible as possible, all the **circuit boards** and connecting wires of the device are plugged into a rear panel, called a backplane.

BASIC: **Beginner's All-purpose Symbolic Instruction Code** (1961); as its name suggests, a simple, direct **language**, good for small home (and now hand-held) **computers**, and designed to simplify **interaction** with a **CRT**. It is not, however, a very powerful language.

batch: Any procedure in which all information is given to the **computer** before *any* operations are performed. Most computers used to be *batch processors*, in that one might turn in a **program** during the day, it would run with all the other programs turned in that night, and the results could be picked up the next morning. With most computers today, to batch means to type in, say, all the invoices for the day; the computer then checks, sorts, and bills them together, rather than dealing with them one at a time. Only very large programs or ones with a great deal of printout are left to run in the overnight mode.

baud: A measure of data-transmission rate, usually one **bit** per second. A teletype (**TTY**) usually prints at 110 baud, for example.

benchmark: A test in which a number of computers are compared in their performance of the same task. Their varying performances then allow comparisons to be made—something like a **computer** gunfight.

binary: Refers to a system of two and only two mutually exclusive components: left-right, up-down, yes-no, 1-0. A binary-number system is made up of only 1's and 0's. This method of data treatment is simple and reliable, but requires vast amounts of space to store some types of information, such as pictures. Videotape, which is an **analog** storage device, is much better at storing visual data.

binary chop: Not a sinister karate blow, but an efficient type of information search. If you have a list in numerical order, you could search for a number in the list basically in either of two ways: You could look at each number until you found the right one—simple, but inefficient. Or you could perform a binary chop: You check the number in the middle of the list first; this tells whether the number you want is in the first or second half of the list; then, you look at the number in the middle of *that* half, and so on, "chopping" the list in ever smaller parts until you find the number you want. Also termed *binary search*.

bit: Short for **binary digit**. The smallest piece

of a **binary** number; that is, a single 1 or 0. (See **byte**.)

block: A division of a **computer**'s memory, that has been divided up into equal areas. These blocks are numbered, and the computer keeps a "map" of which blocks are full, which are empty, and what type of data is associated with which block number. As with a neighborhood, knowing the block and **address** of a particular piece of data gets you to the data's location.

board: the plastic platform upon which **chips** are wired together to create a printed *circuit*. Modern boards are becoming ever smaller; a circuit that would have taken up an entire square foot of space ten years ago is currently a single chip the size of a pencil point.

bootstrap programs: Start-up procedures usually built into the computer by the manufacturer. When a **computer** is started up, it needs a **program** already in place to tell it how to retrieve further program information from its **memory**; this is the bootstrap program.

buffer: A temporary storage area. Different parts of a **computer** handle data at different rates, so buffers are used between fast and slow devices.

burn: A more recent version of **hardwired**. The **chips** on a circuit board are burned if they have been pre**programmed** in the factory to provide one and only one function. (See **PROM**.)

bus: A group of devices may draw their information from a single source, called a bus, which transmits data to and from the devices one at a time. The term originally referred to the actual electrical cable through which the electrical signals were transmitted; this meaning is also still in use.

byte: With early **computers**, a portion of some larger mass of information; the term has now become fairly standardized as referring to a piece of information exactly eight **bits** long—that is, a **binary** number eight digits long—and is essentially synonymous with **character**.

chaining: A large **program** can be broken up into independent parts, with only one part at a time actually taking up space in the **computer**'s **memory**. The different parts are said to be *linked*, and the overall technique is called chaining.

character: A single letter, number, punctuation mark, or mathematical symbol. The **ASCII** code is one method of translating digital characters (**binary** numbers) into *natural language* characters (letters, numbers, punctuation marks). **Computer** devices are rated according to how many characters they can transmit or receive in a second. (See **cps**.)

checksum: Despite the outstanding accuracy of modern **computer** technology, and regardless of manufacturer suggestions to the contrary, nothing, not even a computer, is perfect. A type of irksome error occurs when the data one part of the computer sends is not the data another part receives. One way of checking for transmission errors is to "sum" the data when it is sent, and again when it is received—hence, **checksum**. If the sums don't match, the data is re-sent, rechecked, and so on, until either the sums match or you decide there's a *real* problem. (See **line gremlin**.)

chip: A tiny wafer of silicon, or an equally tiny complete circuit. In the first **analog computers**, cogs were the machine's calculating heart. These were replaced in the 1940s by vacuum tubes, in the 1950s by transistors, and in the 1960s by chips. As of this writing (early 1981), Bell Laboratories has developed a single *bubble-memory chip*, one-tenth the size of a postage stamp, capable of storing 8½ million **bits** of information.

COBOL: Common Ordinary Business-Oriented Language (1959); through extensive use of **subroutines,** COBOL is fast at things **FORTRAN** finds tedious, such as the maintenance and display of data files. However, COBOL is a verbose **language**, and **programs**

written in it tend to be longer than with other languages.

code: The new form created whenever a **language** is condensed and translated into another form. **Computer** code can be **binary** numbers or any of the various levels of **programming languages**.

compiler: A program that takes a *high-level* **language**, such as **FORTRAN**, and translates it into **machine language**. The machine language version is often called a *save file* because it can be saved in **memory** and run over and over again without further recourse to the compiler.

computer: An information-processing system comprised of (at the minimum) a **CPU**, a **memory**, and **input/output** (**I/O**) devices. It is very trite but nonetheless true to say that a computer knows *only* what it is told, and does *only* what it is told to do. Computers are *not* smart. They *are* perfectly retentive (they never forget), and perfectly tireless (they never grow bored). These two qualities describe a device good for storing and moving about vast numbers of on/off electrical impulses in very reliable patterns—patterns the computer itself can modify (but again, only in ways it is *told* to do so). Computers, however, are not very good at being unpredictable or spontaneous, which, considering the apparent inadequacy of the traditional **Turing Test**, seems a fair description of truly *creative* intelligence—that is, the capacity not necessarily to remember or repeat, but to invent and surprise.

computer languages: Any of several numerical and alphabetical languages used to operate and communicate with electronic computers. **Digital computers** can operate only with **binary numbers**—1's and 0's—which tell them what circuits to turn on or off. Instructions written in binary numbers are called *machine language*. Early computers had their instructions entered one binary number at a time, which took months.

Groups of binary numbers that recurred often were given names, such as *JMP, LDA,* or *TXT*. These names constituted *assembly language*, and their development meant **programs** could now be entered in terms of weeks or days.

Next, sets of assembly language names were grouped together and given more English-like designations, such as *WRITE, READ, IF*, and so on. This was the beginning of today's *high-level languages*, of which the following nine are currently the most widely used: **Ada, ALGOL, APL, BASIC, COBOL, FORTRAN, LISP, PASCAL,** and **PL/I**. (See entry for each.)

Each computer language is good at some types of operations, but less good at others. Initially, computer experts expected to be able to design a single programming language that would work well in all possible applications, and would never need to be updated or modified; it has proved an impossible task to date.

LANGUAGE	INSTRUCTIONS
ALGOL	IF X < 0 THEN X: = − X
APL	X ← X $\ulcorner$ − X
BASIC	10 IF X = 0 THEN 30
	20 LET X = − X
	30 CONTINUE
COBOL	IF X IS LESS THAN 0 THEN MULTIPLY X BY − 1 GIVING X
FORTRAN	IF (X.LT.0) X = − X
LISP	(SETQ X(MAX X(MINUS x)))
PASCAL	IF X < 0 THEN X: = − X
PL/I	X: = MAX(X, − X)

(Source: Jerome A. Feldman)

As is true of almost any system, programming languages are combinations of compromises between usability, efficiency, and flexibility. FORTRAN is good at calculating complex mathematical quantities, but a regular Neanderthal at displaying those quantities on a **CRT**. COBOL makes the display of quantities easy, but takes two or three times as many statements to do the calculations. APL is super-shorthand, but that means a person has to know its peculiar shorthand to use it.

Actually, such specialization has worked to programmers' advantage, for now there are at least twenty widely used high-level languages to choose from for solving a given task. The table on page 191 shows how some of these languages would perform a similar operation. The problem is to change a number, X, from its positive value to an unsigned, or absolute, equivalent.

conversational: Refers to either a **CRT**, a **program**, or an entire **computer** system designed to make communication with the machine easier for the user. The computer "responds" to the user's **inputs** as they are entered, and may also ask questions of the user. These questions are short and, wherever possible, of the yes-no variety, which makes it nearly impossible for the system to respond with "does not compute." This is also what is meant when a system is referred to as *user-oriented*. A perfect example of a conversational system is the computerized banking service offered by major banks today.

conversion error: All data, including fractions, must be stored in terms of **binary** numbers—which aren't good at representing certain fractions or percentages. In converting between base 10 (our number system) and base 2 (binary number system), errors can occur. (Yes, it *is* necessary to check your computerized bank statement.)

core: The primary, nonremovable **memory** of a **computer**. The name is derived from early computer memories made of thousands of doughnut-shaped pieces of magnetic material strung along conducting wires. Core memories are rated according to their storage capacity: A core of 32**k bytes** is capable of storing 32,000 individual **characters**, or 16,000 two-character **words**.

cps: characters per second. The speed of **output** devices is rated according to how many **characters**—letters or numbers—they can print per second.

CPU: Central processing unit; the guts of a **computer**, where the computing and instruction-modification actually occurs, as distinct from its **memory** and **peripherals**.

CRT: Cathode ray tube, also called **terminal** or **video peripheral**; basically the same device as a television tube, used to provide a visual display of **input**, data, and other **output**.

cursor: A flashing line or illuminated block on a **CRT** that indicates, like a bouncing ball, just which word you're at.

cybernetics: The study of communications between the human brain and nervous system. It has now come to stand for all efforts aimed at getting electronic devices to function like organic ones—anything from the design of automatically controlled factories to complex computer **programs** relating to large-scale social problems.

cylinders: The areas of information on a **disc** storage device, equal to the number of recordlike grooves, or *tracks*, on the disc.

d/a converter: A device which converts **digital** information to **analog** form. Performs the opposite function of what an **a/d converter** does. A d/a is required so that a computer can drive a motor, produce speech, operate devices, etc., in the "real world."

data base: The amount and type of information necessary for a given **applications program**; the raw information to be stored and/or manipulated by the computer. Business systems are designed to make the entry and maintenance of data bases—such as names, addresses, prices, sales records, credit files—as simple as possible.

decision tree: A graphic representation of the decisions a **computer** has to make during a given **program**. At each *branch* in the tree, the program performs a *test,* or comparison, between two pieces of data, and then proceeds in one direction or the other depending upon the results of the test. There are only two directions possible at each step because a computer can only ask yes-no questions.

dedicated: Assigned to one and only one function. All **burned chips** are dedicated. Larger devices (such as printers, **CRT**s) are dedicated if they deal primarily with only one type of information, such as paychecks or monthly reports.

destructive read: The operation of reading data and by reading, destroying it. Early magnetic **core memories** would be erased every time data was retrieved from them, necessitating the rewriting of the data each time it was used.

diagnostic: This term was taken outright from the medical profession. Certain **compilers** will check through your **high-level language program** and diagnose problems with it, giving fairly specific error messages about where you've put in too many commas, left out a necessary number, and so on. Some diagnostic messages can get pretty insulting—no one likes to be told "GO TO ERROR" by a machine.

digital: Referring to **computer**-based on off/on electrical impulses, which are intrepreted by the computer as 0's and 1's, respectively. Most modern computers are digital machines.

disc: A device like a phonograph record, except that the information it stores is retrieved by *magnetized heads* instead of a stylus. Discs are rated according to their storage capacity, usually in **bytes**. A 5 *megabyte disc* could store one name 5 million letters long. (See **memory, virtual**.)

distributed: Referring to several **computers** in different locations—separate plants, cities, or even countries—that may feed data to a central computer, which stores and processes the gathered information. This is called a distributed system.

documentation: As an architect creates and refers to blueprints to design a physical structure, a **programmer** creates and refers to flow charts and written versions of his **programs**, called documentation, to design **computer** operations. The worse the documentation, the greater the motivation to "start from scratch" when a program needs improvement.

down: Inoperative. Not always a euphemism for "broken," as **computer** systems periodically need to be *taken down*—removed from service—for maintenance and upgrading of their circuitry and **software**.

drive: The equipment that contains and runs a **disc**, roughly equivalent to a phonograph.

drum: Memories for older, large **computers**. These often large magnetic drums were kept spinning constantly, much as magnetic **discs** are today. In principle and design, they were remarkably similar to the first drum phonograph records shown at the Paris Exposition of 1900.

dumb terminal: This is a **CRT** without any added equipment or options, one that simply transmits data to and from a **CPU**. (See **intelligent terminal**.)

dump: A surprisingly literal term, referring to the printout of *all* the information currently in a **computer**'s **core memory**.

EBCDIC: Extended Binary Coded Decimal Interchange Code, pronounced EB-see-dick; IBM's equivalent of **ASCII**.

EDP: Electronic data processing. The use of **computers** to automate accounting systems, files, and other information storage and retrieval, especially in a business context. Many businesses no longer have head accountants, but instead call them *EDP chiefs*.

exception report: Reports are often used to tell people what items of information *don't* conform to specifications or are, in some way, exceptional. Rather than riffling through yards of reports looking for these exceptions, we can ask a *computer program* to report *only* the exceptions, or to report them separately. The ease with which computers can shuffle and reshuffle information to be reported is one of their greatest assets.

file: *Any* related and similar information given a name and stored together, such as lists of addresses, the **binary** code for a **program**, even the computer's index of what files it has in its **memory**. Files are referred to constantly in **computer** literature: *file maintenance, data files, file structure.* How efficiently a **high-level language** searches and maintains files is an indicator of its popularity. (See **record**.)

firmware: Somewhere between **hardware** and **software**; devices that are pre**programmed** in the factory—but, unlike **burned chips**, can be reprogrammed later on to fulfill different functions. The idea is to make some chips hard enough that they do routine tasks automatically, but soft enough that what they do can be altered.

flag: The flag up on your mailbox indicates your mail is in; flag down means it hasn't arrived yet. Flags are used in **programming** in the same way: Set to 1, a flag indicates an event has occurred; set to 0, that it hasn't.

flip-flop: Specifically, a circuit which can store one **bit** of information—that is, a "0" or a "1" —by the absence or presence of an electrical current. The term has worked its way even into our political lexicon, while retaining its original meaning, that is, a complete reverse of direction, either of foreign policy or electrical current. Flip-flops were the names given to individual transistors in "2nd-generation" **computers**.

floppy: Also **floppy disc**, **FD**. A soft **disc** that can be used with **micro-computers**, is about the size of a 45 rpm record, and can store up to 500k **bytes** of information (500,000 **characters**). There are now, of course, *micro-floppies*. (See **micro**.)

format: Before a line of data can be printed out by a **computer**, it must be formatted, which means the **program** producing the informa-

tion must tell the computer whether it will be printing letters, symbols, numbers—and, if numbers, whether they have a decimal point or not—where on the page to print them, and so on. To do such things in **FORTRAN** is tedious, which was a major motivation for the development of **COBOL** and **PL/I**. (See **computer languages**.)

FORTRAN: FORmula TRANslator (1954); one of the oldest and most common **high-level languages**, and the first that allowed people who weren't- experts with *computer hardware* to **program** computers. Used largely in scientific research, FORTRAN is not adept at displaying information, although newer versions of the language are more compact and manageable. There's a good deal of nostalgia connected with this language, and programmers who use it tend to be forgiving of its shortcomings.

garbage: Data that is useless for all practical purposes, data the **computer** has somehow garbled beyond all recognition, or that is too old, too inaccurate, or too something to be worth keeping around any longer. Some **programs** are written exclusively to do *garbage collection,* thus freeing up **memory** space.

gate: A device (occasionally, a **logic** function) that allows the passage of data only when the gate's specific criteria are met. An **AND** *gate* opens *only* for identical data, an **OR** *gate only* for any occurrence of a 1, for example. By wiring various gates together, fairly complex logic operations can be carried out.

handshaking: When a **computer** sends one line of data and asks the receiving machine if the line was received intact before sending another line. Like **checksum**, handshaking (also called **data OK**?) is a technique for guarding against data **transmission errors**. The sending machine gets back either a *data OK* or a *resend* signal. This query/response goes on until all the data has been successfully transmitted.

hardware: The physical components of a machine—**chips**, **drives**, circuitry, the lights and switches, nuts and bolts. The ideal **computer** is one whose hardware automatically takes care of tedious and/or frequently needed tasks, but is flexible enough to be easily modified, repaired, or upgraded. (See **firmware**.)

hardwired: Refers to a function of a device built into the physical components of the system, without need to be **programmed**. A human being's potential for creativity, like his autonomic functions, is hardwired, whereas what he does with the capacity is considered part of his **software**.

high-level language: A **computer language** which resembles English (or any other "natural language"), and can thus be employed more readily by the average computer user.

IC: Integrated circuit. Computer circuits which are usually drawn on materials the size of a blackboard, photographically reduced, then chemically etched on **chips** of silicon the size of pencil points. These ICs are capable of performing all the functions it used to require an entire computer to do.

input: The collective name for all the data that goes into a **computer**, a computer **program**, or an entire computer system. Input is that which the computer, program, or system operates upon.

integer: A quantity that can change only by whole units. For instance, in an integer number system, there is no 1½; we must go 1-2-3-4. Fractional amounts are rounded off to the closest nonfractional number. Integer systems are the source for the word *quantum,* an increasingly popular all-purpose term for describing a whole unit of just about anything.

intelligent terminal: CRTs that have tiny **computers** built into them, and store and manipulate information without using the main computer's time. They are essentially **microcomputers** with their own CRTs.

interactive: Having the capacity for "conversation" between operator and **computer**. (See **conversational**.)

interface: Devices or systems that cannot communicate directly with each other must be connected to an interface, which translates back and forth between them. The United Nations is political interface; a **CRT** or keyboard is an interface between human and **computer**.

interrupt: Computers execute **programs** according to the priority of the received requests. There are low- and high-priority jobs. When a **CPU** is performing a low-priority task and a higher-priority request comes in, the low-priority job is stopped by an interrupt and resumed after the new job is completed.

I/O: Input/output. Either devices or **programs** that handle gathering data from and returning it to the environment outside the **computer** (that is, to the human user or a typed printout or the like).

iteration: The repetition of some task over and over again with one aspect of the task changing gradually. (See **loop**.)

job: The collective name for a **program** and whatever ancillary information the program needs to run, such as lists of names, the results of past calculations, **libraries**, or the like.

jump: Also **go to**. A **programming** command that ends one set of instructions and tells the **computer** to move to a new location in the **program** and start again—usually, moving over (*jumping*) a section of instructions or data not applicable at that time.

K: Short for **kilo**, or one thousand.

languages: See **computer languages**.

library: A collection, sometimes **hardwired**, of functions that the computer refers to frequently but doesn't need continually in its **memory**.

light pens: Light-sensitive rods plugged into a **computer** that transmit signals when they are held against particular spots on a **CRT**. They are used extensively in computer graphics.

line gremlin: When data is transmitted across a connecting wire, or *line,* parts of it sometimes turn up missing—lost to noise or signal drift, or, when there's no other handy explanation, line gremlins.

LISP: LISt Processor (1956); a **language** used largely in work with **artificial intelligence**, LISP seems to thrive on parentheses. This is because the language relies heavily on **looping** through instructions repeatedly whenever possible. The idea behind LISP was that a **programming language** could be syntactically structured with a few hard-and-fast rules that are simply recombined or repeated to handle more complex rules. (LISP *could* mean *L*anguage of *I*nterminable *S*equential *P*arentheses.)

local: Said of a **CRT** ("It's on **local**") if it is not sending to and receiving from the **CPU**, but is instead operating purely as a visual typewriter.

logic: A **computer program** operates through a series of logic decisions. "IF A = B GO TO 1" is a *logic statement* that orders the computer to (1) compare the values of *A and B* and, (2) if they are the same (the statement is then said to be true) to proceed to a statement in the program labeled '1', or (3) if they are not the same (the statement is false) the program goes to the next sequential statement. The logic of a program must be correct for the program to perform its defined task.

loop: A series of instructions in a **program** that are repeated—or *looped through*—until a certain condition is met. For instance:

```
10    I = 1
20    IF I = 101, GO TO 60
30    PRINT I
40    I = I + 1
50    GO TO 20
60    STOP
```

This loop (written in **BASIC**) would print out the number series 1–100, but saves the considerable space and tedium required to write one hundred print instructions. If a loop has a **bug** somewhere, the computer can become trapped, endlessly repeating a series of instructions until it is manually stopped. Making loops as efficient and flexible as possible is a key element in good computer **programming**.

machine language: See **computer languages**.

macro: As in "macrobiotic" or "macrocosm," refers to something applying to an *entire* system. A *macro instruction* might be one that tells a **program** to indent *all* its statements six spaces. Macro can also refer to one instruction that stands for an entire group of **assembly language** instructions, thus saving the time of writing them out individually.

main frame: Originally, the designation of the **CPU** of large **computer** systems. Main frame computers *then* came to mean computers of a certain **core memory** capacity, usually greater than 132**k bytes**. *Now* main frame often means the CPU of a large **time-sharing** system—but not always.

mega: Shorthand for one million.

memory: The data storage area within a **computer** system. Developments in ever smaller, faster, more efficient computer memories have been largely responsible for the startling reduction in computer size and cost. The ideal computer memory is one that stores everything put into it forever, and can retrieve any of it instantly. Short of such perfection, computer memories are arranged hierarchically into *primary* and *virtual* (or secondary) *memories*.

The *primary* (or *core*) *memory* stores the **program** currently running, instructions for retrieving information from other parts of memory, numbers needed to perform ongoing calculations, and so on. However, it would be inefficient and costly to store everything this way.

Virtual memories (meaning memories that aren't "really" memory for they aren't necessarily always accessible) store the greater bulk of information, copies of programs not currently running, reference material, etc. However, it would be too slow to store everything this way. So, most computer systems are a mix, with a primary memory of somewhere under 500**k bytes**, and several virtual memory devices with an overall storage capacity that is limited only by the money available to buy them. Below are different types of memories, with the advantages and common uses:

1. *Bubble memory:* In bubble memories, magnetized bubbles replace the magnetized **chips** of older core memories. The trick in developing them was to make a material pure enough that individual bubbles did not become distorted or lost. Such memories pack tremendous amounts of information into very small spaces, and are used extensively in the latest computer systems, as part of their primary memory.

2. *Disc memory:* **Discs** are the most efficient secondary memory devices, able to store tens of millions of bytes per fourteen-inch disc. They take longer to retrieve information from than core memories, but cost far less per byte than primary memories. The latest discs are written to and read from by laser beams, which decreases the retrieval time somewhat.

3. *Magnetic tape:* Magnetized tape has been around quite some time as an information storage device for tape recorders—but in an application that was **analog**, not **digital**. Magnetic tapes don't store as much information per inch as discs, are harder to find information on, and more costly and difficult to store properly. However, bulk information that is referenced rarely can be stored on "mag tape," and then be made available to the computer only when it is needed.

4. *Punched cards:* Punched cards, though fast disappearing from the world of business computers, are still used by large university facilities—or anyone else who once invested heavily in *card readers, card punch* machines, and other related equipment.

5. *Paper tape:* Imagine you took a roll from a player piano and trimmed it down to perhaps an inch wide and then, instead of recording on the roll instructions as to what keys to activate, you punched a hole for each 1, and did *not* punch a hole for each 0 you wished to enter into the computer. Such are (or were) paper tape memories.

micro: *Micro* originally meant that class of **computer** that used **floppy discs** and could fit on a desk—what are now selling as "home **computers**." *These* computers threaten to become the **main frames** of the future, what with hand-held programmables now hitting the market.

Micro can also refer to a miniature computer within a computer or **CRT** that governs part of the larger device's operations. *Microprogramming* is that branch of computer **programming** responsible for the instructions inside these *microprocessors,* and involves not only putting instructions into the *microdevices,* but also understanding how to interchange them to achieve various functions.

mini: At first, a *minicomputer* was somewhere between a **main frame** and a **micro**—though no one was too sure just where. These days, references to computers as mini, micro, and the like are largely meaningless, and many computer users are calling for the establishment of a standardized scale to rate **computers** purely by their capabilities and not their size.

object program: The version of a **program** the **computer** actually uses, written in **machine language**, as distinct from the *source program,* which is in the original **high-level language**, such as **FORTRAN** or **COBOL**.

OCR: Optical character recognition; using visual information as **input**. Many cash registers in grocery stores now read the product code in the form of little groups of black lines on the packages (called *bar graphics*) and thus automatically keep track of goods sold, inventory, and so on.)

octal: Employing a *base 8* number system. "*Base x*" means that *x* takes the place of 10 in our regular (*base 10* or decimal) number system. Thus, in base 10 we count 1–9, then put a mark in the next place column to the left— the 10's column. In *base 4*, say, we count 1–3, *then* write 10, which would be a 1 in the 4's column, or 4. Base 8 or octal would write the first twenty **integers** as follows:

Decimal (base 10)	Octal (base 8)
1	1
2	2
3	3
4	4
5	5
6	6
7	7
8	10
9	11
10	12
11	13
12	14
13	15
14	16
15	17
16	20
17	21

What's so special about base 8? If **binary** numbers are divided into groups of three digits, and the decimal equivalent of each group is written, the new digits equal the original number in octal. Thus, instead of storing three binary digits, we can store a single-digit octal equivalent. For instance, the decimal number 62 is written in binary 111110. Then:

binary place value	32 16 8	4 2 1
binary number	1 1 1	1 1 0
decimal equivalent of each binary group	7	6
octal place values	8	1

Thus we have a 7 in the 8's place, for $7 \times 8 = 56$, plus 6 in the 1's place, for $6 \times 1 = 6$,

and $56 + 6 = 62$. Octal number systems are central to modern **computer** operations.

off-line: Refers to **programs** that are run in a **batch** mode. A **computer** system is off-line if all its programs are entered in a batch mode.

on-line: Refers to a **computer** system when and if you can communicate with it and run programs on it with almost immediate response. **Time-sharing** systems are on-line. (See **TAT**.)

operating systems: The commercial **programs** that come with a **computer**, and are responsible for running its various devices, giving access to its **memory** and **registers**, and generally governing its operations. These programs are distinct from the ones a **programmer** writes in **FORTRAN**, **COBOL**, or other **high-level languages**.

OR: A **logic** comparison operation, wherein a 1 is produced if *either* of the compared data is a 1.

output: Whatever results from data manipulations, usually fed to the world through one or more output devices, such as a printer, a **CRT**, or a plotter.

pack: Another clever way of squeezing more storage capacity out of a **computer**'s **memory**. Several **characters** can be run through a formula that reduces, or packs, them into a single character, thus requiring a single **storage** space. The data must be *unpacked* to be used, however, and running data in and out of *packing routines* can be irksome. (Even with computers, there is no free lunch.)

parity checking: An error-detection technique, in which an extra **bit**, a 1 or a 0, is attached to a string of data to make the total number of 1's in the data *even*. The receiving end adds up the 1's in the sent data, and if the total isn't even, a **line gremlin** is loose, and the data must be re-sent.

PASCAL: A computer language developed in 1971 in which instructions appear like sentences, making concepts as simple and clear as possible. PASCAL is a fast-growing favorite among home **computer** users. The name derives from Blaise Pascal, French philosopher-mathematician and the inventor, in 1642, of a mechanical "cash register." Used originally with systems analysis, the language has also become widely associated with education and teaching machines.

patch: To tack on a set of instructions somewhere into a **program**—sometimes even while the program is running—just to make things work "for now." Patches are *meant* to be temporary.

peripherals: Those ancillary devices that, if disconnected from the **CPU**, would not stop a **computer**'s operation. **Output** devices are typically peripherals, as are some **virtual memory** devices.

PL/I: Programming Language I (1964). Designed to update and streamline **FORTRAN**, PL/I can also do many things other **languages** specialize in. PL/I, like **COBOL**, makes extensive use of **subroutines** that a **programmer** need not write or worry about, but takes some time to learn. A very powerful language, popular with **computer** programmers.

pointer: Imagine that you have a list of 10,000 items, and that each item is a page of text. You could look through all 10,000 every time you wanted to find a particular page. Or you could create a summary of what was on each page and keep it, along with the page number it referred to, somewhere else. Each summation would then be a pointer to where the full page could be found. Indexes of books are *pointer files*. Thus, **computer files** that contain a large volume of data will use a pointer file to make referencing and sorting easier. Certain types of blocks of information store, as their last piece of data, a pointer to where the next block can be found.

processor: See **CPU**.

program: The detailed sets of instructions that direct a computer to accomplish specific tasks. Simple and repetitive functions are orchestrated by the **hardwired** programs placed in the equipment in the factory. More complex combinations of functions follow **operating system** programs, which are invoked in even bigger groups of instructions by **high-level** programs written in **FORTRAN**, **COBOL**, etc.

programming: The task of orchestrating the way a **computer** will go about solving a problem. Any problem to be solved by a computer must first be subjectable to a formula: Data will be **input**, operations will be performed upon it, and results will be **output**. Next, just what is to be input and output must be defined—and here is where compromises must be made between the desire to input "everything relevant," and the realistic time available for input operations. The programmer must then outline the computer solution in *sequential steps,* defining exactly what decisions the computer will need to make. It is important at this stage to consider *all* the possibilities of a program, so that an unexpected result farther along does not invalidate all the planning done before.

Once the problem has been laid out in terms of input-operations-output, the programmer begins actually writing the task in some **language**. Since different languages are good at different things, he must decide what is the most crucial aspect of the solution, and which language handles that aspect most effectively. While writing the program, he is also interested in making it flexible, so that modification and expansion will be as simple as possible.

Once the program has been written, the programmer is responsible for testing it in all conceivable conditions—and then making the inevitable adjustments such testing brings to light as necessary (this is known as *debugging* a program).

Finally, the programmer has to **document** just how the program does whatever it does —so that, should he get hit by a truck or defect to the Russians the next day, his replacement can deal with the program he has established.

PROM: Programmed read-only memory; A **chip** that has its own set of **hardwired** instructions. PROMs are used extensively in **intelligent terminals** and **microcomputers** to do many of the routine operations. The latest such chips can, under certain conditions, be erased and re**programmed** by their users.

RAM: Random access memory. A method of storing information that allows you to get directly to any data anywhere anytime you want it. In contrast, some computer **memories**, such as the older **drum memories**, were like tape recorders when it came to retrieving information—you had to wind through the entire memory in sequence until you came to the spot you wanted.

real time: Refers to **computers** that operate in response to "real-world" events that are occurring at the same time the computer is processing the information. For example, rocket-guidance controls, airline reservation computers, even some banking computers all perform functions in real time.

reentrant: Refers to a task or subroutine available to many **programs** at the same time, so that multiple copies of it do not have to be stored in **memory**. Reentrant programs are not, however, subject to modification by any of the programs using them.

record: Usually means a single line of data in a **file**. When you type a line of information into a **computer** and then hit the carriage return, this tells the computer you have entered one record of data.

register: A specially assigned section of **core memory** to which data is transferred temporarily to be manipulated. It is, therefore, something like a **buffer**. Today's **computers** have several registers, which are the most readily accessible parts of memory, and thus putting information in and getting data out of a register occurs faster than with any other part of memory.

remote: A transmitting device (such as a telephone) that sends data to a **computer** but is separated from it physically.

ROM: Read-only memory; a **chip** or collection of chips that contain information that can be retrieved, but not erased or changed.

run-time: Any operation that is performed only when a **program** is running—such as looking up information in a table, or calling up a **library** function—is called a run-time operation. **High-level languages** require *run-time interpreters* in order to interact with whatever system they are running on; the interpreters differ according to the equipment.

simulation: The calculation or forecasting of the events, properties, or operation of a system—made by using a theoretical model of that system. Contrary to the myth, a **computer** is not capable of doing anything humans can't do—given enough people, and enough time. Although it is possible to give a large group of people all the data regarding, say, the gradual erosion of the Atlantic Coast beaches, and then ask them to extrapolate the changes in beach structure over the next hundred years, it might take them many years to do it. A computer could produce the same simulation of such ecological processes in probably a thousandth the time, and with far greater accuracy. The computer's simulation would also be more flexible, for you could ask it to vary the yearly average temperatures—or any of the other contributing factors—and then see, in a matter of minutes, just how this change affected the extrapolated system. Computer simulations have worked their way into nearly every field, from political science games (such as "Diplomat") to psycholinguistic models of speech retention, to the design of the space shuttle.

software: Originally referred to the **programs** of a **computer** system, and thus to an abstract rather than a physical construct. However, with **PROMs** and **microprocessors** and **mi-**

croprogramming and firmware, software has become an increasingly "softer" term. Essentially, software is that which instructs the hardware as to how to perform.

source file: The version of a program written in its original language: FORTRAN, COBOL, et al. Source files are important to protect because changes in a program must be made to its source file, which is then retranslated by the compiler into a new object program. If the source file is lost, it *cannot* be reconstructed from the object program.

stack: A list of tasks the computer has to do to execute a given program. The stack tells the computer what to do next according to the LIFO rule—whatever is on top of the stack is dealt with first, and so on down. Organizing tasks this way simplifies some of the computer's decisions, as it can only have access to whatever is on top of the stack.

storage: The entering of data on any level of a computer's memory (primary, secondary). The *storage capacity* of a system tells you how much data it has available *at any one time*. For instance, if a computer system has a core of 62k bytes, and is attached to a disc drive with a five megabyte disc, it has essentially 5,064,000 characters of memory available—although, because other information may be stored on discs that are not currently in the disc drive, the computer has a virtual memory that is unlimited.

structured programming: See top-down.

subroutine: Programs that perform routine or repetitive tasks. Let's say you have a computerized billing system where various dates have to be entered with billing information. Part of the system is responsible for checking these dates to make sure that February 31st is not accepted as a valid date. Although there are probably different programs for different parts of the billing system, they probably all will use the same subroutine to check dates, because the operation is the same regardless of where the data came from. The important idea is that whichever program uses a subroutine, the subroutine performs the same task as it would for any other program.

swap: A programming technique that allows the computer to stop one program in the middle, store it on a disc, run some other program, and, when that one is concluded, restore the original program back into core memory.

TAT: Turn-around time; the time that elapses between the time a program is delivered to the computer (in batch systems) or the computer is told to run a program (in an on-line system), and the time you actually get your results. TATs have become steadily smaller (i.e., faster) since 1955.

terminal: Any device by which one communicates with a computer; now virtually synonymous with CRT.

time-sharing: When several CRTs communicate with a single computer system, and are set up in such a way that any or all of them can be on-line at any one time. Actually, the computer is not paying attention to any more than one CRT at any one instant, but the way in which the CPU juggles demands upon it creates the illusion of responding to all the CRTs simultaneously. Time-sharing systems are expensive to set up, but nonetheless economical to run, and allow a single computer system to be distributed throughout a building, a city, or across the country.

top-down: Programs used to be written in the *bottom-up* method, where first the most general aspects of a task were flow-charted, and only then were the specifics filled in. Now, top-down programming dictates that the specifics are laid out in pseudo-English, even describing charts and *output formats*, and *then* the flow-charting is begun. Such an approach allows the programmer to check that his program works correctly at every step in its development. It also provides for relatively rapid translation from one *high-level language* to another.

TTY: Teletype, a typewriter **peripheral** without a **CRT**.

Turing Test: A traditional method of deciding whether an entity is really intelligent. The entity to be tested is placed in one room, and a person in another room. The two rooms communicate only through a **TTY** or a **CRT**. If, after a given interval, the person is unable to say with certainty that the entity he's been conversing with is *not* intelligent, then the entity is considered to be intelligent—whether it is a **computer** (see **artificial intelligence**), or a chimpanzee, or any other entity that can be **programmed**/trained/encouraged to strike typewriter keys. Actually, the Turing Test is a simple way of dealing with the frustration of realizing we are unable to describe what it is that makes human beings special, and recent "tricky" computer **programs** seem to indicate that the Turing Test is woefully inadequate.

up: The opposite of **down;** working, running, operating. (Who said computer terminology was complex?)

upward compatible: Equipment or **programs** designed to be usable with versions to come later, or that have gone before. When the business and educational communities first showed enthusiasm for **computer** systems, it was immediately recognized that, as newer versions of **hardware** and **software** became available, they would have to fit with whatever versions were already out in the field to be commercially successful. Thus upward compatibility is a major selling point of modern computer systems.

VDT: Video display terminal. See **CRT**.

word: The number of **bits** a particular **computer** treats as storable in a single **memory** location. It used to be the case that **mainframe** computers were those that used 32-bit words, **minis** those that used 16-bit words, and **micros** 8-bit words. **Storage** capacity is sometimes rated in words rather than **bytes**, so you have to know how many bytes the system treats as a single word to know what *word capacity* translates into. For instance, a minicomputer may have 16-bit words; since there are 8 bits to a byte, that means each word is two bytes, or two **characters**.

word processor: Very popular recent arrivals on the office-**computer** scene, essentially **microcomputers programmed** to do text editing on letters, memos, or any other typed text. The idea is that nothing is actually printed on paper until all the editing and corrections have been made in the text as it is displayed on a **CRT**. They are also often capable of making copies, printing mailing labels, **interfacing** with typesetting equipment, and, by the time this description is published, probably several hundred other things.

IV

GOVERNMENT

[15]

Bureaucratese

If thought corrupts language, language also corrupts thought.
—GEORGE ORWELL

Anyone who has had the misfortune to be involved with a state, federal, or municipal bureaucracy knows that there is a variation of the English language used almost exclusively in those realms. Call it Officialese, Government Jargon, Doubletalk, or just Bureaucratese —it is a distinct sublanguage which appears in all government reports, regulations, proposals, studies, and statements. While the untutored individual may react to such works with confusion and frustration, the person fluent in Bureaucratese will understand immediately and fully what (if anything) is being said.

Thus, when a government report states that "the agency is **parameterizing viable** resource **utilization strategies** within the projected personnel/funding **matrix**," the adept comprehends that they're just figuring out what they can do this year with the staff and money they expect to get. Or, when "Phase-two **feasibility studies** indicate that current programs have **impacted** suboptimally upon quality of housing stock in **catchment areas**," the insider knows that the housing program has bombed, and badly.

The language of government agencies has several distinctive characteristics: the use of polysyllablisms and Latinate words whenever possible (**utilization** for use, **implementation** for doing); the use of special government terms and coinages (**Title** IX, **Section** 302, **deinstitutionalization**); the rampant application of abbreviations and acronyms (HUD, CETA, UDAG, LEAA); and the time-honored devices of euphemism, convolution, and ambiguity. This is a style of language that, although impenetrable on first encounter, can be easily learned, and even reproduced, by anyone who acquires the basic vocabulary of Bureaucratese (as detailed in the section that follows) and understands the real purpose of its use.

A statement such as *"Cost-benefit analysis* of **outreach** services indicates that streamlining of field personnel **utilization** could be effected without significant loss of client participation" should be seen not as an imprecise, or ineffectual, use of the English language, but rather as a baroque masterpiece of Intentional Bureaucratese. It has a reassuringly professional tone, is authoritatively multisyllabic, includes several of the current buzzwords, and brilliantly *serves its purpose.* While the average person might translate it into a simple "They're just not getting anything *done* out there!" such crassly adolescent honesty would violate the most cardinal of bureaucratic principles—**CYA**, short for cover your ass. The real purpose of the original statement is to ensure that no one will take the blame for the failure of the outreach program; in fact, the agency head will probably be commended for his businesslike efficiency in conducting the cost-benefit analysis and for (putatively) streamlining his operation.

Bureaucratic language must be viewed, in other words, in light of the interests that it is serving. Both agencies and individuals within them consciously "**structure** the dissemination of information in accordance with **prioritized communications** objectives"—which is to say, they tell you only what they want you to know. Which may be little indeed. The notion of effective language use as the clearest and most direct possible communication of facts and ideas has become—as the bureaucrats would say—**inoperative**. After all, how could you expect to **interface infrastructural** instability, limited-access validation review procedures, **end-user feedback/accountability** matrices, and not eventuate a **scenario** of maximized disinformation?

Herewith, a verbal guide to the world of government agencies and programs—a 71-word vocabulary lesson in basic Bureaucratese.

A Pentagonese Sampler

While the American military establishment has hundreds of specialized terms, abbreviations, and acronyms, which would be impossible to reproduce here in their entirety, the following "sampler" should suffice to provide both some of the most current, and the most revealing, examples. 🍎

ABM: Antiballistic missile.
accidental delivery of ordnance equipment:
Shelling our own guys.
air support: Bombing.

all-out strategic exchange: World War III.
BMEWS: Ballistic missile early warning system.
CBW: Chemical and biological warfare (or **weapons**).

CEP: Circle of error probable; a bomb accuracy measure.

civilian irregular defense soldier: A mercenary.

combat emplacement evacuator: A shovel.

conventional weapons: Everything besides nuclear bombs and **CBW**; these weapons cause conventional deaths.

ECCM: Electronic counter-counter measures.

G and C: Guidance and control.

I and L: Installations and logistics.

ICBM: Intercontinental ballistic missile, with a range of over 3,000 miles.

integrated battlefield: Not one with soldiers of all races, but one with **conventional, CBW,** and nuclear weapons being employed separately or in combination.

JCS: Joint Chiefs of Staff.

limited nuclear war: "You drop just one, we'll drop just one, okay?"

M.A.D.: Mutually Assured Destruction; supposedly a "credible deterrent" to nuclear war.

MBFR: Mutual and balanced force reductions.

MIRV: Multiple independently targeted reentry vehicles. ("Vehicles" are bombs.)

MX missile: Abbreviation for "missile—experimental," currently used to refer to an advanced **ICBM** to be deployed through a multiple protective shelter system (*MPS*), in which 200 missiles will be shifted among 4600 different shelters to preclude destruction by an enemy "counterforce" attack.

NORAD: North American Air Defense Command.

PONAST: Postnuclear attack study.

preemptive strike: Also **protective reaction.** Starting a war; hitting 'em first.

RPV: Remotely piloted vehicles.

SAC: The **Strategic Air Command.**

SAM: Surface-to-air missile.

security assistance: Shipments of arms to other countries.

WIMEX: Easy form of **WWMCCS,** the **World-Wide Military Command and Control System.**

BASIC BUREAUCRATESE

access: Verb, to gain access to, or to develop advantageous relations with. (*Access the private sector:* Get the big companies on our side.)

accountability: Maintenance of the illusion of responsibility and effectiveness. (See **CYA.**)

catchment area: A place where agency services are provided. ("Data base in designated **catchment area** is at present insufficient to provide meaningful evaluation **parameters.**" Translation: "We haven't the slightest idea what's going on out there!")

closely examining: Also, **actively considering, carefully investigating.** This means that your proposal (or complaint, or inquiry, or request) has been received and someone without any power to act on it may respond to you in three to six months—or may not.

communication: Virtually any talking, writing, or entertainment may be elevated by this term. (*In-depth communication:* A long phone call.)

community: 1. People, the public; any place that people live. (*Community-based programs* have their facilities located within cities and towns, as distinct from physically and socially separated institutions such as prisons and mental health facilities.)

2. Defined group; clique. The term takes on this entirely opposite meaning when referring to clearly nonpublic governmental groups: the *intelligence community* (the CIA and related organizations); the *defense community* (the military establishment and related industries); and so on.

consulting: Advising, planning, recommending, analyzing of government programs by outside experts, for scandalously high fees.

consumer demand analysis: Finding out what people want.

cost-effectiveness: The value of a program, product, or agency for dollars expended. The cost-effectiveness of anything is of course determined through a costly *cost-benefit analysis.*

culturally deprived environment: A slum.

CYA: Cover your ass, the quintessential bureaucratic precept. Whatever else a government worker does, he or she must ensure that blame for a program failure, political defeat, or other fiasco is shifted elsewhere, diffused, or otherwise defused.

defunded: Having had funding withdrawn—the ultimate bureaucratic disaster.

deinstitutionalization: The process of reducing the number of persons isolated from society in mental health, corrections, and other state institutional facilities, by the development of halfway houses, group homes, community residences, and other **community-based** services.

development: That stage of a program or **project** after **research** and planning but before **implementation**. A vague term used to euphemize large periods of time in which nothing happens.

economically disadvantaged: Poor.

end-users: The people who are the ultimate recipients of the benefits of a government program.

excluding irrelevant documents: Shredding damaging reports and files.

facilitate: To make easier, to coordinate. ("We've hired a **consultant** to **facilitate** the decision-making process.")

feasibility study: An incredibly expensive research study (six figures are not uncommon), which concludes with a recommendation to undertake the proposed project—or to conduct more research.

feedback: Communication to an agency about its programs; or any other response, usually informal. ("The **feedback** we've been getting from the HUD people is that the proposal won't go through without some changes.")

functional: Literally meaning workable, practical, useful, this is a favorite because it can precede any noun or nominal phrase with impunity—i.e., without any additional meaning whatsoever. Thus, *functional development* **strategy**, **functional prioritization**, etc.

hard funding: Regularly budgeted monies that can be counted on (agency performance notwithstanding).

impact: Verb, to affect or influence. ("Vocational skills training **project** has **impacted** minimally upon employment levels." Translation: "They've been trained but there are still no jobs.")

implementation: Making something happen; actually doing something. The massivity and inertia of government bureaucracies is such that the *implementation phase* (which one would think should be the most important) involves less time and money than that expended upon other stages and functions: **feasibility studies**, planning, **research and development**, **monitoring**, and evaluation.

information: A key word that covers a multitude of mundane things. Usually employed in conglomerate phrases, such as *information transfer* (telling somebody something); *information dissemination* (telling lots of people something); and *information packages* (books, pamphlets, or brochures).

infrastructure: An internal organization, working apparatus, skeleton of effective power. ("We can cut agency staff expenditures by 30 percent without altering our basic **infrastructure**.")

inoperative: No longer applicable; obsolete. Made famous during the Watergate era: ("Previous statements in this matter are **inoperative**." Translation: "We're changing our story.")

input: Contribution, opinion, participation. A computerese term now widely in bureaucratic use. ("Of course we want **community input**, but the final determinations of resource **utilization** certainly can't be left to the **end-users**." Translation: They can squawk all they want—*we* decide where the money goes.")

inservice: Verb, to train those outside the bounds of the bureaucracy to do their jobs better; on-the-job training. The Department of Education, for example, might inservice teachers in testing procedures for first graders. (Also used as a noun: to hold an inservice.)

interface: As a noun, a common ground, boundary, area of interaction. As a verb, to overlap, communicate with, or interact. ("The **intelligence community** has not maintained a strategic **interface** with the consulate." Translation: "They act like we're not even here!")

in the field: Out of the office for a longer period than "at a meeting." The *field* is hypothetically the "real world" where programs are **implemented**.

legitimacy: The right to exist and be funded.

leverage: 1. As a noun, power, connections, or clout.

2. As a verb, to generate large amounts of money through the judicious application of smaller amounts. ("We'll use a $3 million UDAG grant to **leverage** over $20 million in **private sector** investments.")

matrix: A precise-sounding, mathematics/computerese term that has a variety of quite imprecise meanings—making it especially useful in Bureaucratese. It can mean context ("within the **matrix** of ongoing programs"); variety ("The mayor's office provides a **matrix** of services"); or totality ("The program **matrix** includes five modular components").

monitoring function: Keeping track of things.

needs assessment process: Figuring out what has to be done.

needs sensing: Getting **feedback** from the *field;* a variation on **needs assessment**, with a homey touch. Performed by *needs sensors*, naturally.

networking: Forming lots of little mini-bureaucracies throughout the *field* in order to help complicate matters, and get jobs for civil servants. Networking is a form of *linking*, connecting the bureaucracy to the area it is supposed to service. Linking requires *linkers*, who are the people who follow **needs sensors**.

operationalize: To put into effect.

optimize: To increase, improve, raise the odds, make the best of. (**Optimize personnel performance variables:** Get them to do some work.)

outreach: Getting the public involved in an agency's programs; digging up **end-users** when nobody seems to want the "benefits" of a government program enough to apply for them on their own.

parameter: As a noun, a factor, limit, consideration, or boundary. ("Research indicates that the disinclusion of critical sociocultural **parameters** from the planning process has rendered the project non-**viable** in the target **community**." Translation: "The people hate this thing; we've got to drop it.") As a verb, **parameterize:** to establish parameters.

perks: Perquisites; the extra benefits of a government position—agency car or limousine, travel allowances, freebies and emoluments of all kinds. ("The salary's only fair—but the **perks** are terrific!")

pert: From **PERT** (**Program Evaluation and Review Technique**; see entry in BUSINESS MANAGEMENT chapter); to perform a detailed program analysis along specific lines. ("Let's **pert** this one out for fiscal '82.")

phase zero: The beginning stage of a project, especially when the **feasibility study** is being conducted. The phrase has a desirably hard-nosed, military quality.

prioritize: To decide what is most important. "Failure to **prioritize**" serves as a euphemistic misdemeanor covering even the most massive mistakes of judgment and wastes of resources.

private sector: That portion of the economy not

directly on the government payroll; virtually synonymous with business.

proactive: Preemptive reactivity, popularly known as planning in advance—thereby avoiding many of the problems of *reactive* planning (otherwise known as figuring out how to cover up your mistakes). Proper *proactive* planning requires good *think-tanking*, **perting**, **networking**, and **needs sensing**. These requirements help keep the national unemployment rate down.

procedural safeguards: Red tape.

process: A catchword used to legitimize any effort, procedure, or event, no matter how trivial. Thus, deciding becomes *the decision-making process*, doing becomes *the implementation process*, writing becomes *the information dissemination process*, etc.

procurement: Getting. (*Optimization of procurement function:* Getting as much as you can.)

project: A governmental activity with defined objectives and a limited **time-frame**. *Pilot projects* and *demonstration projects* are test runs of a given idea prior to full funding. A project is usually one component of a *program*, which in turn is one part of a *plan*.

quantification: Putting a numerical value on something; reducing a complex situation (such as racial violence) to numerical terms. ("Anecdotal information is insufficient to substantiate continued funding; the agency requires **viable** data **quantification**.")

R and D: Research and development. When not an end in itself, R and D precedes **implementation** of a program or commercial application of a product.

redundancy of human resources: Overstaffing.

RFP: Request for proposals; a bureaucratic formality. Before contractors can be named or grants allocated, an RFP is announced, giving all prospective contractors and applicants a chance to put in their bids. More often than not, the contractor or grantee has already been decided upon, but the RFP is used to maintain the illusion of open competition.

riff: From **RIF** (**reduction in force**); agency personnel cutbacks, due to budget cuts or political changeovers. ("George was **riffed** from the DMH job, but HUD picked him up the next week.")

scenario: A projection, prediction, or hypothetical picture of future events. Originally Pentagonese. ("In the event of detonation of Soviet twenty-megaton nuclear device over Ground Zero Chicago, all **viable scenarios** for Civil Defense response must assume an acceptable civilian loss baseline of three million. . . .")

selected out: Fired.

soft funding: A grant or other financial resource that cannot be depended upon to continue indefinitely.

soft public works: Also **labor-intensive programs**. Government programs that create jobs.

strategy: A large-scale, comprehensive plan of action. Also used in adjectival form, to sound dynamic, realistic, tough-minded. (*Strategic waste disposal plan:* How to *really* get the garbage off the streets.)

structure: Verb, to organize, coordinate, set up, or plan. ("Agency will **structure** the release of **informational** materials within the operative time/**communications matrix**." Translation: "We won't tell them until after the election.")

subsector: A part, portion, or area. Other basic Bureaucratese words with equivalent meanings are **component**, **element**, and **division**.

target: Verb, to aim, specify, earmark, assign. (*Targeting of program resources:* Deciding what to spend the money on.)

task force: A group appointed to work on a specific **project**. The stagnating connotation of *committee* is avoided by the use of this energetic, military phrase. Only the name has been changed, however.

thrust: Purpose, direction, major element. ("The **thrust** of the **communications** program is to maximize agency credibility." Translation: "We've got to get people to believe us.")

time-frame: A period of time. The implication is that the time has been carefully allotted through highly organized and active planning. Needless to say, the profligate wasting of time by government bureaucracies if by far their most notable feature.

title: All bureaucratic activity derives ultimately from some piece of legislation—laws authorizing a War on Poverty, cleanup of the environment, taxation standards (and loopholes), and the like. Title followed by a roman numeral indicates part of a large block of law; each title may be further broken down into *chapters* and *sections*. It is common practice in Bureaucratese to refer to these laws simply by number: "The school expects some **Title** IX funds to come in later this summer, and we're trying to supplement that with our Chapter 766 allocations.")

utilization: Use. (One never uses a short word when the **functional utilization** of polysyllabisms falls within acceptable **communications parameters**.)

viable: Workable, practical, feasible, acceptable, capable of happening. One of the most common adjectives in Bureaucratese. ("In the absence of **viable** alternatives, previous **implementation** procedures will be continued.")

[16]

The CIA and the "Intelligence Community"

In the mid-1970s, those who closely followed events in Washington would have observed a major development: For the first time, Congress made a serious attempt to investigate and control the activities of the American "intelligence community"—a homey euphemism for the spy services and their **covert activity** divisions. In 1975, three separate investigations were undertaken: by the Senate Select Committee to Investigate Governmental Operations with Respect to Intelligence, chaired by Sen. Frank Church; by a similar committee in the House of Representatives, headed by Congressman Otis Pike; and by the President's Special Commission, headed by Nelson Rockefeller. The results of these investigations became available in 1976, and they revealed an appalling series of legal and moral transgressions by the CIA, as well as the FBI and several other agencies. The 1970s also saw the publication of over a dozen books by former CIA officers (Phillip Agee, John Stockwell, Frank Snepp, Victor Marchetti, Harry Rositzke, and others) who exposed in even greater detail the secret activities of the CIA over three decades.

The net result of all this publicity, however, has not been any substantial change in the orientation or the power of the CIA and the other intelligence organizations—the FBI, **NSA**, **DIA**, and Army, Navy and Air Force Intelligence. The budgets of this combined intelligence community are still considered classified information—even most members of Congress are prohibited from knowing how much money they are approving for intelligence and clandestine actions—but it is estimated at over $10 billion yearly. The CIA employs some 16,000 regular staffpersons, as well as tens of thousands more paid **agents** who work for the organization but are not part of the Agency (or the Company, as it is affectionately called); the other intelligence agencies together employ well over 100,000 persons. After a few years during the Carter administration when the intelligence community appeared to be on the defensive —and its **covert activities** were significantly reduced in number and scope—in the 1980s the intelligence agency "spooks" are making a definite comeback.

What has changed, however, is that a large volume of information is now available to the public, by which the actions of the CIA and the other agencies can be understood and evaluated. In this section, through the language of the intelligence services, the reader can begin to gain that understanding. The terms explained below —drawn from books and articles, congressional testimony, and other direct sources—reveal a fascinating and frightening world, quite unlike the romanticized adventures of popular spy novels. We have concentrated mainly on the terms of the CIA, which, although not the largest intelligence agency, is the most aggressive internationally and has the most powerful effect upon world events.

A distinction should be made, moreover, between the functions of **intelligence** and those of **covert** or **clandestine operations**. In the former category are the traditional, legitimate functions of intelligence services: getting all the **information** possible about the military, political, and economic conditions in foreign (especially hostile) countries, and analyzing that information to gauge what actions will best ensure our national defense. This is the purpose for which the CIA was originally chartered by Congress, in 1947. In the latter category, however, fall an incredible array of other activities, most of which are kept totally secret from both Congress and the American people: the manipulation of foreign political situations (rigging elections, bribing public officials, supporting certain trade unions and political groups while crushing others, **disinformation** and propaganda campaigns); the training and support of foreign military and paramilitary forces (not authorized by Congress and often in contradistinction to our stated policies); the assassination or attempted assassination of foreign heads of state; the **destabilization** and overthrow of democratically elected governments (Chile in 1973 being the most salient recent example); the training, at United States taxpayers' expense, of foreign police and security forces in the most modern methods of interrogation, surveillance, and torture (the Shah's infamous SAVAK, for example); experiments in mind control via drugs, hypnosis, electroshock, and brainwashing (see **MKULTRA**); the surveillance and harassment of United States citizens (see **COINTELPRO, CHAOS**); and so on. It is primarily in this area that critics contend the "intelligence" agencies have exceeded their legitimate functions and become the executors of more sinister political directives—both those of the executive branch (such as Nixon's use of CIA, FBI, and NSA to stifle American dissent against his Vietnam policies), the major corporations (ITT in Chile), and the agency chiefs themselves. In the attempt to combat Soviet expansion and other forces deemed "hostile to U.S. interests," the CIA has frequently used methods and supported political forces more ruthless and undemocratic than those we are opposing.

As citizens in whose names, and with whose tax dollars, such things are being done, we need to know more about the intelligence agencies and their role in shaping U.S. policy. We need to know what **executive action** and **black bag jobs** consist of; what **destabilization** of a foreign government really means; what **COINTELPRO** and **HYDRA** and **MKULTRA** and **Operation MONGOOSE** actually were. Once acquainted with such terms—and the facts which they represent—we can debate the issues of the CIA and related agencies as intelligent and informed citizens.

agent: An "outside" person paid by the CIA to accomplish its purposes, but who is not an official employee of the agency (usually called an **officer**). A *career agent* is paid to collect and deliver **information** (the classical espionage setup) to his **case officer** over many years; while a **contract agent** or onetime agent may be hired to perform a limited series of actions —an assassination, a propaganda campaign —after which he is free to sell his services elsewhere. An *agent in place* is a paid agent who occupies a position within the political or military or intelligence apparatus of an "opposition" government or organization: a Cuban government official, for example. An *agent of influence* may not be directly on the CIA payroll but affects events in the same direction as the CIA's operations: usually being an anti-Communist government official or representative of big business. (Note: The term agent has a different meaning in the FBI, where it refers to an official employee of the agency, equivalent to an officer in the CIA).

AID: The **Agency for International Development**; a basic government vehicle for foreign aid disbursements, which has been frequently used as a front for CIA **clandestine operations** and as official **cover** for CIA **officers** abroad.

asset: Anything useful to an intelligence agency, outside of its own employees and materiel. Usually refers to sources of **information** and resources additional to the hired **agent:** "friendly" foreign officials, right-wing generals, cooperative journalists and publishers, wiretaps and surveillance installations, stockpiles of weaponry for paramilitary operations, and the like.

backstopped: When materials an **officer** or **agent** uses for an alias or **cover** identity have been issued with the cooperation or knowledge of the issuing organization, they are said to be backstopped. In other words, if an officer uses an alias driver's license or credit card, if the materials have been backstopped they will check out if someone contacts the DMV or issuing company for verification. The other type of alias materials, not backstopped, are *flash* IDs; if checked, they will not prove valid.

Bay of Pigs: The classic CIA debacle. In 1961, shortly after Fidel Castro came to power in Cuba, the CIA trained a small force of anti-Castro Cubans and engineered their attempt to "liberate" the island. Lacking both popular support for their effort among the Cuban people (who were supposed to "rise up" and join the counterrevolution) and any major military commitment by the United States (a full-scale invasion was contemplated but ruled out), the effort was doomed to failure. The assault force was easily defeated and most of its members captured; the resultant **flap** to the United States government for blatantly interfering in the affairs of another country was immense. The plan, though hatched during the Eisenhower administration, was approved by Kennedy—who later felt that he had been misinformed about its viability and came to regret the venture.

black bag job: Illegal breaking and entering, performed by an intelligence agency (or its **agents**) for the purposes of gathering **information** or installing surveillance devices. The most famous, of course, was the entry into the Democratic Party Headquarters in the Watergate Hotel by the "plumbers" team, employed by the Committee to Reelect the President (Nixon). The FBI has issued directives to its agents to cease such activities, but there is little evidence that any of the intelligence agencies are likely to give up such a common method of obtaining information.

black propaganda: Published reports, leaflets, posters, and rumors that are false or misleading and are attributed to others than their real creators. For example, if the **COS** in a Third World country "leaks" to the local press a secret Soviet document planning the takeover of that country, which document has in fact been written by the CIA and forged to look like an official Russian paper, the procedure is called black propaganda. See also **disinformation**.

blow-back: Adverse repercussions from an agency operation. The term usually refers to the embarrassment that accrues when an operation's true nature is revealed (such as the CIA attempting to "buy" a free election in a democratic country); but also includes an adverse military or political result from even a "successful" operation (such as the hardening of a movement's resolve when their leader has been assassinated).

branch: A subdivision of territory within the CIA organizational system. A branch is smaller than a **division**, larger than a **section**. The Horn and Central Branch would be part of the Africa Division, with the Angola section a subset of that branch.

cables: The largest portion of CIA **information** is transmitted from **officers** to CIA headquarters via cable (telegram) traffic. Hundreds of these cables are received and sent daily between field station officers and their respective **task force** or **division** chiefs in Langley, Virginia. Cables are prioritized in order of their urgency, with a **FLASH** or **CRITIC** cable (the two top priorities) able to reach the CIA from a **COS** anywhere in the world within seven minutes. The cables are, of course, encoded before transmittal and decoded upon receipt. **IMMEDIATE** cables take several hours, **PRIORITY** up to six hours, and **ROUTINE** up to twenty-four hours.

case officer: A staff **officer**, a CIA employee who works on a project of some kind, either **recruiting** and controlling **agents** (spies) for **clandestine collection**, or coordinating a **covert action**, or running some other program. The case officer is, in effect, the liaison between the CIA decision-making bureaucracy in Langley and the actual field operations—either **espionage** or **covert action**.

CHAOS: A secret **operation**, conducted by the CIA from 1969 to 1974. CHAOS was supposed to investigate the extent of foreign support and Communist control of the United States antiwar movement. Although two major CHAOS reports (in 1969 and 1971) concluded there was no evidence of such control or support, nonetheless, at the insistence of President Nixon the operation went on. It ultimately compiled information including the names of 300,000 American citizens and organizations; intercepted mail; maintained over 7,000 separate **201** (personality) **files** on individual American citizens; and established a "security" status that precluded any review or approval process of the operation outside the agency itself. CHAOS was a clear example of the Agency's attempting to fulfill its intelligence/analysis function honestly and accurately, only to be pressured by the executive branch to "produce" the kind of information that the President required for political purposes.

clandestine: Secret, capable of being denied by the government. See **covert**. *Clandestine services* is the inside-CIA term for the **DDO**.

COINTELPRO: A secret FBI program, begun in 1956 to infiltrate and undermine the Communist Party USA, but expanded through the 1960s to include other left-wing parties and ultimately the entire spectrum of peace, antiwar, and black-power and civil-rights movements. COINTELPRO (short for **counterintelligence** program, which was a total misnomer) went far beyond investigation and surveillance, however: Testimony before the Church and Pike Committees in 1975 revealed that the program included wide-scale harassment, intimidation, deception, and **disinformation**. Over 2,000 COINTELPRO actions were approved and taken: Activist couples were split up by means of faked letters purporting infidelities of one

spouse; homes and offices were burglarized; violence was provoked between factionalized groups; extreme activities were provoked by **infiltrated agents**; efforts to prevent black and New Left activists from speaking, teaching, writing, and working were undertaken; group members were anonymously named as informants to their organizations; and First Amendment rights of United States citizens were relentlessly trampled.

collection: The gathering of **information**, which may be **overt** (the source is made aware that he is giving information to the agency) or **covert** (the source is not aware of who is collecting the information—or is unaware that the information is being collected).

compartmentation: Agency term for compartmentalization. The nature of CIA organization is such that many of the departments, especially **covert actions** and other **sensitive operations**, are kept entirely separate from other functions and personnel within the agency, sometimes with locked files and offices. In these cases only the **DCI** or **DDO** may know what is happening within all the separate **sections** and operations.

compromise: When an **officer**'s or **agent**'s **cover** has been blown (exposed), or the nature and extent of a secret facility or **operation** has been revealed, the sources, **assets**, and methods involved are said to have been compromised.

contingency fund: In addition to its normal operating budget, the exact amount of which is classified information which the American public apparently should not know (but which is certainly in the vicinity of a billion dollars yearly for the CIA alone, and many times that for all the intelligence services combined), the **DCI** has at his personal discretion at all times a contingency fund of additional monies, to be used at his personal authorization, amounting to some $50 million (some sources say as high as $100 million). Thus, if a president needs a million in cash to pay someone off, or the **NSC** wants to fund a little $20 million **paramilitary operation** without the approval of Congress, this is where they go.

contract agent: A person hired by the CIA for a specific job; for example, Mafia people paid to arrange the assassination of Fidel Castro.

COS: Chief of station; The head officer of a specific CIA **station**. No figures are available to the public on the number of stations and bases existing around the world, but there are certainly hundreds and most likely thousands.

counterinsurgency: A euphemism for actions taken against grass-roots, popular, or guerrilla-type revolutionary movements that threaten established, pro-American regimes. Much of the CIA's activity in Southeast Asia and Latin America during the 1950s and 1960s went under this rubric.

counterintelligence: Abbreviated **CI**. All those activities taken to counter the work of enemy (or "opposition") intelligence services. This includes discovering foreign **agents** (usually **KGB**) at work in the United States or elsewhere; breaking enemy codes and otherwise intercepting their communications; **penetrating** the other side's intelligence service; planting false **information** through known opposition agents; using **double agents**; and any other activities that will neutralize their effectiveness while maintaining our own.

cover: A visible, plausible identity for an intelligence **officer** or **agent** that does not reveal his true identity or affiliation. *Official cover* is provided by a position with a private company—often, a CIA-created or -controlled entity. (See **proprietary companies**.) Often, a local CIA station chief (see **COS**), especially in a "friendly" political context (the Greek colonels' regime, the Pinochet regime in Chile), makes little or no effort to disguise his identity and is well known to the indigenous political and social circles. See also **deep cover**.

coverage: If there exists a CIA **station** in a given area—which may consist only of an **officer** in a hotel room, or could be a well-established operation with dozens of employees and millions of dollars to dispense—the Company is said to have "coverage" there.

covert action/activities: Any and all **operations** of the agency or its **contract agents**, in which any link to the United States government or its agencies has been disguised or can be denied; secret operations. Into this category fall the most notorious of CIA programs, many of them in direct violation of its original founding charter and often in flagrant disregard of the principles of national sovereignty, democracy, and human rights. Covert actions or operations (also called **clandestine** actions or operations) are generally described as including: (1) *political* and *economic operations* (secret funding of political parties, private training and "support" of individuals, labor unions, police forces); (2) *propaganda activities*, both **black** (covert and false) and *white* (overt, honest); and (3) *paramilitary operations*, including sabotage, military coups, assassinations (or the attempts thereof), raising, training, funding of secret armies, and the like; and (4) **espionage**, the covert gathering of information, which is the original and legal function of the intelligence agencies.

cryptonym: All CIA **officers**, hired **agents, assets**, and **operations** are given code names by which they are designated in all **cable** traffic and memoranda. In general, the first two letters *(digraph)* identify the locale of the operation, or its chief sponsor (MK, for example, indicated a Technical Services Staff program). Some of the better-known cryptonyms, now public knowledge, have been **CHAOS, PHOENIX, MONGOOSE**, and **MKULTRA** (see entries under each of these).

cutout: An intermediary, designed to disguise the link between the CIA and its **covert**

operations. For example, in the case of one of the CIA-sponsored assassination attempts against Fidel Castro (see **MONGOOSE**), there were no fewer than six cutouts between the CIA **case officer** in charge and the actual paid assassin: an American intermediary, three members of the Mafia, a Cuban émigré leader, and a Cuban courier. In most operations, the chain of command is not quite so circuitous, but the use of at least one cutout to mask agency involvement is commonplace.

DCI: Director of Central Intelligence; appointed by the president, he is both the head of the Central Intelligence Agency *and* the representative of the entire intelligence community to Congress and the executive branch. The responsibilities of the position are immense—the DCI must oversee and coordinate a multibillion-dollar intelligence system, plan and approve **covert actions**, and provide the link between all those functions and the upper levels of government. While not officially mandated to formulate policy, inevitably the DCI has become one of the key voices in the creation of the United States' role around the world; thus, additionally he has the responsibility for sustaining American justice and democracy while pursuing **national security**. Few, if any, of the fourteen DCIs who have served since the agency's founding in 1947 can be said to have resolved the moral and political complexities of the job. The best-known DCIs have been Allen Dulles (1953–61), John McCone (1961–65), Richard Helms (1965–1973), and William Colby (1973–1976).

DDCI: Deputy Director of Central Intelligence; the number-two man in the CIA. Generally, the DDCI has assumed most of the responsibilities for direct administration of ongoing CIA activities, while the **DCI** coordinates overall intelligence community functions, establishes policy, and is the liaison to the president, **NSC**, and Congress.

DDI: Deputy Directorate (or **Deputy Director**) **for Information**; that branch of the CIA (or its chief) concerned with gathering **information** and interpreting it. The DDI tends to be somewhat more benign, rational and less aggressive than the **DDO**, and its **clandestine** functions fit more into our classic notion of what "spying" and intelligence agencies are all about. The CIA lists some 10,000 employees in this **directorate**.

DDO: Deputy Directorate (or **Deputy Director**), **of Operations**; that branch of the CIA, and its chief **officer**, in charge of all **covert actions**, fundamentally those activities designed to affect or alter the political/economic/social/or military conditions in foreign countries (and occasionally in the United States as well). The DDO, many critics feel, should not be considered part of the "intelligence community" at all, as its functions have nothing to do with **information collection** and analysis: The DDO is really the covert arm of American foreign policy. It actively and aggressively pursues the perceived interests of the United States government (as defined by the president and the **NSC**) and the major corporations—engineering the overthrow of "unfriendly" governments (Allende's Chile, Mossadeq's Iran), paying off certain political groups, unions, and individuals while sabotaging and undermining others; raising secret armies (Laos) and training others; even teaching Third World despots how to torture and intimidate their people. The justification for such activities is that the United States is in a very real struggle with a ruthless and powerful enemy (or array of enemies), that must be combated by any means necessary. Critics of the CIA hold that while the struggle may be real and the threat genuine, the overthrow of legitimate popular governments and the support of any dictator who proclaims his anti-Communism is the wrong way to defend United States interests and security. Additionally, the budget, decisions, and covert actions of the DDO are almost totally hidden from the Congress and the public (until after the fact, and only then by the extreme pressure of congressional investigation or journalistic pursuit), although the effects of those actions and decisions have a profound impact on world events. The CIA lists some 4,500 employees in the Directorate of Operations; like all other details of this sort that reach the public eye, this is open to question.

DDP: Deputy Directorate for Plans; the name of the **DDO** until March 1973.

DDS and T: Deputy Directorate of Science and Technology; a directorate within the CIA which develops all the technical devices—special weapons, drugs, disguises, poisons and other agents of biological warfare, sophisticated forgeries, "state of the art" surveillance mechanisms, and other James Bondian gimmicks—that the agency may need for its operations or intelligence gathering or may want to have the capability for, should the need arise. **MKULTRA**, the CIA's notorious mind-control experiments project, was conducted under the auspices of the *TSS* (Technical Services Staff; also called the Technical Services Division, or *TSD*) which group is now subsumed within the DDS and T.

dead drop: A method by which **information** can be passed from **agent** to **officer** (or between any two parties). The information (message, photos, microdot texts, etc.) is "dropped" in some prearranged, inconspicuous place (a tree stump, a cemetery) and picked up surreptitiously sometime later.

deep cover: A false identity that is extremely difficult to trace to the CIA. Generally, deep-cover people are **contract** or **career agents**, rather than **case officers**, whose **cover** may be minimal.

destabilize: A euphemism for overthrow. Typically, governments targeted for destabilization are leftist or left-leaning, often democratically elected governments that are not entirely hospitable to United States corporate "development" and do not constitute military allies or bases for United States materiel. Examples include Allende's Chile; Mossadeq's Iran; Goulart's Brazil. Destabilization is accomplished through a variety of means: propaganda, **disinformation**; support of right-wing (occasionally centrist) trade unions and political parties; training of conservative military and police forces; supplying arms and ammunition to same; torture and other interrogation techniques; kidnapping and assassination. Ideally for the CIA destabilization results in a somewhat right-leaning civilian or military regime that welcomes U.S. business on its terms (low wages, high profits, no restrictions) and represents a virulently anti-Communist force both militarily and politically.

devised facility: A business entity run by the CIA as a **cover** for its employees and/or **operations**, but which pursues no real business activities (unlike the **proprietary company**, which does).

DIA: The **Defense Intelligence Agency**; created in 1961 to coordinate the efforts of the three service intelligence agencies (army, navy, air force) and eliminate wasteful duplication. The DIA has not realized that function but does produce **finished intelligence** for the Joint Chiefs of Staff from raw **information** gathered by the three service intelligence agencies.

directorates: There are four major subdivisions of the CIA, known as Directorates: Operations (**DDO**); Intelligence (**DDI**); Administration; and Science and Technology (**DDS and T**). Each Directorate is headed by a Deputy Director, who in turn reports directly to the **DCI** and **DDCI**. See separate entries for each Directorate.

disinformation: False or misleading information, which is deliberately planted or leaked to the public or the opposition intelligence. For example, if the CIA forges documents showing Soviet control of an indigenous left-wing movement in a South American country (when in fact no such control exists), and the fabrication is printed in newspapers and picked up by wire services, the "information" thus created is disinformation.

Division: The largest geographical subset of the CIA; there are eight Divisions (within both **DDI** and **DDO**): Western Europe, Near East, Far East, Africa, Western Hemisphere, Soviet Bloc, Eastern Europe, and Domestic Operations. Each division is then further subdivided into **branches**, **sections**, and **stations** (or bases).

double agent: An individual who is apparently working for one side's intelligence service, while in fact he (or she) is working for the other side. For example, a **KGB** officer in Western Europe might be persuaded or bribed into *turning*, which would mean that he continued in his position with the Soviets but reported all useful **information** to the CIA. Alternatively, he might report everything that transpired with the CIA to his superiors in the KGB, and **penetrate** the CIA's structure as far as he could, in which case he would have become a double agent against the United States (or, strictly speaking, a *triple agent*).

elsur: Electronic surveillance; a euphemism for wiretapping or bugging.

espionage: The secret **collection** of **information**; spying. States have been spying on one another for thousands of years, and while it may not be the most humanistic of occupations, as long as nations threaten one another it is probably a necessary one. The espionage function (and counterespionage, or **counterintelligence**) is thus the one legitimate purpose of the intelligence community; **covert operations** that interfere with the sovereignty of other nations are another story.

Executive Action: A special unit within the CIA, established to eliminate foreign leaders —either politically or physically. Executive Action has thus become a euphemism for assassination or the attempting thereof. At least eight major foreign leaders (and perhaps many more minor figures) have been targeted for such action by the CIA in the past twenty years, including Patrice Lumumba, Fidel Castro, Rafael Trujillo, and General Rene Schneider of Chile.

eyes only: The strictest level of security classification for documents. The next below this is *proscribed and limited*. Eyes-only **cables** and memos are meant to be read only by the person to whom they are sent, and not copied or made available to anyone else.

Farm, the: A major CIA training base, located at Camp Peary, near Williamsburg, Virginia. Here trainees learn the "tradecraft" of **espionage**, **counterintelligence**, and **covert action**.

finished intelligence: The end-product analysis or report made by an intelligence agency (in the CIA, the **DDI**) after having collated raw data from numerous sources (overt and **covert**) and analyzed the results. The CIA, for example, issues finished intelligence reports on a daily and weekly basis for hundreds of cleared government "consumers"; produces a President's Daily Brief on foreign affairs; and does in-depth analyses of special situations (such as, the feasibility of overthrowing the Sandinista government by purely political means).

flap potential: The possibility of embarrassment to the U.S. government or damage to the agency, should a particular project be exposed. Obviously, the more illegal or contrary to avowed U.S. governmental principles an activity is, the greater its flap potential.

flaps and seals: The standard CIA course in mail interception—i.e., how to open and/or read mail without being detected. The CIA ran a mail-intercept program in conjunction with its Operation **HTLINGUAL** for over twenty years.

FLASH: A high-priority **cable** communication designation. FLASH cables can reach a **Divi-**

sion Chief in Langley in seven minutes from a CIA **Station** anywhere in the world.

FOIA: The **Freedom of Information Act;** passed by Congress in 1966 and considerably strengthened in 1975. Under this act, government agencies (including the FBI and CIA) must make their documents and records available to the public through the Federal Register or by special request. Much of what we now know about the intelligence community derives from requests and suits pursued under the FOIA; however some material is still "released" in a heavily censored form—sometimes to the point of total unintelligibility—when the agencies choose to employ exemptions to protect **national security**.

foreign military adviser: A mercenary.

Forty Committee: The previous name for that **NSC** subcommittee (see **OAG**) which is supposed to "review foreign **covert operations** and **collection** activities involving high risk and **sensitivity**." It has existed, under various names, since 1948, and is chaired by the assistant to the president for security affairs, and includes the chairman of the Joint Chiefs of Staff, the **DCI**, and various representatives from the State and Defense departments. There is abundant evidence, however, that the Forty Committee was not always consulted with regard to certain actions or was deliberately misinformed or malinformed on others. A 1974 CIA *Covert Action Manual* states that only 25 percent of all covert operations have been presented to and approved by the Forty Committee. Its previous name was the *303 Committee;* as reorganized by President Ford in 1975, it has been referred to as the **Operations Advisory Group** (**OAG**).

hard target: An **agent** employed by the CIA who is positioned within an enemy (or inimical) political, military, or intelligence system, with good access to strategic **information**.

HTLINGUAL: A secret mail-opening operation which the CIA conducted for twenty years (1950s to 1970s). Over 2 million letters

were photographed and over 200,000 were opened and read—including the mail of Senator Frank Church.

HUMINT: HUMan INTelligence, i.e., information gathered by individuals—as distinguished from **Comint** (COMmunications INTelligence), **Elint** (ELectronic INTelligence), and **Sigint** (SIGnal INTelligence).

Huston Plan: In 1970, at the instruction of President Nixon, White House Assistant Tom Huston, in coordination with the heads of the major intelligence agencies (FBI, **CIA, NSA,** and **DIA**), drew up a comprehensive plan for an accelerated assault on the antiwar movement. It included the "removal of restraints" on electronic surveillance, mail opening, **penetration** of organizations, "surreptitious entry," and authorized a generally stepped-up attack. Nixon approved this so-called Huston Plan, but withdrew his official permission a week later, fearing the political **blow-back** should the plan be exposed. Nonetheless, the agencies involved continued along much the same lines, although without Nixon's official seal of approval.

HYDRA: A secret, computerized file system employed by the CIA during its **Operation CHAOS** in the 1960s and 1970s. The names of over 300,000 American citizens were indexed in the HYDRA system, with over 7,000 individual **201 files**. Although CHAOS was officially terminated in 1974, it appears that the HYDRA files are still intact, awaiting the CIA's next use for them.

infiltrate: To join a group or (organization) as a member and appear to support its purposes. Both the **CIA** and FBI infiltrated scores of civil-rights and antiwar groups during the 1960s. Contrast with **monitor** and **penetrate**.

information: Raw data or reports that have not been "analyzed"—that is, interpreted, verified, and collated with information from other sources. When a mass of information on a subject (say, the likelihood of a Russian invasion of Poland) has been analyzed and conclusions derived, it becomes **finished intelligence**.

KGB: The Soviet secret police/central intelligence system, an immense network that is even vaster and more ruthless than our own. The First Chief Directorate of the KGB is concerned with foreign affairs, and is equivalent to our CIA; the Second Chief Directorate (an internal directorate) spies on Soviet citizens and enforces internal "security" and is roughly equivalent to our FBI, although infinitely more repressive and a pervasive, frightening fact of life for Soviet citizens.

MI-6: The British intelligence service, equivalent to our CIA. It does not, however, engage in **covert actions** on the scale of the CIA or **KGB** and is fundamentally a true "intelligence" organization.

MKNAOMI: A secret twenty-year program by which the CIA (in coordination with the Secret Operations Division of the Army Chemical Corps) developed and stockpiled a variety of chemical and biological warfare (**CBW**) weapons—including deadly shellfish toxin; lethal cobra venom; germs to cause anthrax, encephalitis, tuberculosis, and brucellosis; and devices to spread or inject them surreptitiously. When President Nixon ordered all such CBW weapons destroyed in 1970, the CIA kept its stockpile of shellfish and cobra poisons, enough to kill tens of thousands of people. CIA Director William Colby, testifying about this illegal stockpile before the Select Senate (Church) Committee in 1975, said that what the CIA had kept was really only "a couple of teaspoons" of the poisons.

MKULTRA: A secret CIA program, begun in 1953 and continued through 1964, in which the Technical Services Division pursued the possibilities of mind control through experimentation with drugs (including LSD), electroshock, sensory deprivation, hypnosis, and other methods. In numerous cases, such treatments were administered to completely unwitting subjects, including mental patients, GIs, students, prison inmates, drug addicts, and people picked off the streets. Although officially "terminated" in 1964, MKULTRA projects were subsumed into other more general CIA departments and also into a new project, *MKSEARCH,* which continued until 1972. In two decades these projects funded investigation into an incredible array of techniques for controlling the minds of other human beings, from the use of psychotropic drugs to brainwashing to chemical and biological weapons to inducing social breakdowns. The full extent of the ULTRA project and its continuations will probably never be known, however, as then **DCI** Richard Helms ordered most of the files on MKULTRA destroyed in 1973.

MOLE: An **agent** who has penetrated the enemy intelligence or military service. The term probably originated with spy-novel writers and was picked up by the real-life spooks.

MONGOOSE: A major CIA **covert action** operation begun in November 1961 (at the behest of John Kennedy), the stated purpose of which was to achieve the overthrow of Fidel Castro in Cuba. One spin-off of MONGOOSE was *Task Force W,* which made at least eight separate attempts to assassinate the Cuban leader. In addition to the assassination **task force**, MONGOOSE included a wide range of activities to subvert the Castro government: propaganda, agricultural and economic sabotage, support of anti-Castro exile groups, and periodic paramilitary raids.

monitoring: A minimal form of surveillance of a group or organization, in which operatives attend public meetings and hear only what any other person present would hear. A preliminary stage to **infiltration** and **penetration**.

national security: Taken literally, national security is the legitimate justification for maintaining the armed forces, the intelligence-**collection** and analysis agencies, and an active diplomatic corps. However, the term has been abused by CIA and other intelligence agency officials when applied to the surveillance and harassment of ordinary American citizens protesting their government's policies, or to the refusal to disclose the budgets or details of **covert operations**, or to the support of repressive regimes around the world simply because they are anti-Communist. It is the magic word, invoked when a Helms or a Colby has a secret he chooses not to divulge, a transgression he wishes not to admit.

NSA: The **National Security Agency**; established by a secret presidential directive in 1952, and statistically the second-largest (after Air Force Intelligence) element in the U.S. intelligence community. The NSA is designed to monitor intelligence-related communications from its thousands of listening devices around the world. In the 1960s, NSA also eavesdropped on U.S. citizens targeted by the Nixon administration (*Operation Shamrock*) and employed a **watch list** of 1,200 Americans. NSA lists 24,000 employees and a yearly budget of over $1 billion.

NSC: The **National Security Council**; consisting of the president, the vice-president, the secretary of state, the secretary of defense, and various of their staffpersons. It is concerned with formulating and directing policy and action relative to **national security**. It is to this group that the **DCI** reports and from this group—in theory—that all **covert activities** must gain authorization. In fact, often secret **operations** are not reported fully (or at all) to the NSC; or they may be ordered directly by the president without consulting it.

NSC 10/2: A secret National Security Council directive which in 1948 authorized the creation of the *Office of Special Projects*, later to become the **DDP** (now **DDO**) and authorized it to engage in a wide range of **covert activities**, including propaganda, sabotage, demolition, economic warfare, and other forms of "subversion against hostile states." The CIA

had been created by act of Congress in 1947, which specifically defined its activities as limited to intelligence **collection** and analysis. NSC 10/2, part of the CIA's "secret charter," was thus never authorized by Congress and the American people.

OAG: The **Operations Advisory Group**, formerly called the **Forty Committee**; a subgroup of the **NSC** to which the CIA is directly responsible. See **Forty Committee**.

officer: A generic term for CIA staffpersons, especially those involved in **recruitment**, **collection**, **operations**, or the coordination of same (**case officers**); as distinct from analysts and **agents**.

operations: All those activities the agency undertakes that are not strictly concerned with the **collection** and analysis of **information**. The term has come to apply to all variety of legal and illegal functions, including among the latter the assassination of foreign heads of state; the overthrow of elected governments; the harassment of United States citizens; the training of foreign police in modern methods of torture, surveillance, and propaganda; and the disbursement of monies and munitions to forces and factions in other countries who are considered helpful to United States interests abroad.

OSS: The **Office of Strategic Services**; in many ways the forerunner of the CIA, in existence during W.W. II from 1942 to 1945. The OSS performed both intelligence gathering and analysis and **covert actions**—sabotage, propaganda, counterespionage, support for resistance groups. It played a vital and important role in the war effort against the Nazis, but was disbanded by President Truman shortly after the war ended.

overt collection: Intelligence gathering when the identity of the collecting agency has been disclosed to the source.

paramilitary: Engaged in military-type actions but not as regular armed forces of any nation. The CIA has conducted or sponsored paramilitary operations in dozens of countries around the world—from Guatemala in 1954 and the **Bay of Pigs** in 1961, to Angola in 1975. Paramilitary actions are a method of using force without a formal declaration of war.

PB/SUCCESS: A CIA **covert operation** in Guatemala in 1954, in which the leftist government of Jacobo Arbenz was overthrown by a right-wing military coup, which coup was organized by the CIA. The agency trained the military forces, supplied arms and ammunition, produced propaganda, even flew CIA-supplied fighter-bombers. This relatively bloodless overthrow of a "hostile" government was considered one of the CIA's first real "successes" in Latin America.

penetrate: To gain a position of leadership or high security inside an organization, either for information-gathering or political manipulation purposes. Penetration is both the desired objective of many CIA **operations** and conversely its most feared eventuality—i.e., that the United States intelligence organization will itself be penetrated.

PHOENIX: A major CIA **operation** during the Vietnam War, in which the CIA coordinated an attempt to destroy the "Vietcong infrastructure" through widespread terror, "interrogation centers," and assassination. The CIA's William Colby testified that over 20,000 Vietnamese were killed in the course of this operation in the years 1968 to 1971, although critics have maintained that many of these were innocent civilians, caught in the operations' indiscriminate methods and "kill quotas."

plausible denial: The doctrine that all **covert operations** must not be traceable to the United States government, neither its executive branch nor its intelligence agencies. The use of elaborate **covers**, strings of **cutouts**, **contract agents**, mercenaries, and other such mechanisms enables the government to mask its involvement. Also, the President and the

NSC are often given only vague or watered-down versions of the CIA's actual procedures, so that they can "plausibly deny" having authorized specific deeds, such as the overthrow of a legitimate foreign government. The idea was formally stated as part of **NSC 10/2**, which authorized "covert operations . . . that if uncovered the U.S. government can plausibly disclaim any responsibility for them."

proprietary company: A business operation used by the CIA to provide **cover** for **officers** and perform administrative tasks, without revealing the actual identities or affiliations of those involved. These companies actually operate as real businesses, and some have, in the past, accumulated assets of considerable size. The NorthWest Federal Credit Union, for example, a CIA proprietary, had assets of over $100 million at the end of 1976.

psywar: Psychological warfare; the use of propaganda and other psychological means to neutralize the enemy's influence and gain support for "our side." A bizarre example in the 1950s was the CIA's use of low-flying aircraft with loudspeakers aboard, in which an **agent** flew through thick cloud cover over primitive Philippine villages and hurled amplified curses upon any villagers who cooperated with the Communist Huk rebels; the disembodied voice was taken by villagers to be that of powerful evil spirits.

reading in: When an **officer** is assigned to a new case or project, his first task of reviewing all the written material—the files, **cable** traffic, briefing papers, memoranda, reports—to acquaint himself with the same body of knowledge as other CIA officers.

recruitment: Bringing individuals into the employ of the agency for espionage and/or operational purposes; hiring spies. Recruitment is one of the key functions of a CIA **case officer** abroad.

safe house: A CIA-maintained residence that can be used as a base for secret meetings or activities. Many of the **MKULTRA** experiments on unwitting citizens were conducted from CIA safe houses in New York and San Francisco.

sanitize: To censor (by deletion, revision, or wholesale expurgation) a document for release so that certain elements remain secret. Supposedly the agency is protecting its intelligence "sources and methods" by such procedures.

section: The smallest geographical unit of CIA organization, which may be as small as a single city (Berlin section) or a small country (Angola section). A section is a subdivision of a **Branch**.

sensitive: Possibly embarrassing, scandalous, or otherwise jeopardizing to the agency and/or the United States government. Certain files, for example, are categorized as sensitive, and their contents will never be divulged outside the agency.

sheepdipping: Placing an **agent** in an organization or group where he can attain "credentials" that will enable him to **penetrate** other similar groups. Also refers to the use of military forces under civilian **cover.**

soft file: Records of **sensitive** subjects that are kept unofficially by the agency, and are thus not subject to review by outside sources and not available through the **FOIA (Freedom of Information Act)**. The FBI equivalent is its "Do Not File" file.

SOG: The **Special Operations Group**; a **task force** established within the CIA at various times to carry out usually highly illegal or controversial projects, such as acquiring **information** on domestic dissidents (Operation **CHAOS**, 1967–74), or **paramilitary** adventures not consonant with stated government policy. *Special Operations* is a euphemism for **covert** paramilitary actions.

station: A CIA setup in a foreign country, often under **cover** of the American embassy or consulate. Stations may be old, well staffed, and well established, with the **COS** a recognized and high-profile member of the local diplomatic, social, and political circles; or they may be as small and tenuous as a lone **case officer** in a sleazy hotel room with a trunkful of cables and cash. A station is usually located in a capital city. If located in a smaller city or on a military installation, it is called a *base*.

target of opportunity: A person with valuable **information** who "walks in" to a CIA **station** without having been **recruited**. The term also refers to any useful entity or source of information attained by chance, rather than by active **asset**- building.

task force: A temporary office or group of **officers** put together to plan and/or run a particular program, usually with a limited time frame or objectives. *Task Force W,* part of the CIA's Operation **MONGOOSE**, was specifically created to assassinate Fidel Castro. Although a variety of attempts were planned and some were made—poisoned cigars, exploding seashells, ballpoint pens with poisoned hypodermics—the task force never achieved its "objective."

Track II: The secret CIA program to overthrow the Marxist Salvador Allende, after he had been elected President of Chile in 1970—despite strenuous CIA attempts to block his election by political means (*Track I*). With direct authorization from President Nixon and some $10 million in available funds, the CIA funded and promoted the military coup that brought the brutal regime of Augusto Pinochet to power. One key element in Track II was the "removal" of Gen. Rene Schneider, a strict constitutionalist who supported the elected government and stood in the way of a military takeover. The CIA planned his assassination and passed weapons to certain Chileans to do the job. Schneider was kidnapped and shot to death in 1970; Allende's government was ultimately subverted three years later and Allende himself murdered.

201 file: A separate "personality" file on a single individual, which might list not only the per-

son's political affiliations and activities, but
also his or her habits, weaknesses, family and
friends, etc. The CIA admitted to having developed at least 7,200 of these files on United
States citizens during the course of Operation
CHAOS.

watch list: A list of people (or countries, or organizations) that are to be selected out by a
computer when running through data. For
example, in the 1960s the **NSA** had a watch
list of some 1,200 names of United States citizens, which might be cross-referenced with
mail from Cuba or Russia to determine links
between the antiwar movement and the Communist powers. The CIA in three major studies found no such foreign control, although
both Johnson and Nixon insisted that it be
"found" somehow.

V

SPORTS AND FITNESS

[17]

Basic Jock

While every sport or athletic discipline has its own special terminology (the *carved turn* of skiing, the *slam dunk* of basketball, the *spinning heel kick* of Karate, the *frontside gnarler* of skateboarding), there is a common language that is shared by athletes of all types: the language of training, effort and accomplishment. **Working out** is what every athlete does, whether preparing for Wimbledon or the Golden Gloves, the World Series or the marathon. The language professional **jocks** employ is also the language used by men and women who are exercising not for competition but to get or stay in **shape**; and it can be heard at gyms and Y's, on playing fields and tracks, in showers and locker rooms in thousands of places across the country.

Using Basic Jock not only makes one feel a part of the larger athletic community, but also gives a name to certain phenomena that are commonly encountered by all who strive to improve the body's skill, speed, strength, or endurance. Accomplishing something by brute force, for example (known as **muscling it**), is distinguished in almost every sport from the more efficient, aesthetically pleasing accomplishment in good **form**—also known as good **technique**, *the sweet spot,* or "being in the groove." There are terms for making a maximum effort, beyond the limits of comfort or even tolerable pain: **toughing it out**, **reaching down**, giving **110 percent**. And there are the more unpleasant varieties of athletic experience: **tying up**, **blowing your cookies**, **dying**. But for the confirmed jock, the pleasures of meeting the competition, of **psyching up**, **hustling**, being able to **cruise**, nailing a perfect shot, or just **breaking a good sweat**, are worth all the **burns**, and **shakes**, and **palies**, for in the last analysis, working out is its own reward.

abs: The abdominal muscles. Serious body-builders strive to achieve a corrugated effect, known as *washboard abs,* which results from highly developed stomach muscles with very little subcutaneous fat.

aerobic exercise: Any exercise that raises the pulse rate and oxygen intake above normal levels *and* can be continued for a protracted period of time (generally fifteen minutes or longer). Aerobic exercise—such as running, swimming, cycling, backpacking—is essential for developing cardiovascular conditioning and general endurance.

blow your cookies: Also **blow lunch.** To vomit, especially as a result of extremely strenuous exercise. Usually preceded by the *palies,* in which the face turns a pale color, sometimes tinged with green—signifying that one has overdone it and the body will have no more.

bomb: Also *blitz, blast.* To assault a part of the body with exercise, especially by training in *supersets.* "I really **bombed** my **quads** this week!"

break a sweat: To begin perspiring, especially as a result of strenuous activity. Those who don't break a sweat until they hit the steam room have not really **worked out.**

bulk up: To add muscle size by training with heavy weights (or other heavy resistance exercises), while eating a high-protein, high-calorie diet.

burn: 1. As a noun, the hot, stinging sensation felt in certain muscles (especially the calves) when they have been worked to exhaustion, as by repeated **sets** with extremely high **reps.** The burn is supposedly a sign of catabolic tissue breakdown that will ultimately result in greater strength and **definition.**

2. As a verb, to perform exceptionally, especially in relation to the competition. Also *smoke, blow away.* ("Freddie's gonna **burn** in the 220 tonight, just watch!")

cruise: As a noun, a pace that is fairly fast but can be maintained without strain. Applies mostly to continuous-action sports such as running, swimming, and cycling. Also used as a verb, to maintain such a pace. The ability to cruise for a half hour or more is one of the great pleasures of being in good **shape.**

definition: The degree of muscularity and vascularity in relation to the amount of subcutaneous fat. *Good definition* means that the muscle structures and veins are clearly visible under the skin; in exceptionally good definition, the pronounced separation of muscle parts (known as *cuts*) are revealed—especially in the **abs, delts,** and **quads.**

delts: The deltoid muscles of the shoulder caps.

die: To abruptly lose energy, **form,** will, or (for any reason) the capacity to continue at a previous level of performance. One of the author's most vivid memories is of watching a swimmer in the 1963 New York City championships in the one-hundred-yard butterfly. He was more than a body length ahead of the competition at fifty yards and seemed a sure winner. But as the leader was coming off the third turn, his brother (who knew something that we didn't) announced matter-of-factly from the stands, "He **dies** *now*"—and at that instant the swimmer's arms froze in midstroke, his coordination and strength disappeared, and he barely hung on to finish fifth.

effort level: A subjective estimation of how hard one is exerting oneself, usually expressed as a percentage figure (100 percent being an all-out effort). Thus, a runner might say, "I'm gonna do ten 440s at about seventy-five percent, maybe crank it up to eighty-five or ninety for the last three." Interestingly, researchers have discovered that the subjective reports of effort levels by trained athletes at different speeds (as tested on a treadmill, for example), correspond almost exactly with the objective measurement of certain physiological parameters—especially oxygen uptake as a percentage of possible maximum (VO_2 max).

forced reps: A method used in weight training or other strength-building **workouts** in which several additional **reps** of a given exercise are performed after the normal fatigue point, with the assistance of a training partner, who eases the load slightly while the athlete "forces" out the extra repetitions. No pain, no gain, as they say.

form: The way an athlete looks while performing a movement, usually perceived in relation to an ideal form for that particular sport. Perfect form is not merely an aesthetic abstraction, however, but is meant to be the most efficient use of the body's energy. Often this implies the use of the whole body as a unit (as opposed to the discrete action of arms or legs), and the smooth transition from one muscle group to another (such as from legs to waist to arms in throwing a perfect punch). (See also **technique, muscle it**.)

go for it: The exhortation to another person to take a risk, exert himself or herself fully, throw caution to the winds, and proceed with élan. ("They're having a triathlon race next month—a one-mile ocean swim, fifty-mile cycling, then a thirteen-mile run. I'm thinking of entering; what do you think?" "**Go for it!**")

good hands: The ability to catch a ball, especially under unusually difficult circumstances (such as in midair, body horizontal, having just been struck from behind by a two-hundred-fifty-pound defensive lineman); or the general ability to use one's arms effectively. In boxing, for example, good hands implies speed and unpredictability of punching, though not necessarily with knockout power.

grungy: Dirty and smelly, referring to the condition of certain athletic attire (notably socks and jockstraps) that has been left at the bottom of a gym locker for weeks to molder, fecundate, and decay.

hot-dogging: Showing off or performing exceptionally skillful, difficult, or unusual maneuvers. Hot-dogging occurs in almost every sport but is intrinsically a part of surfing,

freestyle skiing, roller skating, skateboarding, and figure skating.

hustle: To move a lot, to play energetically, to try one's utmost. The term is especially common in ball games (e.g., volleyball, baseball), where a player is said to hustle when he or she does virtually *anything* to reach a ball. "Good **hustle**" is an accolade that signifies a high-energy effort—though not necessarily one of high intelligence or good **form**.

iron: Weights, especially the metal plates added to barbells and dumbbells for weight training. To *pump iron* is to lift weights in order to develop strength: the *iron game* is the world of serious weightlifting.

isometrics: A form of exercise without movement, in which resistance is supplied by tensing against a stationary object or another part of one's body. The child's game of pressing one's arms outward against both sides of a doorway as hard as possible for thirty seconds (and then watching them rise magically on their own) is a familiar example. Isometrics are useful for developing precise muscle control but are limited as a form of exercise and may in fact raise one's blood pressure without steady **aerobic** conditioning.

jock: An athletic supporter, or jockstrap. By extension, a person, male *or* female, who is deeply involved in participation sports, exercises relentlessly, or has a major portion of his or her self-image bound up in athletic prowess. Some would say the adult jock is really a perpetual adolescent; the jock would probably offer to settle the question with a game of one-on-one basketball or a situp contest.

lats: The latissimi dorsi, the muscles of the upper back and sides of the torso, which function to pull the elbows and shoulders down. Highly developed lats look like wings added onto the back, and are one of the most recognizable features of more fanatical bodybuilders.

mental toughness: The attitude enabling one to withstand pain, and overcome any discomfort or resistance in training or competition. One assumes that football players, wrestlers, and other devotees of contact sports develop this quality, but it is in fact found equally in top athletes of any sport. To run twenty-six miles at under five minutes per mile, struggling against the competition, the hills, the weather, and the pain, requires mental toughness if anything does.

muscle it: To perform a move not with optimal **form** but with brute force—usually more than is actually required. Thus, a less experienced Judo player might muscle an over-the-shoulder throw by tensely pulling the opponent with his arms and shoulders, rather than by a smooth, coordinated movement of the legs, hips, and torso.

Nautilus: The most modern form of resistance-training equipment (available to the public only in the last decade), now used by many professional teams as well as in private gyms and clubs. The Nautilus system employs a dozen or more machines that exercise each separate muscle group through its full range of motion, moving circularly against a variable resistance (to accommodate the stronger and weaker areas of a muscle's contractile range). It is thus supposed to promote faster strength gains without the loss of flexibility sometimes associated with weightlifting.

negatives: That portion of any exercise in which the movement of a weight (or other resistance) is gradually resisted, but not stopped; for example, the part of a pushup in which you let yourself slowly down to the floor. Emphasizing the negatives is said to increase strength faster than normal exercising (which concentrates on the positive phase), and is often accomplished by having a training partner help with the positive phase (such as lifting a weight off the chest in the bench press), leaving the athlete on his own to control the weight's descent during the negative phase. Heavily loaded bars have wound up balanced across certain throats as a result of this method.

Olympic set: A regulation barbell used in weightlifting and powerlifting competitions, as well as in serious weight training, consisting of a seven-foot-long cadmium steel bar weighing thirty-five pounds, inside and outside clamps (called *collars*), and an assortment of plates weighing between two and a half and forty-five pounds. In more fanatical gyms, four forty-five-pound plates are welded onto the ends of the bar, making the bar impossible to use by anyone who cannot handle a weight of at least 225 pounds.

110 percent: An effort that is beyond one's apparent maximum, beyond "all out." Often used in an exhortation (*"Give me **110%**!"*) by coaches in their desire to coax superior performance from their athletes. Research has shown, however, that in many sports optimal performance is attained at a perceived **effort level** of 85–90 percent, not 100 percent, and certainly not 110.

pecs: Also **pects**. The pectoral muscles of the chest, which are not of any great usefulness in most athletic endeavors (other than crushing walnuts between your elbows), but which many men seem to consider important, devoting inordinate amounts of energy to developing through bench presses, push-ups, and the like.

psych: 1. As a noun, short for psychology or psychological state. More specifically, it means will or intent or purpose, an attitude that one's spirit will prevail over pain, competition, or resistance. ("I didn't really train enough to finish the marathon, but I had the **psych** and I made it somehow. Couldn't walk for days afterward.")

2. As a verb ("to **psych** someone out"), to intimidate or perplex an opponent in order to break his concentration or undermine his confidence. Also used intransitively, meaning to fall apart under pressure. ("I don't know

what happened in the third set—I just **psyched** out, I guess.")

psyched up: Motivated, highly charged, ready for intense action or competition.

pump: As a noun, the gorging of a muscle with blood through exercising, so that the muscle temporarily increases in size. Getting a good pump and then looking in the mirror is one of the narcissistic pleasures of a weightlifting **workout;** however, the actual, permanent gains in muscle size and vascularity take months or years to achieve. Also used as a verb, to *pump up* one's arms, thighs, etc.

quads: The quadriceps, the large muscles of the front and sides of the thigh, used especially in jumping, sprinting, squatting, and kicking.

reach down: To find within oneself an extra source of energy, strength, or endurance, when one's physical resources appear to be depleted. Muhammad Ali was famous for his ability to reach down at the end of a long, brutal fight and somehow come up with a brilliant last round.

rep: Repetition, the number of times a particular movement is repeated without rest. If a person picks up a barbell and presses it overhead twelve times before setting it down, he or she will have completed one **set** of twelve reps. It is the consensus that training with *high reps* (that is, in sets of twelve or more reps, often up to forty or fifty) increases vascularity, **definition,** and muscular endurance; whereas training with heavier resistance and *low reps* (that is, weights one can handle for only one to five or six reps at a time) produces greater muscle size and single-effort strength.

second wind: A renewal of energy or improved efficiency of motion, usually attained after about ten minutes of continuous exercise (though it may be as early as five minutes or as late as forty-five). Thus, one might be running at seven minutes per mile for one mile without much effort, begin to feel some strain between one and one and a quarter miles, then suddenly feel the same pace become easier at about a mile and an half. Apparently the second wind is the result of a physiological adjustment the body makes to continuous **aerobic exercise**.

set: The basic unit of **working out**—a number of repetitions of a single exercise performed without stopping, as a set of bench presses, a set of squat jumps, a set of situps. A serious calisthenic and/or weight workout generally involves somewhere between ten and forty sets. (See also **reps, superset.**)

shakes, the: Uncontrollable quivering or vibration of the muscles, as a result of their having been exercised to—and through—the fatigue point. Although a strange, disconcerting sensation, the shakes are in fact a sign that a good, high-intensity **workout** has been accomplished and, with proper recuperation, an increase in strength and **stamina** will accrue. A simple way to get the shakes in the thigh muscles: Run up and down football stadium steps two at a time for five to ten minutes (*not* recommended for those with weak hearts).

shape: Physical condition. To be *in shape* implies having good muscle tone (not necessarily big muscles), little body fat, and a reasonable level of **stamina** and endurance. Devotees of different sports and exercise systems of course define being in shape quite differently: For a fairly serious runner it might mean the ability to run ten miles in less than seventy minutes, while for a powerlifter it might be the ability to squat with twice his body weight and bench-press one and a half times body weight. Getting in shape from a condition of being *out of shape* is without question the most grueling and unpleasant of processes, which explains why so many people never really get there; once in shape, however, staying there or improving further is never quite so painful.

stamina: The capacity to perform at a high level of intensity and effort for a sustained (but not indefinite) period of time, and to recover quickly. Thus, good running stamina might be indicated by the ability to run six 880-yard intervals at two minutes, forty-five seconds each (or less), with only two minutes' rest between each. Distinguished from *endurance*, which is the ability to continue going at a moderate level of effort for extremely long periods of time—such as cycling for four hours without stopping.

superset: An intense form of weight training in which one body part or muscle group is worked by two different exercises, performed one after the other without any rest between them. A superset for the thighs, for example, might be a **set** of leg extensions (for the **quadriceps**) followed instantly by a set of leg curls (for the hamstrings).

technique: Correct **form** or method of performing a movement or exercise, with the implication of efficiency and coordination rather than sheer strength. In Olympic-style weightlifting, for example, technique refers to the ability to pull a loaded bar with the legs and back, and then drop under it suddenly —rather than attempting to **muscle it** mostly with arm and shoulder power.

tie up: To lose coordination and muscle control due to fatigue, tension, or actual muscle spasm. Thus, a tennis player might tie up on an important point and not be able to hit freely and smoothly, losing power and accuracy in his strokes.

tough it out: To continue to play or exercise despite pain, exhaustion, or injury. ("He **died** in the third quarter but **toughed it out** anyway. His girlfriend was watching.")

Universal: A weight-training machine with multiple areas that can be used by several people at once. Most Universals include stations for leg press, **lat** pull, bench press, inclined situps, chins, and presses.

workout: A training session; an athletic practice; a mythic journey into the world of sport or exercise. The journeyer sheds the garments of the outside world and puts on special holy clothing (the torn sweatshirt, the ancient sneakers), goes through elaborate preparation rituals (stretching, warming up), and then descends into the Jock World. After reaching the first signpost (**breaking a sweat**), he or she endures a series of trials and tests of character—encounters with impossible weights, interminable distances to be run or swum, fearsome opponents to be met and defeated on the court or field of battle. If the journeyer survives the **burn**, the **shakes**, the **pump**, and manages to **tough it out** through strength of heart and will, he or she is rewarded (the long, hot shower) and may return to the "real world"—exhausted perhaps, but somehow transformed. The true workout is not a routine, mildly unpleasant necessity (as many would have it) but an adventure in the realms of the spirit, played out in the terms of the flesh.

$\lceil 18 \rceil$

Running and Jogging

Current estimates have it that as many as 20 million Americans now run, or jog, regularly; the number that dabble in it, or at least saunter to the supermarket in triple-knit warm-up suits and Adidas running shoes ("the new Jock Chic," proclaims the *Village Voice*) must be far greater. This makes recreational running (as distinct from other forms: running from wild animals, running to catch the bus, running for political office, running a business, running out on someone) one of the major socio-athletic phenomena of modern times. Acolytes of this new religion perceive it as the method by which the overcivilized, technological human being can regain and restore his or her sense of being a primitive, vital creature, an animal capable of covering vast distances (across the dry savannah, the mountain pass, the endless shopping malls) on foot, under its own power.

Anyone who has been **jogging** more than once or twice, and is thus serious enough about it to invest in shoes, books, magazines, nylon running shorts, and other paraphernalia, will balk at the term "jogger" (with its connotation of a bumpy, shuffling trot), preferring to be called "runner," an infinitely more powerful appellation that suggests a certain primal swiftness and grace. The uninitiated observer may fail to notice these qualities among the average motley array of gasping Sunday joggers in the park, but no matter. They are absorbed with **pace** and **distance**, fighting **oxygen debt** and **shin splints**, hoping they don't hit **the Wall**, and don't really care *what* you think. Running, as anyone will expound to you at great length if you're interested, is an extremely personal, introspective endeavor, in which the mind, the will, the consciousness of the runner play by far the most important roles. What deranged human *body*, after all, would choose to race twenty-six miles as fast as it could over hilly Massachusetts roads on an appallingly humid ninety-two-degree day in late April? Would the body not have chosen to lie and lollygag in the shade? To drink mint juleps rather than **ERG**?

Runners (or joggers, or what have you) tend to laconic understatement in their use of language: "I'm doing a little *hill work* today," for example, may refer to the process of hurling oneself up and down, up and down the longest and steepest acclivity available (people often drive long distances to find the optimal incline), until a frothing, pallid exhaustion has been attained. Though the sport (the fad? art? discipline?) is fundamentally solitary and nonverbal, runners have been known to wax quite voluble on occasions—the single word "water," for example, has been delivered with unmatched eloquence. The following lexicon will enable you to converse knowledgeably with any serious runner, or to act the part, until you give up and decide to become a runner yourself.

aerobic: Literally "with oxygen." Any level of exertion in which the body's demand for energy is fully met by the oxygen intake provided by breathing. More generally, any exercise or **pace** in which you do not feel out of breath.

aerobic threshold: The fastest **pace** that an individual can maintain without incurring **oxygen debt**. While for the average health-conscious jogger this is probably somewhere between eight and twelve minutes per mile, top **marathoners** can sustain a pace faster than five minutes per mile, **aerobically**. One's aerobic threshold can be increased through aerobic, **LSD** training.

anaerobic: Literally "without oxygen." Any level of exertion to which breathing is not sufficient to supply energy, and the body temporarily supplies energy without oxygen. Anaerobic running (such as **intervals**) generates an **oxygen debt**, is faster and more exciting, and generally more painful, than **aerobic** running.

Boston: The **Boston Marathon**; held every year in late April, when the weather typically conspires to unseasonal heat and humidity. It is The Race for serious **distance** runners, and —even with severe qualifying restrictions—

attracts fields of over 5,000 runners. Boston is famous for its series of "Heartbreak Hills" around sixteen to seventeen miles.

carbo loading: A widely accepted method for maximizing the amount of *glycogen* (the basic body "fuel" oxidized in the muscles for energy) stored in the body prior to endurance events. Carbo loading consists of three distinct stages: (1) an exhausting workout that depletes the glycogen supply; (2) three to seven days of extremely low-carbohydrate diet; (3) one to three days of extremely high-carbohydrate diet, up to and including the last meal before the event. This process reputedly can result in a stored-glycogen level two to three times the normal maximum.

distance: Generally understood by the running community to mean runs of **10 K** (6.2 miles) or more. Also refers to accumulated mileage logged in a given week or month, as in the piercing question of running one-upmanship: "Doing any **distance** these days?" Top **marathoners** regularly log over 100 miles per week, fifty-two weeks a year.

ERG: Electrolyte Replacement with Glucose; a trade name more generally applied to any of several liquid concoctions taken before, during, and after long-distance runs and races to stave off muscle fatigue and dehydration. Most **marathons** have way stations every few miles, where cups of water and ERG are proffered to the runners; dazed marathoners have been known to drink the water and splash themselves with ERG.

fartlek: Swedish, literally "speed play." Developed in the 1940s by the renowned Swedish coach Gosta Holmer, this is a training method in which a longish run is varied through spontaneous, unplanned changes of **pace**—mixing **LSD**, fast cruise, **shake-ups**, and **sprints**. The point of fartlek is not only physical conditioning but raising the runner's enjoyment and spirit.

fit: A curiously understated term used by world-class runners to refer to absolutely peak athletic condition. (Bill Rodgers to his wife at the start of the 1977 Boston Marathon: "I dunno —Drayton looks **fit**.")

flow: The feeling of energized yet effortless movement that occurs spontaneously during some runs and is the "high" many modern runners seek. It often (but not always) associated with **LSD**-type running; relaxed, noncompetitive psychological states; and the conscious visualization of energizing images.

foot plant: The particular pattern in which the runner's foot touches the ground, absorbs shock, and generates power. The three main foot-plant patterns are: *heel-toe* (heel hits first, weight rolls forward and inward), *whole foot* (sole hits as a unit, less rolling action), and *ball of foot* (heel and midsole never touch; used mainly for **sprints**).

intervals: Also **interval training.** Any of a variety of training methods in which one runs hard for a specified distance, then recuperates (by jogging, walking, or stopping) for a specified amount of time, then repeats the process—often literally ad nauseam. The rest periods are never long enough to allay the insane pain of the next run; in this way, muscle power and **anaerobic** stamina are devel-

oped. Typical interval workout: ten 400-yard **fast runs** with 120 seconds' rest between each.

jogging: A style of moving along, using the legs for propulsion, but without lifting the knees high or stretching the legs far behind; a sort of humble, shuffling gait; considered by various authorities to be any pace slower than eight, or ten, or twelve minutes per mile (depending on their personal **aerobic threshold** and sheer generosity of spirit); any form of bipedal locomotion that does not look like walking, running, or skipping.

kick: A finishing sprint at the end of a middle- or long-distance race, that is, one mile or longer. Certain competitors are known for their astonishing ability to kick past all opponents on the last lap, if they are anywhere near them. (Most notable **kicker** in the world today: Miruts Yifter of Ethiopia.) A burst of speed in the middle of a race is called a *surge*.

lactic acid: The major waste product that accumulates in the muscles during intense or prolonged effort. When lactic acid builds up and is not carried off by the bloodstream, the result is fatigue, pain, heaviness, tightness, and cramps in the limbs. Running on in this condition is said to "build character."

LSD: Long, slow distance running, almost totally **aerobic** and lasting a minimum of thirty minutes. The **pace** is comfortable, never exceeding a 40 to 50 percent level of effort.

marathon: A road footrace of 26 miles, 385 yards, noted as a test of courage and character as well as physical endurance. A form of insanity condoned by society and sanctioned by the AAU. A time of three hours or less is considered good; two hours, twenty minutes is "world class." In the final analysis, however, to finish at all is a major achievement.

masters: Runners over forty. Masters track and field is gaining popularity at a very rapid rate, both in the U.S. and abroad, with many races having awards for a masters' division or even separate masters' events. Two masters age-group records to marvel at: Jack Foster of New Zealand's world-class 2:17:29 in the 1978 New York Marathon, at age forty-six; and Monty Montgomery of California with a 5:42:2 mile—at the age of seventy.

orthotics: Colloquially called *inserts*, these are styrofoam, cork, or plastic devices designed by podiatrists to adjust the interior of the runner's shoe surface to correct abnormalities of the foot, ankle, or leg. The better orthotics are individually constructed from a mold of the runner's foot, and often spell the difference between continual reinjury and pain-free running.

oxygen debt: The inevitable result of prolonged **anaerobic** exercise, marked by gasping, clawing for air, redness or paleness of skin, anguished features, and the obligatory stopping or slowing of **pace**. The **oxygen debt** is always collected.

pace: As a noun, the runner's perceived sense of speed and effort, often defined numerically ("an eight-minute **pace**"), but more often expressed in terms of some subjective quality: a good pace, a smooth pace, a beautiful pace, an impossible pace, a killing pace, etc. As a verb, to establish a speed for another runner in the early portion of a race or workout, making it psychologically easier for him. ("**Pace** me for the first quarter of an 880?")

PR: Personal record; a runner's best time for a given distance. ("I finished 653rd in the Poughkeepsie 10,000 meters, but my 47:42 was a **PR**.")

repeats: A form of **speed work** in which the runner **sprints** hard for a specified distance, then rests as long as necessary to recover completely, then repeats. Compare **intervals.**

runner's knee: Probably the most common malady of the jogging world. Technically called *chondromalacia*, the term applies to several conditions in which pain is experienced in the knee joint or immediately around it. Causes include loosened cartilage, strained tendons and muscle attachments, inflamed nerves, in

turn mostly due to abnormal or imperfect **foot plant**, which stresses the knee joint.

second wind: A physiological phenomenon generally occurring after ten to twenty minutes of steady running, in which the body with some suddenness shifts into a more efficient mode of functioning: The heart rate drops, breathing becomes easier, and the runner experiences renewed ease and energy.

shake-ups: Brief periods in which the runner **jogs** along, bouncing as loosely as possible, allowing the muscles to hang tensionless from the bone structure. An excellent relaxation-and-recovery exercise between hard-run **intervals**.

shin splints: The second of the three most common running injuries, marked by a nasty pain radiating up the front of the lower leg, worsening as the run continues. Generally, shin splints are caused by excessive impact (pounding stride, thin soles, hard surfaces) and/or muscle imbalance between the calves and shins.

speed work: Training done by middle- and long-distance runners to improve their speed and **anaerobic** stamina. Usually practiced on a track, speed work entails **repeats**, **intervals**, or other types of **sprints** and near-sprints.

sprint: The high gear of running, an all-out effort, marked by high knee lift, explosive kick-back of the foot as it leaves the ground, and vigorous arm movement. Full sprinting —as in a one-hundred-meter dash—is almost 100 percent **anaerobic**.

tendonitis: The last of the Big Three running injuries: an inflammation of the Achilles tendon at the back of the ankle, which attaches the calf muscles to the heel. As it is difficult to heal without prolonged rest, many runners learn to live with it. The cry of "tendonitis" is universally acknowledged by fellow runners as sufficient explanation for any limping or hobbling asymmetries of gait.

10 K: Ten kilometers, or 10,000 meters (approximately 6.2 miles); the standard and most common distance for road races, and thus a common measure of a runner's ability. ("Just because you got your **10 K** under forty minutes, doesn't mean you're ready for **Boston!**")

third wind: A psychological breakthrough phenomenon, usually occurring sometime after forty minutes of continuous, **aerobic** running at an unstrained **pace**. Runners report a wide variety of "altered states of consciousness," ranging from deep relaxation, euphoria, or personal empowerment to an almost mystical sense of unity and well-being. The third wind is elusive, and one may run the requisite **distances** for weeks before experiencing it. When one is no longer looking for it, it comes.

ultramarathon: Any race longer than 26 miles, 385 yards; generally, distances of 50 kilometers, 50 miles, 52½ miles (*double marathon*), 100 miles, and how-far-you-can-run in twenty-four hours. The record for the last is 162 miles, held by America's Park Barner.

Wall, the: In **marathoning**, a point generally located at or around twenty miles, when the runner abruptly falls apart and finds it almost impossible to continue; probably caused by the sudden total depletion of the body's store of muscle glycogen. ("I was feeling great until I hit **the Wall**.")

[19]

Tennis

The much-publicized "tennis boom" of the seventies was not merely a media hype: From a relatively small-time sport considered primarily the avocation of the privileged and well-to-do, by the early 1980s tennis had become not only a major spectator sport (exceeded in attendance figures only by the Big Three—football, baseball, and basketball) but the serious hobby of at least 20 million Americans who play tennis at least three times a month, and the occasional athletic diversion of millions more. Top tennis stars such as Bjorn Borg and Jimmy Connors earn several million dollars a year on the pro tennis circuit, and considerably more if their endorsements of tennis racquets, clothes, shoes, and a dozen other products are included. Media coverage of the major tournaments has certainly contributed to the tennis explosion, but there is no escaping the fact that millions of Americans are now playing tennis—on an estimated 150,000 courts—not because they saw the Borg-McEnroe **tie-breaker** at Wimbledon, but because the game is an exciting, challenging test of coordination, skill, strategy, psychology, and stamina.

Much tennis nomenclature has become so familiar to the general public that even the nonplayer is likely to have some notion of what is meant by **ace**, **backhand**, **serve**, **love**, and **deuce**. Those who have followed the game on television during the past few years have probably also acquired a nodding acquaintance with **break-point**, **fault**, **lob**, **volley**, **topspin**, and other fundamentals of **scoring** and play. For the more dedicated player—or spectator—however, there is a far more extensive, and colorful, range of tennis terms and expressions to be learned. Wouldn't you like to be the first on your court to know if you are, have been, or are likely to become a **goomer**, **glooper**, **dinker**, **pooper**, **Johnny Ray**, **turkey**, or **paladin**? Would you like to know the difference between a **chip** and a **chop**, a **cannonball** and an **American twist**, **hitting out** and the **steelies?**

Mere words won't turn you from a **hacker** into a **pro**, of course. But if you work on your **anticipation**, cultivate your **inner game**, **reach up and out** on your **serves**, increase your **backhand follow-through**, and generally **gut it out** for a while, you may develop some **court sense** and wind up, not a **goomer** or **fuzz sandwich**, but a player with a **big game** who can **close off points** and even, now and then, find your way into **the Zone**.

ABC: Not the TV network or something elementary, but a player who has All But a Concluder (or Clincher) shot. The ABC moves convincingly, has lots of good **strokes**, but can't **close off points** and come up with the winners.

ace: A well-**served** ball that completely eludes the **receiver**'s racquet.

ad (service) court: The **service court** to the **receiver**'s left. To **serve** into the ad court, the server must place himself behind the **baseline** and anywhere to the left of the **centerline**.

advantage: Also **ad** and **van**. As early as forty-thirty, canny **servers** will call the **score** as, "**Ad** in," or "My **ad**"—meaning, "I need only one more point to win this game." (Such players are more likely to wait till the **point** after **deuce** to favor an opponent with "**Ad** out," or "Your **ad**.")

all: Even or tied, as in thirty-**all** or six-all. See **points**.

alleys: The four-and-a-half-foot-wide strips added at each side of a singles **court** to make it playable for **doubles**.

American twist: See **serve**.

anticipation: The talent for estimating, imagining, or just plain guessing where the ball is going to go next, as well as with what speed, trajectory, and **spin**. Anticipation is one result of **concentration** and a necessary component of **court sense**.

approach shot: Any **shot** (though usually a **groundstroke**) that enables a player to approach the net, so that he may **cut off the angles** and **close off the point**, usually with a **volley**. An approach shot is often some sort

of **slice** or **chip**, and may also be called (especially when effective) a **forcing shot**.

ATA: Air the armpits; Vic Braden's way of reminding players to **follow through** completely in **stroking backhands**.

ATP: Association of Tennis Professionals; an organization of male **pros**.

ATP computer (or Ranking): A ranking system for male tennis **pros**.

Australian formation: In **doubles**, the **server** and his partner line up on the same side in some variant of an "I" formation, so that the receiver must return **down the line**.

backcourt: The area of each player's side of the **court** that is between his **baseline** and **service line**. Some would limit the backcourt area to include only the four feet in front of the baseline.

backhand: Any **stroke** that right-handers hit on balls to their left, and left-handers vice versa. Against all logic, many remain unconvinced that the backhand is more natural and ought to be easier than the **forehand**.

backspin: Also **slice** and, occasionally, **cut**. Backward rotation of the ball imparted by moving one's racquet **face** vertically down the back of the ball.

backswing: Any preparation for a **shot, forehand** or **backhand**.

baseline: The second line on either side of the net that is parallel to and thirty-nine feet from it.

baseline game: A style of play that relies on hitting **groundstrokes deep** (or otherwise effectively), and waiting for the other player to make an error. Played by a *baseliner*.

"**bend zee knees**": A familiar command, given here in one of **Vic Braden**'s versions. (Another of his is "Sit and hit.") The idea is that if the knees aren't bent, the player is likely to lack both power and control, as well as mobility and flexibility.

big game: The technique of a player who **serves** and moves to the net as fast as he can, in order to **volley** and **close off the point**.

big server: One who **serves cannonballs** or similarly effective serving loads of comparable shocking power.

blow-up: Shadow or no-ball tennis; named with reference to the final scene in the Antonioni film *Blow-Up*. Played with proper **concentration**, the imaginary game may enable intense awareness of one's **strokes**, body movements, the motions of one's opponent(s), the hypothetical flight of the nonexistent ball. Not for the unimaginative. May be played solo, with or without a **court** or wall.

break-point: If the **server** loses the next **point**, he loses the game and his serve. *Double* or *triple break-point* means the server is down (behind) **fifteen-forty** or **love-forty**. See **points**.

broken service: See **serve**.

camels and gypsies circuit: Any of several itineraries taken by touring **pros** rated below, say, 300 on the **ATP Computer**. They say it beats working for a living—and no **fan** would doubt that.

cannonball: A fast, hard, "flat" (no-**spin**) **serve**.

centerline: The line (perpendicular to the net) that divides the two **service courts**.

chip: A ball hit with **backspin**. Some say a chip differs from a **slice** in also having **sidespin**; others accept this distinction but reverse the labels. Either a chip or a slice, with or without sidespin, can make a good **approach** or **forcing shot**. A **chop** differs from a chip or slice in being more sharply **cut** (the racquet generally descending across the back of the ball at an acuter angle), having consequently less velocity, and being more likely to **die** when it hits the opponent's **court**. A chop is usually

called a **drop shot** when hit from behind the **service line**. (In fact, chop has gone so completely out of many players' vocabularies—and games—they may claim no such shot ever existed.)

chipper: A player who thrives on hitting **chips** and **chops**, with here and there a **slice** thrown in, and of course a variety of maddening **lobs**. Chippers are usually also **dinkers**, cordially reviled, and alarmingly successful.

closed: Said of a racquet **face** that is inclined at some angle in the direction toward the playing surface. The opposite of **open** or **spooned**.

close off points: Also **conclude points**. To win points, especially decisively (rather than by the opponent's error). The player who knows how to close off points has the wit and will to move aggressively, hit **forcing shots**, **cut off the angles**, and end **points** quickly. Sometimes called a *closer,* he's no **ABC**.

concentration: In tennis, the ability not only to shut out distractions, but, more importantly, to get into the always-moving center of a game and stay there. The hard part is to not let fear or anxiety keep one from attending to (watching, listening, **anticipating**) the simple essentials: the moving ball (its speed, **spin**, trajectory, its seams; the blur and thunk it makes against and away from the racquet **face**) and one's changing relation to the ball, the **court**, and the opponent. Conditioning and control both help concentration; all, taken together, result in calculated quickness in getting to the ball, as well as fluid ease in dispatching it with power and precision. The player who best concentrates and anticipates is said to be in **the Zone**.

Continental grip: See **grips**.

court: The playing surface; also the area bounded by the **baselines** and **sidelines**. Courts are said to be comparatively *fast* or *slow* depending upon how fast and at what height comparably hit balls bounce from them. Grass and California cement are fast courts, clay (especially red European clay) makes for a slow court; various artificial surfaces are engineered for different combinations of speed and bounce.

court sense: A player's perceptions of exactly where the boundary lines are; and, more importantly, a talent for setting up weak or predictable returns with **forcing shots,** as well as the ability to **close off points** by "hitting 'em where they ain't." (Usually remarked approvingly, as in "The kid's got good **court sense.**")

crosscourt: Shots hit diagonally from the point of contact.

cut: A **stroke** with considerable **backspin** and/or **sidespin**. See **chip.**

cut off the angles: To move toward the net in order to control the angle of the opponent's possible **crosscourt** return.

deep shot: Any **shot,** especially one with considerable velocity, that lands close to the **baseline** or (in the case of **service**) the **service line.** Those who can consistently hit deep find treasure.

deuce: The **score** is **forty**-forty, or any tied score beyond that. Some also call out "**Deuce**" at **thirty**-thirty, since either player/side must still score two more **points** to win.

dies: What happens when a soft **drop** or **chop** splats on the **court.** Also, what may happen to the player who is up against a **dropper** or **chopper.**

dinker: Also **pooper, pusher,** and other far worse names. A player who always tries to get the ball back safely, softly (when in any doubt whatsoever), and with whatever maddening **spins** figure to drive the opponent bonkers. Not without reason, the dinker thinks dinking is percentage tennis. Opponents frequently wish the dinker would grow up, but the wise child knows and loves his own **strokes**.

double-fault: Two consecutive unsuccessful attempts to **serve** a ball into the opponent's **service court.** Server loses the **point.**

doubles: A game played with two players on each side of the **court.** See **mixed doubles.**

down-the-line shot: A **shot** made down a **sideline** near which it is hit.

draw: Each player's position in a tournament schedule, and the process of determining these positions. Draws are theoretically made at random, except for **seeded players.**

drive: Generally synonymous with **stroke** or **shot** or **groundstroke**, though some mean by drive a stroke hit especially hard.

drop shot: A **shot** with excessive **backspin** designed to throw off an opponent's timing (drop shots **die** just over the net when properly executed), tire him with running, and/or demoralize him by winning with what he wants desperately to believe is a dumb low-percentage shot.

drop volley: A **volley** hit softly and usually with extra **backspin** so that it **dies**. More or less interchangeable with **stop volley.**

drum major: A racquet twirler. The drum major's apparent object is to stay loose and rattle the **server** by suggesting he's serving into a propeller or a parade.

Eastern grip: See **grips.**

face: Also **racquet face.** The stringed area of the racquet **head.**

fan: Short for **fanatic.** Not a spectator, though, but a player with *aficion,* a True Believer. The female fan may be a **Joan.**

fault: An unsuccessful attempt to put a ball in the opponent's **service court.** A *foot fault* usually results from the server's touching the **baseline** or stepping into the **court** before his racquet has touched the ball.

FBI: Usually as a question at the very beginning of a friendly match, "**F.B.I**?" means "Shall we play First Ball (i.e., **serve**) In?" One necessarily answers yes.

fifteen: One **point.** See **points.**

finishing shot: Also **winner.** Any **shot** that **closes off the point.**

five: Short for **fifteen**; i.e., one **point,** as in "**five**-Oh" or "**Love-five.**" The logic is not exactly arithmetic, but has to do anyway with saving 50 percent of a **server**'s breath in calling out the **score**.

follow-through: The smooth continuation of any **stroke** past the point of ball contact. A follow-through may be long (as on **groundstrokes** and **serves**) or short (on many **volleys**).

forcing shot: Any **shot** that sets up a weak return and thus leads to being able to **close off the point**.

forecourt: The area of each player's side of the **court** that lies between the net and three or four feet from the **service line** (some say to the service line itself).

forehand: Any **stroke** that left-handers make on balls to their left, and right-handers on balls to their right.

forty: See **points**.

fuzz sandwich: What the unalert player becomes whose racquet is not at the ready; he takes the ball between his teeth.

game: The basic unit of tennis scoring. Except in **no-ad scoring**, a game is complete when **server** or **receiver** has scored four **points**, with an **advantage** of at least two. The first player to win six games (by at least two) wins the **set**.

get: As in *"Good get!"*—meaning "Nice **retrieving** in difficult circumstances!"

glooper: Also **glue pot**. A player who seems stuck to the playing surface, hoping the ball will come right to him.

going for: Taking the chance, believing you can make the **shot**, **hitting out**.

goomer: Also **gomer** (as in Pyle?), **goofer**, and **goober**. A loser, not only in fact and habit, but also by preference or temperament. One who must value the thrill of agony, the victory of defeat. Many a goomer is also a **glooper**, **Johnny Ray**, **turkey**, **turtle**, **winger**, or **nasty**.

Grand Masters: Male players forty-five or over who in their spangled youths won at least one major national tournament. Grand Masters play their own circuit.

grand slam: Winning in one twelve-month period the national championships of France, Great Britain, the United States, and Australia.

grass: See **lawn tennis**.

grips: All the words about grips may make you wonder whether you've lost yours, but the matter boils down to how you hold the racquet in order to get the best results. Simply put, what you want is to optimize your chances to **stroke** the ball where you want it to go and with whatever speed and **spin** you choose. To do any and all of that, the first (and almost only) thing you need to know is that the racquet **face** should dwell as squarely and long upon the ball as you can manage. At the point of contact and beyond, the **sweet spot** (the most effective, responsive string area) should be both vertical to the playing surface and as squarely perpendicular to the **sideline** (i.e., parallel with the **baseline**) as is consonant with the destination you imagine for that **shot**. Why? Because such "squareness" puts more strings on the ball. More strings on the ball means more power and control.

Five or ten minutes of **blow-up** now and then will begin to tell anyone whether a grip change is in order. Should you be "shaking hands with the racquet" (i.e., taking some version of an *Eastern grip*)? Or grabbing it somehow "like a frying pan" (*Western grip*)? Or hanging on pretty much as you might carry a suitcase (i.e., with some variation of a *Continental grip*)? Only you can know for sure by going through swing after swing and paying strict attention to how you best clutch the club for maximum results. You will probably also want to figure out whether and how much you need to move your hand(s) in order to go from a best **forehand** grip to a best **backhand** grip. There's usually plenty of time in which to change.

ground game: That part of a player's game which consists of various **groundstrokes**.

groundstroke: Also **groundies.** Any **stroke** hit after the ball has bounced.

gut it out: Going for the **shot** that's more aggressive, and usually riskier (especially if you're not sure you **own** it).

hacker: An earnest but awkward amateur. A mediocre tennis player who, in weaker moments, imagines the fame, fortune, and love that might have been his had he been born with better tennis genes, or had started playing at age five, or just "had more time to practice." Otherwise known to be sane, sensible, and kind to animals; and often a **fan.**

half-volley: A misnomer for a **groundstroke** taken very close to and not very high above the point where the ball has bounced. Called a half-volley probably because the half-volleyer is characteristically halfway in his progress toward the net, where he wants to **close off the point** with a **volley.**

head: The entire rounded or oval portion of a racquet.

heels up: Some teachers' favorite words (after "**bend zee knees**"), and rightly so; any player is more likely to be leaden unless body weight is balanced forward, toward the toes if not exactly up on them.

hit and giggle: Casual, even slovenly tennis. Sometimes a synonym for club **mixed doubles.**

hitting out: One hitting out is not playing safe or stiff, but **going for** his **shots,** confident that a reasonable number of them will land in; and believing that, in any event, he's better off hitting loose and easy; and that if his shots don't immediately improve, they're more likely to later if he doesn't now fall prey to the **steelies.**

hustler: One who plays for immediate pay, sometimes by betting that his grubby appearance and/or gear will snocker the mark into a foolish wager. At other times, the (known) hustler will offer to handicap himself in one or more ways if the mark will put up a certain amount of cash that says, say, the hustler can't

win if he also has to play in galoshes or drag a Great Dane around on his side of the court.

inner game: Also **Zen tennis.** The internal processes of higher-order **concentration,** awareness, and centering used to improve both one's "performance" on the court and one's experience of playing. Expounded by such teachers as Tim Gallwey and Rick Champion.

ILTF: International Lawn Tennis Federation.

Joan: A female **fan** or **paladin** who, like St. Joan, willingly, eagerly sacrifices her all to the True Faith, though burned out she may become in tennis martyrdom.

Johnny Ray: A weeper, wailer, whiner; a player who can always find something to moan over. See **goomer.**

junk: Also **dump.** As a verb, to take it easy in a **set** already thought lost, in order to save energy for the next one. Not necessarily a bad tactic if in the losing process the junker also tries to loosen up, get his game back, change his game, or do whatever may prove useful in the next set. As a noun, junk refers to soft shots.

killer instinct: What separates the Borgs from the **goomers.**

kill shot: Also a **kill.** Any **shot** virtually unreturnable by mere mortals because of the **spin** and velocity applied to it.

lawn tennis: The original game as played on grass, a mind-expanding if unpredictable surface now largely passed into fabled story or sad disrepair, except at Wimbledon, Longwood, Newport, and similar enclaves of the genteel and powerful.

leaner: Not necessarily also slimmer or fitter than thou, the leaner never misses an opportunity to groan at your **faults,** whoop at your **woodies,** or at least murmur, giggle, or gasp, every time you swerve in the slightest from perfection. Both leaner and **psych-O** add unmistakable tonal spins to "Good try," "Nice idea," and even "Good **get**!" with the general implication of "Astonishing how the klutzes get out of their depth!" They may also inquire, as if earnestly desirous of knowing, how you hold your **backhand**, move your feet on the **volley**, breathe when you serve. The intention here is to make you conscious and clumsy about what would otherwise go on happening smoothly.

let ball: Any ball played over for any reason. Most often, it is a **served** ball (thus, *let serve*) that touches the top of the net and drops into the intended **service court** on the other side. A served ball that touches the net but does *not* land in the intended service court is sometimes termed a **net ball** (usage is divided here), but is also always a **fault**, and thus may not be played over.

line-shrinker: One who calls the lines in his favor in most cases admitting of doubt. Also known as *two-inch eyes* (as in, "It was at least two inches out.") and by other, less generous names.

lingering death: See **tie-breaker**.

lob: A high-arcing **shot**. The *defensive lob* is hit to buy time for a player out of position. The *offensive lob* may be an attempt to throw off an opponent's timing or drive him back from a position near the net. The *topspin lob* is a frequently successful attempt at an outright **winner** over the head of a net-rusher; its **topspin** carries it rapidly up to about twelve feet over the opponent's head, then rapidly down into the **court** before he can catch up with it.

love: In **scoring**, means "zero."

match: A match is won by the first player to win two out of three, or three out of five, **sets**.

match point: The point which, if won by the leading player, will decide the match. Announcing, "**Match point**" or "**Set point**" to an opponent is generally thought to be a courtesy to the possibly dithered; but in doing so, try to keep obvious triumph out of your voice.

mixed doubles: Two teams of one male and one female each, making in all some multiple of four confusions. In (intentionally) *mixed-up doubles*, either the males or the females move on and "couple" with a new partner every

twenty or thirty minutes during a longish weekend evening at certain tennis clubs.

move to the ball: A concept or command, designed to remind you you're playing the ball, not your opponent, and had better stay constantly in motion toward where you think it's likely to appear next on your side of the net.

nasty: A chronic complainer about line calls and things in general.

net ball: A ball that hits the net on any **shot** after the **serve**; it remains in play. See **let**.

net game: That portion of a player's game that consists of **volleys** and **overheads**, shots ordinarily made between his **service line** and the net.

no-ad scoring: In no-ad scoring, a **game** is won by the first player to score four **points**.

not up: Said of a ball that bounces for the second time before it's hit.

open face: Describing a racquet **face** inclined away from the vertical toward the sky. See **grips**.

out: A line call meaning the ball did not land inside the **court**. Other more or less equivalent calls are *long, back,* and *wide.* One also sometimes hears *deep,* but this is frowned upon by the knowledgeable as leading to dreadful ambiguities.

overhead (smash): Any **shot** hit high over one's head after the ball is in play. Some disapprove of adding "smash" to the name, since such a notion may be a partial cause of overheads being hit at considerable velocity—into the net.

overspin: Another name for **topspin**. Imparted by bringing the racquet **face** up the back of the ball so that the ball's top then **spins** in the direction of the opponent. See **backspin**.

own: A player owns a **shot** if and when he can make it successfully with some regularity.

paladin: Has racquet, will travel. A roving knight or Samurai; always a **fan** of sorts, though perhaps pretending to have fallen from the True Faith; in any case, likely to prefer seeming better than a mere **hustler**.

May be found at the more prosperous resorts and on the **camels and gypsies circuit**.

passing shot: Any **shot** that gets past a player coming to net before he can move to cut it off.

poaching: In **doubles**, the netman's moving toward the center of the **court** (as his partner **serves**), in order to intercept and put away the expected **crosscourt** return.

points: In traditional tennis, the points in a game are **love** (zero), **fifteen** or **five** (one point), **thirty** (two points), **forty** (three points), **game** (four points, with a minimum margin of two). In case of a tie—forty-all—the **score** is **deuce**; the next point is an **ad** for one of the players, and the game continues till one or the other gains an **advantage** of two points. In **no-ad scoring**, the first player to win four points wins the game, the seventh point (if necessary) is **served** into the receiver's choice of **service court**, and the server frequently calls the score in the more familiar numbers—one-two-three-four.

pro: A *teaching pro* takes money for helping you improve your game; a *playing pro* tries to take money for making you wish you could.

psycher: A player who tries to upset his opponent's **concentration** and thus his game. See **leaner** and **psych-O**.

psych-O: A clumsier, arguably pathological version of the **psycher** or **leaner**. The sort who might well keep a mummified headmaster in the fruit cellar, or sleep with his racquet.

pusher: One content merely to push (or **poop** or **dink**) the ball back, as he waits for the other guy to blow the **point**. The pusher doesn't necessarily turn out to be a dope.

racket: If the spelling was good enough for Shakespeare, it should be good enough for us, right? Wrong. There's been an incessant waffling back and forth, but *racquet* seems the preferable way to go these days (says *Tennis* magazine, among others), if only because it cuts down the implied decibel level and sepa-

rates the genteel men and women of the tennis world from the boys in La Cosa Nostra.

racquetball: Handball for those who are not into hardening their hands. The chief virtues of racquetball are that it has simultaneously improved the cardiovascular efficiency of the nation and lured fumblers off the real tennis **courts** where, for two or three years in the seventies, they were both an embarrassment to themselves and an aggravation to others.

rallying: Hitting the ball back and forth across the net.

reaching up and out: A verbal formula to inspire that portion of the **service** motion in which one imparts to the ball both maximum force and the requisite amount of **topspin** to make sure that it will clear the net and drop into the opponent's **service court**.

receiver: The person not **serving**; that is, the player who "receives" the serve.

retriever: One adept in chasing down and returning practically every ball that comes over the net.

scoring: See **points**, **game**, **set**, **tie-breaker**, **match**.

seeded player: Also **seeds**. Those thought most likely to succeed by a tournament committee, and distributed throughout a **draw** in such a way as to maximize their chances of growing into quarter-finalists.

serve: Serves are of three or four basic types. A *flat serve* has only the slight **topspin** (**overspin**) it needs in order to get over the net. A *topspin serve* has (of course) a more pronounced topspin, is eminently safe, and kicks high when it bounces. A topspin serve can also be, in part, either a *slice serve* or a *twist serve* (sometimes called an *American twist serve*), depending upon whether its forward **spin** is predominantly to the left (*slice*) or right (*twist*). A service is **broken** (the **receiver** *breaks serve*) when the server loses the **game**; otherwise, he *holds serve*. A player whose serve has been broken is *down a service break*.

service court: That area on the **receiver**'s side

between the net, the first line parallel to it, and the singles **court sidelines**. The receiver's *deuce court* is the rectangle to his right; his *ad* (*service*) *court* the rectangle to his left. The **server** has two chances to put a ball in play as he serves, alternately, into the deuce and ad courts.

service line: The first line on either side of the net that is parallel to and twenty-one feet from it.

set: Unit of tennis scoring. Except when a **tie-breaker** rule is in effect, the player who first wins six or more **games** with a minimum margin of two is the winner of the set. See also **game**, **match**.

set point: The point which, if won by the leading player, will decide the **set**. See **match point**.

setup: A weak return easy to **volley** away to **close off the point**.

shot: Any hitting of the ball with the racquet. See **stroke**, **groundstroke**, **volley**.

short ball: A **shot** that falls short, between the **service line** and the net, and enables the aggressive opponent to come more easily to net and **close off the point**.

sidespin: A **spin** accomplished by moving the racquet **face** across the back of the ball in such a way as to make part of its rotation be lateral (i.e., left to right or right to left); the rest being some amount of **topspin** or **backspin**.

slice: See **chip**, **serve**.

smash: See **overhead**.

spaghetti stringing: Now illegal loose stringing in various patterns and with various materials. The results of spaghetti stringing are unpredictable **spins** and skids.

spin: Rotation of the ball. Spins are generally of three sorts: **topspin** (or **overspin**), **backspin**, and **sidespin**.

spooned: Said of a racquet **face** inclined upward, or **open**.

steelies: Locked-up muscles and responses caused by nervousness, anxiety, and fear.

The cure is to loosen up and **hit out**—or head for the showers.

stroke: Used interchangeably with **shot**, but sometimes preferred as a label for whatever intimations it may have of smoothness and fluidity.

stutter steps: The almost endless half-steps, quarter-steps, and shufflings that the well-articulated player takes in order to adjust and readjust his body in relation to the ball.

thirty: See **points**.

sudden death: See **tie-breaker**.

sweet spot: That area on the racquet's strings that provides maximum power and sensitive responsiveness; the experienced player develops an intuitive feel for it.

tennis elbow: A variety of ailments of the arm and its major hinge, most of which are caused or aggravated by improper (or nonexistent) body movements learned in fly-swatting school.

tie-breaker: A **scoring** device to end **sets** more rapidly than in traditional scoring (where the winner of a set must win by a margin of at least two **games**). At six games–all, either a twelve-point or a nine-point tie-breaker may be used. In the nine-point, *sudden death* version, the winner of the set is the first player to score five points. In the 12-point *lingering death* variety (the apt label is Bud Collins's), the first player to win seven points picks up the marbles *if* he's ahead by two points. If not, the tie-breaker can go on and on, as it did most dramatically at Wimbledon in the 1980 Borg-McEnroe final.

topspin: Forward rotation imparted by moving one's racquet **face** vertically up the back of the ball. Topspin causes a ball to rise in proportion to its **spin** and velocity, then fall more rapidly into the **court** than a **backspin** ball of similar velocity. Upon contact with the court, however, the topspin ball will rise higher on its bounce than the backspin ball.

touch: A stroking style that seems to caress the ball. Some players who profess their reliance upon touch tend to lack somewhat in power and form, however.

turkey: A boaster who deserves basting. Before, and often after, going on the **court**, the turkey tries to convince you he's going to have you for dinner. Ignore his gobbledygook and reach for the carving knife.

turtle: One who tries to make you feel guilty if you don't hit the ball right to him. May plead varicose veins or long-deferred bypass surgery he can't afford. Fall into his trap and he'll knock your ears off with the strength you've helped him to conserve.

US(L)TA: United States (Lawn) Tennis Association. The "Lawn" was pulled out in 1975, partly in recognition of the fact that the U.S. Open is no longer played on grass.

usher: A tournament player excessively given to directing spectators into their seats before he will suffer play to begin.

Vic Braden: A well-known tennis teacher and writer. To "do a **Vic Braden**" is to offer someone a stripped-down, even-cadenced tennis tip, then wrap the advice in epigrammatic hyperbole. (Example: "Keep the racquet high, the ball in your eye. Or you'll end up a **fuzz sandwich**.")

volley: Any ball hit before it bounces. Most players volley from inside the **service line** and close to the net. The aggressive player may volley from farther back, especially against certain opponents. Some balls are easier to hit on the fly than after they've bounced.

Western grip: See **grips**.

WTA: Women's Tennis Association, an organization of female **pros**.

winger: A racquet-thrower. Very bad form.

woodie: A **shot** that caroms off the racquet frame—even if the frame isn't made of wood.

Zone, the: The state of effortless skill and timing. As in, "You were really in the Zone today," meaning, "You were certainly concentrating and moving uncannily well out there." In the Zone, one may lose one's usual sense of ego and ambition, and seem to be directed by an It. In the Zone, one's **concentration** and **anticipation** are close to perfect.

[20]

Sailing

Mankind has been using the wind to transport him over the waters for thousands of years, at least since the time of the ancient Phoenicians and probably long before that. For millennia the sailing vessel was the most efficient—indeed, the only—method of travel over long distances of open sea. In our modern, engine-powered era, sailing is no longer practical, yet it is an anachronism that millions of people find innately satisfying. The old clichés of feeling the salty breezes across one's cheek, watching the spray off the bow and the billowing sails, finding a kind of communion with the wind and the sea—though hackneyed on the page are nonetheless reason enough for large numbers of people to take to the lakes, rivers, and oceans in everything from single-sailed **catboats** to three-masted **barks** and **schooners**.

The language of sailing is old—rooted in the preindustrial days of serious, nonrecreational sailing—and quite complex. There are literally thousands of nautical terms, referring in complete detail to the various elements of the art or science of sailing: names of different vessels (**sloops, yawls, ketches**) and parts of vessels (**keel, ribs, spars, forecastle**); terms describing the various sails and their arrangement, or **rig** (**spinnaker, Genoa jib, mainsail, mizzen**; *gaff-rigged,* **fore-and-aft rigged**); terms for weather, wind, and sea conditions (**fresh breeze, gale, squall, chop**); special terms for ropes, **knots,** and **splices** used on sailing vessels (**halyard, lanyard, sheets, clove hitch, bowline, eye splice**); and phrases describing the most elemental aspect of sailing itself—the relationship of the boat to the wind (**close-hauled, broad reach, starboard tack, running free**).

The following section is by no means exhaustive, but is meant to provide the novice sailor with a basic working vocabulary of several hundred terms that will be used, and understood, on almost all sailing vessels. Having read and digested its contents, the reader will not panic when someone yells at him to **fang the pumps**, or **tail** the

mains'l sheet, or **keep her close-hauled** on a **starboard tack**; he'll know to duck under the **boom** when the skipper yells "**coming about**"; he'll **stow** his **gear** in a shipshape manner; and will generally feel **under way** in his nautical career.

There are scores of different type sailing vessels, and within each major category are countless variations as to size, dimensions, construction, **rigging**, and the like. The dozen most commonly encountered vessels, however, are those defined below. (One note of usage: Smaller vessels, especially open craft with little or no space below **decks**, are termed *boats;* larger vessels, especially those designed for deep-water sailing, are termed *ships*.) 🏵

Vessels

bark: A three-**masted** ship, with the **fore** and **main** masts **square-rigged**, and the **mizzen fore-and-aft-rigged**.

brig: A two-**masted, square-rigged** ship.

catamaran: A sailboat with double **hulls**, joined together.

catboat: A small sailboat with a **centerboard**, one **mast**, and one sail.

cutter: A single-**masted** boat with two **headsails**.

dinghy: A small boat, often used to get from a moored vessel to shore and back; can be rowed or sometimes rigged to sail.

dory: A small, extremely seaworthy rowboat with a high **bow** and flaring sides.

ketch: A two-**masted** boat with a smaller **mizzen** **aft** of the **mainmast** but **forward** of the **rudder** post.

schooner: Any of a variety of vessels with two or more **masts, fore-and-aft rigged**, with the **mainmast** aft of a smaller **foremast**.

sloop: Single-**masted** boat, usually **rigged** with a **mainsail** and a **jib**, the mast being stepped more **forward** than that of a **cutter**.

yacht: An imprecise term applied to a rather expensive sailing vessel, designed and used for leisure or racing (as opposed to work, or the possibility thereof).

yawl: A two-**masted** vessel with the **mainmast forward** and a smaller **mizzen** mast stepped **aft** of the rudder; **fore-and-aft rigged**.

Ropes and other *lines* are used in a hundred ways aboard sailing vessels: to haul in, tighten, support, fasten, raise and lower sails and **spars**, secure cargo, moor vessels, and so on. To these ends, hundreds of knots, splices, and other attachments have been developed; at least the following ten should be part of the novice sailor's vocabulary—and repertory. (*Note*: There are four major types of rope fastenings: *bends* are those which connect one line to another; *hitches* are those which attach a rope to an object, such as a spar or mast; *splices* join two ropes (or two parts of the same rope) into a single line by interweaving the strands; and *knots*, strictly speaking, are all other types of tyings, especially "stopping" knots used to prevent a rope from passing through a **fairlead**—or hole.) 🏵

Ten Most Common
Knots and Splices

back splice: A way of turning the strands of a rope back upon itself, to keep the line from fraying.

bowline: An extremely common knot used to form a secure, temporary loop (or **eye**); often used at the end of **sheets** and **mooring lines**.

clove hitch: The most used knot aboard ship— a way of temporarily securing a line to a **piling**, **spar**, or **belaying pin**.

common whipping: Used at the end of a rope to prevent it from fraying or unraveling; made by wrapping a light **line** or sail thread tightly through and around the end of the rope.

eye splice: A permanent loop made in the end of a **line**, by **splicing** the rope back onto itself.

long splice: A way of splicing two similar **lines** together without increasing the thickness of the rope at the **splice**.

reef knot: A simple square knot; used to tie together two ropes of the same diameter.

seizing: Binding or tying two ropes (or two sections of the same rope) together, using thin **line**.

sheet bend: A knot used to join two **lines**, regardless of whether they are of similar thickness.

short splice: A method of joining together two ropes of the same diameter and material, to form a single **line**; however, the diameter of the rope at the **splice** is increased somewhat.

SAILING TERMINOLOGY

abaft: Behind, in back of; farther in the direction of the **stern**.

abeam: Ninety degrees to the midline of the boat (but not on the boat itself).

about: See **coming about**.

aft: Near, toward, at, or in the direction of the **stern**. (*After*: more aft, i.e., closer to the stern.)

afterguy: The **line** controlling the **spinnaker** pole's fore and *aft trim*.

aground: Touching bottom, or stuck on the bottom.

ahead: Beyond and in front of the **bow**.

ahull: With **sails** furled, pointed on the wind with the **helm** to the **leeward**.

air: The movement or quality of wind, as in *light* or *puffing air*.

alee: Away from the wind (usually said of turning the **helm** or **rudder**; e.g., "hard **alee**").

aloft: Above the **deck** (as, in the **rigging**).

amidships: The middle section of a vessel, between **bow** and **stern**; also, midway laterally, between **port** and **starboard**.

anchor: A device, usually made of steel, fashioned to grip the ocean floor and hold a vessel by chain and/or **line**.

anchorage: A sheltered location at which a vessel can be **anchored** or **moored**.

anchor's apeak: The position of an **anchor** when the anchor **line** is pulled short but before the anchor breaks its grip on the ocean floor.

anchor's aweigh: The position of the **anchor** when it has just broken free and is off the ground.

Annie Oakley: A **spinnaker** sail that is ventilated with several stabilizing holes.

apparent wind: The wind felt aboard a moving vessel and/or indicated by a **masthead** vane or **telltale**. It is the result of the true wind combined with or altered by the speed of the boat.

astern: Behind the **stern** (i.e., off the boat beyond the stern).

athwartships: Across a vessel from one side to another, at right angles to the center line.

awash: Taking water, but not swamped or submerged.

aweather: The direction from which the weather originates; toward the **windward** side of a vessel.

backstays: Rope or wire extending from the top of the **mast aft** to the **deck** of the boat to support the **mast** and prevent it from going **forward**.

backwind: The wind sent off a **forward** sail and onto the **leeward** side of the sail behind it.

bag: Sails and **canvas** that are slack and swelling are said to bag.

baggy wrinkles: Pieces of rope or yarn wound together in such a fashion as to form mop heads used as **chafing gear** on the uppermost wire supports of the **mast**.

bail: To remove water from a vessel, either by hand (i.e., bucket) or pump.

ballast: Weight (usually iron or lead) located and condensed in the lowest part of a boat to help stabilize it by lowering the center of gravity.

bare poles: Term given to a vessel under way without sails set.

batten down: To secure (as gear, cargo, hatches, etc.) in preparation for a storm.

battens: Small, thin wooden or plastic slats that fit into pockets in the **leech** edge of a sail used to stiffen and give more shape to the sail.

beam: The width of a boat at its widest part.

beam reach: To sail at right angles to the wind.

bear down: To turn toward, or approach from, **windward**.

bearing: Direction. To *take a bearing* means to gauge one's direction, either by compass or the stars (*true bearing*) or in relation to a fixed object on land (*relative bearing*).

bear off: To turn the vessel away from the wind, or to sail away to **leeward**.

beat: As a verb, to sail to **windward**, on a series of zigzag **tacks**. Also used as a noun (sailing *on a beat*), meaning a windward course.

Beaufort scale: A system for measuring wind velocity. Numbers from zero to 12 (or 17) indicate a range of wind forces from **calm** to hurricane. For example, 3 refers to a *gentle breeze* (8 to 12 mph), 8 to a *fresh gale* (39 to 46 mph).

before the wind: With the wind coming directly from behind (or **astern**) the boat; i.e., sailing in the same direction as the wind.

belay: To tie or fasten a rope or **line**.

below: Beneath the **decks**. Refers to location or direction ("Go **below**").

bend: To make fast and secure by use of a knot; also, a knot used to connect one **line** to another.

berth: A bunk or bed in which one sleeps aboard a vessel; also, the place where a vessel docks regularly.

bight: A curve; in a **line**, it is the curve before it forms a loop; on land, a curve in the shoreline.

bilge: That part of the interior of a boat below the bottom (floor) boards.

binnacle: A container or stand that supports a ship's compass or other instruments.

bitter end: The free end of a **line** or rope whose other end is fastened; also, the final link of a chain.

block: A pulley; the piece of wood through which a **line** is passed to form a **tackle**.

board: As a noun, the stretch of sea covered in one **tack** of a series. As a verb, to come aboard a vessel.

bolt rope: A rope sewn into the **foot** (lower edge) of a sail for support.

boom: The horizontal **spar** to which the sail is attached, usually by lacing or by a track at the bottom of the sail; the boom is itself attached at right angles to the **mast**.

boom out a sail: To extend a corner of a sail by use of a **boom** or **spar**.

bow: The most **forward** part of the **hull**.

bowsprit: A **spar** projecting forward from the **bow** of a boat.

breakwater: A man-made or natural barrier that protects a harbor or other **anchorage** from waves and storms.

bridle: Usually found on a small sailing boat, a device made of wire or attached to the boat on both ends with a pulley in the middle.

brightwork: Any varnished woodwork or polished metal fittings (usually brass).

broach to: To turn or swing out of control (e.g., **beam**-on when **running free**) due to heavy seas, poor steering, or the like.

broad reach: A **point of sail** when the vessel is sailing with the wind behind the **beam** but not fully **astern**; i.e., the wind is from somewhere near either **quarter**.

bulkhead: A wall or other vertical partition that separates compartments on a vessel.

cable: The **anchor** chain (or rope).

calm: Little or no wind.

canvas: A general term for all the sails of a vessel (which may or may not be made of canvas).

capsize: To overturn (as from storm, collision, extreme **heeling**).

capstan: A cylindrical device (turned by hand or motor) employed for hauling in **line**, raising **anchor**, hoisting heavy weights, etc.

careen: To send a vessel over on its side in shallow water for purposes of cleaning or working on the bottom of the boat.

cast away: To send away or to be forced from a ship by disaster.

cast off: To let go or untie a **line**.

caulk: To seal seams, cracks, or other leakage spots with a waterproof compound; also, the sealant thus used.

centerboard: A movable board or plate, located at the boat's centerline, designed to be lowered below the bottom of the boat as an aid against sideways slippage. Usually operates on a pivot. See also **dagger board**.

chafe: Wear caused by rubbing (of **rigging**, sails, **spars**, etc.).

chafing gear: Windings of rope, yarn, rubber, canvas or other material around any part of a **line**, rope, wire or sail to take the major stress and prevent wear.

chain plates: Metal plates or straps bolted to the **hull** to which the wire **stays** and **shrouds** (wires that support the **mast**) are attached.

charts: Nautical maps of an area complete with navigation aids, water depths, shoals, landmarks, and terrain.

cheater: A small light **staysail** used as a save-all sail when trying to gather any wind at all. Often flown under the **spinnaker** sail.

check: To ease or slack off slowly.

cheek block: A turning **block** whose base is mounted and secure on the **spar** or **deck**.

chock: The metal or plastic casing through which **mooring lines** lead to shore or through which the **anchor** line leads; used to prevent **chafing**.

chop: Unpredictably shifting and breaking waves; rough water due to conflicting tides, current, or waves and prevailing wind.

chute: A parachute **spinnaker** sail.

cleat: A device fashioned to receive and secure a **line** and usually made of metal, wood, or plastic; the standard cleat has two horns around which the line is secured.

clew: The lowermost **aft** corner of a triangular sail.

close haul: The position of sailing as closely as possible to the direction of the wind; the sails are pulled in almost parallel with the centerline.

coaming: A raised rim around the **cockpit** or other parts of the **deck**, to keep water out.

cockpit: The part of a boat from which it is generally sailed, and where the **helm** or **rudder** is located; usually in the **stern**.

coffee grinder: A large two-handed **winch** usually found on racing **yachts**.

coming about: Turning the boat (**bow** first) into the wind so that the bow crosses the wind. Used when changing from one **close-hauled tack** to another.

companionway: A stairway on a boat, leading to or from any of the **decks**.

course: The overall direction a vessel is taking (regardless of what **tacks** may be taken to achieve it).

cringle: A grommet or **eye** in a **sail** covered with light **line** used for securing purposes.

cross trees: Light, horizontal wooden crosspieces atop the **mast**, used to support the tops of and spread the **rigging**.

crow's nest: A lookout platform usually placed high up and **forward**, on the **mast**.

crutch: A **spar** fashioned to receive and support a **boom** or other **spar**.

cuddy: A small cabin, used for shelter on a small vessel.

cunningham hole: An eye not far from the **forward** lower corner of a sail which is used in combination with **tackle** to adjust tension on the sail.

dagger board: A movable type of **centerboard** used to prevent sideward slippage of a vessel; it may be raised or lowered vertically from a housing (but does not pivot).

davits: Small braces projecting overboard, used to hoist small boats (such as lifeboats or **dinghies**).

dead reckoning: Ascertaining the ship's whereabouts without astronomical or visual observation. It is the calculation using the distances run and the courses steered from a previously known position.

deck: Any of a ship's exterior platforms, or floors.

deck plate: A plate bolted to the **deck** usually with a metal ring to accept **blocks**, **shackles**, or **line**.

ditty bag: A small canvas bag that holds a sailor's materials for repairing sails and **line**.

dogwatch: Either of two short duty periods on a ship—4:00 to 6:00 P.M. or 6:00 to 8:00 P.M. (See **watch**.)

dolphin: A **piling**, **spar**, **mooring**, or buoy serving as a marker.

dolphin striker: Also called a **martingale**. A small **spar** beneath the **bowsprit**.

double-headed rig: A vessel with two sails located **forward** of the **mast**.

downhaul: A **line**, sometimes a **block** and line, used to pull in a downward direction on the **boom** to tighten the leading edge of the sail.

draught: Also **draft**. The distance from the waterline to the bottommost part of a vessel; consequently, the minimum depth of water in which the vessel can float without running **aground**.

dry dock: A large basin into which a ship can be floated and from which all water can be drained or pumped out, thus enabling work to be done on all parts of the vessel below the waterline.

ease: To let out, slacken, or release pressure. ("**Ease** off that **sheet**!")

eye of the wind: The precise center of the direction from which a wind is blowing.

eye splice: A **splice** made in the end of a single piece of rope, forming a permanent loop.

fair: Free and unencumbered, without obstacles; said of a rope or **line**, also of weather and sailing.

fairlead: A ring, or wooden **block** with a hole, used as a guide for a **line** to hold it or enable it to run more easily.

fake: Also **flake**. To coil a rope in such a way that it will run freely and not tangle on itself.

falling off: Steering the boat away from the wind.

fang the pumps: To prime the pumps with water.

fast: Secure. To make something fast means to tie it down, attach it to something fixed, or otherwise secure it.

fathom: A nautical measurement equal to six feet; used as a measurement of water depth.

fender: A portable device of rubber, rope, cork, wood, etc., used to absorb the shock of contact between a vessel and any other vessel or wharf.

fetch: To reach an object (or destination) with very little change in **course**; to hold a course.

fid: A cone-shaped piece of wood, iron, or other metal used to spread strands of a rope when making **splices**.

fitting: Any item of marine hardware.

flatten: To **haul** in a **sheet** more closely.

flotsam: The floating wreckage and cargo of a shipwrecked vessel.

fluke: The sharp, triangular blade(s) of an **an-**

chor that "grabs" and holds the sea bottom. There may be one, two, or four.

fly: A wind pennant located on the **masthead**.

foot: The lower edge of a sail.

fore: The front section of a boat. **Fore and aft** means along the line of the **keel** (or centerline); or, at both ends of the vessel; or the entire vessel ("She's **awash fore** and **aft!**")

forecastle: Also **fo'c's'le** (pronounced FOC-sul). **Forward**most section of the upper **deck**; or forwardmost crew's living quarters below the deck.

foreguy: A line used to control the downward tension on the **spinnaker** pole.

foremast: The smaller, **forward**most **mast** on a vessel with two or more masts (with the exception of **yawls** and **ketches**, where the **mainmast** is the most forward).

forereach: To overtake, pass, or gain on (another vessel).

foresail: Sail (or sails) hung to the **foremast** of a **schooner**.

forestay: Wire rope acting as the major support of the **foremast**, leading forward from the **masthead** to the **bow**.

forward: Toward the **bow** (refers to both direction and location).

foul: General nautical term for anything that is not clear (e.g., weather); not safe; jammed, twisted, or entangled (fouled **lines**); or otherwise unfavorable.

freeboard: The distance vertically from the waterline to the **deck** on the side of a ship.

freshen: To pick up strength (said of wind).

furl: To wrap, fold, or roll a sail neatly to a **spar**.

gaff: A small **spar** used to extend the top of a **fore-and-aft** sail. (Thus, **gaff-rigged**.)

galley: A ship's kitchen.

gallows: The frame rising above the **deck** used to stow small boats and extra **spars**.

gear: Equipment of any type.

Genoa jib: Also **jenny**. A large sail rigged to the **forestay** of a boat, overlapping the **mainsail**.

ghosting: Moving forward in little or no wind.

gooseneck: The fitting, usually metal, that attaches and secures the **boom** to the **mast**.

grapnel: A small **anchor** with four or five **flukes**; used on small boats.

grommet: An eye, usually metal but sometimes laced with thin **line**; used as a point of attachment, especially on the edge of a sail.

ground swell: Long smooth waves caused by distant storms.

guard rail: A rail running the length of the boat, bolted to the ship's side and used as a **fender**.

gunwale: (Pronounced GUN-nel.) The edge around a ship's **topside**.

halyard: The **line**, rope, or wire with which a sail is hoisted (and lowered).

hand: Any crew member on a vessel.

hanks: The fittings that attach a **jib** or **staysail** to the **stay** upon which it is hoisted.

hard alee: The order or signal foretelling that movement of the **tiller** that will cause a vessel to turn into the wind.

hatch: The opening in a ship's **deck**, and the cover that closes that opening. ("**Batten the hatches!**")

haul: To pull in a **line**.

hawsehole: The hole through which the **anchor** cable (or other **hawser**) is passed.

hawser: Heavy rope or **cable** used to **moor**, or tow, a ship.

head: The upper corner of a triangular sail. Also, the name given to a boat's toilet.

head off: A command or order to steer the boat in a direction away from the wind.

headreaching: The **point of sail** where the boat has momentum (or **way**) while sailing into the wind.

headsail: (Pronounced HEADs'l.) Any sail **forward** of the foremost **mast**, including **jibs**, **Genoas**, and **spinnakers**.

headstay: The **stay** running from the **masthead** to the **bow** or **bowsprit**.

head to the wind: With sails shaking and pointed into the wind.

head up: A command or order to steer the boat more into or against the wind.

headway: Forward motion.

heave to: To bring a boat to a halt by steering into the wind, with the **helm** to the **leeward** side, either with sails trimmed short or without sails flying altogether. (Past tense, *hove to*.)

heel: As a verb, to tip, tilt, or lay a boat over on its side. As a noun, the amount of tilt, usually expressed in degrees.

helm: The steering device on a vessel, either a **tiller** or a wheel.

hike: To lean back, out over the water, to counterbalance some of a boat's weight when it is **heeling**.

hitch: A knot that ties one rope to another or to a **spar**. (See KNOTS section.)

hold: That part of the inside of a boat that is below **decks**; usually for carrying cargo and equipment.

hull: The main body of a vessel, separate from the **mast** and **spars**, **rigging**, sails, and **decks**.

in irons: Also **in stays**. The condition in which the boat is pointed directly into the wind and has lost all **headway**. This is the natural position for a **moored** boat, but is an embarassing predicament when **coming about**.

jackline: An adjustable **line** on the **mainsail** used to remove the slides of the mainsail on the **mast** when **reefing** the mainsail.

jam cleat: A V-shaped **cleat** that will allow a **line** to pass through it in only one direction.

jib: A triangular sail flown from the **jibstay** (or **headstay**) of a boat **forward** of the **mast**.

jibe: To turn a vessel so that the **stern** crosses the wind (the opposite of **coming about**). Thus, if a boat is sailing with the wind from the **starboard quarter** and turns to **port**, the stern will cross the wind and the sails will shift abruptly to the starboard side of the boat; this is jibing.

jibstay: The wire rope running from the mast to the **bow**, to which the **jib** is attached.

jury rig: A temporary arrangement; makeshift.

kedge: A light **anchor**.

kedging: The process of moving a vessel by pulling on the rope that is attached to a **kedge anchor**. (A kedge anchor is set by having it carried to the desired spot by a small boat.)

keel: The major timber or steel piece that runs the entire length of the bottom of a boat and is designed to counteract sideways slippage.

keelek: A small **kedge anchor**.

keelson: Iron plates or timbers bolted along the length of the **keel**, used to strengthen the keel.

knot: A nautical measurement of speed: 1 nautical mile per hour, the equivalent of 1.15 statute miles per hour.

lanyard: A general name given to any short piece of rope or **line** used for almost any purpose.

lash: To secure by binding closely and tightly with rope.

lay: As a noun, the direction or natural twist of the fibers of a rope. As a verb, to move to a specified position. ("**Lay aloft!**") *Lay to:* To keep a vessel stationary.

layline: The straight **course** on which a boat can reach a given point or destination.

lazarette: A storage compartment generally found on the **stern** of a ship.

leading edge: The foremost edge of a sail.

lee: The side of a boat (or anything else) opposite to the side on which the wind is blowing; the sheltered side. The opposite of **weather**.

leech: The **after** edge of a sail, or either vertical edge of a square sail.

leeward: (Pronounced LOO-ard.) Away from the wind; at, in, or of the direction toward which the wind is blowing. The opposite of **windward**.

leeway: The amount of drift or slippage a boat makes to **leeward**, due to lateral pressure on the sails and **hull**.

let fly: To let go at once.

lifelines: **Lines** strung through **stanchions** running the full length of the boat on either side for safety.

lift: A change in the direction of the wind that allows a boat to sail closer to the wind.

light sails: Any sail made of especially light-weight material (such as a **spinnaker**).

line: The nautical term for rope. Any rope or cordage on board a ship.

list: As a noun, the leaning of a vessel to one side. As a verb, to lean.

log: A record or journal of a ship's voyage, including speeds and distances, winds, ports, and events of the journey. Also, an instrument or device to calculate a boat's speed.

loose-footed: Term applied to a **fore and aft** sail that is not laced to a **boom**.

luff: As a noun, the **forward** edge of a sail. As a verb, to cause a sail to shake, i.e., by sailing more into the wind.

mainmast: The principal **mast** of most larger boats and the only mast of a **sloop** or **catboat**.

mainsail: The sail that is **rigged** to the **after** side of the **mainmast**.

mainsheet: The **line** which controls the **mainsail**.

make fast: To tie, **belay**, or fasten securely.

marconi: Term applied to triangular sails; boats featuring triangular sails are said to be *marconi-rigged.*

marlinespike: A cone-shaped and pointed tool used to separate strands of rope when making **splices**.

mast: The vertical **spar** upon which sails are raised.

masthead: The top of the **mast**.

mast partners: The board across the boat through which the hole is made to house the **mast**.

mast step: The fitting into which the heel of the **mast** is set.

mate: Crew member next in rank below the captain or skipper.

mizzen: A smaller sail, similar in shape to the **mainsail**, **rigged** on its own **boom** and **mast** (the *mizzenmast*) near the **stern** of the ship. Found on **yawls** and **ketches**.

monkey's fist: A decorative knot tied at the end of a heavy **line**, formed around a weight.

mooring: A permanent **anchoring** fixture to which a vessel is **secured** when not sailing.

navigation: The calculation of position and **course**, or the plotting and guiding of a course sailed by a vessel.

offshore: In a direction away from the shore.

off the wind: Any **course** other than in the direction from which the wind is blowing. A **reach** or **run**.

outboard: Extending beyond the **hull**. Usually refers to a small engine mounted on the **stern** of a boat.

outhaul: The **line** used to adjust the tension on the **after** edge of a sail.

overlap: The extension of the **foot** of a sail over another sail.

overstand: To go beyond the direct course to **fetch** a navigation mark or point of land.

painter: A **line** attached to a small boat's (e.g., a **dinghy**) **bow** to tow it or **secure** the boat to another object.

parachute: A colloquial term for a **spinnaker jib**.

part: To break (a rope, chain, etc.).

pay out: To slacken or ease off a **line**.

peak: The **aft** end of a **gaff boom**.

piling: A large log or timber that protrudes vertically from the water.

pinch: To sail a boat too close into the wind.

pitch: **Fore and aft** rocking of a boat.

point: As a verb, to sail a vessel high or close to the wind. As a noun, one-thirty-second ($\frac{1}{32}$) of a circle, or $11\frac{1}{4}°$; one of the thirty-two such divisions on a compass.

point of sail: The direction of sailing in relation to the wind. There are three main points of sail: **beating** (sailing to **windward**); **running** (sailing directly with the wind); and **reaching** (any direction between the two).

port: The left side of a vessel when standing at the **stern** facing the **bow**.

port tack: The **point of sail** when the wind is coming from the **port** side.

preventer: An additional rope or wire used on an overburdened brace or **boom** to take some of the tension, or prevent accidental swings.

pulpit: A platform on the **bow** of a ship to facilitate the handling and changing of sails.

purchase: Leverage or mechanical advantage; increased by means of a **tackle**. Also, the tackle itself.

quarter: Either of the two sections of a vessel (**port** and **starboard** quarters) between the **beam** and the **stern**.

rail: The outer edge of the **deck** running completely around the entire boat, usually made of a varnished wood.

rake: The angle of the **mast** as it differs from the perpendicular.

ratlines: Rope rungs **secured** to the **shrouds** or to the side **stays** for the purpose of going **aloft**.

reach: Any **course** sailed between a **close-haul** and **running** before the wind. (See **close reach**, **beam reach**, and **broad reach**.)

ready about: The spoken signal or order to alert the crew that the boat is going to **come about**.

reef: As a verb, to lessen or shorten a sail's area. As a noun, the rolled and tied-down portion of the sail.

reef points: Short **lines** attached to a sail used to tie the sail, reducing its area.

reeve: To pass a **line** through a **block**.

rhumb line: The straight, unchanging compass **course** steered by a boat.

ribs: The curved timbers that attach to the **keel**, forming the frame of a boat's **hull**.

ride: To be at **anchor**.

rig: As a noun, a boat's sail plan and **mast** arrangements, such as **gaff rig**, **square rig**. As a verb, to equip and fit a ship's sails, **shrouds**, etc.

rigging: The entire complex of fixed and movable **lines**, ropes, **cables**, **shrouds**, etc., on a vessel. See also **running rigging, standing rigging**.

roach: The curved portion of a sail, along its **leech**.

rode: An **anchor line** or **cable**.

roller furling: A mechanical system for rolling the **jib** around its own **luff** wire.

roller reefing: A mechanical system for shortening the sail area, basically by rolling part of the sail around a revolving **boom**.

rudder: The device at the **stern** of a vessel that enables it to be turned; connected to the steering mechanism, or **helm** (either a **tiller** or wheel).

rules of the road: Universally recognized rules of sailing procedure, especially concerning right of way between two or more vessels. For example, sailboats almost always have the right of way over powerboats; a boat on a **starboard tack** has right of way over a boat on a **port tack** on the same **point of sail**; a **close-hauled** boat has right of way over a boat with the wind **aft**.

run: Also **run before the wind**. The **point of sail** almost directly before the wind. To sail with the wind directly, or very close to, dead **astern**; the **mainsail** will then be positioned at almost right angles to the boat's centerline.

runners: The movable **backstays** used on a **yacht**.

running rigging: All **rigging** that is secured at one end and movable at the other, used to control all sails, **booms**, etc. Includes **sheets**, **halyards**, **outhauls**, **lifts**, etc.

sag: An excessive drift **leeward**.

sail stops: Straps made of sailcloth, **line**, or shock cord used to tie and secure a **furled** sail.

scandalize: To reduce sail area by lowering the sail partially.

sculling: Moving a **stern** oar (or the **tiller**) back and forth rapidly to propel the boat forward.

scuppers: Holes on the sides of the **deck**, to allow water to run off.

scuttle: To deliberately sink a ship.

sea anchor: Any device used as a drag.

seaway: Free movement when a vessel is clear

of a **shoal**, land, or other obstruction. Also, rough waters.

secure: To make **fast**; to tie tightly.

seize: To bind with thin rope, **line**, or wire.

shackle: Any of a variety of U-shaped metal **fittings** having a pin or screw to close the opening; used to join two objects together.

shakedown cruise: A test run to see if a vessel is seaworthy.

she: A sailing vessel is always referred to by the feminine pronoun.

sheave: The grooved wheel in a **block**.

sheet: Any rope or **line** used to control a sail.

ship: Technically, a vessel with three or more **masts**; more generally, a large vessel suitable for deep-water navigation.

ship's time: Local apparent time.

shipwright: A boat builder.

shoal: A sandbank, a bar, or other shallow, submerged hazard.

shore: As a verb, to support. As a noun, the edge of land fronting on a body of water.

shore off: To depart, as from a dock or **mooring**.

shrouds: The major side **stays** supporting the **mast**, usually made of wire **cables.** Part of the **standing rigging**.

side lights: Lights on either side of a sailing vessel; the **port** one is red, the **starboard** green.

slack: As a verb, to **ease** off slowly. As an adjective, loose; not **secured**.

slip: The docking area between two small floating piers or sets of **pilings**.

small-craft warning: A weather report indicating dangerous sailing for small boats.

snap hook: A hook with a spring-loaded device for its closure.

snatch block: A **block** hinged at the neck so that it can quickly be opened, to remove or insert a **bight** of **line**

sole: The floor of a boat's cabin.

spar: The nautical term for any pole, wooden or metal, used as a support. Spars include **masts**, **booms**, **bowsprits**, **gaffs**, and **yards**.

spindrift: Spray blowing off the tops of waves in rough weather.

spinnaker: A very large, lightweight sail flown from the **forestay**, swung out opposite the **mainsail** while sailing **before the wind.**

splice: As a verb, to join two ropes (or two parts of a single rope) together permanently, by interweaving their strands. As a noun, the connection thus formed.

spreader: A horizontally placed strut for the purposes of spreading the **rigging** and offering strength, support, and rigidity to the **mast**.

sprit: A **spar** that extends diagonally from the **mast**, to extend a **fore and aft** sail.

squall: A sudden storm or sudden, violent blast of wind and/or rain.

square-rigged: Having mostly rectangular sails which are set **athwartships**. The sails are extended equally on both sides of their **masts**.

stanchions: Upright pillars of wood or metal acting as supports.

standing part: The **secured** end of a rope or **line**.

standing rigging: The permanent, fixed ropes and **cables** used to support the **mast** and other structures. Includes **shrouds** and **stays**.

starboard: The right side of a boat when standing at the **stern** facing the **bow**.

starboard tack: The course sailed when the wind is coming over the **starboard** side of the boat.

started sheets: Eased sheets.

stays: Wire **cable** or heavy rope used to support the **mast** or other **spars**.

staysail: Any of several sails rigged to a **stay**.

stem: The most **forward** beam in a boat's **hull**.

steerageway: The minimal forward motion that allows the **rudder** to be effective in steering the vessel.

stern: The most **aft** part of a boat's **hull**.

sternway: Backward motion of a boat.

stiff: Tending to resist **heeling**.

stinkpot: Sailing people's term for a power boat.

stop: 1. To tie down or make **fast**.
2. A **sail stop**.

stormsail: A heavyweight cloth used in place of a regular-weight sail during heavy weather; usually smaller as well.

stow: To put or store away, especially neatly and compactly.

strike: To lower (a sail).

stuffing box: The device around the propeller shaft to prevent water from coming into the vessel.

swamp: To fill with water; when a boat is swamped, it has sunk to just below the water's surface.

tack: 1. On a triangular sail, the most **forward**, lower corner of the sail.
2. The position of a vessel relative to its sails, or of a ship's **course** relative to the prevailing wind.
3. Each leg of the zigzag course employed for maximum efficiency in sailing any course besides **before the wind**.
4. Changing from one such leg to the next.

tackle: A **block** with **line** running through it.

telltale: A wind indicator, usually a small piece of cloth or yarn attached to a **shroud**.

tender: As an adjective, unstable, offering little or no resistance to **heeling**; the opposite of **stiff**. As a noun, a small boat or motorized **dinghy**.

thimble: A metal-ringed **fitting**, fashioned to receive a rope or **line** in a **splice**.

three sheets to the wind: Drunk, especially with an unsteady gait.

throat: The part of a **gaff boom** that is most **forward** and near the **mast**.

thwartships: Also **athwartships**. Across the ship, at right angles to its centerline.

tiller: A bar, usually made of wood, that moves the **rudder** and with which one steers the boat.

timber: Any large piece of wood that forms part of a boat's **hull**.

topping lift: A line from the **masthead** to outer end of the **boom**; it hoists and supports the **boom**.

topsides: As a noun, the upper parts of a boat, above the waterline. As an adverb, on **deck** or on the upper parts of the ship.

transom: A **stern timber** or beam, often used as a seat.

traveler: A track and sliding device with a **block** or series of blocks used to allow the **mainsheet** to move from side to side.

trim: To adjust the sails in relation to the wind and the **course** steered.

trip: To hoist (the **anchor**).

turnbuckle: A metal screw-**fitting** that is used to adjust tension, usually of **stays**, **shrouds**, and **lifelines**.

turtle: A device that contains a **spinnaker** before it is set.

vang: Any device used to add extra downward pull on the **boom**.

veer: To change direction, to turn away from the wind; also, to let out a **line**.

watch: A division of time on board a ship, especially referring to a shift of duty for officer or crew member. There are seven such watches in a twenty-four hour day, of which five are four hours each and two (the **dogwatches**) are two hours each, 4:00 to 6:00 P.M. and 6:00 to 8:00 P.M. The 4:00 to 8:00 A.M. watch is generally considered both the easiest and the most beautiful.

way: Any movement of a vessel through the water. (See **headway**, **sternway**, **leeway**.) A boat is **under way** when it is in motion and under control.

weather helm: An unbalanced **helm** requiring inadequate tension to **windward** to keep the boat on **course** (opposite is *lee helm*); the tendency of a boat to turn to windward when the **rudder** is **amidships**.

weather side: The **windward** side; the direction toward the wind.

weigh: To **haul** up the **anchor**.

whipping: See knots & splices subsection.

whisker pole: Any light pole or **spar** used to

boom out a **working jib** to the **windward** side to aid the sail in filling with wind.

winch: A drum-shaped device that mechanically increases the advantage of pulling or lifting.

windward: The direction toward the wind.

wing and wing: A sail tactic used when **running before the wind**, whereby the **mainsail** is set on one side while the **jib** is set on the opposite side.

working sails: The term given to everyday sails.

yard: The horizontal **spar** attached to the **mast**, from which a square sail is set.

yaw: A rocking motion from side to side off the intended **course**.

VI

SCENES AND SUBCULTURES

[21]

New Age and New Therapies

The sixties saw the blossoming of what later came to be called "the counterculture"—an interconnecting skein of groups, movements, and ideas that questioned virtually all of the basic assumptions of American life, politics, and culture. The civil-rights and anti–Vietnam war movements, the psychedelic drug subculture, Eastern spiritual movements, religious cults, the ecology movement, health foods, **encounter** and other forms of **group** therapy, mass interest in occult and **parapsychological** matters, and the general pursuit of **personal growth** and **self-actualization**—all these began in the upsurge of creative energy that marked that extraordinary decade.

In the seventies, while the political movements dwindled—or were destroyed—the innovations of the counterculture diffused into the society at large. Two areas did not decline, however, but continued to grow in visibility, numbers of adherents, and impact: the scores of new variations on traditional psychotherapy, generically called the *new therapies;* and an array of spiritual groups and alternative life-style concerns optimistically titled the **New Age**. Though these two phenomena overlap in many instances, and though their boundaries are by no means fixed, the general differentiation between them is this: *New therapies* derive from, and relate to the Western psychotherapeutic mode; their practitioners usually possess advanced academic degrees, and are "professionals" (albeit rogue professionals) not totally removed from the prevailing social/medical/psychological/academic mainstream; they have merely chosen to pursue the more colorful, multifaceted, and contemporary forms of therapy—**Gestalt**, **encounter**, **transactional analysis**, **family therapy**, etc. The New Age, on the other hand, derives more significantly from the Eastern, mystical, and primitive traditions; its practitioners for the most part do not hold academic credentials, nor are they thought to require them. New Age systems such as

Hatha Yoga, **chiropractic**, **Arica**, **TM**, and **Aikido** have their own methods of training and certification; other pursuits—**astrology**, **tarot**, **pyramid power**, and the like—require no credentials whatsoever.

Two related generic terms need to be explained: The **human potentials movement** is almost synonymous with new therapies, except that its emphasis is on personal growth—that is, expanding and improving one's life—rather than correcting or curing disorders, which is the ostensible aim of *therapy*. The **holistic health** movement is a more recent coinage, and refers to the entire spectrum of disciplines relating to health and healing—including both unorthodox systems and progressive mainstream medicine, mental and physical practices, the ancient and the modern. Of the various titles it is probably the most felicitous, implying as it does that a correct concept of human health must include and synthesize *all* factors—diet, exercise, psychology, spirituality, social interactions, physical environment, attitude, and so on. As a result the holistic "concept" appears to be gaining credibility in the established medical and therapeutic worlds, which for the most part have remained hostile to anything smacking of the "occult" or unorthodox.

In New Age circles, language is often employed to show how spiritually advanced or experienced the speaker is—through the liberal use of Sanskrit, Chinese, and occult terminology: "Like, my **energy** was flowing, man, but I was just too attached, y'know? My **guru** gave me this **mantra**, though, that really helped me get **centered**; can't tell it to anybody, though . . . bad **karma**."
Among devotees of the new therapies, catch phrases tend to be used, both in and out of the therapy context, that mimic the word usage of a therapist dealing with a **client** or **group**: "**What I hear you saying is** . . ."; "Let's **process** this out. . . ."; "I just don't feel like **sharing** my **space** right now. . . ."

The double-subject section that follows is subdivided into three main parts: First, a complete lexicon of the various schools, movements, systems, and disciplines that comprise the entire field. Second, the typical jargon of New Age communication—guaranteed to raise your **consciousness**, if not your **kundalini**. And third, the essential verbalisms of new therapy—which should be a **peak experience**, if you're in the right space for it.

Gurus, Heroes, Pioneers: Name-Dropping in the New Age

"**Werner** says . . ." "As **Fritz** once told me . . .", "The **Maharishi** wants. . . ." In **New Age** and New Therapy circles, names are dropped as frequently, and as deliberately, as at any showbiz or media cocktail party. Herewith, the names you've got to know if you want to sound **Aquarian** and **holistic**. 🍒

Aurobindo, Sri: Indian spiritual philosopher and founder of **Auroville**; died 1950. Aurobindo combined a deep spirituality with a passionate commitment to social reform and the relief of human suffering. Rather than escape from mundane existence, he sought to use the "higher" powers attainable through **yoga** for the good of mankind.

Bubba Free John: Young American **guru**, author of *The Paradox of Instruction* and *The Eating Gorilla Comes in Peace*.

Bucky: Buckminster Fuller; brilliant multifaceted scientist, planner, ecologist, architect. Designer of the geodesic dome, innovator of a multitude of plans for the future of the "Spaceship Earth."

Cayce: Edgar Cayce (1877–1945), the "sleeping prophet." An uneducated Tennessee preacher, Cayce had the capacity to enter a trance state, where he received information about people's health, spiritual development, and past lives. He gave thousands of such readings before his death in 1945.

Chinmoy, Sri: A Bengali **guru**, head of the UN Meditation Center in New York City.

Don Juan: The Mexican Indian *brujo* (sorcerer, **shaman**) who is the teacher and guide of Carlos Castaneda in his series of popular books about the "separate realities" discovered through the shamanic way. Whether fictional or real, Don Juan has become a seminal figure whose pronouncements on the way of the warrior are pervasively quoted.

Fritz: Fritz Perls; one of the founders of **Gestalt therapy** and certainly its most famous and flamboyant exponent. Fritz was known for his use of the "hot seat"—where one person from a **group** sat and went through an intense, dramatic therapy process—and for his humorous, charismatic style. An institution himself at the **Esalen Institute**, Fritz died in 1970.

Gaskin, Stephen: American **guru** and spiritual leader of **The Farm**.

Gurdjieff, Georges I. (1877–1949), Greek-Armenian "rascal sage" who traveled all over the world from the 1880s to the early 1900s, seeking knowledge from scores of mystical schools and spiritual traditions. He ultimately developed his own eclectic system of human development, which he called **the work**. Gurdjieff was a brilliant, charismatic, controversial figure who synthesized and translated some of the most ancient, secret methods into a new form for Western individuals.

Houston, Jean: American **consciousness** researcher, lecturer, codirector of the Foundation for Mind Research, and author of *Mind Games: The Guide to Inner Space*.

José: José Silva; Mexican-American who developed **Silva Mind Control** out of his experiments with hypnosis and **meditation**.

Krishnamurti: Jiddu Krishnamurti; Indian philosopher who is unique in wanting no devoted followers and in preaching absolute individuality in all spiritual pursuits. He is the "anti-guru **guru**," and an uncommonly brilliant man: "I maintain that Truth is a pathless land and you cannot approach it by any path whatsoever, by any religion, by any sect."

Laing: R. D. Laing; radical British psychiatrist who introduced the concept that schizophrenia might be a "rational" response to irrational and conflicting life situations, and that the experience of schizophrenia, if allowed to run its course, might be a constructive, enlightening inward journey.

Leary: Timothy Leary; a former Harvard professor who coined the phrase "turn on, tune in, drop out." Leary did just that, becoming the most vocal exponent of **New Age consciousness** in the late sixties. Subsequent experiences, including time in jail and as a fugitive in North Africa, have made him more politically oriented—yet with a "cosmic" perspective.

Lilly: John C. Lilly; unorthodox scientist who pioneered work with the **consciousness** of dolphins and the use of the isolation tank to generate **altered states of consciousness**. Author of *The Mind of the Dolphin, The Deep Self, The Center of the Cyclone.*

Maharaj Ji, Guru: Head of **Divine Light Mission**, who achieved fame in the late sixties as the teenaged **guru**, attracting American followers by the tens of thousands, on one occasion filling the Houston Astrodome with them.

Maharishi: The **Maharishi Maheesh Yogi**; Indian **guru** who founded the system of **Transcendental Meditation** (**TM**), and achieved fame in the 1960s as the Beatles' guru. He was the first to make ancient **meditation** techniques accessible on a large scale to Western society.

Maslow: Abraham Maslow (1908–70); one of the most influential figures in modern psychology. He developed a theory of **humanistic psychology** based not upon normalcy and adjustment to the way most people are, but upon the best and most wonderful in human achievement. He coined the term **self-actualization** to refer to the **process** by which an individual realizes his full potential.

Meher Baba: Indian spiritual master who observed total silence from 1925 until his death in 1969. He was active not only as a spiritual teacher but in aiding the sick and impoverished. His famous statement: "Don't worry, be happy, I love you more than you could possibly love yourself."

Michio: Michio Kushi; the current leader of the **macrobiotic** movement, born in Japan and now a resident of Boston.

Muktananda, Swami: A powerful Indian **guru** who has many followers in the U.S. and Europe. He is known for making astonishing, lightninglike telepathic connections with his students, which transform their **consciousness**, a process called *shaktipat*.

Oscar: Oscar Ichazo; South American spiritual seeker who created the **Arica** school and remains its chief motive force.

Ram Dass, Baba: Formerly **Richard Alpert**; Harvard psychology professor who took LSD, went to India, and emerged as a **guru** without loss of humor or humility. He is the author of the famous *Be Here Now* and one of the most popular American exponents of Eastern spirituality.

Reich: Wilhelm Reich; brilliant rebel student of Freud's in the 1920s, who broke away to develop his own theories and methods of therapy. Reich's major contributions include the idea that neuroses and other psychological disorders are embedded in the body structure; telling insights into the psychology of authoritarianism; the primacy of orgasmic sexual release to psychological health; and the concept of **orgone**, or life **energy**. Although discredited by some for his later extremism, Reich's breakthrough concepts mark him as the key influence in the creation of the new therapy movement.

Rolf, Ida: The developer of **Structural Integration**, commonly called **rolfing**. One does *not* refer to her as Ida when name-dropping.

Sai Baba: A popular Indian **guru** who is famous for materializing a kind of holy ash from thin air, and performing other miracles.

Satchidananda, Swami: Head of the Integral Yoga system, headquartered in New York. A delightful, wise, nondogmatic, compassionate man.

Simonton: Dr. Carl Simonton; a cancer specialist who has pioneered in the use of **meditation**, **visualization**, and other **holistic/New Age** treatments in conjunction with radiation and other orthodox medical methods. At his clinic in Fort Worth, he has reportedly achieved successful cures with patients who were "terminal" by normal medical standards.

Werner: **Werner Erhard** (formerly **Jack Ro-senberg**); the founder of **est**. Werner was a **Scientology** graduate, sales motivation trainer, and student of many Eastern disci- plines before he developed est in 1971. He is good-looking, eloquent, and intelligent, re-vered by his followers, reviled by his critics, and inordinately successful.

Although many people confuse them with the rest of the **New Age** and New Therapy systems, *cults* can, and should, be clearly distinguished. The most salient feature of cults is the tremendous pressure put upon members to remain faithful, and unquestion-ingly obedient, to the system. Adherents are often isolated from other individuals or sources of information outside the cult world, especially in the early period of indoctrination. Information about the true nature of the system's finances, political connections, or lines of authority is often deliberately withheld from the majority of members. The use of violence, threats, isolation, and other unpleas-ant tactics by many cults—both to secure the fidelity of their own people and to resist "attacks" from the outside world—is not uncom-mon.

While opinions will differ heatedly as to which groups are truly cults and which are not, the following list includes the major groups active in the U.S. today that seem to fit the descriptions offered above. Ultimately, of course, one must judge for oneself. 🍎

Cults

Divine Light Mission: Spiritual movement led by **Guru Maharaj Ji** that attracted a tremen-dous American following, numbering at least in the tens of thousands, and considerable media attention, in the early 1970s—when the Guru was still in his teens. The Divine Light organization remains in force, although the number of adherents has dwindled signif-icantly.

Hare Krishna: Spiritual cult whose members have devoted their lives to worship of the Hindu god Krishna. Much of their time is spent chanting and singing, and shaven-headed Krishna acolytes in flowing orange robes can be seen chanting and collecting money in most major American cities.

Scientology: The Church of Scientology is a rather strange organization, devoted to the practice of *Dianetics,* "the Science of Mental Health." Created by L. Ron Hubbard in the 1940s and 1950s, this is a rigidly hierarchical system that uses electronic devices (such as the "E-meter"), group dynamics, and what appears to be a composite of Western and Eastern ideas to effect the psychological growth of its members. After the investment of significant amounts of time and money, one is supposed to become a *clear,* or high-level person who has "mastered the survival of the self."

Synanon: Begun in the late 1960s as a thera-peutic community for drug addicts, in which **group-encounter** confrontation and peer pressure kept members off drugs and cohe-sively united, Synanon seemed for many years to be a positive, progressive model for drug treatment. In the seventies, however, the group degenerated into a violent, fear-ridden cult with only the trappings of its for-mer humanism.

Unification Church: Colloquially known as the **Moonies**. Right-wing pseudo-Christian cult founded by the Korean Rev. Sun Myung Moon and commonly viewed as one of the most sinister. Severe and incessant group pressure, group meetings, group indoctrina-tion amount to a de facto brainwashing pro-cess in the teachings of Reverend Moon—which state that he is the new Messiah and should be followed with unquestioning obe-dience.

NEW AGE AND NEW THERAPIES: SYSTEMS, SCHOOLS, AND METHODS

acupuncture: An ancient Chinese medical sys-tem based upon the theory that the vital force, called **ch'i**, circulates through the body along twelve major routes, called **meridians**. The major form of treatment consists of the insertion of extremely fine needles into *points* along the surface of the body, where meridi-ans are most accessible; the flow of ch'i is thus regularized (either stimulated or reduced) and the disorder rectified. Over 3,000 years old, acupuncture is still a major mode of treatment in the Orient today and is gaining increasing acceptance in the West. A milder, variant method is termed **acupressure**, in which the points are pressed with the thumb or fingertips, but no needles are employed.

Aikido: A modern Japanese martial art based upon spiritual strength (called *ki*) rather than muscular force. Movements are fluid, grace-ful, whirling, yet compellingly powerful; the possibilities for transcendent experience are built into the very nature of the art. Not nearly as popular overall as Karate or Judo, Aikido is definitely the preferred martial art for people with a **New Age** perspective. See also **T'ai Chi**.

Alexander Technique: A system of movement reeducation, in which particular emphasis is laid upon the position of the head and neck and their relation to the rest of the body. It aims at postural improvement and the release of all tension and blocks from the body.

Arica: An eclectic school of psychological/spiri-tual development created by **Oscar Ichazo** in the late 1960s. Arica is ultramodern, slick, highly structured, cliquish—but also quite se-rious about self-transformation through in-tense mind-body training.

assertiveness training: A short-term training method in which participants acquire new patterns of behavior that enable them to as-sert their real needs and feelings in any situ-ation. The goal of AT is to be neither too timid and fearful to express yourself *nor* too aggressive and manipulative when you do so—but rather to be calm, firm, and self-confident.

astrology: Probably the least credible of all **New Age** "sciences" and yet indisputably the most popular. Astrology purports to be a method for understanding facets of a person's char-acter and relationships through computation of the astronomical configurations at the mo-ment of his birth. The astrological world ranges from clichéd newspaper horoscopes (which no one believes) to more serious professional astrologers who will "do your **chart**" for a small fee, using an elaborate sys-tem of books, tables, computations, and inter-pretations.

autosuggestion: Also called **self-programming** or, colloquially, **self-hypnosis**. The conscious mind "plants" a message or instruction in the deeper levels of the mind (variously called the subconscious, the **alpha** level, the hypna-gogic state) to achieve a more effective self-transformation. Autosuggestion is a major technique in almost every system of self-change, both Eastern and Western.

Bach Flower Remedies: A type of **homeopathy**

in which the remedies for all illness are to be found in distillations and infusions of several hundred different wild flowers.

Bates Eye Method: A system for improving vision without glasses through exercises for "relaxation of the mind and eye." Developed by an ophthalmologist over fifty years ago, the system has never been accepted by the medical establishment, although it continues to attract followers who testify to its effectiveness, the most famous of these having been Aldous Huxley.

behavior modification: A method of treatment (based upon behavioral psychology) which aims at direct alteration of a person's behavior, without attempting to understand or deal with the underlying mental or emotional causes. Fear of heights, for example, would be dealt with by gradually accustoming a person to remain relaxed in ever higher locations (a process called *systematic desensitization*), rather than by trying to understand what psychological **pattern** the fear represents. Behavior mod is much more of a "mainstream" psychotherapeutic method, and is generally rejected by the **New Age** philosophy as a mechanistic, non**holistic** approach—unless used in conjunction with other forms of treatment.

bioenergetics: A form of therapy derived originally from the theories of **Wilhelm Reich**, in which the release of physical and emotional **blocks** is emphasized. Through deep breathing, holding stressful body postures, and expressive actions such as kicking and pounding a bed, the **client** is encouraged to give up his or her rigidities of character and let natural **energy** "flow" more freely.

biofeedback: A method by which subjects gain control over supposedly "involuntary" body functions (such as blood pressure, brain waves, muscle tension, blood flow), by having information about those functions "fed back" to them by a machine. Somehow, merely by being accurately informed whenever the blood pressure drops at random (for example), the human body-mind is able to gain conscious control over that function and eventually lower the blood pressure anytime, *at will.* The discovery and development of biofeedback techniques over the last decade has revolutionized our conception of the capacities of human **consciousness** in relation to the reality of the physical body. Biofeedback is now being used in clinical settings around the world to help people control and cure such conditions as high blood pressure, chronic pain, anxiety, and other psychosomatic disorders.

biorhythms: A method of analyzing and predicting how well one will function on a given day, based upon the discovery of three internal cycles in the human body-mind system: a 23-day physical cycle, a 28-day emotional cycle, and a 33-day intellectual cycle. Each cycle includes a peak or high period and a low, or negative period.

Castaneda books: A series of six books, written by Carlos Castaneda, which are hypothetically factual accounts of his apprenticeship and experiences with a Yaquí Indian *brujo* (sorcerer) named **Don Juan.** The books are magical, exquisite immersions in the nonrational world of the native American **shaman**, who moves between the two realms—that of normal, accepted reality, and that of "nonordinary reality." Whether they are fact or fiction is not considered important. With their insistence upon other **dimensions** of existence and their delineation of the "warrior" way of living "impeccably" in *every* reality, the books have become accepted by the **New Age** community as authentic and important spiritual documents.

Cayce material: Over the course of twenty years, **Edgar Cayce** gave thousands of "readings" about the health and spiritual life (including reincarnations) of people he had never seen or met. This remarkable material has been organized, classified, and some of it published, by the Association for Research and Enlightenment (ARE) in Virginia Beach, Virginia.

Children of God: One of the major **New Age** "Jesus people" communes, organized by David Berg in 1969.

chiropractic: A method of treating disorders through manipulation of the vertebrae and other natural physical means. Almost one hundred years old, chiropractic is currently enjoying an explosion of popularity as part of the **holistic health** movement. The basic theory of chiropractic is that nerve impulses determine and maintain the healthy function of all body parts, and that adjustment of the spinal column can regularize nerve impulse transmission when there is a medical problem.

co-counseling: Also called **re-evaluation counseling**. A system of therapy, generally practiced in pairs by two people who are alternately counselors for each other. Co-counseling is almost totally unpublicized and noncommercial. The emphasis in counseling is upon mutual support and appreciation, through trained, sympathetic listening, and on the "discharge" of emotional problems through crying, laughing, action, or energized talk.

dance therapy: A form of **group** and individual therapy in which a wide variety of movement styles are used to help the **client** express feelings, resolve conflicts, get in touch with his or her body, integrate body and mind. Elements of traditional dance training, modern and folk dance, **bioenergetics**, anatomy and physiology, and other body-mind systems are employed to achieve improved physical and emotional well-being.

Do-in: A Japanese form of self-massage, emphasizing pressure at defined **acupuncture** points.

Eckanckar: A small spiritual group, concerned with "the science of soul travel," tracing its lineage through a series of **masters** for thousands of years. The current Eck master is Sri Darwin Gross.

encounter: A form of **group** therapy emphasizing direct, open **communication**, interpersonal interaction and confrontation, and intense, authentic personal involvement. The group experience is not limited to verbal interchange, but may include body-work, nonverbal games, **massage**, dancing, etc. Originated in the NTL (National Training Labs) groups of the late 1940s and expanded by the **Esalen Institute** in its sixties to seventies heyday, the encounter movement has proliferated to such an extent that elements of encounter are to be found in virtually every group therapy situation now extant— of which there are tens of thousands.

est: A high-intensity, authoritarian, large-**group** transformational process in which groups of two hundred or more people spend two weekends in a closed, rigidly structured environment during which time they are expected to "get *it*"—*it* being the spontaneous insight that what is, is. Or something like that. The brainchild of **Werner Erhardt** (formerly Jack Rosenberg), who combined elements of **Scientology**, **Zen** Buddhism, corporate sales and motivation methods, and group dynamics (with a dash of brainwashing), est has become phenomenally successful with nothing but word-of-mouth promotion. Probably as many people swear by est as swear at it.

family therapy: Any of a variety of therapeutic processes in which the whole familial system of a **client** is involved in the therapy process, rather than just the individual, seen in isolation. Family therapy seeks actual changes in the family system itself, not only in the life of a single individual. FT sessions often involve all family members at once, while others may involve only one or two members at a time.

The Farm: A large, uniquely successful **New Age** commune in the hills of Tennessee. The community of over six hundred men, women and children is led by **Stephen Gaskin**, one of the least dogmatic, nonauthoritarian of American **gurus**. In recent years The Farm has moved from being self-supporting to providing famine and disaster relief around the U.S. and the world.

Feldenkrais Method: A system of self-improvement through conscious movement retraining to alter neurological **patterns,** developed by Israeli Judoist Moshe Feldenkrais, the method has gained considerable respect among dancers and other **body-work** therapists and is often incorporated into eclectic therapy practice.

Findhorn: A remarkable community in northern Scotland, where fruits and vegetables of sizes and species inconceivable for that climate have been grown—apparently through the community's spiritual efforts and contact with the indigenous "nature spirits."

Gestalt therapy: A method of **group** and individual therapy developed by **Fritz Perls** and others, using a widely varied array of techniques, many of which are imaginative, dramatic, and partially nonverbal. The prime focus of Gestalt is on deeply and accurately "feeling what you feel"—i.e., applying a deliberately heightened awareness to the emotional realm. Gestalt is probably the best representative of the new therapies: eclectic, energetic, profoundly effective at its best; predictable, inauthentic, faddish at its worst. Elements of Gestalt now figure in many other group and individual therapy methods.

Gurdjieff work: Psychological-spiritual training devoted to the "further evolution" of human beings. Based upon the teachings and writings of **Georges I. Gurdjieff,** charismatic Middle Eastern mystic, philosopher, teacher, the Gurdjieff work is notably noncommercial, · serious, and difficult.

health foods: A major movement that manifests the simultaneous sanity and faddishness of the **New Age.** Every group and every individual defines healthy food differently, but the health-food movement as a whole wisely agrees that food produced without the use of chemical pesticides, insecticides, fertilizers, processing agents, or other additives is better for you than food that contains these toxic ingredients. Beyond this point, disagreement flourishes: Probably a majority of health-food advocates are *vegetarian,* or at least antimeat (fish and eggs may be acceptable); some are rigidly against all animal-derived products (including cheese); some are fruitarians (fresh fruits and leafy vegetables only); others are **macrobiotics** (diet based on brown rice; see entry); **megavitamin** advocates; raw-foods-only types; wheatgrass dieters; fasters; and so on.

homeopathy: A nineteenth-century natural-medicine system that is regaining popularity in the **New Age.** The essence of the system is the application of small quantities of natural minerals, herbs, extracts, and other elements, in specific dilutions determined by the homeopath. The overall philosophy of the system is **holistic** and extremely personalized, with a great deal of time being taken to understand all aspects of the patient before treatment is prescribed.

Huna: The magical-spiritual system of the *Kahunas,* or Hawaiian medicine men. A small number of Huna study groups have sprung up, mainly on the East and West coasts, as part of the **New Age** phenomenon.

I Ching: The ancient Chinese "Book of Changes," a Taoist-Confucian divination system. Through six throws of three coins (originally, a more complex procedure with yarrow stalks), a six-lined **hexagram** is obtained which represents a particular idea, prognosis, and philosophy. The I Ching is consulted for the interpretation of this symbol. "Throwing the **Ching**" is a popular **New Age** procedure when one encounters a major decision, problem, ending, or beginning. The philosophy of the book, whatever the outcome of the throw, is sane, humane, and wise.

ions: specifically, air ions. The earth's atmosphere contains many molecules that have an electrical charge—some positive (fewer electrons), some negative (more electrons). When the concentration of *pos-ions* is high, human beings become fatigued, irritable, illness-prone. When the concentration of *neg-ions* is high, people report feelings of calm, clearheadedness, relaxed well-being. Most of the mechanical devices and physical environments of urban civilization decrease the neg-ions and increase the pos-ions. In response to this, an array of negative-ion generating devices has recently been produced, which alter the electrical quality of the atmosphere in homes, offices, hospital wards, etc.

iridology: The science (or pseudoscience) of diagnosing illness from observation of a person's eyes.

Jesus movement: A term for a wide variety of new religious groups, communes, cults, and nonestablishment churches, most of which share a commitment to the direct experience of Christianity on a more intense and daily basis than that offered by the major Protestant and Catholic churches. Although the term includes many fundamentalist and revivalist churches that have long existed in the U.S. (especially in the rural South), it more properly refers to the welter of **New Age** (late sixties and seventies) Christian communes found all across the country.

Kabbala: A form of Jewish mysticism, in which secret teachings about man, God, and the universe are imbedded in a code involving Hebrew letters and numbers.

Leboyer Method: A method of natural childbirth that focuses on the most gradual, gentle, loving transition from womb to "real world." In the Leboyer Method, the newborn is not subjected to harsh lights, hard surfaces, or violent shocks of any kind, but gently immersed in a warm bath and caressed in a warm, dimly lit room. The theory is that children afforded this more enlightened postnatal experience will avoid many of the traumas that harsh hospital procedures inflict on the infant psyche.

macrobiotics: A dietary system and way of life based upon interpretation of the *Unique Principle:* the continuous interaction of **yin** and **yang** (negative and positive, dark and light, etc.) as found in Oriental philosophy. Created by Georges Ohsawa, the macrobiotic diet centers around brown rice (held to be the most balanced, perfect food), with other foods introduced only in appropriate yin-yang balance. In other respects, macrobiotics is a rather self-conscious life-style, with highly defined sex-role differentiations and an overweening devotion to the teachings of Ohsawa and **Michio Kushi**, its current leader.

massage: No longer the province of ham-handed athletic trainers, massage has come out of sweaty gyms and into private practice. **New Age** variations include **Esalen** massage, *psychic massage*, **foot reflexology**, **Shiatsu**, and **Reichian** deep-muscle massage. In most of these modern variations, the emphasis is not so much on making the **client** feel good at the moment as it is on releasing built-up muscular (and emotional) tension, and promoting **energy** flow.

meditation: Any of a variety of deliberate mind-body **processes** that calm the mind, relax the body, slow brain-wave activity, and generate states of **consciousness** notably different from the normal, waking, anxious or semi-anxious state. There is no single "meditative state," but rather, meditation is the *process* by which one alters consciousness for beneficial mental-physical and/or spiritual purposes. Major varieties of meditation include those found in **Yoga**, **Zen**, **Transcendental Meditation**, **Silva Mind Control**, **Tibetan Buddhism**, **T'ai Chi**, and **Sufism**.

megavitamin therapy: Also known as **orthomolecular psychiatry**. The use of large doses of specific vitamins (and/or minerals) to treat psychological and physical disorders. Megavitamin therapy has been used successfully to treat certain forms of schizophrenia, depression, drug addiction, alcoholism, anxiety, etc. The question of how many such disorders actually represent a biochemical imbalance in the body (which therefore is amenable to megavitamin therapy) remains controversial.

naturopathy: A complete system for health and healing based on **natural** remedies and natural forces. Naturopathic methods include diet (natural foods), fasting, use of light, heat, air, and **massage**, *Hatha Yoga*, breathing exercises, etc. Naturopaths are trained in four-year colleges of naturopathic medicine before being licensed to practice.

Nichiren Soshu: A variant of Japanese Buddhism in which the major practice is the incessant chanting of the **mantra** *Nam myoho renge kyo.* Reasonably popular in the U.S., with groups in all major cities.

numerology: The "science" of numbers—specifically, a method of analyzing a person's character, interactions, and future through key numbers in his life—birth date, number value of letters in the name, Social Security number, etc.

parapsychology: The study of phenomena that are "paranormal"—i.e., do not fit into the known and accepted medical-scientific version of what is real and possible for human beings and what is not. Major areas of parapsychological research have traditionally included: *ESP* (extrasensory perception), *telepathy, clairvoyance,* and **psychokinesis** (moving objects by the mind). More recently, the emphasis of parapsychological research has shifted to examination of voluntary controls of internal states (including blood flow, healing rate, etc.), **psychic healers** and other extraordinary people (Uri Geller, for example), and other objective evidences of previously unknown **bioenergies**.

PET: Parent Effectiveness Training; a system of improving parent-child relations through more open and honest **communication**, mutual respect, and shared decision-making.

PET groups have been organized in all fifty states and have reached tens of thousands of families.

Polarity Therapy: A health system premised upon the balancing of various aspects of the innate life-energy in an individual. Using exercises, special types of **massage**, diet, and re-patterning of life-style, Polarity Therapy seeks the perfect balance of mental, physical, and spiritual **energies**.

Primal Therapy: A therapeutic method developed by Arthur Janov in which screaming, yelling, and crying are used in the reexperiencing of childhood and infantile pain or suffering; thereby (hypothetically) eliminating the neuroses of later life caused by these early traumas.

psychic healing: Any form of healing process that is caused by nonmedical procedures or factors—including prayer, **meditation**, "faith healing," **shamanic** practices, etc. While there are doubtless many charlatans preying upon the vulnerable and gullible in this domain, there remains an abundance of demonstrated cases of "impossible" healings performed by psychic healers under reputable conditions. The **New Age** perspective regards these cases as the utilization of a healing force available for all persons to tap into, if we can only learn how to do so.

psychodrama: A **group** therapy method developed by J. L. Moreno in which conflicts, critical scenes, and other important dynamics of a person's life are acted out, with other members of the psychodrama group playing the roles of key people (mother, father, wife, husband, lover, siblings, etc.).

Psychosynthesis: The eclectic system of Roberto Assagioli, emphasizing the integration of all levels of the self, through **group** and individual work, concentrating on the refinement and use of the will. Psychosynthesis goes beyond ordinary psychological health to include transpersonal and spiritual goals.

pyramid power: The essential concept here is

that the structure of the Egyptian pyramids is one which collects and intensifies certain cosmic and atmospheric **energies**, producing unusual effects upon objects (and persons) inside the pyramid. Scale-model pyramids and other devices utilizing the same principle have been designed—and marketed—that can supposedly keep razor blades sharp and unrefrigerated foods fresh, enhance **meditation**, and "energize" water and other substances.

radical therapy: A therapy that views the individual's problems in the context of an unhealthy, unjust culture/society/civilization. Rather than aiming at the patient's adjustment to such a system, radical therapy includes struggle for social change as an inevitable component of the struggle for personal health.

radionics/radiesthesia: Radionics is the use of instruments and devices to detect natural forces and phenomena as they interact with human beings: finding water with a *dowsing rod,* locating diseased organs with a hand-held *pendulum,* etc. Radiesthesia is the human capacity for detecting such so-called extrasensory information—i.e., the sensitivity of the human body-mind to forces, **energies**, resonances, substances, that is not an accepted capacity in the biomedical model. An example would be a **psychic healer**'s sensation of heat or prickling when passing his or her hands over (but not touching) the disordered organ of a sick person.

Rational Emotive Therapy (RET): A form of psychotherapy developed by Albert Ellis, which emphasizes the role of rational thought and restructuring one's thinking patterns in order to resolve emotional conflicts and problems.

reality therapy: A method developed by William Glasser, used particularly in institutional settings—schools, prisons, hospitals, etc. Reality therapy emphasizes the responsibility of the patient for his or her behavior and feel-

ings, and the primacy of personal morality. The therapy is oriented toward changing behavior, and thereby changing attitudes (rather than the other way around).

rebirthing: A new therapy in which all neuroses and life problems are meant to be eradicated by reliving and reexperiencing the birth process as vividly and realistically as possible. Subjects are immersed in tubs of ninety-nine-degree water, breathing only through snorkels, to duplicate the conditions of the womb, finally emerging to breathe air directly and be **massaged** and welcomed to the world. Supposedly, reliving the birth process consciously and without trauma will undo the psychic damage caused by an unhappy or incomplete "first" birth.

reflexology: Also called **zone therapy**. A system of treating health problems through **massage** of specific points on the feet and ankles (in some variants, on the hands as well). The theory is that all nerves connecting to major organs and limbs of the body have terminals in soles of the feet, the toes, or the sides of the ankles; massage to those terminal points corrects the flow of **energy** to any disordered part.

Reichian therapy: Variously called **orgone therapy**, **vegetotherapy**, and **character analysis**. Based upon the theories and methods developed by **Wilhelm Reich**, this is a body-centered method, using deep **massage**, breathing, hitting, and other violent actions to release energy blocks and restore the free flow of biological **energy** (called *orgone*). A major goal of Reichian therapy is the patient's attainment of *orgastic potency*—the capacity for total and involuntary energy discharge in the sexual embrace—which Reich held as the sine qua non of psychological health.

Rogerian Therapy: Also called **client-centered therapy**. This is a primarily verbal form of psychotherapy premised upon a healthy, positive, supportive relationship between therapist and **client**. A major technique introduced in Rogerian therapy (and now employed in most other modern therapies), is **active listening**, in which the therapist "reflects back" to the client what he or she hears the client saying (rather than analyzing or commenting upon it). The Rogerian therapist presumes the essential goodness and worth of the client, and affirms this as part of the process of the client's self-development.

Rolfing: Also called **structural integration**. A severe, intense form of body reshaping, accomplished over ten often painful sessions. The rolfer's knees, elbows, and knuckles may be used to loosen muscle fasciae and reposition body segments to attain better alignment with gravity and release blocked energy. The aim is to rectify muscle imbalances, tensions, and misalignments that have developed over a lifetime.

Seth material: A series of writings that has been (hypothetically) communicated through author Jane Roberts from a discarnate *entity* named Seth, who inhabits other **dimensions** of **reality**. The material includes a vast amount of information about existence and consciousness on other **planes** or levels of existence than those we know, and has become the subject of study groups and widespread acceptance in the **New Age** community.

Sex therapy: The pioneering work of Masters and Johnson, and other sex researchers of the 1970s, revealed that sexual dysfunction in both males and females is far more widespread than previously imagined. Sex therapy is a method by which the most common sexual dysfunctions—impotence, frigidity (or nonorgasmicity), and premature ejaculation —can be treated with high probability of success. Working with couples—or in the case of single males, with a *surrogate* partner—physical exercises proceed in a graduated manner to restore normal sexual functioning. In the more nearly complete forms of sex therapy, such as that practiced at the Masters and Johnson clinics, attention is also paid to the

psychological dynamics of the individual and the couple being treated.

Shiatsu: Japanese art of finger-pressure **massage** on **acupuncture** points; not only to relax muscles but to rebalance energy flow. An almost synonymous term is **acupressure**.

Silva Mind Control: A system of creative, practical **meditation/autosuggestion** developed by **José Silva** and learned by over a million people in the U.S. and abroad. Through simple mind-body relaxation process, practitioners enter their *level* (state of deep relaxation with high **alpha**-brain-wave production), then use **visualizations**, statements to oneself, and other self-programming methods to improve their lives. Silva is one of the least dogmatic, noncultish, totally practical systems currently being propagated. Its underlying thesis is that the capacity of the mind, at its deepest levels, to receive information is infinite.

stress reduction: In the late 1970s, the medical establishment began to realize the dangerous effects of stress in the generation of disease and disorders of every type, from nervous breakdowns to heart disease. For methods of reducing stress, however (both the physical and psychological varieties), the **New Age** and new therapy systems were far better equipped. Thus the early eighties have seen an upsurge of stress-reduction seminars, workshops, and courses, in which businessmen, executives, and all sorts of decidedly non-**Aquarian** types are learning **meditation**, **biofeedback**, **autosuggestion**, *Hatha Yoga*, aerobics, **massage**, healthy diets, and other forms of relaxation and life-style alteration.

Subud: A spiritual movement begun in Java, in which the major practice is a thirty-minute **latihan**, where groups of Subud followers get together and wait for whatever spontaneous spiritual manifestations (often laughing, crying, shouting, etc.) may occur.

Sufi Order/Sufism: The mystical wing of Islam, characterized by the use of deep **meditation**, teaching stories (especially humorous), ecstatic dancing, and other physical means to attain **enlightenment**. There are several public figures of the Sufi Order who have attained popularity among **New Age** adherents in the West, and others who function (we are told) without being recognized.

T'ai Chi: An ancient Chinese art of **meditation**-in-motion, T'ai Chi is unique in that it is both a combative/exercise system (one of the *internal* martial arts) and a system of spiritual **growth** based upon Taoist philosophy. The basic practice is the *long form,* a ten- to forty-five-minute choreographed exercise in which the practitioner moves in extreme slow motion, as if underwater, breathing deeply and mentally directing the **ch'i** (internal **energy**, life force) along prescribed lines. Practiced daily by millions of Chinese, T'ai Chi is becoming one of the most popular **New Age** body disciplines. Although its techniques look quite different, the internal principles of T'ai Chi are close to those of the Japanese art of **Aikido**.

tarot: A system of divination and character analysis based upon a deck of seventy-eight cards, each with an archetypal image (such as the Hanging Man, the Ace of Swords, the Fool). Tarot originated as a fortune-telling method in fifteenth-century Europe and has survived, almost unchanged, to the present day.

Theosophy: A spiritual-knowledge movement started in the nineteenth century, whose teachings are the basis of most **New Age** assumptions about occult matters. It includes theories of reincarnation, **ascended masters**, **cosmic consciousness**, evolution of the soul, **karma**, etc. Whatever the source of this material—much of it, incidentally, reappears in apparently unrelated contexts, such as the **Cayce** readings—many people in the New Age accept it.

Tibetan Buddhism: The predominant spiritual system of the "mountain kingdom," which has recently become popular in the West. It employs **meditation**, prayer, fasting, and dialogues with the **master**.

Transactional Analysis: Abbreviated **TA**. A form of psychotherapy developed by Eric Berne and Thomas Harris, emphasizing social interactions (viewed in units called *transactions*). The individual is seen as variously acting from three aspects of the self, called the *Parent,* the *Child,* and the *Adult* (roughly analogous to Freud's *superego, id,* and *ego*); the goal of therapy is to act consistently as an adult. Though rarely employed as an in-depth therapy mode, TA has been especially popularized in a series of best-selling books: *I'm OK, You're OK, The Games People Play,* etc.

Transcendental Meditation: Abbreviated **TM**. A simplified yet extremely effective **meditation** system. The essential practice is to sit quietly for twenty minutes, repeating silently to oneself a **mantra** (sacred word) that has been selected for you. Brought to the West by **Maharishi Maheesh Yogi**, a jocular Indian who first attained fame as the Beatles' **guru**, TM has now spread to almost every city in America, and has been embraced by executives, mayors, housewives, and a host of other non-**New Age** types.

wicca: The correct name for witchcraft. Although it has received a *very* bad press for the past five or six hundred years, witchcraft is actually for the most part a benevolent, humane system of natural healing and natural magic. Wicca literally means the "old ways," and is held to be the last remnant of the pre-Christian **shamanic** religions of Europe. Modern practitioners of wicca, as one might imagine, run the gamut from wonderful to bizarre.

Yoga: One of the oldest surviving systems of psychospiritual development, Yoga literally means "union," and refers to the process of the individual spirit unifying itself with the divine, or universal spirit. To this end, there are many varieties of practice, all of which are called Yoga: the most widely known is *Hatha Yoga,* which uses physical practices—postures (**asanas**) and breathing exercises (*pranayama*), among others—to promote health and raise **consciousness**. Others are *Karma Yoga* (the yoga of selfless work), *Bhakti Yoga* (Yoga of devotion), *Kundalini Yoga* (Yoga of divine energy transmitted up the spinal column), and *Raja Yoga* (Yoga of mental control and development). All Yogas have as their basis the religion and philosophy of Hinduism, although in the typical YMCA Yoga class for middle Americans this is downplayed if not discarded. For most people, Yoga has come to mean slow stretching, deep breathing, and **meditation**.

Zen: Formed by the intersection of mystical Indian Buddhism and earthy Chinese *Taoism,* Zen long ago became an integral part of Japanese culture, and remains more a *way* of doing and being than a discrete theology. *Soto,* one of the classic schools of Zen, taught that **enlightenment** could be obtained by "just sitting"—i.e., by the pure **meditative** experience unhampered by instructions and imposed conditions. Other schools (*Rinzai* is the major one) use breath controls, walking meditations, prayers, and the knotty little brain teasers called **koan**; but the base of Zen practice has always been **zazen,** sitting meditation. The special "Zen" qualities—calm **centeredness**, sudden and spontaneous action, and total immersion in the present moment—have expressed themselves in many classical Japanese arts (sword-fighting, brush-painting, tea ceremony) and are now being applied, in name if not in fact, to such nonclassical pursuits as motorcycle maintenance, tennis, and corporate decision-making.

NEW AGE TERMINOLOGY

adjustment: A **chiropractic** treatment or session. In general, the vertebrae are "adjusted" to restore order to the nervous system and hence to every other body function.

Akashic record: The information storehouse wherein every fact, sound, event, and idea since the beginning of time has been recorded. Supposedly the source of information (such as the **Cayce material**) received by people in profound **psychic** states.

Aquarian Age: Era of peace, **enlightenment**, human cooperation; variously said to be now beginning, about to begin, or due in year 2000. Also used to refer to **New Age** ideas, products, etc. ("Flowing all-natural clothing for the **Aquarian** jogger.")

asana: A body posture or position held during practice of *Hatha Yoga.* The most well-known is *padmasana* (the Full Lotus)—sitting with legs intertwined and spine erect.

Ascended Masters: Spiritual greats who have departed from the earthly plane and are playing to packed cosmic houses in the higher realms.

ashram: A spiritual community or practice place, especially in **Yoga** traditions. ("At home she'd never wash the dishes, but she went off to some **ashram** in India and spent six months hauling dung for her **guru**.")

astral body: The "subtle" body, an energy form that is nonphysical and can separate from the physical body during dreams, **meditation**, or **astral projection**, enabling the person's **consciousness** to travel freely in time, space, and all **dimensions**.

astral travel: Also **astral projection, out-of-the-body experience** (**OOBE**). The process by which the **astral body** (including personal **consciousness**) separates from the physical (remaining attached by the *Akashic cord*) and moves in other realms.

Atlantis: Legendary lost continent that supposedly sank thousands of years ago, after having reached a high degree of technological civilization. The existance of Atlantis is a fairly common tenet of **New Age** belief.

atman: The deepest, most essential self, the divine essence within each individual. A major Hindu/**Yoga** saying holds that "**atman** is **brahman**" (God, or universal soul).

aum: Also spelled **om**. A holy word in Sanskrit, often used as sound for chanting aloud.

aura: Radiation, emanation, or other light(s) around the body, said to be visible to certain attuned people. The aura is supposed to show aspects of the nonphysical **energy** bodies of human beings. *Aura reading* (for different color, shape, intensity, etc.) is a method of health and spiritual diagnosis.

Auroville: A major international spiritual community in northern India, organized by **Sri Aurobindo** and *The Mother*.

avatar: A great spiritual leader who is one of the incarnations of God or the Divine Being —e.g., Jesus, Krishna, etc.

bardo: A plane or level of **consciousness** in **Tibetan Buddhist** psychocosmology.

Bhagavad Gita: A major sacred text of Hinduism; literally "Song of the Blessed One."

bioplasma: The Soviet biologist V. I. Inyushin, from his observation of **Kirlian photographic** phenomena and other biophysical studies, has concluded that living things possess a kind of **energy** matrix, composed of an organized system of subatomic particles, which he calls bioplasma. This *bioplasmic body* organizes physical matter according to its form and sounds remarkably like the "subtle body" described in occult lore.

boddhisattva: A highly spiritually evolved person who forgoes his own attainment of **nirvana** (ultimate bliss) in order to assist other living creatures in attaining **enlightenment**. More colloquially, a compassionate, involved spiritual teacher.

brahman: Divinity, world soul, absolute being, God in the Hindu religion.

Buddha nature: Holiness, perfectness, **enlightenment**, which is the true nature of every living being. ("Does a dog have **Buddha nature**?")

center: A key **New Age** term, with many meanings: 1. A place where workshops and classes are offered in **New Age** disciplines (often rendered **growth center**, Center for the Study of . . . etc.).

2. One of the seven **chakras** or other **energy** foci in the human body.

3. The point two to three inches below the navel, considered the most vital energy center in **Aikido**, **T'ai Chi**, and many other psychophysical disciplines (it is also the body's center of gravity).

4. As a verb, to become calm, integrated, relaxed yet energized, physically and psychologically balanced. To be *uncentered*, conversely, means to be tense, frightened, imbalanced, or otherwise out of control of one's energies.

chakra: An **energy** center in the human body. According to **Yoga**, **Theosophy**, and other occult systems, there are seven chakras, roughly corresponding to major nerve plexuses and endocrine glands, which are like energy transformers for atmospheric and basic life energy. As the **kundalini** energy rises from the base of the spine (lowest chakra) to the crown of the head (the highest), each chakra is "opened," releasing tremendous energy and capacity in a given area (sexuality, power, love, communication, understanding, spiritual union, etc.).

chart: In **astrology**, a computation of the astronomical configuration at the moment of a person's birth; the particular combination of *houses*, *planets*, *sun*, **moon**, **rising signs**, etc., is supposed to give detailed information about a person's character, strengths and weaknesses, and destiny.

ch'i: Chinese term for life force, inner **energy**, or breath. Classical Chinese medicine holds that the circulation of ch'i is the predication of all health; such arts as **acupuncture**, **T'ai Chi**, and *Ch'i Kung* are devoted to restoring and maintaining the "flow of ch'i." The concept of ch'i, or life force, exists in many cultures and disciplines other than the Western biomedical (which rejects it): The Sanskrit word is **prana**, the Japanese **ki**; Reich's **orgone** and Inyushin's **bioplasma** are remarkably similar.

consciousness: Awareness, clarity, mental function. This is one of the catchwords of the **New Age** (or, of New Age consciousness), and it can mean almost anything one wants. In **Arica**, a favorite maxim holds that "**consciousness** is everything," and there's even a song entitled "You Are **Consciousness**." At the same time, much attention is paid throughout the New Age spectrum to "raising" or "expanding" consciousness, which generally means becoming more spiritually oriented, less attached to material things and events. *Cosmic consciousness* is a particular variety of consciousness in which the individual mind is in direct contact with the Infinite, or cosmic reality; this is, needless to say, one of the "highest" levels.

dharma: Hindu/Buddhist term meaning truth, way, teaching.

dhayana: Meditation, wisdom.

dimension: Plane, realm, **reality**. Another **New Age** favorite, it can refer to anything from point of view to other worlds.

ego: In most **New Age** spiritual systems, ego is a negative term; it refers to selfishness, attachment to material things and worldly achievements, and limited, unevolved **consciousness**. ("Yeah, his **ego** is getting in the way of really accepting the **master** as his teacher.") Contrast with use of the word in new therapy language.

energy: A favorite catchword, referring to vitality, **consciousness**, spiritual force, but almost never to nonliving forces such as nuclear power. These latter forces would probably be called *negative energies*—which also refers to human anger, cruelty, greed, and violence. To say someone has *good energy* means that he or she is enthusiastic and outgoing without anxiety or anger.

enlightenment: The highest state of **consciousness**, of spiritual attainment, perfectness, absolute knowledge, freedom. This is what everyone in the **New Age** is supposed to be after—though the competition sometimes obscures the goal.

entity: Being, soul, personality. Found frequently in the **Cayce** readings, where the evolution of a single entity through many reincarnations and journeys on other **planes** is chronicled. A useful word for the essential unit of life or **consciousness** that inhabits a physical body but survives beyond the death of the body.

ephemeris: The table or calendar used by **astrologers**, showing daily positions of planets, sun, **moon**, etc. Used in preparing someone's **chart**.

etheric: Of a higher **plane** of existence than the material. The *etheric body* is not synonymous with the **astral body**, however, and is considered a nonphysical "double" body which interpenetrates the physical.

guru: Spiritual teacher or guide. The term is not taken lightly and is applied only to teachers of extremely high **consciousness**. ("My **guru** left the earth**plane** two years ago, but I still contact him every time I go into deep **meditation**.")

hermeticism: A Western occult tradition, hypothetically traced to Hermes Trismegistus, ancient Egyptian **astrologer**, alchemist, magician, sage.

hexagram: A symbol of six horizontal lines, each of which may be broken or unbroken, which is the result of a throw of coins in the **I Ching** divination system. There are sixty-four hexagrams, each with a different interpretation. The author threw the following hexagram on the occasion of writing this entry: ䷭ , which is number 46, *Sheng* (Pushing Upward).

holistic: Whole, complete. Usually refers to a perspective incorporating psychological, physical, and spiritual factors. The *holistic health* movement thus includes everything from **acupuncture** to **negative-ion** generating devices to aerobic exercise, **megavitamins**, **massage**, and **Zen**. *Holistic healing* includes both orthodox Western medicine, unorthodox and non-Western systems (e.g., **homeopathy, chiropractic, acupuncture**), and psychic or "spiritual methods" (prayer, **meditation**, faith healing, etc.)

karma: The spiritual law of cause and effect, sustained through many lifetimes; that is, what you have done in previous lifetimes will affect your fate in this one, and what you do in this one will affect you in lives to come. Often overused by **New Age** people, as explanation for any disaster or personal failing. ("Hey, like, it's your **karma**, man.") *Bad karma* refers to an unsavory or immoral act, which, though nonpunishable in the present, will accumulate a moral debt that will have to be repaid eventually.

kath: An **Arican** term for the physical **energy center** in the lower abdomen, several inches below the navel.

ki: The Japanese term for **energy**, universal life force, spirit. To be *extending* or *pouring forth ki* is to be positive, powerful, energized, healthy; to be *cutting* or *pulling in ki* is to be frightened, **uncentered**, or in ill health.

Kirlian photography: An electrical-photography process developed by Semyon Kirlian in Russia and now being studied and used all over the world. The procedure produces images of lights, flares, streamers, and other apparent **energy** emanations from the bodies of living things, which many believe are visual representations of the nonphysical energies of life: the energy body, **aura**, **astral body**, **bioplasma**, etc.

koan: A brain-teasing or otherwise challenging, rationally insoluble question asked by a **Zen master** of a disciple, to spark an alteration or jump of **consciousness**. The classic example: "What is the sound of one hand clapping?" Often the only "correct" response to one of these koan was a loud shout, an irrelevant retort, or some other spontaneous act.

kundalini: The powerful cosmic energy that lies dormant at the base of the spine, and can be "raised" through **yogic** practices; as the kundalini ascends through the seven **chakras**, their respective powers are released.

latihan: A group religious practice in **Subud**, in which members (divided into men's and women's groups), gather together and await whatever happens spontaneously—which may be shouting, crying, or some genuine spiritual transmission.

level: In **Silva Mind Control**, the basic **meditative** state, attainable quickly and easily through mind and body relaxation, where effective self-**programming** is possible. Biomedically, this state includes a high proportion of **alpha** brain-wave activity.

liberation: As distinct from its use in the therapy world, liberation in the **New Age** commonly means the giving up of attachment to worldly concerns and egotistic goals.

light: This is a big one, meaning truth, ultimate reality, goodness, God, spiritual **energy**, positive energy, or **enlightenment**. Although when used in the abstract this way it can become obnoxiously self-righteous ("Those of us who are striving to realize the **Light**"), the use of light as a **visualization** during certain kinds of **meditation** ("Imagine the injured person completely surrounded by a brilliant **aura** of white **light**, smiling and healthy") is remarkably evocative and effective.

live food: Food that is still growing, such as sprouts; or, more generally, any fruit or vegetable food that is raw and fresh.

mana: Hawaiian/Polynesian word for spiritual boon, life force, **energy**.

mandala: A geometric pattern or visual symbol

that concentrates the attention at a central point; used as a **meditation** device in Asian spiritual systems.

mantra: A Sanskrit word or other sound, or saying, repeated (often silently) as a kind of **meditation**-prayer. In **TM** and other **Yogic** systems, the **vibration** of the word itself is supposed to produce an effect on the **consciousness** of the person pronouncing it. Mantras are, hypothetically, assigned with great seriousness by one's **guru**, and not revealed to others.

master: Strictly speaking, a person who has, after long years of training, study, and personal development, become so spiritually attuned, so personally free of commonplace human games and foibles, so exemplary and wise, that he or she can serve as a teacher, a guide, a spiritual beacon to others. Unfortunately, since anyone can call himself a master who wishes to, we have the sorry spectacle of intelligent people worshiping at the plump feet of spoiled teenagers and prideful, egotistical cranks. True masters—those extraordinary men and women who have indeed transformed themselves into human beings of impeccable morality and spiritual strength—do exist, but they usually don't advertise in the Yellow Pages or appear at the Astrodome.

maya: In Hindu thought, the illusion of the so-called "real world," which is considered meaningless in comparison to the ultimate spiritual **reality**.

medicine: In Native American traditions, spiritual force, healing force, the power of nature, and the system of cultivating them. The *medicine man* or *woman* is the person whose task it is to make such forces available for the benefit of the tribe.

meridian: In classical Chinese medicine, a channel for the circulation of **ch'i**, or vital force. There are twelve meridians, each one emanating from a major organ—heart, lungs, liver, kidneys, etc.

metaprogram: A **program** designed to alter **consciousness** in the direction of spiritual matters or whole systems. Repeating to oneself while in a **meditative** state, "I am **energy**, I am indestructible, I am **consciousness**" would be *metaprogramming;* whereas repeating, "I will be successful, I will be irresistible in my sales campaign, I will attract money" would be programming of a more mundane order. The term was coined by **John Lilly**.

mind: The word crops up at least twice in every **New Age** pronouncement, and is a favorite subject for discussion. The mind is distinguished from the brain, which is merely the physical organ (like a computer) that the mind employs. ("When the individual **mind** touches the **Mind** of the Infinite, then there is bliss; when the individual **mind** asserts its isolation, then there is attachment and suffering.")

moon: In **astrology**, both the current astrological situation ("The **moon** is entering Virgo tonight and we're in for a helluva weekend") and an element of a person's **chart** ("I'm a Leo with my **moon** in Sagittarius").

moxibustion: A technique often used during **acupuncture** treatment in which a small amount of *moxa* (mugwort herb) is placed on an acupuncture point and burned. The mild unpleasantness of singed skin is more than offset (they say) by the therapeutic benefits.

mudra: In **Yoga**, a hand position or gesture that symbolizes—or creates—a specific psychospiritual quality, e.g., such as tranquility or compassion.

muladhara: The lowest, or "root" **chakra**, at the base of the spine, the seat of sexual and procreative/survival **energy** in Hindu body-cosmology.

murshid: A **master** in the **Sufi** tradition.

mushin: "No mind," an altered state of **consciousness** in **Zen** training, in which there is no conscious thought whatsoever, only pure **experience**.

namaste: Sanskrit spiritual greeting, accompanied by a slight bow with the hands joined together as in Christian prayer; seen frequently among serious or wanting-to-appear-serious spiritual types.

natural: Once an honorable and vital word, meaning "as found in nature" or "in accordance with nature," the word has been corrupted and co-opted, often beyond recognition, to sell hairstyles, potato chips, and all manner of exotic behavior. However, in conjunction with other words: *natural healing, natural childbirth, natural foods,* the word retains some credibility and a high degree of approbation in the **New Age**.

New Age: Both the hypothetical new era of "raised **consciousness**" and increased morality, and the movement of people who by their lives and work are ushering it in. In many respects an outgrowth of the radical political movements and "counterculture" of the sixties, in the early 1980s the New Age may be said to include: spiritual and pseudospiritual groups and movements; ecological awareness and action; **natural** foods and health systems; nonindustrial and non-Western cultural elements in general (e.g., primitive, Chinese, Indian, old-fashioned); and a host of other groups and individuals whose work and lifestyle differ significantly from the mainstream, profit-oriented, consumer society. The movement, of course, runs the gamut from the most brilliant and compassionate to the most obsequious and fraudulent.

nirvana: Enlightenment; the ultimate state beyond life and death, beyond all attachment or desire; in Sanskrit, nirvana literally means "extinction." That this should be the "highest" state in certain Oriental religions is revealing.

Om mani padme hum: A famous **mantra** of *Tibetan Buddhism,* which roughly translates as "The jewel is in the lotus."

organic: 1. With respect to food, grown without synthetic pesticides, fertilizers, insecticides, or any other nonnatural agricultural chemicals. Although sometimes abused, the term is more precise and verifiable than **natural** or **health food**.

2. By extension anything that is natural, non-mechanized, and healthy. ("Don't panic, it's **organic**!")

Perfect Master: The top banana in any given spiritual system. Depending on whom you talk to, the identity of the Perfect Master (or **masters**) varies considerably. (The author's personal choice is Louis Armstrong.)

plane: Dimension, level of existence, **vibrational** level. In the classic Hindu and general occult system, the *material* or *physical plane* is the lowest, followed by the **astral**, **etheric**, *mental,* et al.—dimensions of increasing subtlety and spirituality.

prana: In **Yoga**, the life **energy** or vital force, present in the atmosphere and primarily acquired through breathing. The practice of *pranayama* (roughly, breath exercises) is devoted to gaining and storing up a supply of prana.

premie: In the **Divine Light** system of **Guru Maharaj Ji**, an initiate or novice follower.

program: As a noun, a habitual unconscious mental pattern, which may have existed since childhood or may be consciously created through **autosuggestion**. As a verb, to create such a pattern in a person. ("Society has **programmed** us to fear being alone.")

psi: A recently coined word for **psychic** faculties and other phenomena that cannot be explained through orthodox biology and physics. Fire-walking, spoon-bending, telepathy, and premonitory dreams would all be considered manifestations of psi phenomena.

psychic: Of the mind. Generally applied to all occult and paranormal matters in which an exceptional function of the human mind is involved: *psychic healing, psychic reading, psychic surgery, psychic information.* Of course, the past decade has seen such appropriations as psychic dating services, about which we will not deign to comment.

psychokinesis: Abbreviated **PK**. The ability to move objects solely by the action of the **mind**; or, in general, the ability to affect material **reality** via the mind.

pulse diagnosis: A major element in traditional Chinese medicine (see **acupuncture**) in which each of twelve different pulses (six at each wrist) is felt to give information about the condition of the twelve major internal organs.

reality: It is a major tenet of **New Age** thought that there are many different "realities," consisting not only of what an individual thinks, perceives, feels, and strives for, but also of many different levels and **planes** of existence that are totally removed from our familiar worldly existence, some of which can be reached during **meditation** or other spiritual experiences. Thus, in contrast to the psychotherapeutic realm, where there is usually an assumed objective reality that people can make of what they will, in New Age parlance reality is far more variable and plastic, the cliché of choice being "You create your own **reality**."

rising sign: An important element in a person's birth horoscope—the **sign** that was in ascendance (i.e., on the eastern horizon) at the moment of birth. Those who are au courant **astrologically** never answer the question "What's your sign?" with a simple "Aquarius" or "Sagittarius," but say, "I'm a Virgo—but with Scorpio **rising**."

roshi: A **master** or teacher in **Zen** Buddhism.

samadhi: A state of bliss, **enlightenment**, full realization beyond all striving, **ego**, or duality; the highest state of **consciousness** in Hindu/**Yoga** tradition. See **satori**.

satori: **Enlightenment**, full awakening, sudden realization; the high point of **Zen** discipline. Unlike the **Yogic samadhi**, which is a state of mind far removed from worldly **realities**, the Zen satori is a revitalized, intensified return to "normal" reality. (A classic Zen story: When the disciple, having attained satori, rushes in to tell the **master** the good news, the master smiles and hands him a broom with which to sweep the monastery floor.)

seiza: A classic Japanese position, sitting on the heels with the knees apart and the back perfectly straight. The position is common to **Zen** and martial arts training and is conducive to a calm, stable mental state.

shakuhachi: A wooden flute fashioned from the base of the bamboo. The haunting, deep, mournful tones of the shakuhachi have long been associated with Far Eastern spirituality.

shaman: In primitive cultures, the person who moves between the "real world" of the tribe's daily life and the "other world" of spirits and spiritual forces. The shaman traditionally uses **meditation**, fasting, wilderness isolation, and occasionally drugs to alter **consciousness** and experience other **dimensions** of **reality**. He or she then returns with knowledge or power to benefit the people of the tribe.

shanti: Peace; the greeting (often expanded to *Om shanti*) of those who are involved in **Yoga** and other Indian-derived disciplines.

siddhi: A paranormal power gained through spiritual practice—e.g., telepathy, clairvoyance, the ability to materialize objects. The adept is not supposed to be distracted by the accumulation of these powers en route to true **enlightenment**.

sign: In **astrology**, one of the twelve zodiacal signs into which the solar year is divided: Aries, Taurus, Gemini, Cancer, Leo, Virgo, Libra, Scorpio, Sagittarius, Capricorn, Aquarius, and Pisces. A person's sign is determined by the date of his birth and is supposed to indicate predispositions of character—especially in conjunction with other astrological factors. "What's your sign?" is perhaps the most widely recognized—and least meaningful—of **New Age** clichés.

sitting: **Meditating**. ("I've been **sitting** three hours a day since I got back from the **ashram**.")

spiritual materialism: Spiritual practices that repeat the same flaws as most other, material striving: competitiveness, greed, egotism, desire for security. The term was coined by Tibetan Buddhist Trungpa Rinpoche.

swami: Lord; a title given a **guru** or other spiritual teacher, in the Indian tradition.

t'an t'ien: In **T'ai Chi** and other Chinese systems, the **energy center** in the lower abdomen, where the **ch'i** is stored through breathing and other body-mind practice.

Tantra: A form of **Yoga** that employs physical sensations to raise **consciousness** (as opposed to many other forms, which seek to reduce or ignore physical sensations). Tantric Yoga may include a prolonged, conscious sexual act as a form of **meditation**; inevitably, Tantra has come to mean spiritual or pseudospiritual sex in the popular imagination.

Tao: The way, or order of the universe; nature; the essence of any system when realized perfectly. ("Our special seminar this weekend will be 'The **Tao** of Loving.' ")

Tao Te Ching: The classical text of Chinese Taoism, attributed to the sage Lao Tzu, circa 600 B.C. It is a paradoxical, brilliantly simple book about nature and mankind that can be read and understood on many levels.

Thetan: In **Scientology**, the deep self, the perfect being within each person.

third eye: The spiritual organ, located in the forehead above and between the eyes; held to be the organ of intuition and spiritual "seeing." Often related to or synonymous with the pineal gland, a primitive light-sensing organ within the brain; also generally considered to be the sixth **chakra**.

triune function: In **Polarity Therapy**, the inter-

action of positive, negative, and neutral **energies** within the human body-mind.

Vedanta: Classical Hinduism, as expounded in the 5,000-year-old scriptures, the *Upanishads.*

vibration: Often shortened to **vibes**. A catchall word for feeling, **energy**, quality, impression, state, level, or idea. ("I'm picking up some very negative **vibrations** from some of you.")

wellness: See following section.

whole: An almost meaningless word with nonetheless positive connotation in **New Age** parlance: *whole person, whole earth, whole body,* etc. Originally a reaction to the traditional split of mind and body, psychology and medicine, man and nature in Western culture.

The Work: The **Gurdjieffian** discipline and self-transforming practice.

wu wei: Chinese, literally "not-doing." A central concept in Taoism and **T'ai Chi**, meaning to act effortlessly, to be so perfectly attuned that one's actions are natural, spontaneous, and without strain. The full phrase is *wei wu wei,* which literally means to "do without doing" —i.e., to accomplish without trying.

yin and yang: In Taoism and other Far Eastern thought, the basic duality of all things. Yin is feminine, dark, yielding; yang is masculine, light, active. Yin and yang refers to the continuous interplay of these opposites, their interconnection, mutual attraction, etc. It is also a euphemism for sexuality, especially among spiritual types who don't want to admit to mundane passions.

zazen: The practice of seated **meditation** in **Zen** Buddhism. This is the central method of spiritual practice, and is employed for many hours every day in serious **Zen** training.

NEW-THERAPIES TERMINOLOGY

active listening: Also called **reflecting back**. A method developed by Carl Rogers in which the *therapist* (or other active listener) restates what he has just heard the **client** say, in order

to make the client aware of himself more fully and to assure him that he is being understood.

alpha: Specifically, the type of brain wave associated with relaxation, dreaming, and **meditation**. More generally, a deeply relaxed mental state in which there is still an awake **consciousness**. ("I want you to breathe deeply three times . . . get into **alpha** . . . and **visualize** yourself as a four-year-old child. . . .")

altered states of consciousness: Abbreviated **ASC**. This term includes virtually every type of mental state other than "normal," waking **consciousness**—everything from simple dreaming and imagining to drug-induced hallucinations, **meditation** insights, runners' euphoria, etc. Masters and Houston, at the Foundation for Mind Research, have even developed an *Altered States of Consciousness Induction Device,* acronym *ASCID.*

block: Anything that inhibits **communication**, the flow of **energy**, health, personal **growth**, or **self-actualization**. Blocks may be psychological (anxiety, inhibition), physical (muscle tension, rigidity), sexual, spiritual, etc.

body work: Schools of therapy (**bioenergetics**, **rolfing**, *sensory awareness*, etc.) or specific therapy techniques that deal with the body—not so much for physical improvement per se, as to enhance the mind-body connection.

client: In the old, medical-model schools of psychiatry and psychotherapy, the person receiving treatment was called the *patient;* in the new, post-1960s therapies, the preferred word is "client." This is in keeping with the **human potential** philosophy that the therapist does not "cure" the patient, but provides a service (or, *creates a* **space**) through which the client can resolve his own conflicts and heal himself.

communicate: To talk, express oneself, interact meaningfully. This is a key word, for in the new therapy world, improved communication is seen as the sine qua non of improved relations with others—one's real differences of opinion and style notwithstanding. ("I never really **communicated** with my father.")

dialoguing: A therapy technique in which the subject recreates a conversation between two (or more) parts of his own personality. For example, the hedonistic inner child might dialogue with the repressive, "adult" self. In **Gestalt therapy,** dialoguing may be taken farther, and conversations enacted between parts of the body, characters or objects from a dream, etc. ("I dreamed I was flying over the city on a beautiful white horse." "Okay, be the horse. Tell the rider how you feel.")

dyad: A group of two people. ("Let's work in **dyads** on this exercise.")

ego: For the most part, used in somewhat the Freudian sense—as the adult, conscious personality; or more generally, the self or sense of self. Ego is not the bad word it is in the **New Age** spiritual thinking—in fact, to have a small ego (i.e., low self-image) is far worse than having a large ego (well-developed sense of self, self-confidence, self-importance).

Esalen: A **growth center** in Big Sur, California, founded in the early 1960s. Esalen was *the* place for **human potential** work in the 1960s, and was the locus for much of the work of human potential luminaries such as **Fritz Perls**. Although now one of hundreds of such centers, Esalen is still synonymous with an eclectic, exciting, state-of-the-art approach to new therapies and growth techniques.

experience: As both noun and verb, this is the quintessential **human potentials** term: One does not meet people—one "**experiences**" them; one does not try something new (whether hang gliding or **primal therapy**)— one "has an **experience**" of it; etc. The combinations of this word—**peak experience**, *meaningful experience, experience of being;* etc.— remain similarly imprecise in meaning. You just have to experience them.

feedback: Any opinion rendered about anything, especially someone's words or actions. ("I'd like everyone to give Jim a little **feedback** about what he just **shared** with us.") Feedback, of course, can be *positive* (compliments, flattery, encouragement), or *negative* (criticism, attack, discouragement).

grounding: In **bioenergetics**, as a noun, the quality of feeling connected to the ground through one's feet, which affords greater balance and physical stability, and also a feeling of personal strength and competence. As a verb, exercises in grounding one's **energy** usually involve standing with the knees bent for extended periods of time.

group: A method of therapy or **growth experience** in which a number of individuals (generally between five and twenty) work with a therapist (or *group leader,* or *facilitator*); in almost all groups, the real interaction between members of the group forms at least a portion of the "material" that is worked on. ("You'll have to make your own dinner, honey, I've got **group** tonight.")

growth: Used as a noun and an adjective. Generally, applies to **group** work, courses and workshops, or other life changes that enhance one's enjoyment and capacity for living; the term is distinguished from *therapy,* which is designed to solve specific problems. A major characteristic of the **human potentials movement** is that people are involving themselves in all sorts of schools and therapies (**Gestalt**, **encounter**, **bioenergetics**, **est**, **T'ai Chi**) not because they have a problem, but rather to improve themselves and enhance their enjoyment of life—in short, for personal growth.

guided fantasy: A therapy technique in which **clients** are led through an imaginary sequence of events, which they are to **visualize** as vividly as possible, adding details of their own that reveal inner psychological material. ("You are walking down a long, dark, narrow tunnel. At the end of the tunnel is a tiny, flickering light. As you gradually approach, you realize the light is a candle. As you approach further, you can make out a person sitting in front of the candle. You address the person and ask him or her one question. . . .")

here: Present, aware, actively involved, supportive. A shortening of the formerly popular "in the here and now." ("I don't want to work with Karl on this **process**. I just don't feel that he's **here** for me.")

humanistic psychology: A "Third Force" movement (as distinct from both Freudian and behaviorist) begun by **Abraham Maslow** and based upon the characteristics of the most positive, creative, and healthy human beings. The emphasis in humanistic psychology is upon **self-actualization** and personal **growth**.

human potentials movement: The concatenation of therapies, therapists, **growth centers**, theories, methods, and individuals, begun in the late 1960s and flowering through the 1970s and into the 1980s, devoted to what **Maslow** termed **self-actualization**—i.e., the development of the fullest and finest capacities of human beings. The term includes virtually all of the new therapies described in this section, and overlaps to some degree with the **New Age** groups; orthodox Freudian and behavioral modes of treatment, however, fall outside the movement.

information: A great word, because virtually anything under the sun can be considered information: a word, a look, the color of a sunset, a childhood memory, a newspaper statistic. The connotation is that there is no subjective distortion of the material in its transmission. ("Don't get so defensive, I'm just **sharing** some **information** with you.")

inner game: The application of **human potential** and **New Age** techniques—many of them drawn from Eastern spiritual disciplines—to Western sports. The inner game of tennis, for example, would include **Zen** concentration, **T'ai Chi** effortlessness, and pregame **visualization** practices.

I statement: A way of phrasing something that begins with "I"—generally as opposed to "you." When John says, "Mary, you treat me like a little child," he will be encouraged to restate this as "I feel like a little child when I'm encountering Mary"—thus **owning** the feeling rather than blaming Mary for it. Whether or not Mary *is* actually to blame is another question entirely.

it: In **est**, what everyone is after. Paradoxically, one cannot "get **it**" as long as one is trying to do so. Further, once you do get it, what you get is the realization that there was nothing to get—that, as **Werner** says, "everything that is, is—and everything that isn't, isn't." If this revelation doesn't seem worth $300 and two weekends of being called a **tube**, then you obviously haven't got it.

marathon: A **group** therapy session that lasts for several days without letup. The intensity of interaction, and the likelihood of confrontations, breakthroughs, and genuine encounters, are heightened by the length of the session.

open: Used in conjunction with certain nouns to form terms such as *open marriage, open relationship, open classroom,* and the like. It is supposed to mean free, uninhibited, unrestricted—but is often a euphemism for unstructured, unprincipled, or chaotic.

orgone: In **Reichian** theory, the cosmic life **energy** that manifests itself on all levels, from the formation of galaxies to the sexual embrace of man and woman. Reich developed several devices (*orgone box, orgone blanket*) and therapy methods to enhance or regularize the *orgone energy* of his clients. See also **ch'i** and **bioplasma** entries in NEW AGE section.

own: To take responsibility for, admit to, accept. ("Fred, you've been saying that Angela is driving you crazy. I want you to **own** your own feelings about your sanity, and give the **group** an **I statement** about those feelings.")

peak experience: A term coined by **Abraham Maslow** to mean a period of deep insight, breakthrough perception, euphoria, or mystical transcendence. The peak experience is one in which feeling, meaning, and well-

being are at a much higher level of intensity than during "normal" experience.

pre-orgasmic: An optimistic euphemism for what was once termed "frigid"; generally refers to a woman who has not (yet) attained orgasmic satisfaction from heterosexual activity, though she may have done so through masturbation.

process: As a noun, any sequence of events, procedures, or cycles—as the *growth process,* the *maturation process,* the *therapeutic process.* As a verb, to go over things, especially to talk out one's reactions to an exercise (or process!) in a therapy situation. ("We'll leave twenty minutes after the nonverbal **experience** to **process** it out.")

program: Any unconscious psychological pattern. ("You've got **programs** operating in your mind since your childhood—we're going to make them conscious so that you can eliminate or change them.")

role-playing: A therapy technique, common to **Gestalt** and many other schools, in which a scene in the **client**'s life (remembered, imagined, or anticipated) is acted out, by the client and therapist, or client and other **group** members. A woman who fears a confrontation with her boss, for example, might be called upon to role-play the scene with someone acting the part of the boss, in order to reveal her underlying feelings and explore possible different strategies for handling the situation.

self: The personality, the **ego**, the essential aspect of a person, the "real" you. Often compounded—the *inner self,* the *deep self,* **self-actualization**, and so on. In *new therapies,* "self" is a positive word that implies the healthy, integrated personality. (Contrast this with its usage in **New Age**, where the self —as distinct from God or the All—is negative.)

self-actualization: The **process** of improving oneself, becoming more creative, more fulfilled, more loving, more successful in **hu-**

manistic (not material) terms. Coined by **Abraham Maslow**, the term has now diffused in meaning to refer to almost any activity—however selfish or foolhardy—undertaken to alter one's life.

share: To speak, express oneself, or do virtually anything in a therapy situation. (A **group** member may blurt out, "I think this whole thing is a pile of shit and that you don't know what the hell you're doing!"—to which the group leader is likely to respond, "I'd like to thank John for **sharing** his feelings with us. That was beautiful.")

space: Opportunity; occasion; room; context; freedom. ("What I'm hearing is that you need Jenny to give you more **space** to **experience** other women." "Like, this **space** makes me feel un**centered**." "I'm in kind of a mellow **space** right now.")

stroke: In **TA**, any expression or act from one person to another—positive or negative. The term has a generalized use, outside of TA, meaning a compliment or other positive **feedback**. ("I'm sensing that Jack could use some **strokes**.")

transpersonal psychology: A term coined by Stanislav Grof to refer to that branch of psychology concerned with the individual's experience of, and relation to, spiritual, cosmic, and other transcendent **realities**. It is the study of ecstasy, **peak experiences**, bliss, mystical **experience**, **meditation**; the expansion of human capacity beyond the personal and social realms.

tubes: What people are called during **est** training. (When they graduate, they are *est-holes*.) The term implies that one has no power to shape one's own experience—only to eat and excrete.

visualization: An extremely effective technique employed in many forms of therapy, in which scenes or pictures are vividly imagined, in order to affect the subconscious mind; if done correctly, a visualization can be as profound and "real" as a dream or even a real event.

wellness: A recent coinage meaning a positive, vital state of health—more than the mere absence of disease. The **wellness movement** is virtually synonymous with the **holistic health** movement, but with more emphasis on enjoyment and growth than on curing illness.

"What do you feel right now?": The traditional query of **Gestalt therapy**, premised upon the idea that being in touch with one's feelings in the present moment is the sine qua non of psychological health and **growth**. The question is asked repeatedly, relentlessly, at various junctures in a **group** or individual therapy session.

"What I hear you saying is": The classic therapy response to someone else's emotional statement, indicating that the listener is practicing **active listening** and is about to restate what the speaker has just said.

BARRY: This is ridiculous! Nobody in this **group's** really being honest about their feelings. We're all just playing games!

PHIL: **What I hear you saying**, Barry, is that you're upset right now.

BARRY: Damn right I'm upset! I'm fed up with this shit!

PHIL: Can you describe how it feels to be fed up?

[22]

Gambling

The fierce urge to gamble has manifested itself in all human societies since there was anything of value with which to wager. A form of backgammon was played in the ancient Mesopotamian city of Ur, dice games not unlike **craps** were played in the Egypt of the pharaohs, the "casting of lots" (akin to our current office **pools**) was common among the twelve tribes of Israel in Biblical times. Amazon Indians, West African Pygmies, Australian Bushmen, the ancient Aztecs, Phoenicians, Greeks, and Romans—all cultures have gambled, from the most "primitive" to the most "civilized."

In America today, estimates have it that all forms of gambling pursued by our citizens—casino gambling, racetrack betting, sports and horse betting through **bookmakers**, private **poker**, dice, and backgammon games, office and factory pools, private wagering, bingo and bridge—if totaled together represent an astonishing *$400 billion* exchange, exceeding by a huge margin the financial activity of any multinational corporation or industry! This unbelievable figure becomes more comprehensible if we recognize that a single thoroughbred racetrack may have a daily **handle** (total of money wagered) of over $1 million; or that the illegal **numbers game** accounts for over $5 billion per year by itself! We are a nation of gamblers—some coolly professional, some driven and compulsive, most casual but nonetheless fascinated.

What is it that intrigues and seduces us about gambling? One element, to be sure, is the thrill, the risk-taking, the tension and excitement of not knowing (and betting), followed by the resolution of winning or losing. For most people, this entertainment is the major reason they gamble, rather than any realistic expectation of winning a significant amount of money. For the somewhat more serious and expert gambler, there is the challenge of self-control, of calculating coolness and unshakability in the face of wildly fluctuating fortunes and the mercilessness of chance. This is a virtue men have always sought, and gambling—more than any other test of "grace under pressure" besides actual combat—puts it on the line. Finally, there is a kind of reverse social mobility. People love gambling because it carries the patina of crime, the forbidden, the underworld, the lawless but vital, sexual, present-oriented subculture.

Gambling talk   It is in the language of gambling that this aura of the illicit is most evident: suburban matrons **shooting**, **fading**, **crapping out** at Las Vegas **craps** tables; respectable doctors and lawyers raising, calling, **sandbagging** in Friday-night poker games like Mississippi riverboat gamblers; the clerk or carpenter donning a fedora and checking the **morning line** before he puts two dollars on the **combination ticket** at the track. In the language we can all partake of the exciting, the mysterious, the forbidden world; we can pretend to be what we are not. And who knows? If we hit the **exacta** on a couple of **long-shot fillies**, back into a **pat hand** on a no-**limit** card game, hit a lucky streak on the dice, roulette, or 21—what we pretend and hope for might come true. It is both the illusion and the hope that makes gamblers of us all. 🦃

action: Also called the **play**. The betting climate, or volume. ("The *action's* good at Joe's tonight.")

ahead: Also **up**. Winning. ("I'm two hundred **ahead**.") The opposite is *down*. The way a player uses these terms can often reveal the extent of his gambling pathology: One tall tale has it that an inveterate gambler walked into a Vegas casino in rags, bet his last five dollars, ran it into the tens of thousands until his streak finally broke and he lost it all. Asked by a friend at the door as he was leaving how he had fared, he replied coolly, "I'm *down* five bucks."

angle: An idea on how to "beat the game"—especially, a method of cheating.

ax: The cut taken out of a player's bet by a game operator, usually in private gambling. Casinos normally avoid such a charge by never paying off at correct **odds**. (See **percentage**.)

baggage: Also **kibitzers**, **lumber**, **wood**. People who watch gambling games (*craps*, *poker*, etc.), but do not play.

banker: In private gambling, the player who accepts the bets of the other players. In a casino, the employee who pays off the winners.

big nickel: Race and sports **bookies**' term for five hundred dollars. A *small nickel* is fifty dollars.

big one: Also **a yard**. A thousand dollars. A *small one*, also called a *C-note*, is a hundred.

big order: The stuff that big-time **bookies** are made of. They can handle a bet (*order*) of fifty thousand dollars or more.

bite: Also **touch**. A request for a loan. ("He put the **bite** on me for a **yard**.")

book: A bookmaking (i.e., illegal bet-taking) establishment. There are both *race* (horse racing) and *sports* (sports-betting) books.

bookie: Also **bookmaker**. A person who takes race and sports bets, usually just outside the laws of a state.

cold deck: Also **cooler**. Cards prearranged for cheating.

even money: Also *toss-up*. Odds of one to one; payoff will be twice the amount of the bet.

extension: The money limit a **bookie** will accept on an event. If he receives additional bets, he may try to *lay off* these with other bookmakers. When he reaches his extension, the game is **off the board**—no more bets accepted.

fish: A dollar bill.

gaff: A cheating device or technique, as in *gaffed dice*.

handle: The total amount of money changing hands in a casino, track, or other gambling enterprise.

high roller: A gambler with plenty of money, prepared to bet high stakes.

hot: Said of a gambler on a winning streak that defies the odds. Even though casinos know the mathematics of their profession, they are not beyond a superstitious fear of the hot player.

ice: Also **fix money**. Money paid to "keep the heat off"—that is, to pay off police and other officials in order to keep illegal gambling operations going.

line: The stated odds for a particular bet (at the track or through a **bookmaker**)—the odds at which bets can be placed. *Five-cent line, ten-cent line, forty-cent line* are bookies' *price lines* that include a percentage margin for the bookie. For example, a **toss-up** sports bet might be quoted as "six to five, **pick 'em**."

long shot: A horse with little chance to win. More generally, any bet with slight chances of winning.

mark: Also **pigeon, patsy,** or **sucker**. A novice gambler, someone easy to cheat, hustle, or outgamble. ("This guy's an easy **mark**.")

marker: 1. Any of various kinds of numbered chips used to indicate money owed by a player during the game.

2. An IOU.

3. A bill or coin laid on a space on the layout to indicate a player's bet.

mechanic: A skilled cheat who traffics in **gaffed dice, cold decks,** or other sleight of hand.

numbers: An illegal daily lottery, found in all large cities in the United States and extraor-

dinarily popular among poor people; one three-digit number wins every day.

nut: A gambler's or casino's overhead.

odds: *Correct odds* are the ratio of unfavorable chances to favorable. *Payoff odds* are usually less than correct odds, allowing casinos to tip the scales in their favor, extracting their **percentage** for operating the game.

off the board: A **bookie**'s term for when betting on a particular event is closed, and no more bets will be accepted.

paperhanger: Someone who passes bad checks, *not* by mistake.

percentage: Also **PC**. The price paid in one form or another to the game operator for the privilege of playing. It can be levied either by direct charge to the gambler or by the more popular method of the casinos: to pay off at less than **correct odds**.

pick 'em: A **bookie**'s term for a sporting event thought to be evenly matched. (See **toss-up**.) Often the bookie will extract his percentage by quoting odds of "five and one-half to five, **pick 'em**."

point shaving: A kind of fix in team sports events. Players try to keep the point-scoring differential (or *spread*) between the teams down below a certain level.

pool betting: A type of sports betting common in offices, clubs, factories, and among other groups of people. Each person pays a certain amount into the pool (on the outcome of the World Series, for example) and one bettor ultimately wins the entire lot.

readers: Any type of marked cards; they can be read by the cheater but not by the other players.

rundown: A **bookie**'s line for the day. (The phone rings: "**Run** me **down**." "Guidry and Fingers six to five, **pick 'em**, Falcons and Rams **off the board**."

runner: One who makes pickups for the **numbers** racket.

screen-out: A cheating technique, involving misdirection or covering up. For example, the cover-up might come when a cheating player leans over the table to block the view of others while his friend, the dealer, switches to a **cold deck**.

short slip: In the **numbers** game, when a bet listed on a slip is not properly covered; the payoff is usually adjusted to compensate for the shortage.

side bet: Wagering peripheral to the actual game being played. In poker, for example, side bets might be made between individual players in addition to standard play for the **pot**.

sucker bet: A stupid bet, a bet with extremely poor odds; a bet that gives the hustler or expert gambler a great advantage over the *sucker*, or novice.

system: A "scientific" method of betting (or *handicapping*) in which the bettor follows a formula rather than his "hunches" or feelings. Most well known is the *Martingale Progressive system*, in which the bettor doubles his wager after each loss. This system would be foolproof were it not for the betting limit imposed by almost all casinos and games.

telephone numbers: Big money.

toss-up: A race or event in which each bet is given equal chance. ("The Knicks game tonight looks like a **toss-up**.")

tough money: Money needed for the essentials of living—rent, food, children's clothing. Only the most desperate or compulsive gambler plays with tough money.

HORSE-RACING TERMINOLOGY

across the board: Also **combination ticket**. A **win**, **place**, and **show** bet on one horse in one race. ("Fifty bucks **across the board** on Lazy Susan in the third at Belmont.")

chart: Published race results. ("He's been studying the **charts**.")

colt: A male horse four years old or younger.

combination ticket: A bet that covers **win**, **place**, and **show** options on one ticket.

daily double: A bet in which to win you must pick the winners of two successive horse races, usually the first and second or fifth and sixth.

exacta: A bet in which to win the bettor must pick the first- and second-place finishers in a single race.

filly: A female horse less than five years old.

form player: A bettor who considers a horse's past performance before wagering. He studies the **racing form**, the daily digest with all facts and figures.

front runner: A horse that takes the lead early and sets the pace.

furlong: One eighth of a mile (220 yards). The measure of distance in thoroughbred horse racing.

gelding: A male horse (any age) that has been castrated.

handicapper: The track official who rates the horses. Also, a writer who publishes a list of projected winners. More generally, anyone who takes the time to study horses' records and make intelligent bets based on them.

"if"-money bet: A bet in which the **bookie** is instructed to place a second bet at the track only if the first horse **wins**.

in the money: Finishing a race in first, second, or third place.

late line: Also **morning line** or **revised line**. A revised forecast of the odds published in the track program.

maiden: A horse that has never won a race.

mare: A female horse five years old or older.

odds-on favorite: A horse that is such an overwhelming favorite that the odds sink below **even money**.

off-track betting: Wagers made on horse or dog

racing at betting parlors instead of at the track. Such betting is illegal in many areas. The Off Track Betting (OTB) Corporation in New York is a government-sponsored attempt to diminish illegal **bookmaking**, with profits going to the city.

on the nose: Betting on a horse to **win**, as distinguished from **place**, **show**, or **combination-ticket** bets ("Two *C*'s on Hot Legs, **on the nose**.")

pari-mutuel: A racetrack betting system in which the winners on any particular race receive all the money bet on that race, after the track's share has been taken out.

parlay: A preplanned series of several bets, premised on winning the first; the original bet plus the winnings go on the second bet, and so on.

perfecta: Same as **exacta**. The first- and second-place horses must be picked, in correct order to win. The payoff is always big.

quinella: A bet in which the first- and second-place finishers must be picked in order to win; their order of finish does not matter.

racing form: An information sheet on the horses.

scratch: To remove a horse from the day's race.

stooper: Also **ticketpicker**. Someone who literally "stoops" to find some winners among the discarded tickets at the racetrack.

stretch: Also **home stretch**. The final straightaway to the finish line. The straightaway on the opposite side of the oval is the **backstretch**.

tote board: The track scoreboard that flashes the changing money totals and odds on the horses as the betting continues at the windows. At the race's end, it indicates the payoffs on the first three horses.

tout: Also **tipster**. Anyone trying to sell supposedly "inside" information on the horses.

win, place, show: Racetrack categories that pay off on the horses. A win ticket pays off only if your horse finishes first. A place ticket pays if she runs first or second. A show ticket rewards the holder for a first-, second-, or third-place finish.

wire: The finish line. ("It's down to the **wire**.")

CASINO TERMINOLOGY

carpet joint: Also **rug joint**. The plush casinos often attached to well-known hotels. *Sawdust joints* are their unpretentious counterparts.

croupier: A casino employee who deals, collects, and pays off at **roulette**, **baccarat**, and other games of French derivation.

floorman: A casino employee responsible for spotting and correcting irregularities, and supervising the gaming tables.

front man: A person, usually with no criminal record, who is the nominal owner of a gambling house. This permits underworld figures to get their enterprises licensed.

house: The operators of the gambling game. Can be casinos, illegal joints, or merely a player who extracts a percentage for his role.

juice joint: A gambling house with crooked dice or roulette games, maintained by concealed electromagnets.

keno: A game resembling bingo, played in separate rooms (*keno lounges*) or alcoves of most casinos.

ladder man: In **craps** or **baccarat**, a casino employee who overlooks the play for dealers' mistakes and cheating from an elevated vantage point.

Las Vegas total: Any Las Vegas casino employee will tell you that the Las Vegas total is what most male visitors are after: gambling, entertainment, and women.

let it ride: To combine your original bet with all additional winnings and to wager them again, you tell the dealer or **croupier** to "**let it ride**."

limit: The maximum amount a player can bet on any game or event. In casinos, the tables will often show a sign indicating minimum and maximum bets: "$5 to $500." The limit insures that so-called **system** players cannot beat the house.

one-armed bandit: A slot machine. The casinos don't hide the fact that the "slots" are their easiest money.

pit boss: The man who supervises the action at a number of tables, corrects for errors, and watches for cheating.

side game: Any of a number of casino games of chance with a carnival flavor and a whopping **percentage** favorable to the house. These are primarily of the "wheel of fortune" variety like the Big Six, Money Wheel, Race Horse Wheel, etc.

Poker

back to back: Also **wired**. In **stud poker**, when an *up card* and the **hole card** are of the same denomination. Other players moan, "He's got 'em **back to back**" or "He's got aces **wired**."

bluffing: Deceiving other players as to the true nature of one's hand; making a weak hand appear strong (to force them to **fold**), or a strong hand appear weak (to encourage betting). Bluffing is not only legitimate but is the major psychological ploy of **poker**, accomplished not only through one's betting pattern, but also through gestures, expressions, and calculated "reactions."

draw poker: A type of **poker** in which players are first dealt five cards, then given the option of exchanging one to four of them by drawing new ones, in order to improve their hand.

fold: To drop out of a hand; to withdraw from the betting. Usually signified by putting down one's cards and announcing "I'm out."

Gardena: A town south of Los Angeles, which features legalized "**poker** palaces."

high-low: A poker game in which the high hand splits the **pot** with the lowest hand; usually played as a variation of **seven-card stud**.

hole card: In **stud poker**, the facedown card (or cards).

jacks or better: A variation of **draw poker** in which betting cannot be *opened* (cannot begin) until some player holds at least a pair of jacks.

pat hand: A hand such as a full house, which a player decides not to improve by drawing new cards.

poker: Game played by from two to seven players, the object of which is to hold the most favorable combination of 5 cards. There are innumerable variations of betting poker, of which the two major types are **draw** and **stud**. Betting usually occurs with each new round of cards dealt, which may occur as many as five or six times in a single game. It is a game of skill, strategy, and psychology at least as much as it is a game of chance.

pot: The accumulated amount of money bet on any single hand; the chips (or cash) are placed in the middle of the **poker** table, until the end of the hand, when they are collected by the winner. (A player's internal monologue: "I can't **fold** now—there's over a hundred bucks in the **pot** already!")

pot limit: A limitation on the betting in a **poker** game. The maximum bet or raise allowable is determined by the amount of money in the **pot** at the time of the bet.

sandbagging: A ploy in which a player with a strong hand passes in order to raise when another player opens.

stud poker: One of the major varieties of **poker**. One or more cards are dealt facedown (**hole cards**), the rest face up (**up cards**); the hole cards are revealed only at the end of the game. *Five-card stud* and *seven-card stud* are the two most common versions.

Roulette

column bet: A bet on one of the three columns of twelve numbers; a win pays two to one.

corner bet: A bet on four adjacent numbers, made by placing a chip on the juncture of all four.

even-money bet: A bet on red or black, odd or even, or one to eighteen or nineteen to thirty-six; these bets are, obviously, one to one.

line bet: A bet placed on six numbers in two rows of three numbers each; pays five to one.

roulette: A game begun in France and now popular in American casinos, played by placing bets on a *layout* whose numbers and colors correspond to those contained in a bowl called the *wheel*. The **croupier** spins the wheel counterclockwise, then quickly sends the ball clockwise on the wheel's back track. The ball rests in any one of thirty-eight compartments (*canoes*), separated by metal partitions. Bets can be placed on thirty-six of thirty-eight numbers, or on several combinations and other possibilities.

split bet: A bet in which the bettor's chip is placed on the line between any two numbers, meaning the bet covers both; pays seventeen to one.

straight bet: A bet on any single number. Pays thirty-five to one.

Craps

big six, **big eight:** A bet in which the player wagers that six (big six) or eight (big eight) will be thrown before a seven.

blanket roll: A controlled throw of the dice, onto a rug or blanket. Expert hustlers under these conditions can throw any number they choose.

boards: The raised edges around a **craps** table against which the dice must be thrown. This prevents control of the dice by skillful cheats.

box man: The person in charge of the **craps** table; he supervises the game and collects the money.

come-out: The **shooter**'s first throw of the dice. He wins immediately if he rolls a seven or eleven.

crap out: To roll a two, three, or twelve on the **come-out** roll; the shooter who craps out loses immediately.

craps: A gambling game played with a pair of six-sided dice; it is a fast, noisy, exciting game played illegally on streetcorners and in basements, and legally in all major casinos. See **crap out.**

fade: To bet against the **shooter** before the **come-out.** The shooter bets that he will **pass**; fader bets that he will not.

floating game: An illegal game that moves (*floats*) from one location to another, in order to avoid the police.

hard way: A craps bet that four, five, eight or ten will be rolled with matching numbers on the dice. To make those same numbers in another fashion is, of course, the *easy way*.

natural: A seven or eleven on the **come-out** roll. An immediate win for the **shooter.**

pass: To win, either by throwing a 7 or 11 on the **come-out** roll or by making one's **point.**

pass-line bet: An **even-money bet** that the **shooter** will win.

point: If the **shooter** does not roll seven or eleven on his first roll but does not **crap out**, the number rolled becomes his point. If he makes his point on any succeeding roll *before* rolling a seven, he wins. Point numbers are four, five, six, eight, nine, and ten.

shooter: The person throwing the dice. Other players bet he will win or lose.

stick man: A casino employee who runs the **craps** table, wielding the stick and calling out the numbers. ("That's eight the **hard way**.")

Blackjack

anchor man: Also **third base**. The **blackjack** player to the dealer's right and the last to play a hand. This is the best vantage point for the **case-down player**.

blackjack: Also **twenty-one**. 1. A casino card game in which players try to come as close to twenty-one as possible on the total number value of their cards.

    2. A hand totaling twenty-one; this wins immediately unless the dealer also has twenty-one.

bust: To go over twenty-one; the player loses.

case-down player: Also **counter**. A person who can mentally keep track of all cards that have already been dealt, thus computing the changing odds as the deck is dealt out. Counting, when done correctly, can be a successful **system** for winning at **blackjack**. Most casinos bar known **counters** from playing at their blackjack tables.

double down: To double one's bet, by turning both cards up and drawing one additional (down) card.

hit: As a verb, to get an additional card—or cards—after the original two cards dealt. ("**Hit** me.") As a noun, each additional card dealt. ("I'll take a **hit**.")

push: A tie between player and dealer; nobody wins.

split a pair: When dealt a pair, the player has the option to split it—i.e., to turn both cards up and make two separate hands, taking a **hit** on each.

stand: To play with the cards you already have; not to take a **hit**.

standoff: The situation that exists when the dealer and the player have the same count. Nobody wins, there is no payoff.

Baccarat

baccarat: A card game of French origin played in the larger and more luxurious casinos in America, known for its high stakes. The game is somewhat similar to **blackjack**, the object being to have one's cards total nine or as close to nine as possible.

banco: In **chemin de fer**, a bet to cover the entire amount of the player's bank.

chemin de fer: Known colloquially as **shimmy**.

A variation of **baccarat** in which the banker plays against only one opposing hand and must follow certain prescribed rules of play.

coup: One hand or round in the game.

natural: An eight (*La Petite*) or 9 (*La Grande*) in the first two cards, which wins immediately unless matched or beaten.

shoe: The box from which cards are dealt by the **croupier**, two to each player.

[23]

Wine

Humankind has been delighting in the fermented juice of the grape for millennia, and will no doubt continue to do so far into the future, provided that the vodka vs. bourbon drinkers do not carry their crude dispute into the thermonuclear alley. In the good old USA, wine consumption has more than doubled in the past decade —though still only a small fraction of the 135 bottles per year consumed by the average citizen of France or Italy. Nonetheless, we appear to be in the midst of a "wine boom," not only of bottles quaffed but of vineyard acres planted (in California, up 300 percent since 1960) and media attention rendered.

Oenologists, or wine experts, have developed a unique vocabulary for expressing their enthusiasms and dismays about all manner of wines. Describing a simple alcoholic beverage as "**mature** and **complex**, with a cherry-berry **nose**, **leggy** and **full-bodied**, though a bit on the **fat** side, but with a remarkably smooth **finish**" may seem a trifle excessive to some, but others might like to know what they're talking about. The Swedes, after all, have fifty-three words for cold; the Eskimos even more for the varieties of ice and snow.

But before you can talk about the wine, you've got to taste it, and before you taste it, you've got to buy it. Understanding a wine from its label is an equally fascinating, and clearly more practical, aspect of oenological semantics. Each of the wine-producing nations has its own distinctive terminology for classifying the character and quality of a wine. Some of these systems are comprehensible with a little effort; others are quite insane. Two California wines, for example identically labeled except for the designation "**Produced and Bottled By** . . ." on one and "**Made and Bottled By** . . ." on the other, will be two totally different wines, not nearly of comparable caliber.

A good wine, it is said, "transcends taste, transcends language, and approaches enlightenment." In order to guide you in your search for the transcendental wine experience, however, a basic knowledge of wine terms and label-reading is indispensable. We have subdivided the chapter into five sections: "Wine Tasting"; "Reading the Label: France"; "Reading the Label: Germany"; "Reading the Label: California"; and "Reading the Label: Italy."

A *votre santé, prosit, salud,* and cheers.

WINE TASTING

Wine tasting (and oenophilia in general) is the wellspring for a flowery and arcane aesthetic jargon; a bastion for the cognoscenti who delight in ritual, employing a lexicon that is equal parts denotation, connotation, and pure fancy. The following example is a composite derived from a recent issue of a popular wine magazine: "An interesting molasses and raisin **nose** with a hint of cantaloupe; intense and **leggy**, but not overly **chewy**; an expanding **bouquet**, seemingly presumptuous at first, but **full-bodied** with a surprisingly graceful **finish** that subdues some of its youthful awkwardness. A **young**, racy, likable brat."

Buried beneath the wine taster's verbal foppery, however, lies a core of *relatively* clear descriptive terms. These terms are an attempt to create a basic shared understanding of the range and depth of the wine experience. Beyond these initial definitions, though, you're on your own. As any oenophile will tell you, tasting a wine involves combining the individual's character with the **character** of the wine —a unique, one-of-a-kind experience. Expressing such a special interaction requires more of the artist than the technician; creativity and metaphor are, therefore, a very large part of the language of wine tasting.

It pays to remember that the conscientious wine taster tries to achieve a Zen master's concentration, to make an entire universe out of a single swallow of fermented grape juice. This can actually become a religious experience. (I have heard one wine described as "the baby Jesus in velvet"!) Transcendental or not, the ritual will follow some or all of the following steps:

1. Concentrating. You focus in on the task at hand: no talking or frivolity from here on.
2. Scrutinizing the label (in order to see and remember what exactly it is that you're drinking; and to connect the coming wine experience with other wines in the past).
3. Uncorking the bottle, observing the cork for any clues it can give to the nature (particularly the defects) of the wine at hand.

4. Pouring or decanting the wine (after a suitable time for letting the wine breathe).

(These four steps are the preliminaries; what follow are stages in the actual sensory vinicological experience.)

5. Looking at the wine. Swirling it around in the glass, tilting the glass away from the viewer, and observing the liquid under a bright light, with a white background. This procedure is for perceiving color and brightness or cloudiness. Color is the first facet of the wine gestalt.
6. Smelling the wine. A true oenophile will sniff it a few times, then bring his nose over the edge of the glass and slowly, deeply inhale; most often more than once. This is done to appreciate the wine's **nose**, and to savor the **bouquet**.
7. Tasting the wine. Our intrepid wine connoisseur draws the (hopefully) celestial liquid into his mouth, slurps it, swooshes it around for a while, and lets it rest on his tongue and totally inundate the inside of his mouth. Tasting for the first time gives one a sensory combination of sweetness, sourness, acidity, tannicity, weight (the feel of the liquid), and harmony.
8. Swallowing the wine. This is not an important stage in the ritual; it does, however, provide a certain kind of base satisfaction on a primitive level.
9. Aftertasting the wine. All wines leave a certain distinct sensation on the palate *after* they've been swallowed. This aftertaste is known as the **finish**, and is often clearly quite different from the initial aroma, flavor, and feel.
10. Talking about the wine, is, arguably, a part of the degustation process, helping to fix the experience in one's memory. This last step is particularly pleasurable when one is among either fellow cognoscenti—who will appreciate your baroque, flowery descriptions as you appreciate theirs; or the untutored hoi polloi—who will be impressed and intimidated, or at least incredulous, and won't have the faintest idea what you're talking about.

The following are some wine-tasting terms that are commonly bandied about, and clearly divide the oenophile from the wino. Terms with an asterisk should have a fairly consistent meaning from taster to taster; all other terms are associative, reminiscent, and evocative. Remember, this is a field in which self-assured subjectivity rather than precision is the name of the game. This is also the *only* refined, complex, erudite, even noble method for imbibing alcohol. Once you learn how to talk like this, you'll never be a rummy again.

*acetic: Sour, smelling like vinegar. The odor of a bad or ruined wine.

acid, acidy, acidic: The opposite of alkaline—i.e., tending toward the lower end of the Ph scale. Many wines have a desirably acid quality (especially when balanced by an equivalent sweetness) without tasting sour. See **astringent**; **tannic**.

*aroma: 1. The smell of the wine before tasting (almost always connotes a single distinct flavor).

2. The smell of the wine when it is in the mouth.

3. The grapelike smell of a young wine. This term may or may not be synonymous with **bouquet**, except that the latter is a more prestigious term, and implies more **complexity**.

astringent: Sharp; too **acidic** unless modified by an adjective; for example, "a pleasant and surprising, subtle astringency." Almost always a negative term. See also **tannic**.

austere: Simple and possibly harsh; not **complex** (enough). Usually used as an uncomplimentary term.

*balance: The interrelationship among all the aspects of a wine. A *well-balanced wine* is one in which there is a harmonious orchestration of the senses. What this really means is that no single sensation sticks out and overwhelms the others. Occasionally, balance will be used simply, to mean the **acid**-alkaline base, such as "a clean, soft acid **balance** in a raisin-berry taste." (N.B.: A balanced wine is the same as a well-balanced wine.)

big: Having a full, **rich**, ample *weight*. A big wine is one that does not feel **thin** or watery in your mouth, but has a good **body**. This term is almost a synonym for body, but is most usually used to describe red wines, such

as Chateauneuf-du-Pape, or a California Zinfandel or Petite Sirah.

*body: The feel of a wine in the mouth and on the palate; its *weight* or volume, of which a contributing factor is alcoholic strength. A wine can have body, or be *big-bodied*, or have a *good body*—the meaning is the same in each case.

*bouquet: The smell of a **mature** wine, **complex** and **complete**. Bouquet is the standard terminology for describing the scent of a good wine; other terms are **nose** ("fresh apple-fruit **nose**"), *perfume, fragrance,* and *smell.* "Smell" is never used except as a term of disapprobation ("contained an antiseptic, vinegary smell. Totally undrinkable.") See also **aroma**.

*brown: A wine color that indicates the wine is too old or is **oxidized**, that is, aging improperly, or has already been ruined by exposure to air during bottling. Brown coloring is *not* a sign of defective wine, however, when one is talking about Madeira or sherry. See also **Maderized**.

character: Character in a wine is somewhat similar to character in a person; it all depends on who is perceiving that character. In general, a wine with character is one that has positive and distinctive traits that make it special; or, as an oenophile might put it, a wine with character is a wine that has a unique *personality*.

clean: A term more often applied to white wines, and always complimentary. It can best be defined as pure and uncontaminated to the nose and palate; well-made and refreshing; not flawed.

*cloudy: Describing a wine which in the glass does not appear clear and bright—there seems to be some kind of suspension within the wine itself. Cloudiness is the sign of an unsound wine; it also ruins the *intensity* and *brilliance* of the wine's color.

coarse: Rough, **hard**, poorly made; a bad example of the vinifier's art. A coarse wine may also be bitter, **acidic**, and **thin**.

complete: Well-balanced and **mature**; describing a wine that has aged well and is enjoyable to drink. See **balance**.

complex: Possessed of a multiplicity of subtle scents, many of which are described in terms of fruits, flowers, spices, and sweeteners, with some vegetables and other assorted odors thrown in. Complex almost always refers to the **bouquet** of the wine; a complex wine therefore is one with a **rich**, deeply variegated smell, usually an older and more **mature** vintage.

Uncomplicated is a complimentary term almost always reserved for **young** wines, meaning light, simple, fresh, and "fun."

*corky, corked: A wine is corky if it gives off an unpleasant, musty odor, due to the disintegration of the cork as a result of mold. A corked wine is one that has been ruined by such a process.

depth: A wine with depth is a wine that has a full, **rich** flavor; most commonly applied to red wines, particularly Bordeaux.

dry: Not sweet, without sweetness, not very sweet (when applied to sherry). Dryness is the opposite of sweetness, but it does *not* mean **acidic** or sour or bitter. Dryness is also not the distinguishing factor for a good wine. There are bad dry wines, and good sweet wines (German eiswein or Auslese, for example).

earthy: Literally, tasting of the earth. This can be a compliment or a criticism, depending on the context. Certain mineral salts in the soil will be picked up by the wine, especially in warm climates, such as that of Italy; when tasted they can add "masculinity" or **body** to a wine, or they can ruin it.

elegant: Having excellent breeding; describing a good, carefully made wine, usually prestigious to begin with.

fat: Also **flabby**. **Rich** and full-bodied, but missing the necessary sharpness or **acidity** to make it **balanced**. Not firm (young and without decisive **character**). It's not a compliment.

finesse: On a par with **elegant**, but this word is becoming overused. It means class, distinction, high quality. A wine with finesse is probably not quite as good as a wine with great nobility. Elegance probably lies somewhere between the two, with an added element of *je ne sais quoi.* Any questions?

*finish: Along with **bouquet**, **body**, and color (which is not defined here because it is what it says it is), one of the major facets of wine tasting: the aftertaste once the wine has been swallowed. Wines are said to have a *short, medium,* or *long finish,* depending on how long the flavor lingers after the wine is gone. Often the finish of a wine provides a different sensation from the original tasting.

flinty: This is usually a form of praise, describing the subtle taste reminiscent of the way flint sparks smell—a kind of unique, **clean**, clear, **hard** sensation. The usual example of a flinty wine is Pouilly Fumé. The term refers only to white wines.

flowery: Possessing a perfumed **bouquet**, particularly reminiscent of fresh flowers; fragrant. German Rieslings are good examples.

foxy: This is a term applied specifically to native American grapes, more specifically (and almost exclusively) those grown in New York State. The Concord grape is the sine qua non of foxiness, great for grape jelly, horrible for wine. It is that Concord grape jelly smell that is defined as foxy when detected in a wine. The term is commonly (but not always) pejorative.

fruity: Describing a wine that has the scent of fruits and is ripe tasting. Raspberries, apples, black currants, plums, cherries, and peaches are some of the fruits most often evoked besides grapes.

grapy: Having a fresh, pronounced grape flavor, a good sign in a **young** wine. Older wines should not be grapy, but more **complex**. A wine made from the **Muscat** grape such as Beaumes-de-Venise might be considered the pinnacle of grapiness.

hard: Having too much tannin; possessed of a harsh, bitter, **astringent** quality that makes the inside of your mouth pucker (like drinking a glass of very strong tea). Young red wines generally become **softer** (less hard) with age. See **tannic**.

legs, leggy: A wine that, when swirled in the wineglass, seems to stick to the inside of the glass and *slowly* descends in smooth, thick drops. Usually a complimentary term, describing a wine's viscosity and glycerine content. A leggy wine, when experienced in the mouth, is often referred to as *chewy*. The path the wine drops follow down the inside of the glass are, as you might have guessed, known as the *legs*.

*Madeirized: Turning brown, or already brown due to oxidation or excessive aging. A Madeirized wine is so called because it smells like Madeira (a sweet Portuguese dessert wine), as well as exhibiting a distinct color change.

*mature: Optimally aged so as to bring out the best qualities of the wine, and to minimize its negative qualities (such as **tannicity**). A *ripe* wine is one that should be drunk immediately, before it turns *old;* that is, a wine at the peak of *maturity*.

noble: Magnificently made, **mature**, **balanced**, with an excellent **finish**; *harmonious*.

*nose: The **bouquet** of the wine; more generally, the olfactory **character** of the wine when it is smelled in the wineglass. ("An intense, heady **nose**, brilliant garnet with orange edges, **smooth** and **well-balanced** with an aged-berry flavor and an appealing **soft acid finish**.")

*oxidized: Bad smelling; **Madeirized**; ruined due to exposure to air during bottling or because of a faulty seal by the cork.

piquant: Having a pleasant sharpness; a detectable **acidity** that seems to add to the wine's **character**.

rich: In red wines, having **depth**; in sweet wines, having sweetness. Not used for dry white wines. Also used to enhance a description: "a **soft**, **rich**, supple berry and wood taste."

*robe: A term sometimes used as a metaphor for the color of the wine. ("**Leggy**, with a marvelous **bouquet** of black raspberries and violets, and a rich, black ruby **robe**.")

rough: Uneven, not **smooth** or well-**balanced**, although a rough wine may still possess some good qualities. See **coarse**.

silky: Specially, marvelously **smooth** in texture in the mouth; most often used to refer to **mature** reds, but can be applied to whites as well. Probably *the* superlative, after which (in descending order) come *velvety* (more on the tongue than the palate), and **smooth**. Often all three are thrown in together: "a **silky-smooth** texture and a **velvety finish**." (This is just a test to see if you can maintain your sanity under trying conditions.)

smooth: Nicely textured; neither too sharp nor too **flabby**. See also **silky**.

soft: Not harsh; having a pleasant sensation on the palate and tongue. Not necessarily the same as **smooth**.

spicy: Distinctively flavored with herbs and spices found in both white and red wines. The Traminer and Gewurztraminer grapes, particularly in the Alsace region of France, produce wines that are notably *spicy*.

sulfury: Smelling of sulfur, feeling prickly in one's nose. Often, after airing, the smell will disappear.

tannic: Harsh and **astringent**, puckering the inside of the mouth as does a cup of very strong tea. At the far extreme, a tannic wine tastes *bitter*. Many **young** wines are initially quite tannic and **smooth** out as the wine **matures**.

tart: Too sharp and **acidic**; similar to *severe*, but not quite as bad.

thin: Watery, with little substance; without **body** or taste.

vigorous: Along with *nervy, firm, racy,* and *lively,* generally means fresh and young, with a good **nose,** and lots of promise; a likable and presumptuous brat, a talented adolescent.

yeasty: Having the smell of yeast, usually indicating that a slight secondary fermentation may be taking place. The term is not complimentary except in the case of champagnes— for example, "a sweet **yeasty nose** billowing with fruit."

young: Not yet **mature;** of a relatively recent vintage. This is *not* a term of opprobrium; many young wines are excellent drinking wines, particularly certain whites and Beaujolais.

WINE LABELS

The purpose of a wine label is to describe the nature and quality of the wine to be consumed. To understand the semantics of labeling, it is important to note that there are five distinct ways to describe a wine: place of origin, specific grape **varietal** or combination of grapes from which it is made, year in which the grape was harvested (*vintage*), national rating of quality (applicable only in France, Germany, and Italy), and bottling procedures. All or some of this information will be found on a particular bottle of wine.

Reading the Label: France

French children are brought up on watered wine and cheese instead of milk and cookies; to the French, wine is not merely a popular refreshment, it is a national liquid aesthetic. No wonder that, despite greater wine production levels in other countries, France remains the vital center of the winemaking art.

Many French wines imported to the U.S. are not always what they seem, however, and at first glance the French labeling system may appear too arcane to master. The following is a concise explanation of the most important terms, which will enable even the novice to understand and select well from the wines of France. 🐛

appellation contrôlée, appellation d'origine contrôlée: A term indicating that the wine is guaranteed by the French government to conform to geographical and varietal standards, and to production method. Although this is not necessarily an indication of quality, all of France's top-quality wines have an *appellation contrôlée.* The key to real quality is how localized the *appellation* is. For example, an *appellation Beaujolais* is inferior to an *appellation contrôlée Beaujolais Villages* (from the northern half of the Beaujolais region), which, in turn, is inferior to a *Moulin-à-Vent appellation contrôlée* (one of the villages in the Beaujolais district). This hierarchy is generally valid. Of course, if a local village or vineyard produced terrible wine one year, and the rest of the area flourished, then this rule would no longer be applicable. For French government ratings, see also **V.D.Q.S., V.D.P.**

blanc de blanc: A white wine made from all white grapes; sometimes also used for champagne made from all white grapes.

blanc de noir: A white wine made from black grapes. (This is not an impossible achievement. The length of time the grape skins are left in after the pressing determines the darkness of the wine.)

brut: The driest of champagnes, and other sparkling wines. (Although a new, drier term is *brut intégrale,* or *brut zéro*). Less dry is **sec**, and even sweeter is **demi-sec**; the sweetest is labeled *rich. Extra-sec* is a term interchangeable with brut.

cave: Cellar. See **mis en bouteilles dans nos caves**.

champagne: A sparkling wine from the Champagne region of France produced by the rigorous **méthode champenoise**, reputedly the best sparkling wine in the world. Champagnes are rated, in descending order of dryness: (1) **Brut intégrale** or **brut zéro** (both rarely seen); (2) **brut** or *extra-sec* or extra dry; (3) **Sec** or dry (which is really slightly sweet); (4) **Demi-sec**; (5) Rich (rarely seen here). It should be noted that, the drier the wine, the less the quality of the grape used can be masked.

Luxury versions of name champagnes are either vintage champagnes (e.g. Veuve Clicquot La Grande Dame 1973) or are indicated by such terms as **cuvée, tête de cuvée**, *reserve, private reserve, certificat,* etc.

There are primarily two types of champagne designated by grape—**blanc de blanc** (from the Chardonnay grape), and **blanc de noir** (from Pinot Noir and Pinot Meunier grapes, usually with some Chardonnay mixed in).

château: A wine-producing property in Bordeaux, not necessarily containing a beautiful and stately château upon its grounds. It is im-

portant to note that a wine labeled "Château ———" does not necessarily contain wine from grapes grown on the property! See **appellation contrôlée**.

clos: An enclosed vineyard, not necessarily under one ownership, but usually carrying some status. (For example, in the village of Fixin, Clos du Chapitre). Usually clos is used for vineyards or properties in Burgundy; **château** for those in Bordeaux.

commune: A wine-producing area or district, fairly well localized and delimited by the French law. It may include a specific area surrounding a village, or a grouping of villages.

côte: Hillside. On a label it means "locale" or "district." For example: Côte de Nuits, Côtes-du-Rhône.

crémant: Literally "creamy." When used on **champagne**, it means half-sparkling, that is, slightly less bubbly than normal champagne.

cru: Growth or vineyard. Prefixes and suffixes to this word are used to describe the best wines France has to offer. Unfortunately, the cru classifications differ in different French wine-growing areas; and in the Médoc (a major wine-producing region in southwestern France) where the cru classification was first established in 1855, the 125-year-old rating system has never been changed!

In descending order of quality, the Médoc classifications are: *premier cru, deuxième cru, troisième cru, quatrième cru, cinquième cru, cru exceptionnel, cru bourgeois supérieur, cru bourgeois.*

In other wine-growing areas of France, the general classification is *grand cru* (the best) followed by *premier cru.* Of course, there could be no Gallic charm to this system without exceptions to the exception. In Saint-Emilion, there is *premier grand cru classé,* and *grand cru classé.* Sauternes are classified *grand premier cru, premier cru,* and *deuxième cru.* In Pomerol, the tiniest of the top wine districts in Bordeaux, no classification system has ever been established. It's a cru, cru world.

cuvée: The literal meaning is "within the vat or wooden cask." Cuvée on a **champagne** bottle means a blend (the various wines mixed in the same vat); cuvée with a prefix is a loose denotation of quality. *Premier cuvée* and **tête de cuvée** are both terms for premier-quality wines; tête de cuvée is often seen on top-of-the-line champagnes, and on some wines from the Côte d'Or.

(N.B. In Burgundy, this term is sometimes used as a substitute for **cru**; on occasion it is also used simply to indicate the origin of the wine, cuvée de ———. Obviously, a word for all seasons.)

demi-sec: Literally, "half-dry." For **champagne**, moderately sweet.

domaine: A property (a vineyard or collection of vineyards) that produces wine; an estate. The rough equivalent of a **château**.

doux: Sweet.

éleveur: The individual or company who purchases the wine from the grower and matures it himself before selling it to the **négociant**. When the négociant performs this function, he may be listed on the bottle as *éleveur et négociant*.

estate bottled: A denotation that the wine described has been bottled where it was produced, and therefore is guaranteed to be authentic. If the words describing estate bottling are not in the language of the host country, this statement is not legally binding. Another way to get around this declaration is through the **appellation contrôlée**. If Château Fou-Fou has an appellation contrôlée of Bordeaux and nothing more, then the owner of the château can purchase wine from anywhere in the Bordeaux region, bottle it on his estate, and declare **mis en bouteilles** *à la propriété*.

(See also **mis en bouteilles** listings, the French statements of **estate bottling**.)

frais: On a wine label, frais means chilled. Anywhere else, it means fresh. See **servir très frais**.

generic wines: Wines with extremely non-specific names. Although this is not a French term, it is important to understanding the language on the Gallic wine bottle. A generic wine such as Bordeaux Blanc or Côtes-du-Rhône will be a mixture of various wines from the general area for which they are named, without much distinction or character. A generic wine is never anything more than a **vin ordinaire**.

grand cru: Best or great growth. See **cru**.

grand vin: Literally a "great wine." Actually, in terms of the quality of the wine, this phrase has no meaning whatsoever.

marque déposée: Trademark.

méthode champenoise: A long and costly production process for creating a sparkling, clarified wine. Although the technique is used elsewhere, no wines outside the Champagne region may call themselves "**Champagne**." (Freixenet, for example, a sparkling Spanish wine, also uses the méthode champenoise.) See also **mousseux**.

mis au domaine: See **mis en bouteilles**. . . .

mis en bouteilles . . . : Bottled on the property. *A la propriété*, literally "on the property"; *au domaine*, the same; *au château*, at the château. The term means "home-bottled"—i.e., a declaration that the grower saw to it that his wine, and only his wine, went into his labeled bottles. There are, for the unscrupulous, ways of getting around this statement. See **estate bottled**.

mis en bouteilles dans la région de production: Literally "bottled in the region in which it was produced." This is a step down from **dans nos caves,** and is no guarantee of anything.

mis en bouteilles dans nos caves: Strictly translated, "bottled in our cellars." A statement frequently used by the shippers and wine-merchants, and relatively meaningless as a guarantee.

monopole: Literally "monopoly." An individually owned vineyard, or a wine producer who has exclusive rights to the wine on the label.

mousseux: A term used to define any sparkling wine other than **champagne**. Some examples are: Mousseux de Vouvray, Mousseux de Touraine. In 1975 another term was created: **crémant** (e.g., Crémant d'Alsace). Other sparkling wines are labeled neither mousseux nor crémant, and are not **champagnes** either. These wines are just to keep you on your toes: Blanquette de Limoux, Saint-Péray, and one or two others.

négociant: A wine merchant who functions as a blender, maturer, bottler, and shipper of the wines he buys, and whose name is often connected to the wine he sells. (See also **éleveur**.) Often on a wine bottle you will see: "Albert Carrefour, **négociant** à Santenay," meaning Albert Carrefour is the merchant at Santenay for this wine, and his reputation goes with it.

nouveau: New. A wine to be drunk immediately, as a fresh, **young** wine, almost always seen in this country as a suffix to Beaujolais. Beaujolais Nouveau is a wine to be drunk in the fall in which it was fermented, usually beginning with celebrations on or around November 15. See also **primeur** and (**vin**) **de l'année**.

ordinaire: Table wine. See **vin ordinaire**.

pétillant: Semi-sparkling or crackling. See **crémant**.

petit: Used in front of the name of a wine, this indicates a lesser version of that wine, such as Petit Chablis.

premier cru: Strictly translated, "first growth." In terms of the French wine-rating system, the best (in Bordeaux), but rated second best in Burgundy and elsewhere. See **cru** for further complications.

primeur: "The first," ready to be drunk now. Applied almost exclusively to Beaujolais. See **nouveau**.

propriétaire: Owner of the vineyard or wine-producing property.

récolte: Harvest, or crop. The word is also used to mean vintage. When used in the past tense (*récoltée*) it can also mean "produced" (e.g., "11,238 *bouteilles* **récoltées**").

sec: Dry, except when on **champagne**, where it signifies that the wine is not very sweet.

servir très frais: Serve well chilled.

supérieur: An indication of a 1 percent higher alcohol content than a wine without such a suffix. It does *not* mean that such a wine is of any greater quality.

tête de cuvée: Literally, "at the head of the vat." The "best of the vat" might be a better interpretation, but this terminology is not dependable. Seen on some **champagnes**, and some wines from the Côte d'Or (Burgundy) region. See also **cuvée**.

(**vin**) **de l'année:** "Wine of the year," meaning not the best wine of the year, but the wine to be drunk in that year, preferably as soon as possible after fermentation. An "early" wine, almost always a Beaujolais. (See also **primeur** and **nouveau**.)

Vin Délimité de Qualité Supérieure (V.D.Q.S.): A classification indicating that the wine has passed certain government requirements for type of grape, origin, alcohol content, and maximum quantities produced; but not for quality per se. V.D.Q.S. wines do not have the same status as **appellation contrôlée** wines do; but a very general appellation contrôlée wine may very well not be as good as a more localized wine with a V.D.Q.S. marking. (See also **V.D.P.** and **appellation contrôlée**.)

Vin De Pays (V.D.P.): A classification one step below **V.D.Q.S.**, established to raise the quality of wines in the south of France (the Midi region). Some of these may be on their way up, but they're starting at the bottom. The official term *vin de pays* on a label should not be confused with *vin du pays*, meaning the "local wine," or "what the locals drink." Depending upon where you are, le vin du pays can be very classy indeed.

vin ordinaire: Table wine.

The Germans have a distinctive approach to wine: They concentrate almost exclusively on the production of white wines, and in the accepted German hierarchy, the higher quality a wine, the sweeter it is. Many of the German whites are considered among the finest in the world, with a delicacy and exquisite balance unduplicated elsewhere. For the initiated, the German classification system is quite logical, with strict stipulations for each geographical, qualitative, and varietal category. But unless *you* know the difference between a **Bereich** and an **Einzellage**, or a **QmP** and a **Liebfraumilch**, you're up the Rhine without a paddle. 🍎

Amtliche Prüfungsnummer: Abbreviated **A.P. Nr.**, sometimes only **AP**. The official German government certification of the wine's quality, given only to wines rated **Qualitätswein** or higher. The figures within the number show the grade, vineyard, test-batch number, and year in which the wine was bottled.

Anbaugebiete: One of the eleven geographical areas into which German wines have been divided. The most well known here are Rheingau, Rheinhessen, Rheinpfalz, and Mosel-Saar-Ruwer. One of these regions must be named on every bottle rated **Qualitätswein, QbA,** or **Qualitätswein bestimmter Anbaugebiete** (all meaning exactly the same thing). A QbA wine is a wine of quality with the traits of the vineyards from its region. Unlike a **QmP** wine, sugar has been added to the QbA wine to bring it up to standard.

Occasionally, Anbaugebiete is shortened to **Gebiet**. In order of increasingly localized wine-producing areas, the terms are: **Bereich, Grosslage, Einzellage**. In general, the more localized the area, the better the wine.

aus eigenem Lesegut: "From the harvest of the grower." The wine has been bottled on the premises. The equivalent of the French **estate bottled**. (See also **Erzeugerabfüllung**.)

Auslese: A **QmP** wine of very high quality (and therefore high sugar content), made from very ripe grapes in an excellent vintage year. In the hierarchy of the five levels of superlative German wines, auslese is precisely in the middle: **Kabinett, Spätlese, Auslese, Beerenauslese, Trockenbeerenauslese**. See also **QmP** and **Eiswein**.

Beerenauslese: A high-quality **QmP** wine, between the **Auslese** and **Trochenbeerenauslese** levels.

Bereich: A designated subregion or district, one step more localized than a **Gebiet**. A wine labeled *Bereich Johannisberg* is a composite wine gathered from anywhere within the entire Rheingau district, sort of an **appellation contrôlée** Rheingau. (This is because only one Bereich has been delineated for the Rheingau: Johannisberg.)

In order to keep the foreign oenologists on their toes, Johannisberger Erntebringer is the name of one of the ten **Grosslages** in the Rheingau. And, yes, there is a vineyard in the area called . . . Schloss Johannisberg! Other vineyards in the area are Johannisberger Klaus, and Johannisberger Hölle. It's enough to make you weep into your **Trockenbeerenauslese**.

If your courage and determination have not yet been dampened, see also **Grosslage, Einzellage** and **Anbaugebiete**.

Deutscher Tafelwein: Vin ordinaire or table wine, the second-lowest ranking in the German wine system, but still subject to quality controls under German law. Deutscher Tafelwein differs from ordinary **Tafelwein** in that it must, by law, contain only the juice of German grapes.

Deutsches Weinsiegel: A seal on the neck of the wine bottle indicating that the wine is judged to be superlative by an independent testing body—the German Agricultural Society.

diabetiker wein, diabetiken: A denomination indicating the driest of the wines (i.e., with the most minimal sugar content). In ascending order of sweetness, the denominations are: diabetiker, **trocken, halb-trocken.** These denominations have only recently been developed, and have not been widely exported. Nevertheless, dry wines rated as high as **Auslese** are now being produced.

Domäne: The equivalent of the French **domaine,** but often much larger. (See also **Weingut, Verwaltung, Staatlich Weinbaudomäne.**) Just as in France, a Domäne may gerrymander through a number of separate vineyards or villages, and in such a case the name and reputation of the owner-producer will be a salient factor in determining the quality of the wine.

Einzellage: A single local vineyard, the most specific designation in the German labeling system by geographic location. Almost always, the name of the vineyard is shown on the label *following* the name of the town in which the vineyard is located, for example, Erbacher Marcobrunn. (The town is Erbach, the vineyard is Marcobrunn. The "**-er**" is added as a suffix to the name of each town.)

Unfortunately, not only are there exceptions to this rule, but the rule itself requires certain inside information. A Rauenthaler Baiken and a Rauenthaler Steinmacher are two very different wines. Rauenthaler Baiken comes from the Baiken vineyard within the town limits of Rauenthal. Rauenthaler Steinmacher is the legal term for the **grosslage** in the Rauenthal area. One wine is from an Einzellage, the other from a Grosslage; but there is no way to tell unless you are familiar with the names beforehand. See also **Grosslage, Schloss, Bereich, Anbaugebiete.**

Eiswein: Literally "ice-wine." A very special wine made from grapes frozen on the vine, intensely sweet, quite rare, and quite expensive. Considered a great delicacy.

-er: A suffix added onto the name of a town listed as the wine's place of origin. For instance, if the town is Piesport, the label would say "Piesporter." Thus, a wine made from the Riesling grape grown within the town limits of Piesport would be a Piesporter Riesling. See also **Grosslage.**

Erben: Heirs.

erzeugerabfüllung: Estate bottled; wine from the single vineyard listed; wine bottled by the grower. See also **aus eigenem Lesegut.**

Gebiet: See **Anbaugebiete, QbA.**

Gemeinde: A commune or other localized wine-producing area.

Graf: Count.

Grosslage: A grouping or collection of **Einzellages,** all of which supposedly produce wines of a similar caliber and status. Grosslages within a small geographical area can vary considerably—e.g., Niersteiner Gutes Domtal (fair, unreliable), and Niersteiner Rehbach (highly reputed).

Despite Germany's tight quality controls and labeling rules, the only way to tell the difference between a Grosslage and an Einzellage is to recognize the names. Since there are 150 Grosslages and 3,000 (approximately) Einzellages, this is a rather hefty proposition. Still, the distinction is important since, as a general rule, the smaller the specified area, the better the wine. See also **Einzellage, Bereich.**

Gutsverwaltung: See **Verwaltung.**

halb-trocken: Literally "half-dry." From a recent new German appellation series: **diabetiker** (very dry, suitable even for a diabetic); **trocken** (dry but not as dry as diabetiker); halb-trocken (somewhat drier than the same wine without such an appellation, but not as dry as trocken).

This terminology indicates somewhat of a

trend toward making German white wines more palatable during a meal. (Usually, because of their sweetness, they are drunk before or after.) See also **diabetiker, trocken,** and **QmP**.

Kabinett: The lowest of the five quality ratings of **QmP** wines, and also the driest of these wines. A Kabinett-rated wine is still sweeter than an average **Liebfraumilch,** but is also richer and better **balanced.** See **QmP, Spätlese, Auslese**.

Keller: Cellar. Also used to mean a place in which wine is is produced. Exactly the same meaning as **Weinkellerei,** meaning "winery," although a Weinkellerei can also act as a shipper.

Liebfraumilch: A **QbA** wine, semisweet, and very popular in the United States. Wines from Rheingau, Rheinhessen, Rheinpfalz and Nahe can legally be termed Liebfraumilch. About 50 percent of all German wines produced for export are Liebfraumilch.

Perlwein: Semisparkling, the equivalent of French **pétillant,** or, in the case of French **champagne, crémant**.

Prädikat: A special attribute, roughly translatable as "with distinction." Wines designated *mit Prädikat* are created only in very good vintage years when the harvest produces grapes that ripen fully on the vine (and therefore need no added sugar for proper fermentation and **balance**). See **Qualitätswein mit Prädikat (QmP)**.

Qualitätswein bestimmer Anbaugebiete: Abbreviated **QbA.** The first level of government-designated quality wines, often shortened on the label to **Qualitätswein.** These wines can by law come from only one of the eleven official German wine-producing areas (**Anbaugebietes**), such as Rheinhessen, Mosel-Saar-Ruwer, or Nahe; and the name of one of these areas must appear on the label.

QbA wines are basically dry, and always drier than *QmP* wines. Under German law both *Tafelweins* and QbA wines are allowed to add sugar to the *must* (unfermented wine) in order to bring them up to standard. This is an important and necessary concession, since in northerly Germany, wines must often be harvested before they have reached a proper state of ripeness.

See also **tafelwein, QmP**.

Qualitätswein mit Prädikat: Abbreviated **QmP.** Literally "quality wine with distinction." A wine possessing some special characteristics that set it apart from other wines. This is the highest general quality level for German wines, and is divided into five gradations, each one sweeter than the last: **Kabinett, Spätlese, Auslese, Beerenauslese, Trockenbeerenauslese**.

In addition, there is another QmP designation that is unique: **Eiswein.** Usually of Auslese or Spätlese level, this wine is an exceptional balance of intense sweetness and acidity, and is quite rare. See also **Prädikat, Eiswein, Kabinett**.

Roseewein: Rosé wine.

Schloss: Castle. Originally a term for a vineyard or estate; in the current system it can designate either a large geographical district (**Bereich** Schloss Böckelheim), a village (Schloss Böckelheim as well), or an estate (Schloss Vollrads).

Schlossabzug: Bottled on the grounds of the castle (**Schloss**).

Sekt: Sparkling wine with a **QbA** designation.

Spätlese: A category of **QmP** wine, one step up in sweetness and intensity from a **Kabinett.** See **QmP, Kabinett,** etc.

Staatliche Weinbaudomäne: The domain of the state; a state-owned wine-producing estate. See also **Domäne, Staatsweingüt**.

Staatsweingüt, Staatsweingüter: State-owned vineyard; same as above.

Tafelwein: The lowest general classification level for wines, below **QbA** and **Deutscher Tafelwein.** A Tafelwein may legally be composed in part of non-German-grown wines.

trocken: "Dry." A wine that is supposedly dry enough for diabetics, although there is another rating with an even lower sugar content: **diabetiker**. A wine with one of the three "dryness" ratings may be of the **Auslese** or **Spätlese** quality level, with excellent **body** and **complexity**. See also **halb-trocken, diabetiker**.

Trockenbeerenauslese: Abbreviated **TBA**. The pinnacle of German wines. Very rare, made of grapes that have attained an advanced level of ripeness, and have begun to dry on the vine; the resulting juice is highly concentrated and extraordinarily rich. The result is a **rich, noble** wine of superb taste, **body**, and **balance**.

(N.B. **Trockenbeerenauslese** does not mean a "dry" or **trocken** beerenauslese. The "trocken" here refers to the fact that the grapes are partially dried on the vine before they are pressed, making the juice concentrate even sweeter. This is *the sweetest* of German wines.)

Verwaltung: Property, property of. Often followed by the name of the vineyard or estate owner.

Weingut: The estate or domain at which wine is produced. See also **Domäne, Staatlich Weinbaudomäne**.

Weinkellerei: Literally, wine cellars. Usually means a winery.

Weissherbst: A rosé **QbA** wine.

Winzergenossenschaft: A cooperative organization of wine growers; also one of the longest words you'll see on a label that may well be covered with them. (Runner up is the **Grosslage** Schlossböckelheimer Bugweg, or any wine from the village of Schlossböckelheim perhaps from the vineyard of Kupfergrube. Hopefully such a wine is also **erzeugerabfüllung**, and of course would be at some level of **Qualitätswein mit Prädikat**, perhaps even **Trockenbeerenauslese**.)

Winzerverein: A wine growers' collective or cooperative; exactly the same as above, but eight letters shorter.

Reading the Label: California

The development of wines and wine-growing areas in the last decade in California can be compared to that of no other area in the world. In 1960, there were 116,500 acres of grape **varietals** planted in the state for the production of wine; by 1980 this number had grown to 332,500. Such "higher-class" grapes as Cabernet Sauvignon increased in acreage at an astounding rate. (For Cabernet Sauvignon, 615 acres in 1960 to 23,592 in 1980; for Chardonnay, 295 acres to 15,956 in the same time period!) These figures are an indication not only of the increased American consumption of wine, but of a demand for more "quality" wines (as opposed to **jug wines**).

The late 1960s and particularly the 1970s have seen a profusion of new wineries specializing in fine wines. Many of them are no larger than a **château** in Bordeaux or an **estate** along the Rhine. Some recently produced wines are considered not only the best California has ever produced, but on a par with the best in the world. Baron Philippe de Rothschild, owner of one of the most distinguished French appellations, likened American wines to Coca-Cola only ten years ago; today he is a partner in the Robert Mondavi winery in the Napa Valley.

Because growth has been so explosive, the situation in terms of wine description (on the label) can best be described as fluid. Even such basic standards as the French **appellation contrôlée** and the German **Qualitätswein** have not been established for California. Many vineyards have their own microclimates, and so standardizing by geographic location is unreliable; vintners throughout the state are still experimenting with harvesting, fermentation, and bottling processes, so even a particular wine from a particular vineyard may change from one year to the next, and even from one batch or **lot** to the next. Nevertheless, the ability to accurately interpret the language of the California wine label can be a great help in distinguishing between fine wines, table wines, and wines masquerading as something other than what they are. The difference between **produced and bottled by** and **made and bottled by** on a label, or between California vintage Cabernet Sauvignon and Napa Valley Martha's Vineyard Cabernet Sauvignon 1974, can be extremely important in determining the quality of what you will be drinking, and whether the price is justified. Some wines labeled Rhine Wine or California Chablis have as much similarity to a German white wine or a French Chablis as they do to Kool-Aid. Many of them are closer to vintage Kool-Aid (with alcohol added) than to anything else.

Herewith, a guide to the confused and confusing language of the label in California. Press on. ❦

appellations of origin: Wines labeled by county (e.g., Napa, Sonoma, Lake, San Luis Obispo) or smaller areas (Alexander Valley, Russian River Valley, and Rutherford) are subject to certain legal strictures if the area is specifically named. If you buy a wine labeled Napa Valley Zinfandel 75 percent of the grapes must come from that area; if you buy a 1979 Napa Valley Zinfandel (that is, with the vintage date on the label), 95 percent of the grapes must come from the area. In general, the most general geographic area listed on the label will indicate the origin of the grapes used:

American: (*American Burgundy* for instance) the wine's grapes come from at least two different states.

California: The wine is a grape blend from anywhere within the state of California.

Napa County: The wine comes from within the legal limits of the county.

Freemark Abbey (or any other specific vineyard within Napa County): With the additional designation **grown, produced and bottled by** that same vineyard, the wine comes from the Freemark Abbey (or specified) vineyard.

See also **vintage**, **varietal**, **generic**.

barrel fermented: Wine that has been fermented in wooden casks (usually oak) instead of larger stainless steel tanks. Wines *aged in wood* take on some of the qualities of the wood, and gain additional **complexity** and **body** (according to some vintners). Barrel fermentation is more often used with red rather than white wines. Some wineries have opted for indigenous California redwood instead of the traditional oak.

Botrytis cinerea: A beneficial mold or fungus that attacks white grapes when they reach a certain level of ripeness, and the climatic conditions are conducive (warm and moist). Grapes harvested after this mold has worked on them have an intensified flavor and character found in no other wines. They also have a high concentration of both sugar and acid, and are richly aromatic. Known as *pourriture noble* in France (Sauternes) and *Edelfäule* (the best **Auslese** and above) in Germany, Botrytis has been induced on California grapes since 1969.

Wines labeled **late harvest** or **selected late harvest** made from the *Johannisberg Riesling* grape can occasionally reach the intensity of a **Beerenauslese** or even **Trockenbeerenauslese**. Other botrytized American grapes include *Sauvignon Blanc* and *Sémillon* (the grapes used in France to make Sauternes) and others.

Unfortunately, since there is no legal definition of the level of botrytization, or any rating of how widespread the fungus is on the harvested grapes, you make your bet and take your chances with wines indicating the presence of Botrytis in their grapes. The name and reputation of the vineyard is one of the best indications of quality.

brix: An American measurement of the amount of sugar in harvested grapes; occasionally also used to indicate the sweetness of the finished product. Brix numbers range from about fifteen (very dry) to twenty-eight (very sweet).

brut: As in France, brut should, and usually does mean "dry," and refers to the driest version of **champagne** available from a particular producer. Since there is no legal definition, brut in the United States can mean anything the producer wants it to.

bulk process: The cheapest and simplest method for creating **champagne**, also called *Charmat* (which sounds French and much more prestigious). In this technique the wine is removed from the bottles and placed in a large sealed vat for secondary fermentation (which produces the bubbles).

In order of preference, the three champagne production methods are: (1) **méthode champenoise** (traditional method); (2) **transfer process**; (3) *Charmat* or bulk process.

cask, cask number: A wine labeled with a cask number is a broad hint that the wine has been made with care, in small quantities, and may be defined by the cask in which it was fermented. Sometimes this is the case; sometimes it's merely an advertising gimmick.

cellared by: This implies that the wine was aged or matured or treated in some way in the winery mentioned. By itself, the term probably means that the wine was produced somewhere else and then stored (and possibly matured) at the vineyard mentioned. Occasionally this term can actually mean that the wine was carefully attended to at the vineyard. As usual, though, because there are no legal requirements as far as the amount of time or the nature of the cellaring process is concerned, "cellared by" is a relatively valueless term.

champagne: In France, **champagne** can only be sparkling wine from the Champagne region made by the **méthode champenoise**. Here, champagne means only "sparkling wine." It can be American (from U.S. grapes), California (from California grapes), or New York State (from New York State grapes). Again, grapes from the designated area need comprise only 75 percent of what you get in the bottle. If it's *vintage champagne,* 95 percent.

Champagne from California may be made by any of three processes: **bulk process** or *Charmat process*; **transfer process**; or **méthode champenoise**.

classic: Probably stolen from the Italian denomination **classico**, meaning the best of its type (such as Chianti Classico). In the United States, however, the term has no meaning whatsoever.

cooperage: This originally meant storing in

wooden vats or barrels; now it just means storing (in vats, tanks, stainless steel, plastic, Dixie cups or anything else.)

crackling: The equivalent of **crémant** in terms of carbonation. In terms of production technique, if crackling is the only term on the label indicating how the sparkling wine was created (no **bulk process**, *Charmat*, and so on), the wine was probably artificially carbonated *after* fermentation.

crush: A vintage or harvest (such as the 1982 Zinfandel crush).

cuvée: In France, cuvée means "vat." Here it usually signifies a special lot, implying higher quality. Sometimes used interchangeably with **vintage** or **crush** to give the vintage date (such as, cuvée 1979).

demi-sec: Moderately sweet (not "half-dry," as the French translation would indicate).

estate bottled: This term is at present unregulated in the United States, and has no specific meaning. (This will probably change after 1983.)

extra dry: May well mean "dry"; might also mean "not too sweet." Used exclusively for **champagnes**. Use your imagination.

filtered: A process of using filters to remove impurities from a wine; *microfiltration* is a superfine filtration sometimes used in lieu of pasteurization. A filtered wine gains clarity and filtering removes harmful yeast growths and microorganisms; but some vintners believe it also diminishes the character and body of a wine. Some wines, therefore, are labeled **unfiltered** or **unfined**.

fined: The process of removing suspended particulate matter in the wine by adding egg white, gelatin, or clay to the wine vat. The additive slowly sinks to the bottom, collecting the particulate as it goes. Some wines are described as **unfined** because it is believed that this process also removes some of the wine's flavor.

generic wine: A wine not listed according to its grape **varietal**, but most often simply named after certain geographic locations in Europe: Burgundy, Chablis, Chianti, Sauterne, Rhine Wine, Champagne; or named for a particular *type* of wine: rosé, claret (red Bordeaux), sherry, etc.

Generic is also a term sometimes used to include **proprietary** names, which are titles a particular wine-producing company will give to a particular wine blend: Vino da Tavola, Rubion, Rustico, Emerald Dry, Insignia, Rhinegarten, and the like.

The vast majority of American table wines consumed are generic wines (most of which are sold as **jug wines**).

grown, produced, and bottled by: This is the true equivalent of **estate bottled** or **Erzeugerabfüllung**. It means that the wine in the bottle comes from the named vineyard, and has been fermented and bottled there.

jeroboam: Three liters; a metric measure for **jug wines**, equalling just over three quarts.

jug wine: A poor to palatable "table wine" labeled mostly as a **generic**, sold in large-size containers (**magnums** and **jeroboams** now replacing half-gallons and gallons). Inexpensive but often hardly worth the price.

late harvest: A term indicating that the grapes were very ripe when harvested, and may even have been *botrytized* (see *Botrytis cinerea*). It can apply to red or white wines, and almost always means a more than usually sweet wine of high quality.

limited bottling: Anything from a small, fine batch of the vineyard's special blend to a bottling run limited by the vineyard's having run out of glass containers. A meaningless term.

lot, lot # : Intimations of special treatment notwithstanding, lot does not mean a lot, although scrupulous vintners and vineyards may use it to mean a particular batch of wine that was bottled separately. Roll your own on this one.

made and bottled by: This means only that the named producer fermented a minimum of 10 percent of the wine in the bottle on his property. None of the grapes have to be his grapes; 90 percent of the wine can be processed elsewhere. A very different designation from **produced and bottled by**.

Vineyards interested in further confusing the issue like to put on their labels such terms as *perfected and bottled by, vinted by, developed and bottled by, created and bottled by, cellared and bottled by*. Obviously, these growers have their Bacchus against the wall.

magnum: A metric term now adopted for **jug wines**. A magnum equals 1.5 liters, or approximately one-and-a-half quarts.

méthode champenoise: Fermented entirely in the bottle (see description in French label section). N.B. If a bottle says *bottle fermented* and does *not* say méthode champenoise, the wine was probably produced by the **transfer process**.

natural: Also **natur**, **naturel**, and other variants. Used in sparkling wines to mean very dry. Like **brut**, not totally reliable; but probably more reliable than brut.

private reserve: A term that could mean that, in private, the vintner is quite reserved in expressing praise for this wine; or it could mean anything. It *used* to signify a rather special product of that vineyard: mature, rich, full-bodied, and so on. Somewhere, someplace, it probably still does.

produced and bottled by: This term means that the winery or vineyard mentioned on the label crushed (not harvested), produced (fermented and matured), and bottled at least 75 percent of the wine in the bottle. Do not confuse this term with **grown**, **produced**, **and bottled by** (grown, harvested, fermented, and bottled) or **made and bottled by** (and other variants).

proprietary name: See **generic wine**.

proprietor's reserve: If you've seen **private reserve**, you've seen it all; the term does not necessarily mean anything. (The same goes for **reserve**, **selection**, **special cask**, **special**

selection. Many of these terms *may* indicate a wine of very high quality; none of them, however, are required by law to do so. It all depends on what you know about the scruples of the particular winery.)

reserve: See **selection**.

residual sugar: The amount of sugar remaining in the final, bottled product. Over 1 percent is very slightly but noticeably sweet; over 5 percent is very sweet. Under 1 percent is generally considered dry.

sec: This term, which in French means "dry," in most **champagnes** in the United States means "sweet," or at least semisweet. This is to keep people who know French on their toes, ha ha.

select: This term is almost as precise as **proprietor's reserve**.

selected late harvest: From a trusted vineyard, this means a riper, often more *botrytized* grape than that indicated by **late harvest**. From those whose semantics are somewhat looser, it can mean "harvested later than usual," or anything else.

selection: Although not prescribed by law, this often means a choice wine of that vineyard. Often it doesn't. You're leaning on the conscience of the vintner and vineyard. (See **private reserve**, **proprietor's reserve**.)

special cask, **special selection:** See **selection**.

transfer process: A process used in sparkling wines in which, *after* the second fermentation in the bottle, the wine is removed and placed in a large vat where filtration and some additional sweetening occur (known in France as the *dosage*). Wines labeled "individually fermented in the bottle" are transfer-process wines; those labeled "individually fermented in *this* bottle" (emphasis added) are made by the **méthode champenoise**.

unfiltered: See **filtered**.

unfined: See **fined**, **filtered**.

varietal: A wine named after its chief component grape. Current, outmoded laws require only that a named varietal contain at least 51 percent of the grape on the label; the rest is up to the discretion (or indiscretion) of the vineyard/winery. When you're drinking a glass of Napa Valley Zinfandel, in other words, you may only be drinking half a glass. In 1983 the new regulations will require that a named varietal contain at least 75 percent of that grape.

Scrupulous and highly reputed wineries will, it must be noted, use 100 percent of the grape listed, or else give information as to the composition of the wine blend by grape (e.g., 60 percent Cabernet Sauvignon, 30 percent Zinfandel, 10 percent Pinot Noir).

vintage, vintage date: A vintaged wine (that is, one with a vintage year on the label) must contain 95 percent wine from grapes which were crushed in that year.

Reading the Label: Italy

Italian wine labels (and the classification of Italian wines) make the French and German systems seem utterly clear and simple by comparison; to the uninitiated, Italian wine classifications may seem like the creation of a mad Italian oenologist who took a composite of the French and German systems and threw in the Dewey decimal system and Grimm's fairy tales for good measure. There is a kind of wild abandon that seems inappropriate for the world's largest wine producer (and consumer: Italian wine consumption stands at about thirty gallons per person per year!). Nevertheless, for the individual with a sense of adventure (and a sense of humor), the following is a healthy introduction to the language of Italian wine labels.

A brief overview of the variety of classification methods is necessary before we embark upon a list of specific terms. Italian may be named by the grape varietal (Barbera), the location (Soave), a combination of grape varietal and location (Barbera del Monferrato), or simply by a name that has been created for a particular wine (Lacrima Christi, Est!Est!!Est!!!, Santa Maddalena), a title that may be whimsical, proprietary, or of religious significance. Even if you have a wine of a specific name, that wine may be red, white, or rosé, sparkling or still, sweet or dry. The name of the shipper, producer, "house," or **consorzio** may also determine the quality of the wine; Bolla, Folonari, and Ruffino, for example, are three of the better-known producers. There is no really clear hierarchy of region, district, village, vineyard; nor is there a rating system for vineyards or delimited areas (as in France, with its **cru** system). In addition, wines produced in different years from the same area may be aged different amounts of time, depending on the judgment of the individuals producing them.

So much for the bad news; for a more optimistic picture, see **D.O.C.**, **riserva**, **classico**, **superiore**, and **consorzio**. And *buona fortuna.* ●

Italian Wine Names

HOUSE	GRAPE VARIETALS	TOWNS, DISTRICTS	NAMES
Antinori	Aleatico	Asti	Buttapuoco
Bertani	Barbera	Barbaresco	Est! Est!! Est!!!
Bigi	Bonarda	Bardolino	Freciarossa
Bolla	Cabernet	Barolo	Sangue di Guida
Bosca	Cortese	Capri	Santa Maddalena
Cantin Masi	Dolcetto	Carema	Sfursat, Sforzato
Cavit	Fiano	Castelli Romani	
Ceretto	Lagrein	Chianti	
Fabiano	Lambrusco	Colli Orientali	
Faza-Battaglia	Malvasia	Donnaz	
Folonari	Merlot	Gattinara	
Fontafredda	Monica	Gavi	
Giacobazzi	Moscato	Ghemme	
Lamberti	Montepulciano	Grumello	
Melini	Nebbiolo	Inferno	
Riunite	Picolit	Ischia	
Rivera	Pinot Blanco	Lugana	
Rufino	Pinot Grigio	Manduria	
	Pinot Nero	Montalcino	
	Primitivo	Montefiascone	
	Prosecco	Montepulciano	
	Sangiovese	Oltrepo Pavese	
	Schiava	Orvieto	
	Sylvaner	Piave	
	Teroldego	Piemonte	
	Tocai	Ravello	
	Traminer	Rufina	
	Traminer Aromatico	Sassella	
	Trebbiano	Soave	
	Verdicchio	Trentino	
	Verduzzo	Valgella	
		Valpantena	
		Valpolicella	
		Velletri	
		Venegazzu	

Opposite is a partial list of some of the most common names found on Italian wine labels, and their categories of meaning. The most popular wines imported into the United States are Chianti, Lambrusco, Bardolino, Soave, Valpolicella, and Asti Spumante. Some of the top-quality red wines are Barolo, Barbaresco, and Gattimara.

abboccato: Semisweet. (See also **amabile**.)

amabile: Literally "amiable." Semisweet, but a little sweeter than **abboccato**.

amarone: Wine made from late-harvested, overripe grapes that have been fermented until they lose their sweetness—that is, until the wine becomes "dry". This category can produce some very fine wines, notably Recioto Amarone della Valpolicella. (See also **recioto**.)

asciutto: Dry. (See also **secco**.)

azienda vinicola: A wine-producing company.

bianco: White. Toscano Bianco, for example, is white wine from Tuscany, a kind of white Chianti.

cantina: A winery or wine cellar. (See also next entry.)

cantina sociale: A winegrower's cooperative (for example, Cantina Sociale di Soave, the winegrower's cooperative from the town of Soave).

casa fondata nel . . . : Business founded in. . . .

casa vinicola: A winery; the equivalent of **cantina**.

classico: A geographical "inner" zone within a **D.O.C.**, usually indicating a superior wine from that region; for example, Chianti Classico, Orvieto Classico, etc.

colli, collio: Hills. A number of **D.O.C.** wines have an appellation beginning with this term, such as Colli Albani, and Colli Orientali del Friuli. Frascati is a well-known white wine from the Colli Albani area; twelve different wines are produced under the Colli Orientali del Fruili aegis, each named after its grape varietal.

consorzio: An organization or association of wine producers (growers and shippers) who have established their own standards for the wine they produce. Often an emblem is placed on the neck of a wine bottled by a specific consorzio. The most famous of these is the *gallo nero* (black rooster), the seal of the Chianti **Classico** region consorzio. The gallo nero is accepted as an indication of a superior Chianti Classico, a step up from a **D.O.C.** Chianti Classico. Similarly, a Chianti Classico **Riserva** produced by the consorzio (indicated by a black rooster within a red inner circle and a gold outer circle on the neck of the bottle) indicates a superior-quality Riserva, probably the best available.

D.O.C.: Denominazione di Origine Controllata. In 1967 the first nationwide law pertaining to wine standards, districts, and names was put into effect in Italy. D.O.C. is the Italian equivalent of the French **appellation contrôlée**, or the German **Qualitätswein** and **Qualitätswein mit Prädikat**.

For each named (and strictly defined) geographical area, the D.O.C. laws stipulate the maximum amount of wine that can be produced per acre, grape varietals that make up that wine, standards of taste, regulations on simplicity and clarity of labeling, and even required aging. A D.O.C. appellation on a wine label is a guarantee of basic quality—it indicates that you are getting the wine you pay for, from the delineated area, and states that the wine has achieved acceptable quality standards for a wine of its type. Depending upon the wine, however, those standards may indicate an outstanding wine (e.g., Brunello di Montalcino) or one that is not particularly noteworthy (Est! Est!! Est!!!). In this the D.O.C. system differs drastically from the

French and German systems, which contain a clearly delineated hierarchy of quality. It is important to remember that the D.O.C. laws only set basic quality standards for each particular wine in a specifically circumscribed area—they do not necessarily indicate that that wine is a wine of high quality to begin with. Venegazzù, for example, is a wine of high repute from northwestern Italy that does *not* have a D.O.C. status.

Another problem with the D.O.C. appellation is that it allows certain districts to add a maximum of 15 percent of wines from outside the district named. Thus, a Valpolicella may be only 85 percent Valpolicella, a Bardolino only 85 percent Bardolino.

Before the prospective Italian wine jargoneer runs screaming off into the mists of the Colli Albani, a few words of cautious optimism are in order. Although it is difficult to distinguish quality *between* one wine and another unless you know the wine to begin with, *within* each wine D.O.C. appellation there are certain ranking systems. **Classico** implies a favored inner geographical area. **Superiore**, **vecchio**, **riserva**, **riserva speciale**, and **stravecchio** indicate, in ascending order, the amount of time the wine has been aged. (**Superiore** also indicates a higher alcohol content.) **D.O.C.G.**, a new, more stringent national name and origin delineation, will eventually come into wide effect, stipulating wines that are a "step above" the D.O.C. wines. Last but not least, the **consorzio** system acts as a general indicator of higher quality wines within a particular D.O.C. Beyond all this, as is the case to a lesser degree in France, Germany, and certainly California, you have to know the name and reputation of the wine (and its vintage, and, often, its shipper) in order to determine its quality.

Ah, well. Living *con brio* requires a certain touch of madness, does it not? Avanti!

D.O.C.G.: Denominazione di Origine Controllata e Guarantita; a new, more stringent government selection system, one step above **D.O.C.** Only a few high-quality wines have been granted this appellation so far, among them Brunello di Montalcino, Vino Nobile di Montepulciano, and Barolo. (See also **D.O.C.**)

dolce: Sweet.

fattoria: Estate.

frizzante: Slightly sparkling, the Italian equivalent of **pétillant**. Lambrusco is the best known here.

imbottigliato: Bottled. "Imbottigliato da" means "bottled by . . ." and usually refers to the wine's producer. "*Messo in bottiglia al castello*" means "estate-bottled."

liquoroso: Very sweet, usually high-alcohol-content wine; occasionally fortified, sometimes with brandy. (See also **vinsanto**, **passito**.)

passito: An intense, sweet wine that is made from grapes that have been dried in order to intensify the sugar content of the must. Best known are Caluso Passito and Vinsanto Toscano. (See also **vinsanto**.)

recioto: A wine made from selected (that is, riper, with higher sugar content) grapes that are allowed to dry partially after harvest. The result is a strong (high-alcohol-content) wine, full-bodied, and usually semisweet. It may be red (Recioto della Valpolicella), or white (Recioto di Soave, Recioto di Gambellara). A dry version, in which a larger proportion of the sugar has been allowed to ferment out, is called Recioto della Valpolicella Amarone. Recioto wines are not as sweet as **passito**, **vinsanto**, or **liquoroso** wines.

riserva: A term of stipulated aging under **D.O.C.** laws. The amount of aging varies with the wine; usually, the longer it is aged, the higher the quality. Refosco (Colli Orientali del Friuli) is riserva after two years; Chianti **Classico** and Barbaresco after three years; Barolo requires four years; Brunello di Montalcino and Aglianico del Vulture five years. The stipulated aging time, it must be noted, is not always in wood (i.e., in a cask), but often partially in the bottle.

riserva speciale: Wine aged slightly longer than a **riserva**. Usually a very special wine of high quality. Barolo, for instance, requires four years of aging for riserva, five years for riserva speciale.

rosato: Rosé. Rosato del Salento is a rosé, but so is Riviera del Garda Chiaretto. Sometimes the label will tell you, sometimes it won't.

rosso: Red. Rosso Conero, for example. Of course, most Italian wines are red, and they don't bother to tell you about it on the label.

secco: Dry. The equivalent of **asciutto**. (See also **abboccato**, **dolce**, **liquoroso**, ascending orders of sweetness.)

spumante: Sparkling. The most famous Italian wine with this appellation is Asti Spumante (spumante from the town of Asti). Many other Italian wines are produced in sparkling versions, such as Soave, Lacrima Christi, and Nebbiolo, but few of them are imported here. The most popular exported Italian sparkling wine (actually **frizzante**, or semisparkling) is Lambrusco, which usually accounts for over half of all such wines brought into the United States in a particular year. Most of the Lambrusco shipped here is sweeter, and generally inferior to the wine drunk around Bologna. Most of it is also not **D.O.C.** wine, and may therefore be from the Lambrusco grape grown anywhere in Italy.

stravecchio: Very old. Aged for a long period of time.

superiore: A wine with superiore on the label must, under **D.O.C.** laws, be aged slightly longer than a wine without such an appellation; it also must have a somewhat higher minimum alcohol content. White superiore wines require a much shorter aging, however, than do the reds.

tenuta: A wine estate.

vecchio: Old. Aged for a specified period of time under **D.O.C.** laws, but always less than a **riserva**. A Chianti aged for two years may be labeled vecchio; aged for three years, it becomes a riserva.

vendemmia: A vintage year; grape harvest year.

vinsanto: Rich, dense, almost always sweet or semisweet white wine made from grapes that have been harvested and then dried to intensify sugar content. (See also **passito**.)

[24]

Drugs

The issue of drug abuse in our society is a complex and disturbing one. To begin with, the dimensions of drug use are far greater than most people imagine: **Heroin**, a $10-billion-a-year industry; **marijuana**, the single largest cash crop in the state of California; 44,000 tons of **cocaine** smuggled into the U.S. every year; five *billion* prescription doses of **tranquilizers** taken every year, many of them abused or overused; billions in legal profits from the sales of **Valium** alone; thousands of deaths from **overdose**, from both legal and illegal drugs; half a million **heroin** addicts, spending $100 to $400 a day to support their habits, the vast majority of this money obtained criminally; 20 million or more regular **marijuana** smokers (including one-tenth of all high-school seniors, who smoke **pot** *daily*); alarmingly widespread use of **PCP**, **barbiturates**, and **hallucinogens** among high school and even grade school children. We are concerned in this chapter with the language of drug abuse—both the illegal drugs such as **heroin**, **cocaine**, **marijuana**, and **LSD**, and the nonmedical usage of prescription drugs such as **barbiturates, tranquilizers**, **sedatives**, and the like. Although not included in the scope of this section, the widespread use of caffeine, nicotine, and alcohol—which in heavy use especially produce many of the characteristics of drug abuse syndromes, with equally deleterious effects —should be considered in examining, objectively, the overall phenomenon of substance abuse in America today.

The argument has been made that most human beings have some kind of innate drive to alter their normal psychophysiological state, whether for pleasure, relaxation, stimulation, escape, enhancement of perception, or simply for the sake of change. Given the fact that virtually all human cultures evidence the use of both **psychotropic** substances (from wine to hallucinogenic fungi to coca leaves to double martinis) and other means of psychophysiological change (ecstatic dancing, music, fasting, meditation, prayer, and other religious or mystical practices), this argument seems to have some validity. However, the realities of drug abuse in America today —in both the harmful nature of the substances being used and the criminal subculture controlling their distribution and sale—go far beyond any "natural" need for experimentation and change: ten-year-old kids **freaked out** on **PCP**, college students snorting **heroin**, housewives hooked on **barbiturates**—these are clearly abusive and damaging, frequently deadly patterns of behavior.

Blame for the drug situation in America today falls in four areas: (1) on the criminal underworld, which peddles **addiction** and misery for inconceivable profits ($5,000 worth of wholesale heroin goes for $1 million on the streets of New York); (2) on the drug industry, which spends over a billion dollars yearly promoting and marketing the sale of prescription drugs, many of which are overused or find their way into illicit use; (3) on the state and federal governments, which by maintaining an antiquated set of policies have not solved the drug problem but only exacerbated it (the legal dispensation of heroin in England, for example, has virtually eliminated both the illegal traffic in that drug and the horrendous social disorder caused by addicts' need for cash); (4) on the parents, friends, and relatives of drug-abusing children, adolescents, and adults, who either care too little or are too afraid to intervene.

In the chapter that follows, we will examine the language of drug abuse in four categories: "The Major Abused Drugs and Their Characteristics"; "Street Names for Abused Drugs"; "The Terminology of Illegal Drug Sale and Use"; and "Medical/Psychological Terms Relating to Drug Use."

For the parent, friend, teacher, counselor, psychologist, or just plain concerned citizen, this glossary may be of use.

THE MAJOR ABUSED DRUGS AND THEIR CHARACTERISTICS

I. Opiates

Opium, morphine, codeine, heroin, methadone, Demerol, Dilaudid. The opiates generally are derived from the poppy plant, and are legally defined as **sedative narcotics**. **Opium** is the raw product from which **morphine** (its **alkaloid**) and **codeine** are drawn, and from which **heroin** and **Dilaudid** are chemically converted. **Demerol** and **methadone** represent completely synthetic opiates. Morphine (ten times as strong as opium, one-third to one-half the strength of heroin) and the other opiates have similar effects when taken in equivalent doses, although each has its own particular characteristics.

The opiates all cause euphoria and indifference to pain. While local anesthetics block sensations of pain, opiate users may be aware of pain but are detached from their own sensations, and thus unconcerned. Nonaddicted users tend to emphasize the pleasurable aspect of the drugs, which in the stronger opiates has been compared to orgasm. Serious dangers common to use of all opiates, however, are the high likelihood of **tolerance**, **addiction** and **withdrawal** symptoms and side effects such as itching, nausea, runny nose, constricted pupils, joint pains, hiccups, and constipation. Opiate **withdrawal** symptoms include violent chills, increased blood pressure, vomiting, fever, and insomnia. However, unlike alcohol or **barbiturate** withdrawal, opiate withdrawal is never fatal, and even long-term use does not appear to permanently impair physical or mental functioning. Perhaps the greatest danger, however—particularly of heroin—is the ruthless criminal subculture that controls its distribution and sale—a function, many say, not of the drug but of its illegality. 🍎

OPIUM

Also **black stuff**. This oldest of the **opiates** can be eaten or smoked, but not injected. It was once infamous for its intoxicating effects in *opium dens,* and was praised as a medical panacea before being replaced by **morphine** for medical use. Such medicines as laudanum, containing 10 percent opium, were sold over the counter throughout the nineteenth century and were employed for a variety of symptoms including babies' colic and teething pains. Today, however, it is strictly a black-market drug.

MORPHINE

Also **cube**, **dope**, **hard stuff**, **junk**, **M**, **morf**, **mud**, **white stuff**. The main **alkaloid** of **opium**, morphine can be injected or taken orally. It was originally used as an **analgesic**, especially for wounded soldiers since the Civil War (which sent home 45,000 addicts). War has since been a major source of morphine addiction. (In 1900, there were estimated to be over 300,000 morphine addicts in the U.S.)

CODEINE

Also **schoolboy**. Codeine is always taken by mouth, is famous as a cough suppressant, and is also used in treatment of diarrhea. Doctors will often prescribe cough medicines containing some percentage of codeine for chronic or serious coughs, but they are reluctant to prescribe straight codeine because of its potential for abuse. However, even cough medicines with codeine added can cause intoxication and have often been used for that purpose.

Also **H**, **big H**, **blanks**, **boy**, **brother**, **brown**, **brown sugar**, **caballo**, **Chinese red**, **China white**, **dope**, **doojee**, **hard stuff**, **junk**, **horse**, **smack**, **skag**, **schmeck**. Heroin is the most potent and most common **opiate** available on the street, and can be inhaled, injected, or less often, smoked. Its use and trade are responsible for an enormously high proportion of underworld "business" and urban property crime, and have infiltrated virtually all social classes. Although it is a more potent **analgesic** than **morphine**, its potential for addiction and abuse is so high that it is never legally used. In 1976, the Drug Abuse Council estimated that there were 4 million heroin users of one degree or another in the U.S., and of these over half a million have been estimated to be true **addicts**. The numbers of users have taken a sudden rise in the last year or two, as high-potency heroin (20 to 40 percent pure), mostly from the middle East, has become available in the illegal market.

Heroin sales constitute a major black-market industry, which is largely controlled by the Mafia, but which includes a large number of inner-city black and Hispanic dealers as well. Drug enforcement agents confiscate only an estimated 2 to 5 percent of all heroin entering the U.S., and the remainder yields an estimated $10 *billion* or more a year in black-market sales—more than most of the corporations listed in the *Fortune* 500. Corruption has been rampant among those responsible for controlling heroin as well: In 1969, for instance, three-quarters of the eighty Bureau of Narcotics and Dangerous Drugs agents (BNDD) assigned to New York were fired for their involvement in heroin traffic. Only about fifty of the estimated approximately 10,000 dealers of heroin are prosecuted each year.

A typical heroin addict spends between $100 and $400 a day supporting his **habit**, most of this gained through sale of stolen goods. Heroin-related theft is thought to be responsible for 50 percent of all inner-city property crime. The economic cost of these damages, combined with treatment costs, is well over $20 billion a year; the social and personal costs—to addicts and their victims alike —are incalculable.

While some claim that more efficient enforcement of narcotics laws would restrict illegal sale and use of the drug, others point to the example of England, where heroin is legally controlled and dispensed to registered addicts, cutting drug-related crime to almost nothing. *Fifteen cents'* worth of legal heroin in England sells for $15 to $30 on the U.S. streets. While a British type of system has been suggested for the U.S., it has so far gained little support here.

Most heroin enters the U.S. today through New York, Miami, Seattle, New Orleans, Phoenix, and San Diego, while Southwest Asia (Turkey, Afghanistan, Iran), Mexico, and Southeast Asia constitute the major sources.

METHADONE

Also **dollies**, **biscuits**, **medicine**. Methadone's major use has been in the legal treatment of **heroin addiction** in the U.S., in programs similar to the British (heroin) **maintenance** system. Although methadone is actually more addictive than heroin, in equivalent doses its effects last for twenty-four hours (while heroin lasts only four to six hours) and its use blocks the effects of, or need for, heroin. Thus, the addict need be seen only once a day without danger of his taking heroin. However, methadone has now become a black-market street drug, with an illegal traffic and nonsupervised addict population of its own. As with **morphine** (the "cure" for **opium** addiction) and heroin (the "cure" for morphine addiction) before it, the methadone cure has become a new problem in its own right. It remains, however, the only viable medical (as distinct from psychological) treatment for seriously addicted individuals in the U.S. as the drug situation obtains today.

DEMEROL

Also **junk**, **stuff**, **white stuff**, **demis**. This synthetic **opiate** has been used as the major **analgesic** in child delivery for forty years, despite the fact that there is some suggestion that it causes prenatal sedation, the danger of respiratory depression in the mother, and even the possibility of infant brain damage. It is also prescribed for pain in other cases, and is the most often chosen opiate of addicts in the medical professions.

DILAUDID

Also **D**, **big D**, **dillies**, **junk**, **stuff**, **white stuff**, **footballs**. A synthetic painkiller, used for postoperative and other severe or chronic pain. It is also prescribed for such illnesses as cancer, heart attack, and severe coughing. As with **Demerol**, most **addicts** are connected to the health industries.

II. Sedatives ("downs")

Barbiturates, tranquilizers, analgesics, and other sedatives, and related drugs. While each has its own character and uses, all depress the central nervous system, causing relaxation through slowing of metabolic functions and associated effects. With the possible exception of **marijuana**, sedatives are the most widely used drugs in our society today. They are legally available by prescription for psychological and medical ailments (such as insomnia, stress, anxiety, muscle tension), but have been shown to cause mental and physical damage, harming, in the aggregate, more people than **heroin**. Overuse and abuse of these drugs constitutes a devastating problem in the U.S. and often has fatal consequences. In 1977, for instance, there were 30 million prescriptions written (approximately 700 million doses) for the painkiller **Darvon**, and in that year this one drug was connected to 1,100 deaths. Between 1976 and 1977, approximately 57 million prescriptions for **Valium** were filled (over 3 *billion* pills), and in that period of time there were 54,000 Valium-related emergency-room admissions, with 900 deaths connected to its use. Because of **potentiation** the taking of such drugs with alcohol is the major cause of sedative **overdose**. Even normal use of sedatives, however, can create undesirable side effects—sometimes the opposite of their intended effects. Despite this, the pharmacological treatment of pain and mental distress, largely with sedatives, has become increasingly prevalent among doctors and psychiatrists alike. 🐝

Seconal (phennies, reds, redbirds, pinks, pink ladies, red devils, seggy, seccy); Nembutal (nemmies, nimbie, yellowjackets, yellows); Amytal (amies, blues, bluebirds, blue devils, blue heavens); Tuinal (rainbows, tooies, reds-and-blues, double trouble); Luminal (purple hearts); sodium pentothol ("truth serum"). The barbiturates are strong central nervous system depressants, which can be injected or taken orally in capsules. Long-acting ones, such as **Luminal** (eight to sixteen hours), are used to control disorders such as convulsions. The very short-acting ones, such as **sodium pentothol**, are often used in conjunction with vaporous anesthetics to induce general anesthesia. (Sodium pentothol has also been used for interrogation, as it lowers a person's psychological resistance, and has been known as "truth serum.") The most widely abused barbiturates, however, produce effects for four to six hours, and include **Amytal, Seconal, Nembutal**, and **Tuinal**. Legally used as sleeping pills, sedatives, and pain relievers, they are regularly abused by an estimated one million people, and are responsible for 3,000 deaths a year, half of which are suicides. Although they are as addictive as **heroin** and actually more harmful to the body, barbiturates are present in one-third of U.S. households. The common practice of washing the pills down with liquor is responsible for a large number of overdoses, as barbiturates (and almost all other sedative-type drugs) are **potentiated** by alcohol.

Reactions to barbiturates are unpredictable and range from drowsy calm to aggressive, hostile behavior. Blurred vision, lack of coordination, and insensibility are common effects, but the drugs have also been associated with violent assaults. The long-term barbiturate user may become chronically exhausted, uncoordinated, and emotionally unstable, suffering from loss of memory and concentration. Personality changes may include development of paranoia and tendencies toward violence.

Withdrawal from barbiturates may be the harshest and most dangerous of all drug experiences. Lasting two to three weeks, it involves severe sweating, nausea and vomiting, hyperactivity, shaking and cramping, racing heart, hallucinations, fever, convulsions, and seizures. Psychosis may develop and last up to two weeks, leading to exhaustion, metabolic collapse, and even death. An estimated 5 to 7 percent of barbiturate withdrawals are fatal without medication to ameliorate the severity of their effects.

TRANQUILIZERS

Thorazine, **Compazine**, **Mellaril**, **Miltown**, **Librium**, **Valium**, **Equanil**. The tranquilizers are most used for psychotherapeutic purposes, reducing anxiety and tension, and preventing excitable behavior. These drugs are divided into the *major tranquilizers,* used for more severe symptoms, and the *minor tranquilizers,* available by prescription for simple nervous tension and other minor ailments. It is this second class that is most abused, and the abuse is often deceptive, since it may have a valid prescription to back it up. Both classes of tranquilizers have been surrounded by controversy in recent years.

The major tranquilizers are used in treatment of a wide variety of severe disorders, such as cancer, surgery, labor, and delivery, but are mostly used for schizophrenia, manic depression and psychosis, and related psychological problems—including **LSD flashbacks**. Thorazine is the drug most used in treating psychosis. Compazine is often used to control nausea. **Tolerance** develops to all these drugs, but they are basically nonaddictive. The treatment of psychotics with Thorazine has been criticized by some because of side effects and the possible heightening of symptoms. Others complain that massive doses of the major tranquilizers simply "mask" the problem by reducing the patient's ability to respond, thus eliminating the problem —and the personality.

The minor tranquilizers, including Miltown—the strongest—

and Valium, Librium, and Equanil—similar in effect but less potent —cause mild euphoria and sedation in small doses. While businessmen and others account for much minor tranquilizer use, the advertising campaigns for Valium and related drugs have mostly been directed toward women and, until the mid-seventies, were strongly oriented toward "anxious housewives." Typical advertising in professional medical journals depicted women who were everything from exhausted and anxious to sloppily dressed or even frigid. Valium (or an equivalent) was shown to be the solution to these problems. The "bored, overeducated housewife," the "woman who has trouble relating to others"—all were advised to take minor tranquilizers. Since the mid-seventies, however, advertising strategies have changed, in accordance with the incredibly widespread use of minor tranquilizers by ordinary people: One ad depicts a pretty, well-groomed young woman, calm, alert, and ready to type (even she needs tranquilizers!). Americans relying on minor tranquilizers or "abusing" them to some extent number in the millions. Aside from the large number of hospital emergencies and deaths associated with Valium, the drugs can cause a chronic inability to concentrate, higher probability of birth defects, and, in the opinion of some researchers, the possibility of permanent brain damage from prolonged heavy use.

Darvon, **Talwin**, **Percodan**. These resemble the **anesthetics** but are not as strong, not usually causing unconsciousness. They are used for mild sedation and as painkillers. Darvon is the major analgesic: the third most used drug in the U.S. today, with the highest death rate of any pill. Causing **tolerance** and **dependence**, its side effects include dizziness, headaches, and stomach problems. In high doses it may cause convulsions, respiratory depression, coma, and death. Strangely, many do not find it an effective pain reliever. It is chemically similar to **methadone**, and has been reclassified in recent years as a **narcotic**. ANALGESICS

Talwin, one of the stronger analgesics, is prescribed for moderate to severe pain. Continued use causes tolerance and may lead to addiction. Its side effects include nausea, dizziness, blurred vision, and it may even cause hallucinations and a variety of physical difficulties. Its major danger is when taken in conjunction with the antihistimine PBZ (as **T's and Blues**) with potentiated effects similar to those of heroin. Percodan, prescribed for mild to moderate pain, also causes dependence, and severe **withdrawal** symptoms may accompany sudden removal of the drug from the system.

OTHER SEDATIVES

Methaqualone (Quaaludes, ludes, quacks, quads, 714s, soaps, soapers, wall bangers); chloral hydrate (knockout drops); Doriden (CB, ciba). Methaqualone is similar to the **barbiturates** in effect, but causes the user a more euphoric and energetic affect, and promotes amiability, laughter, sexual excitation, and uninhibited behavior. High doses, however, cause grossly uncoordinated behavior and loss of muscular control. Regular use can cause addiction, and the alcohol it is often taken with can lower the amount that constitutes a lethal dose. Side effects include blurred vision, headaches, numbness, and nausea. It is used by young people to enhance drunkenness and sexuality, and is often thought of as a "party drug."

Chloral hydrate is chemically related to methaqualone. It can cause a drunken **high** similar to that of alcohol, but is far more harmful and addictive.

Doriden is used in insomnia and as a general sedative. Physical **dependence** develops quickly and **withdrawal** symptoms are severe —they may include seizures, and are fatal in 20 to 25 percent of all cases without additional treatment. It produces euphoria and long-term symptoms similar to those of the **barbiturates**. It is particularly difficult to remove this drug from the system, making **overdose** more dangerous than with many other drugs.

III. Central nervous system stimulants

Cocaine, amphetamines. These are drugs that **potentiate** the effects of natural nervous system chemicals, causing increased nervous and metabolic activity. Cocaine is the milder of the CNS stimulants, while the amphetamines have a much stronger overall effect. All of them cause a sense of excitation, increased nerve signals, and heightening of experience. The user feels **rushes** of energy, and, especially with the amphetamines, an inability to keep still, with the tendency to talk or perform activities rapidly or incessantly. The amphetamines in particular do serious damage to the body and nervous system. &

COCAINE

Also **C, coke, big C, blow, cholly, dust, happy dust, lady, nose powder, snow, white, white girl, Bernice, Bernies.** A favorite of the wealthy and the "hip," cocaine is known as the "champagne of drugs," both because of the light euphoria it causes and because of its price. It is less harmful than the **amphetamines**, has no physical withdrawal symptoms—though **coming down** from the cocaine **high** may produce mild depression; and its stimulative effects are generally subtle, generally lasting fifteen to thirty minutes per dose.

It is believed to intensify the sex drive in some and generally increases psychic energy. When injected, cocaine is much more dangerous, and serious users may **shoot up** as much as twenty to thirty times a day.

Among cocaine's undesirable effects may be included anxiety, rapid heart and pulse, raised blood pressure, nausea, and vomiting. Overuse may cause hallucinations, paranoid psychosis and other amphetamine-type effects. Chronic cocaine users tend to have destroyed nasal tissue and runny noses. Some develop perforated septums or blocked nasal passages, but in general psychological **dependency** on the drug is the greatest danger.

Cocaine is exported from Peru, Bolivia and Colombia, where it is rather cheaply produced from the coca leaves chewed by the local Indians. In the U.S. the best-quality cocaine sells for about $2,500 an ounce, and an estimated 44,000 pounds are smuggled into the U.S. per year.

Also **speed**; **ups**; **uppers**; **methamphetamine/Methedrine**   AMPHETAMINES
(speed, meth, crystal); **Benzedrine (bennies, benz, benzies, pep pills, whites)**; **Dexedrine (copilots, dex, dexies)**; **Biphetamine (black beauties)**; **Diphetamine (footballs)**; **diet pills**. These CNS stimulants can be taken in pill form such as Benzedrine and Dexedrine, or intravenously in the form of crystal methamphetamine or other injectable types. Legal uses include the treatment of narcolepsy (sleeping sickness), epilepsy, and Parkinson's disease. They have also been used in the treatment of hyperactive children, and as a dieting aid because of their depressive effects on appetite, taste, and smell.

A favorite among students, truck drivers and others who need to work without sleep for some period of time, amphetamines make it possible to stay awake, move or work rapidly, and they may provide a euphoric **rush**; but they actually decrease efficiency with prolonged use and may ultimately destroy nervous system functions.

The **speed freak** culture is known for its antisocial behavior, probably stemming from the drug's side effects: irritability, anxiety, insomnia, aggressiveness, tremors, loss of appetite, and stomach problems. Taken regularly, definite personality changes take place. The long-term user may develop paranoid delusions and compulsive behavior, such as endless repetition of meaningless acts. Controls on these drugs have been inadequate: In one case, two New York doctors were indicted for prescribing 700 patients a week with liquid amphetamine without supervision (cited in *Tranquilization of America*, Warner Books, 1979).

IV. Hallucinogens

Synthetic hallucinogens and natural hallucinogens. These are nonaddictive drugs that produce **hallucinations** or other abnormal or delusional states of mind. Similarities have been drawn between the effects of these drugs and psychosis, including vivid perceptual changes, heightened colors and sounds, and time-sense distortion and **kinesthetic experiences**. Shortly after the drug is taken, anxiety and/or exhilaration may be experienced, along with nausea, rapid pulse, and dilated pupils. After this the hallucinatory experience (or **trip**) may begin.

In a small number of cases, hallucinations may continue beyond the normal duration of effects, or they may recur suddenly long after the initial drug experience (see **flashback**). However, the usual experience lasts from three to ten hours. More frequently, users may experience **bad trips**, in which subjective distortions take on a terrifying aspect. This usually occurs with high doses or in negative settings (as many of the effects of these drugs are based upon psychological reactions). Complications also arise frequently from the ingestion of hallucinogenic drugs **cut** with **PCP**, strychnine, or **amphetamines**. 🍎

SYNTHETIC
HALLUCINOGENS

LSD (**acid, blue cheer, California sunshine, Christmas tree, clear light, blotter, cubes, cupcakes, dots, microdots, paper acid, purple microdots, purple Owsley, sunshine, white lightning, windowpane**); **STP**; **DMT**; **MDA**; **THC**. Among the chemical hallucinogens produced and popularized within the 1960s youth subculture, LSD was and is the most widely used. Once promoted by such "spokesmen" as Timothy Leary and the former Richard Alpert (now Baba Ram Dass), it has been credited at one time or another with everything from revealing the presence of God to causing permanent chromosome damage—neither of which claim has ever been proven. It has been used by such psychologists as Stanislav Grof in "LSD therapy," and by the CIA in brainwashing experimentation. Whether hallucinogens constitute a potentially useful tool for opening untapped regions of the mind, or are simply destroyers of normal mental functioning is still subject to debate.

Among the other synthetics, DMT is an hour-long **trip** otherwise similar to LSD; STP is an eight- to twenty-four-hour trip that tends to be quite intense; MDA lasts about eight hours and combines effects from LSD and the **amphetamines**; and THC is either the extracted or synthesized version of the active principle in **marijuana**, which at high levels of dosage causes hallucinogenic effects. Aside from these and other relatively minor variations, the drugs have similar properties.

Peyote (buttons, cactus, mescalito); mescaline (mesc); psilocybin (magic mushrooms, mushrooms); morning-glory seeds (flying saucers); ayahuasca (yage); datura (jimson weed). Such natural hallucinogens as peyote have been known to Native Americans and non-Western peoples for centuries. They were used not for kicks or escape, but as a deep-rooted part of their culture and religions—connected to their ideas of God and the sacred. Through the "hallucinatory" action of the natural hallucinogen, occurring in cacti, mushrooms, and other plants, the practitioner would be taken out of the mundane sphere of ordinary events into the intensified dimension of religious meaning. It is interesting to note that although hallucinogen use is illegal almost everywhere in the Western world, its ritual use in American and Mexican religions is respected and allowed by our modern legal systems.

Among the natural hallucinogens, peyote and psilocybin are the most popular in street use, along with mescaline, the active principle of peyote. Mescaline and peyote have been compared to **LSD**, but this is often because LSD has frequently been sold under the name of mescaline; in general, mescaline and peyote are not as often associated with negative experiences among users.

Marijuana, hashish, hash oil, kif. These drugs derive from the various parts of the **cannabis sativa** or hemp plant, particularly the resin-filled top flowers and leaves. All of the various cannabis products have been known to peoples throughout the world for millennia; they have become increasingly popular in the West and the United States during the last few decades for their sense-distorting and euphoric effects, and in some circles have become a social drug akin to alcohol. ❧

Also **dope, gage, ghanja, Gainesville green, grass, gold, ragweed, herb, Mexican green, Panama red, pot, rope, sinsemilla smoke, supergrass, superweed, tea, Thai sticks, weed, Colombian, Jamaican. Marijuana**, the dried flowers or leaves of the female

NATURAL
HALLUCINOGENS

V. Marijuana and other cannabis derivatives

MARIJUANA

hemp plant, is the most widely used **cannabis** product. Found in a variety of types and potencies, marijuana use in the U.S. was confined through the 1950s mainly to blacks, jazz musicians, and the "beatniks." It became a mainstay of the "hippie" movement of the 1960s, but during the 1970s the drug came into much more widespread use. It is now popular within many walks of life and all social classes; estimates have it that at least 20 million Americans use marijuana with some frequency, while easily twice that number have at least tried it.

While high doses may cause hallucinations, normal quantities cause a lightheaded euphoria, giddiness with some loss of coordination, heaviness, warmth, and increased heart rate. A dreamlike sense of altered perception that arises may be interpreted as pleasant or frightening. Detachment and distortions of body image combine with sensual feelings and the enhancement of colors and sounds, along with broken thought processes and a decrease in short-term memory. It has been suggested that the pleasant side of the marijuana **high** must be learned, by internalizing the interpretations of other users. While moderate marijuana use apparently does not cause serious physical problems for most people, long-term heavy users may experience chronic disruptions of thought processes, a persistent decline of memory and energy, and may slip into a passive and uncaring attitude. Heavy users may smoke as many as ten **joints** per day, but only a small percentage of marijuana smokers do so; even at this level there is no physical **dependence** on the drug, only a psychological one.

Marijuana is being used experimentally in the treatment of glaucoma, anorexia, hypertension, migraine, and epilepsy, and to ameliorate the nausea and other adverse effects of chemotherapy treatment of cancer.

OTHER CANNABIS
DERIVATIVES

Hashish (**hash, blond, Lebanese, black Russian, Afghani**); **hash oil** (**oil, black oil, red oil, cherry leb**); **kif.** Among the other **derivatives** of the **marijuana** plant are **hashish, hash oil,** and **kif**. Hashish is the most common, and is made from marijuana by a cooking process that concentrates the **resin** containing the active ingredient, or **alkaloid**. Hash oil is extracted from hashish and has an even higher concentration of resin. The liquid is heated and the vapor inhaled from a hash oil pipe. Kif is a mixture of tobacco and specially grown marijuana which is rather rare in the U.S. but is extremely common in Morocco. It is interesting to compare with the black American practice of rolling **joints** of marijuana mixed with tobacco; tobacco seems to **potentiate** the effects of marijuana somewhat.

Anesthetic inhalants; **petroleum-based inhalants**, **and others**; **PCP**; and **amyl nitrate**. 🍎

VI. Deliriants and other drugs

Nitrous oxide (**nitrous**, **gas**, **laughing gas**); **chloroform**; **ether**. The **anesthetic gases** include **nitrous oxide**, **ether**, and **chloroform**. They produce giddiness and euphoria and desensitize the user to pain, but may kill by causing respiratory failure. Their effects last no more than five or ten minutes.

ANESTHETIC INHALANTS

Cleaning products, **glue**, **gasoline**, **benzine**, **lacquer**, **thinner**, **Freon**, **aerosols**. When a user inhales the fumes of the various **petroleum products**, which include **glue** (with the active ingredient toluene), **cleaning products**, **gasoline**, **benzine**, **lacquer**, **thinner** and **aerosol sprays**, coordination is lost, the user becomes disoriented and confused. While the **high** is similar in some ways to that from alcohol, solvents often cause delirium and may lead to coma, while the inhaling of freezer preparations (e.g., **Freon**) has been proven to cause death in some cases. Glue sniffing and other inhaling of petroleum products is limited in frequency compared to use of **marijuana** and the **sedative drugs**, but the effects can be far more severe—metabolic changes, possibly organ and brain damage. What is more, use seems to be confined to those least able to judge its dangers—children, teenagers, and educationally impoverished urban "street people."

PETROLEUM-BASED INHALANTS AND OTHERS

Also **angel dust**, **angel hair**, **Cadillac**, **CJ**, **crystal**, **DOA**, **elephant**, **elephant tranquilizer**, **hog**, **horse tranquilizer**, **killer weed**, **KJ**, **mist**, **peace pills**, **pig tranquilizer**, **rocket fuel**, **sheets**. Originally a human tranquilizer, PCP's use has become restricted to anesthetizing animals because of its dangerous side effects. Technically termed phencyclidine but commonly called **angel dust** on the street, it is inhaled, injected, swallowed or smoked, often in combination with **marijuana**. PCP's one- to six-hour **trip** causes **hallucinations**, disorientation, lack of coordination and **analgesia**, and has been passed off as various true **hallucinogens**. However, it is far more dangerous.

PCP

Soon after taking PCP, the user may experience body-image changes, such as alteration of body size and weightlessness. Both euphoria and panic may occur at this time. Then hallucinations and space-time distortions begin, followed by feelings of detachment and isolation. While **coming down**, thoughts of death, despair, extreme paranoia, and depression may set in. PCP may cause detachment from any sense of right and wrong, and has been credited with causing a range of antisocial behavior, from public nudity to murder. Its use is unfortunately common among school-age American children.

AMYL NITRATE

Also **amys**, **pearls**, **poppers**, **snappers**. This drug is known for its immediate **rush** and disoriented **high**, and is popular among users for its enhancement and supposed prolongation of orgasm. Used medically to relieve the pain of angina, it is taken by breaking a small glass vial or ampule and inhaling the released gas. It acts by dilating blood vessels leading to the heart for two to three minutes, causing a warm and euphoric rush. It is popular in the gay community for its relaxation of sphincter and other involuntary muscles. Although its permanent effects are open to dispute, it is extremely dangerous for those with low blood pressure, as it lowers the blood pressure further. *Butyl nitrate*, a close equivalent of amyl nitrate, is often sold legally as a liquid room deodorizer, but is reported to produce the same range of effects as amyl nitrate.

STREET NAMES OF DRUGS

A: Amphetamines.

Acapulco gold: Especially potent Mexican marijuana.

acid: LSD.

Afghani: Hashish or hash oil from Afghanistan.

amies, amys: Amytal, a barbiturate; or, amyl nitrate.

angel dust: PCP (phencyclidine).

angel hair: PCP.

barbs: Barbiturates.

bennies, benz, benzies: Benzedrine, an *amphetamine*.

Bernice, **Bernies:** Cocaine.

big C: Cocaine.

big H: Heroin.

biscuits: Methadone.

black beauties: Biphetamine, an amphetamine.

black oil: Hash oil.

black Russian: A dark type of extremely potent hashish.

black stuff: Opium.

blanks: Heroin.

blockbusters: Barbiturate pills, possibly Nembutal.

blond hash: Light-colored, less potent hashish.

blotter, blotter acid: A dose of LSD impregnated in a small segment of paper.

blow: Cocaine.

bluebirds: Sodium amytal, a barbiturate.

blue cheer: A type of LSD.

blue devils, **blue heavens:** Sodium amytal, a barbiturate.

blues: 1. Numorphan (a derivative of morphine). 2. Sodium amytal, a barbiturate.

bomb: High-potency heroin; also, a large **joint** of marijuana.

bombita, **bombido:** Desoxyn or other amphetamines.

boy: Heroin.

brother: Heroin.

brown, **brown sugar:** Heroin.

brownies: Probably Dexedrine, an amphetamine.

browns: Amphetamine.

buttons: Peyote.

C: Cocaine.

caballo: Spanish for **horse**, i.e., heroin.

cactus: Peyote.

Cadillac: PCP.

California sunshine: LSD.

candy: Barbiturates.

chalk: Amphetamines.

cherry leb: Hash oil.

Chinese red: Heroin.

Chinese white: High-potency heroin.

cholly: Cocaine.

Christmas tree: A type of LSD.

CJ: PCP.

clear light: LSD.

coke: Cocaine.

Colombian, **Colombo:** High-potency marijuana.

copilots: Dexedrine, an amphetamine.

crank: Amphetamines.

crystal: 1. Crystalline desoxyn or methamphetamine, to be snorted or injected. 2. PCP.

cubes: LSD soaked into sugar cubes.

cupcakes: LSD.

cyclones: PCP.

D: Dilaudid.

demis: Demerol.

dex, **dexies:** Dexedrine, an amphetamine.

dillies: Dilaudid.

DOA: PCP.

dollies: Methadone.

domestic: Low- to medium-potency American marijuana.

doobie: Marijuana.

doojee: Heroin.

dope: Heroin; grass; morphine; also used for virtually any drug.

dots: LSD microdots.

double trouble: Tuinal.

downs: Barbiturates and other sedatives.

dust: Cocaine; also PCP.

dynamite: Cocaine.

elephant: PCP.

elephant tranquilizer: PCP.

eye-openers: Amphetamines.

fives: Amphetamines.

flake: Cocaine.

flying saucers: Morning-glory seeds, an hallucinogen.

footballs: Diphetamine, an amphetamine; Dilaudid, synthetic opiate.

fours: The strongest of the four types of Tylenol with codeine tablets.

gage: Marijuana.

Gainesville green: Low-potency American marijuana.

gas: Nitrous oxide.

ghanja: A potent form of marijuana in India.

girl: Cocaine.

gold: Any of several very potent varieties of marijuana.

goofballs, **goofers:** Barbiturates or sedatives.

gorilla pills: Barbiturates or sedatives.

grass: Marijuana.

H: Heroin.

happy dust: Cocaine.

hard stuff: Heroin, morphine.

hash: Hashish.

Hawaiian: High-potency marijuana grown in Hawaii.

hearts: Amphetamines.

herb: Marijuana.

hog: PCP.

horse: Heroin.
horse tranquilizer: PCP.
idiot pills: Barbiturates.
Jamaican: High-potency marijuana from Jamaica.
joy juice: Chloral hydrate.
junk: Heroin, morphine.
kif: A marijuana-tobacco mixture specially prepared in Morocco; also, the Moroccan marijuana grown for this mixture.
killer weed: PCP.
King Kong pills: Sedatives, barbiturates.
KJ: PCP.
lady: Cocaine.
LA turnabouts: Amphetamines.
Lebanese: Hashish from Lebanon.
lightning: Amphetamine.
ludes: Quaaludes (Methaqualone).
M: Morphine.
magic mushrooms: Psilocybin.
medicine: Methadone.
mesc: Mescaline.
mescalito: Peyote.
meth: Methedrine, an amphetamine.
Mexican green: Common, low-potency marijuana from Mexico.
microdots: Weak LSD doses of approximately 100 micrograms each, usually in small blue beads.
mikes: Micrograms (of LSD).
mist: PCP.
morf, morpho: Morphine.
mud: Morphine.
mushrooms: Psilocybin.
nemmies, nimbie: Nembutal, a barbiturate.
nitrous: Nitrous oxide gas.
nose powder: Cocaine.
oil: Hash oil.
oranges: Amphetamines.
orange sunshine, orange wedges: LSD.
Owsley: Popular purple California LSD during the 1960s.
Panama red: High-potency marijuana from Panama.
paper acid: LSD (**blotter acid**).

paraquat: A poison added to Mexican marijuana to prevent sale and/or use.
peace pills: PCP.
pearls: Amyl nitrate.
pep pills: Amphetamines.
perks: Percodan.
phennies: Seconals.
pig tranquilizer: PCP.
pink ladies, pinks: Seconal, a barbiturate.
poppers: Amyl nitrate.
pot: Marijuana.
purple hearts: Luminal, a major tranquilizer.
purple microdots: LSD (see **microdot, Owsley**).
purple Owsley: LSD (see **Owsley**).
quacks: (Quaaludes: Methaqualone).
quads: (Quaaludes: Methaqualone).
ragweed: Low-potency marijuana.
rainbows: Tuinal, a barbiturate.
red devils: Seconal, a barbiturate.
red oil: Hash oil.
reds and blues: Barbiturates (Tuinals).
reds, redbirds: Seconal.
rocket fuel: PCP.
rope: Marijuana.
schmeck: Heroin.
schoolboy: Codeine.
seccy, seggy: Seconals.
714s: Quaaludes (Methaqualone).
sheets: PCP.
sinsemilla: Seedless super-high-potency northern California marijuana.
skag, scag: Heroin.
sleepers: Barbiturates; sleeping pills.
smack: Heroin.
smoke: Marijuana.
snappers: Amyl nitrate.
snow: Cocaine; heroin.
sopors, soapers, soaps: Methaqualone.
speckled birds: Amphetamines.
speed: Amphetamine.
speedball: Injection of heroin mixed with cocaine or amphetamine.
stuff: Any drug; often heroin.
sunshine: LSD.

supergrass, superweed: Marijuana cut with PCP, formaldehyde, or other strong sense distorters; also, any extremely high-potency marijuana.

super Quaalude, super soper: Highest-strength Methaqualone tablets.

T's and Blues:: Potent combination of **Talwin** and PBZ (an antihistamine), used as a cheap heroin substitute.

tea: Marijuana.

tens: Amphetamines.

Thai sticks: One of the strongest grades of marijuana; consists of dried top flowers from Thailand marijuana plants wrapped around a stick.

tooies: Tuinal.

truck drivers: Amphetamines.

turnabouts: Amphetamines.

25: LSD.

uppers, ups: Amphetamines.

wall bangers: Methaqualone.

wedges: LSD.

weed: Marijuana.

white lightning: LSD.

white, white girl: Cocaine.

whites: Benzedrine.

white stuff: Any and all opiates (heroin, morphine, etc.).

windowpane: Small, transparent LSD dose to be dissolved on the tongue.

yellowjackets: Barbiturates (Nembutal).

yellows: Nembutal.

ILLEGAL DRUG SALE AND USE: TERMINOLOGY

acid head: One who habitually uses LSD, or who regards LSD as an important aspect of his life.

acid freak: One who habitually uses LSD and exhibits bizarre behaviors resulting from its use.

acid trip: The experience triggered by taking LSD. Acid trips vary immensely, from pleasurable, subjective perceptual changes (intensification of colors and sounds, etc.) to ecstatic, mystical revelations to horrific, nightmarish **freak-outs**. Most users report a rough "travel" sequence, however, of **getting off** (exhilaration and/or anxiety as the drug takes effect); **peaking** (the drug reaches its height of noticeable effect); **tripping** (the body of the experience, lasting from several hours to a full day or more); and **coming down** (the fading of the drug's effects and a return to normal sense of reality).

A-head: A habitual amphetamine user.

back up: To repeatedly inject and withdraw blood mixed with heroin while the syringe is in the vein, so as to heighten and lengthen the initial **rush**.

bad: Good; potent, with reference to drugs. The exception is *bad acid*— LSD that contains toxic additives or is in fact not LSD at all but PCP or some other drug.

bag: A unit of drug sale on the street level. A *dime bag* of marijuana, for example, is ten dollars' worth. Bags of heroin are usually small glassine envelopes.

bang: As a noun, a shot of heroin or other narcotic. As a verb, to **shoot up**.

bent: High on drugs, usually hallucinogens, sometimes narcotics.

bhong: A pipe for smoking marijuana.

big man: A narcotics dealer on the next level up from the street **pusher**; any large-scale narcotics dealer. See **the man**.

blow: To smoke marijuana or its derivatives.

blow it: To accidentally bypass the vein in a heroin injection and thus lose some in the skin.

blow your mind: To feel the effects of a strong dose of a mind-altering drug (especially an hallucinogen), implying that the reality of the user is transformed.

bogart: To take too long with, or too much

from, a marijuana **joint** that is being passed around and shared by several people.

bomb: High-potency heroin.

bombita: Any amphetamine prepared to be injected.

booting: See **back-up**.

brick: A pound or **key** (kilogram) of marijuana pressed into a brick shape for transport and sale.

bring down: 1. To use medical/pharmacological methods to return a drug user to a more normal state, e.g., by means of major tranquilizers, B vitamins, or the like.

2. To cause anxiety, discomfort, or an undesired return to "reality" from the **high** of a drug experience.

3. As a noun (a bring-down), any depressing, unfortunate, or soberingly real experience or event.

bummer: Also **bum trip**. A negative reaction to a drug (see **bad trip**) or, by extension, any unpleasant situation or experience. ("Yeah, I dropped out—school was a **bummer**.")

bundle: A tied bunch of twenty-five small **bags** of heroin, sold from **dealer** to **pusher** and then sold individually on the street.

burn: 1. To cheat someone in a drug deal by giving less than the promised amount or quality.

2. To turn a drug user over to the authorities.

burned out: Exhausted or damaged (physically and/or psychologically) through prolonged drug use.

bust: An arrest for illegal activities, especially drug possession or sale.

buy: As a verb, to purchase drugs. As a noun, the purchasing of drugs (to "**make a buy**").

buzz: The initial, lightheaded effect of smoking marijuana; the effect of any drug.

carrying: Having illegal drugs on one's person. See **holding**.

chasing the dragon: A method of taking heroin originated in Hong Kong, involving inhaling fumes from a heated heroin-barbiturate mixture; named for the mixture's snakelike appearance and movement as it is heated.

chipping: Also **chippying**. Nonhabitual, occasional narcotics use for pleasure, among nonaddicts. See **weekend habit**.

clean: 1. With no drugs on one's person.

2. No longer taking drugs.

3. As a verb, to remove the twigs, stems, and seeds from marijuana for easier smoking.

coming down: The last phase of a drug experience when its effects begin to wear off. See **acid trip**.

connection: 1. The person from whom one regularly gets one's drug supply.

2. Any drug **pusher**.

3. A high-level source of narcotics (e.g., *The French Connection*).

contact high: Experiencing the effects of marijuana or hashish without using any, either through being exposed to the exhaled smoke of users, or the apparent "communication" of the intoxicated mental state from one person to another.

cook, cook up: To dissolve the heroin-water mixture in the **cooker** by heating it with a lit match, thus preparing it for injection.

cooker: A spoon or other small container in which the heroin-water mixture is heated.

cop: To buy drugs. See **score**.

cotton: Also **satch cotton**. The small piece of cotton through which heroin is filtered into the syringe in order to remove any impurities.

cotton shooter: One who collects and **shoots** the residual heroin from leftover **cottons**.

crash: To **come down** from a long **speed** or **acid** (LSD) jaunt and suddenly experience the exhaustion and other physical effects that the drug had masked; to fall deeply asleep after *coming down*.

cut: To mix a drug with a less expensive but seemingly similar substance in order to increase one's profits and/or reduce the drug's potency. For example, heroin is often cut with quinine, or with milk sugar.

deal: To sell drugs.

dealer: A drug seller. There are many types and levels of dealers, from the college student who buys a few ounces of **grass**, which he sells to his friends, to the high-level underworld dealers who import heroin on a massive scale.

dealer's band: The rubber band by which heroin **bags** are tied to a **dealer's** wrist so that they can quickly be thrown away if he is approached by the police.

deck: Bag.

dime, **dime bag:** An envelope containing ten dollars' worth of heroin, or of marijuana.

dirty: Uncleaned marijuana. (See **clean**.) Also, having drugs on one's person.

do, **do up:** To take a drug. ("I used to **do** a lot of drugs, but I'm **clean** now.")

dope fiend: A user of **hard drugs**; often used by addicts to refer to themselves.

doper: A person avidly or deeply involved in drug use (usually not **hard drugs**).

downs head, **downs freak:** A heavy user of sedatives, barbiturates, and the like; a person who inclines that way in his typical choice of drugs.

dried out: Having completed detoxification, or *withdrawal*, from a drug.

drop: To take a pill, particularly **acid** (LSD).

dropper: Eyedropper used in **shooting** narcotics. See **works**.

dummy: Fake heroin.

duster: A cigarette composed of heroin mixed with tobacco.

dynamite: 1. High potency (less diluted) heroin.

    2. Potent marijuana.

    3. Any potent drug (also an adjective, as "some **dynamite** *Colombian*.")

eat, **eat some:** To take drugs orally.

eighth: Approximately one-eighth ounce of heroin prepared for sale.

fall out: To **nod out**.

feds: Federal narcotics agents. See **narco**.

fives: A five-milligram tablet of Benzedrine or other amphetamines.

fix: An injection of a narcotic, particularly heroin.

flash: See **rush**.

flashback: The recurrence of effects from a previously taken drug, especially LSD or other hallucinogens. Flashbacks can sometimes occur months after a person's drug use has been terminated.

flip out: To experience extreme anxiety, disorientation, or panic in reaction to the effects of a drug, particularly LSD. Flipping out has sometimes led to temporary or prolonged psychosis.

flowers: The highly **resinous** top buds of the marijuana plant.

flying: The condition of being extremely **high**.

freak: One who uses drugs, particularly the hallucinogens or marijuana, as an important aspect of his life, and/or adheres to the associated life-style and manners.

freak out: Originally referred to the alterations of consciousness inherent in LSD use, as well as being used synonymously with **flip out**; it has now come to refer mainly to the latter effect—i.e., an experience of deep anxiety, panic, or temporary psychosis engendered by a drug experience.

fucked up: Extremely **high**; implies being high to the point of being unable to function competently. This does not necessarily have a negative connotation among drug users, however.

garbage: Extremely weak heroin.

garbage drugs: Glue sniffing, **PCP**, and other drugs that have a high likelihood of adverse effects.

get off: To experience a drug taking its effect. See **rush**.

gone: Extremely **high**.

goods: Drugs, usually in reference to sale or purchase.

gutter: Those veins of the elbow area used for **shooting** heroin.

habit: A physical and/or psychological dependence on a drug, especially one of the opiates;

addicts speak of a specifically priced habit, depending on how much must be spent to satisfy it, e.g., a "$200-a-day **habit**." This amount defines the amount of stealing, **dealing, hustling**, or other money-raising activity the addict will have to perform *every day*, in order to sustain his addiction.

hard drugs, hard stuff: Heroin or other narcotics.

hash pipe: A special pipe used to smoke hashish.

head: 1. A regular user of a drug who is, however, not an addict; the term does not generally refer to physically addictive drugs. See **A-head, acid head**.

2. The particular state of being **high**, or, by extension, any state of consciousness or subjectivity. ("She's been in a really weird **head** lately.")

head shop: A store where drug paraphernalia are sold, such as **hash pipes, roach clips, rolling papers**, and various legal drug substitutes.

high: In a state of euphoria or otherwise nonnormal condition, usually from drug use. Qualifiers such as *a little high* or *really high* often accompany the pronouncement of this state. To *get high* often refers to the act of smoking marijuana, but is used for almost every form of drug use as well. A *natural high* is one obtained without drugs—as, from music, meditation, sex, running, wilderness, and beauty.

hit: As a noun, a dose of a drug, especially an inhalation of marijuana or hashish. ("Let me get a **hit** off that **joint**.") As a verb, to get the needle successfully into the **mainline** when **shooting** heroin.

holding: Carrying drugs on one's person.

hookah: A water pipe for smoking marijuana; the water cools the marijuana smoke, which can be quite harsh, as it bubbles through the pipe.

hooked: Addicted.

hustle: As a verb, to sell contraband, steal, or otherwise raise cash to support a drug **habit**. As a noun, an illegal or other business enterprise put together to raise quick cash.

jag: An extended drug experience; the equivalent of a **trip** with reference to drugs other than hallucinogens or marijuana; may particularly refer to cocaine and amphetamine experiences.

Jefferson airplane: A **roach clip** made of a split paper match; the **roach** is inserted in the V formed by the split.

jerk off: Back up.

joint: A marijuana cigarette.

jones: 1. A **hard-drug** addiction.

2. The effects of *withdrawal* from a drug.

junkie: A heroin addict.

key, kilo: A kilogram, particularly of marijuana (2.2 pounds), which forms the basic unit of wholesale marijuana distribution.

kicking: Going through *withdrawal* to free oneself of an addictive drug habit—i.e., "**kicking the habit**."

kicks: The pleasurable sensations derived from drug use; to use drugs "for kicks" is to do so simply for pleasure, not for escape or relief from pain.

layout: 1. **Works**.

2. Equipment for smoking opium.

lid: A unit of marijuana sale, referring to approximately twenty-two grams (about three-quarters of an ounce) of marijuana, or about the amount that would fit into a small tobacco tin.

line: A dose of **cocaine** powder, laid out in a thin line for **snorting**.

luded out: Extremely high on **Quaaludes** (Methaqualone) to the point of jeopardizing performance of basic functions, such as walking, talking, and standing.

mainline: 1. As a verb, to inject heroin into one of the major veins. (See **hit**.)

2. The vein into which heroin is injected.

make: To purchase (drugs). ("I just **made** some **downs**.")

make a buy: To purchase drugs.

the man: 1. The **pusher** or **dealer** from whom one purchases drugs.

2. Any pusher or dealer, especially on a large scale, removed from on-the-street peddling.

3. The police or other authorities; the system of authority in general which bears down on the user's or **hustler**'s life-style.

maryjane: One of many alterations of the word "marijuana."

monkey: A drug habit. See **jones**.

monkey on my back: 1. An opiate drug habit.

2. Undergoing the effects of withdrawal from heroin or other opiates.

munchies: Intense, continuous craving for food consequent upon smoking marijuana.

narc, narco: An undercover narcotics officer, or any narcotics officer.

nickel, nickel bag: A package of five dollars' worth of a drug.

nod, nod out, go on the nod: To fall asleep or be in a state of constant half-sleep or a pattern of dozing and waking, because of the strong effect of an opiate or depressant drug; so named because the head of the drug user bobs up and down regularly as he experiences the effects of the drug.

number: A **joint**.

OD: Short for **overdose**. Used as both noun and verb.

on the needle: Being a narcotics injecter.

panic: A general heroin shortage; may be due to a series of large **busts** in the area, or a lack of supply from the source country outside the U.S.

peak: That point in an LSD **trip** in which its continuously increasing effects reach their height. See **acid trip**.

the people: Distributors of heroin at the higher levels.

pillhead: A heavy pill user, referring to use of either barbiturates and other sedatives, or amphetamines.

pipe: 1. A large vein to use for **mainlining**.

2. A smoking pipe, used to ingest marijuana or hashish.

poke: A drag of a marijuana cigarette.

pop: 1. To take a pill.

2. To shoot heroin under the skin, rather than in a vein; a practice that gives a milder **rush** and **high** and does not leave as obvious **tracks**. Also called **skin-pop**.

puff: To smoke opium.

pull: Also **poke, toke, hit**. A single drag of a marijuana **joint**.

pusher: A **dealer** of heroin or other **hard drugs**; generally *not* used to refer to sellers of marijuana, hallucinogens, cocaine, or the like.

quarter: Twenty-five dollars' worth of drugs, as a *quarter bag* of heroin.

reefer: 1. A **joint**.

2. **Marijuana**.

resin: The sticky or gummy substance in marijuana or poppy plants, which contains their active ingredients.

righteous: High-potency (drugs).

roach: The leftover butt of a marijuana **joint**. Roaches can be smoked using a **roach clip** or collected and smoked in a **pipe**; or the contents of the roaches can be spilled out, collected, and rerolled into a new joint. Roaches are particularly strong because of the additional **resin** that has built up through smoking.

roach clip: A paper clip, tie clip, or specially designed clip used to hold the small **roach** in order to smoke it without burning the fingers or lips.

rolling papers: "Cigarette" papers used to roll marijuana into a smokable **joint**. Sold not only in **head shops** but at newsstands and drug stores everywhere.

rush: The sudden onslaught of euphoria after heroin is **mainlined**; also refers to many other drug-related sensations when they first appear or suddenly increase in intensity.

satch cotton: See **cotton**.

schmecker: Heroin user or addict (**schmeck** = heroin).

score: To make a purchase of a desired drug. ("He's trying to **score** some **coke** for this weekend.")

set of works: See **works**.

shit: Heroin or other drugs.

shooting gallery: A place used by addicts to **shoot up**; usually an apartment in an abandoned building or inner-city tenement.

shoot, shoot up: To inject heroin or any other drug in liquid form.

skin-pop: See **pop**.

snort: To take a drug by inhaling it, in a powdered form; usually refers to cocaine, heroin, or **crystal**.

spaced out: Disoriented or otherwise **high** to the point of sensory and cognitive distortion; in a dreamlike, out-of-touch mental state due to drug use. The term applies both to the immediate drug experience and to a more chronic mental pattern. ("After that last **trip**, he was **spaced out** for months.")

speed freak: A habitual user of amphetamines, especially one who **shoots** the drug.

spike: A hypodermic needle used to inject drugs. See **works.**

spoon: 1. A wholesale unit of pure heroin, to be **cut** and sold by the **street pusher**; roughly about one-sixteenth of an ounce.

2. A teaspoon used to dissolve heroin in water and heat it.

3. A tiny spoon used for **snorting** cocaine (*cokespoon*).

stash: As a noun, an individual's supply of drugs, particularly marijuana. As a verb, to hide drugs, such as heroin, and associated paraphernalia, in a safe place.

stoned, stoned out: **High** (or very high).

straight: 1. Not **high** at the moment.

2. Off drugs.

3. Never using or having used drugs.

4. Part of the nondrug ("mainstream") world.

street pusher: The lowest level of drug **dealer**, who sells individual units of the **cut** product (usually **hard drugs**) on the street.

strung out: 1. In need of a **fix**

2. Badly **hooked**.

3. Physically deteriorated because of drug use and associated effects.

tab: A dose of LSD in tablet form, although it may not be a tablet proper but a small **cut** section of LSD-impregnated paper, sugar cube, or the like.

taste: 1. A shot of heroin, or a portion taken of any drug by any means.

2. A small dose of a drug given without charge from one user to another.

tie off: To apply a tourniquet (using a belt, surgical tubing, or the like) to the arm above the **mainline** so as to distend the vein and make the injection of a drug easier.

toke: A single inhalation of a marijuana **joint** or other smoking concoction.

tracks: The tiny holes that form a permanent or semipermanent scar around the area of the **mainline** on an addict's arm.

trip: A prolonged drug experience, generally of hallucinogens. See **acid trip**.

turn on: 1. To get **high**.

2. To give some of a drug to another user as a gift.

3. To supply someone with a first drug experience, as applied to a particular drug he or she has never used, or to the first experience of drugs in general.

4. To give someone marijuana or LSD.

5. To become aware of the effects and lifestyle of drug use, particularly that of the psychedelics and marijuana (mainly 1960s; now archaic except in the past tense).

wasted: **High** to the point of exhaustion or incompetence.

water pipe: See **hookah**.

weekend habit: The occasional use of **hard drugs**: it is possible to use a drug such as heroin on a restricted basis without becoming addicted. See **chipping**.

wiped out: Wasted; extremely tired, as after a long **trip**.

wired: 1. Having a heroin habit.

2. Under the influence of amphetamines.

works: Also **kit**. The equipment used by addicts to inject heroin (or other drugs)—consisting of a hypodermic needle (or a regular needle with eyedropper and bulb), a spoon or bottle-cap **cooker**, a belt or cord for **tying off**, and a bottle of distilled water. The addict dissolves the drug in water, heats it with a match in the cooker, ties off his arm and injects the drug into a vein using either a syringe or an improvised needle-and-eyedropper arrangement.

zonked, zonked out: Spaced out, wiped out, wasted.

MEDICAL/PSYCHOLOGICAL TERMS RELATING TO DRUG USE

addiction: A complex syndrome of intense, compulsive involvement with a drug and its effects, including components of both physical and psychological **dependence**, developed **tolerance** to the drug's effects, and **withdrawal** symptoms if the drug is removed from the addict's system. The term is usually reserved for the typical syndromes connected with **heroin**, other **opiates**, and **barbiturates**.

alkaloid: A class of basic organic compounds that have an active effect on human metabolic functions. Alkaloids are usually derived from plants, may be toxic, and include such substances as **morphine**, nicotine, caffeine, **cocaine**, quinine, **codeine**, strychnine, reserpine, and **LSD**.

analgesics: Drugs that reduce or relieve pain but do not cause loss of consciousness. Analgesics include aspirin (and other salicylates), as well as Demerol, Darvon, **morphine**, and other **narcotics**.

anesthetics: Drugs that reduce or eliminate sensation, especially pain. Include ether, sodium pentathol, **nitrous oxide**, novocaine, halothane, and cyclopropaine.

antidepressants: Drugs used to treat depression, especially when biochemically based; some are central nervous system stimulants (e.g., amphetamines), while others are actually sedatives. Frequently successful in combating depressive symptoms, although there are frequent undesirable side effects.

benzodiazepines: The chemical basis of the minor tranquilizers, such as Valium and Librium.

controlled substances: Drugs subject to legal regulation, listed under five basic categories, known as *Schedules I–V*. (I: abusable, medically useless drugs such as **heroin**, **LSD** and **marijuana**; II: abusable drugs with some legitimate uses, such as **morphine**, **Demerol**, **Quaaludes**, and **amphetamines**; III: not much abuse potential, including some **barbiturates**: IV and V: similar to III but with even less abuse potential.)

cross-tolerance: A tolerance developed to a drug that is chemically related to a different drug one has used; as, between **LSD** and **mescaline**, or **heroin** and **methadone** (the basis of methadone treatment for heroin addiction).

dependence: An intense and chronic need for a drug, which may be *physiological* (as in the case of **narcotics addiction**, where lack of the drug will produce painful and dangerous **withdrawal** symptoms) and/or *psychological* (as in the case of some marijuana and cocaine users, who feel they cannot function without the drug but are not biochemically **addicted**).

detoxification: The process of **withdrawing** an **addict** or other drug-dependent person from drug habituation.

drug automatism: The condition in which a drug user becomes unaware of how much of a drug he has taken, or is taking, and continues to ingest more; usually due to intoxication and/or **tolerance**; considered a major cause of **barbiturate overdose**.

hallucination: A "false" perception by any of the senses that has no matching cause in the physical world.

kinesthetic experience: The experience of perceiving cross-sensory phenomena, such as "seeing sounds," "tasting colors," etc. Associated with **LSD** use.

MAO inhibitor: Certain **hallucinogens**, nonstimulant **antidepressants**, and blood pressure medications that depress the activity of the enzyme MAO, an important metabolizer of otherwise poisonous food components. Most **psychoactive** drugs either are, or **potentiate** with, MAO inhibitors.

maintenance therapy: The legal dispensing of drugs to **addicts**, both to prevent the onset of **withdrawal** symptoms, and to control their habit toward either **detoxification** and/or transformation of their life-style.

multihabituation: The development of two or more simultaneous drug habits that are related to one another. The best-known is the **amphetamine-barbiturate** or **amphetamine-barbiturate**-alcohol multihabituation, in which the amphetamine user cannot sleep without taking a depressant, and then must take a stimulant in order to wake up and function. However, multihabituation may also form in order to **potentiate** the effects of two somewhat similar drugs, such as **heroin** and barbiturates.

Nalline test: Nalline, a **narcotic antagonist,** is used to test whether or not an **addict** has been using a narcotic, and to what extent. After Nalline is administered, the effects of the narcotic are blocked and *withdrawal* symptoms corresponding to the extent of physical **dependence** quickly take place.

narcotic antagonist: Any drug that blocks the effects of a **narcotic**.

narcotics: Addictive, painkilling, and sensory-depressing drugs, particularly the **opiates** (morphine, codeine, heroin, etc.).

overdose: A somewhat imprecise term referring to any of a variety of severe physical symptom-complexes, caused by the ingestion of more of a drug than a person's system can tolerate; some typical aspects of overdose include respiratory depression or failure, coma, heart failure, and shock. Death is not uncommon in the absence of medical treatment. Most overdoses are the result of excessive dosages of heroin, other opiates, barbiturates and other sedatives (especially when **potentiated** by alcohol), and some stimulants.

potentiation: The increase in the effects of a drug through interaction with another substance in the system which intensifies its biochemical action. The most pronounced and prevalent potentiation syndrome is that of alcohol with barbiturates and other sedatives.

phenothiazines: The pharmacological group from which the **major tranquilizers** (such as Thorazine) are derived.

psychoactive: Having the effect of altering the normal state of the psyche; affecting both perception and cognition.

psychotropic: Causing a change in consciousness or mood.

tolerance: The gradual adaptation to the biochemical effects of a drug, such that the user must take increasing dosages in order to achieve the same subjective effect. A major danger in the use of **barbiturates**, for example, is that while tolerance to the drug develops with prolonged heavy use (such that the user takes ever-higher quantities), the amount that constitutes a lethal dose does not also increase; thus, the chronic user may **overdose** simply as a product of the tolerance syndrome.

withdrawal: A complex of painful and often dangerous symptoms that result from the cessation of drug use by a person who has developed a *physical* **dependence** on a drug. Possible symptoms include anxiety, aching, cramps, nausea, weakness, convulsions, and other conditions dependent upon the particular drug and the length and dosage level of the addiction. Particularly in the case of barbiturate-type drugs, untreated withdrawal can be fatal.

Index

The numbers in parentheses are chapter numbers.

The numbers in parentheses are chapter numbers.

The numbers in parentheses are chapter numbers.

The numbers in parentheses are chapter numbers.

The numbers in parentheses are chapter numbers.

The numbers in parentheses are chapter numbers